# THE PENAL SYSTEM

First published 2002. Reprinted 2002, 2003

SAGE Publications Ltd
6 Bonhill Street
London EC2A 4PU

SAGE Publications Inc
2455 Teller Road
Thousand Oaks, California 91320

SAGE Publications India Pvt Ltd
32, M-Block Market
Greater Kailash - I
New Delhi 110 048

**British Library Cataloguing in Publication data**

A catalogue record for this book is
available from the British Library

ISBN 0-7619-4742-6
ISBN 0-7619-4743-4 (pbk)

*Library of congress control number available*
Typeset by Keystroke, Jacaranda Lodge, Wolverhampton
Printed in Great Britain by The Cromwell Press, Trowbridge, Wiltshire

# THE PENAL SYSTEM

## An Introduction

*Third edition*

Michael Cavadino and James Dignan

**SAGE Publications**
London • Thousand Oaks • New Delhi

# Contents

# Preface to the Third Edition

This is the one you have all been waiting for (until the next edition becomes due that is). Once again the pace of penal change has been swift since our second edition (informally subtitled 'The Michael Howard Years') came out in 1997 – just in time for New Labour to take over following the General Election of that year. So this third edition (unofficial subtitle: 'The Jack Straw Era') again represents a major revision – and of course a vital purchase for all students of the English penal system. For the most part, this book is as up-to-date as we could make it in April 2001, although you may notice the occasional later detail if we manage to sneak it in at the proof-reading stage. One development since then has been the replacement of Jack Straw as Home Secretary by David Blunkett, and of course there could be other changes by the time you read this. We may not be able to predict the future, but we have included a new self-study guide that should make it easier for you to keep track of such changes as they unfold by consulting the growing number of relevant penal policy sites on the Internet.

Thanks are again due to colleagues in the Centre for Criminological and Legal Research and the Faculty of Law at Sheffield and in the wider criminological community, who are either too numerous or too embarrassingly few to mention individually (you guess which). We again have to thank the team at Sage, especially Miranda Nunhofer, who have been as helpful as ever. Thanks also, as always, to Lucille Cavadino and Angela Dignan for their understanding, tolerance, patience and loving support during the writing of this book.

# Introduction

This book is about the penal system – the system that exists to punish and otherwise deal with people who have (usually)[1] been convicted of a criminal offence. More precisely, we are centrally concerned with the 'English' penal system, by which we mean the system in England and Wales. (Scotland and Northern Ireland have separate systems.) However, much of what we say (especially about penal philosophy and penal sociology in Chapters 2 and 3) is of relevance to more than one country; and we have referred to other penal systems at times to help illuminate the English (and Welsh) experience.[2] While we have tried to be factually correct, to outline differing viewpoints and to be as comprehensive as is possible in a book of this size, we have not felt any need to be shy about expressing our own opinions. In a nutshell, these are that the English penal system is unjustly and irrationally harsh, and that our penal practices and attitudes towards punishment require radical revision.

## THE CRIMINAL JUSTICE SYSTEM

The penal system is part of a larger entity known as the *criminal justice system*, a term covering all those institutions which respond officially to the commission of offences, notably the police, prosecution authorities and courts. It is often misleading or unsatisfactory to examine the penal system in isolation from the larger criminal justice system. Consequently, at times in this book – for example in Chapters 4, 9 and 10 – we deal with the criminal justice system as a whole.

There now follows a very brief and basic guide to the criminal justice system as a whole, to assist readers who may not be familiar with the system or its terminology. Figure I.1 is a simplified diagram of the criminal justice system up to the point where an offender is sentenced by a court, which is the moment when the offender enters the *penal* system.

In many cases when a crime is committed, the agencies of criminal justice never respond at all. For the criminal justice process normally starts to operate only when a crime is reported to the police, and by no means all crimes are reported. In 1999 only 41 per cent of all the crimes uncovered by the official British Crime Survey were reported to the police, and only 23 per cent were officially recorded as crimes by the police (Kershaw et al., 2000: 5–6). If an alleged offence is reported, or otherwise comes to the attention of the police, the police may then investigate it. The police have a wide range of powers

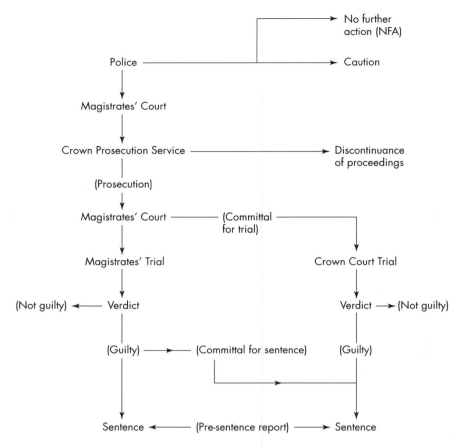

FIGURE I.1   *The criminal justice system in England and Wales, up to the point of sentence*

(notably those contained in the Police and Criminal Evidence Act 1984) to carry out searches and to arrest and question suspects in pursuit of their investigations. If the police believe that there is sufficient evidence to put the suspect on trial, they may charge an arrested suspect with the offence: this is the first stage in the prosecution process. The police then 'lay an information' before the local magistrates' court alleging that the suspect has committed the offence. The prosecution is then taken over by the Crown Prosecution Service (CPS), a state agency independent of the police which was created by the Prosecution of Offences Act 1985.

There are two alternatives to the charging procedure. One (accounting for about two-thirds of all prosecutions) is for the police to seek a summons issued by a magistrate. Under this procedure the alleged offender remains at liberty for the time being but is ordered to attend court. Another possibility is to dispense with prosecution entirely and for the police instead to administer an official warning. In the case of an offender of 18 or over, this is known as a *caution*. A caution should not be given unless the offender admits guilt. No formal punishment ensues, but the caution will form part of the offender's official criminal record. Since 1 June 2000 (and earlier in some places), cautions for young offenders under 18 have been replaced by *'reprimands'* and *'warnings'* (also known as 'final warnings'), which are explained more fully in Chapter 9. In 1999, 33 per cent of known offenders were 'diverted from court' by being cautioned, reprimanded or warned rather than prosecuted.

When the alleged offender reaches the magistrates' court (and becomes a 'defendant'), the court may have to decide whether to grant the defendant *bail* (conditional release prior to the actual trial) or whether the defendant should be *remanded in custody* for the time being. Custodial remands are usually to prison, or to a remand centre run by the Prison Service.[3]

Criminal offences fall into three categories: indictable only, summary only, and triable either way.[4] This categorization determines at which court – magistrates' court or Crown Court – the trial will be held.[5] Offences which are indictable only (for example murder, rape and robbery) must be tried at the Crown Court before a judge, with a jury of 12 randomly selected lay people to decide on the verdict if the defendant pleads not guilty. In these cases the magistrates' court sends the case to the Crown Court for trial 'on indictment'. Offences which are summary only (for example, common assault, minor criminal damage and most motoring offences) must be tried 'summarily' at the magistrates' court before at least two and normally three lay justices of the peace or a single district judge (a professional magistrate, formerly known as a 'stipendiary'). Offences which are 'triable either way' include theft, arson and most burglaries. If a defendant charged with one of these offences pleads guilty, the case will stay in the magistrates' court at least for the time being.[6] But if the defendant pleads not guilty, the magistrates then decide whether to 'commit' the defendant to be tried in the Crown Court trial or whether the case may be tried in the magistrates' court. A defendant who intends to plead not guilty at present has the right to insist on a Crown Court trial for an offence which is triable either way.[7] In practice, the great majority of triable either way offences are dealt with in the magistrates' court.

Defendants have the choice of pleading either guilty or not guilty in both the magistrates' court or the Crown Court. If the plea is not guilty the burden rests on the prosecution to prove to the magistrates or jury that the defendant is guilty 'beyond reasonable doubt'. But the great majority of defendants plead guilty: around 90 per cent in the magistrates' court and over 70 per cent at the Crown Court.

If the defendant pleads guilty or is found guilty (or in other words is convicted of the offence), the magistrates or judge then pass *sentence*. The sentence is the punishment (or other order of the court) which is imposed upon the defendant as a consequence of committing the crime. A few offences have mandatory or semi-mandatory penalties attached: for example, there is a mandatory penalty of life imprisonment for murder, while for driving with excess alcohol in the blood disqualification is semi-mandatory (i.e. automatic unless there are exceptional circumstances). The Crime (Sentences) Act 1997 introduced new semi-mandatory and minimum sentences (under the 'three strikes and you're out' principle) for repeated serious violence, domestic burglary and Class A drug trafficking (see Chapter 4). Most offences, however, have a statutory maximum penalty – for example, seven years' imprisonment for theft – but no statutory minimum. The magistrates' court also has statutory limits on its sentencing powers: it cannot sentence an offender to more than six months in prison for a single offence or to more than 12 months in total, nor can it normally impose a fine of more than £5,000. However, a magistrates' court can commit an offender it has convicted to the Crown Court for sentence if it feels that its sentencing powers are inadequate. As long as the statutory maxima are not exceeded, the court usually has a wide range of sentences to choose from. These include the *custodial* sentences of imprisonment (for adults), detention in a young offender institution (at present, for offenders aged 18 to 20) and detention and training orders (for young offenders under 18). *Non-custodial* penalties (to which we devote Chapter 5) include suspended prison sentences, fines, compensation orders, community rehabilitation orders (formerly known as probation orders), community punishment orders (formerly community service orders),[8] and absolute and conditional discharges. The court may be assisted in its choice of sentence by a pre-sentence report (PSR) prepared by a probation officer (or, in the case of juvenile offenders, by a member of the youth offending team: see Chapter 9). Pre-sentence reports provide the sentencer with information about the offender's behaviour and social and family background, and usually include a proposal for what the sentence should be.

Convicted defendants may appeal to a higher court either against their conviction or against the sentence which has been passed, or both. The Attorney General (a government law officer who is a Member of Parliament) additionally has the power to refer certain sentences passed by the Crown Court to the Court of Appeal on the grounds that they are too lenient.

A sentence of imprisonment means that the offender is allocated to a prison by the Prison Service.[9] (We examine prisons and imprisonment in Chapters 6 and 7.) Under present arrangements, prisoners do not usually serve the full term of the sentence pronounced by the court: for example, an offender sentenced to two years' imprisonment will normally be released after one year, and at the discretion of the prison authorities may be released up to two months earlier still under a 'home detention curfew'. Shorter-term prisoners are released automatically at a certain point of their sentence, but for longer-term prisoners their early release may take the form of *parole*, which is discretionary release decided upon by a body such as the Parole Board. For many prisoners, early release is combined with compulsory supervision by a probation officer in the community and released prisoners can under certain circumstances be returned to prison to serve the unexpired portion of the sentence. The most recent innovation, home detention curfew, involves both supervision and a home curfew enforced by electronic monitoring or 'tagging' of the offender. (For fuller details of the system of *'early release'* from prison sentences, see Chapter 8.)

Non-custodial sentences usually require the offender to carry out some action, such as pay a fine or compensation or perform community service. Alternatively, the offender may be required to *refrain* from acting in certain ways, in particular to avoid re-offending within a given time limit (for example, if the sentence is a conditional discharge or a suspended sentence). Offenders who 'breach' the terms of their sentences either by disobeying their requirements or by re-offending can be brought back to court as a result, and the court will then have a range of sanctions available. These sanctions often include the power to pass custodial sentences, which may be additional (or 'consecutive') to any custodial sentence imposed for a fresh offence.

A recent legislative change which may prove to be of major importance to the whole criminal justice system is the Human Rights Act 1998. This Act, which came into force on 2 October 2000, incorporates the European Convention on Human Rights into English law. Previously, the United Kingdom government was bound by treaty to respect and defend the human rights set out in the Convention, but it was not directly binding in domestic law. Those who considered that their human rights had been violated could only gain redress by the long drawn-out procedure of petitioning the European Court of Human Rights in Strasbourg. If the Court found that UK law was incompatible with the Convention, a duty lay on the government to introduce legislation through Parliament to rectify domestic law. (This arrangement has at times had important effects on English penal law, for example in altering arrangements for early release – see Chapter 8.) Under the 1998 Act, all public bodies – including, for example, criminal justice agencies such as the police, probation service and Prison Service – are under a legal duty to act in accordance with the Convention. Furthermore, English courts are bound *where possible* to interpret English law so that it is compatible with the Convention. (This has already had an impact in encouraging the Court of Appeal to reconsider its interpretation of the law regarding 'two strikes and you're out' sentences: see Chapter 4.) If the court decides that English law is unequivocally incompatible with the Convention it must make a formal declaration to this effect; the government then has the power to 'fast-track' legislation through Parliament to remove the incompatibility.

## STRATEGIES FOR CRIMINAL JUSTICE AND THE PENAL CRISIS

This book is largely concerned with the 'crisis' in the English penal system and the policies which governments have developed in response to this crisis. We introduce the penal crisis in general terms in Chapter 1. In Chapter 11 we provide a history of the strategies adopted by national governments up to the present day, but a brief summary is appropriate here to set the scene.

We find it helpful to use a general, three-fold categorization of criminal justice policies which we call '*Strategies A, B and C*' (based on Rutherford, 1993; see also Cavadino et al., 1999). Strategy A is a *highly punitive* approach embodying what we call 'law and order ideology' (see Chapter 1): the attitude that offenders should be dealt with as severely as possible. A governmental strategy based on this attitude would involve making criminal justice harsher and more punitive at every stage and in every respect. Strategy A embodies an '*exclusionary*' approach to offenders, tending to reject them as members of the community (see Cavadino et al., 1999: 48–50). The '*managerialist*' Strategy B seeks to apply administrative and bureaucratic mechanisms to criminal justice in an attempt to make the system as smooth running and cost-effective as possible. Strategy C seeks to protect and uphold the *human rights* of offenders, victims and potential victims of crime. It seeks to minimize punishment and to ensure fairness and humane treatment within the criminal justice system, and is *'inclusive'*, seeking to maintain offenders within the community and reintegrate them as law-abiding citizens. Proponents of Strategy C are not all of one mind: some favour measures to rehabilitate and reform offenders, while some advocate *'restorative justice'* measures which seek to ensure that offenders perform reparation to their victims and to the community (see Chapters 2, 5 and 9). Others, while still being motivated by humanitarianism and a wish to lessen the harshness of punishment in general, propound the view that offenders should be punished according to their *'just deserts'* (see Chapter 2).

In the early 1980s, the Conservative government of Margaret Thatcher injected a heavy dose of 'Strategy A' into penal policy. This meant being deliberately harsher in punishing offenders (although as we shall see, especially in Chapters 9 and 11, this was by no means entirely the case across the board). From around 1987 onwards, however – a period we refer to as 'the Hurd era', after Home Secretary Douglas Hurd (1985–9) – the Thatcher government's penal policy became less dogmatic and more pragmatic, although still tinged with punitive 'law and order' rhetoric. The centrepiece of this new strategy was the Criminal Justice Act 1991, which represented the most radical legislative reform to the penal system since the Second World War. This Act combined elements of all three strategies. Philosophically, the Act was influenced by the ('Strategy C') notion of 'just deserts'; in practical terms it was hoped that it would reduce the prison population and make it more easily manageable (a 'Strategy B' aim). The idea was that more offenders than hitherto should undergo *'punishment in the community'* rather than being sent to prison. Punishments were also in general to be in proportion to the seriousness of the crime – in other words, offenders were to get their 'just deserts'. But some categories of offender (notably violent and sexual offenders) were to receive harsher punishment than hitherto, and 'punishment in the community' was to take on a tougher and more punitive aspect (thus incorporating elements of 'Strategy A').

The 1991 Act was brought into force in October 1992. However, within months the Conservative government (now headed by Mrs Thatcher's successor, John Major) had abandoned the strategy embodied by the Act. From 1993 to 1997, in a development we have termed *'the law and order counter-reformation'*, the Conservative government – especially in the person of Michael Howard, Home Secretary from May 1993 to April 1997 – pursued ever harsher Strategy A policies, including the hasty repeal of some central provisions of the 1991 Act. Mr Howard famously declared to the Conservative Party Conference in October 1993 that *'prison works'*.

Following their victory in the General Election of May 1997, the 'New Labour' government of Tony Blair – and his Home Secretary Jack Straw – sought to implement its famous campaign promise to be 'tough on crime and tough on the causes of crime' (Labour Party, 1997) by pursuing a mixture of policies with elements of all three of our 'ideal-type' Strategies. This has included introducing some new measures based on 'restorative justice' (see especially Chapter 9) – in line with one version of Strategy C – and an emphasis on assessing the effectiveness and cost-effectiveness of penal measures (which fits with the managerialism of Strategy B). Strategy A is also well represented in the New Labour policy mix, as the government favours the increased use of imprisonment for persistent offenders and policies of *'zero tolerance'* (see Cavadino et al., 1999: 28–30) towards various categories of wrongdoing.

Having introduced the penal crisis in Chapter 1, we discuss facets of the crisis and the responses to it throughout this book. Chapters 2 and 3 may be heavily theoretical, but unashamedly so, for they are also intimately connected to the crisis theme. Chapter 3's exploration of penal sociology underpins our analysis of how the crisis should be explained, while our investigation of the philosophy of punishment in Chapter 2 should contribute to an understanding of why the penal system suffers from its crucial 'crisis of legitimacy'. Chapters 4 to 10 deal with various aspects of the system and its crisis. Chapter 4 identifies the decisions of courts – not only their sentencing decisions but also their actions in relation to bail and mode of trial – as the crux of the crisis. Chapter 6 investigates the troubled prison system, while Chapters 5, 7 and 8 deal with three developments which have so far had less than total success in relieving pressure on the prisons: the proliferation of non-custodial penalties, the policy of prison privatization and mechanisms for early release. Chapter 9, on young offenders, provides contrasting object lessons from recent history on how to exacerbate a penal crisis and how to relieve one. Chapter 10 investigates the burning issue of bias within the criminal justice system. Finally, in Chapter 11 we discuss whether the crisis is likely to be solved, and we put forward our own agenda for change.

## A NOTE ON TERMINOLOGY: 'SYSTEM'

Perhaps the title of this book is misleading. Arguably, one of the salient features of the English penal and criminal justice *'systems'* – at least until recently – has been their highly *unsystematic* nature, with different agencies working in relative isolation from each other, exercising wide and unaccountable discretionary powers, and subject to no overall coordination or strategic control. Some writers have even described criminal justice as a 'non-system'. Whether that description is still an accurate one is one of the major issues we will be considering in the light of recent attempts at reform: see in particular Chapters 4 and 9. In any event, we do have penal and criminal justice 'systems' in the sense that they are composed of different agencies which are *interdependent*: their activities intimately affect each other and they need to be studied within this context of interdependency (see, for example, Feeney, 1985). We see this kind of 'systems analysis' as an important tool in understanding the penal system and attempting to bring about positive modifications. (This is a particular theme of Chapter 9.)

## NOTES

1   There is one very important exception to this. *Remand prisoners* accounted for 19 per cent of the total prison population in 1999. Most of these are prisoners who are remanded in custody while awaiting trial; a minority have already been convicted and are awaiting sentence.

2   The subject of 'comparative penology' is explored more fully in Cavadino and Dignan (forthcoming).

3   For many years it was common for remand prisoners to be held in cells in police stations because of prison overcrowding, but this practice ceased in 1995.

4   Unless otherwise stated, statistics for offences and offenders which we present in the book normally relate to 'indictable' offences, which include offences triable either way.

5   At the time of writing Sir Robin Auld is reviewing the whole system of criminal courts in England and Wales (see Chapter 4) and is expected to make radical proposals for change, possibly involving the creation of a third, intermediate level court between the existing magistrates' and Crown courts.

6   The defendant will be *convicted* (found guilty) in the magistrates' court. It is still possible, however, for the defendant then to be committed to the Crown Court for *sentence*.

7   The government currently intends to introduce legislation to remove this right to Crown Court trial for defendants charged with 'either way' offences. See Chapter 4.

8   Probation and community service orders were renamed as from 1 April 2001 by ss. 43 and 44 of the Criminal Justice and Court Services Act 2000.

9   The Prison Service (formerly the Prison Department of the Home Office) is headed by a Director General (Martin Narey in 2001) who is answerable to the Home Secretary. The Home Secretary's (and Home Office's) other responsibilities include the police and the probation service.

# 1

# Crisis? What Crisis?

'Martin Narey, the head of the Prison Service, last night named six jails as "hellholes" and warned that he would quit his job unless conditions throughout prisons in England and Wales improved . . . Mr Narey's threat to quit follows last week's clash between the Lord Chief Justice and the Home Secretary over the corrosive effects of the ever-rising prison population . . . Mr Narey said that he was not prepared to keep on apologizing "for failing prison after failing prison". He said he had had enough of trying to "explain the very immorality of our treatment of some prisoners and the degradation of some establishments".' (Alan Travis, 'Jails Chief Threatens to Resign', *The Guardian*, 6 January 2001)

At times like this, it might not seem controversial to claim that the penal system is in a state of crisis. Nor would most people in Britain imagine that this 'penal crisis' is either new or sudden. For many years, media reports have acquainted everyone with the notion that rocketing prison populations, overcrowding, unrest among staff and inmates, escapes and prison riots – like the riot at Strangeways Prison in April 1990 – add up to a severe and deepening penal crisis. The term 'crisis' has been common currency in both media and academic accounts of the penal system for well over 20 years now; the word recurs in newspaper headlines and in the titles of learned books and articles (for example, Bottoms and Preston, 1980; Rutherford, 1988). Evidence for the existence of a crisis seems to be constantly in the news. Recent years have seen – to mention just a few out of many possible illustrations – embarrassing escapes from two high-security prisons (Whitemoor and Parkhurst) in 1994 and 1995; the dramatic sacking of Prison Service Director General Derek Lewis by Home Secretary Michael Howard in 1995; scandals about the manacling of pregnant and dying prisoners when they receive treatment in hospitals; record numbers of suicides in prisons; the jailing in 2000 and 2001 of six prison officers from Wormwood Scrubs for planned and sustained attacks on inmates; and the disturbing racist murder of Zahid Mubarek by a fellow inmate in Feltham Young Offender Institution in March 2000. All this is set against the background of a prison population scaling ever higher, all-time record levels and a continuing deep malaise running through the penal system as a whole.

Yet is it really a 'crisis'? A cynic could be forgiven for finding the penal crisis uncannily reminiscent of the supposed 'crisis of capitalism', which some Marxists used to constantly insist was real, severe, ever-worsening and likely to prove terminal in the near future. Yet both capitalism and the penal system seem to keep going somehow, unlike those regimes, parties and theories which were founded on Marxism. Perhaps few would dispute that the penal system has serious problems – but is it really in a state of *crisis*? Then again, how long can a crisis last while remaining a crisis rather than business as usual? Surely there is something paradoxical in claims that the crisis has lasted for decades, or even that the system has been 'in a perpetual state of crisis since the Gladstone Committee report of 1895' (Fitzgerald and Sim, 1982: 3).

If to be in crisis means that the whole system is on the brink of total collapse or explosion, then we probably do not have a crisis. (Although it should not be forgotten that when systems do collapse or explode – like the communist system in Eastern Europe in the late 1980s and early 1990s, or the system of order within Strangeways Prison in April 1990 – they can do so very suddenly.) But it can be claimed validly that there is a crisis in at least two senses, identified by Morris (1989: 125). First, we have 'a state of affairs that is so acute as to constitute a danger' – and, we would add, a moral challenge of a scale which makes it one of the most pressing social issues of the day. Second, we may be at a *critical juncture*, much as a seriously ill person may reach a 'turning point at which the patient either begins to improve or sinks into a fatal decline'. In other words, either the present situation can be used as an opportunity to reform the system into something more rational and humane, or it will deteriorate into something much worse even than the present. In this book we will be using the 'C-word' in these senses to refer to the present penal situation in England and Wales, albeit with slight embarrassment and the worry that it has been used so often and for so long that there is a danger it may be losing its dramatic impact.

Whether or not we choose to use the word 'crisis', what are the causes of the state the penal system is in, and how do its different problems relate to each other?

## THE ORTHODOX ACCOUNT OF THE CRISIS

The *orthodox account* of the penal crisis is probably still the kind of analysis most often encountered in the mass media. At least until Lord Justice Woolf's[1] 1991 report into the Strangeways riot (Woolf and Tumim, 1991) versions of it were also regularly found in official reports purporting to explain phenomena such as prison disturbances. It is well summarized by the following extract from a newspaper article of 1977 (Humphry and May, 1977):

> Explosive problems remain in many of Britain's prisons – a higher number of lifers . . . who have nothing left to lose; overcrowding which forces men to sleep three to a cell and understaffing which weakens security. Prisons, too, are forced to handle men with profound psychiatric problems in conditions which are totally unsuitable.

This passage gives us almost all the components of the 'orthodox account' of the penal crisis. The crisis is seen as being located very specifically within the *prison* system – it is not seen as a crisis of the whole *penal* system, or of the criminal justice system, let alone as a crisis of society as a whole. The immediate cause of the crisis is seen as the combination of different types of difficult prisoners – what has been called the 'toxic mix' of prisoners (Home Office, 1984a: para. 124) – in physically poor and insecure conditions which gives rise to an 'explosion'.

The orthodox account points to the following factors as implicated in the crisis:

1   The high prison population (or 'numbers crisis').
2   Overcrowding.
3   Bad conditions within prison (for both inmates and prison officers).
4   Understaffing.
5   Unrest among prison staff.
6   Poor security.
7   The 'toxic mix' of long term and life sentence prisoners and mentally disturbed inmates.
8   Riots and other breakdowns of control over prisoners.

These factors are seen as linked, with number 8 – riots and disorder – being the end product which shows there is a crisis. Figure 1.1 shows how the different factors interact according to the orthodox account. The high prison population is held responsible for overcrowding and understaffing in prisons, both of which exacerbate the bad physical conditions within prison. The combination of poor conditions and inadequate staffing have an adverse effect on staff morale, causing unrest which (through industrial action, for example) serves to worsen conditions still further. The four factors of bad conditions, overcrowding, understaffing and staff unrest are blamed for poor security. Finally, the combination of the 'toxic mix' of prisoners with these deteriorating conditions within which they are contained is thought to trigger off the periodic riots and disturbances to which the prison system is increasingly prone.

We do not believe that the orthodox account provides a satisfactory explanation of the crisis, for reasons we shall be giving shortly. But most of the factors this account points to are real and important, as we shall now detail.

### The high prison population (the 'numbers crisis')

It is widely agreed – although perhaps not by either the current Labour government or its Conservative predecessor – that the number of prisoners in England and Wales is alarmingly high. It is also rapidly rising. Table 1.1 shows how (despite occasional dips, such as the one which followed the implementation of the Criminal Justice Act 1991 in 1992) the prison population has increased to around 65,000 from under 40,000 since 1975, a year in which prison numbers were already causing serious concern. On an average day in 1998 there were 65,298 people in prison in England and Wales; numbers in prison reached their highest ever peak in July 1998 when 66,500 people were in prison.[2]

There was a slight reduction in the prison population in 1999, thanks to the introduction of 'home detention curfew' (see Chapter 8) in January 1999. This scheme is likely to effect an ongoing reduction in the population of around

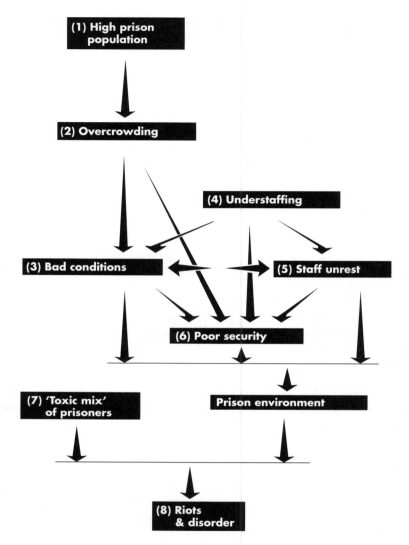

FIGURE 1.1   *The orthodox account of the penal crisis*

2,000 prisoners if it remains in its present form, but only to create a small one-year dip in the figures. On the other hand, the introduction of 'three strikes and you're out' semi-mandatory prison sentences for domestic burglars (see Chapter 4) could add 5,000 to the prison population in the longer term (White and Cullen, 2000; see Chapter 4). So the figures are set to continue to regularly break all-time records, as they have since 1995. Official Home Office projections estimate that by 2007 the prison population could be as high as 80,000 if current trends continue (White and Cullen, 2000).

There are several factors involved in this increase in prison numbers in recent years. In Chapter 4 we discuss the relationship between some of these factors, and conclude that the most crucial is the pattern of decisions by the

TABLE1.1    *The Prison Population[3] of England And Wales, 1975–1999*

| 1975 | 39,820 |
|------|--------|
| 1980 | 43,109 |
| 1981 | 43,346 |
| 1982 | 43,754 |
| 1983 | 43,773 |
| 1984 | 43,349 |
| 1985 | 46,278 |
| 1986 | 46,889 |
| 1987 | 48,963 |
| 1988 | 49,949 |
| 1989 | 48,610 |
| 1990 | 45,636 |
| 1991 | 45,897 |
| 1992 | 45,817 |
| 1993 | 44,565 |
| 1994 | 48,794 |
| 1995 | 51,047 |
| 1996 | 55,281 |
| 1997 | 61,114 |
| 1998 | 65,298 |
| 1999 | 64,770 |

*Sources:* Home Office 1986; 1995b; 1996a, 1996c; White and Woodbridge, 1998; White, 1999; Cullen and Minchin, 2000a

courts. The most important of these is the *sentencing decision* – whether convicted offenders should be sent to custody and, if so, for how long – which we call 'the crux of the crisis'. Also important, however, are decisions about which courts defendants should be tried in and whether they should be remanded in custody in the meantime.

These court decisions can in their turn be greatly influenced by government policies, actions and rhetoric. For a long time both Conservative and Labour governments generally attempted to keep the size of the prison population under control by a mixture of legislation, executive action and exhortations to courts. However, from 1993 onwards John Major's Conservative administration reversed this stand and pursued policies whose explicit aim was to increase the numbers of people in prison. Most notable was Home Secretary Michael Howard's declaration at the Conservative Party conference in October 1993 that 'prison works' and that he did not flinch from measures which would increase the prison population.

The 'New Labour' administration of Tony Blair which took power in 1997 may have dropped the slogan 'prison works',[4] but has shown little interest in trying to encourage reductions in sentences to custody. Indeed, Home Secretary Jack Straw said that he wanted to see tougher sentences for robbery (*Daily Telegraph*, 26 June 2000) and for petty persistent offenders (*The Guardian*, 1 February 2001) and criticized magistrates for freeing too many defendants on bail before their trials. Not surprisingly, therefore, the rise in the prison population has shown little sign of abating under New Labour.

For many years now England and Wales has consistently had one of the highest proportionate prison populations in Western Europe. Table 1.2 shows

TABLE 1.2    *Prison Populations in Western Europe, 1999*

| Country | Total prison population | No. of prisoners per 100,000 pop. |
| --- | --- | --- |
| Portugal | 13,086 | 130 |
| ENGLAND AND WALES | 65,993 | 125 |
| UNITED KINGDOM | 73,195 | 125 |
| Scotland | 6,010 | 120 |
| Spain | 44,197 | 110 |
| Turkey | 64,907 | 100 |
| Germany | 79,666 | 95 |
| Luxembourg | 392 | 90 |
| France | 53,948 | 90 |
| Italy | 51,427 | 90 |
| The Netherlands | 14,057 | 90 |
| Austria | 6,877 | 85 |
| Switzerland | 5,950 | 85 |
| Belgium | 8,135 | 80 |
| Ireland | 2,929 | 80 |
| Northern Ireland | 1,192 | 70 |
| Greece | 7,525 | 70 |
| Denmark | 3,496 | 65 |
| Sweden | 5,270 | 60 |
| Norway | 2,695 | 60 |
| Finland | 2,389 | 45 |
| Cyprus | 247 | 40 |
| Iceland | 103 | 35 |

*Source*: Walmsley (2000)

that in 1999 (in proportion to the total number of people in the country as a whole) the English prison population was second only to Portugal, with Scotland not far behind. It is true that proportionate prison populations are even higher in some countries outside Western Europe: indeed, the United States and Russia both have over five times as many prisoners relative to their population as do England and Wales.[5] Nevertheless, within the Western European frame of reference Britain does seem to be strikingly punitive, having maintained a high position in the prison population league table for many years now. This relatively high prison population does not seem to be because the UK has more crime, or more serious crime, than comparable countries;[6] rather it is because more offenders are sent to custody, and for longer periods, in the UK than elsewhere in Western Europe (see, for example, Barclay and Tavares, 2000; NACRO, 1998b; Pease, 1992).

There should be little doubt, then, that the present and future size of the prison population is a major problem. If drastic steps are not taken to reduce prison numbers – and there is currently little sign of such steps being seriously considered by the government – they seem set to grow even more alarmingly in the coming years.

## Overcrowding

On 31 May 2000 the prison population was 64,837, whereas English prisons officially had room for a total of 63,420 inmates,[7] making the system as a whole overcrowded by a factor of 2 per cent. This may not sound too drastic, but these overall figures do not do justice to the overcrowding problem. For prisoners are not spread evenly throughout the system. The top-security 'dispersal prisons' (see Chapter 6) are frequently not filled to capacity, while overcrowding is concentrated in local prisons (which predominantly house remand prisoners and those on short-term sentences). On 31 January 1999, for example, male local prisons were on average overcrowded by 20 per cent; while in some cases the situation was even worse, with one prison even having 90 per cent overcrowding (Penal Affairs Consortium, 1999).[8] As a result, in 1998–9 12,024 prisoners were sleeping two to a cell designed for a single inmate (White, 1999), an increase of 4 per cent over the previous year and up from 8,700 in March 1995 (a rise of 38 per cent). These are not – yet – the worst ever figures for overcrowding in English prisons, for the prison building programme which commenced in 1982 (see Chapter 6) has added greatly to the capacity of the prison system; but the situation has been worsening. It is likely to deteriorate further in the immediate future if the current expansion in the prison population continues.

### Bad conditions

Overcrowding, of course, contributes to bad physical conditions in prisons. (It has also led in recent years – although not at the moment of writing – to hundreds of remand prisoners being kept in even more inadequate conditions in police cells.) But there are other causes of bad conditions as well as overcrowding: many prisons are old and decaying, and newer prisons have often turned out to be so badly designed that they are not a noticeable improvement.

The particular issue of sanitary facilities in prison (or the lack of them) is something of a cliché. The fact that many prisoners routinely had to spend long periods in their cells without access to a toilet, having to use chamber pots and queue up to 'slop out', was a potent symbol of the squalor of British prisons. Perhaps it was this symbolic importance which led the then Home Secretary Kenneth Baker, when responding to the Woolf Report in February 1991, to announce a programme to provide all prisoners with access to toilet facilities. This project was officially completed in April 1996, although it seems clear that some prisoners still do not have adequate 24 hour per day access to toilets.[9]

In any event, the problem of prison conditions is hardly limited to slopping out. As we shall see in Chapter 6, other elements of prison life are equally important, such as the amount of time prisoners are kept cooped up in cells and the lack of opportunities for activities of all kinds. In these respects, there has been a general and continuing decline in prison conditions over a long period of time (King and McDermott, 1989).

The poor conditions in prisons affect staff as well as inmates, contributing to low staff morale and unrest. At times they have become an overt issue in industrial disputes; for example, prison officers at Wandsworth once threatened industrial action partly over the issue of the prison's infestation by rats and cockroaches and the methods used to combat it (*The Guardian*, 24 January 1987).

## Understaffing

There are essentially two views about understaffing in prisons. One view is that it is the result of government parsimony in paying for prison staff and their wages; the other is that any staff shortages are due to restrictive practices deployed by the Prison Officers' Association (POA).

Several developments have affected the staffing and resourcing of prisons in recent years. In 1985 a new system of individual budgets for each prison – in effect cash limits on what can be spent on staff in each prison – was introduced. 1987 saw a new wage structure known as 'Fresh Start', designed to limit staff overtime. Prison officers claimed that this led to understaffing because not enough new prison officers were recruited. Whatever the rights and wrongs of Fresh Start, it is worth noting that research on its effects found twice as many examples of deterioration in prison regimes as of enhancement (McDermott and King, 1989). There followed a round of Treasury-inspired cuts in Prison Service running costs announced in 1995 (to the tune of 13.3 per cent over a three-year period). The Prison Service budget has since been substantially increased by the New Labour government – although, of course, any extra funding has to go around a fast-rising number of prisoners. Increasingly state-run prisons have had to justify their spending levels in comparison with privately-run prisons, which limit their running costs by economizing on staff (see Chapter 7). The pressure is on prisons to keep staff numbers to a minimum.

If prisons are understaffed (or if those running the prison believe they are understaffed) this affects conditions. Prisoners may be left locked in their cells for longer, because there are not the staff to supervise out-of-cell activities or to escort them from place to place. Visits to prisoners may be restricted or cancelled. And prison staff may become restless.

## Staff unrest

For many years the relationship between the prison staff and the Home Office has been – at its very calmest – one of simmering discontent. Local and national industrial action by prison officers has been a recurrent event. In 1978 widespread disruptive action led to the setting up of the May Inquiry (May, 1979). But May's report failed to satisfy the POA. 1986 saw the most alarming disruption yet: protest action including a national overtime ban by prison officers over the issue of staffing levels sparked off the worst sequence of riots by inmates that had occurred up to that date. Industrial action over staffing arrangements continued, most notably at Wandsworth Prison in 1989, when police officers were drafted in to replace prison officers. More recently, severe legal restrictions have been placed on the ability of prison officers to undertake industrial action,[10] although this has not put an end to protest actions of varying degrees of legality and illegality. In any case, legal limitations on action cannot prevent staff *unrest*, which is as bad as it has ever been (see Chapter 6) and shows every sign of having become a permanent feature of the British penal scene. Indeed, it has been exacerbated by developments which prison staff (including governor grades) see as threatening, such as budget cuts and privatization of prisons (see Chapter 7).

## Security

Security lapses always seem to have the potential to create more public uproar than any other event surrounding the penal system. This was well exemplified by the ructions which followed the breakouts from two high-security 'dispersal' prisons, Whitemoor and Parkhurst, in 1994 and 1995. Two official reports (Woodcock, 1994 and Learmont, 1995) exposed 'a chapter of errors at every level' (Learmont, 1995: para. 2.257) which had facilitated these escapes, and the Parkhurst breakout led eventually to the dismissal of the Director General of the Prison Service and a furious political row in October 1995.

Yet despite the air of moral panic which surrounds such incidents, it remains the case that since the 1960s the English penal system has not had a bad record overall for 'security', in the sense of managing to keep prisoners inside prison. Escapes are currently neither common nor increasing: indeed, they have decreased in recent years (see Chapter 6). Breakouts from the high-security 'dispersal prisons' had been extremely rare prior to the Whitemoor escape, and no top-security 'Category A' prisoner has escaped since 1995.

The word 'security' is often used in a different sense, to refer to the degree of *control* exercised over prisoners. Particular concerns voiced in this regard are the use of illicit drugs and assaults by prisoners on prison staff and on other inmates. Prison staff often complain that understaffing (combined sometimes with other deficiencies in material resources) reduces 'security' in prisons, making assaults, breakdowns in control and even escapes more likely. It is often 'security considerations' – *fears* about security and control – which exacerbate the physical conditions of prisoners; for example, they may be kept locked in their cells almost all day because they are not trusted to be let out without a high degree of staff-intensive supervision. In the wake of the Woodcock and Learmont inquiries into the Whitemoor and Parkhurst escapes there was a noticeable and damaging shift of emphasis towards security (see Chapter 6). Such shifts have the natural tendency of diverting resources towards ensuring 'security' and changing staff practices in ways which adversely affect prison conditions and regimes still further.

## 'Toxic mix' of prisoners

We can agree with the orthodox account on many details concerning the component factors of the crisis. But the notion of a 'toxic mix' of prisoners is an issue on which we definitely part company. We do not deny that some characteristics of prison inmates may make them more or less likely to cause problems – if the prisons predominantly housed old people or nuns rather than young men with past records of anti-social behaviour they would doubtless experience fewer riots. But there are several difficulties with 'toxic mix theory', as we shall see.

It is often said that one important constituent of the so-called 'toxic mix' is *lifers* – prisoners serving sentences of life imprisonment. Such prisoners are often said to have 'nothing left to lose' (for example, Humphry and May, 1977). Yet (while there are more lifers than there used to be)[11] most of them have a great deal to lose. A 'life sentence' does not usually mean that the prisoner is kept in prison until he or she dies (although it may: about a dozen lifers die in prison each year), but lifers are only released at the discretion of the Parole Board (and in some cases the Home Secretary – see Chapter 8). Few things jeopardize a prisoner's parole chances more than misbehaviour within prison, and especially participation in riots and protests. (Similar logic applies to other prisoners who are serving long 'fixed-term' sentences but who are eligible for early release.) Yet ironically, recent policy developments have threatened to create a situation whereby some lifers and other long term prisoners do have relatively little to lose. For example, there are now some lifers whom the Home Secretary has decided should never receive parole, and who have been told as much. If provision for early release becomes less generous, it becomes all the more likely that prisoners serving long sentences will feel that they have rather less to lose.[12]

There is widespread agreement that there are many *mentally disturbed* people in prison who would be better off in hospital. Various surveys over the years have estimated that up to 90 per cent of prisoners could be categorized as having some form of mental disorder (Singleton et al., 1998; see also, for example, Gunn et al., 1991). The surveys which find the highest incidence of mental disorder among prisoners tend to include not only mental illness but also diagnoses over which some scepticism is arguably warranted, such as 'personality disorder' and alcohol and drug misuse. Even discounting such categories, however, it is clear that many prisoners suffer a dispro- portionate amount of mental distress and disturbance. And it is equally clear that the quality of psychiatric services for mentally ill prisoners is woefully inadequate (Reed and Lyne, 2000). As human beings we are suitably horrified by this state of affairs; but as penologists we wonder cynically how great a contribution this factor really makes to the penal crisis. Despite popular stereotypes, most mental illness makes the sufferers, if anything, more amenable to control rather than less, and mentally ill prisoners have not been prominent in organizing riots.

In any event, as we shall see shortly, this 'toxic mix' cannot always be implicated in causing riots for it is often simply not present in prisons which experience disorder.

One interesting feature of the Woolf Report into the Strangeways and other riots of 1990 (Woolf and Tumim, 1991) was its implicit rejection of the 'toxic mix' theory. Although some prison staff claimed to the Woolf inquiry that there had been a worsening 'mix' of prisoners in their prisons prior to the disorders, Woolf's report did not say that this was a cause of the riots. He also recommended that most prisons should be 'community prisons' catering for a wide variety of prisoners from their locality, a prescription which does not seem readily compatible with the notion that this sort of mixture is conducive to disorder.

### Riots and disorder

To the general public, one of the most noticeable symptoms of the penal crisis – along with the occasional spectacular escape – is the prison riot. Apart from a riot at Parkhurst in 1969, disturbances were comparatively infrequent in British prisons until the year of 1972, which saw a major wave of rooftop demonstrations in many prisons. Subsequently – just to select some of the outstanding incidents – there were major riots at Hull in 1976, Gartree in 1978 and Albany in 1983. Since the mid-1980s there have been more prison riots in Britain than in any other European country. In 1986 a national overtime ban by prison officers sparked off riots in eighteen prisons. April 1990 saw the worst ever series of prison riots, including the 25-day riot and siege at Strangeways Prison, Manchester. More riots have occurred in the years since Strangeways, for example at Full Sutton in January 1997 and April 1998, and at Portland Young Offender Institution in May 2000. The overall incidence of disturbances within the prison system has risen substantially in recent years. And, like staff unrest, inmate disorder shows no sign of disappearing from the scene.

### Criticisms of the orthodox account

Generally speaking, then, most of the factors emphasized by the orthodox account are genuine enough (with the exception, in our opinion, of the 'toxic mix' idea). Where we believe the orthodox account to be seriously misleading is in the *causal relationships* it postulates between the different factors, and especially its explanation of prison riots.

One problem with the orthodox account is that it simply does not square with the facts about prison riots – and in particular, about where in the prison system they occur. If riots are caused by overcrowding, understaffing, bad physical conditions and poor security, one would expect them to occur exclusively in the local prisons and remand centres which are the most overcrowded and understaffed, where conditions are worse and security less tight than in many longer-stay establishments. Yet prior to the 1986 riots, major disorder was almost entirely confined to 'dispersal prisons' – prisons which house prisoners on long sentences, which are not overcrowded or under-staffed, where conditions are relatively good, and where security is at a maximum. After 1986 the pattern was largely reversed, with most major disorders occurring in local prisons (such as Strangeways), remand centres and lower-security establishments. But these riots are not satisfactorily explained by the orthodox account either, for such institutions lack the particular 'toxic mix' of prisoners which is supposed to be an important causative factor in inmate disorder. In a nutshell, the worst conditions and the supposedly most toxic mixes simply do not coexist in the same prisons. Then again, the prisons which experienced riots in 1986, 1990 and subsequently were not all overcrowded (for example Northeye in 1986 and Dartmoor in 1990) or the worst in terms of physical conditions (Wymott and Wayland in 1986).

One could try to modify the orthodox account to accommodate these factual discrepancies. Indeed, such a modified version appears in Sir James Hennessy's (1987) official report into the 1986 disturbances (which, as we shall see, contrasts interestingly with Lord Justice Woolf's report into the 1990 riots). Hennessy partly blamed the mix of offenders in the prisons affected by riots in 1986; but in doing so, he stood the traditional 'toxic mix' theory on its head by claiming that prison order was rendered unstable by young inmates serving *short* sentences, rather than long term prisoners with 'nothing left to lose'. But such an explanation could not of course account for the riots in dispersal prisons in earlier years (or indeed for more recent disturbances in dispersal prisons such as Full Sutton).

The very phrase 'toxic mix', with its pseudo-scientific ring, indicates a more fundamental deficiency in the orthodox account. As we have portrayed it in Figure 1.1, the whole process of the crisis on this account seems very mechanistic (or *'positivistic'*, a term explained in Chapter 2). One thing leads automatically to another: prisoners and prison staff both seem to react to conditions in a mindless manner. The prisoners in particular seem to behave like molecules in a test tube: place such a combination in such a physical environment, agitate, apply heat, and an explosion is the automatic result.[13] We do not believe that people are like that. Rioting is not mindless behaviour; it is meaningful human action. Lord Scarman said in his famous report on inner city riots that 'public disorder usually arises *out of a sense of injustice'* (Scarman, 1986: xiii; our italics), and as the Woolf Report rightly recognized, this is as true in prisons as it is in the inner city. And this crucial sense of injustice is not a mindless automatic reaction, but an active interpretation of a situation. So for an adequate description and explanation of the penal crisis, we need to explore why there is this perception of injustice, and even to ask whether this perception is correct. In our opinion this is the main flaw in the orthodox account, and one we hope to go some way towards rectifying.

## IMPROVING ON THE ORTHODOX ACCOUNT

We think a more adequate account of the penal crisis can be developed by taking on board and integrating into our explanation the insights of a variety of penal commentators. In what follows we draw upon the Woolf Report (Woolf and Tumim, 1991); the radical account furnished by Mike Fitzgerald and Joe Sim in their book *British Prisons* (1982); the contributions of Tony Bottoms (1980a, 1983, 1995a; Bottoms and Stevenson, 1992); and Stuart Hall's work on the politics of law and order (1979, 1980; Hall et al., 1978). To begin with, we shall highlight certain aspects of the crisis which the orthodox account either ignores or fails to address adequately.

### The crisis of penological resources

It is implicit in the orthodox account that there is a problem of limited resources such as space within prisons and numbers of prison officers. But the problem is wider and deeper than that. Tony Bottoms (1980a) has identified a general *crisis of penological resources*, affecting not only prisons (to which the orthodox account is limited) but extending to the entire penal system, including those agencies (such as the probation service) which provide and run non-custodial penalties and what might be called 'post-custodial' provision such as parole supervision. 'This crisis takes two forms: the size of the prison population' (combined with the lack of prison places and the running expenses of locking up and catering for such a large number of prisoners) 'and the demands on the probation and after-care service' (Bottoms, 1980a: 5). This twofold crisis of resources has generated an imperative to limit the numbers in prison and to deal with more offenders outside the prison 'in the community', but without overloading the probation service. Another aspect of this crisis is the lack of resources to keep the prison officers sufficiently materially satisfied to defuse industrial relations problems within prisons, and to provide prison inmates with constructive and fulfilling ways of occupying their time.

This *material* aspect of the crisis – the ever-present issue of scarce material resources such as buildings, staff, equipment and money – is one which always needs to be borne in mind when seeking to understand the state of the penal system. As we shall see, however, this is only one side of the picture.

### The crisis of visibility

Perhaps the crisis of visibility (so named by Fitzgerald and Sim, 1982: 6–11) does not deserve its own heading, but it is an interesting example of an aspect of the crisis which the orthodox account fails to encompass. It concerns the secrecy that surrounds prisons and what goes on inside them. Developments in recent years have meant that 'slowly, but surely, the secrecy behind the prison walls is being breached, as alternative sources of information about the prisons are more securely established' (Fitzgerald and Sim, 1982: 11). A good example of such a breach of secrecy followed an incident in 1979, when the until-then-secret 'MUFTI' team of specially trained prison officers in riot gear (see Chapter 6) broke up a protest demonstration by prisoners in D Wing of Wormwood Scrubs. The Home Office originally announced that no prisoners had been injured, but it eventually had to admit that 54 had been, and that there had been criminal assaults on prisoners by staff. The wall of secrecy and official disinformation had been effectively breached by prisoners smuggling information to their outside contacts, together with dissident members of the system including two official prison visitors (Stern, 1993: 70–2). Other cracks in the wall of secrecy have appeared in recent years, as we shall see in Chapter 6.

Fitzgerald and Sim seem to see the *existence* of secrecy as a 'crisis' in itself. Morally speaking, we have no doubt that it is; but again reverting to our cynical sociological standpoint, we suspect that on the contrary it is often the *dispelling* of secrecy that causes problems for the system and exacerbates the crisis. For if we assume that there is much in prisons that will not bear being exposed (and if not, why keep it secret?) then opening up the prison is likely to decrease the legitimacy of the system. If 'knowledge is power'[14] then there is a danger that the system will lose much of its power if it loses control of information about itself. (It may also increase staff unrest by leading prison officers to feel that their authority is further threatened.) On the other hand, if greater visibility should lead to prisoners being better treated (for fear of abuse being exposed) then visibility rather than secrecy could help to defuse the crisis. It is also noticeable that many incidents of prison disorder – especially the popular form of demonstration on the prison rooftop – are clearly motivated by the very desire to make prisoners' grievances and allegations *visible* in a way that would never normally happen. So, while we have no doubt that prison secrecy should be dispelled, it seems as if (paradoxically) both secrecy *and* openness can contribute to the crisis – as long as there are secrets to hide.

The problem with secrecy is that the secret information is typically of a discreditable nature which, if it gets out, can damage '*legitimacy*'. This means that the 'crisis of visibility' is only a part of what has justly been termed 'the final and most crucial aspect of the crisis in British prisons' (Fitzgerald and Sim, 1982: 23), to which we now turn.

### *The crisis of legitimacy*[15]

Whereas the crisis of penological resources is a *material* crisis, the crisis of legitimacy is *ideological* in nature: it exists in the minds of human beings. Sociologists use the term 'legitimacy' to mean *power which is perceived as morally justified*. The penal system wields power over its subjects, but its moral right to do so has been coming under strong attack. Fitzgerald and Sim, who first identified the 'crisis of legitimacy', related it to 'calls for the abolition of imprisonment' and to 'a more fundamental political crisis which transcends the prison walls' (1982: 23–4). There may have been an element of revolutionary wishful thinking here: if all the system had to worry about was the minority of people who seriously call for the abolition of prisons or the prospect of the imminent overthrow of capitalism there would not be much of a crisis.[16] Nevertheless, even among non-abolitionists (and across most of the political spectrum) there has been grave disquiet about the state of prisons. Even conservative commentators can regard the conditions within some prisons as morally intolerable to a civilized community (some examples are given by Stern, 1993: 2, 4). The squalor produced by prison overcrowding is perhaps the issue which most scandalizes the public conscience, but there are others. These include the rising incidence of suicides among prisoners (see Chapter 6); the state of the prison health service (Sim, 1990); the presence in prisons (as noted previously) of large numbers of people with mental health problems; and the over-representation within prisons of members of ethnic minorities (see Chapter 10).

Tony Bottoms (1980a) also sees the penal system as suffering from a crisis of legitimacy (though he does not use the term), as well as from the crisis of resources discussed earlier. He identifies as an important cause of the crisis of legitimacy *the collapse of the rehabilitative ideal*. Prior to the 1970s, the penal system could plausibly legitimate itself by claiming as its *raison d'être* the rehabilitation of offenders: the provision of training and treatment which would cure them of their criminality, benefiting both them and society as a whole. As we shall see in Chapter 2, this claim subsequently became less plausible and less acceptable, with a general belief arising that 'nothing works' in the treatment of offenders. This undermines the legitimacy of the penal system: not only of the prisons (whose claim to be providing effective rehabilitation was always shaky in many eyes) but equally for other components of the penal system, notably the probation service which has for some years now been demoralized and uncertain about what its proper rationale and direction should be. The system has found itself in dire need of new ways of legitimating itself, and this need has given rise to a variety of responses. We discuss these further in the following section; but they have included, most potently, the rise of what we shall be calling 'law and order ideology'.

It is not only the system's legitimacy with outside observers and the general public which is important. The system will also suffer severe difficulties if it lacks legitimacy with its own employees, including prison staff and probation officers. Perhaps most important of all is *the legitimacy of the system with those who are its subjects* – in our opinion, the crucial factor in the genesis of prison riots and of many of the system's other problems. After all, a penal system can only run with the acquiescence of offenders. No prison could run for long if not for the fact that most prisoners most of the time are prepared simply to cooperate with the staff and 'do their bird'. This is not to say that they normally have no sense of injustice. They may bear grievances about the fact that they are locked up in prison, perhaps for longer than they feel they deserve or for longer than other offenders whom they regard as comparable. (We shall see in Chapters 2, 4 and 10 that they may well have good grounds for this belief.) They may have other grievances concerning the prison regime, early release, the behaviour of prison staff and the prison disciplinary system (see Chapters 6 and 8). Even so, prisoners do not normally riot unless this sense of injustice has been somehow inflamed beyond its normal simmering state.

Prisoners' sense of injustice was highlighted by the Woolf Report (Woolf and Tumim, 1991) on the prison riots of April 1990, which has become established as a historic and classically liberal account of what is wrong with English prisons, what causes prison riots and what should be done to prevent them. Woolf's central finding was that:

> there are three requirements which must be met if the prison system is to be stable: they are *security, control and justice* . . . 'security' refers to the obligations of the Prison Service to prevent prisoners escaping. 'Control' deals with the obligation of the Prison Service to prevent prisoners being disruptive. 'Justice' refers to the obligation of the Prison Service to treat prisoners with humanity and fairness, and to prepare them for their return to the community in a way which makes it less likely that they will re-offend. (paras 9.19–9.20; our italics)

'Security' and 'control' are hardly novel concepts, figuring significantly in both the orthodox account and in Fitzgerald and Sim's 'crisis of containment'. Woolf also acknowledged as relevant, factors such as overcrowding and insanitary physical conditions, but did not regard these as crucial. Their significance for Woolf was in contributing to *prisoners' sense of injustice*.

Woolf did not use the word 'legitimacy', but it is clearly the prison's lack of *legitimacy with inmates* which he saw as of central importance. He showed a keen awareness that, on the one hand, legitimacy is in the mind; but on the other hand what is in people's minds usually depends on the external reality: 'It is not possible for the Inquiry to form any judgment on whether the specific grievances of these prisoners were or were not well-founded. What is clear is that the Prison Service had failed to *persuade* these prisoners that it was treating them fairly' (para. 9.25). Despite not committing himself about specific grievances, Woolf believed that genuine injustice contributes to a lack of legitimacy which in turn makes disorder more likely. A substantial number of prisoners participated in the riots 'at least in part, because of the conditions in which they were held and the way in which they were treated. If a proper level of justice is provided in prisons, then it is less likely that prisoners will behave in this way. Justice, therefore, contributes to the maintenance of security and control' (para. 1.151). Woolf's humanistic attention to the subjective interpretation by prisoners of their situation marks a distinct departure from the orthodox account.

While talking about the need to keep security, control and justice in 'balance', Woolf appeared to emphasize the importance of justice, and the imbalance he was most concerned about was the prospect of security and control measures exacerbating prisoners' sense of injustice. Although Woolf stated that 'there is no single cause of riots' (para. 9.23) it may not be too great a distortion to say that he saw the lack of legitimacy of the prison for its inmates as the key factor in explaining the disorders. For this reason he stressed in his recommendations not only measures to improve prison conditions but also reforms of grievance and disciplinary procedures (see Chapter 6) which might both improve the objective standard of justice within prisons and be seen as fairer by prisoners.

The penal system's legitimacy problems are – of course – by no means all related to feelings that the system is excessively harsh and inhumane. Rather more common among the general public is the perception (regularly encouraged by tabloid newspapers and many politicians) that the penal system is on the contrary over-lenient, lax and insecure. It is bound to be difficult for the system to achieve legitimacy with all its different audiences – public, press, politicians, penal practitioners and penal subjects – under these circumstances.

## RESPONSES TO THE CRISIS

How have governments responded to the penal crisis? And not only governments, but other actors in the penal arena, such as practitioners, commentators, Home Office civil servants and Opposition politicians? Their responses can be roughly allocated into two categories: *ideological* (or philosophical) responses to the crisis of legitimacy in particular; and *practical* responses to the management problems caused by the material crisis of resources.

On the *ideological* side, Tony Bottoms (1980a) listed a number of varying responses to the collapse of the rehabilitative ideal and the consequent dire need for the penal system to find new ways of legitimating itself. These responses included the revival of the philosophy of 'just deserts' (see Chapter 2) between the 1970s and 1990s. But the most prominent ideological response, amounting to a massive shift in penal ideology, has been the rise and rise of what we call '*law and order ideology*' – the appeal to a harsh, '*Strategy A*' programme of 'toughness' which is represented as being an effective remedy for crime. (See the Introduction for an explanation of 'Strategies A, B and C'.) In the sense in which we use the phrase, 'law and order ideology' is more than just the unexceptionable belief that society should be governed by law, and that crime should be effectively controlled. It is a complex if naive set of attitudes, including the beliefs that human beings have free will, that they must be strictly disciplined by restrictive rules, and that they should be harshly punished if they break the rules or fail to respect authority, and of course it naturally leads its adherents to favour a 'Strategy A' approach to criminal justice policy. (The phrase 'populist punitiveness', coined by Bottoms (1995a), means much the same thing.)

The ideology of law and order has been notably and provocatively analysed by the Marxist theorist Stuart Hall (1979, 1980; Hall et al., 1978). Hall sees law and order ideology as an important component of what he calls 'authoritarian populism', which in turn constituted an important strand in the political phenomenon of 'Thatcherism'. However, not only did the 'drift into a law and order society' in Britain[17] begin well before the accession to power of the Conservative Party under Mrs Thatcher in 1979 – although that was something of a defining moment – but it accelerated significantly under her Conservative successor John Major, especially after he appointed Michael Howard as Home Secretary in 1993 (see Chapter 11). For Hall, law and order ideology forms part of a pro-ruling-class response to a wider crisis of social order whose roots lie partly in the problems of the British economy and of Britain's declining role in the world.

This is far from a full explanation, however. It does not account for the parallel developments in other countries, or for the reinvigoration of law and order ideology since early 1993, at a time when Britain's role in the world may have continued to decline but her economy was not getting any worse. Other long-term social and political developments have led to a greater degree of 'populism' in politics, in Britain and elsewhere, especially in respect of criminal justice policy. One likely explanation for this is that the decline of traditional communities has led to both an increase in crime and a general feeling of insecurity in the psyche of the modern individual which feeds into a fear of crime and a tendency to favour punitive fixes for the perceived threat it poses. 'In such a context, a politician seeking popularity can reasonably easily tap into the electorate's insecurities by promising tough action on "villains"' (Bottoms, 1995a: 47). Further, modern politicians increasingly attune their policies according to the results of opinion polls and focus groups, which seek to identify policies which are (often very superficially) attractive to voters. It is largely along these lines – essentially, by reference to the calculations of politicians seeking to retain or gain power in the modern social context – that would explain, for example, the 'law and order counter-reformation' under John Major from 1993 to 1997 and the persistence of a high dose of 'toughness' in criminal justice policy under Labour since 1997. As Hall (1979: 15) says, law and order ideology is not an automatic 'reflection of the crisis: it is itself a *response* to the crisis'; in other words it is created by human beings operating in their own real environments; which for politicians is the world of politics.

This does not necessarily mean that pursuing 'Strategy A' will be a genuine recipe for political success; let alone that it will solve the problems of crime and punishment. The fate of John Major's government – defeated by a New Labour landslide in the General Election of 1997 – suggests that 'playing the law and order card' is by no means a sure ticket to electoral success. For one thing, although politicians currently tend to see law and order ideology as ruling public perceptions about criminal justice, and consequently calculate that it is to their own advantage to be perceived as 'tough', research suggests that the public may be nowhere near as 'law and order' minded as is generally supposed (see, for example, Mattinson and Mirrlees-Black, 2000). And even assuming they were, there would be no way of satisfying constant media calls for ever tougher criminal justice policies. So – on the ideological side of things – Strategy A will not solve the crisis of legitimacy. Moreover, pursuing ever harsher policies and indulging in 'law and order' rhetoric inevitably worsens the crisis of penological resources (on the material side of the equation). Recent history bears out what one would expect, that 'tough' policies and rhetoric have had the natural result of increasing the harshness of punishment – and consequently the size of the prison population and the scale of the penal crisis. Thus, Worrall and Pease (1986: 186), examining the steep rise in prison numbers in 1985, found that the most plausible explanation was that 'a general penal climate in Great Britain has permeated sentencing practice and made it harsher'. Other surges in the prison population, in 1991–2 and from early 1993 onwards, have also coincided with an increase in the intensity of 'law and order' rhetoric emanating from government ministers (Travis, 1993).

For a long time – certainly until the Major government's 'law and order counter-reformation' of 1993 – it could be said that the overall response of the British state to the penal crisis had been mostly directed towards the material crisis of resources rather than the ideological crisis of legitimacy. The response largely took the form of *penological pragmatism*: responding to developments and attempting to manage the resources crisis 'with no clear or coherent philosophical or other theoretical basis' (Bottoms, 1980a: 4). This pragmatism – which is still a vital strand in policy even in these more ideological times – has not been completely shapeless. One strong theme was identified and christened by Tony Bottoms in a highly prescient paper back in 1977: the strategy of *bifurcation* (Bottoms, 1977, 1980a). 'Bifurcation' refers to a dual-edged approach to the problem of offending: differentiating between 'ordinary' or 'run of the mill' offenders with whom less severe measures can be taken on the one hand, and on the other hand 'exceptional', 'very serious' or 'dangerous' offenders who can be made subject to much tougher measures. In this way 'a bifurcated policy allows governments to get tough and soft simultaneously' (Pitts, 1988: 29).

This 'twin-track strategy', as government ministers took to calling it in the early 1990s, was a growing trend in the English penal system for a considerable time, and was well exemplified in the Criminal Justice Act of 1991. On the one hand, the Act tried to encourage judges and magistrates to sentence more petty offenders to punishments in the community rather than to custody; but on the other hand, the Act allowed people convicted of violent or sexual offences to receive harsher sentences than hitherto. From the point of view of the resources crisis, this looks like a rational response: because there are so many more 'run of the mill' than 'serious' offenders, a bifurcated policy should save many more resources than it costs. In terms of legitimacy with the general public such a strategy could also be effective, since the public can be reassured that the really 'serious' offenders about whom they are most concerned will be kept locked up for long periods. Bifurcation can thus be seen as a pragmatic response to the combined crises of legitimacy and resources, with constraints imposed by law and order ideology. But in terms of *legitimacy with prisoners* – and in terms of preventing prison riots – bifurcation runs the risk of proving seriously counterproductive since it seems so unfair to those who are singled out as the 'very serious' cases in what they may see as an arbitrary manner.[18]

As the politics of punishment have grown harsher, the other limb of bifurcation – being less harsh to less serious offenders – has also come into conflict with law and order ideology. The Criminal Justice Act 1991 embodied what we have termed 'punitive bifurcation', a version in which even lesser offenders were to be treated with apparent 'toughness'. For although under that Act's policy of 'punishment in the community' more offenders were to be kept out of prisons they would be *punished* in the community; non-custodial penalties were to be more punitive and controlling than hitherto. But even this harsher version of bifurcation did not survive the law and order counter-reformation, and as Michael Howard declared that 'prison works' and that more rather than fewer offenders should go to prison, both pragmatism and bifurcation were sacrificed on the altar of ideology.

Perhaps a more robust strand of the pragmatic approach to penal policy – and certainly one which seems to keep growing in strength over the long term – is the element known as *managerialism*. This is what we call the '*Strategy B*' approach to criminal justice (Cavadino et al., 1999: 41–5). This approach is based on the notion that modern managerial techniques, as used in private sector businesses, can be successfully applied to the problems of crime and punishment, both to control crime and to deploy penal resources effectively and efficiently. Its influence can be observed in such diverse developments as the 'systems management' approach to dealing with young offenders (see Chapter 9), the pursuit of 'crime prevention' strategies, the conversion of the Prison Service into an executive agency (see Chapter 6), and the current Labour government's interest in seeking and applying evidence of 'what works' to control crime and prevent criminals from re-offending (see Chapters 2 and 11). Managerialism – like penological pragmatism more generally – is primarily directed at the material crisis of resources rather than the crisis of legitimacy. Pragmatism and bureaucracy may have their place in the practical running of things but are hardly likely in themselves to inspire minds sufficiently to defuse the legitimacy problems of the penal system.

Eagle-eyed readers may have noticed that we have mentioned both Strategy A-type (harsh and punitive) and Strategy B-type (managerial) responses to the crisis, and wondered: have there been no Strategy C-type (humanitarian, human rights-based) responses? To be fair, there have – although in recent years they have tended to take a poor third place to the other two strategies. But the Criminal Justice Act 1991 was largely based on the philosophy of 'just deserts' – a particular interpretation of what human rights require in the penal context – that offenders have a right to punishment in proportion to the seriousness of their offences. More recently there has been a revival of interest in measures that can be taken to reform and rehabilitate offenders, an aim which, while very different from giving offenders their just deserts, can also be filed under the general heading of humanitarianism. And, perhaps most significantly of all, the current Labour government has been showing much greater interest than any government hitherto in the idea of *restorative justice* (see Chapters 2, 5, 9 and 11), especially for young offenders. We will give more details about all these responses to the crisis throughout this book, and in Chapter 11 we return to provide a general overview and give our own opinions on what kind of responses we ourselves favour.

## A RADICAL PLURALIST ACCOUNT OF THE CRISIS

We said earlier that one problem with the orthodox account of the penal crisis is that it is *positivistic*: it sees the crisis in terms of mechanistic causes and effects and ignores the place of subjective human experience, perception, reflection and meaningful human action. It sees the crisis in overwhelmingly material terms – it recognizes the material crisis of resources but ignores the ideological crisis of legitimacy. In the previous two sections, by contrast, we have sought to emphasize that, although material circumstances are indeed of vital importance in explaining the penal crisis, they are only one side of the story. The other side, equally crucial, is the realm of ideas and ideology. Material and ideological factors interact with each other in a manner which could be described (in unfashionable Marxian terminology) as 'dialectical'.

In seeking to explain and understand the penal crisis, we wish to go further than just widening the orthodox account and adding the ideological dimension to it. We think the crisis can be analysed within the context of a general theoretical framework which is both intellectually respectable and useful, a theory we call *radical pluralism* (Cavadino, 1992). The nature of this theory will be explained in greater detail in Chapter 3, but it is a composite, compromise theory which is capable of incorporating those elements of the crisis which the orthodox theory rightly identifies while also drawing upon the insights of commentators such as Fitzgerald and Sim, Bottoms, Hall, and Lord Woolf.

The word 'pluralism' in the title of this theory means that we recognize that a large number of varied elements (including a variety of interest groups with greater or lesser power) are involved in the penal system and its crisis, and that these elements interact in a highly complex manner. We see a need to analyse the crisis in the context of the relationships between politics and economics, ideology and material conditions. We do not believe that this kind of analysis can be politically or morally neutral – and nor should it, for our understanding of the situation is that the penal system is morally indefensible and is in dire need of a programme of radical reform which would inevitably be highly political. On the other hand, the penal crisis is not simply a by-product of a 'crisis of capitalism', and it could be largely solved without a complete political and social revolution.

Our account is represented in diagrammatic form in Figure 1.2. The most striking feature of the diagram is its complexity; and yet Figure 1.2 is vastly oversimplified. An arrow in the diagram means that one factor affects (often this means 'exacerbates') another in the direction shown. Some of the connections pictured have already been discussed or mentioned. For example,

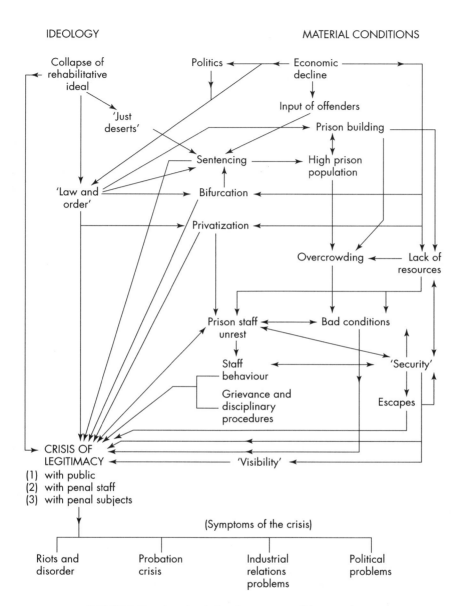

FIGURE 1.2    *A radical pluralist account of the penal crisis*

we have already indicated how economic decline, political developments and the collapse of the rehabilitative ideal helped to give rise to a resurgence of 'law and order ideology'. Similarly, bifurcation can be seen as having been produced by a combination of law and order ideology and the practical need to do something about the high prison population in a situation of scarce penal resources and general economic stringency. Other factors and relationships will be dealt with in later chapters.

A few more points are worth stressing about this kind of account. First, it is crucial to emphasize again that the crisis is composed of both material and ideological elements, and we have consequently tried to organize Figure 1.2 accordingly. These interact in a complex fashion: indeed certain features of the system, for example bifurcation, cannot be neatly placed on one side or the other of the (ultimately artificial) material/ideological divide since they are both ideologies and material practices at the same time.

The penal crisis is sometimes described as not one but several interlocking crises; indeed, we ourselves talk about, for example 'the crisis of resources' and 'the crisis of legitimacy' as if they were quite separate things. But ultimately it may be best to think of the penal system as one highly complex system and the penal crisis as a single entity – albeit with multiplex causation and a variety of symptoms. For there is a single unifying factor of the penal crisis, into which all the exacerbating elements flow and from which most of the symptoms of the crisis proceed (as Figure 1.2 shows). This key factor is the *crisis of legitimacy*, which is ignored by the orthodox account, but which we see as crucial. Riots, staff unrest, the malaise in the probation service and the political problems caused by the penal system are not the *direct* results of a high prison population or a lack of money or of decent prison buildings (although these do contribute to the crisis), but result from what people believe and how they feel – from the *moral reactions* of people within and outside the penal system to the material situation. (In sociological jargon, the effects of the objective material conditions are 'mediated' through the subjective perceptions of human actors which are structured by ideology.)

The crisis of legitimacy, it is worth repeating, is at least threefold. The penal system needs to legitimate itself with different groups of people: with the public (including politicians, commentators etc.), with penal staff (including prison staff and probation officers) and with penal subjects (prisoners, probationers and others who are subject to penal treatment). Failing to satisfy the sense of justice of these different audiences leads to the alarming visible 'symptoms' of the crisis: political problems, industrial relations problems, malaise among prison and probation staff, and disorder among prisoners.

In saying that the crisis of legitimacy is central, we are saying that the penal crisis is in essence a *moral* crisis. By this we do not just mean that many people *believe* that the system is unjust. As we hope to make clear (especially in Chapter 2, but also throughout the whole of this book), the penal system is indeed in our opinion the source of very substantial injustice, and the crisis is unlikely to be solved unless this injustice is mitigated.

Finally, we are at pains to stress that, despite all the arrows in Figure 1.2, we do not believe that human actions and beliefs are mechanistically determined. For example, bifurcation was a policy which was *occasioned* and *encouraged* by the conjunction of overcrowding and lack of resources in an ideological atmosphere of 'law and order' and legitimacy crisis, but it was not inevitable: policy-makers could (and probably should) have decided to do something else instead. Nor were Michael Howard's law and order policies between 1993 and 1997 inexorably brought about by economic decline and the collapse of the rehabilitative ideal; nor are New Labour's current policies determined by iron laws of history. All of which means that the crisis was not inevitable and is not insoluble. But it cannot be solved unless we change people's ideas about punishment.

## NOTES

1   The Woolf report was co-authored by Her Majesty's Chief Inspector of Prisons, Judge Tumim. It is for convenience, and not out of any wish to disregard Judge Tumim's contribution, that we refer to 'Woolf' in the singular throughout this book.
2   This is a 'seasonally adjusted' figure (see below, n. 3), from Cullen and Minchin (2000a).
3   These figures represent the *daily average* prison population – the figure for all prisons (including remand centres, young offender institutions and prisoners held in police cells) for an average day in the calendar year. The prison population fluctuates seasonally, and at times in the year the daily average population is significantly exceeded.
4   Home Secretary Jack Straw declared in October 1997 that he had 'no interest in chanting a simplistic mantra that prison works'. (Quoted in *Prison Report* No. 41, Winter 1997, p. 3.)
5   In 1999, 730 people were in prison out of every 100,000 people in the general population in Russia, while the United States imprisoned 680. The US figure has since risen even higher to over 700: in February 2000 its prison population topped 2 million for the first time. The United States, which contains 5 per cent of the planet's population, now accounts for 25 per cent of the world's prison inmates.
6   It is sometimes claimed that these figures can be explained by taking into account different countries' crime rates (for example, Barclay et al., 1995: 54; see also Pease, 1994). The most recent international survey of victims of crime (van Kesteren et al., 2001) does show the English rate for certain crimes in 2000 to be higher than those of several other countries. However, the relatively high English prison population dates back to times when similar surveys (for example Mayhew, 1994) found the level of crime in Britain to be similar to the European average for most offences.
7   This is the official figure for 'certified normal accommodation' (CNA) (see Chapter 6). The Prison Service also identifies a higher 'operational capacity', which was 71,170 on 31 May 2000 (Cullen and Minchin, 2000b). This higher figure gave rise in 2000 to claims by some journalists and politicians that there are 'spare places' in the prison system. However, this is only true in the sense that more prisoners *could* be crammed in at the cost of greater overcrowding.
8   Similarly, on 31 March 2000, Preston Prison was overcrowded by 75 per cent, Northallerton by 72 per cent and Leeds by 57 per cent (Hurd, 2000).
9   See, for example, *Prison Report* No. 44, Summer 1998: 21. Since 1996 prisoners have had to slop out at Dartmoor, Gloucester, Exeter and Bristol prisons, at Portland Young Offender Institution, and possibly at others as well.
10   Section 127 of the Criminal Justice and Public Order Act 1994 forbids anyone to induce prison officers to withhold their services or commit a 'breach of discipline'.
11   On 31 March 2000 there were 4,469 life sentence prisoners (*Prison Report* No. 51, June 2000, p. 9). This compares with figures of 140 in 1957, 730 in 1970, 1,535 in 1980, 2,795 in 1990 and 3,095 in 1993.
12   Another supposed element in the 'toxic mix' has been said to be Irish Republican prisoners (thus the toxic mix could be summarized as comprising 'the mad, the bad and the Irish'). Whatever the past effect on the volatility of prison populations of Irish Republicans – and we are sceptical – this has now been relegated to the past as the Northern Ireland peace process has led to the release or transfer to Ireland of all such prisoners in English prisons.

13 Hennessy (1987: para. 9.06) says almost exactly this in a passage which reads as not entirely metaphorical: 'It can perhaps be explained in terms of a chemical reaction. When a number of elements are brought together and a suitable catalyst is added, an explosion may result.'

14 This slight misquotation of Francis Bacon serves to paraphrase (also slightly inaccurately) Michel Foucault, whose ideas are discussed in Chapter 3.

15 The legitimacy of prisons has recently received attention from Sparks (1994) and Sparks and Bottoms (1995).

16 See however Sim (1992, 1994a), where he explains that 'abolition' does not entail a total end to the confinement of people however anti-social or dangerous they may be, but merely the abolition of the institution of prison as we know it. He also outlines the important part which 'abolitionists' have played in campaigns which have raised public awareness about the iniquities of the existing system.

17 There is a strong resemblance between the rise to prominence of 'law and order' during the 'Thatcherite' period in Britain and its continuance thereafter, and its similar rise under Ronald Reagan's presidency in the United States (1981–1988) and persistence since; other countries also provide partial parallels.

18 Indeed, bifurcatory changes in the parole system seem to have contributed to two riots in Scottish prisons in the 1980s: see Chapter 8.

# 2

# Justifying Punishment

In Chapter 1 we argued that the most crucial factor in the current malaise in the penal system is the 'crisis of legitimacy'. A social institution is 'legitimate' if it is *perceived as morally justified*; the problem with the penal system is that this perception is lacking and many people inside and outside the system believe that it is morally indefensible, or at least defective. We need to investigate whether such moral perceptions are accurate, if only to know what should be done about them. If they are inaccurate, then the obvious strategy would be to try to rectify the perceptions, by persuading people that the system is not unjust after all. But if the perceived injustices are real, then it is those injustices which should be rectified. This chapter accordingly deals with the moral philosophy of punishment and attempts to relate the philosophical issues to the reality of penal systems such as that of England and Wales today.

The basic moral question about punishment is an age-old one: 'What justifies the infliction of punishment[1] on people?' Punishing people certainly needs a justification, since it is almost always something which is harmful, painful or unpleasant to the recipient.[2] Imprisonment, for example, causes physical discomfort, psychological suffering, indignity and general unhappiness along with a variety of other disadvantages (such as impaired prospects for employment and social life). Deliberately inflicting suffering on people is at least *prima facie* immoral, and needs some special justification. It is true that in some cases the recipient does not find the punishment painful, or even welcomes it – for example, some offenders might find prison a refuge against the intolerable pressures of the outside world. And sometimes – for example when the punishment takes the form of a sanction whose main aim is to reform the offender – any suffering involved may not be deliberately caused. But even in these cases punishment is still something *imposed*: it is an intrusion on the liberty of the person punished, which also requires a moral justification.

The two most frequently cited justifications for punishment are *retribution*, and what we call *reductivism* (following Walker, 1972). Retributivism justifies punishment on the ground that it is *deserved* by the offender; reductivism justifies punishment on the ground that it helps to *reduce the incidence of crime*. Various other theories also exist, some of them combining elements of both retributivism and reductivism. In the following discussion, we shall be making use of Hart's (1968) distinction between the *general justifications* (or 'general justifying aims') put forward for having a *system* of punishment, and the *principles of distribution* which it is claimed should determine how severe the punishment of individual offenders should be.

## REDUCTIVISM

Reductivism is a *forward-looking* (or 'consequentialist') theory: it seeks to justify punishment by its alleged *future consequences*. If punishment is inflicted, it is claimed, the incidence of crime will be less than it would be if no penalty were imposed. Reductivist arguments can be supported by the form of moral reasoning known as *utilitarianism*. This is the general moral theory first systematically expounded by Jeremy Bentham (an important figure in penal thought and history) which says that moral actions are those which produce 'the greatest happiness of the greatest number' of people. If punishment does indeed reduce the future incidence of crime, then the pain and unhappiness caused to the offender may be outweighed by the avoidance of unpleasantness to other people in the future – thus making punishment morally right from a utilitarian point of view. But it is not necessary to be a utilitarian to be a reductivist. Indeed, at the end of this chapter we will be arguing an alternative position (based on human rights) which although non-utilitarian nevertheless takes account of the possible reductivist effects of punishment.

How is it claimed that punishment reduces crime? There are several alleged mechanisms of reduction, which we shall discuss in turn.

### *Deterrence*

Essentially, deterrence is the simple idea that the incidence of crime is reduced because of people's fear or apprehension of the punishment they may receive if they offend – that, in the words of Home Secretary Michael Howard addressing the Conservative Party conference in 1993, 'Prison works . . . it makes many who are tempted to commit crime think twice.' (More recently, Conservative leader William Hague also endorsed deterrence theory in calling for a criminal justice system that 'scares the hell out of criminals' – *The Guardian*, 19 May 2000.) There are two kinds of deterrence, known as 'individual' and 'general' deterrence.

*Individual deterrence* occurs when someone commits a crime, is punished for it, and finds the punishment so unpleasant or frightening that the offence is never repeated for fear of more of the same treatment, or worse. This sounds a plausible idea, but unfortunately it seems not to work too well in practice. If individual deterrence was effective, we would expect that if we introduced a new kind of harsh punishment designed to deter, the offenders who suffered the new punishment would be measurably less likely to re-offend than similar offenders who underwent a more lenient penalty. This was the alleged rationale behind the introduction of the 'short, sharp shock' detention centre regime for young offenders by Mrs Thatcher's Conservative government in the early 1980s (see Chapter 9). As had been widely predicted by criminologists and other commentators, the detention centres with the new harsher regimes were no more successful than detention centres with unmodified regimes in terms of the reconviction rates of their ex-inmates (Home Office, 1984b). Indeed, there is some research which indicates – quite contrary to what the notion of individual deterrence suggests – that offenders who suffer more severe penalties are *more* (not less) likely to re-offend (West, 1982: 109; Brody,

1976: 14–16). And one particularly thorough research study on boys growing up in London concluded that if a boy offends, the best way to prevent him from offending repeatedly is *not to catch him* in the first place (West, 1982: 104–11)!

This research evidence seems contrary to common sense, but such findings are not as incomprehensible as they look at first sight. They do not show that punishment has no deterrent effect on offenders, or that no offender is ever deterred. But they suggest that *overall*, punishment has other effects which cancel out and even outweigh its deterrent effects. These anti-deterrent effects of punishment are known as 'labelling effects'. 'Labelling theory' in criminology claims (and is supported by research studies such as those just mentioned) that catching and punishing offenders 'labels' and stigmatizes them as criminals, and that this process can in various ways make it more difficult for them to lead a law-abiding life in future. They may find respectable society and lawful opportunities closed to them while unlawful ones are opened up (custodial institutions are notoriously 'schools for crime' where offenders can meet each other, learn criminal techniques and enter into a criminal subculture), and their self-image may change from that of a law-abiding person to that of a deviant. Harsher penalties in particular could help to foster a tough, 'macho' criminal self-image in the young men who predominate in the criminal statistics. (For a fuller discussion of labelling theory, see Taylor et al., 1973: ch. 5.)

So the notion of individual deterrence seems to be of little value in justifying our penal practices. But there is another, perhaps more promising category of deterrent effect: *general deterrence*. This is the idea that offenders are punished, not to deter the offenders themselves, but *pour encourager les autres*.[3] General deterrence theory is often cited to justify punishments, including those imposed on particular offenders. One faintly ludicrous example is a 1983 case[4] where the Court of Appeal said that a particular sentence would 'indicate to other people who might be minded to set fire to armchairs in the middle of a domestic row that if they do, they were likely to go to prison for as long as two years'.

Now, there can be little doubt that the existence of a *system of punishment* has some general deterrent effect. When, during the Second World War, the German occupiers deported the entire Danish police force for several months, recorded rates of theft and robbery (though not of sexual offences) rose spectacularly (Christiansen, 1975; Beyleveld, 1980: 159). And if, for instance, on-the-spot execution were to be introduced for parking on a double yellow line, there might well be a significant reduction in the rate of illegal parking. But short of such extreme situations, it seems that *what punishments are actually inflicted* on offenders makes little difference to general deterrence. For example, in Birmingham in 1973 a young mugger was sentenced to a draconian 20 years' detention amid enormous publicity, and yet this sentence made no difference to the incidence of mugging offences in Birmingham or in other areas (Baxter and Nuttall, 1975; Beyleveld, 1980: 157). Similarly, studies have found little if any evidence that jurisdictions with harsh levels of sentencing benefit as a result from reduced crime rates (von Hirsch et al., 1999: ch. 6).

This does not mean that deterrence never works, but it does mean that its effects are limited and easy to overestimate. There are several reasons for this.

First, most people most of the time obey the law out of moral considerations rather than for selfish instrumental reasons (Tyler, 1990; Paternoster et al., 1983). Second, people are more likely to be deterred by the likely moral reactions of those close to them than by the threat of formal punishment (Willcock and Stokes, 1968). Again, potential offenders may well be ignorant of the likely penalty, or believe they will never get caught. Some recent research has found that those who carry out robberies on enterprises such as banks and building societies tend to be dismissive of their chances of being caught even when they already have been caught and sent to prison, and as a result most do not think twice about the kind of sentence they might get (Gill, 2000). Much the same seems to be true of burglars (Bennett and Wright, 1984: ch. 6). Or the offender may commit the crime while in a thoughtless, angry or drunken state. There is some good evidence that general deterrence can be improved if potential offenders' *perceived likelihood of detection* can be increased[5] but little to suggest that severer punishments deter any better than more lenient ones.

These truths were officially recognized by the then Conservative government in 1990, before Mr Howard's announcement that 'prison works'. The 1990 White Paper *Crime, Justice and Protecting the Public* (Home Office, 1990a: para. 2.8) stated: 'There are doubtless some criminals who carefully calculate the possible gains and risks. But much crime is committed on impulse, given the opportunity presented by an open window or unlocked door, and it is committed by offenders who live from moment to moment . . . It is unrealistic to construct sentencing arrangements on the assumption that most offenders will weigh up the possibilities in advance and base their conduct on rational calculation. Often they do not.'

All of this suggests that, while general deterrence might form the basis of a plausible *general justification* for having a *system* of punishment, it is more difficult to argue that the *amount of punishment* imposed by our system is justifiable by deterrent considerations. In terms of its deterrent effects, it seems almost certain that the English penal system is engaging in a massive amount of 'overkill'. As we saw in Chapter 1 (especially Table 1.2), England has more prisoners proportionate to its population than most other countries in Western Europe. For example, contrast England with Finland, which in 1999 had 55 prisoners per 100,000 population compared with England and Wales's 125. Unlike England, Finland in recent years has as a deliberate matter of policy sought to reduce its prison population (Törnudd, 1993), without noticeably poor effects on its crime rate which has risen at a similar rate to that of other European countries. Similarly, a significant reduction in the West German prison population in the 1980s did not lead to an increase in major crime or make the streets less safe (Feest, 1988; Flynn, 1995).

A utilitarian deterrence theorist ought to conclude from this that the English penal system is an immoral one. Jeremy Bentham (1970: 179) himself propounded the principle of 'frugality' (or 'parsimony'), which states that punishments should be no more severe than they need to be to produce a utilitarian quantity of deterrence. 'Overkill' causes unnecessary suffering to the offender, and all suffering is bad unless it prevents a greater amount of suffering or brings about a greater quantity of pleasure.[6] So, although for a utilitarian deterrence might justify having a penal system, it does not justify the one we actually have. We shall argue later that the same is true for our preferred approach based on human rights.

## Reform

Reform (or 'rehabilitation')[7] is the idea that punishment can reduce the incidence of crime by taking a form which will improve the individual offender's character or behaviour and make him or her less likely to re-offend in future. Reform as the central aim of the penal system was a highly popular notion in the 1950s and 1960s, when penological thought was dominated by 'the rehabilitative ideal'. Many proponents of reform (of a kind known as 'positivists': see later in this chapter) have favoured a particularly strong version of this ideal called the 'treatment model'. This views criminal behaviour not as freely willed action but (either metaphorically or literally) as a symptom of some kind of mental illness which should not be punished but 'treated' like an illness.

For some advocates of rehabilitation, optimism about reforming offenders has included the sentence of imprisonment, with incarceration being seen not so much as a retributive or deterrent punishment but as an opportunity to provide effective reformative training and treatment. For most rehabilitationists, however, the conventional wisdom has long been that 'prison doesn't work' in reforming offenders, and so cannot be justified in these terms. Figures showing high rates of re-offending following release from custody are often quoted as bearing this out; for example a Home Office study of prisoners released in 1994 found that 56 per cent of offenders released from prison in 1994 (and 75 per cent of young males released from custody) were reconvicted within two years. After seven years, 73 per cent of released prisoners have been reconvicted (Kershaw, 1999). Statistics such as these led the government to state in the White Paper which preceded the Criminal Justice Act 1991 (Home Office, 1990a: para. 2.7) that imprisonment 'can be an expensive way of making bad people worse'.

Although once dominant in penal discourse, the ideal of reform became discredited in the early 1970s, partly as a result of research results which suggested that penal measures intended to reform offenders were no more effective in preventing recidivism than were punitive measures. The received wisdom about reform came to be that *'nothing works'*, that 'whatever you do to offenders makes no difference', although this was always an exaggeration. It is true that in the 1970s extensive reviews of research in the United States (Lipton et al., 1975) and in Britain (Brody, 1976) found it to be *generally* the case that different penal measures had equally unimpressive outcomes in terms of re-offending. Similarly, recent studies (for example Kershaw, 1999) have found that, when account is taken of the differing characteristics of offenders[8] sentenced to custody and various types of community sentence, the type of sentence they receive seems to make no discernible difference to whether they reoffend or not.[9] However, studies from the 1970s onwards – including those most often quoted as evidence that 'nothing works' – have also found examples of reformative programmes which seem to work to some extent with certain groups of offenders (see Palmer, 1975). The generalized conclusion (associated with the American Robert Martinson)[10] that 'nothing works' became widely accepted – not so much because it had been shown to be true, more because the disappointment of the high hopes invested in reform led to an over-reaction against the rehabilitative ideal.

In the past few years there has been something of a revival of the reformative approach. The new attitude – sometimes associated with the 'Strategy B' approach to criminal justice (see the Introduction) – has been that *something works*, that systematic experimentation, research and monitoring can identify effective methods of dealing with offenders. A burgeoning literature (for example Gendreau and Ross, 1987; McGuire, 1995) asserts that certain programmes and techniques have already been proved to have a significant effect in reducing reoffending. The current Labour government (and especially Home Secretary Jack Straw) has expressed particular interest in eliciting evidence as to *'what works'* to reduce offending and applying the results of research evidence in practice: an 'evidence-based' policy of trying to increase the effectiveness of the criminal justice system. (Although, as we shall see, especially in Chapter 11, it is arguable that government policy is still based more upon ideological and political considerations than upon any dis-passionate consideration of the evidence.)

The claims which are now made for the effectiveness of reformative measures are usually more modest than those which were put forward during the period of rehabilitative optimism. Few nowadays hold to the 'medical' or 'treatment' models of punishment, or claim that science can provide a cure for all criminality. Reform tends now to be seen not as 'treatment' which is imagined to work independently of the will of the offender, but as measures which enable or assist rather than force offenders to improve their behaviour – what has been called 'facilitated change' rather than 'coerced cure' (Morris, 1974: 13–20). Many of the currently fashionable programmes attempt to improve the cognitive and reasoning skills of offenders (for example, Ross et al., 1988), often by confronting them with the consequences and social unacceptability of their offending in the hope that they will as a result, decide to change their attitudes towards breaking the law. This 'cognitive behavioural' approach (which we discuss further in Chapter 5) does not deny the offender's free will, rather it appeals to it. It follows that reform can never be guaranteed to work (as, of course, research well and truly confirms). But it may still be well worth trying, even though we remain sceptical about some of the more enthusiastic recent claims for the effectiveness of reform. The empirical evidence may have destroyed the reformative aim as a plausible *general justification of the penal system*, but reform remains a reductivist aim which it may well be right to pursue *within* a system of punishment.

## Incapacitation

Prison works, according to Conservative Home Secretary Michael Howard in 1993, not only by deterrence, but also because 'it ensures that we are protected from murderers, muggers and rapists' – apparently a reference to the reductivist mechanism known as 'incapacitation'. Incapacitation simply means that the offender is (usually physically) prevented from re-offending by the punishment imposed, either temporarily or permanently. The practice in some societies of chopping off the hands of thieves incapacitates in this way (as well as possibly deterring theft). Similarly, one of the few obviously valid arguments in favour of capital punishment is that executed offenders never reoffend afterwards. Lesser penalties can also have some incapacitatory effects. Disqualification from driving does something to prevent motoring offenders from repeating their crimes. Attendance centres may be used to keep hooligans away from football matches. And imprisonment normally ensures that the offender is deprived of the opportunity to commit at least some kinds of offence for the duration. Not all crimes, by any means: many thefts and assaults (on staff and other inmates) take place in prison, as do drug offences, while headlines such as 'Bootlegger ran £23m empire from prison' (*The Guardian*, 2 December 1999) exemplify some of the other criminal opportunities open to the incarcerated felon. But it is true that offences such as domestic burglary and car theft become somewhat more difficult when you are locked up in prison.

Life imprisonment is one sentence which is specifically used in many cases for the purposes of incapacitation. A 'life imprisonment' sentence would be more precisely described as a *potentially* lifelong prison sentence, since most 'lifers' are eventually released; but the life sentence means that they will not be released as long as it is believed that they pose an unacceptable risk of serious reoffending (see further Chapter 8). Life sentences may be imposed, and lifers kept in prison, even though this exceeds what would be a normal length sentence proportionate to the seriousness of the offence.

It is certainly a plausible claim that incapacitation could be a justification (or partial justification) for punishments such as disqualification from driving and attendance centre orders. As to whether and how far incapacitation can serve to justify imprisonment, one key issue is the factual question of how effectively prison reduces crime in this way. Although only rough estimates are possible, the best calculations suggest that the incapacitation effects of imprisonment are only modest. This is largely because most 'criminal careers' are relatively short, so that by the time offenders are locked away they may be about to give up crime or reduce their offending anyway. The most authoritative estimate, by the former head of the Home Office Research and Planning Unit, Roger Tarling (1993: 154), is that 'a change in the use of custody of the order of 25 per cent would be needed to produce a 1 per cent change in the level of crime'. On the other hand, the prison population could be substantially *reduced* without creating a massive crime wave: if the numbers in prison were cut by 40 per cent, this could be expected to lead to an increase in criminal convictions of only 1.6 per cent (Brody and Tarling, 1980).

Nor is there much evidence that incapacitatory sentences can be targeted with any great success or efficiency on more selected groups of repeat offenders who are particularly likely to reoffend (Tarling, 1993: 154–160; Hagell and Newburn, 1994). Nor can we accurately predict which offenders are likely to commit particularly serious crimes if they do reoffend (Levi, 1997): our powers of prediction are simply not up to the job, whether we use impressionistic guesswork, psychological testing, statistical prediction techniques or any other method. If we do try to pick out individuals in any of these ways and subject them to extra-long sentences on the basis of our predictions, we will be imprisoning a large number of people who would not in fact reoffend; typically at least twice as many as those who actually would offend again. And even if it was possible to target potential recidivists or those likely to commit grave crimes, this would run into the ethical objection that we were punishing people not for what they have done but for what they *might* do in the future – punishment for imaginary crimes in the future rather than real ones in the past – which might not be fundamentally wrong in principle to a utilitarian, but is a serious objection for most moral codes, including retributivism and human rights theory.

It seems unlikely, then, that incapacitation can provide a general justification for our present practice of imprisonment, let alone justify increasing our use of imprisonment,[11] or for introducing any new incapacitatory measures. Nevertheless, the current trend in both England and the United States is for governments to create new sentences explicitly aimed at achieving incapacitation.[12] Most US jurisdictions now have so-called 'three strikes and you're out' laws, whereby repeat offenders are automatically jailed for life for a third offence. Under these laws, people have literally been sent to prison for life without parole for offences such as stealing a slice of pizza, which was the third offence of the unfortunate Jerry Williams in California in 1995 (*The Guardian*, 13 October 1995). In England, provisions introduced in the Criminal Justice Act 1991 (sections 1(2)(b) and 2(2)(b)) permit extra-severe custodial sentences for violent and sexual offenders if the court thinks this is necessary 'to protect the public from serious harm'. And the Crime (Sentences) Act 1997 imported the 'three strikes and you're out' principle, with semi-mandatory prison sentences for adult domestic burglars and drug dealers convicted for a third time, and semi-mandatory life imprisonment for serious violent offenders who offend a second time (see Chapter 4).

## RETRIBUTIVISM

The retributivist principle – that wrongdoers should be punished because they deserve it – is in some ways the complete antithesis of reductivism. Where reductivism is forward-looking, retributivism looks backwards in time, to the offence. It is the fact that the offender has committed a wrongful act which deserves punishment, not the future consequences of the punishment, that is important to the retributivist. Retributivism claims that it is in some way morally right to return evil for evil, that two wrongs can somehow make a right.

Retributivism is sometimes combined with reductivism to produce a compromise theory. Often these compromise theories state, in effect, that punishment is only justified if it is both deserved *and* likely to have deterrent effects (for example von Hirsch, 1976: chs 5 and 6).

If people are to be punished because they deserve it, it is natural to say that they should also be punished as severely as they deserve – that they should get their *just deserts*. Retributivism thus advocates what is known as a *tariff*, a set of punishments of varying severity which are matched to crimes of differing seriousness: minor punishments for minor crimes, more severe punishments for more serious offences.[13] The punishment should fit the crime in the sense of being in proportion to the moral culpability shown by the offender in committing the crime. The Old Testament *lex talionis* (an eye for an eye, a life for a life, etc.) is one example of such a tariff, but only one: a retributive tariff could be considerably more lenient than this, as long as the proportionate relationship between crimes and punishments was retained.

This is a point which needs stressing, because it is a common mistake – certainly among our own students – to assume that retributivists are those who advocate the harshest punishments, and to equate retributivism with a draconian, 'Strategy A' approach to criminal justice. In fact, it is often the case that retributivists (for example, those who follow the 'justice model' of punishment we discuss later in this chapter) actually favour relatively *lenient* punishment. (But punishment which is ultimately justified by the fact that it is deserved and proportionate.) On the other hand, some notable exponents of Strategy A – such as Michael Howard – have attempted to justify their harsh penal policies by appeals to their supposed effectiveness in controlling crime by reductivist mechanisms such as deterrence and incapacitation. The mistake is understandable, and there may be a certain psychological truth behind it. Maybe many advocates of Strategy A are primarily motivated by a hatred of criminals and a wish to see them 'get what they deserve' rather than by a desire to pursue rational steps to reduce crime, whatever their proclaimed motives. But retributivism is not inherently harsher than other philosophies, and indeed it has certain attractive features to those of a humane disposition.

One of these attractive features is its consonance with what is generally acknowledged to be one fundamental principle of justice: that *like cases should be treated alike*. ('Like' for retributivists means alike in the intuitively appealing sense of 'similarly deserving'.)

Another attractive feature of retributivism is that there is a natural connection between the retributive approach and the idea that both offenders and victims have *rights*. Reductivist theory (at least in its utilitarian form) has always found it difficult to encompass the notion of rights, even when it comes to providing entirely innocent people with a right not to be punished. (For if we could achieve the desired reductive consequences by framing an innocent person, and if these effects are all that is needed to justify punishment, what would be wrong with punishing the innocent?) Retributivism has no such problem, since it follows automatically from the retributive principle that it must be wrong to punish non-offenders. Nor may we punish criminals to a greater extent than their crimes are felt to deserve (for example in the hope of reforming or incapacitating them or deterring others): under the retributivist principle offenders have a right to go free once they have 'paid their debt to society'. Life imprisonment for stealing a pizza would be ruled out as disproportionate, for example. Retributivism thus fits in well with our common-sense intuitions which insist that it is indeed morally relevant whether the person punished has behaved well, badly or very badly in the past. Probably for this reason, it has proved a remarkably resilient idea. Although for many years retributivism was regarded (at least in academic circles) as outmoded and even atavistic, it has enjoyed a major revival in recent years, notably in the form of the 'justice model' discussed later in this chapter.

But retributivism is not without its own philosophical difficulties. One problem is how to justify the retributive principle itself. It may accord with some of our moral gut reactions, which seem to tell us that wrongdoers should be made to suffer. But maybe these reactions are merely irrational vindictive emotions (akin to vengeance) which, if we are to be moral, we ought to curb rather than indulge. A related objection is that it is not immediately clear how the retributivist principle relates to any general notion of what is right or wrong. At least utilitarian reductivism has the virtue that it can be derived from the general moral and political theory of utilitarianism.

Some theorists have attempted to counter these objections by reference to the 'social contract', a theory which provides a general account of political obligation (see especially Murphy, 1979). The idea is that all citizens are bound together in a sort of multilateral contract which defines our reciprocal rights and duties. The terms of this contract include the law of the land, which applies fairly and equally to all of us. The lawbreaker has disturbed this equilibrium of equality and gained an unfair advantage over those of us who have behaved well and abided by the rules. Retributive punishment restores the balance by cancelling out this advantage with a commensurate disadvantage. It thus ensures that wrongdoers do not profit from their wrongdoings, and is justified because if we failed to punish lawbreakers it would be unfair to the law-abiding.

This 'modern retributivism' was highly influential for a time, although it was always far from universally accepted and it eventually became discredited even in the eyes of some of its foremost former advocates (Murphy, 1992: 24–5, 47–8; von Hirsch, 1986: ch. 5; and 1993: ch. 2). But even if we assume that it is sound at an abstract philosophical level, it would be extremely dubious to assert that this theory can justify our present practices of punishment or anything like them. The main difficulty is that the theory only applies if our society is a just one in which all citizens are genuinely equal; otherwise there is no equilibrium of equality for punishment to restore. If – as appears to be the case – detected offenders typically start from a position of social disadvantage (which means that the obligation to obey the law weighs more heavily upon them than on others) then punishment will tend to increase inequality rather than do the opposite. In fact, this was exactly the conclusion once reached by the modern retributivist Jeffrie Murphy (1979: 95), who stated that 'modern societies largely lack the moral right to punish'.[14] Even if such a sweeping conclusion is not warranted, retributivists should be strongly critical of many aspects of our penal system. Not least among these are the lack of consistency in sentencing practices (see Chapter 4) and the use of incapacitatory sentences, which mean that offenders are to a great extent not dealt with in proportion to their just deserts. So despite its resilient popularity, retributivism remains an implausible justification for our actual practices of punishment.

## OTHER JUSTIFICATIONS

Reductivism and retributivism do not exhaust all the possible justifications for punishment, or the aims which it has been suggested punishment can rightly pursue. We now proceed to deal with a few of these: denunciation, reparation, and the associated notions of disqualification, requalification and reintegrative shaming.

## Denunciation

Giving evidence to the Royal Commission on Capital Punishment in the 1950s, Lord Denning (Gowers, 1953: para. 53) made the following statement:

> The punishment for grave crimes should adequately reflect the revulsion felt by the great majority of citizens for them. It is a mistake to consider the objects of punishment as being deterrent or reformative or preventive and nothing else . . . The ultimate justification of punishment is not that it is a deterrent, but that it is the emphatic denunciation by the community of a crime.

The idea that punishment does and should demonstrate society's abhorrence of the offence, and that this in some way justifies punishment, is quite a popular one. It was explicitly cited as a rationale for the sentence in the 1981 case of Marcus Sarjeant, an unemployed teenager who fired blanks at the Queen during the Trooping the Colour ceremony. Sentencing Sarjeant to five years' imprisonment, Lord Lane (the Lord Chief Justice) said: 'The public sense of outrage must be marked. You must be punished for the wicked thing you did' (*The Times*, 15 September 1981). Similarly, the 1990 White Paper *Crime, Justice and Protecting the Public* (Home Office, 1990a: para. 2.4) stated that 'punishment can effectively denounce criminal behaviour'.

Denunciation might be advocated for more than one reason. What we term *instrumental denunciation* is actually a form of reductivism (which we discuss at this stage for convenience). This is the idea that denunciation can help to reduce the incidence of crime – a notion which may at first seem somewhat obscure, but which has a distinguished intellectual pedigree. Émile Durkheim (1960: vol. 1, ch. 2; see below, Chapter 3) argued that one function of the criminal law and punishment was to reinforce the *conscience collective* of society and thereby ensure that members of society continued to refrain from crime. Punishment, Durkheim thought, has an educative effect. It does not only teach people to obey the law out of fear and prudence (which is deterrence); it also sends a symbolic moral message that the offender's action is socially abhorred, and therefore wrong.

As with general deterrence, it is difficult on the evidence to make very strong claims about the effectiveness of denunciation. Research suggests that members of the public are not influenced in their moral attitudes towards offences by the punishments which are imposed (or which they believe are imposed). People seem to have sufficient *respect for the law* to disapprove more strongly of an action when a law is passed against it, but they do not have sufficient *respect for the criminal justice system* to be influenced by the severity of punishment inflicted (Walker and Marsh, 1984; cf. Tyler, 1990: 44–7). This suggests that (like general deterrence) instrumental denunciation cannot justify any particular level of severity of punishment; nor can the penal system (as is sometimes fondly imagined)[15] 'give a lead' to public opinion about the rights and wrongs of how people should behave.

A different version of denunciation theory (and the one we suspect Lords Denning and Lane subscribe to) is what we term *expressive denunciation*. This is the (non-forward-looking) notion that punishment is justified *simply* because it is the expression of society's abhorrence of crime. Sometimes this is explained in terms of the community showing its recognition of and commitment to its own values (for example, Lacey, 1988).

The claim is therefore that denunciatory punishment is justified *even if it has no good consequences* such as educating the public conscience and thereby reducing the amount of crime. When posed in such stark but accurate terms it becomes difficult to see why this is supposed to amount to a distinct moral justification for punishment. It looks suspiciously like knee-jerk retributivism, spuriously ennobled by reference to the 'community'. Perhaps it is right that the official institutions of a community should express moral judgements on behalf of its law-abiding members – but why should it have to take the form of *punishment*? Why – unless perhaps we are closet retributivists or reductivists – should not offenders simply be formally denounced with words and ceremony and then set free? Unless we care nothing for human freedom and are impervious to human suffering, denunciation seems an implausible *general justification* for a system which deliberately inflicts punishment on people.

Nevertheless, there may be something to be said for the notion of denunciation. Whether or not things could be otherwise in a radically different society, as things are, the conviction and punishment of an offender necessarily carries a moral, condemnatory message and is seen as so doing. Perhaps, as we have seen, members of the public are currently not greatly influenced by such messages; but there is still something morally wrong about making incorrect moral statements (cf. von Hirsch, 1986: ch. 5). It follows that it is wrong to convict and punish someone who has done nothing morally wrong. And if it makes sense to punish at all, there is some point in trying to punish offenders at least roughly in proportion to the moral gravity of their offences. Denunciation may not on its own provide a general justification for having a penal system, but it may help provide us with one[16] acceptable *principle of distribution* for punishment.

A theory which resembles denunciation (but which also contains elements of reform and reintegrative shaming) is the 'communicative theory' of punishment put forward by Antony Duff (1986). Duff sees punishment as an attempt at moral dialogue with offenders, censuring their actions and hoping to secure their 'contrition', with the result that they mend their ways. We doubt whether this theory can on its own provide an adequate justification for punishment, let alone for our current practices. But the idea that penal practices can and should be designed to foster this kind of moral dialogue is an attractive one. It fits in well with the 'cognitive behavioural' approach to reforming offenders (see above), and with the ideas and practices we discuss next – reparation and reintegrative shaming.

## Reparation

Reparation is the notion that people who have offended should do something to 'repair' the wrong they have done, and in so doing acknowledge the wrongness of their actions. This can take the form of compensating the victim of the offence or doing something else to assist the victim. If there is no individual or identifiable victim (or the victim is unwilling to accept it), reparation can be made to the community as a whole by performing community service or paying a fine into public funds. The idea of reparation is associated with the wider notion of '*restorative justice*', which seeks to restore and repair relations between offenders, victims and the community as a whole, and which has come very much to the fore in discussions about punishment in recent years. We shall have more to say about restorative justice and about various reparative forms of punishment in Chapter 5.

Reparation is a sound and valid principle which we strongly favour (Dignan, 1994; Dignan and Cavadino, 1996; Cavadino and Dignan, 1997b); one of its virtues is that it could be of great value in assisting the 'reintegration' of offenders, as we discuss shortly. Reparation can be seen either as a desirable aim in its own right, or as a valuable but secondary aim which may be pursued when imposing punishment which is justified on other grounds (such as reductivism). If punishment is to be inflicted, it is surely better that the punishment should directly benefit the victim or society than that it should merely hurt or restrict the offender. It is obvious, however, that the reparative principle cannot begin to justify the penal system that we have, since most punishments (and most notably imprisonment) contain little or no reparative element, and may even make it difficult or impossible for the offender to make amends. But if reparation were more consistently pursued, we should have a much more civilized and morally acceptable penal system than the present one.

### Disqualification, requalification and reintegrative shaming

Michel Foucault (1977: 130) says of penological 'classicists' such as Beccaria (of whom more shortly) that they 'saw punishment as a procedure for requalifying individuals as subjects, as juridical subjects'. Lawbreakers have placed themselves outside of society by committing their offences, but the penal process should ultimately aim at returning them to society as full members. Tony Bottoms (1983: 176–7) has compared this notion to that of the 'sin-bin' in ice hockey: the player who has committed a foul is excluded (or 'disqualified') from the game for a while and symbolically marked out as an offender, but after a term of fixed duration the player is allowed to rejoin the game as a full participant or 'requalified subject'.[17] The process therefore has two stages, the disqualification stage in which the offender is publicly and symbolically shamed by punishment, and the requalification stage when the punishment comes to an end and the offender is reintegrated into society as a full citizen.

The disqualification stage in this bears some resemblance to denunciation, which we found to be of limited value as a justification of punishment. Requalification of the offender, on the other hand, strikes us, like reparation and reform of the offender, as one valid aim which a penal system should pursue. At present, however, it cannot be said that our system does this very effectively. The stigma of disqualification tends to linger on well past the point where offenders have served their official punishment, and they often continue to be excluded from law-abiding society rather than being reintegrated into it. This (as labelling theory rightly suggests) is bad not only for the offenders but for the rest of society, because it makes reoffending much more likely. The trouble with our system is that we overdo the disqualification and pay insufficient attention to requalification.

John Braithwaite (1989) has put forward a general theory of crime and punishment which has some affinities with these notions of disqualification and requalification. He claims that successful societal responses to crime are those which bring about the *reintegrative shaming* of the offender. Offenders should be dealt with in a manner that shames them before other members of their community. But the shaming should not be of a 'stigmatizing' nature which will tend to exclude them from being accepted members of the community; it should be of a kind which serves to reintegrate them within it, by getting them to accept that they have done wrong while encouraging others to readmit them to society. (As we said above – and see also Dignan (1994) – reparative measures may be particularly suitable in pursuing reintegrative shaming, for the performance of reparation shames the offender symbolically while seeking to set matters right between the offender, the victim and the community.) If such a strategy were to be an effective one – and the jury is still out, although it seems a promising idea – then reintegrative shaming would be a valuable method of reforming offenders, which we see as a valid reductivist aim which could be pursued within a morally defensible penal system.

## SCHOOLS OF PENAL THOUGHT

The various justifications for punishment we have outlined have waxed and waned in relative popularity over time. In this section we provide a brief history of the development of penal thought in the West to show how different combinations of penal justifications have found favour in different eras.

### The classical school: deterrence and the tariff

The year of 1764 saw the publication of one of the most influential works of penal philosophy of all time: *Dei Delitti e delle Pene* (On Crimes and Punishments) by the Italian, Cesare Beccaria (Beccaria, 1963). This book, the seminal work of the 'classical' schools of criminal law and penology, provided a thoroughgoing critique of the criminal justice systems of eighteenth-century Europe along with a blueprint for reform along more rational and humane lines.

To understand the classicists it helps to have some understanding of what they were reacting against. Punishment under the *ancien régime* of eighteenth-century Europe was both arbitrary and harshly retributive, dominated by capital and corporal penalties. Moreover, 'due process' in the form of effective legal safeguards against wrongful conviction, was all but absent in the criminal justice system of the time, and even the laws which defined which actions were criminal were vague and extremely wide. On the other hand, the existence of wide discretion in the hands of judges and of the sovereign (notably in the form of the pardon, which was extensively used) meant that the guilty were as likely to go unpunished as were the innocent to be wrongly convicted and harshly dealt with. The classicists claimed that such a system was not only inhumane and unfair, but profoundly irrational and inefficient for the task of controlling crime.

Beccaria's blueprint called for clarity in the law and due process in criminal procedure combined with certainty and regularity of punishment. There should be a definite, fixed penalty for every offence, laid down in advance by the legislature in a strict tariff. These penalties should be proportionate to the gravity of the offence, but as mild as possible in contrast to the 'useless prodigality of torments' which characterized the existing system. Once an offender was found guilty, however, the sentence should follow automatically; in the strict classicism of Beccaria there was no room for clemency by way of pardons, reduction of sentences because of mitigating circumstances, or early release from the punishment laid down. All people were to be treated as fully responsible for their own actions, including their own offences.

The intellectual influence of classicism, and of Beccaria in particular, was enormous. Its principles were praised by reforming monarchs such as Frederick II of Prussia, Maria Theresa of Austria and Catherine the Great of Russia; the French Code introduced by the revolutionary regime in 1791 was an attempt at direct implementation of his plan for a rigid tariff of punishments; and Beccaria also greatly influenced such English jurists as Romilly and Blackstone. Its greatest impact was, however, on the framing of codes of criminal law rather than on penal systems. Beccaria's blueprint was never implemented in full.

Classicism grew out of the Enlightenment, the eighteenth-century philo-sophical movement which stressed the importance of human reason and which undertook the critical reappraisal of existing ideas and social institutions. Beccaria made particular use of the Enlightenment notion of the 'social contract' as the source of legitimate political authority. He argued that rational people drawing up a just social contract would only be willing to grant governments the power to punish to the extent that was necessary to protect themselves from the crimes of others. It followed that punishments should be no harsher than was necessary to achieve reductivist ends by means of deterrence; from this he derived his proposal for a tariff of fixed, certain penalties, proportionate to the offence but relatively mild by the standards of his own day. (Thus, like retributivists he advocated a proportional tariff, although he was himself a reductivist.) Beccaria opposed capital punishment as being cruel and inefficient as a deterrent. Punishments should, he said, be public and of a kind appropriate to the type of offence: corporal punishments for crimes of violence, public humiliation for 'crimes founded on pride' and so on. This would, he thought, assist in deterrence because 'in crude, vulgar minds, the seductive picture of a particularly advantageous crime should immediately call up the associated idea of punishment' (Beccaria, 1963: 57). But as we have seen, Foucault and Bottoms detect in classicism a concern not only with deterrence but also with 'requalifying individuals as juridical subjects'. Once they have suffered punishments fitting to their crimes, the social contract dictates that offenders have a right to re-enter society as citizens.

In general, Beccaria's philosophy exhibits what could be regarded as a curious combination of concern with the rights of the individual under the social contract on the one hand, and utilitarian reductivism on the other – curious because rights theory and utilitarianism are often thought to be philosophically incompatible. Yet he explicitly appeals to both concepts. (Indeed, not only did Beccaria use the concept of utility, but Bentham himself acknowledged his intellectual debt to Beccaria in the most fulsome terms and is even believed to have first encountered the phrase 'the greatest happiness of the greatest number' in Beccaria's master work: see Beccaria, 1963: x–xi, 8.) This intriguingly attractive blend of rights theory with forward-looking reductivism is perhaps one of the features that make Beccaria a continually fascinating and influential penal thinker even today.

### Bentham and neo-classicism: deterrence and reform

The Englishman Jeremy Bentham (1748–1832), the main founder of the utilitarian philosophy, was also a major penal thinker and reformer. His penal thinking was an application of his general philosophy that law and government should pursue 'the greatest happiness of the greatest number', which logically led him to espouse a purely reductivist approach to punishment, with no place for retributivism of any description. Despite the intellectual debt he acknowledged to Beccaria, his ideas differed from those of his Italian predecessor in several respects. At a philosophical level he had no time for notions of the social contract or human rights (he famously described the idea of natural rights as 'nonsense upon stilts'.) Nevertheless, like Beccaria he regarded clarity and due process in the criminal law as desirable, but from a purely utilitarian point of view. Similarly, he followed Beccaria in advocating a proportionate tariff of punishments for offences. Like Beccaria he said that punishment should be primarily justified because of its deterrent effects, but he also proclaimed that punishment of the right kind could serve a further reductivist aim: that of reform.

His model of utilitarian punishment was exemplified most famously in the Panopticon – a prison he designed and narrowly failed to persuade the British government to let him build. The Panopticon was designed in such a way that prisoners were under constant surveillance by inspectors in a central observation tower. Prisoners were to be made to perform productive work within the prison in a consistent and regular manner in order that they should acquire rational work habits which they would retain after release instead of returning to crime. Thus, whereas classicism's image of human nature portrayed all human beings as being fully responsible for their own actions, Bentham saw criminals as having limited rationality and responsibility, but thought that they could be made more rational by the correct application of reformative techniques in his 'mill for grinding rogues honest', as he called the Panopticon. His thinking also took account of limited human rationality on the question of responsibility for offences; unlike Beccaria he allowed for mitigating circumstances such as duress, infancy and insanity to reduce or even remove an individual's liability to punishment.

Beccaria's ideas had been fated to win great praise but achieve less by way of practical influence in the running of penal systems. Bentham's success was greater but far from total. Utilitarian reductivism became a prominent rationale for punishment but never displaced retributivism entirely. Criminal justice systems in the nineteenth century developed along *neo-classical* lines. This meant that criminal laws were clarified and in some countries codified, as both Beccaria and Bentham advocated, but leaving a greater degree of flexibility and judicial discretion than either would have found congenial. For example, the highly Beccarian French Code of 1791 was soon revised to reintroduce recognition of mitigating circumstances, judicial discretion in sentencing and the prerogative of mercy.

The Benthamite approach had its greatest impact in respect of one of its greatest points of difference from Beccarian classicism: the *form* punishment should take. Beccaria's scheme had no place for imprisonment as a punishment. (He only discussed imprisonment as the temporary incarceration of a suspect before trial. He did advocate penal servitude as a punishment for certain offences, but this was not to be served in prison.) Bentham by contrast saw prison, in the shape of the Panopticon, as a useful method of dealing with offenders. Although the Panopticon was never built exactly as he designed it (a modified version was constructed at Millbank on the Thames and opened, with extremely poor results, in 1817), imprisonment rapidly became the pre-eminent method of punishment. As Foucault (1977) famously observed, the end of the eighteenth century and the early nineteenth century saw a massive shift (sometimes called 'the great transformation') from *corporal* to *carceral* punishment (see Chapter 5). Moreover, this was a new form of imprisonment whose aims were not confined to containing offenders for a period and deterring the populace from crime. It also set out to retrain (or 'discipline' to use Foucault's word) the inmates, along the kind of lines Bentham advocated. As Foucault (1977: 16) put it, punishment no longer addressed itself to the body of the criminal, but to the soul.

### *Positivism: the rehabilitative ideal*

A century after Cesare Beccaria's *Dei Delitti e delle Pene* saw the light of day there came the publication of another work by an Italian called Cesare, equally seminal and revolutionary but in most respects diametrically opposed to Beccaria's way of thinking. This was Cesare Lombroso's *L'Uomo Delinquente* (The Criminal Man) (1876). Lombroso is best known for his theory, an extension of Charles Darwin's ideas, that criminals were atavistic throwbacks to an earlier stage of evolution. But more important than this particular theory (which he was later to modify substantially) was Lombroso's role as the founder of the *positive school of criminology*. The positivist view is that crime, along with all other natural and social phenomena, is *caused* by factors and processes which can be discovered by scientific investigation. These causes are not necessarily genetic, but may include environmental factors such as upbringing in the family, social conditioning and so on. Positivists believe in the doctrine of *determinism*: the belief that human beings, including criminals, do not act from their own free will but are impelled to act by forces beyond their control. Thus, where Beccaria's vision of human nature had been one of untrammelled free will while Bentham had admitted that the responsibility of some humans was limited, positivism denies responsibility altogether.

It follows (for the positivist) that it is wrong to hold people responsible for their crimes and punish them in ways that imply that their crimes are their own fault. Criminality is no more the fault of the offender than illness is the fault of the invalid, and both require treatment not blame. So retributivism is clearly excluded as a justification for punishment. Positivism is also typically sceptical about deterrence, on the grounds that empirical evidence scientifically assessed demonstrates that punishment is ineffective as a deterrent. The reductivist methods favoured by positivism are incapacitation, and especially reform. Criminological science should be able to predict which offenders (and perhaps even which people who have not yet offended) are likely to commit further crimes. Such people should be diagnosed by experts and given appropriate treatment which will prevent them from re-offending; if necessary they can be detained to incapacitate them in the meantime.

Positivism in its purest form rejects two important doctrines common to both classicism and neo-classicism, namely due process and proportionality. Due process is not appropriate in the diagnosis and treatment of crime any more than it is in medicine, since the scientific investigative process does not and should not proceed along legalistic lines. Proportionality is similarly seen as a mistaken notion, since there is no reason why the treatment needed by the offender should be in proportion to the gravity of the offence. Instead of the punishment fitting the crime, the treatment should fit the individual criminal. (For this reason the positivistic approach is sometimes referred to as the 'individualized treatment model'.) Positivism particularly favours the *indeterminate sentence*: it is premature to decide at the time of sentence how long the offender should be detained for, since this may depend on how quickly the treatment works; ideally, therefore, the release decision should be left in the hands of treatment experts to take at a later date.

Positivism, and the *rehabilitative ideal* associated with it, gradually came to dominate criminological thinking and rhetoric, reaching its zenith in the 1950s and 1960s, especially in the United States. For example, indeterminate and semi-indeterminate sentences (such as 'one year to life') became more and more common in the US, with release dates dependent not upon the sentence passed at trial but upon the parole process. This was a time of 'rehabilitative optimism': there was a widespread belief that criminology and other behavioural sciences would progressively discover the causes of crime and the way to cure all offenders of their criminality. In the 1970s, however, the positivist approach was dealt a series of severe blows which led to the collapse of the rehabilitative ideal. One of these blows (mentioned in the section on 'Reform' above) was cruelly self-inflicted: positivistic criminological research, far from demonstrating the effectiveness of treatment measures, seemed instead to show that treatment did not work. At much the same time, positivism came under a powerful and sustained political and theoretical critique associated with the 'justice model'.

*The justice model: just deserts and due process*

The justice model (Bottomley, 1980; Hudson, 1987) first emerged in the US as a critique of the positivistic 'individualized treatment model'. The first book-length statement of the justice model in the 1970s was the American Friends Service Committee's report *Struggle for Justice*, published in 1971. The authors claimed that the treatment model was 'theoretically faulty, systematically discriminatory in administration, and inconsistent with some of our most basic concepts of justice' (American Friends Service Committee, 1971: 12). Theoretically faulty, because the individualized treatment model identified the cause of crime as a pathology within the individual, whereas the authors saw the true causes of crime as structural, resulting from the way in which society is organized. Systematically discriminatory, because the wide discretion which positivism vested in supposed experts within the criminal justice system operated in practice to disadvantage offenders from poorer sections of society. And inconsistent with justice, because the lack of due process and proportionality in the treatment model offends our moral intuitions about the rights of the individual and the unfairness of treating offences of similar gravity in possibly widely varying ways. It was also felt that the positivistic notion that offenders were not rational and responsible agents, and that they should be reprogrammed until they conform to society, was a profound insult to human dignity.

The justice model asserts two central principles, both of which harked back to the classicism of Beccaria. The first is due process in procedure, and the general limitation of official discretion within the criminal justice system. The second is proportionality of punishments to the gravity of offences – or in other words, that offenders should receive their *just deserts*.[18] Disproportionate sentences with the alleged purpose of reforming the offender are to be rejected. This is so whether the reformative sentence would be disproportionately long or disproportionately short, although most adherents of the justice model in the 1970s (who tended to be liberal or moderately radical in political persuasion) wanted a just deserts system which would punish less harshly overall – again like Beccaria two centuries previously.

It is not only reform as an aim of punishment that the justice model eyes with suspicion. Justice model writers are also mostly sceptical of the effectiveness of deterrence and even more so of the validity of deriving a just tariff from deterrent considerations (as Beccaria and Bentham claimed to do). The justice model's philosophy consequently relies heavily on either retribution or denunciation as at least a partial justification for punishment. The most definitive justice model statement of the 1970s, the Committee for the Study of Incarceration's *Doing Justice* (von Hirsch, 1976: chs 5 and 6), adapted Jeffrie Murphy's (1979) modern retributivist theory and concluded that retribution and deterrence in combination provided the general justification for punishment. More recently, Andrew von Hirsch (1986: ch. 5, 1993: ch. 2) has claimed that punishment is justified on the two grounds of reductivism (which he calls 'the preventive function' of punishment) and denunciation (or 'the blaming function'), the latter being the basis for adopting proportionality as the principle for the distribution of punishment.[19]

The justice model made its impact on both sides of the Atlantic and else-where.[20] In the US many states moved substantially away from indeterminate sentences and positivistic devices such as parole.[21] The high water mark of the justice model's influence in Britain was the 'just deserts' strategy which was pursued by the British Conservative government prior to early 1993 and which centred around the Criminal Justice Act 1991 (see the Introduction and Chapters 4 and 11). Although by no means representing the justice model in a pure form,[22] the 1991 Act sought to establish a principle of 'just deserts' (based on retributivism and denunciation[23]) as the primary aim of sentencing. The White Paper which preceded the Act repeatedly stressed 'just deserts'[24] as the aim of criminal justice, and stated that 'punishment in proportion to the seriousness of the crime ... should be the principal focus for sentencing decisions' (Home Office, 1990a: paras 2.1–2.3). The 1991 Act provided that custody should normally be reserved for offenders who had committed offences whose seriousness justified such a sentence, and that both custodial and non-custodial sentences should remove or restrict the offender's liberty to a degree proportionate to the seriousness of the offence.

## FROM 'JUST DESERTS' TO 'LAW AND ORDER' – AND BEYOND?

It is often said that the agenda of the justice model, although originally proposed by liberals and radicals who wished to reduce the overall harshness of punishment, was 'co-opted' from the late 1970s onwards by the political Right (for example, Bottoms, 1980a: 11; Hudson, 1987: 72). Whether or not this is the best way of describing the situation, it is true that one can identify some important strategies and approaches to punishment in this period which combined certain aspects of the justice model with a generous dash of the populist, punitive ideology of 'law and order', which we discussed in the first chapter and which has been gathering ever greater influence since the 1970s. Indeed, the 'just deserts' strategy for the English penal system discussed above can be seen as a hybrid of this kind, for along with pursuing a greater proportionality in sentencing in general, the government insisted that community penalties should be made more toughly punitive (a policy known as 'punishment in the community') and that custodial sentences for violent and sexual offenders should be increased.

Other just deserts/law and order hybrid approaches have been considerably more punitive than this. (After all, the government at the time did hope that the 'just deserts' package would *reduce* the English prison population.) It is possible to discern – for example in the United States for much of the late 1970s and 1980s – a kind of 'right-wing just deserts' approach which shares with the liberal version a retributivist approach and a preference for proportionate, 'just deserts' punishments, but advocates *more severe* fixed-term sentences. Reformative measures are disfavoured by this approach not because they might be disproportionately harsh, but because they may be too soft. This approach departs from the liberal justice model markedly in its attitude to due process: if anything it *disapproves* of excessive procedural safeguards on the grounds that they are likely to act as an obstacle to ensuring offenders receive their just deserts.

From the vantage point of the present day, these more punitive versions of 'just deserts' assume the appearance of temporary staging posts on a rapid journey heading towards a 'law and order society'. In Britain, we have heard little about 'just deserts' – certainly from either Conservative or Labour politicians – since the 'law and order counter-reformation' of 1992–1993. In terms of the philosophy of punishment, the Conservative government of John Major (especially in the person of Michael Howard) then abandoned the retributivism which was central to the Criminal Justice Act 1991 in favour of the assertion that 'prison works' by incapacitation and deterrence[25] – although this was perhaps not so much philosophy as a rationalization designed to legitimate a populist set of 'tough' ('Strategy A') penal policies. Arguably, the historical role of the justice model – entirely contrary to the intentions of its progenitors – was to pave the way for the transition to a more punitive penal system and a more authoritarian society. As we shall see throughout this book, much of this punitiveness lives on under the New Labour government elected in May 1997, which is as little influenced by the philosophy of 'just deserts' as its immediate predecessor. One illustration of this is the government's insistence that the penalty of imprisonment is appropriate not only for serious offenders but also for persistent petty offenders, a policy which offends against the idea that the punishment should fit the crime.[26] Indeed, Jack Straw has said explicitly that he wants to end the 'just deserts' philosophy underlying the 1991 Criminal Justice Act and that it is time to make the sentence fit the offender rather than the offence (*The Guardian*, 1 February 2000). More generally, government policies are currently being justified not on the basis that they provide a fair amount of punishment for offenders, but because they are claimed to be effective in controlling crime – which is of course reductivism. For the moment at least, 'just deserts' is out of fashion with those who have most power to determine the shape of criminal justice. What reigns in its place at the moment is not simply 'law and order', however, but a combination of philosophies and strategies.

## STRATEGIES AND PHILOSOPHIES

It is not as simple as one might imagine to relate these philosophies and schools of thought to the broad 'Strategies' ('Strategies A, B and C') we detailed in the Introduction. (To recap briefly, Strategy A is harshly punitive, Strategy B is managerialist, and Strategy C is humane and rights-based.) Newcomers to the subject tend to assume that retributivism (with its traditional overtones of 'an eye for an eye') is the harshest philosophy and the one underlying the punitive 'Strategy A'. It is indeed possible to espouse Strategy A and call for maximum punishment on the basis of a harsh interpretation of retributivism. But, as we have seen, some notable proponents of Strategy A (such as Michael Howard) have justified their policies on *reductivist* grounds, claiming for example that 'prison works' to deter and incapacitate. On the other hand, the retributivist philosophy insists not only that punishment should be proportionate to the offence, but that it should *not be disproportionately severe because this would be undeserved*. This is, indeed, a central message of the justice model, most of whose proponents we would place under the heading of Strategy C, because they were concerned to minimize the violation of human rights involved in the infliction of excessively severe punishments.

So Strategy A can be based – although not necessarily with any great intellectual coherence – on either retributivism or reductivism (or indeed on the theory of denunciation). Proponents of the lenient, human rights-based Strategy C can also draw on any of these philosophies and justifications for punishment. Those whose humanitarianism takes the form of advocating reformative measures invoke reductivism (and the belief that reformative treatment can help reduce future crime); while, as we have seen, proponents of the justice model can appeal to either retributivism or denunciation, typically combined with reductivism in a hybrid justification for punishment. Those who favour restorative justice could be reductivists (believing that this kind of justice is the most effective at controlling crime) or may appeal to the desirability of reparation as an independent aim in its own right.

There is, therefore, no simple equation between the *philosophies* of punishment and what we term *strategies*. Both reductivism and retributivism can be either harsh or humane. However, when it comes to consider Strategy B – the managerialist strategy – there is one general philosophy which fits it very neatly. This is the philosophy of *utilitarianism* – the notion that one should always act in the interests of the 'greatest number' of people. The emphasis managerialism places on effectiveness and cost-efficiency has a decidedly utilitarian tinge. So does the way in which managerialism is not greatly concerned about the human rights of individual offenders or about ensuring that offenders get their 'just deserts' (however much or little that is conceived to be). It follows that a proponent of Strategy B should, if consistent, espouse utilitarian *reductivism* as the basic aim of punishment. And indeed, the rise of managerialism in criminal justice has occurred in conjunction with an increasing interest in 'what works' to reduce crime (both by general crime prevention measures and penal sanctions aimed at reducing recidivism, including reformative treatments) – and, significantly, what works most efficiently and cost-effectively. This utilitarian (Strategy B) agenda has been very prominent in the policies of Jack Straw as Labour's Home Secretary, combined with the punitive legacy of his (Strategy A) predecessor and a dash of Strategy C, notably in the introduction of 'restorative justice' measures for some young offenders.

## CONCLUSIONS: PUNISHMENT AND HUMAN RIGHTS

This chapter has been a complex one, but it has nevertheless been an exercise in oversimplification. As well as reducing some sophisticated philosophies down to some relatively crude statements, we have probably also given the impression that penal systems 'in the real world' at different stages in history possess a consistency and coherence that is in fact largely lacking. The philosophies we have described do exert a very real influence on the shaping of penal systems and penal practices, but none of the various schools of thought has ever been totally dominant, even at the height of its popularity. No penal system has ever been entirely retributivist, or entirely reductivist, or thoroughly Beccarian. This impurity of the real world can be seen in the existing English system: the justifications for punishment accepted by the Court of Appeal include retribution, deterrence, denunciation and reform (and probably all the others as well) in a promiscuously eclectic mixture.[27] Government policies have been similarly eclectic, as a variety of penal aims and philosophies have been cited (often simultaneously) to justify policies whether harsh or relatively lenient.[28] Reductivism rather than retributivism is currently in the ascendancy as a general principle, but with deterrence, incapacitation, reform and reparation all finding favour to various degrees.

Given this confusing welter of competing and combining philosophies, can we reach any valid conclusions about the rightness or otherwise of punishment? We think we can, although any such conclusions (which we can only sketch out here) will inevitably be inherently controversial.

Any verdict we pass on punishment must be soundly based on an acceptable general moral philosophy. This does not necessarily mean that a diversity of penal aims is ruled out, but each of the different aims must be justified by the same general philosophy if our position is to be coherent. Our preferred philosophical basis is *human rights theory* rather than utilitarianism. Along with theorists such as Ronald Dworkin (1978) and Alan Gewirth (1978) we would hold that each individual human being has certain fundamental rights which we possess equally by virtue of being human. These fundamental rights are variously described and vindicated by a variety of philosophical arguments to which we cannot do justice here. Suffice it to say that we think that at least one important human right can be described as a right – belonging equally to each human individual – to maximum 'positive freedom', by which we mean the ability of people to make effective choices about their lives.[29]

If there is a right to positive freedom, then punishment (which reduces the freedom of the person punished) is *prima facie* wrong and requires special moral justification. It is difficult to see how punishment could be justified on purely retributivist grounds consistently with the positive freedom principle, and the same would seem to go for expressive denunciation as a general justification of the system. For if retribution and denunciation were all that punishment achieved, the criminal's freedom would be gratuitously diminished without this doing anything to improve anyone's prospects for exercising choice. However, rights theory allows for one person's *prima facie* right to be overridden in the interests of other individuals' more important 'competing rights' (see Dworkin, 1978). The relevant competing rights here are those of the potential victims of crime in the future. The commission of crimes against them will have the effect of diminishing their positive freedom, to which they also have a right. For example, crimes of injurious violence reduce the victims' freedom to operate physically free from pain, while property offences will deprive them of resources and thereby remove their freedom to choose to act in ways which require the use of those resources.[30] *The general justification for having a system of punishment must therefore be forward-*

*looking and primarily reductivist*: based on the claim that punishment does something to reduce the incidence of crime, and thereby prevents the diminution of some other people's positive freedom. The most plausible mechanism by which punishment may be thought to achieve this aim is general deterrence, although other reductivist effects such as instrumental denunciation and incapacitation may make a secondary contribution.

The reductivist aim must, however, be pursued in a manner consistent with the human rights of the offender (or suspected offender). We think that retributivists and denunciationists are right to insist that there is no justification for punishing someone who has not deliberately and wrongfully broken a just law and thereby exercised a freedom to which they are not entitled (because to do so has diminished other people's freedom or has threatened to do so). Rights theory therefore provides a basis for a principled compromise between reductivism and retributivism. It also follows that, although offenders do forfeit some portion of the rights citizens should normally enjoy, they still retain the status of human beings and therefore retain important human rights (Richardson, 1985), a point on which we are closer to some retributivist thinkers than to classical utilitarianism.

We further agree with retributivists, denunciationists and justice model theorists that one valid general principle for the *distribution* of punishment is that offenders should be punished at least roughly in proportion to the moral gravity of their offences. Our main reason for this is the argument we referred to when discussing denunciation: that to punish disproportionately is to convey incorrect moral messages about the relative gravity of offences. (The principle of justice that like cases should be treated alike is also relevant here.) But this principle – called by Hart (1968: 9) 'retribution in distribution' – is only one valid principle among others,[31] and is hardly inviolate in every single instance. We would take some convincing that it can often be right to depart from it by punishing more harshly than an offender 'deserves' on a standard tariff, for example by sentencing an offender to an exceptionally long custodial sentence for purposes of reform or incapacitation.[32] But we see no reason why it should not be acceptable (and consistent with our human rights philosophy) for aims such as reform,[33] reparation and requalification to be considered and pursued when it has to be decided what punishment (if any) should be allocated to individual offenders, as long as this does not have the result of making the punishment harsher. The operative principle should therefore be one of a 'retributive maximum' as advocated by Norval Morris (1974: 75): while an individual offender may be punished up to the level indicated by the tariff, there is no obligation to do so if other valid considerations indicate that a more lenient course will be more constructive or humane. As Morris says, 'deserved justice and a discriminating clemency are not irreconcilable'.

This human rights-based approach leads, naturally enough, to a 'Strategy C'-type approach to criminal justice: one, indeed, which incorporates the concerns of the different varieties of Strategy C which we have identified. There is a place in this approach for proportionality in punishment – 'just deserts' at least in setting the 'retributive maximum' – and also for reformative measures, and for restorative justice where it is possible and appropriate to apply it (cf. Cavadino, 1997b: chs. 2 and 3; Cavadino and Dignan, 1997b).

We particularly favour the restorative justice approach, for a variety of reasons. For example, one virtue of many reparation schemes is that they afford both offender and victim a say in determining the nature of the offender's punishment. This increases the positive freedom of the victim as well as the offender, a consideration which should normally justify a downwards departure from the proportional tariff. (See Cavadino and Dignan (1997b); Dignan (forthcoming).)

Strategy A is, as one would expect, anathema to this human rights approach for at least two reasons. First, it leads to punishments – such as 'three strikes and you're out' sentences – which are unfair to individual offenders because they are disproportionately excessive for the crime committed. And second, the general levels of punishment called for by Strategy A are also grossly excessive, because of the amount of 'overkill' involved: the suffering and loss of liberty caused is outweighed by the relatively small amount of crime which is prevented by such heavy penalties compared with a more lenient regime (Cavadino et al., 1999: 37–41). There is, however, room in our approach for 'Strategy B'-type managerial techniques, provided these are used in the pursuit of human rights-based aims (Cavadino et al., 1999: ch. 2). For example, there is nothing wrong with using techniques such as research and monitoring to discover and apply 'what works' to reform offenders, and indeed we strongly favour such an 'evidence-based' approach.

If our rights-based theory is the correct moral framework for punishment, how should we judge our current penal practices? Our own judgement is a severely negative one, and for one central reason: *we punish too much* – and in particular, we imprison far too much. For the 'principle of parsimony' applies as much to our forward-looking human rights theory as it does to utilitarianism: offenders have a right not to have their freedom gratuitously diminished to a degree greater than is necessary to produce the desired reductivist results. We would go so far as to argue that a thoroughgoing application of the principle of parsimony means that imprisonment should be used very sparingly indeed. It should be reserved for those few offenders who represent a serious danger to others and need to be 'incapacitated', and perhaps also – for very brief periods only – for offenders who intransigently refuse to co-operate with non-custodial measures. Otherwise, there is no morally legitimate aim of punishment which cannot be achieved just as well and more humanely by the use of non-custodial punishment (Cavadino et al., 1999: 117–20). But it is not necessary to follow us as far as this to accept the evidence that – as we saw in the section on deterrence – the penal system is engaging in a massive overkill operation. This amounts to a scandalous infringement of the human rights of those who are punished excessively. And as punishment levels continue to increase, so does the immorality of our penal practices.

It is not necessary to subscribe to human rights philosophy to agree with this conclusion. Indeed, we find it impossible to imagine a plausible and consistent moral philosophy which could justify our present penal practices or anything like them. (We have already seen that utilitarians and retributivists should also condemn our existing system.) It is difficult to resist the implication that our penal system is morally unjustifiable – morally bankrupt might not be too strong a phrase. Of course, not everyone is well versed in moral philosophy.

But this is hardly necessary in order to make valid observations about how the penal system treats people unfairly, causes unnecessary suffering, does little to reduce crime and fails to punish offenders in accordance with their moral deserts. So perhaps it is no wonder that we are not the only ones who perceive the system as unjust, and that it finds itself with a crisis of legitimacy on its hands.

## NOTES

1   By *'punishment'* we mean any measure which is imposed on an offender in response to an offence, even if it is intended to help the offender (or victim) rather than to hurt or harm. However – and for want of a better word – we use the word *'punitive'* in this book as an adjective referring to measures whose primary purpose is to confine offenders or otherwise make their lives less pleasant, for purposes such as retribution or deterrence. Thus, in our terminology there are 'punitive punishments' such as imprisonment and 'non-punitive punishments' which have aims such as the reformation of the offender or providing reparation to victims. Both types of punishment, however, stand in need of moral justification.

2   'What form should punishment take?' is a regrettably neglected question in debates about punishment. It is normally simply assumed that punishment consists of some form of 'hard treatment' which it is often further assumed 'censures' the offender (expresses moral disapproval of their actions). One of the merits of the restorative justice approach to punishment, which we favour, is that it reopens the debate about the form punishment should take; and also about the most effective and morally justifiable means of censuring offenders (Dignan, forthcoming).

3   This famous phrase is from Voltaire's *Candide* (1947: 111), in which the hero witnesses the execution of the luckless English Admiral Byng who lost Minorca to France in a sea battle. An Englishman explains to Candide that 'in this country we find it pays to shoot an admiral from time to time to encourage the others'.

4   *R. v. Fairman* [1983] *Criminal Law Review* 197. It is quite possible that the court's tongue may have been in its collective judicial cheek.

5   See Beyleveld (1980: 147–9, 209–11); von Hirsch et al. (1999: 13, 45). It is the offenders' subjective *perceptions* of the risk of detection which counts. It is often difficult to affect this perception even by increasing the real risk (Maguire, 1982: 88). On the other hand it is sometimes possible to deter people by merely increasing the *apparent* risk, as when the Copenhagen police succeeded in reducing speeding offences by 33 per cent by placing cardboard cut-out policemen by the side of the road (*The Guardian*, 9 February 1988). Similar results have been claimed for devices such as plastic cut-out police cars positioned beside roads and on flyovers (*The Guardian* 6 May 1992).

6   Nor should the utilitarian overlook the economic cost of punishments such as imprisonment. Each place in an English prison cost on average £25,096 in 1998/99 (HM Prison Service, 1999c: 9), so each unnecessary prison place represents significant resources which could have been deployed for any number of more utilitarian purposes such as health or education.

7   We shall be using the words 'reform' and 'rehabilitation' interchangeably, although some writers have defined them in different ways (for example Bean, 1981: 46).

8   This adjustment needs to be made because offenders who are sentenced to custody are usually more likely to have those characteristics (especially extensive previous records of offending) which make reoffending more likely in any event.

9   The two-year reconviction rates were 56 per cent for custody, 43 per cent for

conditional discharges, 51 per cent for community service, 45 per cent for fines and 60 per cent for probation orders: all within 4 per cent of what might have been predicted for these offenders. Although the results for some of these community sentences can be seen as disappointing, they nevertheless also suggest that punitive measures such as prison are no *more* effective than reformative ones in preventing re-offending, although typically more expensive. It has been estimated that keeping an offender in prison for three weeks is more expensive than probation or community service for a year (NACRO, 1995a).

10  In fact Martinson (1974) never actually said '*nothing* works', and he later (1979: 244) revised his views and asserted that 'some treatment programs *do* have an appreciable effect on recidivism'.

11  Not only does imprisonment provide little incapacitation at enormous cost, it also seems likely that alternative, non-custodial measures can often be equally effective at preventing or at least postponing re-offending at much lower cost (see, for example, Ashworth, 1983: 32; Raynor, 1988: 111).

12  'Three strikes and you're out' sentences have also been defended on the grounds that they enhance deterrence; potential offenders are supposedly deterred by the knowledge that if caught and convicted they will receive an automatic prison sentence. Given what we have already said about deterrence, this seems unlikely. In any event, studies of 'three strikes' laws have demonstrated that, like so much else in criminal justice, they make no measurable difference to crime rates (Stolzenberg and D'Alessio, 1997) whether by deterring or incapacitating.

13  Standard retributivist theory leads to the logical conclusion that punishment should be proportional to the seriousness of the *current offence*, and therefore that it is generally wrong to increase a sentence on the grounds of the offender's *past record* of previous convictions (for offences for which the offender has previously been punished). In practice, however, courts tend to operate two tariffs in tandem: an '*offence-based tariff*', and an '*offender-based tariff*' which punishes recidivists more severely. (See Cavadino, 1997b: 35–40.) This distinction between the two kinds of tariff will become important in Chapter 4.

14  However, Murphy suggested (1979: 107) that retributivism might justify punishing some offenders, for example business executives who commit tax fraud, who start off in a position of equality or better. It is also arguable that criminals who offend against victims who are less well off than themselves, or whose actions leave their victims in a situation of severe disadvantage, could have their punishments justified in a similar manner.

15  See, for example, *R. v. Sargeant* (1974) 60 Cr App Rep 74, where Lord Justice Lawton said that 'society, through the courts, must show its abhorrence of particular types of crime, and the only way in which courts can show this is by the sentences they pass. The courts do not have to reflect public opinion. On the other hand courts must not disregard it. Perhaps the main duty of the court is to lead public opinion.' (The Sargeant in this case was not the Marcus Sarjeant who shot blanks at the Queen, but an over-enthusiastic disco bouncer.)

16  The 'justice model' theorist Andrew von Hirsch (1993: ch. 2) argues in effect that what he calls 'the blaming function of punishment' requires that punishments should in general be *strictly* proportionate to the gravity of the offence, so that proportionality is not just one, but the only or paramount principle of distribution. In our opinion this approach is both over-rigid in practice and unjustified in principle (Cavadino and Dignan, 1997b).

17  If we wanted to be pedantic, we would point out that it may be dubious to attribute the concept of 'requalification' (as explained by Bottoms) to either Foucault or Beccaria. It is not clear what Foucault means by his use of the word, while Beccaria

does not discuss what should happen to the offender when the punishment is over. Nevertheless, the concept as explained by Bottoms is an important one whatever its exact historical antecedents.

18 For justice model theorists, this usually means that there should essentially be an offence-based rather than an offender-based tariff (see n. 13 above), although they are not always entirely consistent on this point (see e.g. von Hirsch, 1976).

19 See above, n. 16.

20 Other countries where similar developments occurred include Canada, Australia and Sweden.

21 However, many of these American developments, although moving towards more predictable and often fixed-term sentences, did not adhere to the 'just deserts' principle of proportionality between offence gravity and sentence severity (see von Hirsch, 1993: ch. 10). Thus in our terms these developments can be seen as owing more to 'law and order' than to the justice model.

22 As we have already seen, the 1991 Act also provided for incapacitation, in the form of disproportionately severe custodial sentences for some violent and sexual offenders. The 1990 White Paper (Home Office, 1990a: ch. 2) also allowed for reform and reparation to the public as legitimate, though subordinate, aims of sentencing along with retributivism and denunciation. Deterrence, however, was damned with faint praise as an aim of punishment.

23 See the White Paper preceding the Act (Home Office, 1990a: para. 2.4): 'Punishment can effectively denounce criminal behaviour and exact retribution for it.'

24 The effect was, however, unfortunately somewhat spoilt by the fact that the phrase was misspelt as 'just desserts' on each of its many appearances in the White Paper.

25 For example, 'three strikes and you're out'-style semi-mandatory sentences (see Chapter 4) are incompatible with the principle of a retributive tariff.

26 The idea that there should be 'progression' in the sentencing of petty offenders so that persistent offending will earn them custody means espousing the kind of 'offender-based tariff' (see n. 13 above) which offends against 'just deserts' philosophy.

27 See *R. v. Sargeant* (1974) 60 Cr App Rep 74.

28 For example, the White Paper which preceded the Criminal Justice Act 1991 stated that 'the first objective for all sentences is denunciation of and retribution for the crime', but continued: 'Depending on the offence and the offender, the sentence may also aim to achieve public protection, reparation and reform of the offender' (Home Office, 1990a: para. 2.9). (Deterrence received less support, but was not totally disapproved.)

29 This 'positive freedom principle' is discussed more fully in Cavadino (1983; 1989: ch. 10; 1997a); cf. also Gould (1988). Some rights theorists, including Dworkin (1978), justify rights on the relativistic ground that people in our society happen to accept that such rights exist. We find more interesting the non-relativistic argument of Alan Gewirth (1978) to the effect that human reason can establish that human beings in any society possess certain definable fundamental rights. A similar argument for the positive freedom principle is put forward by Cavadino (1983 and 1997a).

30 Not all crimes have individual victims; but many crimes that do not, have indirect effects which threaten to reduce the positive freedom of (perhaps many) individuals. For example, defrauding the Inland Revenue depletes the public purse, which may have the effect of reducing public provision and thereby removing choices of various kinds from members of the public. Punishment cannot be justified on this basis if the law which the offender has broken itself violates the positive freedom principle. The law should not forbid harmless actions which do

nothing to reduce anyone's positive freedom, however indirectly. More generally, if society is to be just it should be organized so as to uphold everyone's equal right to positive freedom. The less just society is in these terms, the less just its penal system will tend to be.

31  See Cavadino and Dignan (1997b).

32  In the case of 'protective sentences' – exceptionally long custodial sentences for the purpose of incapacitating supposedly dangerous offenders – we would adopt the rights-based reasoning of Bottoms and Brownsword (1983). This rules out protective sentences for all but the most 'vividly dangerous' offenders.

33  Not all methods of attempted reform are acceptable, however. To be consistent with the positive freedom principle, reform must take the shape of 'facilitated change' rather than 'coerced cure' (Morris, 1974: 13–20). Coerced cure is inconsistent with the offender's right to freedom.

# 3

# Explaining Punishment

Why do we have a penal system? Why does punishment take different forms in different societies and at different stages in history? Why, for example, have penal ideas and practices altered over time in the West in the ways described in the 'Schools of Penal Thought' section of the previous chapter?

The *sociology of punishment* is the area of inquiry which seeks to answer questions like these. The answers put forward are often controversial. Like many areas of sociology, the sociology of punishment lends itself to (often radically) differing approaches which provide rival explanations of penality. (We shall be using the word 'penality' to include *ideas* about punishment as well as concrete penal practices (cf. Garland and Young, 1983a; Garland, 1990b).) Again like other fields of sociology, these approaches can be conveniently located within competing traditions which each owe their orientation to one of the three great 'founding fathers' of the discipline of sociology: Karl Marx, Émile Durkheim and Max Weber. It is equally convenient for us to divide this chapter accordingly.

## THE MARXIST TRADITION

Karl Marx (1818–1883) was not only the founder of modern communism but also originated one of the most influential traditions in sociology. His message was that societies had to be understood in terms of their economic structures, and in particular their social relations of production and the conflicts between the different economic classes which exist as a result of those relations. He claimed that capitalist society was polarizing 'into two great hostile camps, into two great classes directly facing each other: Bourgeoisie and Proletariat' (Marx, 1977: 222). The bourgeoisie or capitalist class (the ruling class under capitalism) is the class of people which owns the means of production (including factories, industrial machinery etc. in an industrialized society), while the proletariat or working class comprises those who need to sell their 'labour power' (their ability to work) to the capitalists in order to live. The struggle between these two classes was for Marx the key to understanding modern society and its future, which he envisaged as the revolutionary overthrow of capitalism by the proletariat leading ultimately to a classless communist society.

In a key passage, Marx wrote (1977: 389):

> The sum total of these relations of production constitutes the economic structure of society, the real foundation, on which rises a legal and political superstructure and

to which correspond definite forms of social consciousness. The mode of production of material life conditions the social, political, and intellectual life process in general. It is not the consciousness of men that determines their being, but, on the contrary, their social being that determines their consciousness.

This passage is the source for one of the most debated features of Marxist social theory, known as the '*base and superstructure* metaphor': the idea that the economic 'material base' of society determines developments in the 'super-structural' realms of law, of politics and of people's ideas generally. Marx described the consciousness of people in a situation of class conflict as *ideological*, meaning that although they might represent and believe their ideas to be objective and of universal validity, in reality these ideas express and serve class interests. In particular, Marx claimed that 'the ruling ideas of each age have ever been the ideas of its ruling class' (Marx, 1977: 236).

Marxist penology applies this method of analysis (known as 'historical materialism') to the study of penality. It relates punishment to the economic structure of the society in which it takes place and to the class interests furthered by penal practices and ideologies. A general point is that punishment is inflicted by the state for breaches of the law. Marxists see both state and law as operating in the interests of the ruling class rather than society as a whole. Punishing people for disobeying the existing laws – which maintain the status quo and the position of the ruling class – functions to reinforce the power and privilege of that class.

Historical materialism can also be used to explain the history of penal thought sketched in the previous chapter. For example, it has often been observed (by no means only by Marxists) that the ideas of Beccaria – and the Enlightenment generally – were linked to the interests of the bourgeois class who were gaining in economic and political power at the time but still needed legal protection against the old ruling class, the landowning aristocracy who retained a corrupt control of the levers of state power (Beccaria, 1963: xxi; Taylor et al., 1973: ch. 1). Similarly, Bentham's penology – and utilitarianism generally – were functional to the interests of the bourgeoisie at a slightly later historical stage (Ignatieff, 1978; Hogg, 1979). Positivism in turn can be seen as a set of ideas tending to reinforce the ideological domination (or 'hegemony') of the bourgeois class at a yet later stage when it had become the ruling class in Europe: if criminal actions can be described as the result of mindless pathology rather than rational choice this both absolves capitalism of any blame for crime and helps to delegitimize protest against the existing order (Taylor et al., 1973: ch. 2). Conventional histories of punishment tend to represent these developments in thought and practice as rational, progressive, scientific and humane; Marxists are sceptical of such claims and see the furtherance of class interests as of prime importance. When we come nearer the present with the recent rise of 'law and order ideology' – especially as fomented by politicians of the Right – Marxists are likely to have little difficulty perceiving whose interests are being served by the notion that crime is entirely the fault of individual, predominantly working class offenders who should be punished as severely as possible (Hall et al., 1978; Hall, 1979, 1980).

While much of the above would probably be unobjectionable to most Marxists, there are some important fissures within the Marxist tradition itself, especially in relation to the 'base and superstructure metaphor', which have an important bearing on the nature of the explanations of punishment offered by different kinds of Marxists. It will be instructive therefore to examine some of these different strands within Marxism.

### Economic determinism: Rusche and Kirchheimer

In the minds of many people, Marxism means simple economic determinism: the idea that economics determines everything, that the 'superstructure' of law, politics and ideology merely reflects the state of the economic 'base'. Few Marxists today believe this (and certainly Marx himself never believed anything so crude), but the misconception is understandable since this simplified version of Marx's message was communist orthodoxy for a long time. The 'economic determinist' approach produced one classic, pioneering work of Marxist penology: Georg Rusche and Otto Kirchheimer's *Punishment and Social Structure* (1939).

Rusche and Kirchheimer attempted to demonstrate that penal practices in any society were directly connected to the mode of production. 'Every system of production tends to discover punishments which correspond to its productive relationships' (1939: 5). For example, 'it is self-evident that enslavement as a form of punishment is impossible without a slave economy; that prison labour is impossible without manufacture or industry, that monetary fines for all classes of society are impossible without a monetary economy'. Moreover, 'if a slave economy finds the supply of slaves meagre and the demand pressing' it will be likely to introduce penal slavery. But once society had advanced from a slave economy to feudalism, penal slavery was no longer an option. Nor were fines an option for punishing the majority of (thoroughly impoverished) offenders, so feudalism relied instead on capital and corporal punishments (1939: 6).

A similar economic explanation was offered for the rise of the 'house of correction' (the forerunner of the modern prison) from the end of the sixteenth century on. Early capitalism needed more labour power, so it became uneconomic to kill and mutilate offenders. It was better for capitalism that offenders should be incarcerated and set to productive work (whose profits would, naturally, be pocketed by the capitalist class in the usual manner). Punishment could therefore be used to 'fill out the gaps in the labour market' (1939: 7). Even where this was not the case, Rusche and Kirchheimer argued that the choice of methods of punishment is largely influenced by fiscal interests, such as how much a punishment costs to administer.

This analysis of punishment is inadequate for at least two reasons. Firstly, it fails to explain the mechanisms linking an economic imperative with a penal practice. Capitalism needed the house of correction, and somehow it magically came into being as a result. Unless the capitalist class was engaged in a conspiracy which was simultaneously crudely self-interested, brilliantly well hidden and (remarkably) informed by economic analyses of a kind which had never been published at the time, it is hard to see how and why this occurred.

It is also hard to see in this theory any picture of real human beings (capitalist or otherwise) operating with limited rationality and knowledge in a recognizably real world. Or to put it another way, the analysis lacks both humanism and a theory of ideology – a theory about why people have the ideas they have, and what effects they have.

A second problem is that the theory embarrassingly fails to fit the facts of history. Rusche and Kirchheimer themselves admit (1939: 102) that imprisonment became the standard method of punishment at a time when the demand for prison labour had *fallen* as a result of technological and other developments. Again, a theory of ideology seems necessary to explain this seeming disjuncture between base and superstructure (Garland and Young, 1983b: 25).

This is not to say that economic imperatives play no part in penal developments. For example, it seems very likely that pragmatic considerations including economic ones have played their part in the expansion of the parole system (see Chapter 8). It has also been argued strongly, especially by Andrew Scull (1977), that the move towards creating 'alternatives to custody' in the 1960s and 1970s was primarily a product of fiscal calculation (see Chapter 5). And the current 'crisis of resources' in the penal system is an economic reality which certainly has had its effects on penal policy. But economics do not determine penal practices in a simple and direct manner; if they did we should hardly have the extremely wasteful penal system which exists in this country today, with its needlessly and expensively high prison population. Economic considerations are mediated through the minds of human beings who live in a social world, which means that the impact of economics is crucially conditioned by ideology – a notion which has been explored and expanded by the Marxist theorists to whom we now turn.

### Ideology and hegemony: the legacy of Gramsci

Antonio Gramsci (1891–1937) was not a penologist, but he was, famously, a prisoner. Imprisoned by the Italian fascists for his communist affiliation and activities from 1926 until his death, his contribution to Marxist theory was written inside prison (Gramsci, 1971).

Gramsci's writings marked a major shift away from the one-sided economic determinism of writers such as Rusche and Kirchheimer. For Gramsci, the 'superstructure' of ideology, law and politics was of great significance in the revolutionary struggle in an advanced capitalist society. Central to his ideas was the notion of *hegemony*, the ideological domination exercised throughout society by a successful ruling class. Hegemony meant that one class has persuaded the other classes to accept its own moral, political and cultural values. This was important because the ruling class (and the state which was its instrument) did not merely rule by coercion – which for our purposes means in particular by punishing people for breaking its laws. Equally important was the ideological factor of *consent*: in a situation of hegemony, subordinate classes 'consent' to the existing social relations because they are effectively represented as being universally beneficial. The production of this consent is one vital task for the state, and one necessary component of the continual reproduction of existing social relations.

Thus ideology and the 'superstructure' are not merely reflections of the material economic 'base', but interact with it in a two-way relationship. The economics of the base could not explain everything that existed or occurred in the superstructure; as Marx's collaborator Engels had suggested, the economy was only the mainspring of history 'in the last analysis' (Gramsci, 1971: 162). And the superstructure could make a difference to the base. If consent were not successfully produced and reproduced, this could ultimately affect the condition and prospects of the economic base, not least by making a great deal of difference to the likely success of the revolutionary struggle.

Importantly, Gramsci did not believe that consent was produced as the result of a ruling class conspiracy to hoax the workers; for him, ideologies arose out of the material realities within which human beings live and work. Or, as Marx said, people's consciousness was determined by their social being (albeit not entirely determined by their *economic* position). Nor was hegemony an inevitable or universal phenomenon, and conscious efforts to combat it at the ideological level were a necessary part of the socialist project. (These ideas of Gramsci's have been notably developed and applied to modern criminal justice policy by Stuart Hall, whose account of 'law and order ideology' we touched on in Chapter 1.)

There is much more to Gramsci than this: for example, Marxist theory is indebted to his pioneering use of concepts such as 'praxis', 'civil society', 'class fractions' and the 'historical bloc' and his analysis of the nature, role and composition of the state in class societies. Perhaps above all, Gramsci injected a sense of humanism into Marxism: for him, history was made by human beings. He believed that socialism would not come about as the inevitable result of impersonal laws of economic development but would have to be built by active human beings working purposively and creatively. However, it is in his treatment of ideology that Gramsci's legacy has been most pervasive and where he is the unmistakable precursor of all the Marxist and post-Marxist theorists we now proceed to discuss.

### 'Structuralist Marxism' and Althusser

The French philosopher Louis Althusser (1918–1990) created a sophisticated reinterpretation of Marxism often referred to as 'structuralist Marxism'. Although Althusser himself disclaimed the label 'structuralist' it is at least loosely apt to describe his ideas, since he regarded the structure of the social system (and in particular the relationships between its different 'levels' or 'instances') as central to the task of understanding society.[1] Among the important features of Althusser's 'structuralism' is a rejection of humanism as a valid element in Marxism. He claimed to detect an 'epistemological break' in the writings of Marx in the year 1845, discarding Marx's (undoubtably humanist) early works as juvenilia and constructing a non-humanistic 'scientific' Marxism on the basis of his later works only (Althusser, 1969). History, according to Althusser, is not made by freely acting human beings but by 'structural causality'.

Society, according to Althusser, is a complex unity of different, unevenly related 'levels' or 'instances'. The economy is the ultimately determining instance, but the superstructural instances of ideology and politics are not mere reflections of it: they possess a 'relative autonomy' (Althusser, 1969: 111, 240; 1971: 135). Indeed, the different instances are mutually determining: there is a 'reciprocal action' of the superstructure on the base (Althusser, 1971: 135), and the ideological and political instances are part of the essential conditions of existence of the entire social formation. It is still the case that the economy is determinant 'in the last instance', but the economy never functions in isolation from the other instances. As Althusser put it (1969: 113): 'the economic dialectic is never active *in the pure state*; in History, these instances, the superstructures, etc. – are never seen to step respectfully aside when their work is done . . . From the first moment to the last, the lonely hour of the "last instance" never comes.'

It is difficult to see how, on this account, the economy is supposed to retain its ultimately determining role. Since the political and ideological instances are just as necessary for the existence of a social formation, they seem to be equally determining, and the economic 'base' no longer looks to be especially basic. Perhaps Althusser was unwilling to acknowledge this outright, because to do so would be to run the risk of departing from the fundamental Marxist doctrine asserting the primacy of economics in social explanation. Consequently Althusser denied the logical conclusion of his own theory by continuing to invoke 'economic determination in the last instance' as a dogmatic but essentially metaphysical, almost religious assertion.

Be that as it may, it is clear that ideology was at least as important to Althusser as it was to Gramsci. All societies (not only class societies, according to Althusser) need ideology as part of their conditions of existence. And a society's ideology must be constantly reproduced if the society is to survive, just as (for example) an industrial society must continually renovate and update its machinery and ensure that the next generation of workers is produced, kept alive and prepared for productive labour. For production could not continue unless the proletariat were ideologically conditioned in each generation to submit to the rules of the established order within which production occurs.

Althusser stressed the role in this reproductive process of what he called 'Ideological State Apparatuses' (ISAs) (Althusser, 1971: 127–84). Among these he included the educational system and also many institutions that are not usually thought of as part of the state, such as the family, churches, the media, trade unions and political parties.[2] These ISAs were to be distinguished from the more instantly recognizable 'Repressive State Apparatus' (RSA), consisting of 'the Government, the Administration, the Army, the Police, the Courts, the Prisons, etc.'. As the names suggest, the RSA functions predominantly by overt coercion to ensure that the conditions of production are maintained, while ISAs function predominantly to reproduce existing ideology, which is the ideology of the ruling class.

For our purposes it is interesting that although Althusser locates the penal system logically enough within the Repressive State Apparatus, he also makes it clear that there is no such thing as a purely repressive apparatus, and that the RSA also functions (if only secondarily) by ideology. (Similarly, he identifies the law as both an ISA and part of the RSA since it functions both to coerce and to reproduce ruling class values.) This provokes the consideration that the penal system may perform a dual function in the reproduction of the social formation. On the one hand, and most obviously, it comprises a set of repressive practices which among other things may help to preserve the conditions of production by deterring crime. But it may also function ideologically, by conveying conservative moral messages. For example, retributive punishment might help inculcate law-abiding ideology in the populace by telling them that breaking the law is wicked and deserves punishment. Reformative punishment could assure people that the existing state was effectively combating crime to the benefit of all, including even the offender – disguising the truth that the capitalist state in fact operates for the benefit of the ruling class. A Marxist approach which takes the role of ideology seriously needs to analyse punishment in terms such as these.

In the last analysis (as it were) we doubt whether Althusser's theory represents a significant step forward from the work of Gramsci. In some important respects – particularly Althusser's dogmatism, determinism and anti-humanism – we think it represents a definite step in the wrong direction. But aspects of his work, especially his insistence on the importance of ideology, have been a positive influence on modern Marxism and on some Marxist studies of crime and punishment. For example, Stuart Hall's analysis of 'law and order' owes much to Althusser as well as to Gramsci. Fitzgerald and Sim's *British Prisons* (1982) is another example of radical analysis which pays at least as much attention to ideology as to economics. Whatever the overall balance sheet, Althusser's impact has been undeniable.

### Post-structuralism, discipline and power: Michel Foucault

Michel Foucault (1926–1984), who studied under Althusser, took the step his teacher never did and distanced himself from Marxism while remaining politically radical. Perhaps even more than Althusser, Foucault represents a decisive move away from economic determinism. Like Althusser, Foucault was once called a structuralist, but although he showed great interest in structures (including the structures of thought and of 'discourse' in different ages) he differs significantly from both Althusser and other structuralists, often being described consequently as 'post-structuralist' – and also as 'post-Marxist' and 'post-modernist'. He shares structuralism's anti-humanism, but has a much more dynamic conception of structures. The structuralist account portrays structures as relatively unchanging and self-reproducing; the post-structuralism of Foucault discerns and investigates a continual flux and change in society and in structures themselves. As Alan Sheridan (1980: 90) says, 'there is a sense in which his work is profoundly anti-Structuralist. Far from wishing to "freeze" the movement of history in structures, his whole work has been an examination of the nature of historical change.'

For penology, Foucault's most important examination of historical change is his great work *Discipline and Punish: The Birth of the Prison* (1977). In this book Foucault investigated the massive shift (mentioned in Chapter 2) from *corporal* to *carceral* punishment between the late eighteenth and mid-nineteenth centuries (see also Chapter 5). His explanation for the coming of the prison at that time was that this was 'the moment when it became understood that it was more efficient and profitable in terms of the economy of power to place people under surveillance than to subject them to some exemplary penalty' (Foucault, 1980: 38). The new industrial social order required new techniques of power and new institutions to control the subordinate classes. The prison was one of these new institutions, along with the factory, asylum, school and workhouse, all of which shared certain common features with the prison.

Two central concepts here are *discipline* and *power*. Discipline was the new feature of the Benthamesque industrial-age prison, whereby the inmate was 'normalized' or schooled into conformity by constant surveillance and the imposition of a highly regulated physical routine including repetitive forced labour. Where the earlier forms of corporal punishment were directed at the body of the convict, disciplinary punishment aimed, via the body, at the 'soul' of the offender. Not that 'prison worked' in its intended goal of reforming criminals; on the contrary its failure in this respect was almost immediately apparent. But the prison was (and is) paradoxically successful in a different way precisely because of this. It successfully *produces delinquents*, creating a criminal section of the population and thereby dividing the subordinate classes into mutually antagonistic factions. The criminals created by prison could be used by the bourgeoisie for a variety of political purposes, for example as informers, *agents provocateurs* and strike breakers (Foucault, 1977: 264–92; 1980: 40–2) – essentially a 'divide and rule' strategy.

The concept of *power* for Foucault is intimately connected with that of 'knowledge', which in turn is not a matter of objective truth separable from power relations. 'Power and knowledge directly imply each other . . . there is no power relation without the correlative constitution of a field of knowledge, nor any knowledge that does not presuppose and constitute at the same time power relations' (Foucault, 1977: 27). Thus, the disciplinary surveillance of the prison created a new kind of 'knowledge' of the convict's body which created a new kind of power. However, power for Foucault is not merely exercised in a simple manner by the state or by one class over others via punishment and other mechanisms, but is a ubiquitous and many-sided phenomenon; there exists a 'multiplicity of power relations' in society which are the constant focus of negotiation and struggle. It follows that punishment – or indeed any social phenomenon – is an inevitably highly complex phenomenon which should require extremely subtle analysis. Ironically, however, one criticism of Foucault is that his penology is actually too crude and simple, reducing the complex phenomenon of penality to questions of power and little else, and postulating what looks suspiciously like an old-fashioned class conspiracy theory to explain the advent and historical persistence of the prison (Garland, 1990a and 1990b: ch. 6).

Foucault's cryptic style leaves the nature of his theory obscure in many respects. The traditional Marxist 'base and superstructure' is conspicuous by its absence in Foucault, but it is less clear what he thought the role of economics is in social and penal change. As Stan Cohen (1985: 24) remarks, Foucault 'veers between a materialist connection between prison and emerging capitalism and an idealist obsession with the power of ideas'. Clearly though, he was more concerned with the ideological genesis and effects of punishment than with its relationship with economics.

Foucault has been much analysed, and criticized by some on both theoretical and historical grounds (Ignatieff, 1981; Garland, 1985, 1990a, 1990b: ch. 7), although even his critics in the field of penal sociology have been profoundly influenced by Foucault. Foucauldian concepts such as 'normalization' and 'discipline' have become standard tools of analysis; for example, there is one major debate (discussed in Chapter 5) as to whether we are witnessing a 'dispersal of discipline' emanating from the prison and spreading throughout society (Cohen, 1979; Bottoms, 1983). Foucault's contribution has certainly transformed the sociology of punishment.

### Humanistic materialism: the case of E.P. Thompson

The English historian E.P. Thompson (1924–1993) represents a humanistic current of Marxism far removed from either Althusser's structuralism or Foucault's post-structuralism. He contributed not only to general Marxist theory, but also directly to penology in *Whigs and Hunters* (1977), his painstaking historical study of the passing of the 'Black Act' of 1723, a penal statute of extraordinary scope and ferocity.

Thompson's *The Poverty of Theory* (1978) is an extended polemic against Althusser and his disciples. Above all, Thompson insisted that history is made, not by the inevitable operation of impersonal structures, but by the actions of real human beings. 'For all these "instances" and "levels" are in fact human activities, institutions, and ideas. We are talking about men and women, in their material life, in their determinate relationships, in their experience of these, and in their self-consciousness of this experience' (Thompson, 1978: 289).

He also accused Althusser of covert 'idealism' in that his structuralism in effect denies the genuine role of the economy in constraining legal and ideological forms. Thompson claimed, for instance, that when he was researching *Whigs and Hunters*, 'on several occasions, while I was actually watching, the lonely hour of the last instance *actually came*' (Thompson, 1978: 288). A change in the mode of production from feudalism to agrarian capitalism required and forced the emergence of new forms of law and punishment appropriate to the new economy, such as Enclosure Acts and laws to penalize poor foresters who attempted to exercise their customary rights of grazing and timber-cutting in the forests.

Thompson had much to say about law. He accepted that law is 'relatively autonomous' of the economy, but he found little use for the 'base/ superstructure metaphor', rejecting what he saw as Althusser's rigid division of social formations into different 'instances' or 'levels'. Law, he said, is to be found 'at *every* bloody level'.[3] Law can function ideologically, to legitimate the existing order and 'mystify' subordinate classes into acquiescence (what Gramsci called 'consent'). But 'people are not as stupid as some structuralist philosophers suppose them to be. They will not be mystified by the first man who puts on a wig . . . If the law is evidently partial and unjust, then it will mask nothing, legitimize nothing, contribute nothing to any class's hegemony'

(Thompson, 1977: 262–3). So law was never the exclusive possession of the ruling class; rather it provided 'an arena for class struggle, within which alternative notions of law were fought out' (Thompson, 1978: 288). The foresters' view that customary law vindicated their rights to use the forest conflicted with an emerging capitalist version of law under which these customary rights were extinguished; thus a class battle was fought in the forum of legal debate.

Much of what Thompson said about law can also (we think usefully) be applied to punishment. Penality can also be found 'at every bloody level', although it can perhaps be roughly divided into (material) penal *practices* and (ideological) penal *rhetoric*. The relationship between the two is not necessarily straightforward; for example, penal rhetoric might be predominantly positivistic at a time when actual penal practice is predominantly classicistic and deterrent. (Arguably this was the case in the English penal system during the supposed reign of the 'rehabilitative ideal'.) Yet such discrepancies are not caused by the logic of structures but by the messy and often far from inevitable ways in which people come to understand the world around them and their own practices. Again, like law, punishment and ideas about punishment can serve to mystify and legitimate oppression, but can also afford 'an arena for class struggle'; and as we suggested earlier in this chapter, the history of penal thought can be fruitfully viewed in these terms. Readers will doubtless have already gathered that, if forced to choose a version of Marxism, we should favour one similar to Thompson's.

## THE DURKHEIMIAN TRADITION

Émile Durkheim (1858–1917) addressed himself directly to the question of punishment to a much greater extent than either Marx or Weber ever did. He did this especially in two works: *The Division of Labor in Society* (Durkheim, 1960, first published 1893) and the article 'Two Laws of Penal Evolution' (1973, first published 1900).

*The Division of Labor* expounds Durkheim's theory about the development of specialized work in society. Durkheim distinguishes between simple, pre-industrial societies in which there is little division of labour (sometimes referred to as *Gemeinschaft* societies) and more advanced (*Gesellschaft*) societies in which people perform specialized jobs. The central question for Durkheim was *social solidarity*, or 'the bonds which unite men one with another' (cited in Lukes, 1975: 139). This solidarity took different forms in the two different kinds of society, but in each case Durkheim saw punishment as playing an important role in the creation and maintenance of the solidarity which was a necessary condition for social order and the continued existence of society.

Durkheim said that simple societies were held together by 'mechanical solidarity through likeness': people were united by the similarity in the labour and the general social roles they performed, which also gave rise to a homogeneous *conscience collective*. *Conscience collective* is variously translatable as 'collective conscience' or 'collective consciousness', and means 'the totality of beliefs and sentiments common to average members of the same society'.

Crime, for Durkheim, could be defined in terms of the *conscience collective*: 'an act is criminal when it offends strong and defined states of the collective conscience' (Durkheim, 1960: 79–80). Criminal acts call forth a collective hostile response in the shape of punishment, and the punishment serves to restore and reinforce the outraged *conscience collective*. So punishment is not primarily deterrent or reformative; it is produced by collective *retributive* emotions and has a useful *denunciatory* effect. 'Its true function is to maintain social cohesion intact.' The *conscience collective* 'would necessarily lose its energy, if an emotional reaction of the community did not come to compensate its loss, and it would result in a breakdown of social solidarity' (Durkheim, 1960: 108).

In *The Division of Labor*, Durkheim claimed that the *conscience collective* played only a small part in maintaining social cohesion in more advanced, industrial societies. Differentiated labour meant that people now differed from each other to a much greater extent, including in their consciences. Social solidarity was now 'organic', deriving from the interdependence of people who were no longer largely self-sufficient as a result of their own labour alone. The *conscience collective* became weaker, vaguer, less religious and more humanistic in character. Punishment would consequently also dwindle in importance as the division of labour progresses, and punitive law would come to be replaced by 'restitutive law' which requires lawbreakers to make reparation to their victims rather than suffer retributive punishment.[4]

By the time Durkheim came to write *Two Laws of Penal Evolution*, he had modified his theory about the decline in importance of the *conscience collective* (a phrase he ceased to use) and had come to believe that collective sentiments were a crucial factor in any society. However, he still held that the nature of these collective sentiments differed at different stages of society's development, being of a predominantly religious character in simple societies but much more secular, humanistic and individualistic in industrial societies.

His first 'law of penal evolution' was a two-pronged 'law of quantitative change': 'The intensity of punishment is the greater the more closely societies approximate to a less developed type – and the more the central power assumes an absolute character' (Durkheim, 1973: 285). The first part of this law he explains as follows. In simple societies, whose collective sentiments are based on religion, all crimes (even crimes such as murder) are essentially 'religious criminality': they are seen as offences against God or the gods. Consequently punishments tend to be severe because any sympathy for the offender is overwhelmed by the need to appease the God. But as collective sentiments change, it is 'human criminality', comprising only offences against other people, which shocks collective sentiments and attracts a punitive response. The shock value, however, is less.

> The offence of man against man cannot arouse the same indignation as an offence of man against God. At the same time, the sentiments of pity which he who suffers punishment evokes in us can no longer be so easily nor so completely extinguished by the sentiments he has offended and which react against him; for both are of the same nature. (Durkheim, 1973: 303)

The same humanistic sympathy which causes crimes against people to be criminalized also serves to mitigate the punishment; so in general the severity of punishment should diminish as societies develop. But this progression will not continue indefinitely until punishment disappears; on the contrary, Durkheim predicted that the tendency would reverse, and less serious crimes against the person would come to be criminalized.

A second independent factor on severity of punishment is the degree of absolutism in government. Where government takes the form of absolute power 'the one who controls it appears to the people as a divinity . . . this religiosity cannot fail to have its usual effects on punishment' (Durkheim, 1973: 305), making punishment more severe than one would expect for a society of the same level of development but a less absolute government. For Durkheim this explained the harshness of punishment in the seventeenth and eighteenth centuries, when absolute monarchy was at its height.

Durkheim's second 'law' was: 'Deprivations of liberty, and of liberty alone, varying in time according to the seriousness of the crime, tend to become more and more the normal means of social control' (1973: 294). Durkheim saw the centrality of the prison as largely brought about by the operation of the first part of his first law: prison was a milder penalty than capital and corporal punishments and so became adopted as collective sentiments became more sympathetic to the criminal's suffering. (This account obviously stands in marked contrast to Foucault's explanation of the same historical phenomenon, discussed previously. What Foucault saw as a self-interested, indeed cruel strategy for exercising power, Durkheim saw as motivated by sympathy for the criminal; see Garland, 1990a.)

Durkheim's social theory differs sharply from Marxism in several respects. One of these is the role of economics. Although Durkheim did not see economic developments as unimportant, for him they were in no way basic. The most important determining social force to Durkheim was collective sentiments, and especially religion – a factor which some would describe as 'cultural' and Marxists tend to characterize as 'ideological'. In this respect, the more recent Marxist theories which give greater explanatory weight to ideology have narrowed (but far from closed) the gap between Durkheim and Marxism.

Another difference from Marxism is the stress Durkheim places on the existence of consensus and the need for order in society (and for change to be of a peaceful and evolutionary nature), where Marxism stresses the centrality of class conflict and the necessity of revolution. To some extent this can be seen as a matter of political temperament determining which side of the coin one emphasizes. Even a Marxist like Gramsci, who spoke of the 'consent' of the subordinate classes, saw consensus as false consciousness and hoped for revolutionary change. On the other hand Durkheim, a reformist socialist of sorts, was passionately opposed to violent revolution and agitation, and was concerned to identify and encourage the social consensus that made possible a peaceful social order for the benefit of everyone.

One of Durkheim's main legacies is the sociological tradition known as *functionalism*. Functionalism analyses social phenomena in terms of their functions – that is, their positive effects in helping the entire social system to continue operating. (The two most eminent functionalists to follow Durkheim were Robert Merton (1968) and the 'structural-functionalist' Talcott Parsons

(1937, 1951).) Like Durkheim, functionalists assume that a certain degree of order is necessary for societies to survive, and see shared social values as vital in securing this order. They see society and human action as being structured by social rules and values, and portray social systems as reproducing themselves via socialization – the transmission of social values to new generations through the family, the educational system and so on. Another functionalist concept, present in Durkheim's work and elaborated by his successors, is *social control*, a term which encompasses all the methods whereby society keeps it members obedient to its rules.

Although functionalism has often been attacked as a conservative sociological tradition, some of its terminology and certain aspects of its analysis have been appropriated by Marxist and radical theorists. Clearly, for example, Althusserian structuralism has at times a quite tangible functionalist flavour, especially in its account of the reproduction of capitalist relations of production. Most notably, the concept of 'social control' has been taken over wholesale by radical criminologists with little apparent sense of embarrassment (see Cohen, 1985) – but for radicals 'social control' is usually a term of abuse denoting capitalist repression.[5]

The Durkheimian tradition remains a source of influence for non-Marxist penologists as well. Tony Bottoms (1977) used Durkheim's 'two laws of penal evolution' to offer an explanation of the trend towards 'bifurcation' in British penal policy, whereby less severe punishments for the majority of offenders is combined with harsher measures for the minority of really serious offenders (see Chapter 1). The trend towards greater leniency for most offenders can be explained by the operation of the first part of Durkheim's first law, which postulates increasing leniency as collective sentiments become more secular. On the other hand, Bottoms saw the central power of the British state as having become more absolute in recent years, which part two of law one says should lead to harsher punishment. This duly transpires, but only for the more serious offenders. The concentration of punitive attention on more serious and violent offenders is an 'attempt to reassert an agreed *conscience collective*, or other kind of consensus, in a time of great social and moral doubt and confusion. Such a reassertion will, in the criminal field, result in the attempt to create consensus at any rate around the crimes which we almost all abhor, such as serious violence' (Bottoms, 1977: 90). Whether or not Bottoms' analysis was correct – and clearly it would now need some modifying to explain the later partial shift away from bifurcation with the rise of law and order ideology – the Durkheimian concern with shared social values and sentiments as an explanatory factor remains highly relevant to sociology, and to the explanation of punishment in particular.

## THE WEBERIAN TRADITION

Despite being one of the major streams of modern sociological thought, the theoretical tradition founded by Max Weber (1864–1920) has to date produced little explicitly Weberian penology.[6] But this probably reflects negatively on penology and penologists rather than on Weber and his thought. We shall concentrate briefly on those aspects of Weber's sociology which have the most obvious relevance to penology.

Weber's sociology is sometimes described as 'a debate with the ghost of Marx' (MaCrae, 1974: 52). Weber recognized the importance of economics in shaping social reality, but was concerned to demonstrate that culture and religion influenced economic development just as much as economics influenced culture. He explored this theme most famously in *The Protestant Ethic and the Spirit of Capitalism* (1930) and related works, arguing that Calvinistic Protestantism's individualistic ethos and positive attitude to the accumulation of private wealth provided the key to understanding why capitalism first arose in the West rather than in Asia where the economic conditions for capitalist development existed to at least an equal extent. But he also accepted that economics in turn influenced culture; it was the version of Marxism which saw culture as a mere 'reflection' of the economic base that Weber was concerned to refute. The difference between Weber's position and the more sophisticated Marxisms which see culture as relatively autonomous and interacting with the economy in a reciprocal (or 'dialectical') relationship is perhaps not great.

Another important contribution of Weber's was his analysis of different kinds of power in society (Weber, 1968: chs. 1 and 3). He distinguished between simple *power* (the ability to make one's will prevail against the resistance of others), *domination* (enduring power associated with a habit of obedience on the part of the subordinate person or group), and *legitimacy* (power which exists and endures because those subject to it believe it is morally right to obey). All governments and powerful groups seek to acquire legitimacy, for the very good reason that it is the most efficient and stable basis for exercising power. As we saw was true of Durkheim, much of this analysis and terminology of Weber's has been adopted by radical and Marxist theorists; thus we find radicals such as Fitzgerald and Sim (1982) identifying a 'crisis of legitimacy' in the penal system (see Chapter 1).[7]

Weber went on to distinguish three types of legitimate authority: traditional authority, charismatic authority and 'legal authority'. He saw legal authority as characteristic of modern Western societies. A person who wields authority in such a society does not do so typically by virtue of traditional rules (about kingship or hereditary authority, for example) or because of that person's supposed special charismatic qualities, but as a result of an impersonal rule which has been consciously created by a rational legislative process, Weber says that the appropriate administrative form for a system of legal authority – because it is the most efficient form – is *bureaucracy* (Weber 1968: chs. 3 and 11). Characteristics of bureaucracy include impersonality, the interchangeability of officials, routinization of procedure and a dependency on the existence of recorded information.

In Weberian vein, Kamenka and Tay (1975) suggest that advanced capitalist societies tend to develop 'bureaucratic-administrative law' which increasingly regulates human activities for impersonal collective purposes such as general economic efficiency. Tony Bottoms (1983) suggests that this analysis may explain some recent developments in penal systems, such as the rise in importance of relatively impersonal and standardized penalties such as the fine. Other penal developments can also be seen in this light. Obvious examples are the emergence of fixed penalties for certain motoring offences, the (highly bureaucratic) parole system (see Chapter 8), the move towards standardization in sentencing by means such as sentencing guidelines (see Chapter 4), and the general trend towards 'managerialism' in criminal justice (see Chapters 1 and 5). One recent manifestation may have been the 'blizzard of paper' which the Learmont report (1995: para. 3.125) complained had been engulfing a Prison Service 'strangled by bureaucracy'.

Finally we should mention Weber's general importance in the development of humanism in sociology. For Weber, the sociologist needed to understand (*verstehen*) the subjective experience of 'ideal-typical' human individuals located within particular societies, classes and cultures – not, of course, denying that social forces shape and influence individuals, but insisting that individual human beings and the meanings they use to interpret their social world are of prime importance in understanding society. This must be as valid an insight in the penal field as in any other.

## PLURALISM AND RADICAL PLURALISM

In our opinion the most satisfactory framework for explaining penal phenomena is one which draws on several different sociological traditions.[8] We call this a *radical pluralist* position,[9] since it represents a compromise between Marxism and the pluralist tradition in sociology.   •

Pluralism (for example, Dahl, 1961) holds that, at least in modern Western democracies, power is not monopolized by a single ruling class but is distributed between a plurality of interest groups of different kinds, which are represented in the political arena by a variety of organizations including political parties. Politics is a process of competition, bargaining and compromise between the different interest groups in which the state plays an impartial and independent role as 'honest broker' between the various parties. This vision of society contrasts with that of Marxism, which sees power in capitalist society as concentrated in the hands of the (bourgeois) ruling class, and society as primarily divided into two great opposing classes rather than a motley of interacting interest groups. Similarly, the state for Marxists is by no means neutral and independent, but is, in the words of Marx and Engels 'but a committee for managing the common affairs of the whole bourgeoisie' (Marx, 1977: 223). Although the state might operate as an honest broker between different sections of the ruling class and may seek to give the appearance of neutrality to mystify its class nature and role, it will never be neutral as between the general interests of the bourgeoisie and the proletariat.

Neither traditional Marxism nor conventional pluralism seems adequate to us. Marxism's main flaw is its insistence on economics and the economic category of class as the one fundamental explanatory factor. This has meant, for example, that despite some valiant efforts, Marxism has been ultimately unable to deal with other important social dimensions such as race and gender differences without reducing them to a mere aspect of class oppression and class struggle. We are not convinced that the penal realities concerning race and gender outlined in Chapter 10 can be satisfactorily explained in this manner.

Nor can all the groups involved in penal developments and penal conflicts and struggles be easily defined in terms of economic classes (although an attempt could perhaps be made to analyse them as representing 'alliances of class fractions'). We might mention non-state 'groups like PROP, the prisoners' group which for many years campaigned for prisoners' rights . . . Radical Alternatives to Prison (RAP) which successfully campaigned against control units [see Chapter 6] . . . Women in Prison (WIP) which explored conditions in Durham's maximum security wing as well as drawing attention to the high incidence of self-injury among female offenders . . . [or] Inquest which has bullied the Prison Department into setting up a suicide prevention unit' (Ryan, 1993: 401; see also Ryan, 1978; Sim, 1994a).

Again, as all viewers of the classic BBC television comedy *Yes Minister* are aware (Lynn and Jay, 1981; see also Kellner and Crowther-Hunt, 1980; Chapman, 1978), the state bureaucracies and their members have their own organizational and personal interests to pursue which are often at variance with those of their supposed political masters, which in turn are not invariably identical with those of either the electorate or of any coalition of interest groups. This would appear to be true, for example, of the Home Office, which for many years (at least prior to the advent of Michael Howard as Home Secretary) was largely successful in getting its strategy of 'penological pragmatism' implemented (see Chapters 1 and 11; Bottoms, 1980a; Fitzgerald and Sim, 1980). Joanna Shapland (1988) has shrewdly likened both non-state groups and the state agencies involved in the criminal justice system (such as the police and the courts) to feudal 'fiefdoms'. While of course we do not live in a feudal society, this analogy is in some ways highly apt: such fiefdoms represent partially autonomous concentrations of power and interest not readily reducible to class analysis.

Pluralism on the other hand is unembarrassed by the existence of a plurality of important social divisions. But conventional pluralism has its own defects, chiefly its 'honest broker' conception of the state. It seems clear, at least to us, that the state is by no means fully independent of, and impartial between, all groups and classes in society. ('Relative autonomy' is not perhaps a bad description.) For one thing, the personnel of the state are members of some of these interest groups themselves, and the more powerful state personnel will tend to be members of, or sympathetic to – or sharing the ideologies of – the more powerful and entrenched classes and groups. In the penal field, certain kinds of (more respectable) interest and pressure groups have at times been allowed a degree of influence on official policy[10], while others – especially those which challenge ruling ideologies – have had to struggle much harder to make an impact (Ryan, 1978).

However, the chasm between the pluralist and Marxist views has been narrowing encouragingly in recent years (McLennan, 1989). Marxists have discovered the state to be relatively autonomous and classes to be composed of 'class fractions' which seem to interact in a manner curiously reminiscent of the pluralist account. (They have also recognized the political virtues of pluralistic multi-party democracy, which pluralism appeared to celebrate while Marxists previously derided it as 'bourgeois democracy' which merely served to mystify the reality of class oppression.) The modified Marxism of E.P. Thompson approaches even closer to pluralism. For Thompson (1978: 298–9), classes are not the inevitable creation of economic relations, but 'arise because men and women, in determinate productive relations, identify their antagonistic interests, and come to struggle, to think, and to value in class ways'. Furthermore, law and the state afford 'an arena for class struggle' (1978: 288) in which victory for the ruling class is not necessarily assured. If this is true of classes, why should it not also be true of other interest groups, and what ultimately differentiates this from pluralism? Especially since there has been convergence from the pluralist side as well. Some pluralist writers have accepted that class division and class competition are pervasive factors in modern society, and that not all interest groups are equal in power or equally able to compete in the political arena (for example Dahl, 1985).

A radical pluralism could build on the common ground emerging between these two traditions. It could also incorporate some features of the Weberian and Durkheimian traditions – and perhaps not only the ones which, as we have seen, have already been purloined by Marxism. Equally, it could avail itself of the insights of 'systems analysis', a mode of examining the penal system which we explain in Chapter 9. There are some who would object on philosophical grounds to this kind of synthesizing approach. Different theoretical traditions, it is sometimes claimed, belong to 'incommensurable paradigms' (Kuhn, 1962); one can work within only one of them at a time. But there is no good reason, philosophical or otherwise, why a synthesis of different theories should not be sought, as long as the assembled components do not actually contradict each other. (It would be incoherent, for example, to amalgamate wholesale the theories of E.P. Thompson and Michel Foucault since the humanism of the former is incompatible with the anti-humanism of the latter.)

We think that a coherent radical pluralism can be constructed on the basis of a humanism which accepts, as Marx put it, that human beings 'make their own history, but they do not make it just as they please; they do not make it under circumstances chosen by themselves' (Marx, 1977: 300). These constraining circumstances on human agency include the economic, political, cultural and ideological factors which shape our social world, but neither economics nor ideology is 'basic'. The economic situation may set limits on what is socially possible, but (as Weber for one insisted) this is equally true of the prevailing ideological situation. Economics and ideology are thus both 'determining' in a weak sense, and they interact with each other, but neither makes a single future inevitable. Indeed, much of what happens in human affairs, including the realm of penality, depends on the 'swarming circumstances' (Garland, 1990b: 285) which hold sway at any particular moment, and on how the people subject to those circumstances make sense of them and respond to them.

As we said in Chapter 1, we think that the current 'penal crisis' should be seen in terms such as these. Material factors (such as the shortage of penal resources) interact with ideological developments (such as 'law and order ideology' and the all-important 'crisis of legitimacy') in a complex and some-times unpredictable manner. Much of this complexity and unpredictability is precisely because the intersection between the material and the ideological occurs in the practices of living human beings: offenders, sentencers, employees of the penal system, politicians, penal campaigners and members of the public. This vital human element makes the study of penality a complex and uncertain business. But it also means that people can, by their efforts, have a positive (or, of course, a negative) effect on the reality of punishment.

## NOTES

1   Althusser disclaimed the label 'structuralist' to distance himself from other theorists (notably the anthropologist Lévi-Strauss), for whom the structures of thought and language are determining. For Althusser, by contrast, it is the structure of the entire social formation, including the economic and political instances, which determines history.

2   Althusser's remarkably broad concept of the state relates to an important intra-Marxist debate which we cannot explore here. Many of the institutions which Althusser categorizes as part of the state would be viewed by Gramsci as part of 'civil society'. For what it is worth, we prefer the Gramscian approach.

3   This may be unfair on Althusser, who as we have seen described law as both part of the Repressive State Apparatus and as an Ideological State Apparatus, and who said that the different instances never exist or function in a pure manner independent of each other.

4   Durkheim got his penal anthropology wrong on this point. Bottoms (1980a: 23n) notes that Durkheim was 'ignorant of the great extent of the role of restitution in primitive societies'. His thesis in *The Division of Labor* also seems inconsistent with his later prediction in *Two Laws of Penal Evolution* that more and more offences against the person would come to be criminalized in the future.

5   One of us has argued elsewhere (Cavadino, 1989: ch. 2) that although social control is inherently conservative in the sense that it tends to preserve the existing state of society, this does not make all social control objectionable even from a radical's point of view, because there is much in existing society which radicals should want to preserve. (Durkheim would undoubtedly have agreed with this!)

6   However, Garland (1990b: ch. 8) argues convincingly that Weber has been a major influence on some significant penological work, including that of Foucault, often without receiving due acknowledgement.

7   We suspect that Fitzgerald and Sim borrowed the idea of a crisis of legitimacy from the German Marxist theorist Jürgen Habermas (1976), who in turn was profoundly influenced by Weber. We might also note that Gramsci's concept of hegemony has much in common with the notion of legitimacy.

8   Our position has much in common with that of David Garland (1990a, 1990b), who similarly wishes to synthesize the contributions to penology of the different traditions. However, Garland avoids making any attempt to link the sociology of punishment to any wider social theory, such as our radical pluralism. See Cavadino (1992: 13–14).

9   Unfortunately, there is no generally accepted term for such a position, nor is there a generally accepted meaning for 'radical pluralism'. For example, McLennan (1989) uses this term to refer to a position which is emphatically not ours, namely the 'post-modernist' philosophy which rejects any notion of universal reason. McLennan would call our position 'critical pluralism'.

10  However, in the recent climate of 'law and order' even these respectable organiza-
    tions (which include the National Association for the Care and Resettlement of
    Offenders (NACRO) and the Howard League for Penal Reform) have been finding
    it difficult to have much effect on policy-making, despite the formation of a joint
    body (the Penal Affairs Consortium) to give voice to their collective viewpoint.

# 4

# Court Decisions:
# the Crux of the Crisis

There is nothing inevitable about the penal crisis which we described in Chapter 1. Nor is it merely the result of 'law and order' ideology, although that is one potent factor. To a large extent the prison numbers crisis, and many of the problems that are associated with it, are the unintended outcome of a series of uncoordinated decisions taken, independently, by the various institutions that make up the criminal justice system in England (see Figure I.1 in the Introduction).[1] These have been likened (Rutherford, 1986) to a series of filters which between them determine who gets embroiled in the criminal justice system, and for how long. One feature that is peculiar to criminal justice agencies in England is the extent to which they are encouraged to exercise discretion under conditions of low visibility and subject to minimal restraint by other bodies. If we want to understand the current penal crisis we need to examine the way this discretion is exercised, its consequences for the rest of the penal system and the reasons for the continuing failure over the years to subject it to more effective control.

Although the police and the Crown Prosecution Service have a vital rôle in determining which alleged offenders proceed to subsequent stages of the criminal justice system, the most direct and immediate impact on the penal system is exercised by the courts themselves. In many respects the courts epitomize the 'unsystematic' nature of the English criminal justice system. Responsibility for deciding how offenders should be dealt with is currently allocated to three different tiers of courts: magistrates' courts, Crown Court and the Court of Appeal. Each court is staffed by different sets of judicial officials, and both the powers at their disposal and the parameters within which they choose to exercise them vary considerably. The criminal justice legislation within which these powers are delineated is itself highly complex, frequently irrational and lacks coherence.

Indeed, the confusion and irrationality extend even to the heart of government and are reflected in the highly idiosyncratic arrangements for allocating political responsibility for the different parts of the criminal justice system. In sharp contrast with many other countries, which have a unified Ministry of Justice, in England and Wales responsibility is shared between three separate government departments. Responsibility for the judiciary and the courts rests with the Lord Chancellor's Department, though the Home Office is responsible for drafting the criminal justice legislation which they have to apply, and also for the police, prisons and probation. Responsibility for the Crown Prosecution

Service, meanwhile, comes under the remit of the Attorney General. This muddled set of constitutional arrangements makes at best for an absence of 'joined up government'[2] at the heart of criminal justice and penal adminis-tration. At worst it can result in an undignified turf war between contending criminal justice 'fiefdoms' (Shapland, 1988; see Chapter 3). Most seriously of all, however, it makes the task of reforming 'the system' much more difficult in the absence of a unified and integrated policy-making process.

In short, the picture we will paint in this chapter is a fairly dismal one of a system that is largely out of control. The one constant feature, to which we have already referred, is the degree of discretion that is enjoyed by all criminal justice agencies, including the courts, and the tendency for this to be exercised with almost total disregard for the impact which a given decision may have on other parts of the system. One key theme we intend to address is the effect of this virtually unregulated decision-making process on the broader penal crisis which we outlined in Chapter 1. We will consider why it has proved so resistant to change so far and will assess whether recent attempts at reform are likely to ameliorate the many pressing problems to which we will be referring. We will also set out proposals for future reforms which we ourselves favour.

We begin, however, by examining three of the most crucial sets of decisions for which the courts are responsible: *remand* decisions (whether accused persons are freed on bail or remanded in custody); *jurisdiction* decisions (whether they are tried in the magistrates' court or committed for trial in the Crown Court); and *sentencing* decisions.[3] In each case we will outline the legal framework and organizational context in which each set of decisions is taken, before assessing their impact on the overall penal crisis. We will also say something about the decision-makers themselves, and the relatively limited mechanisms that are available for controlling the way they exercise their considerable discretionary powers.

## THE REMAND DECISION

Suspects are presumed innocent until proved guilty, an important principle which is undermined by the practice of imprisoning a person before trial. Nevertheless there are circumstances in which the individual's general right to liberty is deemed to be overridden by other considerations such as the protection of the public. The recent history of bail law in England and Wales reflects a continuing tension between these two rival sets of imperatives. Latterly, as we shall see, it has also become another battleground in the increasingly bitter conflict between those seeking to adhere to the Strategy C notion of individual rights and exponents of a Strategy A 'law and order' approach. But one of the most fascinating unanswered questions concerns the extent to which the 'rules of engagement' may be changed in the light of the Human Rights Act 1998, which came into force on 2 October 2000, while the current edition of this book was being written.

The decision to imprison suspects before trial or convicted defendants before they are sentenced can contribute to the penal crisis in two main ways: by exacerbating the prison numbers crisis when people are remanded in custody unnecessarily, and by fuelling the crisis of legitimacy. The legitimacy of custodial remands may be called into question if suspects or defendants are remanded in custody inappropriately, or if the conditions in which they are remanded do not reflect their special legal status.[4] The current legal framework regulating the circumstances in which a person can be remanded in custody is laid down in the Bail Act 1976 (as amended; see Cavadino and Gibson, 1993), which was prompted by concerns on each of these counts.

The 1976 Act sought to reduce the number of defendants remanded in custody by introducing a statutory presumption in favour of bail. It also sought to improve the quality of the decision-making process both by structuring it, and by requiring not only that decisions be recorded, but that reasons be given where bail is denied. The Act sets out the criteria which have to be satisfied before bail can be refused. This is permitted where there are substantial grounds for believing that, if released on bail, the defendant would fail to appear for trial, would commit an offence while on bail, or would obstruct the course of justice. In addition, bail may also be denied if the court thinks it necessary for the defendant's own protection, if there has been insufficient time to enable the court to obtain enough information to reach a decision, or if the defendant has previously failed to answer bail. Even where bail is granted, conditions may be imposed; the use of such conditions seems to have been increasing recently (Hucklesby, 1994).[5]

The same decision-making framework applies whoever is responsible for deciding whether a person should be remanded on bail or in custody. In England and Wales, this responsibility is shared between the police[6] and the courts. Where criminal proceedings are commenced by way of charge,[7] the police must decide whether to hold a suspect in custody or to grant 'police bail' pending the first court appearance. Relatively few defendants are refused bail by the police,[8] though research has shown (Simon and Weatheritt, 1974; Jones, 1985) that there is a very close correlation between court decisions on bail and earlier decisions taken by the police. So the latter can have important repercussions at a later stage.

Once a case has reached the magistrates' court, responsibility for granting or refusing bail becomes a matter for the court itself, but only after hearing representations from the Crown Prosecution Service. There are three main stages at which a decision on bail may need to be taken. One is where an adjournment is sought before or during the course of a summary trial. A second is at the 'committal stage', in cases that are to be tried on indictment in the Crown Court. The third occurs after conviction, whereupon a court may request an adjournment so that reports on the defendant may be obtained before passing sentence.

Following the implementation of the 1976 Act, there was a steady decline in the proportion of defendants who were refused bail while awaiting summary trial: only about 6 per cent in 1994, compared with 16 per cent in 1978 (Home Office, 1999a: para. 34). However, this was still not sufficient to avert an explosion in the remand prison population, which in turn has contributed substantially to the prison numbers crisis over the intervening years. In 1999, the average remand population was 12,520, which is more than double the 1976 figure of 5,090 (Home Office, 1977b, 2000b; Cullen and Minchin, 2000a).

Consequently, remand prisoners in 1999 accounted for 19 per cent of the average population in custody, compared with just under 12 per cent in 1976, though as recently as 1994 the proportion was as high as one quarter.[9] This may seem surprising since the Bail Act is thought to have contributed not only to a fall in the proportionate use of custodial remands, as we have seen, but also a fall in the number of defendants who are remanded in custody each year.[10]

Part of the increase in the remand population is a result of greater numbers of offenders coming before the courts. But one of the main causes of the recent remand explosion has been a tremendous increase in the *length of time spent on remand* (NACRO, 1993). Between 1978 and 1986 the average length of time spent in custody by male prisoners awaiting trial for indictable offences more than doubled, from 24 days in 1978 to 57 days, before falling to 46 days, the lowest for a decade in 1999 (Home Office, 2000b).

The government has responded to the problem by trying in various ways to reduce the time it takes for cases to complete their progress through the courts. They include the introduction of statutory time limits under the Prosecution of Offences Act 1985, which limit the length of time for which a person may be held in custody awaiting the start of summary trial or committal for trial.[11] For indictable cases the custody time limit in magistrates' courts is normally 70 days between first appearance and the start of the trial or committal proceedings, while for summary offences the limit is 56 days. Where the accused is committed for Crown Court trial the time limit is 112 days before the start of the trial. Under the Crime and Disorder Act 1998, however, different time limits may be set for different types of cases.[12]

A variety of case management techniques (sometimes referred to as 'fast-track' initiatives) have also been introduced, as recommended in the Narey report (1997). And defendants who are charged with either way offences are now encouraged to enter a plea (of guilty or not guilty) *before* a decision is taken as to which venue the case should be tried in, instead of afterwards (see below).[13]

Some progress has been made, as we have seen, in that the average time spent in custody by male untried prisoners during 1999 – at 46 days – was the lowest for a decade (Cullen and Minchin, 2000a: p.2). However, the reduction in the overall average masks considerable disparities in the time it takes to process cases in the different courts. Although delays are far from negligible even in magistrates' courts, the problem is particularly acute in relation to Crown Courts where the average waiting time for those denied bail is around nine and a half weeks from committal to trial (Lord Chancellor's Department, 1999, 2000). It follows that any significant increase in the number of defendants who are committed for trial to the Crown Court instead of being dealt with by the magistrates will itself engender further delays and so add to the growing remand problem.[14]

Trial delay is only part of the problem, however, since not all of those remanded in custody are awaiting trial.[15] Another factor contributing to the stubbornly high remand population relates to the level of custodial remands, prompting concerns that some offenders may be remanded in custody unnecessarily. Anxiety on this score is fuelled by evidence relating to the outcome of proceedings in cases where bail has been denied by magistrates at some stage in the proceedings. A disturbingly high proportion of these defendants – over one in five – are acquitted altogether or have charges against them dropped (Home Office, 2000a: ch. 2), and all of these could be said to have suffered a double injustice. For the initial violation of the presumption of innocence in such cases is compounded by a complete absence in Britain[16] of any entitlement to compensation for wrongful detention before conviction. Moreover, of those who are remanded in custody in either court, fewer than half (42 per cent) are sentenced to immediate custody (Home Office, 2000a: para. 8.10). The latter statistics do not necessarily mean that bail was improperly denied in the first instance.[17] However, they do cast serious doubt on the need and justification for pre-trial detention on the present scale, particularly in view of the deplorable conditions in which most remand prisoners are held (see also Cavadino and Gibson, 1993 and Morgan and Jones, 1992). They also serve to remind us that excessive or inappropriate use of custodial remands calls into question the legitimacy of the process itself, particularly in the eyes of those who may be denied bail.

Concerns about the legitimacy of the process are aggravated by the possibility that for some of those remanded in custody, the outcome of the trial itself and ultimately the choice of sentence may also be affected by earlier remand decisions. First, a defendant who is remanded in custody is likely to find it much more difficult to prepare an adequate defence than one who is free on bail. Second, the change in a defendant's domestic circumstances which is liable to result from such a decision – eviction from rented accommodation, dismissal from work, loss of family ties – could well have an adverse effect on the choice of sentence following conviction. Other things being equal it appears that those who are remanded in custody are more likely to plead guilty, substantially less likely to be acquitted and very much more likely to receive a custodial sentence on conviction than their counterparts who are remanded on bail (see, for example, Bottomley, 1970; Davies, 1971).[18] Figures relating to those who were tried in the Crown Court for example, show that during 1998 the acquittal rate in England and Wales for those remanded on bail was nearly *five times* that of those remanded in custody. Moreover, those who pleaded guilty after being remanded in custody for trial in the Crown Court were almost twice as likely to receive an immediate custodial sentence as those who pleaded guilty after being remanded on bail (79 per cent and 40 per cent respectively: Home Office, 2000a: ch. 8 and Table 8.7).

Concerns about the fairness of the decision-making process are also fuelled by evidence of persistent and widespread disparities in the rate of custodial remands in different parts of the country. Early studies by Winfield (1984), Jones (1985) and Gibson (1987) first drew attention to the seemingly random process which can result in a custodial remand rate as low as 5 per 1,000 indictable proceedings in Liverpool and as high as 698 per 1,000 in Lambeth (Gibson, 1987). More recent research by Hucklesby (1997) suggests that the phenomenon of '(in)justice by geography' continues to characterize the remand decision-making process.

One obvious reason for the persistence of pronounced regional anomalies on this scale is the fact that the guidance contained in the 1976 Act still affords massive scope for the exercise of discretion by magistrates, thereby enabling different policies to be pursued in individual court areas. To that extent the Bail Act's attempt to structure the decision-making process by requiring reasons to be given has so far failed to eliminate even the grossest of inconsistencies. It remains to be seen whether the Human Rights Act will succeed where the Bail Act has failed, since the standards of procedural fairness that are required by the European Convention on Human Rights are likely to require more detailed and robust reasons for depriving unconvicted defendants of their right to liberty and security. For example, it may no longer be sufficient in future for courts simply to tick a box indicating that bail has been denied because of a perceived 'risk of reoffending' or 'risk of absconding'. Instead of this mechanical or 'stereotypical' reasoning process, it seems probable that courts will be required to specify the facts relating to the case in question that resulted in a particular conclusion being reached.[19]

Improving the quality of the remand decision-making process is highly desirable, but it is only likely to succeed in promoting consistency and avoiding unnecessary use of custodial remands if courts have access to accurate and adequate information which can help them to assess the defendants' chances of absconding or reoffending while on bail. In the past, courts have lacked the relevant and reliable information they need relating to defendants, their home circumstances, or the circumstances in which their offence had been committed. However, in 1987 a small number of experimental 'bail information schemes' successfully demonstrated that the provision of verified information enabled the Crown Prosecution Service to be more selective when opposing bail, as a result of which bail was granted more generously in those areas operating the scheme, without any increase in the failure rate (Mair, 1988; Stone, 1988; Lloyd, 1992; Mair and Lloyd, 1996). By mid-1993 (the latest figures available) there were 192 court-based and 31 prison-based schemes in operation.[20] Until their coverage is extended nationwide, however, which is still some way off, large numbers of defendants will continue to be remanded in custody unnecessarily because of a lack of adequate information.

Another way of reducing the number of defendants who are unnecessarily remanded in custody involves the provision of hostel accommodation for those who have no permanent residence and who, for that reason, may be thought less likely to attend their trials.[21] The number of bail and probation hostels expanded considerably during the late 1980s and early 1990s, but since then there has been a decline in the number of hostels and places that are available. In January 1994 there were 115 approved bail and probation hostels in England and Wales, providing 2,690 places, but by 1998 there were only just over 100 hostels, providing a little over 2,000 places (Home Office, 1998a). Because of the absence of nation-wide coverage, it is probable that many offenders continue to be remanded in custody who might otherwise have been released on bail but for the lack of accommodation.

So far we have been concentrating on complaints that the law relating to bail and its operation affords inadequate protection to defendants, and have examined some of the strategies that might address such concerns. However, both the law and practice relating to bail have been subject to intensive criticism of a rather different kind in recent years, alleging that bail is granted too readily (thus affording inadequate protection to potential victims) and that the 'failure rate' is unacceptably high. References to the alleged 'failure rate' associated with bail decisions usually relate to the level of absconding and the incidence of offending while on bail (by so-called 'bail bandits').

The proportion of defendants who fail to appear at court after being released on bail was 12 per cent in 1998 (Home Office, 2000a: para. 8.11), though in some cases the reasons are likely to be legitimate or at least excusable; and in most of these cases the decision to grant bail on the information available at the time would have been entirely correct. The level of offending while on bail has generated much more controversy in recent years. A survey conducted by Morgan (1992) concluded that the percentage of bailed defendants who were convicted of a further offence while on bail in 1988 was around 10 to 12 per cent, about the same as in 1978. However, a more recent Home Office study has suggested that the problem may be much more acute, particularly in respect of juvenile defendants (Brown, 1998). The latter study reported that the proportion of defendants who committed an offence while on bail was as high as 24 per cent, taking into account both those who are bailed by the police and those bailed by a court. Moreover, the rate of offending while on bail was higher still in the case of juveniles, for whom it was 38 per cent, compared with 18 per cent for adults. The difference between the two sets of findings – at least with regard to the overall offending rates – may be attributable in part to the different sets of 'counting rules' that were used to calculate the figures. For example, Morgan excluded offences which resulted in a caution (as opposed to a conviction in court) or those 'taken into consideration', whereas these were included in the later study.[22]

Concerns over the problem of offending while on bail have generated three rather different sets of responses. One was an experimental scheme involving a variety of measures to improve the quality, accuracy and timeliness of information available to decision-makers. The aim was to enable them to make more realistic assessments of the risk of reoffending while on bail, and thereby 'target' the use of custodial remands more effectively (Morgan and Henderson, 1998). The project had mixed results, however, with only one of the five areas reporting both a lower level of offending while on bail and a reduced use of custodial remands. The only other area to achieve a reduction in the offending level did so at the expense of a substantial increase in the custody rate for defendants, particularly among those who fell within the higher risk categories.

A second response has been to try and reduce the risk of reoffending on the part of those who have been released on bail. One way of doing this involves the use of bail support schemes that are often aimed at young offenders who are liable to be remanded in custody because they are considered likely to reoffend (NACRO, 1998a). Bail support schemes involve a variety of interventions (for example those intended to help control anger and aggression, reduce alcohol or drug misuse, tackle difficulties with family relationships, schooling or accommodation) in the hope of avoiding a custodial remand. The development of bail support schemes for young offenders in particular was given a major boost in the Crime and Disorder Act 1998, which required all local authorities to provide bail support for alleged and convicted young offenders.[23]

Another way of trying to reduce the risk of reoffending and thereby reduce the rate of custodial remands involves the release of defendants on bail but subject to surveillance in the form of electronic monitoring. An experimental scheme was established to electronically monitor or 'tag' defendants on bail for a six-month period in 1989. Although claimed by the government to be a success, the Home Office evaluation report (Mair and Nee, 1990) suggested otherwise, with a much lower than expected take-up rate by the courts matched by a high failure rate on the part of defendants (see also Muncie, 1990; Nellis, 1991).[24]

The third, and most controversial, response to the problem of offending on bail has been to restrict the availability of bail to those perceived as falling within 'high risk' categories, which formed part of the Conservative government's 'Strategy A' approach to criminal justice and penal policy during much of the 1990s. However several of these restrictions now look vulnerable to challenge under the Human Rights Act. The most obvious example relates to the outright denial of bail to persons charged with serious offences such as murder, manslaughter and rape who have previously been convicted of any such offence.[25] In anticipation of the Human Rights Act this total ban was replaced by a 'rebuttable presumption' that bail should not be granted in such cases unless there are 'exceptional circumstances which justify it'.[26] Even in its amended form, however, the Law Commission (1999: paras 9.10–9.23) has expressed doubt as to its compliance with the European Convention on Human Rights, and has recommended that section 25 be further amended to ensure that courts retain real discretion in such cases, even if they are required to give special consideration to factors counting against the granting of bail. The normal presumption in favour of bail is also withheld from defendants who are charged with an indictable offence that appears to have been committed while they were on bail facing an earlier charge.[27] The Law Commission concluded (1999: para. 6.14) that this provision also contravenes the European Convention and should accordingly be repealed, but recommended that offending on bail should be added to the list of factors to be taken into account when deciding for or against bail. The Law Commission also reached a similar conclusion in respect of a third recent restriction on the availability of bail, which relates to those who are arrested under section 7 of the Bail Act for breach of bail conditions.

If the law relating to bail were to be amended in order to ensure that it is compliant with human rights legislation along the lines proposed by the Law Commission this would provide a welcome shift from a Strategy A approach, to one that is more consistent with Strategy C, reversing recent trends. However, in our view further reforms will also be required to prevent the law and practice relating to bail and remand from exacerbating the penal crisis.[28] First, the Bail Act needs to be amended to prevent courts from remanding in custody cases that are unlikely to result in a custodial sentence. This would not only help to reduce the number of custodial remands but would also address the current anomaly whereby courts are obliged to consider the seriousness of an offence before imposing custodial sentences (see below), but not when imposing custodial remands. Second, bail information and bail support schemes and also bail hostels need to be established and adequately resourced on a national basis. Third, time limits should be further tightened and more rigorously enforced in order to reduce trial delays (and therefore the length of any custodial remands).[29]

## MODE OF TRIAL DECISIONS

In December 1999 the government set up a wide-ranging review of the criminal courts – the Auld Review (2000a) – whose extensive terms of reference encompass the organization and work of the courts, and also include their rules of procedure and evidence. We will return to this and other recent initiatives relating to mode of trial decisions towards the end of this section, but begin by setting out the existing legal framework, its implications for the penal crisis and the way it has operated in practice.

Under the existing two-tier system of criminal courts, one of the most critical decisions relates to the mode and venue of trial. For certain kinds of offences the venue and type of trial are determined by law. This applies to the most serious offences such as murder, manslaughter and rape, which are triable only on indictment. Magistrates have no option but to commit such cases for trial to the Crown Court, though they are relatively few in number. A much more numerous group, comprising the least serious offences, are designated as 'summary only', which means that they have to be tried by magistrates themselves. However there is a third and much more contentious category of offences for which there is no prescribed mode of trial. This includes offences that, relative to the other two categories, fall into an intermediate or variable degree of seriousness: for example, theft, handling stolen goods and burglary. A considerable degree of discretion is built into the system for determining how and where these so-called 'triable either way' cases (see the Introduction) will be tried.

Following a recent change in the law,[30] the procedure for determining the venue and mode of trial with regard to triable either way cases is determined in part by the defendant's plea. Previously the mode of trial decision came before the plea was taken, but under the new 'plea before venue' procedure, if the defendant indicates an intention to plead guilty then the magistrates are obliged to try the case themselves. Only if the defendant indicates an intention to plead not guilty (or gives no indication either way) is the following discretionary decision-making process activated.

In cases such as these, magistrates have first to decide which venue would be more appropriate for trial of the offence, in the light of representations made by the prosecution and the defence, though at present defendants are entitled to insist on being tried in the Crown Court if they so choose. Among the factors which magistrates are required to take into account in reaching a decision are the seriousness of the offence, and whether their own powers of punishment would be adequate if the defendant were to be convicted (section 19, Magistrates' Courts Act 1980). National guidelines relating to mode of trial decisions[31] have also been issued in an effort to promote greater consistency and also reduce the level of unnecessary committals. Even where triable either way cases are tried summarily, magistrates still have the power to commit a convicted defendant to the Crown Court for sentence where they feel that their own powers are inadequate.

As with bail decisions, the exercise of both these sets of powers can have profound consequences, not only for the defendant but also for the rest of the penal system. Decisions as to mode of trial and sentencing venue can affect *inter alia* the likelihood and duration of a remand in custody, the probability of an acquittal, the type and severity of any sentence imposed (and thus, indirectly, the size of the prison population) and the cost to the public purse. They also likely to influence public perceptions of fairness (particularly with regard to the (non-)availability of jury trial), and thus have a crucial bearing on the wider crisis of legitimacy that continues to affect the criminal justice system as a whole.

In recent years, there has been a dramatic increase, amounting to a veritable explosion, in both the number and proportion of defendants who are committed for trial at the Crown Court in respect of triable either way offences. In 1998, 73,300 persons were committed for trial, which represents a 25 per cent increase on the 1979 figure of 55,300 (Home Office, 1980: Table 4.5; and 2000a: para. 6.14). However, the number of committals for trial was 16 per cent fewer than in 1997. This recent reduction is directly attributable to the introduction of the plea before venue procedure. Another direct consequence of the new procedure, however, has been to drastically increase the proportion of defendants who are committed to the Crown Court for sentencing after trial by the magistrates' court. The number of committals for sentence in 1998 rose by more than 160 per cent compared with the previous year, from 7,300 to over 19,000 (Home Office, 2000a: para. 6.14).

Turning now to the way the remand decision-making process operated in practice, at least before the 'plea before venue' system was introduced, the predominant influence on the way magistrates exercised their discretion was found to be the attitude of the Crown Prosecution Service. In one study (Riley and Vennard, 1988) the degree of correspondence between prosecution recommendations and the court's decision as to venue was as high as 96 per cent, raising concerns that magistrates might be improperly delegating their responsibility for these decisions to the CPS instead of exercising their own independent judgement. Alternatively, it could be argued (see for example, Ashworth, 1998: 245) that both prosecutors and magistrates were independently applying the same criteria and, not surprisingly, frequently came to the same decision. However, this explanation is rendered somewhat less plausible by the evidence in the same study of pronounced regional variations in the proportion of defendants who are committed for trial (another example of 'justice by geography').

Other studies (notably Hedderman and Moxon, 1992, 1994)[32] confirmed that a majority of the triable either way cases (64 per cent) that were tried in the Crown Court were committed because the magistrates declined jurisdiction rather than because the defendant had elected that form of trial. Moreover, a majority of these committals by the magistrates (62 per cent) received sentences that magistrates would have been empowered to impose, suggesting that the committal may not have been necessary in such cases. Both the Mode of Trial guidelines and the new plea before venue procedure were introduced in order to reduce the number of unnecessary committals. But although the number of committals for trial has fallen, as we have seen, CPS statistics for 1998 reveal that the proportion of triable either way cases that are committed for trial at the behest of the magistrates rather than at the request of the defendant has in fact continued to increase steadily, from 63 per cent in 1992 to 72 per cent in 1998.

In spite of the recent developments we have outlined, and the partial easing of the pressure on the Crown Court to which they have contributed, the demand for reform has, if anything, intensified rather than abated. There are now two rival and, to some extent, contradictory sets of initiatives which are being promoted by different government departments,[33] each of which is likely to have far-reaching implications for the present system of determining how and where different types of criminal cases are tried. The first set of proposals emanates from the Home Office and would remove the defendant's right to insist on trial in the Crown Court in triable either way cases.[34] If this is enacted, decisions as to venue will become the sole responsibility of magistrates, after considering representations from the prosecution and the defence. It is also proposed to reclassify certain triable either way offences such as minor theft involving goods valued at less than £5000 as summary only.[35]

The government estimated that the effect of these changes would be a reduction in the number of Crown Court trials of around 14,000 per annum, generating net savings of £128 million. The main cost would be a substantial curtailment in the rights of citizens who are charged with either way offences to insist on trial by judge and jury if they choose to. They would be forced to accept a mode of trial with an inferior acquittal rate.[36] (Defendants who intend to plead guilty would not be disadvantaged by these proposals since they appear willing to waive their right to Crown Court trial. They would, of course, remain liable to be committed to the Crown Court for sentence.) Whatever one's views on the merits of the proposal, it is unlikely to result in more consistent sentencing than at present, in view of the known disparities in sentencing between local benches, and the extremely limited influence of the Court of Appeal on the sentencing practices of magistrates (see below).

The second initiative emanates from the Lord Chancellor's Department: the potentially even more far-reaching review of the criminal courts under Lord Justice Auld, to which we referred earlier. Although the review was not expected to report until some time in 2001, Auld was known to be considering still greater restrictions to the right of jury trial, including cases involving technical or complex evidence such as fraud cases, and those involving children as defendants or principal witnesses. However, the proposals relating to the structure and jurisdiction of the courts themselves could prove to be yet more radical, as we will see in the next section.

## THE SENTENCING DECISION

In deciding what sentence to impose, sentencers may take a variety of factors into account. They include factors relating to the offence, including any aggravating or mitigating circumstances; factors relating to the offender; and factors relating to the aims or purposes that a sentencer might hope to achieve in selecting a particular sentence. We begin this section by outlining some of the main sources of information that are available to assist sentencers in reaching their decision. However, the single most distinctive feature of the English sentencing system is the breadth of discretion – in respect of each of those factors – that is conferred on sentencers at all levels within the system. That is why it is also important to understand who the sentencers are. For under conditions of largely unrestricted discretion, factors such as the character, attitude, training and social background of sentencers may make a considerable difference to the way their discretion is exercised. We will conclude this section by assessing the different forms of 'constraints' to which sentencers may be subject in exercising their discretion, now and in the past.

### Aids to sentencing

In order to assist sentencers in their task, various reports may be supplied to the court. In the Crown Court the prosecution is responsible for producing a statement, known as 'the antecedents', which contains brief details of the offence and any previous convictions and sentences relating to the offender. However, the most important source of information consists of *'pre-sentence'* reports (or PSRs, formerly known as social inquiry reports), which are prepared for the court by probation officers (or in the case of young offenders, by other members of the local youth offending team; see Chapter 9). As the task of sentencing has increased in complexity in recent years the rôle of this report has become steadily more important. At one time it simply commented on an offender's suitability for probation, but following the recommendations of the Streatfeild Committee in 1961, the probation service was encouraged to make more general recommendations as to sentence, in addition to the provision of more factual information concerning the offender's character and personality, social background, educational record, employment and prospects.

The position of the pre-sentence report was made even more pivotal within the original sentencing framework introduced by the Criminal Justice Act 1991 (Cavadino, 1997c), though subsequent changes blunted the thrust of these reforms as well as many of its other provisions. The intention was for pre-sentence reports to assist sentencers by focusing principally on the seriousness of the offence rather than, as in the past, the welfare needs of the offender;[37] and by considering an offender's suitability for a community sentence. To this end, National Standards for Pre-Sentence Reports were introduced in 1992 (Home Office et al., 1992; later revised, in 1995 and 2000), which prescribed a uniform format and listed the contents to be covered.

The 1991 Act also stipulated that pre-sentence reports should normally be considered before imposing either a custodial sentence or one of the more restrictive 'community sentences' (see Chapter 5). This would have ensured that reports were prepared for virtually all offenders at risk of imprisonment.[38] However, this met with resistance on the part of some members of the judiciary who objected to their loss of discretion (Gelsthorpe and Raynor, 1995). Subsequently the Criminal Justice and Public Order Act 1994 allowed courts to dispense with reports which they deemed 'unnecessary' whenever the offender is aged 18 or over, and thus to deprive themselves of the benefit of what could be relevant information and an independent assessment of the case and the various sentencing possibilities. This raised concerns, first that offenders might be sent to prison when there could be a genuinely viable non-custodial option available (Penal Affairs Consortium, 1995f). Second, there were fears that this could have a discriminatory impact on black offenders, since research had shown that such offenders were disproportionately liable to receive custodial sentences after pleading not guilty in the Crown Court (Moxon, 1988; Hood, 1992: 156; see Chapter 10). Subsequently, it has been found that around 15 per cent of adult offenders (irrespective of court) are given custodial sentences without a PSR, but community sentences are rarely imposed in the absence of such a report (Charles et al., 1997).[39]

More recently, the Crime and Disorder Act 1998 introduced a new shortened form of pre-sentence report, known as the 'specific sentence report', for courts to use when contemplating the imposition of a reparation or action plan order. These new measures are currently only available for young offenders and are described in more detail in Chapter 9.

### Who are the sentencers?

The English criminal justice system is unusual in conferring the power to pass sentence on two completely different sets of sentencers who contrast not only in the powers at their disposal, but also in their social background, composition, mode of selection, training and much else besides. Adult offenders who are convicted in the magistrates' courts will normally be sentenced by a bench of lay (meaning unpaid, and largely untrained) magistrates, though in some of the larger conurbations lay benches are supplemented by full-time professional magistrates known as District Judges (Magistrates' Courts),[40] who sit alone. Magistrates are responsible for handling around 96 per cent of criminal cases, although a growing number who are convicted of triable either way offences (31,034 in 1999, which is just over 6 per cent of all indictable offenders proceeded against in the magistrates' courts) are then committed to the Crown Court for sentence (Lord Chancellor's Department, 2000). However, the review of criminal courts under Lord Justice Auld (2000b), to which we referred earlier, was known to be contemplating a radical overhaul of the existing structure and jurisdiction of the criminal courts. One option under consideration would involve the introduction of a unified three-tier court in which 'either way cases' are tried by a single district judge flanked by two lay magistrates, who would presumably have increased sentencing powers, thus obviating the need to commit so many offenders to the Crown Court for sentence.[41]

Although magistrates are officially supposed to be broadly representative of the communities they serve, in reality they conform much more closely to Lord Devlin's cliché about the composition of the jury in earlier times. In 1956, when eligibility for jury service was still limited by a property qualification, he described jurors as 'predominantly male, middle-aged, middle-minded and middle-class'. Although women now account for 49 per cent of the lay magistracy, successive studies (notably Baldwin, 1976; but see also Burney,

1979; Raine, 1989; and Dignan and Wynne, 1997) have shown them to be overwhelmingly middle-aged and middle-class. They also tend to be middle-minded, not just because of the selective (and, until recently, highly secretive) recruitment procedure by which they are appointed, but also because in the course of their training and socialization they are imbued with a particular self-perception about their rôle that amounts almost to a consistent ideology (Parker et al., 1989), aspects of which we shall discuss shortly.

Lay magistrates are given a small amount of training, in which sentencing matters feature fairly prominently, and are assisted in the exercise of their powers by a legally qualified clerk.[42] However, studies have shown (Hood, 1962, 1972; Parker et al., 1989) that the chief formative influence on sentencing practice in magistrates' courts is not the law, their training or the advice they receive from other professionals, nor even the way similar cases have been decided by that particular court in the past.

Instead the principal influence is the 'sentencing culture' of a particular bench, into which new recruits are gradually socialized by watching their more experienced colleagues at work. The ideology which gives substance to this culture is based on a twin belief in the uniqueness of the magisterial rôle itself, and also the individuality of each particular case. The latter belief explicitly rejects consistency as a virtue in its own right, while the former demands a balancing of public interests against those of the particular defendant in the light of moral judgements that only the magistrate is deemed qualified to make. Because sentencing is viewed by magistrates as a craft or mystery, whose rites are known only to initiates (as opposed to a rational enterprise dedicated to the pursuit of externally defined goals), this renders it both impervious to criticism from outside, and highly resistant to attempts at external control.

Defendants who are convicted in the Crown Court are sentenced by a Crown Court judge. Crown Court judges differ from lay magistrates in a number of important respects (though it could be said that their ideologies are similar). One important difference between them is that judges are not only legally trained but have invariably spent most of their working lives as practising barristers (or, less often, solicitors). It is important to note, however, that they receive little training for their rôle as *judges*, in marked contrast to most Western European jurisdictions which adopt a professional career structure for judges who are recruited immediately on graduating from law school. The Judicial Studies Board provides training for Crown Court judges, consisting of short (four day) induction courses for new recruits, and continuation courses for more experienced judges. Although judicial attitudes towards training are becoming somewhat less dismissive than they were in the past, it remains the case that the main method of 'perfecting the art' of sentencing is by practising on actual offenders.[43]

The fact that English judges are recruited almost exclusively from the ranks of successful practising barristers has also had the effect of narrowing considerably the background from which judges are drawn, even in comparison with the far from representative magistracy. Judges who sit in the Crown Court tend to be slightly older than magistrates on average (around age 60 for judges and age 56 for lay justices). However, in contrast to magistrates, judges are not just predominantly male, they are almost exclusively so. In 1999, only 6 per cent of circuit judges (who sit in the Crown Court) were women (Home Office, 1999a: 67). In terms of race the position is even worse for, again in 1999, there were only five black circuit judges (0.9 per cent).

As for the social composition of the judiciary, the many surveys that have been carried out in recent years show an overwhelming predominance of upper and upper-middle-class backgrounds (see, for example, Griffith, 1997: 18; House of Commons Home Affairs Committee, 1995). The figures on schooling and educational background are particularly revealing, not just because they disclose that roughly 80 per cent of the country's judges received a public school education, or that over three quarters had attended either Oxford or Cambridge universities, but because they also confirm that this social profile has remained virtually unaltered over the last four decades or more. The significance of these social and occupational characteristics of the judiciary is twofold. In the first place they draw attention to the enormous social distance that exists between those who pass sentence in the Crown Court and those on the receiving end. This might call into question the legitimacy of the proceedings, not least in the eyes of many defendants. But even more importantly they also help to explain the uniqueness of English judicial culture compared with that elsewhere.[44] Part of this has to do with the lack of systematic training to which we have already referred. But – particularly in the absence of a coherent professional philosophy – social and occupational origins have also played an important part in shaping judicial attitudes in England.

The restrictive social and occupational background from which almost all senior judges in England are drawn has provided a fertile medium in which an alternative and extremely powerful indigenous judicial culture has been able to develop. This is founded on a set of shared ideas that have, at least until recently, constituted the ruling ideology in both legal and political circles, at any rate on matters of sentencing policy. The cornerstone of that ideology is *the doctrine of judicial independence*, to which we now turn.

## The doctrine of judicial independence

A restricted version of the doctrine of judicial independence prevails in most legal systems whose constitutional arrangements and traditions provide for a separation of powers between the legislative, executive and judicial branches of government. There it is interpreted simply and uncontroversially to mean that governments are not permitted to influence the decision of the courts *in individual cases*. However, in England the principle has been inflated into a much more extreme dogma which might be termed the 'extravagant version' of the doctrine. This relies on a constitutional sleight of hand to claim not only that judges should be free to administer the law (and sentences) without fear and favour in respect of a particular case; but also that it would be unconstitutional for governments to seek to regulate the total amount of discretion that judges should exercise by formulating broad sentencing policies (Ashworth, 2000: 46).

This curious distortion of the doctrine that has taken place in England cannot be explained by the mere presence of constitutional arrangements based on a separation of powers or other countries would have experienced a similar phenomenon. A much more plausible explanation might be found in Weber's distinction (1968: ch. 11) between those countries that developed formally rational judicial systems under the influence of Roman and ecclesiastical law, in which the demand for predictability encouraged measures to control judicial discretion; and countries such as England, in which a historically powerful cadre of lawyers successfully resisted such demands and jealously guarded their traditional independence. Although he did not refer to sentencing practices as such, the traditional English approach to sentencing certainly provides an excellent example of Weber's *'khadi justice'* which 'knows no rational "rules of decision"' and eschews the giving of reasons for decisions. Weber's analysis also suggests that as they develop and become more bureaucratic (see Chapter 3), societies are likely to replace *'khadi justice'* with more rational and predictable forms of justice. As we shall see, there have been some moves in this direction, even in England.

It has been persuasively argued by Ashworth (1983: 59–68; 1995a: 40–46; 2000: 46–51) that the extravagant version of the doctrine of judicial independence has no foundation in constitutional law, for Parliament is at liberty to legislate on any aspect of sentencing should it choose to. Nevertheless, during the twentieth century governments came in practice to accept the extravagant version; and, like many such myths, its influence over the years has been in inverse proportion to its constitutional validity. We will be tracing its pervasive effects below, first in relation to the largely untrammelled sentencing powers that have been enjoyed by the courts in England for most of the last century; and secondly in contributing to the policy vacuum that continued to characterize the English sentencing system, at least until the enactment of the Criminal Justice Act 1991.

### Constraints on the powers of sentencers

In discussing the extent to which sentencing discretion in England and Wales has been subject to control in the past, or is likely to be in the future, we will adopt the threefold classification elaborated by K.C. Davis (1969): that is, *'confining'* discretion (restricting the scope of discretionary power that is available); *'structuring'* discretion (regulating its exercise in advance); and *'checking'* discretion (reviewing the way it has been exercised by an appeal process). Another useful preliminary distinction is that between external control over sentencing discretion as opposed to *self-regulation* practised by sentencers themselves. For, as we shall see, one of the most obvious effects of the myth of judicial independence on sentencing practice over the years has been the extent to which sentencers have been left to police themselves according to their own rules and principles.

Although not totally unfettered, the sentencing powers that are available under the English penal system are still subject to only minimal external constraints on the way they are exercised. Wide discretion on the part of sentencers has long been a hallmark of the system, and in the recent past this extended both to the initial choice of general sentencing *aim* which the sentencer thought it appropriate to pursue[45] and to the selection (and severity) of a particular sentence from the extensive range that is available. These conditions fostered a 'pick-and-choose' or 'supermarket' approach to sentencing on the part of the courts which was encouraged by the Court of Appeal, and which governments did not seek to overturn until the introduction of a new sentencing framework in the Criminal Justice Act 1991 (see below).

CONFINING DISCRETION   Compared with other jurisdictions, little attempt has been made in England and Wales to confine the exercise of sentencers' discretion by limiting the extent of their powers. There are statutory *maximum* penalties for particular offences, but many of these were devised so long ago, and in such different circumstances, as to render them largely irrelevant for the control of judicial sentencing today. Moreover, the tendency during the present century has been to create broadly-defined criminal offences (such as theft), with a sufficiently generous maximum to cater for the worst contingency. There are still relatively few mandatory sentences. For a long time the only major exception was the mandatory life imprisonment sentence for murder. Even this is unpopular with the judiciary as an infringement on their discretion to do justice in individual cases, and there have been repeated calls for its abolition (for example, Nathan, 1989; Lane, 1993; Penal Affairs Consortium, 1994). There is also a 'semi-mandatory' sentence of disqualification from driving for the offence of driving with excess alcohol in the blood; 'semi-mandatory' meaning that the sentence is required unless the court finds that there are exceptional circumstances in the individual case. A number of new semi-mandatory and minimum sentences were introduced by the Crime (Sentences) Act 1997, as we shall see below. The sentencing powers of magistrates are more closely confined by law. For example, they cannot impose a custodial sentence that is longer than six months in respect of a single offence. Nor can they normally impose a fine of more than £5,000. Nevertheless, they also enjoy a considerable degree of discretion within these upper limits.

There are a few additional restrictions on the use or combination of certain measures, but apart from these limited inroads little attempt has been made to *confine* the discretion of sentencers by statute. One notable (and short-lived) exception was a provision in the Criminal Justice Act 1967 compelling courts to suspend all sentences of imprisonment of up to six months. This provoked fierce opposition from the Magistrates' Association which viewed it as an unwarranted attack on the independence of magistrates, and just five years later the measure was repealed as a result.

STRUCTURING DISCRETION   One of the best-known techniques for *structuring* discretion, which has gained special favour in America and Australia during the last decade, is based on the adoption of comprehensive sets of sentencing guidelines for the courts. These can take various forms,[46] but they all prescribe in advance (with varying degrees of precision) the appropriate penalty for a whole range of offender/offence combinations. This approach allows a much tighter and more consistent control of sentencing than could ever be achieved by a system of appellate review of the kind that has been favoured in England and Wales until recently (see below). By providing sentencers with one set of criteria relating to the circumstances of the offence in question, and a different range of criteria taking into account relevant characteristics of the offender, guidelines can operate rather in the manner of a road mileage chart, enabling the appropriate penalty to be simply 'read off' from the matrix supplied. Or they can be less mechanical than this, simply providing a range of standard sentences for different kinds of typical offence, along with guidance on roughly how much to adjust the standard sentence in the light of common aggravating and mitigating circumstances. This is the form that sentencing guidelines have taken in England. In either case, guidelines normally only provide a 'presumptive sentence' or starting point, from which the sentencer is free to depart if this is thought appropriate in an individual case, provided reasons are given for doing so.

In general, sentencers seem to respond better and more willingly to the structuring of their discretion by guidelines than to having it confined by maximum, minimum and mandatory sentences. They resent the latter, which constrains their power to do justice as they see it in individual cases. But sentencers often welcome external *guidance* as to how they should make their (often difficult) sentencing decisions, whether this comes from official guidelines or the informal sentencing culture of the bench or advice from more experienced colleagues.

At least until the Crime and Disorder Act 1998 (see below), attempts to structure sentencing discretion in England and Wales have been extremely limited in scope. One early example (dating from 1948) took the form of statutory provisions discouraging the use of custodial penalties for young offenders unless it appeared that no other method was appropriate. Since 1989, the Magistrates' Association has issued its own national guidelines setting out a scale of recommended penalties covering the 25 commonest offence types likely to come before the magistrates, together with guidance on the approach to be adopted for different degrees of seriousness. These guidelines have been revised periodically.[47]

The most ambitious legislative attempt to structure the exercise of sentencing discretion during the twentieth century was made by the Criminal Justice Act 1991. This established broad criteria – relating to both sentencing aim and the amount of punishment – that courts should apply when deciding on a sentence. The general framework established by the 1991 Act is still in force although, as we shall see, its effects on sentencers' discretion have been substantially watered down since its introduction. We shall be examining the provisions and fortunes of the 1991 Act later in this chapter. Otherwise, the only guidance that is available comes from the past practice of the courts themselves in determining the 'going rate' for particular offences, and in particular the *checking* and *structuring* functions of the Court of Appeal.

CHECKING AND STRUCTURING DISCRETION: THE ROLE OF THE COURT OF APPEAL    Although there is no such thing as a 'correct' sentence, there is a notional scale of penalties familiarly known as the '*tariff*', which is based on the 'normal range' that has been developed by courts in the past, under the guidance of the Court of Appeal. The key principle underlying the tariff is that the severity of a sentence should be proportionate to the gravity of the offence and the degree of culpability on the part of the offender (or in other words the offender's 'just deserts'). The main sentencing aims reflected in the tariff are those of general deterrence, retribution and, possibly, denunciation. Where a sentence is imposed that clearly exceeds the tariff it is liable to be reduced on appeal, and traditionally the rôle of the Court of Appeal was confined to *checking* a sentencer's discretion retrospectively in this way.

However, once its sentencing decisions came to be regularly reported in the *Criminal Law Review* (from 1954 onwards), the way was then open for the Court of Appeal to start laying down general sentencing principles for lower courts to apply in similar cases in the future. This *structuring* function of the Court of Appeal was further strengthened by the appearance in 1970 of D.A. Thomas's *Principles of Sentencing* (2nd edn, 1979), which provided an accessible digest of a great many of its decisions, both reported and unreported. Other developments include the introduction in 1979 of a series of law reports devoted exclusively to sentencing decisions – *Criminal Appeal Reports (Sentencing)* – and an encyclopaedia – *Current Sentencing Practice* – which makes it easier to locate relevant decisions. In addition, the regularly updated *Sentencing Referencer* (Thomas, 2000) clearly sets out the main requirements for each main form of sentence, drawing attention to the key sentencing principles that are involved in applying it.

Since the mid-1970s, the Court of Appeal itself has sought to provide more systematic guidance for sentencers by laying down so-called '*guideline*' *judgments*. These go beyond the immediate issues raised by a particular case and spell out, for example, the range of penalties felt to be appropriate for varying degrees of seriousness within a given offence category.[48] In the early 1980s the Court of Appeal also sought to formulate more general guidance on overall sentencing levels by attempting to 'talk down' the level of custodial sentencing for ordinary 'run-of-the-mill' offences.[49]

Although this self-regulatory mechanism sounds as if it might be quite an effective constraint on the exercise of discretion by sentencers, in practice it is subject to a number of serious limitations. The most obvious of these relates to the tariff itself, which is inherently vague. While the Court of Appeal is ultimately responsible for establishing the tariff, this is far from being a cut-and-dried list of appropriate penalties. It is merely a rough guide to the general sentencing levels that this court feels is appropriate, and allowance needs to be made for inconsistency on the part of the Court of Appeal itself (Thomas, 1983; Ashworth, 2000: 29), plus the considerable 'latitude' which is normally allowed before it will interfere with a sentence passed by the Crown Court.

There is even disagreement among judges as to whether the tariff should properly be based on the seriousness of the *current offence*, as the Court of Appeal affirmed in the case of *R. v. Queen*[50] or whether it is permissible for a court to sentence primarily on the basis of the offender's *previous record*, for which, as Ashworth (1990; 1995a: 153) has pointed out, there is also Court of Appeal authority.[51] In practice it is clearly the case that petty persistent offenders have often been given sentences that were quite disproportionate to the offences they had currently committed.[52] In cases such as these, trial courts have clearly operated with an *offender-based* tariff rather than one that was *offence-based*. The original intention embodied in section 29(1) of the Criminal Justice Act 1991 was that the penalty imposed should be commensurate with the seriousness of the current offence. The section explicitly stated that offences should not be regarded as more serious 'by reason of any previous convictions of the offender or any failure of his to respond to previous sentences'. Although there was nothing new in this principle, it was hotly contested by members of the judiciary including the Lord Chief Justice (Taylor, 1993), and the resulting clamour contributed to the government's decision (as part of its 'law and order counter reformation' in 1993; see below) to reword section 29(1) to read:

> In considering the seriousness of any offence, the court may take into account any previous convictions of the offender or any failure of his to respond to previous sentences.[53]

It has been persuasively argued (Wasik and von Hirsch, 1994: 413; Ashworth, 1995a: 161) that this reformulation is still consistent with the principle affirmed in *Queen* that sentencers should essentially apply an offence-based rather than an offender-based tariff (while allowing for a measure of mitigation for a *good* previous record), but there has been no Court of Appeal pronouncement in favour of this interpretation. In practice, sentencers seem to have taken the 1993 amendment as an invitation to increase sentences substantially if the offender has previous convictions (see below).

Another difficulty with the tariff is the fact that there are probably at least as many different tariffs in practice as there are levels of court (Court of Appeal, Crown Court and magistrates' court).[54] Consequently, the guidance handed down by the Court of Appeal is frequently way out of line with the levels of sentence that are typically imposed for similar offences by the lower courts. One notable example of this gap in sentencing levels (Ashworth, 1983) was the 1980 case of *R. v. McCann*,[55] in which the Court of Appeal reduced the sentence for a relatively minor burglary by an offender who had only one distant previous conviction, from two years' imprisonment to nine months. Even this reduced sentence exceeds, by a considerable margin, the *maximum* penalty which could have been imposed in a magistrates' court (which is where the majority of burglars of this type would normally have been tried). And indeed in the magistrates' court in 1980 less than a third of such cases would have received a custodial penalty at all (Home Office, 1981a).[56]

It seems, then, that the Court of Appeal is out of touch with actual sentencing practices operating elsewhere in the system, and especially in magistrates' courts. This should not be a surprise. For appeals against sentences imposed by magistrates are heard not by the Court of Appeal, but by the Crown Court. The only appeals against sentence that the Court of Appeal gets to hear are those imposed by the Crown Court which operates a harsher tariff than does the magistrates' court.[57] This was confirmed in a very thorough study which compared differences in sentencing patterns between the two levels of court in respect of six common triable either way offences (Hedderman and Moxon, 1992).[58] When a sample of cases in which defendants had elected for trial (and which magistrates would therefore have considered suitable for summary trial had they consented) was compared with a matched sample of similar cases tried by magistrates, it was found that those sentenced in the Crown Court were almost three times as likely to receive a custodial sentence, and that such sentences were on average two and a half times as long.

Until recently, the rôle of the Court of Appeal in structuring the discretion of Crown Court sentencers was further constrained by the fact that only the defendant could appeal against sentence. This had the effect of limiting the range of sentences that were likely to be appealed mainly to prison sentences in the upper reaches of the tariff and, as a result, relatively little guidance was available on the use of non-custodial penalties. Since 1988 the prosecution has in effect been given a limited right of appeal, at least in cases where the Attorney General can be persuaded to refer an 'unduly lenient' sentence to the Court of Appeal. But this has done little to improve the quality of guidance emanating from the Court of Appeal as there are a number of restrictions surrounding its exercise.[59] There are now around 60–70 references by the Attorney General each year (mainly involving cases of rape, robbery, grievous bodily harm, malicious woundings and causing death by dangerous driving), though not all of these result in an increased sentence (Ashworth, 2000: 31).

One of the most serious weaknesses in the self-regulatory capacity of the Court of Appeal remains its continuing failure to provide much-needed sentencing guidance in respect of 'ordinary' offences such as theft, burglary[60] and dishonesty. And given the existence of the three different tariffs we identified above, this deficiency appears to be systemic and probably irremediable by the Court of Appeal if it is left to its own devices.

This illustrates the point that the problems of sentencing will not all be automatically solved by introducing structuring mechanisms such as guidelines. It is also necessary for sentences to be structured in the right way and set at the right level.

## SENTENCING OUT OF CONTROL: THE CRUX OF THE CRISIS

### Pre-1991: the laissez faire approach

For much of the post-war period, continued deference to the principle of judicial independence resulted in a virtual abdication of responsibility for developing a coherent sentencing policy on the part of successive English governments. As a result, courts were left with considerable discretion which was only marginally constrained by the guidance emanating from the Court of Appeal. Such was the strength of this self-denying ordinance that very few attempts were made by governments during this time to fill the policy-making vacuum, and even these were met by implacable opposition on the part of the judiciary. One short-lived and singularly ill-fated example was the Royal Commission on the Penal System which was set up in 1964 'to re-examine the concepts and purposes which should underlie the punishment and treatment of offenders'. Just eighteen months later it achieved the dubious distinction of being the only Royal Commission to be wound up without producing a report when it collapsed over internal differences as to the scope of its report and how it should proceed.

In the wake of this débâcle, subsequent attempts at policy-making were less ambitious, if not conspicuously more successful. For example, as we shall see in Chapter 5, the main response of successive governments to the growing prison numbers crisis from the 1960s to the 1980s was what we call *'the strategy of encouragement'*: providing a range of additional penal measures and then, out of deference to the principle of judicial independence, relying on exhortation[61] rather than legislative direction in an attempt to change the sentencing practice of the courts. The early 1980s saw the culmination of this approach with Home Office ministers and the Lord Chief Justice working together to press the case for restraint in the use of custody, albeit with very limited success.

The result of this 'softly softly' approach was that sentencers were effectively allowed a free rein in developing their own sentencing practice, leaving official policy-makers to respond and adapt to an agenda over which they had little control. The policy vacuum which was allowed to develop in this way was inadequately filled by leaving it up to the courts to formulate their own guiding principles. This was partly because, as we have seen, the Court of Appeal showed no inclination to formulate a coherent set of sentencing aims for the guidance of sentencers, and partly because the self-regulatory mechanisms on which it sought to rely in the pursuit of its more limited policy objectives were themselves seriously defective. As a result, the discretionary powers of sentencers remained largely unconstrained and out of control while the penal crisis intensified.

**THE 1991 REFORMS: A NEW SENTENCING FRAMEWORK**

During the late 1980s, following the appointment of Douglas Hurd as Home Secretary in 1985, there were signs of a growing recognition within the government that legislation to widen sentencers' options, even when backed by executive exhortation, was insufficient to change sentencing outcomes and that, unless sentencing discretion was restricted, there was little hope of modifying sentencers' own objectives in the pursuit of the government's goal of reducing the use of custody (Sabol, 1990).

There followed a toning-down of the law-and-order rhetoric of the early 1980s and, while the development of penal policy during this period was increasingly influenced by pragmatic considerations – how to deal with the growing penal crisis – there were also welcome signs of a willingness to engage in fresh thinking about crime and the way offenders are dealt with. This was reflected very vividly in changing government attitudes towards the use of imprisonment. A Green Paper published in 1988 (Home Office, 1988a) stated bluntly that 'imprisonment is not the most effective punishment for most crime' and that it should be reserved only for very serious offences involving significant risks to the public. At the same time there was growing support for the policy of dealing with a much larger proportion of offenders in the community. Mindful perhaps that previous attempts to limit the use of custody had not been particularly successful, this time the government made it clear in its White Paper *Crime, Justice and Protecting the Public* (Home Office, 1990a) that it was prepared to risk the wrath of the judges by setting out for the first time a new policy framework for sentencing which would give much clearer policy guidance to sentencers than at any time in the past. The key element in this strategy was the Criminal Justice Act of 1991.

Part I of the Act, which dealt with sentencing, reflected four key themes that were set out in the White Paper, although they were not articulated as clearly as they might have been. The first was a welcome *reinterpretation of the doctrine of judicial independence*, which asserted government responsibility for formulating sentencing policy while affirming the principle of non-interference in individual cases. The second theme was the adoption of a *'just deserts'* approach, based on the principle of proportional punishment as the primary aim of sentencing. This was intended to play a vital rôle in limiting the use of custody, especially for minor property offenders. However, the principle of proportionality was subordinated to the aim of incapacitation, in respect of a restricted category of more serious cases. This 'twin-track' or *bifurcatory* approach to sentencing constituted the third key theme underlying the 1991 reforms. The fourth and final theme was concerned with the means by which these ends should be pursued, which was to be a *partnership between the legislature and the judiciary*. Under the terms of this partnership, Parliament would confine itself to establishing a framework consisting of general principles, leaving it to the courts themselves to decide how these principles should apply in individual cases, and to the Court of Appeal to develop more detailed guidance where appropriate.

The sentencing framework that was introduced in the 1991 Act is set out in Figure 5.1 (Chapter 5). The basic framework is still in force despite the partial backtracking that soon followed. It can be thought of as a set of filters designed to ensure that the severity of the penalty appropriately reflects the seriousness of the offence. The Act established two 'proportionality thresholds' that have to be satisfied before an offender can be dealt with by any of the more restrictive sentencing measures. The first proportionality threshold – the *custody criterion* – restricted the use of imprisonment to offences that are 'so serious that only such a sentence can be justified for the offence'.[62] The second threshold[63] governed the use of 'community sentences', which are non-custodial penalties that nevertheless entail some restriction of liberty (see Chapter 5 for further discussion). These were reserved for offences which are 'serious enough to warrant such a sentence'. Where either a custodial or community sentence is passed, the deprivation of liberty involved should normally be 'commensurate with the seriousness of the offence'.[64]

In this way the 1991 Act sought to prioritize the 'just deserts' proportionality principle as the primary sentencing aim for the great majority of offenders and bring to an end the 'pick-and-choose' or 'supermarket' approach that had previously prevailed. However, the overall coherence of the new sentencing framework was seriously undermined by the incorporation of an important exception to the principle of proportionality in the case of violent or sexual offences. In these cases, the use of custody and of long custodial sentences was authorized where the court[65] considers it necessary 'to protect the public from serious harm from the offender', even though the sentence is out of proportion to the seriousness of the current offence. Consequently, the principle of proportionality is subordinated to the aim of incapacitation in these cases. This gave a further twist to the bifurcatory spiral, and sanctioned the use of harsher penalties on a group of offenders who were already severely dealt with within the existing system (Wasik and von Hirsch, 1990). Quite apart from its obvious implications for the prison numbers crisis, such a strategy means that certain offenders are being incarcerated on the basis of what it is feared they might (speculatively) do in the future rather than what they have been proved to have done in the past. When similar proposals have been made in the past they have been greeted with well-founded objections on both moral and empirical grounds, given the known inaccuracy of existing prediction techniques and the tendency for violence to be 'over-predicted' (see Bottoms, 1977; Monahan, 1981; Radzinowicz and Hood, 1978; Bottoms and Brownsword, 1983; Cavadino, 1989: 99–100). Moreover, the Act does not even require sentencers to consider such predictive techniques as do currently exist before passing sentence.

An even more serious weakness with the Act was its failure to spell out with sufficient clarity the radical new framework it was seeking to introduce (Ashworth, 1995b: 259–60). The language used was opaque and frequently clumsy and, in the light of previous experience, far too much faith was reposed in the constructive partnership that was envisaged between legislature and judiciary. This misplaced trust rendered the Act highly vulnerable to a process of 'destructive interpretation' at the hands of an often hostile or at best unsympathetic judiciary, sections of which were openly resentful at their perceived loss of independence.

One clear instance of this judicial obstructionism concerned the keystone around which the new sentencing framework was constructed: the primacy that was intended to be accorded to the principles of desert and proportionality and the downgrading of some other penal aims, notably deterrence. Although not explicit in the Act itself, the preceding White Paper had come close to dismissing deterrence as a permissible sentencing aim (Home Office, 1990a: para. 2.8). And yet in one of its first rulings[66] on the wording of the new Act, the Court of Appeal, led by the Lord Chief Justice, refused to allow an appeal against a four year sentence for robbery even though this had been specifically referred to by the trial judge as a 'long deterrent sentence'. Instead, the Court of Appeal took advantage of this early opportunity effectively to rewrite the Act by stipulating that the phrase 'commensurate with the seriousness of the offence' in section 2(2)(a) means 'commensurate with the punishment *and deterrence* which the seriousness of the offence requires' (italics supplied). This 'flagrant misreading' of the statute enabled the judges 'to continue largely with "business as usual"' (Ashworth, 1995a: 83).

Judicial non-cooperation with the intentions of the Act was also manifested in the continuing reluctance by the Court of Appeal to take the lead that was envisaged for it in developing clear guidance for the lower courts in relation to the custody threshold – showing the danger in leaving this crucial term to be defined and developed by the judges themselves. Ashworth (1995a: 237) cites numerous examples in which frequently lengthy custodial sentences have been upheld for relatively minor thefts,[67] in clear contravention of the proportionality principle enshrined in the Act. Although there have been other decisions in which the Court has been prepared to quash the use of custodial sentences for minor offences,[68] its overall response has been unhelpful and has betrayed the trust that was placed on it to exercise the wide discretion vested in it constructively and responsibly. Particularly disappointing has been the adoption by the Court of an impossibly vague test for determining seriousness, which refers to what any 'right-thinking member of the public' would regard as serious.[69] The effect has been to preserve maximum discretion for individual sentencers rather than offering them guidance consistent with the underlying (and widely recognized) spirit of the Act, however inadequately this may have been expressed in its wording (Ashworth and Hough, 1996).

In spite of these defects, the 1991 Act was by no means the unmitigated disaster that it has sometimes been portrayed as by its opponents (see Crow et al., 1995; Cavadino et al., 1999: 68–9). Although far from perfect, the strategy that lay at the heart of the 1991 reforms was at least reasonably coherent, particularly when compared with the policy vacuum which preceded it. And it did address a number of important political and penological realities, not least of which are the finite supply of prison places and the seemingly insatiable judicial demand for them if given a free rein.

In some important respects, indeed, the Act was at first achieving precisely what had been intended. Immediately following its introduction there was a reduction in the proportionate use of custody and an increase in that of non-custodial sentences (Flood-Page and Mackie, 1998: 13; and see Chapter 11). Even the much-maligned unit fine was achieving many of its original aims, as we shall see in Chapter 5. But these penological successes were soon to be undone by a political backlash that wreaked much more damage to the strategy represented by the 1991 Act than any destructive interpretation at the hands of the judiciary.

### Post 1991: the law and order backlash

The 1991 reform strategy began to unravel in spectacular fashion from late 1992 onwards in what has been described as 'one of the most remarkable *volte faces* in the history of penal policy in England and Wales' (Ashworth and Gibson, 1994: 101). We discuss the general political factors responsible for this dramatic U-turn in Chapter 11, although we may note here that one factor (albeit in our opinion a relatively minor one) was a measure of public and judicial disquiet over aspects of the 1991 Criminal Justice Act itself, particularly section 29 (discussed earlier) and the provisions relating to unit fines (which we discuss in Chapter 5).

The response from John Major's Conservative government was 'the law and order counter-reformation': a conscious policy decision to 'play the law and order card' for all it was worth. Hastily prepared amendments were added to the Criminal Justice Act 1993, the effect of which was to water down the 1991 Act's restrictive criteria for imposing custody. Sentencers were given greater scope to pass custodial sentences in cases that might otherwise not be thought of as sufficiently serious where the offender had a bad previous record, and were allowed to take into account all the offences with which an offender had been charged.[70] The same Act also precipitately abolished the entire system of unit fines that had been introduced only months earlier (see Chapter 5). Even more important than these legislative amendments, however, were the drastic changes in political rhetoric which accompanied them, the most notable instance being Home Secretary Michael Howard's 'prison works' speech to the 1993 Conservative Party Conference (see Chapters 2 and 11). The government now stridently renounced many of the ideals underlying the 1991 reforms, such as the principle of restraint in the use of custody, and a preference for punishment in the community as the preferred response to minor offending. The result of this 'counter-reformation' was a marked increase in both the proportionate use of custody and also the average lengths of prison sentences, starting in 1993, as we shall see later in this chapter.

The Strategy A-inspired 'law and order counter-reformation' reached its climax in the adoption of American-style mandatory and minimum sentences for certain categories of offenders in the Crime (Sentences) Act of 1997 (see Cavadino et al., 1999: 74); although importantly, this Act's provisions are only 'semi-mandatory' in that they include limited exceptions allowing the court to avoid passing the prescribed sentences in certain cases. The Act requires the imposition of a life sentence after an offender is convicted of a second serious violent or sexual offence ('two strikes and you're out'), unless there are exceptional circumstances.[71] It also requires the imposition of a minimum sentence of at least seven years imprisonment on an offender who is convicted of a Class A drug trafficking offence for the third time ('three strikes and you're out'), unless the court considers this to be 'unjust in all the circumstances'.[72] And (subject to the same qualification) a court is now similarly required to impose a minimum sentence of at least three years on an offender who is convicted for a third offence of domestic burglary.[73] Despite being enacted by the outgoing Conservative administration, the Labour Party had been broadly supportive of the proposals while in opposition, and all three sets of provisions were ultimately implemented by the New Labour government which took office in 1997.

New Labour's support for these 'two strike' and 'three strike' penalties was not shared by the judiciary, who resented the intrusion on their sentencing discretion and felt that they would lead to injustice in many individual cases while proving ineffective as deterrents. Shortly after the Human Rights Act 1998 came into force in October 2000, the Court of Appeal under Lord Woolf (who, is in 2001, the Lord Chief Justice) took the opportunity to reinterpret and broaden the meaning of 'exceptional circumstances' in the 'two strike' penalty for serious offences. It ruled that a case was sufficiently 'exceptional' if the offender did not present a significant risk to the public, and therefore the court was not obliged to pass a life sentence in such a case.[74] This judgment will presumably allow sentencers to avoid passing life sentences in many – possibly most – of these 'two strike' cases. The 'three strike' sentences have proved equally unpopular with sentencers, who in these cases already had the benefit of a wider 'get-out-clause' in the original legislation, being empowered to pass a lighter sentence if the one prescribed is 'unjust'. As a result, by December 2000 not a single 'three strikes' sentence had been passed on a domestic burglar since the provision was implemented a year previously, and only four persistent drug dealers had received the 'mandatory' seven-year sentence since the section relating to them was introduced in October 1997 (*The Guardian*, 27 December 2000). On this showing, it seems likely that the original predictions that the new two- and three-strike sentences would eventually add over 5,000 to the prison population (White and Cullen, 2000) may not be fulfilled. We saw previously how governments have failed to bend sentencers to their will when seeking to reduce sentencing levels. This episode shows that, although government rhetoric can successfully exhort the judiciary to sentence more harshly in general terms, they can be just as resistant to legislation which removes their discretion to be *less* harsh than the government desires in cases where the merits of the individual case seems to them to warrant it.

It should not be assumed that the 'law and order counter-reformation' has necessarily run its course, despite the change of government in 1997. We have already made the point that, even though sentencing *practice* may have become much more punitive during the 1990s, and despite the legislative forays that have been made since the 1991 Act, the just deserts-based sentencing *framework* which it introduced has so far remained substantially intact. However, in May 2000, Home Secretary Jack Straw announced a fundamental review of the existing sentencing framework itself. (The review was published on 5 July 2001, after the proofs for this book had been sent to the publisher. See Halliday, 2001.)

The main aim of the review is to explore the scope for more flexible sentencing options 'which join up custodial and community penalties' (see Chapter 5).[75] In a speech accompanying the announcement, the Home Secretary spoke of the need for a framework 'which sends a clear, tough message about sanctions for persistent re-offending. It must be made far clearer to offenders what the consequences of their actions will be, without ambiguity.' It is too soon to say what the outcome of the review might be. But the fact that it is taking place at all casts further doubt on the longer-term viability of the entire sentencing reform programme that was adopted in the 1991 Act and, in particular, on the principle of offence-based proportionality that formed its cornerstone. At the very least the review seems likely to herald a further retreat from an offence-based to an offender-based sentencing tariff: one that incorporates the notion of 'progression' from less serious to more serious forms of punishment the more an offender reoffends (see Home Office, 2001: 28). This would be in accordance with Mr Straw's often-stated view that prison is the appropriate penalty, not only for those who commit serious offences, but also for those who persistently commit minor crimes. At worst , the review could result in the complete dismantling of the existing sentencing framework, and a return to something more like the far less principled 'supermarket approach' that prevailed before 1992.

The New Labour government's other main initiative in the field of sentencing reform has been much more constructive, however, and involves a major change in the rôle and responsibility of the Court of Appeal, though its impact to date remains very modest. Under the 1998 Crime and Disorder Act,[76] the Court of Appeal has been given a much more proactive role and it now has a duty to consider whether to frame much more general sentencing guidelines relating to whole categories of cases, whenever it hears an individual appeal (section 80). When it frames guidelines, the Court is required to have regard to the need to promote consistency in sentencing; to the sentences currently imposed for offences in this category; to the cost of different sentences and their relative effectiveness in preventing re-offending; and to the need to promote public confidence in the criminal justice system.

Even more importantly, section 81 of the 1998 Act established a new body, called the Sentencing Advisory Panel, with responsibility for advising and assisting the Court of Appeal on the issuing of sentencing guidelines. The Sentencing Advisory Panel is not only entitled to express its views on any guidelines proposed by the Court of Appeal, but can also (either on its own undertaking or when directed by the Home Secretary) take the initiative and propose that the Court of Appeal should frame or revise guidelines for a particular category of offence. When communicating its views to the Court of Appeal, the Panel is also under a duty to pass on information to the Court of Appeal concerning the current level of sentencing for this category of offences and about how expensive or effective the available sentences are.

The Sentencing Advisory Panel quite closely resembles the Sentencing Council that many reformers have advocated in recent years (Ashworth, 1983: 447; 1987: 81; 1995a: 342; Penal Affairs Consortium, 1995g: 7; Cavadino and Dignan, 1997a: 106–7). However, its impact will inevitably be determined by the extent to which the Court of Appeal is willing to engage in a more proactive process of sentencing reform than it has shown enthusiasm for in the past, and early indications are not that promising. The Sentencing Advisory Panel met for the first time in July 1999 under the chairmanship of Professor Martin Wasik.[77] During its first nine months the Panel carried out consultation exercises in respect of four distinct categories of offence:[78] environmental offences, offensive weapons, importation and possession of opium and racially aggravated offences. In respect of the first of these issues, however, the Court of Appeal concluded that it was unable to usefully formulate guidelines – despite the fact that the topic had been referred to the Panel by the Home Secretary, and in spite of its undoubted relevance to an environmental pollution case before the court involving the *Sea Empress* at Milford Haven.[79] This apparent reluctance to take its statutory responsibilities seriously once again calls into the question the suitability of the Court of Appeal as an appropriate body to undertake the increasingly urgent need for wholesale sentencing reform.

## FUELLING THE PENAL CRISIS

It should be evident by now that, at least until recently, the very considerable discretionary powers of English sentencers were largely exercised in a policy vacuum. As we have seen, they received little guidance as to the aims they should be pursuing, few broad policy directions, and only minimal direction as to the principles they should apply in approaching their task. Even when attempts have been made, more recently, to replace the sentencing policy vacuum with a relatively loose framework of broad sentencing principles, the courts have responded with disdain, either subverting or ignoring them at will. The end product of this highly devolved system of decision-making is a persistent and escalating penal crisis. Like the other two sets of decisions we have examined in this chapter, the sentencing decisions of the courts have severely aggravated both the prison numbers crisis and also the crisis of legitimacy.

### The prison numbers crisis

The precise relationship between penal policy and sentencing practice is a matter of some complexity, but we may begin by noting that the size of the sentenced prison population at any given time is determined by three key variables, two of which are the direct responsibility of the courts. One is the number of people who are sentenced by the courts and the proportion of those who are given custody (referred to as the rate of *imprisonment*); the second is the *length of sentence* actually imposed by the courts; and the third (over which the courts have no direct control) is the operation of the various forms of *early release* which we examine in Chapter 8. The sentenced prison population is a function of the number of people received into prison and the average length of sentence that they actually serve (sometimes known as *effective sentence length*: Fitzmaurice and Pease, 1982: 575). It follows that the courts can contribute to the prison numbers crisis either by sending more people to prison than they need to, or by sending them there for longer than is necessary. In our view there is convincing evidence that the courts are doing both.

In 1999, just under 1.5 million offenders were sentenced for summary and indictable offences (Ayres, 2000), which is marginally lower than the figure a decade earlier. However, the number of offenders who were sentenced to immediate custody for all offences was a massive 71 per cent higher than it was in 1993. Overall, 23.4 per cent of those who were sentenced for indictable offences in 1999 were given a custodial sentence, which was the highest rate for over 40 years (Ayres, 2000: 1). In the Crown Court the custody rate increased from 49 per cent in 1993 to 63 per cent in 1999. Moreover, the average length of custodial sentences was also substantially higher in the Crown Court – 24.1 months for males aged 21 and over – compared with an average of 20.5 months in the early 1990s.[80] Responsibility for the massive increase in the prison population following the onset of the law and order counter-reformation thus rests largely in the hands of sentencers, albeit aided and abetted by politicians of a 'law and order' persuasion.[81] Conversely, it is not attributable to an increase in the number of offenders coming before the courts, which has actually declined somewhat, nor to decisions of other criminal justice agencies such as the police or Crown Prosecution Service.

In terms of their overall impact on prison numbers, it is also possible to apportion responsibility fairly precisely between the two levels of court in England and Wales, though the data need to be interpreted with care. Prison statistics show that, of the total prison population in 1999, only 11 per cent of prisoners were sentenced by magistrates' courts, compared with 89 per cent who were sentenced by Crown Court judges,[82] in spite of the fact that very many more indictable offenders are tried and convicted in magistrates' courts than in the Crown Court (77.3 per cent and 22.7 per cent respectively in 1999: Elkins et al., 2000: Table 6). However, the proportionate use of custody is very much lower in magistrates' courts (at 12.5 per cent for adult indictable offenders in 1999[83]) than it is in Crown Courts (where the corresponding figure was 63 per cent). And since (as we have seen) the custodial sentences imposed by Crown Courts also tend to be longer than those passed by magistrates' courts, the sentencing practice of the Crown Court is clearly a much more potent factor in generating the prison numbers crisis.

Such figures help to explain why it is that the average length of custody imposed by the higher courts is a historically proven index of prison population generally, once allowance has been made for changes in the level of recorded crime (Home Office, 1956; but cf. Bottomley and Pease, 1986: ch. 4). However, it is also worth noting that there are various other ways in which both magistrates and judges may contribute, either directly or indirectly, to the prison numbers crisis. One example is by imposing a fine without taking sufficient account of a defendant's ability to pay, with the result that imprisonment is imposed for default (see Moxon, 1983). Another is by imposing additional restrictions to community penalties in respect of offenders whose lifestyles make it unlikely that they will be able to comply, thereby increasing the risk of default if they do breach the order (which is what criminal justice practitioners call 'setting them up to fail').

So far we have established that the unprecedented recent increase in the size of the prison population is chiefly the product of changes in the sentencing practices of the courts following the 'law and order counter-reformation'. More direct evidence that many English courts use custody excessively relates to three different aspects of the *differential* use of imprisonment.

The first relates to growing evidence of marked differences in the use of imprisonment between England and Wales and comparable jurisdictions, even when courts are dealing with similar offence types (Collier and Tarling, 1987; International Bar Association, 1990; NACRO, 1998b). Although international comparisons need to be interpreted with care, they do show that the United Kingdom has, over a long period of time, maintained a high prison population relative to its overall population compared with many other Western European states (see Chapter 1). It can be objected that geographical comparisons of this sort are not entirely compelling because of important differences between the criminal justice systems, and the levels of crime, in the countries concerned (Pease, 1994; Ashworth, 1995a: 228–9). However, it would be unwise to press these objections too far.

For one thing, Rutherford (1986) has argued convincingly, on the basis of detailed historical and geographical evidence relating to England and Wales, Japan and the Netherlands, that there appears to be no consistent relationship between levels of recorded crime and rates of imprisonment, which suggests that the latter are largely determined by the decisions of courts in the different countries. Again, a recent study comparing England and Wales and Australia (two countries whose criminal justice systems are not too dissimilar) offers even firmer evidence that differences in the use of imprisonment in the recent past between these two jurisdictions were largely the outcome of decisions for which the courts themselves are responsible. In 1986 the number of people in prison per 100,000 of the population was appreciably higher in England and Wales than in Australia (at 93 compared to 70 respectively). In a detailed and thorough analysis of possible factors which might account for this difference, J. Walker et al. (1990) ruled out differences in crime rate or detection rate or the use of different definitions of imprisonment. Instead, the evidence strongly suggested that the higher imprisonment rate in England and Wales at that time was brought about by the courts' decisions to commit a greater number of people to prison, both on remand and also under sentence.

Finally, studies by the International Bar Association (1990) and the International Comparisons in Criminal Justice Project (see NACRO, 1998b), in which judges and other representative legal practitioners from different countries were asked to assess the range of sentences which should be imposed in respect of various offences, have found that the English response was more punitive than that of most other jurisdictions (and than almost any other European country involved in the studies). These findings may not be conclusive, but they certainly suggest strongly that sentencing in England and Wales is harsher than in many other comparable countries, and that this is one of the most important causes of our relatively high prison population.

Second, there is evidence of excessive use of immediate custody *by the Crown Court* compared with the magistrates' court in respect of minor property offenders. A study by Moxon (1988: 15) showed that as many as two-fifths of those who were convicted in the Crown Court of offences involving less than £200 received unsuspended custody[84] in spite of persistent concern at the time about the need to restrict custody to only the most serious property offenders. These findings are also in line with figures which we cited earlier (Hedderman and Moxon, 1992), suggesting that for a given range of offence types, Crown Courts are very much more likely to resort to custody than magistrates' courts, and to pass longer sentences. Once again this points to excessive use of imprisonment, certainly on the part of the Crown Court. More recently, Flood-Page and Mackie (1998) have shown that whereas magistrates were likely to treat breach of trust as a factor meriting a community sentence, Crown Courts were more likely to impose custodial sentences in such cases.[85]

Third, as we shall see in the next section, even after allowing for differences in the mix of offenders or offence types, there is also considerable *geographical* variation in the use of custody on the part of both magistrates' courts and Crown Courts in different parts of the country. This suggests that those courts making relatively heavy use of imprisonment 'frequently have no reason to do so if the experience of other courts is any criterion' (Hood, 1962: 122). While the courts may not be *solely* responsible for the prison numbers crisis, we would argue that the recent relentless increase in the population of sentenced prisoners is largely attributable to the persistent practice of 'over-sentencing'. By this we mean using custody unnecessarily for minor property offenders and others, and of imposing longer sentences across the board than is required for strictly reductivist purposes. Moreover, responsibility for this practice rests mainly, but not exclusively, with the Crown Court. However, the differential use of imprisonment by the courts also helps to fuel the continuing crisis of legitimacy, to which we now turn.

### The crisis of legitimacy

A marked degree of disparity in the way similar offenders are dealt with in different parts of the country is an inevitable consequence of operating a highly discretionary judicial decision-making process. A succession of research studies (Hood, 1962, 1972; Tarling and Weatheritt, 1979; Tarling et al., 1985; Prison Reform Trust, 1997a) has demonstrated the extent of this disparity on the part of magistrates' courts. A Home Office (1994c) survey, involving 21 magistrates' courts, found that the proportionate use of custody in late 1993 ranged from 3 per cent of sentences in a number of courts to 15 per cent in Bolton. The proportionate use of the fine also varied widely from 17 per cent in Derby to 63 per cent in Newport. An earlier study (Tarling et al., 1985) had shown that similar variations could not fully be explained by differences in either the kind of offences with which each court had to deal or the offenders coming before them; in other words the disparities were real. This is not surprising given the insistence by magistrates on the uniqueness of every case they judge and the need for them to deal with each case on its own particular merits, which is their justification for utterly rejecting calls for consistency (Parker et al., 1989).

Attempts to conduct rigorous investigations into possible similar disparities in sentencing at the Crown Court level have in the past been met with judicial opposition and refusal to co-operate (Ashworth, 1984). However, wide disparities in the use of custody between Crown Courts were disclosed in 1992 when the Home Office published sentencing profiles for each court as part of a series of volumes on the costs of the criminal justice system (Home Office, 1992), and more recently in statistics published by the Penal Affairs Consortium (1995a). The latter show that, in respect of first-tier Crown Courts only (those dealing with the most serious indictable offences) the proportion of offenders given custodial sentences for indictable offences in 1993 ranged from 38 per cent in Sheffield to 66 per cent in Winchester. The average length of sentence also varied from 13.9 months in Kingston upon Thames to 29.2 months in Isleworth.

Findings such as these are significant in relation to the wider penal crisis since even apparent disparities in the way offenders are treated will fuel resentment and are likely to contribute to the feelings of injustice which lie at the heart of the penal system's crisis of legitimacy. (The same may be equally true of other apparently arbitrary decisions taken by the courts in relation to remand and trial venue.)

**THE WAY AHEAD?**

As we have seen, both the prison numbers crisis and the crisis of legitimacy remain stubbornly intractable, despite some recent attempts at reform. The most urgent task is to tackle the worsening problem of over-sentencing. But how is this to be accomplished? In our view, the answer is emphatically not to dismantle or water down the existing sentencing framework on the ground that it no longer accurately reflects the sentencing practices of the courts. To do so would be rather like a driver responding to acute brake failure by pressing the accelerator pedal in order to match the speed of the runaway vehicle. This might give the illusion of being in control but patently ignores the fact that the vehicle is careering unstoppably in the wrong direction.

One simple step which could be taken in order to tackle the problem of over-sentencing would be to repeal the semi-mandatory and minimum sentences that were introduced by the Crime (Sentences) Act 1997. Perhaps the courts' lack of enthusiasm for applying these provisions as originally intended means that this would have relatively little direct effect on sentences, but it would make a symbolic statement that the government is no longer keen to ratchet sentencing levels in an upwards direction whatever the inclinations of sentencers themselves. We would also favour the scrapping of the remaining mandatory life sentence of imprisonment for murder, which encompasses such a wide range of intentional killings as to render inappropriate the current 'one-size-fits-all' sentencing response. This restoration of *discretion to be lenient* would doubtless be popular with the judiciary.

However, some constraints on the discretion to sentence *harshly* are clearly needed if the problem of over-sentencing is to be resolved. Although we do not favour mandatory sentencing provisions, we believe that there is a very strong case for confining the discretion of sentencers by drastically restricting, if not removing altogether the power to impose custodial sentences on minor property offences. In our view it is seldom, if ever, justifiable to send someone to prison for offences such as trivial forms of criminal damage (for example, spraying graffiti) or minor acts of shoplifting, however persistent an offender might be. It follows that – unlike the Labour Party in recent years – we do not favour the idea of 'progressive' sentencing whereby petty persistent offenders are given only one chance, or only a very limited number of chances in the form of relatively lenient disposals before moving on to a 'tougher' sentence. Instead, sentencers should be required to follow a policy of 'horizontal' sentencing in such cases, which means that they should be obliged to make use of the most appropriate form of non-custodial penalty that would meet the needs of any victim while tackling, if possible, the cause of the offending behaviour. This would mean strengthening, not weakening, the offence-based 'proportionality' provisions of the 1991 Criminal Justice Act.

In the longer term, however, the problem of over-sentencing calls for more effective ways of structuring, rather than confining, the discretion of sentencers. The creation of the Sentencing Advisory Panel represents a welcome but limited step in the right direction, and could potentially help to achieve more consistency in the sentencing of particular offence categories. This in turn would address one of the key elements in the current crisis of legitimacy, which relates to the huge disparities in the way comparable offences and offenders are dealt with. However, the Panel's capacity to do so is crucially dependent on the willingness of the Court of Appeal to accept its recommendations and, as we have seen, the early omens on this score are not wholly encouraging.

Even if the new arrangements were to succeed in reducing *disparities* in sentencing, this would probably do little to address the even more pressing problem of *excessive* sentencing. Indeed, it might even worsen it by bringing about a 'levelling up' of more lenient sentences to reach the norm set by the guidelines. Attacking over-sentencing would require a much more proactive role for the Panel,[86] which, in our view, should be given a much more clearly articulated responsibility to devise a systematic set of guiding principles to give effect to the current sentencing framework contained in the 1991 Criminal Justice Act. The primary aim in formulating these principles should be to bring about a drastic reduction in both the number and length of custodial sentences. In determining which offences need to be punished by means of custody, and for how long, the Panel would need not only to have regard to the principle of offence-based proportionality, but also to ensure that the expensive commodity of imprisonment is not used for cases that could safely and satisfactorily be dealt with by non-custodial measures.[87] And in formulating its guidance, the Panel would need to take into account not only the known relative costs of different sentencing measures, and their effectiveness in preventing reoffending, but also the known harmful consequences associated with imprisonment. These include the risk of harm to inmates, the negative consequences for their families and the risk to the wider community[88] that imprisonment may all too often make offenders worse rather than better. This may seem a bold and radical agenda. It would certainly require a considerable degree of political skill and courage to effect it, and to do so in such a way that a rebellious judiciary do not once again find ways of undermining the entire enterprise. However, we believe that it provides the most effective way of addressing one important root cause of the current penal crisis. We also believe that it should be possible for an enlightened government to reach an understanding and accommodation with the judiciary whereby their sentencing discretion was in some ways less *confined* (by mandatory sentences) but more rigorously *structured* (by guidelines). In order to assess the scope for the kind of approach we have advocated, and the prospects for its success, we will need to take a closer look at the full range of sentencing options that is currently available to the courts, which we do in Chapter 5.

**NOTES**

1   The study of the relationships *between* the various criminal justice agencies (or systems analysis) is attracting increasing interest from policy-makers and commentators alike. The present chapter is largely an exercise in systems analysis, but see also Chapter 9 for further discussion.

2   A phrase which was frequently used in the early days of the Blair government, particularly when making the case for reform of the youth justice system.

3   The other major decision for which the criminal courts are also responsible – determining the guilt or innocence of a defendant – is one that lies outside the scope of this book. It is worth pointing out, however, that continuing doubts over the courts' ability to deliver justice fairly and consistently when trying defendants contributes to the wider crisis of legitimacy that still suffuses the entire criminal justice system.

4   In the case of untried suspects, at least, their status is still that of an innocent citizen.

5   One study found that the proportion released on conditional bail was as high as 38 per cent (East and Doherty, 1984).

6   In 1995 the power to release defendants on conditional bail was extended to the police for the first time, under section 27 of the Criminal Justice and Public Order Act 1994.

7   Where proceedings are commenced by way of summons, the question of pre-trial detention does not normally arise.

8 In 1998, 15 per cent of those arrested and charged with indictable offences were held in custody until their first court appearance, which is similar to the level recorded in 1991, following a slight fall in the intervening period (Home Office, 2000a: para. 8.5).

9 Between 1987 and 1997, the size of the remand population increased by 9 per cent, but this was dwarfed by a 29 per cent increase in the size of the sentenced population over the same period (Home Office, 1999a: 51). This represents a significant change since the 1980s, when the increase in the overall prison population was chiefly driven by an increase in the number of remand prisoners.

10 Shortly before the Bail Act came into force, the number of remand prisoners received into custody was 68,388 (NACRO, 1993). In 1999 the number was less than half this figure, at 34,100 (calculated from figures contained in Cullen and Minchin, 2000a).

11 See the Prosecution of Offences (Custody Time Limit) Regulations 1987 (SI 299), SI 1991/1515, SI 1995/555 and SI 1999/2744.

12 Section 43. This would enable more exacting time limits to be imposed, for example, in respect of juvenile cases or, conversely, more generous time limits in respect of serious fraud cases. The section also restricts the criteria governing a court's decisions to grant extensions to the limits. However, it also relaxes the sanctions for failing to comply with the limit, by enabling proceedings to be stayed rather than acquitting the defendant.

13 S. 49 Criminal Procedure and Investigations Act, 1996.

14 Among those committed for trial at the Crown Court the proportion remanded in custody has risen from 22 per cent in 1986 to 27 per cent in 1998. This compares with a custodial remand rate of 15 per cent for those charged with indictable offences who are tried by the magistrates themselves, though this rate has itself more than doubled since the 7 per cent of custodial remands recorded in 1986.

15 The proportion of convicted but unsentenced remand prisoners, as opposed to those awaiting trial, was 37 per cent in 1999 (calculated from figures contained in Home Office, 2000b: ch. 2).

16 Almost uniquely – see Shelbourn (1978) – but probably not for much longer. Article 5(5) of the European Convention on Human Rights confers an enforceable right to compensation on anyone who is detained in contravention of Article 5, which safeguards an individual's right to 'liberty and security'. Damages may be awarded against the Crown where a court acts in breach of Article 5 of the Convention, regardless of good faith (Law Commission, 1999: paras 1.17–1.23).

17 See Ashworth (1998) for more detailed discussion of this issue.

18 See also Moxon (1988); Crow et al. (1989), especially Chapter 3.

19 See Law Commission (1999: paras 4.2–4.15).

20 Parliamentary written answer by Earl Ferrers to Lord Hutchinson, 24 June 1993.

21 Although they may be preferable to custodial remands, it should not be overlooked that bail hostels also entail a restriction on liberty and are themselves therefore capable of being abused if used for offenders who would not otherwise have been remanded in custody. See Lewis and Mair (1989).

22 If Morgan's figures had been calculated on the same basis as Brown's, the overall offending rate would have come to about 17 per cent, which narrows the gap considerably between the two sets of findings.

23 Section 38. The Youth Justice Board which was also created by the 1998 Act (see Chapter 9) has committed £35m over the three years from 1999 to the development of new bail support projects.

24 Despite this initial failure the idea has not been abandoned, and more recent attempts to introduce electronic monitoring for sentenced offenders, and also as a

conditional form of early release for certain categories of short sentenced prisoners, are discussed further in Chapters 5 and 8 respectively.

25  Section 25 of the Criminal Justice and Public Order Act 1994.

26  Section 56 of the Crime and Disorder Act 1998. Moreover, courts are required to state their reasons for granting bail in such cases, by virtue of paragraph 9A of Part I of Schedule 1 to the Bail Act.

27  Section 26 of the Criminal Justice and Public Order Act 1994.

28  The reforms we favour are also advocated by the coalition of 40 voluntary sector penal reform organizations that make up the Penal Affairs Consortium (2000).

29  Though care is needed to ensure that this does not prejudice the interests of victims with regard to consultation procedures and any entitlement to reparation; see Chapters 5 and 9.

30  Section 49 of the Criminal Procedure and Investigations Act 1996, which came into force in October 1997.

31  National Mode of Trial Guidelines were first issued as a Practice Direction [1990] 3 All ER 979. The guidelines were subsequently amended, in 1995, but the later version was not officially promulgated. See Ashworth (1998: 243–5, 260); White (1996). N.B. the guidelines themselves can be found in Watkins et al. (1998) and Watkins and Gordon (2000).

32  See also Riley and Vennard (1988) and Bottoms and McClean (1976).

33  This is one of the clearest illustrations of the undignified 'turf wars' between rival criminal justice fiefdoms to which we referred earlier. Conflict between rival governmental power bases is more likely to occur within chronically unsystemic policy-making processes of the kind that characterize the English and Welsh system, but is rarely visible on this scale.

34  Such a change was recommended by the Royal Commission on Criminal Justice (1993). Two Criminal Justice (Mode of Trial) Bills were introduced by the government in 1999 and 2000, but failed to proceed due to fierce opposition in the House of Lords. The government currently plans to introduce a third Bill along the same lines.

35  This was one of the options put forward in a Home Office Consultation Paper in 1995 (Home Office, 1995c).

36  The comparative acquittal rates for contested cases are as follows: for summary only cases that are tried in the magistrates' court: 19 per cent; for triable either way cases that are tried in the magistrates' court: 32 per cent; for triable either way cases that are tried in the Crown Court: 45 per cent. The overall acquittal rate for defendants tried in contested cases in the magistrates' court is 26 per cent, which compares with an acquittal rate of 43 per cent for those tried in contested cases in the Crown Court. (Figures based on CPS statistics for the year ending June 1999, and the Narey pre-pilot research as cited in Home Office, 2000c.)

37  A change of emphasis that was symbolized by dropping the name 'social inquiry report'.

38  There was a limited exception in the case of offences triable only on indictment, where the court considered it unnecessary to obtain a report as, for example, where it was clear from the facts that a custodial sentence is unavoidable (section 3(1)).

39  No evidence was found of any differential tendency to dispense with PSRs in respect of non-white defendants but, as the researchers point out, the numbers involved were too small to enable any firm conclusions to be drawn as to any ethnic differentials.

40  Formerly known as 'stipendiary' magistrates, until August 2000. The change of name was brought about by s.78 of the Access to Justice Act 1999, and can be seen as part of the Blair government's attempt to modernize the criminal justice system. See also Seago et al. (2000).

41 Sanders (2001) has also advocated the use of 'mixed panels' (comprising a single professional judge and two lay magistrates who would be drawn from a broader cross-section of society, sit less frequently and be given less training) for the trial of contested minor cases, or either way cases provided the defendant consents. Mixed panels would also be responsible for sentencing in both indictable-only and either-way cases. However, single professional judges would replace the current combination of lay magistrates assisted by legally trained clerks for less complex, 'technical' decisions including bail hearings, mode of trial decisions and uncontested summary cases.

42 In theory the clerk's rôle is confined to advising magistrates on what sentences are available to them, rather than on which sentence to choose in individual cases, though in practice this distinction is sometimes a difficult one to sustain. See Darbyshire (1999).

43 See the Howard League (1993) for recommendations to improve the quality of training available for senior practitioners from all criminal justice services and professions including the judiciary.

44 See Downes (1988) for an interesting contrast in judicial cultures between England and the Netherlands.

45 The case of *R. v. Sargeant* (1974) 60 Cr App R 74 is a classic illustration of the policy free-for-all that prevailed before the Criminal Justice Act 1991. Here the Court of Appeal expressly endorsed the four classical principles of retribution, deterrence, prevention and reform, despite their apparent mutual incompatibility (see also Chapter 2).

46 See von Hirsch (1987) for details. Some are enacted in legislation, while others (like the Magistrates' Association Sentencing Guidelines which we will mention below) are drawn up by representatives of the sentencers themselves, as a voluntary guide to practice.

47 See Magistrates' Association (1997) for the latest version. The guidelines are issued with the blessing of the Lord Chancellor and Lord Chief Justice. Although they are also endorsed by the Justices' Clerks' Society, individual courts are free to adapt them as they see fit.

48 Examples are *R. v. Billam* (1986) 8 Cr App R (S) 48, concerning sentences for rape; *R. v. Aramah* (1982) 4 Cr App R (S) 407 (importation of drugs); *R. v. Boswell* (1984) 6 Cr App R (S) 257 (causing death by dangerous driving); *R. v. Stewart* (1987) 9 Cr App R (S) (social security fraud).

49 See in particular the cases of *R. v. Upton* (1980) 71 Cr App R 102 and *R. v. Begum Bibi* (1980) 71 Cr App R 360. Although the Lord Chief Justice's pronouncements were followed by reductions in the average length of prison sentences in both the magistrates' court and the Crown Court, these were relatively modest and, in the case of the Crown Court at least, were soon reversed.

50 (1981) 3 Cr App R (S) 245 – a case which was cited approvingly by the government in its 1990 White Paper *Crime, Justice and Protecting the Public* (Home Office, 1990a: para. 2.18), and later received legislative endorsement in section 29(1) of the 1991 Criminal Justice Act (see below). The *Queen* principle does not mean that no account whatever can be taken of the offender's past record since a *lack* of previous convictions can be a mitigating factor.

51 *R. v. Gilbertson* (1980) 2 Cr App R (S).

52 See, for example, the sentences originally imposed in the cases of *Queen* (see above note 50) and *R. v. Bailey* (1988) 10 Cr App R (S) 231, both cited in Ashworth (1995a).

53 As amended by section 66(6) of the Criminal Justice Act 1993. But see now section 151 Powers of Criminal Courts (Sentencing) Act 2000 (hereafter abbreviated to PCC(S)A 2000).

54 There is also evidence that professional district judges (formerly known as stipendiary magistrates) sentence offenders more severely than their lay colleagues, even when other relevant factors affecting the types of cases dealt with are taken into account (Flood-Page and Mackie, 1998: 69).

55 (1980) 71 Cr App R 381.

56 The position has not changed that much over the intervening years. In 1999 only 25 per cent of *domestic* burglars were sentenced by magistrates to immediate custody. However, it is possible that a higher proportion of these cases are now dealt with in the Crown Court, where the custody rate in such cases is higher, at 75 per cent. See Sentencing Advisory Panel (2001).

57 Moreover, the Court of Appeal usually hears appeals from defendants who are aggrieved at the severity of their sentences, and in consequence is most familiar with the *upper range* of sentencing in the Crown Court.

58 See also the Justices' Clerks' Society (1982) whose comparative survey of the use of custody in the two levels of court for a selected range of offences revealed even greater differentials.

59 It was originally limited to indictable-only offences, but has now been extended to certain triable either way offences. They include indecent assault, cruelty to children and making threats to kill: Criminal Justice Act (Review of Sentencing Order) 1994. New powers were introduced on 21 August 2000 covering drug trafficking and certain sexual offences involving children: SI (2000) 1924.

60 For example, in *R. v. Mussell* (1990) 12 Cr App R (S) 607, the Court of Appeal declined to set proper guidelines for burglary, stating that 'each offence has to be judged individually'. Guidelines for domestic burglary were issued in *R. v. Brewster and Others* [1998] 1 Cr App R (S) 181, but in March 2001 the Sentencing Advisory Panel (see below) indicated that it would invite the Court of Appeal to revise these, taking into account the findings of a public opinion survey commissioned by the Panel. See Sentencing Advisory Panel (2001) and Russell and Morgan (2001).

61 See, for example, the Advisory Council on the Penal System's 1977 interim report, *The Length of Prison Sentences*, which invited judges to think about imposing shorter prison sentences as a contribution towards relieving the problem of prison overcrowding, a copy of which was sent to every judge and every bench of magistrates (Ashworth, 2000: 49).

62 Originally section 1(2)(a), Criminal Justice Act 1991. But see now PCC(S)A 2000 section 79.

63 Originally section 6, Criminal Justice Act 1991. But see now PCC(S)A 2000 section 35(1).

64 PCC(S)A 2000 sections 80(2)(a) and 35(2)(b) respectively.

65 PCC(S)A 2000 sections 79(2)(b) and 80(2)(b).

66 *R. v. Cunningham* (1993) 14 Cr App R (S) 444.

67 Among the most notable are *R. v. Costello* (1993) 15 Cr App R (S) 240 in which a custodial sentence of six months was upheld for aiding and abetting an attempt to obtain money by drilling the coin box of a public telephone; and also the cases of *R. v. Keogh* (1994) 15 Cr App R (S) 279 and *R. v McCormick* (1995) 16 Cr App R (S) 134, in which custodial sentences were also upheld for offences of minor deception and minor theft by an employee respectively, both of them involving very small amounts of money. See also Thomas (1995: 146).

68 For example, in relation to minor indecency (see *R. v. Orriss* (1993) 15 Cr App R (S) 185) and non-domestic burglary (see *R. v. Carlton* (1993) 15 Cr App R (S) 333).

69 The test had been formulated before the 1991 Act (in *R. v. Bradbourne* (1985) 7 Cr App Rep (S) 180) but was affirmed in *R. v. Cox* (1993) 14 Cr App R (S) 479.

70 Under the 1991 Act, sentencers had only been permitted to take account of the 'principal' offence and one other, when assessing seriousness. This judicially unpopular 'two-offence rule' was abolished by the 1993 Act.

71 Originally section 2 of the Crime (Sentences) Act. But see now section 109 PCC(S)A 2000.

72 Originally section 3 of the Crime (Sentences) Act 1997. See now section 110 PCC(S)A 2000.

73 Originally section 4 of the Crime (Sentences) Act 1997; see now section 111 PCC(S)A 2000.

74 *R. v. Offen* (2000) 1 Cr App R (S) 565, a case in which a socially inadequate man made a wholly ineffectual attempt to rob a building society after a previous conviction for a similar offence.

75 Press release 129/2000, issued on 16 May 2000.

76 See Cavadino et al. (1999) for a fuller account of the shifts in Labour Party thinking on the issue of sentencing reform prior to the implementation of the Crime and Disorder Act.

77 The ten other members include academics, sentencers (both magistrates and a Crown Court judge), those with knowledge of the criminal justice system (including prisons and probation) and independent members (one management consultant, a County Education Officer and a Professor in Ethnic Health).

78 Sentencing Advisory Panel *First Annual Report* (2000). See also www.sentencing-advisory-panel.gov.uk/info.htm

79 *R. v. Milford Haven Port Authority* (2000) 2 Cr App R (S) 423. It remains to be seen whether it is any more receptive to the Panel's views in respect of the sentencing of opium cases, where the reference came from the Court itself.

80 The average length of custodial sentences also increased in the magistrates' court immediately after the implementation of the 1991 Criminal Justice Act, reaching a high of 3.1 months in 1994. But by 1999 it had reverted to the early 1990s figure of 2.6 months.

81 Either directly, by introducing new mandatory or minimum sentences under the Crime (Sentences) Act of 1997, or indirectly, by adopting harsher rhetoric in pronouncements on sentencing – for example Michael Howard's notorious 'prison works' speech.

82 The figures relate to prisoners received under sentence, including those committed to prison for non-payment of fines, but excluding remand prisoners, and are calculated from figures published in the Prison Statistics for 1999 (Home Office, 2000b: Table 1.11).

83 Though this compares with a rate of only 5 per cent in 1992 (Ayres, 2000: para. 29).

84 In many cases the custodial sentences seemed to be largely the result of past offending or of the offender being in breach of an existing court order. This suggests that a genuine switch in sentencing practice away from an 'offender-based tariff' to an 'offence-based tariff' in which sentences were primarily determined by the seriousness of the current offence could have significant effects in reducing the number of custodial sentences.

85 Though unlike the Moxon and Hedderman and Moxon studies cited earlier, they did not make any attempt to compare offences within a given range of seriousness.

86 Alternatively, this task could be given to a separately constituted Sentencing Council.

87 This would mean repudiating the doctrine to which former Home Secretary Jack Straw (like several of his Conservative predecessors) subscribed that – unlike virtually all other publicly funded institutions – imprisonment is essentially a 'demand-led service'. 'Within the sentencing framework set by Parliament,

who is sent to prison and for how long is a matter for the courts', HC Deb. 2 March 1998.

88 Victims may also be disadvantaged if offenders are imprisoned unnecessarily in cases that could more appropriately be dealt with by a non-custodial measure that might also enable the offender to provide compensation or some form of suitable reparation for either the victim or the community.

# 5

# Community Penalties and the Future of Punishment

The initial response to the rapidly escalating prison numbers crisis in England and Wales since the war relied heavily on various techniques of 'demand management', to try to restrict the use of custody by sentencers and ensure that a higher proportion of offenders are dealt with outside the prison system. The prevalent technique to date has been what we call the *'strategy of encouragement'*: extending the range of non-custodial options that are available to sentencers, and encouraging (but not directing) them to use these instead of imprisonment. This policy of favouring non-custodial sentences is of interest for both theoretical and practical reasons. In terms of penological theory it has been cited as evidence of a possible radical shift in the kind of social control techniques that are currently being deployed by modern industrial states, and as a pointer to probable future developments in which there may be less reliance on traditional forms of punishment such as incarceration. At a more practical level it is obviously of interest to penal reformers who wish to make the penal system more humane or effective by reducing the use of imprisonment.

Whatever the intention might have been, however, the strategy of encouragement has in the past not only failed to reduce the size of the prison population significantly, but for much of the time it has even seemed incapable of preventing an increase in the use of custody. And in more recent years, the entire strategy has increasingly given way to an alternative 'supply-side' approach,[1] in which the aim is not to manage or suppress the judicial demand for custodial measures, but to attempt to meet the demand by building more prisons. However, this strategy is extremely expensive, takes time, and may still not be sufficient to satisfy the seemingly insatiable demand for ever more prison places.

In this chapter we will begin by providing a brief historical account of the main policy developments with regard to non-custodial penalties and attempts to limit the use of custody, before considering each of the principal measures, the way they have been used and their impact on the use of imprisonment. Then we will critically examine three rival theories that offer contrasting interpretations of the significance of these developments for the future of social control systems before drawing our final conclusions.

## THE STRATEGY OF ENCOURAGEMENT AND THE CRIMINAL JUSTICE ACT 1991[2]

English courts probably have a wider (and faster growing) range of disposals available to them than in any other comparable jurisdiction. Although the quest for alternatives to imprisonment dates back almost a century, with the introduction of probation and an expansion in the use of the fine, most non-custodial penalties have been introduced comparatively recently in response to growing anxiety over the seemingly remorseless rise in post-war prison numbers. During the 1960s and 1970s it became apparent that traditional 'alternatives to custody' were unable to contain the prison numbers crisis, and it was in this context that suspended sentences of imprisonment and community service orders were introduced (in 1967 and 1972 respectively), and steps taken to encourage the use of compensation orders. However, the prevailing strategy was still heavily influenced by continuing deference on the part of governments towards the 'extravagant version' of the doctrine of judicial independence (see Chapter 4), and this was reflected in a lack of clear guidance to sentencers as to how the new measures should be used. An increase in the proportionate use of imprisonment for adult indictable offenders – which rose from 13.4 per cent in 1975 to 21 per cent in 1986 – provided convincing evidence of the failure of this '*laissez-faire*' approach, and contributed to a radical shift in government policy towards the use of non-custodial penalties during the late 1980s.

As we saw in Chapter 4, this involved the introduction of a new sentencing framework in the Criminal Justice Act 1991. But in spite of the attempt to *structure* the decision-making processes of sentencers, it still relied heavily on the strategy of encouragement, since sentencers' discretion remained wide. The new approach was symbolized by an important change in terminology, in which the terms 'punishment in the community' and 'community penalties' were substituted for the more traditional phrase 'alternatives to imprisonment'. The switch was intended to emphasize the government's initial desire that non-custodial measures should be seen as demanding penalties in their own right, and therefore appropriate for all but the most serious of offences. Efforts were also made to give substance to this tougher image for community penalties, as we shall see, by greatly intensifying the restrictions they imposed on the liberty of offenders. This, too, was intended to make them more attractive to sentencers for the less serious offenders whom the government at that time wished to see being diverted from custody. We have described this as the policy of '*punitive bifurcation*' since, although it is based on a differentiation between serious and not so serious offenders (bifurcation), it also involves a more overtly punitive approach across the whole range of punishments, lest the non-custodial options be seen (and dismissed by sentencers) as a 'soft option'.

Another major change brought about by the 1991 reforms was the way in which punishments of all kinds were ranked for the first time as part of a graduated tariff of measures designed for different levels of seriousness and linked to the concept of 'just deserts'.[3] The absence of an agreed scale by which they could be ranked in order of severity[4] had been another weakness associated with the older 'alternatives to imprisonment' approach and, together with the absence of any clear legislative guidance for sentencers, has been blamed for the failure of the strategy of encouragement (for example by Ashworth, 1995b: 252).

The current sentencing framework is set out in diagrammatic form in Figure 5.1, and can be seen as a series of filters in which the more restrictive measures are intended to be progressively reserved for offences of increasing seriousness. There are three levels of penalty. The highest level – custodial sentences (Level 3) – is normally reserved for offences which are 'so serious that only such a sentence can be justified'.[5] At the second level, 'community penalties' (more restrictive non-custodial penalties such as probation and community service) are to be reserved for offences that are 'serious enough to warrant such a sentence',[6] and any restrictions on liberty that are associated with a particular community penalty should themselves be 'commensurate with the seriousness of the offence'. Subject to this overriding 'proportionality principle', sentencers are also obliged to consider what type of order(s) would best meet the needs of the individual offender, so there is still some scope for rehabilitative aims to be pursued by sentencers. At the lowest level (Level 1) of this desert-based hierarchy of measures, the least serious offences are intended to be dealt with mainly by means of either financial or warning penalties.[7]

In spite of the U-turn on penal policy which followed in the wake of the 1991 Act, the sentencing framework which it introduced has remained largely intact until now – apart from the system of unit fines, which we discuss later. However, the pivotal rôle that was originally accorded to community penalties (and indeed the whole strategy of punitive bifurcation) was seriously undermined by the pro-custodial rhetoric that accompanied these more recent changes. In discussing the impact of the various non-custodial options available to the courts, we shall be referring to Table 5.1, below, which indicates their changing pattern of usage over the last half century.[8] In the next section we examine the principal penalties that are currently available to the courts when dealing with adult offenders. We will follow the order suggested by the 1991 sentencing framework, starting with the most lenient and culminating in the use of custody.

## LEVEL 1: NOMINAL AND WARNING PENALTIES

### Absolute and conditional discharges

Where a court is satisfied that it would be 'inexpedient to inflict punishment',[9] it may discharge an offender instead. This discharge can take one of two forms. The first is an absolute discharge, which is the most lenient response a court can make following a conviction. It requires nothing from an offender and imposes no restrictions on future conduct. Absolute discharges are rarely used, and account for only around 1 per cent of disposals. In part this may be because cases that are likely to be dealt with by means of a purely nominal penalty tend to be discontinued or dealt with by means of a caution instead of being prosecuted.

| LEVEL 3 | CUSTODIAL MEASURES |
|---|---|
| **Age** | **Type of sentence** |
| 21+ | Imprisonment |
| 21+ | Suspended sentence of imprisonment |
| *18–20* | *Detention in a young offender institution/imprisonment* |
| *12–17* | *Detention and training order* |

## CUSTODY THRESHOLD

*Criterion*: offence is 'so serious' that only a custodial sentence can be justified (s. 79(2)(a) Powers of Criminal Courts (Sentencing) Act 2000) *or*
there is a need for 'public protection' in the case of violent or sexual offences (s. 79(2)(b) Powers of Criminal Courts (Sentencing) Act 2000).

| LEVEL 2 | COMMUNITY SENTENCES |
|---|---|
| **Age** | **Type of sentence** |
| 16+ | Probation order ('community rehabilitation order') (with or without additional requirements) |
| 16+ | Drug treatment and testing order |
| 16+ | Community service order ('community punishment order') |
| 16+ | Combination order ('community punishment and rehabilitation order') |
| 10+ | Curfew order |
| *10–20* | *Attendance centre order* |
| *10–17* | *Supervision order (with or without additional requirements)* |
| *10–17* | *Action plan order* |

## COMMUNITY SENTENCE THRESHOLD

*Criterion*: offence is 'serious enough' to warrant such a sentence (s. 35(1) PCC(S)A 2000) *and* such a sentence is 'suitable' for the offender in the opinion of the court (s. 35(2)(a) PCC(S)A 2000).

| LEVEL 1 | FINANCIAL PENALTIES | | OTHER NON-CUSTODIAL PENALTIES | |
|---|---|---|---|---|
| *Age* | *Type of sentence* | | *Age* | *Type of sentence* |
| All | Fines | | All | Conditional discharge |
| All | Compensation | | All | Absolute discharge |
| | | | *10–17* | *Reparation order* |

**N.B. Measures that are restricted to non adult offenders are denoted in italics and are dealt with more fully in Chapter 9**

FIGURE 5.1   *The sentencing framework established by the Criminal Justice Act 1991 (as amended)*

TABLE 5.1   *Adult indictable offenders: types of sentence*[10]

| Type of sentence | Percentage of offenders | | | | | |
|---|---|---|---|---|---|---|
| | 1938 | 1959 | 1975 | 1989 | 1994 | 1999 |
| Imprisonment | 33.3 | 29.1 | 13.4 | 17.5 | 18.2 | 26.0 |
| *Supervisory penalties* | | | | | | |
| Probation | 15.1 | 11.9 | 7.0 | 9.0 | 12.0 | 12.7 |
| Community service | N/A | N/A | 0.5 | 5.4 | 10.7 | 8.8 |
| Combination order | N/A | N/A | N/A | N/A | 2.4 | 3.4 |
| Curfew order | N/A | N/A | N/A | N/A | N/A | 0.2 |
| *Total* | *15.1* | *11.9* | *7.5* | *14.4* | *25.1* | *25.1* |
| *Non-supervisory penalties* | | | | | | |
| Suspended sentence | N/A | N/A | 11.2 | 10.5 | 1.1 | 1.1 |
| Fine | 27.2 | 44.8 | 55.3 | 41.4 | 34.9 | 29.5 |
| Discharge | 23.4 | 13.1 | 12.0 | 14.1 | 18.2 | 15.1 |
| Other penalties | 1.0 | 1.1 | 0.6 | 2.1 | 2.4 | 3.2 |
| *Total* | *50.6* | *57.9* | *78.0* | *68.6* | *56.6* | *48.9* |
| Number | 38,896 | 75,358 | 209,709 | 216,400 | 215,500 | 229,900 |

Most discharges are conditional, which means that the offender is required not to commit a further offence within a given period, which is specified by the court and may be up to three years in duration. If this condition is breached the offender may be dealt with not only for the fresh offence, but also in respect of the one for which the conditional discharge was originally imposed. In essence the conditional discharge represents a threat, or warning, of future punishment and the sentencing aim with which it is most closely associated is thus deterrence (see Chapter 2). Even within the just deserts-based framework introduced by the 1991 Act, however, there is still a place for conditional discharges since they do not fall foul of the proportionality principle that was enshrined in the Act. Indeed, of the two forms of discharges, conditional discharges are far more frequently used by sentencers. Their use for adult indictable offenders increased sharply during the 1980s, but declined somewhat during the following decade, having reached a peak in 1991.[11] Since the popularity of the conditional discharge over the years appears broadly to have been inversely related to that of the fine, one explanation for this might be that conditional discharges are seen as a useful substitute for financial orders in respect of unemployed offenders, particularly since the use of the fine itself also appears to have been sensitive to the prevailing rate of unemployment, at least in the past (see below).

A somewhat anomalous measure that is also available to sentencers is the ancient common law power to 'bind offenders over', though its use is not restricted to convicted offenders. Indeed, a Law Commission survey undertaken in 1987 suggested that nearly three-quarters of bind-overs were directed against non-offenders, including witnesses, complainants or anyone else involved in the proceedings. A bind-over is in effect a suspended fine since an offender stands to forfeit a specified sum of money unless s/he abides by an undertaking to be of good behaviour and keep the peace. Although the

Law Commission (1994) recommended the abolition of this increasingly anachronistic power, its flexibility and popularity among sentencers may yet ensure its survival for a while longer.

## LEVEL 1: FINANCIAL PENALTIES

### The fine

The fine is by far the oldest of the regular non-custodial penalties available to the courts, and in terms of its impact on the rate of imprisonment, has almost certainly had the greatest effect over the years. Throughout its history, however, its potential impact in performing this rôle has been limited both by the poverty of most offenders, which renders them unable to pay a substantial fine, and by the fact that the ultimate sanction for non-payment is imprisonment. Relatively few offenders were fined in the early twentieth century, even in the magistrates' courts (Bottoms, 1987: 180); and of those who were, many still ended up in prison because payment of the whole sum was required immediately the fine was imposed. However, its usage increased dramatically during the course of the last century as a result of two major reforms. The first, in 1914, enabled magistrates' courts to allow offenders to pay their fines in regular instalments.[12] This resulted in a spectacular reduction in the number of people who were received into prison for non-payment of fines, from 75,000 in 1913 to 5,300 in 1918–19 (Bottoms, 1987: 178). An even more important reform was brought about by the Criminal Justice Act 1948,[13] which greatly extended the range of indictable offences that were punishable by fines, regardless of the court of conviction. This paved the way for the spectacular post-war increase in the use of the fine which can be seen in Table 5.1.

After 1948 the fine quickly established itself as the most frequently used sanction even for dealing with more serious offences, and since then no other community penalty has bettered it as a means of displacing custody – though it should also be noted that much of its success has been at the expense of other non-custodial penalties such as probation and the conditional discharge (see Table 5.1). The fact that the early post-war years coincided with an era of near-full employment meant that the fine offered an attractive alternative for straightforward, run-of-the-mill offenders who lacked obvious social problems requiring the assistance of a probation officer. Another factor that may help to explain its popularity in recent years is the internal difficulties that have been experienced by the probation service (see below), and the fact that the fine, unlike probation, was not tarnished by any association with the discredited treatment model. Moreover, fines not only generate revenue instead of consuming scarce penal resources, but also have reconviction rates that are no higher than – indeed if anything are marginally lower than – those associated with other penalties.

However, since 1979 the dramatic advance of the fine has been very largely reversed. This appears to have coincided both with an increase in the proportionate use of other non-custodial penalties and also, at the same time, a significant increase in the use of custody. One obvious factor that might help to account for the down-turn in fortunes experienced by the fine during the

1980s is the relatively high level of unemployment that was sustained through-out that decade and beyond, and indeed there is plenty of evidence of a link between these two trends, illustrated in Figure 5.2 below (see, for example, Softley, 1978 and Moxon, 1983).[14] The study of Crow et al. (1989: 48) disclosed an interesting bifurcatory tendency in the case of those who were unemployed. Some, for whom a fine might otherwise have been expected, were dealt with instead by way of discharge or compensation only, while others received probation, a community service order (CSO), or even a custodial penalty instead. This finding appears to confirm the impression conveyed by Table 5.1 that in recent years the fine has itself been displaced to some extent by warning sanctions such as the discharge, but also by 'higher tariff' (and more intrusive) penalties such as probation, community service and imprisonment. And this trend seems to be continuing, for the proportionate use of the fine has continued to decline in the last few years despite reduced rates of unemployment.

The marked decline in the use of the fine during the 1980s led to growing pressure for further reform in two key areas: first the need to ensure that the level of fine that is imposed is related more precisely to an offender's ability to pay; and second in relation to the problem of enforcement.

UNIT FINES   One reason why sentencers were often reluctant to contemplate financial penalties for unemployed offenders was their unwillingness to reduce the amount imposed to levels that they considered to be derisory, and their reluctance was compounded by a lack of accurate information about offenders' means. Other countries (notably Germany and Sweden) had successfully addressed these problems by developing a system of 'day fines' in which the primary aim is to achieve 'equal impact'[15] on offenders regardless of their means by depriving them of so many days' pay. These models

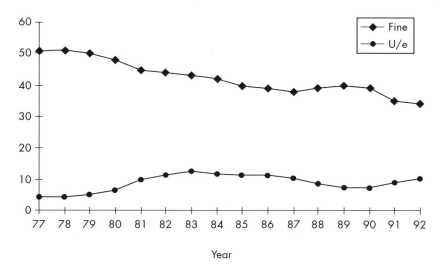

FIGURE 5.2   *Unemployment rate (adjusted to OECD concepts) and use of the fine for indictable offences*

provided the inspiration for a series of experiments which were conducted in four magistrates' courts during the late 1980s. The success of these pilots (Gibson, 1990a; Moxon et al., 1990) convinced both government and – equally importantly – the magistracy (Home Office, 1990a: para. 5.2), that such a system could be successfully adopted in England and Wales. Accordingly, the Criminal Justice Act 1991 introduced a new system of '*unit fines*' for magistrates' courts only, which came into force on 1 October 1992.

In many respects the unit fine system was ideally suited to the new sentencing framework that was introduced at the same time. Not only is the fine itself straightforwardly punitive, and therefore in keeping with the just deserts philosophy that underpinned the rest of the sentencing framework, but the new system of unit fines offered a formula for giving effect (within certain limits) to the proportionality principle which the philosophy also incorporated.[16] This formula involved two sets of calculations, the first being based on an assessment of the seriousness of the offence, on a scale from 1 to 50 units. The second calculation was based on an individual offender's weekly disposable income, which is the amount that is left after making standard deductions to reflect ordinary living expenses. This balance represented the 'multiplier' which determined the value of each unit for that offender. Depending on the means of the offender, the monetary value of these units might range from a minimum of £4 per unit in the case of unemployed offenders, who are dependent on benefits from the state, to £100 per unit for very wealthy offenders.

In the end, however, neither its broad compatibility with the philosophy of 'just deserts', nor the vast sums of money that had been spent on training and publicity were enough to ensure the survival of the unit fine. Instead, it was peremptorily abolished in the summer of 1993 by the then Home Secretary, Kenneth Clarke, in perhaps the most astonishing and unjustified *volte face* in the history of the English criminal justice system.

There were genuine problems with the unit fines system, though these stemmed mainly from the way it was implemented in practice rather than the principle of securing equal impact itself. In the first place it incurred the wrath of a vociferous minority of magistrates, who resented the level of prescription it involved as an unwarranted fetter on their independence. There were one or two highly publicized resignations from a few benches, though nothing like the mass exodus that some had forecast. A survey of magistrates conducted in four court areas in the north of England six months after the implementation of the Criminal Justice Act 1991 (Crow et al., 1994b) found that a majority of magistrates (57 per cent of those responding) *agreed* with unit fines in principle, and that the high level of dissatisfaction related mainly to the way they had been implemented in practice (mentioned by 54 per cent of respondents).[17]

A second and much more potent focus of opposition to the system of unit fines was to be found among sections of the mass media. They seized on one of the virtues of the Act – which was its aim of securing equal impact by scaling the amount of the fine according to the offender's ability to pay – and portrayed it as a vice by deliberately contrasting the amounts imposed for very similar offences while glossing over or ignoring the often huge income differentials involved.[18] They also objected to the fact that relatively well-paid, middle-class motoring offenders were being fined substantial sums while the unemployed and low paid were in their view 'let off' with derisory fines for offences which they considered to be much more serious.

In part this over-reaction (and in some cases wilful misinterpretation) on the part of sections of the media may well have been the result of an 'own goal' by those responsible for framing the unit fine legislation, since the highly successful pilot schemes had managed to avoid all such controversy. The main difference between the pilot scheme and the one that was eventually introduced was the value of the units. Because of a general increase in the standard scale of fines at the same time as unit fines were introduced, the value of each unit increased dramatically from a range of £3 to £20 per unit in most of the pilot schemes to a range of £4 to £100. This increase in the amount per unit led to the much greater differentials which so fuelled the resentment of some newspaper journalists and editors.

Setting aside these practical and political shortcomings, how successful was the unit fine in achieving its primary aim, which was to reverse the decline in the proportionate use of the fine and to increase its use for the unemployed? Here the balance sheet was much more positive. Home Office monitoring[19] showed that in the period following the implementation of the Criminal Justice Act 1991, the steady decline in the use of the fine in magistrates' courts was temporarily reversed, only to be resumed after unit fines were abolished by the Criminal Justice Act 1993 (Home Office, 1994c: Table 7.2). However, the use of the fine for unemployed offenders rose especially sharply, from 30 per cent in the summer of 1992 to 43 per cent of indictable offences in 1993; but it too fell back sharply (to 32 per cent) by late 1993 (Home Office, 1994c). Moreover, the average fine for the unemployed decreased (from £88 to £66) during the period that the unit fine was in operation, while it increased for those in employment (from £144 to £233). However, these differentials also narrowed once more after unit fines were abolished, and by late 1993 the averages were £158 for employed offenders and £78 for the unemployed.

At first glance it seems paradoxical that a measure which was successfully piloted and seemed likely to achieve most of its primary aims should have been unceremoniously scrapped so soon after its implementation while other equally controversial provisions such as electronic tagging (see below) or prison privatization (see Chapter 7) have been persevered with despite comparable setbacks. To account for the paradox it is necessary to look beyond the shortcomings of the unit fine system to the wider political context that prevailed in the period following its implementation. A politically enfeebled government, making a deliberate strategy decision to 'play the law and order card', decided to make the dramatic gesture of abolishing a measure that was known to be unpopular instead of simply reforming it (Cavadino and Dignan, 1992: 297). As such, the episode represents a short-term triumph of political expediency over principle, though the long-term cost is likely to be considerable.

Unit fines were abolished by section 65 of the Criminal Justice Act 1993 and, as a result, magistrates now have more discretion when determining how much an offender should be fined. The effect of this was not a complete return to the pre-1991 status quo, however. Courts are now required to enquire into an offender's financial circumstances before fixing the amount of a fine,[20] and may make a 'financial circumstances order',[21] which obliges the offender to furnish the court with such details as it requests or risk a further fine for non-compliance.[22] In fixing the amount of a fine, magistrates are still required to ensure that it reflects both the seriousness of the offence and the offender's financial circumstances. Moreover, the size of the fine may be either increased or decreased in the light of the offender's means[23], whereas before 1991 the general practice was that fines were only adjusted downwards in the case of less well-off offenders. After the abolition of the unit fine, the Magistrates' Association issued revised guidelines for fines, and the most recent version (April 1997) recommended a more structured approach when relating fines to means, with fines being set according to three broad income bands.[24] Whether this is sufficient to halt the continuing decline in the use of the fine remains to be seen however; so far there is no sign of this happening.

Under this looser formulation it is nevertheless quite permissible for magistrates' courts to retain a non-statutory version of the original unit fine system,[25] and a Home Office survey[26] of local fining practices found that 17 per cent of courts did employ a form of 'unit fine' approach. A majority of courts (55 per cent) indicated that they followed the Magistrates' Association Guidelines then in force, while 28 per cent used a modified version of the Guidelines. The wide range of responses obtained by this survey suggests that a reversion to a discretionary approach for fixing the amount of a fine is likely to result in a return to the disparity and chaos that characterized the pre-1991 system (see Carlen and Cook, 1989; Flood-Page and Mackie, 1998: 50). Indeed, the situation could now be even worse since the differences between those areas that persist with a non-statutory form of the unit fines system and those that revert to a more discretionary approach are likely to be even greater than before. This will almost certainly exacerbate the problem of 'justice by geography' and could contribute, indirectly, to the continuing crisis of legitimacy.

THE PROBLEM OF FINE DEFAULT   Another legacy of the 1993 counter-reforms was a rekindling of the type of concerns that had preceded the introduction of unit fines: fine default, enforcement methods and, in particular, the imprisonment of fine defaulters. The ultimate sanction for offenders who default is imprisonment, and the maximum periods for this are prescribed by statute according to the amount outstanding[27]. However, it is generally recognized that poverty and debt rather than wilful refusal are the principal factors associated with non-payment of fines (Penal Affairs Consortium, 1995d). A Home Office survey (Moxon and Whittaker, 1996) of imprisoned fine defaulters confirmed that three quarters of imprisoned fine defaulters were unemployed and in receipt of benefit.[28]

In the past, as we have seen, huge numbers of people were imprisoned each year for non-payment of fines. Indeed, as recently as 1994 fine defaulters accounted for 26 per cent of all prison receptions of sentenced offenders (Home Office, 1996a). But, since the average time they actually spent in prison was around seven days (Barclay, 1995: 27), they accounted for just 1.5 per cent of the prison population at the time.[29] Although their contribution to the prison numbers crisis may appear to have been minimal, they did pose other problems, not least of which were the administrative (and financial) strains which their rapid turnover imposed on local prisons which are among the most stressed institutions of the whole system. However, the greatest hardship was of course borne by the offenders themselves (most of whom were women[30]) – who all too often found themselves being imprisoned for an offence that was not originally deemed serious enough for either a custodial or a community penalty – and also by their families.

Since 1994, however, a number of developments have contributed to a significant reduction in the number of people who are imprisoned for non-payment of fines. The first was a High Court ruling in November 1995,[31] which stated unequivocally that magistrates and their clerks are acting unlawfully where imprisonment is imposed for non-payment of a fine without considering all alternative remedies first. The extensive range of alternatives that were available at that time included the imposition of money payment supervision orders on offenders who find it difficult to manage their finances, attachment of earnings orders (which require employers to deduct payments from earnings and remit them directly to the court), deductions from an unemployed defaulter's benefits[32] or civil enforcement through the County Court.

A second significant development took the form of a range of measures initiated by the Government's Working Group on the Enforcement of Financial Penalties. They included the issuing of good practice guidance for the courts covering timetables for reviews of payments, better monitoring of enforcement methods, greater use of money payment supervision orders, and fines clinics. And third, the existing range of alternative enforcement provisions was expanded still further.[33] The Crime (Sentences) Act 1997 allowed courts to impose a community service order of up to 100 hours on fine defaulters (section 35),[34] or a period of disqualification from driving (section 40), and authorized the use of attendance centre orders for fine defaulters up to the age of 25 instead of 21 as previously (section 36). The Act also provided for electronic monitoring to be used as a way of dealing with fine defaulters after piloting the measures experimentally during 1998. Provisional findings from two pilot areas (Elliott et al., 1999) showed that the most popular enforcement measure (with sentencers and offenders alike) was community service (which made up over three quarters of the total). However, the new arrangements do not appear likely to significantly increase the number of fines collected.

As a result of these various initiatives, the use of imprisonment as a default sanction for non-payment of fines has declined considerably, and in 1999 fine defaulters accounted for only 3,700 prison receptions (Home Office, 2000b), compared with 22,723 just five years earlier (Home Office, 1996a). This was equivalent to just 4 per cent of all prison receptions, compared with 26 per cent in 1994. And because of the short time served, fine defaulters comprised an even smaller percentage of the total sentenced population than before (0.2 per cent in 1999 compared with 1.5 per cent in 1994).

There has also been legislation aimed at avoiding the use of repeated fines for petty offenders who may be likely to default as a result. A provision in the Crime (Sentences) Act 1997[35] allowed courts to impose community service or a curfew order instead of a fine (even if the offence would not normally be serious enough for a community sentence) where the offender has outstanding fines and does not have sufficient means to pay a further fine.

Although there has been some progress in reducing the use of imprisonment for fine defaulters, this is likely to have only a limited impact on the prison numbers crisis, for the reasons we have explained. Meanwhile, the more serious problem relating to the chronic under-use of the fine remains as intractable as ever, despite a substantial reduction in the unemployment rate in recent years, and in spite of calls by the Home Secretary for greater use to be made of the fine, just after New Labour came to power in 1997. Unfortunately, the experience of sentencing reform initiatives in England and Wales since the war has shown that relying on a 'strategy of encouragement' to 'talk up' the use of the fine is unlikely to be sufficient by itself. It will need to be combined with effective constraints on the discretion of sentencers if it is to succeed. And in our view, only a reintroduction of the unit fine principle (suitably modified to remedy the teething problems associated with the 1991 reforms) that is clearly enshrined in legislation will be capable of reversing the steady decline in usage over the last few decades. However, the fine is not the only financial penalty to suffer from disenchantment on the part of sentencers. As we shall see in the next section, the same is also true of compensation orders, and this is despite the consistent and explicit statutory support they have received over the years.

### Compensation and reparation

Reparation, or making amends for the damage that has been caused by the offence (see Chapter 2), is an aim of sentencing which in recent years has been given much greater prominence following a long period in abeyance.[36] Reparation, as we shall see, can take various forms, but the most obvious of these involves the payment of financial compensation either instead of, or in addition to, some other form of punishment. The development of victim compensation schemes, and the related rise of reparation as a distinctive penal philosophy are both important contemporary penal trends (Bottoms, 1983). We deal with reparative measures in this section, as their main manifestation in relation to adult offenders at present takes the form of the compensation order, which is a 'Level 1' penalty.[37] But reparative measures in the shape of 'action plan orders' have also been introduced as 'community penalties' at Level 2 of the sentencing framework in respect of young offenders (see Chapter 9), and there is no reason why in principle they could not operate at this level for adult offenders too.

As far as compensation is concerned, the needs of victims were for a long time seriously neglected by the criminal justice system. Until 1972, the power of the courts to award compensation was limited, and consequently few orders were made. In the Criminal Justice Act 1972 a general provision was introduced allowing compensation to be awarded as an ancillary order additional to the main sentence without the victim having to apply for it, provided injury, loss or damage had resulted. This greatly increased the number of compensation orders granted each year. Ten years later courts were given the power to award compensation in its own right, rather than simply as an addition to some other penalty (Criminal Justice Act 1982). Moreover, where both a fine *and* compensation were felt to be appropriate, but the offender had insufficient means to pay both, courts were directed to give preference to compensation.[38] This was taken a stage further in the Criminal Justice Act 1988, which required courts to give reasons for not awarding compensation. In theory, at least, this means that courts are obliged to consider compensation in every case where there has been loss or damage to personal property or personal injury.[39]

All these developments are indicative of growing official enthusiasm for the idea that courts should take victims' interests into account when passing sentence.[40] In spite of this official support, however, courts remain strangely reluctant to give effect to this clearly expressed legislative intention, and the use of compensation orders, like that of the fine, has also declined in recent years. Between 1990 and 1999, at a time when living standards generally were rising and unemployment levels were falling, the proportionate use of compensation orders fell in both sets of courts. In the Crown Court the proportion of offenders who were ordered to pay compensation fell from 29 per cent to 17 per cent in respect of violent offences and from 13 per cent to 7 per cent in respect of minor property offences.[41] Similar falls were also recorded at magistrates' courts, from 60 per cent to 43 per cent in respect of violent offences, and from 22 per cent to 15 per cent in respect of minor property offences.[42] Why might this be?

A recent Home Office study (Flood-Page and Mackie, 1998: 62, 111) found that one of the main reasons sentencers gave for not awarding compensation was that the offender lacked the means to pay, and some felt reluctant to award compensation if the amount that could be afforded would appear too derisory. (As with fines, courts are obliged to relate the amount of any compensation awarded to the offender's means.) Sentencers also complained that information about the value of the loss or harm caused is often lacking.[43]

One solution would be to extend the ambit of the existing criminal compensation scheme, as mooted in the 1988 Green Paper *Punishment, Custody and the Community* (Home Office, 1988a: para. 3.10). This would enable courts to make immediate payment of the full sum awarded in the compensation order, and then recover money from the offender at a later date according to the latter's ability to pay. Although the suggestion was favourably received, the government later back-tracked on the idea (Home Office, 1990a: para. 4.25), in view of its financial implications. As a matter of principle, however, it hardly seems fair that a victim's entitlement to court-ordered compensation should entirely depend on an offender's ability to pay, particularly while the state currently benefits exclusively from the revenue raised by fines. We would therefore favour a scheme in which the revenue from fines is used to fund a reformed criminal compensation scheme of the kind we have described.[44] Indeed, this could form an important part of a more radical reformulation of our existing system of punishments in which the elements of reparation for victims and the reintegration of offenders are given far greater prominence (see Chapter 11).

In the meantime, other urgent reforms are required to ensure that sentencers start to take more seriously their legal responsibilities to prioritize victims' entitlement to compensation, instead of relegating this to a subordinate consideration, as so often seems to happen. For example, it is still all too common for compensation to be withheld, or reduced in amount, not simply because the offender lacks the means to pay, but because the court insists on imposing fines or awarding costs against an offender, despite clear legislative directions to give precedence to compensation in such circumstances (Flood-Page and Mackie, 1998: 127). Once again, this will require clear constraints to be imposed on sentencers' discretion, to prevent them from flouting the policy laid down in legislation, since it is clear that exhortation by itself will not be sufficient. Likewise, the statutory obligation to give reasons for not awarding compensation is frequently ignored altogether. This may be an area that is ripe for review under the Human Rights Act, since current practice falls far short of the standards imposed by the European Convention on Human Rights.

Even if the existing compensation scheme were to be reformed along the lines we have suggested, it would remain inherently limited in scope. One obvious limitation is that it is only capable of providing for material needs, whereas victims may well experience serious emotional difficulties as a result of the offence, not to mention the possible damage that might have been caused to an existing relationship between offender and victim. (On the needs of victims within the criminal justice system generally, see Christie, 1978; Shapland et al., 1985; Shapland, 1984; Marshall, 1985; Zehr, 1985; Blom-Cooper, 1988.) A second limitation follows from the fact that courts alone have the power to order compensation to be made, which means that compensation is normally unlikely to be forthcoming where the offender is diverted from prosecution, for example when they are cautioned instead.

During the mid-1980s a number of experimental 'victim offender mediation and reparation schemes'[45] were set up in England and Wales (some of them with government funding) which appeared to offer a solution to these problems. Although they differ in a great many respects, two distinct approaches can be identified (see generally Marshall and Merry, 1990). The first type of scheme was court-based, and usually operated at the point of sentence or immediately prior to sentence when the court referred a case to the probation service for a pre-sentence report. The possibility of mediation leading to some form of reparation was then explored, and, if the parties agreed, a proposal might then be presented to the court as part of a package involving some form of non-custodial sentence instead of imprisonment. Many of these schemes were only concerned with less serious 'low-tariff' offences, in which case their potential to divert offenders from custody was obviously limited. A notable exception, however, was the very ambitious Leeds Mediation and Reparation Service, which deliberately targeted 'high tariff' offenders with the aim of providing an alternative to custody, and which has survived long after many of its contemporary projects closed down (Wynne, 1996).

The other type of scheme operated at the pre-court stage and aimed to divert offenders away from the criminal justice system altogether. Most schemes of this kind depended on a high degree of co-operation between the police and a reparation/diversion bureau. The initial aim was to identify cases that were suitable for diversion and then, provided the offender admitted the offence and the bureau agreed to take the case on, the offender was cautioned instead of being prosecuted. Mediation between victim and offender was one possible outcome, and could lead to some form of reparation being negotiated, though this was not invariably the case.

The findings from these early experimental schemes were largely disappointing, however (see Marshall and Merry, 1990), particularly in relation to the pre-trial schemes (see, for example Davis et al., 1988, 1989), and appeared to cast doubt on the extent to which the interests of victims could be reconciled with those of offenders, at least within the context of the existing criminal justice system. In the light of these findings the government lost interest in the idea of direct reparation to victims, which consequently did not feature in the 1991 Act. However, these 'first-generation' schemes were aimed exclusively at juvenile offenders, for whom the principle of cautioning with the aim of 'diverting' the young person from court was already well-established (see Chapter 9). So it was not altogether surprising that within such schemes diversion remained the primary objective; that reparation tended to be used selectively, as just one option among others in a pre-prosecution 'tariff' of measures; and that, even where it was attempted, the reparation agreement was often purely 'token' in character, and had little to offer victims.

Only when the concept of pre-trial diversion based on reparation was extended to *adult* offenders could the potential effect of reparation on diversion be properly put to the test. One such scheme was the Kettering Adult Reparation Scheme, which began operating on an experimental basis in 1987. Although not entirely problem-free, the preliminary findings were sufficiently encouraging (see Dignan, 1991, 1992) for the scheme to be extended to the rest of the county during 1990–1.[46] The scheme helped to demonstrate, first, that where a philosophy of 'even-handed' reparation is pursued, it is possible to ensure that victims' interests need not be prejudiced by the diversion of adults from prosecution; second that such a scheme is capable of achieving a reasonably high level of victim and offender participation; third that the great majority of victims and offenders appear satisfied with both process and the outcome; and fourth that, at least in the short term, it is possible to secure police support for a significant increase in the rate of adult diversion from prosecution.

We have argued (1992, 1997a) that this type of scheme offers a way of combining diversion from prosecution with constructive reparation for victims, thereby ensuring that their interests are not sacrificed in the pursuit of cost savings or administrative convenience. Indeed, experience elsewhere (notably in New Zealand and Australia)[47] gives ground for cautious optimism that this kind of approach might assist in the development of a more restorative system of criminal justice in general, with the potential to ameliorate many aspects of the current penal crisis. Although the development of restorative justice measures in England and Wales has been slower and more cautious, progress has nevertheless been made since the early experimental schemes in the 1980s. For example, initiatives such as the Northamptonshire Diversion Unit helped to encourage the development of 'caution plus' schemes, which were commended in two highly influential reports by the Audit Commission (1996, 1998). Moreover, the reform of the youth justice system by the New

Labour government led by Tony Blair after the 1997 General Election was also influenced in part by the philosophy of restorative justice, notably with regard to the introduction of reparation orders, action plan orders and referral orders. We will examine all these developments more closely in Chapter 9.

However, they also accentuate the curious neglect of both compensation and reparation within the 1991 sentencing framework. This is highly regrettable since the legislation and case law that pre-dated it provide an inadequate basis for reconciling the often conflicting interests between restorative and desert-based principles of justice.[48] Consequently, if the sentencing framework is to be revised (see Chapter 4), this remains one of the most important issues that needs to be addressed.[49]

### LEVEL 2: COMMUNITY SENTENCES

The 1991 Criminal Justice Act introduced the concept of 'community sentences', which are medium tariff penalties that are regarded as sentences in their own right rather than as 'alternatives to custody', as they were previously.[50] Community penalties have proliferated in recent years,[51] and the Powers of Criminal Courts (Sentences) Act 2000 designates no fewer than eight specific 'community orders': probation orders; community service orders; combination orders; curfew orders; drug treatment and testing orders, attendance centre orders; supervision orders and action plan orders.[52] The last three of these are not available for adult offenders and will not be dealt with here (but see Chapter 9). All community orders are subject to a 'seriousness threshold'; that is, the offence must be 'serious enough to warrant such a sentence'.[53] Finally, another change that reinforced the reformulation of community penalties as punishments in their own right was the abolition of the requirement to seek consent on the part of an offender before imposing such a measure.[54] In the next section, we will deal with each of these adult-focused community orders in turn, before moving on to the Level 3 custodial penalties.

### Probation (community rehabilitation orders)

Probation orders are officially renamed '*community rehabilitation orders*' as from 1 April 2001 by section 43 of the Criminal Justice and Court Services Act 2000. In what follows, and elsewhere in this book, we refer to these orders by their more familiar and traditional name.

ORIGINS AND EARLY DEVELOPMENTS  For much of the twentieth century probation – along with the fine – was the main alternative to a custodial sentence. The official probation system as we know it today was first introduced by the Probation of Offenders Act 1907. Garland (1985) has described how this Act transformed what had previously been an amateur, *ad hoc* practice performed by well-meaning notables and evangelical reformers – such as the Church of England Temperance Society's 'police court missionaries' – into a comprehensive statutory service provided by professional probation officers who were employed by local authorities. Under the terms of the 1907

Act, probation was established as an important alternative to custody where either the character of the offender or the nature of the offence were such as to persuade the court that 'punishment' was 'inexpedient'.

Because a probation order did not technically count as a 'sentence', it could not, in its original form, be combined with any other penalty in respect of a single offence; nor did a conviction 'count' against the offender for certain purposes. Both of these restrictions were removed by the Criminal Justice Act 1991, which converted the probation order into both a sentence of the court and a 'conviction'. The Act also spelt out[55] more detailed criteria for making a probation order. Courts now have to be satisfied that probation would be desirable 'in the interests of a) securing the rehabilitation of the offender; or b) protecting the public from harm from him or preventing the commission by him of further offences'.

Any probation order entails some restriction on an offender's liberty by virtue of being placed under the supervision of a probation officer, with a duty to report as required and to receive visits at home for a prescribed period of between six months and three years. Over the years, however, there has been a tendency for the range of conditions which may be imposed by the court to be extended, and for the restrictions which they impose on an offender's liberty to be intensified. There are now five specific kinds of additional requirements (or 'conditions').[56] They include requirements as to residence; requirements to attend a 'probation centre' (formerly known as a 'day centre') for up to 60 days;[57] requirements to take part in (or refrain from) other specified activities for up to 60 days;[58] requirements to submit to appropriate psychiatric treatment for a mental condition; and, finally, similar requirements to submit to appropriate treatment for drug or alcohol dependency.

In terms of its impact on the use of imprisonment by the courts, probation's record of achievement has been wildly variable. In its early days it appears to have made a major contribution to the substantial reduction in the size of the prison population that was sustained until the beginning of the Second World War. For example, in the 30 years following its introduction the proportionate use of imprisonment declined by considerably more than half, while that of probation more than quadrupled from 7 to 31 per cent of all indictable offenders (Rutherford, 1986: 129). The year 1938 proved to be the high-water mark for the probation order, however, for the following four decades witnessed a spectacular decline in its proportionate usage for adult offenders, as can be seen from Table 5.1. Its nadir was in 1977 when a mere 5 per cent of adult indictable offenders were given probation orders, though proportionate usage picked up again thereafter, and by 1994 it had recovered to 11 per cent, where it has remained. The post-war decline seems all the more remarkable because it began during a period of rehabilitative optimism. Moreover the decline continued throughout the 1970s, in spite of substantial investment in the probation service and considerable increases in manpower during that decade.[59]

There are a number of possible reasons for the declining use of probation in the post-war period. These include organizational and ideological changes within the service which may have affected its relationship with the courts; the impact of other non-custodial sanctions on the sentencing practices of the courts, and finally, the collapse of confidence in the rehabilitative ideal which took place in the 1970s. The most important organizational change to affect the probation service during its formative years was its continuing quest for professional status during the pre-war and immediate post-war period. McWilliams (1981) has argued that this *professionalization* had a profoundly detrimental effect on the relationship between the service and the courts which might help to explain why there was a serious loss of confidence in the value of probation despite the general sense of rehabilitative optimism which still pervaded penal thinking at the time.

Among the important milestones on the road to professional status since 1907, the following are of particular importance: the creation in 1912 of a professional body, the National Association of Probation Officers; the beginnings of a specialist training programme at about the same time; the gradual development of a more bureaucratic form of organization following the adoption of a national set of rules in 1926; and the subsequent evolution of a hierarchical career structure. Finally, but just as important according to McWilliams (1981: 100), was the gradual acquisition during the 1930s–1950s of a body of specialized theoretical knowledge based on the adoption of American-style social casework techniques.[60] This was to have a marked effect on relationships between the probation officer and the bench, not just because they no longer seemed to be speaking the same language, but because they no longer appeared to share the same values or priorities either.

One symptom of this changing relationship was that individual probation officers began to spend less time actually in court as the increasingly bureaucratic nature of the job imposed additional demands on their time. This was accompanied by a much more fundamental switch of priorities on the part of the service as a whole, as it extended its interest in casework to the needs of a rather different group of offenders – those who had been sentenced to custody – following their release from prison (see also Raynor, 1993). The assumption of new responsibilities in the field of after-care[61] also coincided with a general down-grading of the service's more traditional commitments, a process that was accelerated by the abolition of probation for juveniles in 1969,[62] and a resulting transfer of supervisory responsibility for some juveniles from the probation service to local authority social workers.

McWilliams suggests (1981: 110) that as a result of all these changes, the relationship between probation officers and the courts became much more problematic: from being 'friends of the court', they became 'mere acquaintances', losing both stature and influence in the eyes of sentencers in the process.[63] McWilliams' account offers a plausible explanation for the otherwise unexpectedly early decline in the use of probation by the courts. The continuing steady decline that took place during the 1970s is less surprising, being related partly to the ready availability of a variety of alternative measures such as the fine, suspended sentence and community service order (see below), but also to the collapse of the rehabilitative ideal after 1970 (see Chapter 2).

The collapse of confidence in the 'treatment model' of rehabilitation had particularly serious and far-reaching consequences for the probation service. For having pinned its colours so unambiguously to the treatment mast over the previous four decades, as part of its unending quest for professional status, the withering theoretical and empirical assault that was sustained by the treatment model during the 1970s left the probation service without a coherent sense of purpose or even a clear *raison d'être* (Rumgay, 1989). The probation service responded to the dilemma in which it found itself by embarking on a lengthy and continuing (if largely inconclusive) debate about its future rôle and direction (see Harris, 1977; Haxby, 1978; Bottoms and McWilliams, 1979; Rumgay, 1989; Shaw and Haines, 1989; James, 1995; Nellis, 1995, 1998; Cheetham, 1998; and Pease, 1999).

At the heart of the debate was a deep-rooted philosophical conflict between the rival 'welfare' and 'control' functions which probation may be made to serve. On the one hand, probation officers were traditionally exhorted to 'advise, assist and befriend'[64] their probationers, and this was how many still defined their primary role. On the other hand, however, probation officers had always been expected to discharge an explicitly law-enforcing rôle, and among the duties which they owed to the court were those of supervising offenders with a view to preventing further offences, and also reporting any breaches to the court. As we shall see, the latter perspective has become ever more dominant over the last two decades, as central government has systematically sought to redefine the rôle of probation in line with its increasingly managerialist and punitive instincts.

MANAGERIALISM AND THE ASSAULT ON PROBATION'S TRADITIONAL ETHOS   Three key themes can be identified in government policy towards probation since the late 1980s, each of which poses a serious threat to the service's more traditional ethos. The first is a brand of *'managerialism'* which combines a bureaucratic quest for greater cost-efficiency and more effective planning with a more overtly political quest for more effective forms of social regulation.[65] The second is directed more to the substance and 'image' of the probation order, which the government has sought to recast as a tougher and more demanding measure. As we shall see, managerialist techniques have also been pressed into service in pursuit of this aim. The third relates to the recruitment and training of probation personnel.

The election of a Conservative government in 1979 unleashed on the probation service a managerial revolution, which assumed a variety of forms.[66] The first, which we have labelled *'technocratic managerialism'* (Cavadino et al., 1999: 103) involved the zealous application of various managerial techniques and philosophies borrowed from the private sector in order to raise standards of service, promote greater accountability and increased 'value for money'. An early manifestation of this new orthodoxy in respect of the probation service took the form of a Statement of National Objectives and Priorities (SNOP) which was issued by the Home Office (1984c) as part of the government's Financial Management Initiative (Humphrey, 1991). SNOP urged local probation committees and chief officers to ensure that probation resources were managed 'efficiently and effectively' in pursuit of clear objectives with a view to delivering value for money to the taxpayer. It also signalled clearly that the old *laissez-faire* approach to probation policy which placed a high value on the professional autonomy of individual caseworkers was about to be replaced by a much more assertive form of centralized control. Moreover, the SNOP initiative was reinforced by a barrage of measures designed to increase the degree of central oversight and control of local service provision. The Audit Commission, National Audit Office and Her Majesty's Inspectorate of Probation were all pressed into service to assess local services against a standard range of 'key performance indicators'[67] designed to measure their quality and effectiveness.

A second form of managerialism, which is often referred to as *systemic managerialism*, sought to integrate the probation service much more closely into the wider penal system, of which it has always been an important, if somewhat detached component (Cavadino et al., 1999: 105). This aim was spelt out most clearly in a government Green Paper on the reorganization of the probation service (Home Office, 1990e), which stressed that the primary rôle of the probation service should be to serve as a criminal justice agency, complementing the work of other agencies such as the police, prisons and, principally, the courts, rather than as a separate social work agency. Its distinctive contribution was defined in terms of preventing or reducing reoffending by those under supervision, with a view to reducing overall levels of crime (Home Office, 1990e: para. 3.2).

However, the Conservative government's ambitions for the probation service were not simply confined to the promotion of the largely abstract and rational values that are often associated with technocratic managerialism – efficiency, effectiveness and value for money. Nor were they sated by securing a 'systemic realignment' of the probation service as an integrated component of the broader criminal justice system. For the Conservatives also held equally forthright views regarding the *nature* of the interventions undertaken by the probation service and, especially after 1993, were prepared to use managerial techniques as a means of promoting their increasingly hard-line policy objectives. We have referred to this as *'punitive managerialism'* (Cavadino et al., 1999: 106).

An early manifestation of this approach was a clear attempt to redefine probation in terms of 'punishment and control' rather than welfare objectives, which was spelt out in the 1988 Green Paper *Punishment, Custody and Community* (Home Office, 1988a). This new approach was also embodied in the Criminal Justice Act 1991, which converted the probation order into a 'sentence' (or 'punishment') and meant that for the first time it was possible to use it in combination with other penalties,[68] even for the same offence. The 1991 Act also crystallized earlier attempts to focus the work of the probation service on more serious offenders who would otherwise be at risk of custody, by categorizing probation as a 'community sentence', occupying an inter-mediate position within the hierarchical framework of penalties which the Act established. The process was taken a stage further by the drawing up of National Standards (Home Office et al., 1992, 1995, 2000) which prescribe in some detail the various aims of the probation order and how they should be put into practice. As well as dealing with enforcement and breach proceedings (see below) they emphasize the need to develop a supervision plan, the aims of which include the need to identify the causes of the offending behaviour and seek to address them, and to make offenders aware of the impact their offence has had on the victim.[69] They also require offenders to be issued with expected standards of behaviour including the avoidance of offensive language or behaviour.

Within the context of the 1991 Act, probation was initially expected to play an important part in developing and delivering 'credible' community penalties to the courts as part of the drive to limit the use of custody for less serious offences. In the wake of the ensuing 'law and order counter-reformation', however, this pivotal rôle for the probation service was abandoned, and Michael Howard began to complain (Home Office, 1995d) that probation was poorly understood, was widely regarded as a 'soft option' and lacked credibility with the courts.

Mr Howard also opened up a new front in the long-running assault on the probation service's more traditional ethos and values by attacking the service's recruitment and training policies (Home Office, 1995e). This culminated in the controversial and hotly contested removal of the legal requirement for all new probation officers to hold a Diploma in Social Work,[70] and a bid to encourage recruitment from a 'broader base', including those who were perceived to have relevant experience and skills, even if they lacked the formal qualifications. One group of potential applicants whom Michael Howard particularly wished to encourage were those from the armed services, many of whom have traditionally been recruited as prison officers in the past.[71] Jack Straw subsequently reinstated a university-based training programme for the probation service in 1997 as one of his first acts as Home Secretary. This involves a mixture of university teaching and work-based assessment, but leads to a Diploma in Probation Studies, instead of the social work qualification that had previously antagonized Mr Howard. Moreover, a press release issued at the time (Home Office, 1997a) reaffirmed the aim of attracting a wider range of recruits than previously.

THE PROBATION SERVICE UNDER NEW LABOUR   Following the General Election of 1997 the future of the probation service was for a time shrouded in uncertainty as the incoming New Labour government launched a series of wide-ranging reviews, many encompassing issues that extended far beyond the probation service itself.[72] Other reviews have focused much more specifically on the probation service, and have resulted in a variety of proposals and changes affecting its structure and organization, funding, future rôle and even its very identity and image. In July 1997 the government established the 'Prisons–Probation Review' (Home Office, 1998b) in order to examine the structure and organization of both the prison and probation services, including options to establish closer links between them. A consultation paper – *Joining Forces to Protect the Public* (Home Office, 1998c) – which coincided with the publication of the review rejected the idea of a merger between the two services, which some had feared,[73] and settled for a more modest organizational reform of the service.

The ensuing Criminal Justice and Court Services Act 2000, restructured the probation service and created a unified national service for the first time,[74] and one that is directly accountable to the Home Secretary. The previous conglomeration of 54 separate and, to some extent, autonomous local probation services were reorganized into a single service that is divided up for administrative purposes into 42 local areas. The boundaries for the service exactly match those of the corresponding police forces (another example of *systemic managerialism*; see above), and each local area is to be served by a board composed of representatives of the local community. However, the main thrust of the provisions is to convert the service into a centrally controlled service, removing most of the autonomy traditionally enjoyed by local services.[75]

The Criminal Justice and Courts Services Act sets out the aims of the probation service in the following terms: to protect the public, to reduce offending and to provide for the proper punishment of offending. It also defines the purpose of the service in terms of assisting the courts in sentencing decisions and providing for the supervision and rehabilitation of offenders. The formal name for the new service, which is also set out in the Act, is the National Probation Service for England and Wales. This nomenclature was adopted after the abandonment of an earlier and increasingly farcical attempt to push through a more radical 'rebranding' exercise aimed at making probation sound 'tougher'. Having rejected options such as the Community Justice Service, the Home Office announced that the service was to be known in future as the 'Community Punishment and Rehabilitation Service'. However this was quietly dropped after a brief but successful campaign based on an all too obvious anagram of the acronym by which the service would undoubtedly have become known and, all too probably, derided. The desire to give a makeover to the image of the service and its activities was not entirely extinguished, however, and the Criminal Justice and Court Services Act pressed ahead with the renaming of certain community orders including the probation order itself. This is renamed[76] the 'community rehabilitation order' (section 43) 'in order to reflect better the nature of certain community orders, and make them more easily understood'. A further development (which we discuss later in this chapter) has been the introduction of new rules to make the probation order 'tougher' by ensuring that the sanctions for offenders who fail to comply with the requirements of their orders are applied more strictly.

The Criminal Justice and Courts Services Act accomplishes many of the technocratic and systemic managerialist objectives with regard to the probation service to which (as we have seen) a succession of earlier Conservative Home Secretaries had also aspired. Many will lament these developments,[77] fearing that the traditional humanitarian and moral impulses that have long characterized the service are incapable of being sustained in the face of these newer and blunter managerial and pragmatic imperatives. For ourselves, we are not opposed to all forms of managerialism, since we accept that some managerialist techniques do have a part to play in ensuring that the service pursues important new goals (such as meeting the needs of victims), and in promoting better standards, greater fairness and increased efficiency, all of which may help to improve the quality of the service for its clients (see Cavadino et al., 1999). However, we remain implacably opposed to all forms of *punitive* managerialism, by which we mean the use of managerialist techniques in pursuit of harsher, punitive measures, of the kind that are associated with Strategy A. This is therefore the yardstick by which we would seek to judge the reform of the probation service under New Labour. What conclusions can we draw from the changes that have been made to the rôle and future direction of the probation service, as opposed to the way it is structured and administered?

As with other aspects of the government's criminal justice policies, there have been both positive and negative developments with regard to the rôle and responsibilities of the service since New Labour came to power. Among the positive developments, we would single out in particular the key rôle which probation officers were given in implementing the government's 'Welfare to Work' programme, resulting from its commitment to extend the benefits of the programme to offenders on their release from prison (Cavadino et al., 1999: 115). Using the probation service to help tackle the problem of social exclusion in this way represents a rare and commendable extension of its traditional welfare and supervisory functions. Likewise, the creation of new multi-agency youth offending teams under the Crime and Disorder Act 1998 (see Chapter 9) could help to stimulate probation staff and others to assist in the development of various restorative justice initiatives, including victim consultation and the delivery of a variety of reparative measures. Ultimately, it is possible that such developments could pave the way towards a more extensive rôle for restorative justice-based approaches within the criminal justice system as a whole, especially if similar measures are extended from younger age ranges to the adult criminal justice system. Developments such as these appear to represent a welcome departure from the punitive managerialism that characterized many of the previous Conservative government's policies towards the probation service.

However, other policies relating to the probation service appear to be just as heavily influenced by punitive managerialist sentiments as any that emanated from the Conservative governments of the previous two decades; for example, in relation to the increasingly draconian enforcement strategies that are being developed to deal with non-compliance. Moreover, many of Jack Straw's policy pronouncements on the subject of probation still contain the same punitive rhetoric associated with his predecessors.[78] In view of these mixed messages – and the policy contradictions which they appear to embody – the future rôle and direction of the probation service remains uncertain. One thing that is abundantly clear as a result of the Criminal Justice and Court Service Act reforms is that the way these tensions are ultimately resolved will owe far more to the policy predilections of whatever government is in power at the time than to any preferences on the part of the service itself.

### The community service order (community punishment order)

The community service order (CSO) is officially renamed the 'community punishment order' as from 1 April 2001 by section 44 of the Criminal Justice and Court Services Act 2000, but again we shall mostly refer to it by its more familiar name. The CSO originated from a recommendation of the Advisory Council of the Penal System (1970) and was first introduced in England on an experimental basis by the Criminal Justice Act 1972. After a brief trial period in six selected areas it was made available nationally in 1975, since when it has quickly established itself as an important measure, both in England and elsewhere. Part of its initial popularity probably derived from its appeal to a range of different sentencing philosophies since it combines elements of reparation, rehabilitation and retribution although, as we shall see, there has been a tendency lately to augment its punitive aspects at the expense of the other two aims. Its proportionate use by the courts for adult male offenders has remained around 9 per cent since 1994, compared with 11 per cent for the probation order during the same period.

A community service order requires an offender to undertake between 40 and 240 hours unpaid work in the community within a twelve month period. The work is provided by an approved agency and is organized and supervised by the probation service. It may consist, for example, of outdoor conservation projects, construction of adventure playgrounds, or decorating houses and flats for elderly and disabled people. It can be highly tailored to the individual offender, as in the case of footballer Eric Cantona, probably the best-known recipient of a community service order to date, who was ordered to help coach local children as his penalty for assaulting a spectator. Failure to attend and perform the work as directed can lead to the offender being 'breached', i.e. taken back to court and penalized for non-compliance with the order (see below).

Although it was introduced as a promising alternative to custody, there has never been any legal stipulation that a CSO should only be used as an alternative to a custodial sentence.[79] Early empirical studies on the impact of CSOs on other court disposals estimated that only between 45 per cent and 50 per cent of those receiving CSOs would otherwise have been sentenced to custody (see in particular Pease et al. 1977; Pease, 1980: 35), and consequently that at least half would otherwise have received non-custodial penalties.

Within the context of the 1991 sentencing framework, the community service order is subject to the same threshold requirement relating to seriousness as the other community sentences. Furthermore, the number of hours ordered to be worked must be commensurate with the seriousness of the offence. Prior to the 1991 Act, however, there was a lack of Court of Appeal guidance on the number of hours that were appropriate for individual cases. Moreover, it appears (Flood-Page and Mackie, 1998: 126) that in spite of the sentencing framework there is still a lack of consensus among sentencers as to whether the concept of a tariff applies to community sentences, or whether, conversely, such sentences are selected simply according to the needs and circumstances of the offender.

Finally, as with the probation order, steps have been taken in recent years to strengthen the punitive element in CSOs, principally through the introduction of National Standards for the Supervision of Offenders in the Community, though these have also sought to promote greater consistency in the execution of the orders. The first set of National Standards was introduced in 1988, ostensibly with a view to encouraging the adoption of accepted forms of 'best practice' including type of work to be performed, standards of performance and action to be taken on breach. However, the rules also incorporated more exacting procedures for dealing with lateness, non-compliance and unsatisfactory behaviour, and required every offender who is subject to an order of more than 60 hours to perform at least 21 of those hours in a group placement doing work of a manual nature. The 1995 version of the National Standards (Home Office et al., 1995) reaffirmed that work placements should be 'demanding in the sense of being physically, emotionally or intellectually taxing'. Enforcement procedures have subsequently been tightened up still further (see below), and the constant attempts to project a much tougher, more punitive image for the order culminated in the adoption of a tougher-sounding name – the community punishment order – in the Criminal Justice and Court Services Act 2000.

### The combination order (community punishment and rehabilitation order)

Prior to the 1991 reforms, probation and community service were both available only as an alternative to dealing with an offender in any other way, and consequently they could not be combined with any other penalty, or with each other, at least for a single offence. Following the 1991 Act, most previously prohibited combinations involving these two penalties were removed, thereby opening up a new range of possible sentencing permutations. However, some restrictions were retained in the way that probation and community service can be combined. Under the current sentencing framework this is only possible by means of a 'combination order', which was introduced by section 11 of the Criminal Justice Act 1991 (and which was renamed the 'community punishment and rehabilitation order' as from 1 April 2001 by section 44 of the Criminal Justice and Court Services Act 2000 ).

The combination order is available for offenders over the age of 16 who are convicted of an imprisonable offence. The probation element carries a higher minimum period (12 months instead of six) than does probation by itself, though the maximum period is the same for both (3 years). The community service element has the same minimum of 40 hours work, though the maximum is lower than for community service by itself (100 hours instead of 240 hours). Probation supervision has to continue for at least as long as community service is being performed, which is why the minimum period is higher than for probation alone.

The apparent aim of the combination order was to provide a particularly demanding non-custodial measure for some of the petty persistent property offenders who had hitherto all too often been sentenced to custody (Home Office, 1990a). However, its official aims as set out in the 1995 National Standards (Home Office et al., 1995, 2000) simply repeat those of its constituent parts. Because of the severe restriction on liberty that is involved, informal attempts were initially made by the probation service and some magistrates' clerks to restrict its use to relatively 'high tariff' offences in the Crown Court, but of the 12,400 orders made in 1999, just under three quarters (73 per cent) were in fact made by magistrates (Ayres, 2000: Table 7). The order now accounts for 4 per cent of all indictable offenders. It is the only community sentence to have increased in usage at the Crown Court since 1994, while in magistrates' courts it appears to have contributed to an increase in the overall use of community sentence, albeit partly at the expense of the ordinary community service order (Flood-Page and Mackie, 1998: 15).

### Curfew orders, exclusion orders and electronic monitoring

At the same time as steps were being taken to 'beef up' probation and community service, another even more intrusive form of control was being developed which did not depend on the co-operation (or even involvement) of the probation service. This was the 'curfew', a modified form of house arrest. A power to impose 'night restrictions' as part of a juvenile supervision order had already been introduced by the Criminal Justice Act 1982. This was opposed and disliked for its emphasis on surveillance and control by the probation service and social workers who were responsible for enforcing it, and it was little-used by magistrates (Nellis, 1991: 170). But the idea was to resurface in the Criminal Justice Act 1991, and when it did the provisions for enforcing curfews broke new ground.

The 1991 Act introduced the curfew order[80] as a penalty that could either be used in its own right or in combination with other community or financial penalties. Offenders can be ordered to remain in a specified place (usually their own homes) at specified times of between two and twelve hours in the day. Provision was also made[81] for curfews to be enforced by means of *'electronic monitoring'* or *'tagging'* as it has come to be known (Lilly, 1990; Nellis, 1991) – with offenders being obliged to wear an electronic device attached to their ankles or wrists which alerts a remote computer if the curfew is broken. Provision was also made for private sector agencies, rather than the probation service, to be given responsibility for the monitoring. Despite its somewhat outlandish origin – in a 'Spiderman' cartoon[82] – electronic monitoring of offenders was introduced in a number of American states from 1983 onwards[83] and, following a favourable recommendation from the House of Commons Home Affairs Committee in 1987, an experimental scheme designed to test the technical feasibility of the idea for suspects on remand was introduced in England in August 1989.[84] Although there were a number of well-publicized set-backs to the scheme, involving both technical malfunctioning of the equipment and clear evidence of 'consumer resistance' to the idea on behalf of both courts and taggees (including a high 'breach' rate[85]), the government's enthusiasm for tagging seemed little diminished.

The Criminal Justice and Public Order Act 1994 made provision for curfew orders with electronic monitoring to be introduced for sentenced offenders[86] on an area by area basis (Schedule 9, para. 41). A series of trials ensued,[87] which showed that overall completion rates were relatively high, equipment failures were rare and sentencers began to make more frequent use of the orders after a very low initial take-up rate (which persisted in some trial areas). However, tagging is not cheap in comparison with other community sentences,[88] and there are doubts as to the kind of offender for whom tagging might be most suitable. Nevertheless, encouraged by these findings, the government extended the power to make curfew orders backed by electronic monitoring to all courts in England and Wales in December 1999. The Criminal Justice and Court Services Act 2000 extends these powers still further, and will enable courts to allow the conditions of other community penalties to be monitored electronically. (Electronic monitoring also forms an integral part of the 'Intensive Supervision and Surveillance Programme' for persistent young offenders introduced in 2001: see Chapter 9.) The 2000 Act also creates a new community order – the exclusion order – which will require an offender to stay away from a certain place or places, either at particular times or at all times (section 46). The new disposal will be available either as a free-standing sentence or in combination with another community penalty or a fine, and could again be monitored by electronic means when suitable technology is developed.

Despite the evident enthusiasm with which tagging has been greeted by politicians of both main political parties,[89] the whole idea of curfews and tagging is nevertheless open to a number of serious ethical and practical objections. The main ethical objection is that such highly intrusive forms of supervision may be degrading, and so restrictive of individual freedom as to threaten the values of democratic society (Rutherford, 1986: 168). The main practical objections relate to the ways in which the measure could be (mis)used by the courts. In the United States, for example, experience has shown that the most suitable candidates for monitoring are socially stable offenders with a job, who have committed non-violent offences (Whitfield, 1995; Baumer and Mendelsohn, 1992). This highlights the risk of the scheme being used to supplant other non-custodial measures rather than imprisonment, particularly since the offence for which it is imposed need not be imprisonable. Even if this were not the case, and tagging were to be used in the way the government appears to envisage (Home Office, 1990a: para. 4.9) – in an attempt to help control the personal behaviour of those with a 'disorganised and impulsive' lifestyle – it is still likely to be more intrusive than the most probable alternative, which would be a probation order. In addition, there is also the danger of this strategy backfiring if (as seems highly probable) the kind of offenders for whom curfews are used were to breach the order in significant numbers, and end up in prison as a result.[90]

### Drug treatment and testing orders; drug abstinence orders

Drug treatment and testing orders were introduced as additional community orders by the Crime and Disorder Act 1998.[91] They are aimed at those who commit crimes to fund their drug habit, and who show a willingness to co-operate with treatment. The order can be given to offenders aged 16 and over, either on its own or in conjunction with another community order; it lasts for between six months and three years. Provided the offender consents, the order requires a person to undergo treatment, and specifies the frequency of the mandatory drug testing that is also part of the order. There are regular court reviews to monitor the offender's progress.[92] Information about the suitability of offenders is presented to the court in a pre-sentence report. The orders themselves are administered by multi-agency teams that may draw on the services of probation officers, community psychiatric nurses, psychiatrists, psychologists, drug workers and GPs.

Drug treatment and training orders were piloted in three areas for a period of eighteen months beginning in October 1998 (Turnbull et al., 2000a & b) prior to national implementation in 2000. The pilot areas experienced a slow initial take-up, and some implementational problems, but also reported substantial reductions in the amount spent on drugs (and also in the self-reported level of acquisitive crime) for those completing the programme. However, the National Association of Probation Officers has cautioned (*The Guardian*, 31 October 2000) that the schemes were very selective and only accepted 'low risk' offenders. The Criminal Justice and Court Services Act 2000 introduces an additional free-standing community order – the drug abstinence order – which requires offenders who are over the age of 18 to abstain from misusing specified Class A drugs for a period between six months and three years (section 47).[93] They are also required to provide samples when requested, for the purpose of monitoring compliance with the order.

### Reform of the 1991 framework of community sentences?

As we were completing this book, the government was poised to announce the outcome of a wide-ranging review of the 1991 sentencing framework (see below and Chapter 4). Although the detailed proposals were unclear at this stage, the review was known to be considering the case for adopting a 'more flexible' structure for community sentences (see now Halliday, 2001; see also Home Office, 2001: 42). One option under consideration would involve a shift from the existing extensive range of relatively discrete and self-contained community sentences to a more generic approach in which sentencers might be invited to concoct a more individualized community sentence comprising components adapted to both the offender and the offence. For example, a given community sentence might comprise a 'punitive component' (such as a curfew or exclusion condition); a 'reparation component'; an 'offending behaviour component' (for example a drugs or alcohol treatment programme); and an 'ill-gotten gains component' (for example a confiscation order).[94] The most obvious danger with such a strategy, if adopted, is that it could foster an 'aggregative' approach to sentencing that might easily result in community sentences becoming even harsher than they are already. The review was also known to favour the adoption of a more active supervisory rôle for judges which would encourage them to monitor an offender's progress and, if necessary, adjust the content of the order (as in the case of the drug treatment and testing order). One probable consequence would be a further increase in the number of offenders who end up being given a custodial sentence after breaching a community sentence (see below).

### Enforcement of community sentences: breach provisions

One of the main aims of the National Standards which exist for all forms of community penalty is to provide clear guidance on the standard of compliance that is expected. The 1995 version (Home Office et al., 1995) required probation officers to record any failure to turn up for a supervision meeting or community service session for which they fail to receive a satisfactory explanation, and instructed them to initiate 'breach' proceedings after three such failings at most. However, a national audit of 10,000 cases undertaken on behalf of the Association of Chief Probation Officers (*The Guardian*, 28 September 1999) showed that only 44 per cent of offenders who fell into this category were in fact breached.[95] New National Standards for the probation service (Home Office et al., 2000), which came into force on 1 April 2000 were intended to tighten up on enforcement by directing probation services to initiate breach proceedings after only a second unacceptable failure.

Moreover, the government has also strengthened, in two respects, the sanctions that are likely to be imposed on offenders who fail to comply with a community order. First, the Criminal Justice and Court Services Act 2000 now imposes a statutory duty on probation services to issue a warning to offenders after the *first* unacceptable failure to comply with an order, and to return offenders to court after the second unacceptable failure (section 53). In addition, the Act also introduces a presumption of imprisonment in such cases, unless the court is of the opinion either that the offender is likely to comply with the order during the remaining period, or that there are exceptional circumstances.[96] It has been officially estimated that the revised National Standards alone will add 1,000 on to the numbers in prison (White and Cullen, 2000), but the combined impact of the new standards and the 2000 Act could be considerably greater than this. Of the 130,000 or so offenders who are supervised annually by the probation service, approximately 23 per cent (around 30,000) breach their orders, but in recent years the custody rate for those in breach has been declining, and in 1993 was only 37 per cent for those on community service orders, and 18 per cent for those on probation. If an additional 20,000 offenders in receipt of community orders were to be imprisoned for three months for breaching them, this could add 5,000 to the annual prison population.

A second attempt to strengthen the enforcement regime for community sentences is contained in the Child Support, Pensions and Social Security Act 2000, the relevant provisions of which come into play once a court has determined that a community sentence has been breached. The effect of such a determination is to reduce the level of benefit to which a claimant is entitled (in the case of a person eligible for income support),[97] or to remove it altogether (in the case of a Jobseeker's Allowance) for a fixed sanction period (section 63). The measures, which apply to the whole of Great Britain, are to be piloted in a number of areas with a sanction period set at four weeks (though the maximum allowable period is 26 weeks). The measures will apply initially to offenders aged between 18 and 59, at least for the duration of the pilots. The provisions also entitle 'vulnerable claimants' to apply for hardship payments.

### Effectiveness of community sentences?

In our opinion, community sentences should always be used in preference to custodial punishment unless the offender represents a serious risk to the safety of others, or (exceptionally and for brief periods only) where confinement is the only possible means of gaining the co-operation required to make the appropriate community sentence work. This opinion is founded on moral, rights-based considerations (see Chapter 2) rather than purely practical calculations. Nevertheless, whatever one's angle on the morality of punishment, we would also argue that community punishment is capable of serving almost all the purposes that are conventionally associated with imprisonment at least as effectively as, and in some cases more effectively, than custody itself (see Cavadino et al., 1999: 117).

The relative 'effectiveness' of penal sanctions (in terms of their success in reforming or individually deterring offenders) is conventionally measured by comparing reconviction rates, despite their well-known shortcomings as a measure of 'penal success'.[98] When the reconviction rates that are associated with custody and community penalties are compared after allowing for factors that are known to influence the risk of reconviction (such as age at first offence, type of offence, criminal history and gender) the differences between them are usually found to be negligible.[99] However, it has been claimed (McGuire and Priestley, 1995) that community sentences which conform to certain principles – for example those focusing on social skills or training or cognitive behaviour – can have measurable, positive effects on recidivism, whereas those with strong punitive effects can increase recidivism by some 25 per cent.[100] Research evidence also seems to show that comparable reformative programmes are more likely to be successful in community settings rather than in custody.[101]

Moreover, there is no reason in principle why community penalties should not also serve denunciatory or retributive ends, just as custody is assumed to. As for the pursuit of other punitive purposes such as reparation and reintegrative shaming, it also seems highly probable that these are more likely to be successful (for obvious reasons) where offenders are kept in the community instead of being locked up. Indeed, restorative justice processes such as mediation and conferencing have the added advantage, if conducted properly, of denouncing an offender's conduct without at the same time denigrating and stigmatizing the offender as a person, in the way that conventional penalties (and particularly custodial ones) do. Consequently, the main apparent advantage that custody has over other penal measures derives from the 'protective' impact it appears to offer the public at large in 'incapacitating' offenders from committing certain kinds of offences.[102] We accept that there are some serious violent and sexual offenders who present such a clear and vivid threat to the safety and well being of others that custodial incapacitation is both justifiable and right. For the great majority of less serious offenders who are routinely incarcerated, however, it is highly doubtful whether the temporary 'gain' in public protection that custody appears to offer can be justified in view of the known economic, social and personal costs that are associated with such an extreme sanction. The fact that community penalties appear to be at least as effective as custody in preventing reconvictions in such cases, while at the same time affording greater opportunities for the needs of victims to be addressed, should in our view be conclusive.

## LEVEL 3: CUSTODIAL PENALTIES

Under the 1991 sentencing framework, the third and most severe level of penalty is custody itself. Strictly speaking, custody comprises not only immediate imprisonment (or detention and training orders in respect of those under the age of 18) but also suspended sentences of imprisonment[103] (which are only available in the case of adults). In addition, as we shall see, the government has recently signalled a revival of interest in the idea of various forms of 'intermittent' custody, which seek to combine elements of custodial and community penalties within the same disposal.

### The suspended sentence

Courts may, in circumstances which we will describe below, suspend the activation of any prison sentence of two years or less for a prescribed period – known as the 'operational period' – which may be between one and two years. If, during this operational period, the offender commits a further imprisonable offence and is convicted, the court is then obliged to activate the suspended sentence in full unless it is of the opinion it would be unjust to do so.

The history of the suspended sentence is instructive since it was the first post-war attempt to restrain the use of custody by means of a specially designated 'alternative to imprisonment'. By the mid-1960s it was becoming increasingly apparent that the English prison system was facing a growing problem as the prison population rose to three times its pre-war level, in spite of the drastic reduction in the *proportionate* use of imprisonment (compared to other sentences) which had been brought about largely by the impressive expansion of the fine (Bottoms, 1987). Previous proposals to introduce such a measure had twice been decisively rejected by the Advisory Council on the Treatment of Offenders in 1952 and 1957, on the grounds that it was 'wrong in principle and to a large extent impracticable' (1952: para. 23). However, by 1967 the urgent need for practical remedies had largely overcome these scruples and the suspended sentence was introduced (by the Criminal Justice Act 1967) in the confident expectation that it would relieve pressure on the prison population. Unfortunately, as is often the case when products are pressed into service on the basis of inadequate 'research and development', the measure soon began to exhibit a number of serious design faults and malfunctions which stubbornly proved impossible to eradicate completely.

One design fault was a failure to provide sentencers with sufficiently clear guidance as to the circumstances in which the sentence was to be used. In particular, the original legislation failed to emphasize that it should only be used in cases considered serious enough for a sentence of immediate imprisonment. This was a serious weakness because, as Bottoms (1981) showed, many sentencers were attracted to the measure not as an alternative to custody but as offering a more immediate and credible deterrent (the 'sword of Damocles' effect) than other non-custodial measures did. Consequently, it quickly became apparent that the measure was not only being used as a substitute for immediate custody, as intended, but also in place of other 'alternatives' such as the fine and probation. Indeed, calculations by Home Office researchers suggested that of those given suspended sentences in the years before 1970 'only between forty per cent and fifty per cent would, but for the new provisions, have been sentenced to imprisonment for the original offence' (Oatham and Simon, 1972: 233).[104] As a result, more people were put at risk of a custodial sentence, on reconviction, than would otherwise have been the case. On this occasion the Court of Appeal did try to make good

Parliament's omission, by stressing that the sentence should only be used in respect of offences that would otherwise justify the use of immediate custody,[105] and this ruling later received legislative endorsement.[106]

A second 'malfunction' relating to the suspended sentence (discovered by Bottoms, 1980b: 5) was that magistrates' courts (but not Crown Courts) tended to increase the length of suspended terms of imprisonment compared with those taking immediate effect. However, the most serious design fault associated with the suspended sentence was the draconian sanction that was applied in the event of a breach, whereby courts were normally obliged to activate the suspended sentence in full.[107] This problem was further compounded by an early Court of Appeal ruling,[108] to the effect that any custodial sentence that is imposed for the subsequent offence should run consecutively to the activated sentence (rather than concurrently). Largely as a result of these features, the suspended sentence in England did not reduce the prison population as it has in other jurisdictions such as Japan and the Netherlands, where breach only rarely leads to imprisonment (Rutherford, 1986: 159), and this failure to achieve its primary aim was apparent long before the 1991 reforms.

Following the introduction of the 'just deserts' package in the 1991 Act, the position of the suspended sentence became even more precarious since the sentencing aim with which it is most closely associated is based on a form of deterrence, and deterrent justifications had been disparaged in the White Paper preceding the Act (Home Office, 1990a: para. 2.8). Moreover, although in theory it remained the most severe penalty that could be imposed short of immediate imprisonment, in practice this was not how it was always perceived whether by sentencers or offenders, many of whom saw it as a 'let off'. Within the 1991 sentencing framework the high-tariff position of the suspended sentence was rendered even more anomalous following the deliberate 'toughening' of the community penalties in Level 2. Although this anomaly was acknowledged in the 1990 White Paper (Home Office, 1990a: paras 3.20–3.21) the government drew back from outright abolition of the suspended sentence, possibly fearing that it would result in a greater use of immediate custody. Instead, steps were taken to severely curtail its use by prohibiting it unless the case would otherwise have qualified for a sentence of immediate imprisonment, and even then only where its use could be justified by exceptional circumstances.[109] In addition, courts were also obliged to consider giving 'added bite' to the suspended sentence by combining it, where appropriate, with either a fine or compensation order, neither of which would normally be available where immediate custody is imposed.

The effect of these restrictions has been dramatic, as can be seen from Table 5.1. For whereas before 1992 the suspended sentence accounted for 10 per cent of adult males and 8 per cent of females, these figures were down to 1 per cent and 2 per cent respectively by 1994, and the measure is now hardly used at all by magistrates. It seems probable that initially most of those who would previously have been given a suspended sentence were being dealt with by means of a community sentence instead (Flood-Page and Mackie, 1998: 125), but that this was no longer true following the law and order counter-reformation of the mid-1990s, which appears to have resulted in a drastic lowering of the custody threshold. Consequently, there is little doubt that many offenders who are presently being sentenced to immediate custody would have received a suspended sentence of imprisonment prior to 1992. This has called into question the rationale for retaining the severe restrictions that were imposed on the use of suspended sentences at a time when the custody threshold was arguably much higher than it is today (Flood-Page and Mackie, 1998: xiii).

### 'Alternatives to imprisonment' and their impact on the size and composition of the prison population

Prior to 1991, the policy of widening the sentencers' repertoire of non-custodial sanctions had notably failed to alleviate the prison numbers crisis (except perhaps in the realm of juvenile justice: see Chapter 9). The general experience appeared to be that non-custodial alternatives supplemented, rather than supplanted, existing custodial measures and largely functioned as alternatives to each other rather than to custody. Thus, as we have seen, even when touted as direct alternatives to custody, new non-custodial penalties such as the CSO or suspended sentence replaced other non-custodial penalties at least half the time. The proportionate use of custody by the courts actually increased significantly during much of the period in which the various new alternatives were available.

Some commentators had high expectations of the new strategy embodied in the 1991 reforms, with one even predicting the end of the 'carceral era'.[110] While accepting that it was a step in the right direction, other liberal commentators such as ourselves were sceptical about whether it had gone far enough, even though it was partially and temporarily effective in reducing the proportion of custodial sentences and increasing the use of the fine. Following the 1993 counter-reforms, however, these short-term gains were reversed as the government abandoned its erstwhile commitment to curtailing the use of custody, while retaining the policy of toughening community penalties. As a result, courts were encouraged to use custody more freely for offenders who might have avoided it under the 1991 reforms, and those who did escape a custodial sentence were liable to be dealt with by means of a very much tougher range of non-custodial disposals.

These changes were also reflected in the statistics relating to the use of immediate custody over the last decade. By 1999 the proportionate use of immediate custody for indictable offences at all courts had reached 23.4 per cent, which was the highest for 40 years. The proportionate use of immediate custody increased in both sets of courts. In the Crown Court the custody rate in 1999 was 63 per cent, which was 19 percentage points higher than in 1991, and the highest level recorded since 1998 (Ayres, 2000: para. 35). In the magistrates' court the proportionate use of immediate custody was 12.5 per cent, compared with only 5 per cent in 1992 (Ayres, 2000: para. 29).[111] As for the composition of the prison population itself, the feature that has attracted most comment (Home Office, 2000b) is the increase in the proportion of longer sentenced prisoners (serving over four years), which in 1999 accounted for more than 40 per cent of male sentenced prisoners, compared with just 32 per cent in 1989. Just as significant, however, has been the rapid increase in the proportion of the prison population serving sentences of up to six months, which accounted for 52.4 per cent of the prison population in 1999 (Home Office, 2000b: Table 1(f)), compared with just 37.2 per cent in 1995 and just under 7 per cent in 1989. This represents an average increase of over ten per cent in each year between 1995 and 1999, and a more than sevenfold increase since 1989.

### Immediate and intermittent custody: towards the 'seamless sentence'?

In May 2000 the then Home Secretary, Jack Straw, announced a fundamental review of the 1991 legal framework for sentencing under John Halliday and, in particular, its impact on the sentencing of repeat offenders (Home Office, 2000d). This marked a potentially decisive break from the official policy of seeking to curb the use of imprisonment for less serious offenders by promoting the use of community punishments instead. In announcing the review, Mr Straw indicated his strong disapproval of the offence-based proportionality principle that formed the cornerstone of the 1991 reforms, and signalled support for the rival principle of 'progressive sentencing'. The latter is more closely related to the offender's criminal history, and pays much less regard to the seriousness of the current offence.

One of the aims of the sentencing framework review is to explore the possibility of 'seamless sentences', or 'more flexible sentencing options which join up custodial and community penalties'. Several possibilities are known to be under consideration. They include an option described as 'Custody Plus', which is envisaged as a substitute for existing custodial sentences of between three and twelve months' duration. The sentence would consist of a set period in custody (of up to three months, to be served in full), followed by a further period of 'community punishment', which could last up to an overall maximum sentence of twelve months. A second option is described as 'Suspended Sentence Plus' whereby, in addition to sentencing an offender to some form of community sentence, a court would also prescribe a custodial sentence of a set length, which would form the starting point for any re-sentencing that might be called for in the event of breach proceedings. A third option, referred to as 'Intermittent Custody', is based on the principle of periodic detention (for example for so many hours per day) in some form of appropriate accommodation while allowing an offender to participate in designated activities. These might include employment, treatment programme or educational component.

There are a number of possible objections to these latest ideas for sentencing reform. Some of these objections relate to how fair or effective it is to 'target' petty persistent offenders with harsher penal measures as is proposed, issues which we discuss further in Chapter 11. Suffice it to say at this point that these new proposals are disturbingly vague about the *kind* of persistent offenders for whom they are intended. Consequently, they are likely to increase the use of custody considerably for relatively petty offenders who pose no serious threat to society, however much of a nuisance they might be. As a result, the new measures will almost inevitably drive the prison population to new heights, particularly in the current sentencing climate. Even if the new measures would be subject to the existing 'custody threshold' requiring a 'serious' offence, this would probably have little effect given the steady erosion of this threshold that has taken place in sentencing practice since the 'counter-reformation' of 1993. It is also likely that the flexibility of 'seamless sentences' would in practice (in the present punitive climate) be used less to move offenders from prison into the community and rather more to shift them in the opposite direction since they are liable to be deemed to have behaved unsatisfactorily while on supervision in the community.

Consequently, the most probable effect of these impending proposals will be to ratchet up still further the general severity of the system of penalties now in operation without any credible prospect of compensating benefits in the form of reduced prison numbers, lower expenditure or increased levels of public protection. We turn now to the question of whether it is possible to make sense of these and other recent developments; and what light, if any, theories of penality can shed on such changes, and on the nature and future direction of social control mechanisms in general.

## SHIFTING PATTERNS OF PENALITY: THEORETICAL REFLECTIONS

Although, as we shall see, there is considerable debate at present concerning the exact nature and significance of recent developments within the penal system, there is also much common ground between the protagonists regarding the context within which these changes are said to be taking place. All are agreed that the starting point for the current debate lies in the so-called 'great transformation' of punishment which has been most notably chronicled by Foucault (1977) (see also Ignatieff, 1978 and Rothman, 1971). This original 'transformation' was the major shift in the form of punishment from 'corporal' to 'carceral' punishment, which occurred around the end of the eighteenth and beginning of the nineteenth centuries (see Chapter 2).

There is also a broad measure of agreement on the part of contemporary penal commentators that a number of significant changes affecting the penal system have occurred since then, and particularly since the mid-1960s. But opinions differ as to whether these amount to a 'second transformation', and, if so, what form it is taking or how exactly it should be characterized.

### Scull's 'decarceration' thesis

The opening shot in the present debate was fired by Andrew Scull in 1977 with the publication of his book *Decarceration: Community Treatment and the Deviant – A Radical View*. Although he has subsequently revised some of his ideas (Scull, 1984), Scull originally argued very strongly that we are now experiencing a major shift in the ideology and apparatus of social control that amounts to at least a partial reversal of the original 'great transformation'. Scull used the word '*decarceration*' to refer to 'the state-sponsored policy of closing down asylums, prisons and reformatories' (Scull, 1984: 1). (The term is also used more broadly by those seeking to analyse the interrelationship between prisons and alternatives such as probation, community service orders and other community penalties, and the use made of other diversionary strategies including both pre-trial initiatives and early release mechanisms.)

The term thus encompasses two parallel tendencies: one is the so-called 'community corrections movement' whereby offenders are increasingly dealt with in the 'community' instead of locking them up in custodial institutions; the other is the move towards 'community care', which extends the same principle to the treatment of the mentally ill and mentally handicapped, and which results in the systematic closure of large-scale psychiatric institutions. As well as lumping together policies for dealing with the 'mad' and the 'bad' in this way, and using the same term – 'decarceration' – to cover both tendencies, Scull also illustrates his thesis with reference to both British and American developments since, as we shall see, he also believes that the forces that are ultimately responsible for decarceration policies are at work throughout the contemporary capitalist system.

According to Scull, the most potent of these forces are economic considerations, which now favour decarceration whereas at the time of the original transformation of the penal system a policy of incarceration made greater economic sense. In brief, he suggests that by the turn of the nineteenth century, the old 'poor law' system for the relief of poverty was quite unable to cope with a massive increase in the number of desperately poor people, many of whom were economically unproductive for much of the time, and who lacked the means to provide for their own subsistence. Moreover, traditional methods of social control (based mainly on a feudal pattern of social obligations between rich and poor) were losing their effectiveness at this time. Consequently, the most economically efficient way of dealing with the problem of poverty and its attendant risk of social disorder was to move to a system of large-scale institutions within which the unproductive and the deviant could be provided for and controlled.

But by the late twentieth century, these economic and social considerations no longer apply. Instead, the cumulative effects of increased public expenditure over the years (on welfare, housing and industrial assistance programmes, among others) have plunged the state into a serious and worsening fiscal crisis, making it imperative for public expenditure to be drastically curbed. One way of doing this is by using welfare payments and social services to enable many of the so-called 'problem populations' (Scull, 1984: 135) who were previously incarcerated in institutions to be looked after and controlled in the community instead. From the state's point of view it is now relatively much more expensive to keep people locked up in institutions than it is to subsidize others to look after them in the community. Scull is not convinced that community alternatives *are* necessarily cheaper to operate in practice than the institutions they displace – because of opposition from vested interests and the difficulty of achieving more than marginal cost-savings unless whole institutions can be closed down. But he does strongly maintain that decarceration has more to do with cost-saving imperatives than with the development of more effective forms of treatment, or any genuine commitment to humanitarian improvements in the lives of the incarcerated.

Indeed, far from being humane, he considers that decarceration is not in the interests either of the deviants themselves, or of the community into which they are unceremoniously decanted. In the case of the elderly and the mentally ill, for example, he argues that such a policy results in many ex-inmates being herded into 'newly emerging "deviant ghettoes", sewers of human misery . . . within which . . . society's refuse may be repressively tolerated' (1977: 153). As far as offenders are concerned he speaks of 'burglars and muggers . . . being left to walk the streets', and even 'the perpetrators of violent crime' as being 'turned loose under conditions which guarantee that they will receive little or no supervision'. As a result, he considers that decarceration 'forms yet one more burden heaped on the backs of those who are most obviously the victims of our society's inequities. And it places the deviant in those communities least able to care or cope with him.' (1977: 1–2).[112]

Scull is surely right to insist that we should look behind the façade of official rhetoric when examining the reasons for major penological change. But, in other respects, Scull's thesis is open to criticism: partly on theoretical grounds because it is based on an over-simplistic form of economic determinism (see Chapter 3); partly because it fails to fit the facts in a number of crucial respects; and partly because Scull himself fails to probe sufficiently deeply behind the rhetoric of decarceration to expose the real consequences of the changes to which he refers. We will now deal briefly with each of these charges in turn.

One major difficulty with Scull's 'fiscal crisis' argument is its rather simplistic assumption that because traditional methods of treating and controlling 'problem populations' are becoming relatively more expensive to operate, the state is obliged to adopt decarceration rather than seeking savings elsewhere, for example through cuts in welfare programmes. In fact, as critics such as Matthews (1979: 106) have noted, this is precisely what the state has done. Cuts in public expenditure over the last few years have been very selectively distributed, with the result that spending on law and order has actually increased substantially during this period[113] at the expense of other public expenditure programmes, notably welfare spending. What the 'fiscal crisis' argument fails to take into account is that in any given period, penal policy is a product of the complex interplay between political and ideological pressures, in addition to the economic forces with which Scull was almost exclusively concerned.

Another serious problem that results from Scull's economic determinism is a tendency to over-generalize from the available data in a way that is not supported by the facts. Many commentators (see, for example, Cohen, 1979; Matthews, 1979; Burton, 1983; Hudson, 1984) agree that his thesis applies quite well to developments in mental health policy in recent years, but he is almost universally criticized for assuming that because the same economic pressures presumably apply to the treatment of offenders as well, it follows that recent developments in penal policy must necessarily be part of the same phenomenon. In fact, as we shall see, this contention is fatally undermined by empirical evidence drawing on geographical, historical and contemporary data relating to trends in the use of imprisonment.

Geographically, the 'fiscal crisis' theory is seriously weakened by evidence relating to the Dutch experience since the war.[114] For although the Netherlands is almost a textbook example of decarceration in the penal sphere, it spectacularly fails to conform to the fiscal crisis argument – in fact, quite the reverse. Downes (1988: 58) has pointed out that the main reduction in the prison population – both in terms of daily average population and also in proportion to crime rates – was experienced during the period from the mid-1950s to the early 1970s. This was a time of unprecedented prosperity which preceded the onset of the fiscal crisis to which Scull refers. Conversely, later plans which envisaged a doubling of the 1975 prison capacity by 1990 coincided with a period of heightened economic uncertainty.[115]

Scull's decarceration thesis is also undermined by historical evidence relating to the use of imprisonment. This quickly dispels the notion that decarceration is a uniquely distinctive feature of post-war penal policy as it seeks to respond to novel economic constraints. For example, there was a remarkably rapid decline in the prison population from 1908 to 1918 (see Ruggles-Brise, 1921: ch. 17; Fox, 1934: ch. 17; Rutherford, 1986: 122–31; Bottoms, 1987: 178–9). During this period the prison population more than halved from 22,029 to 9,196.[116] By comparison, during the post-war decarceration era described by Scull, his own figures show a near doubling of the prison and borstal population from 21,370 in 1951 to 38,382 in 1972.

It could be argued that such increases in the absolute number of people imprisoned are misleading unless account is taken of changes in the crime rate and, in particular, of the total number of convicted defendants (Bottoms, 1983: 183). When the *proportionate* use of imprisonment for all sentenced offenders is examined (see Table 5.1), it can be seen that there was indeed a fall in the proportion of the sentenced population who were imprisoned between 1960 (when it was 25 per cent) to 1971 (when it was 18 per cent). But thereafter it rose again, and in the case of adult male offenders the rate of imprisonment almost doubled between 1974 and 1999 (15 per cent and 27.9 per cent respectively). So even on this weaker definition of decarceration, Scull's thesis was not borne out by events, at least at the level of penal practice. Barbara Hudson (1984) has suggested that decarceration during this period occurred only at the level of rhetoric,[117] in official discourse about the use of imprisonment, and that Scull failed to probe behind this rhetoric to see what was really happening.[118]

Scull's original assessment of the *consequences* of decarceration has also been criticized (see in particular Cohen, 1979: 361) for taking at face value claims that decarceration would result in non-intervention, and complaining that this would lead to a weakening of sanctions against offenders. In his more recent work, Scull (1983, 1984) acknowledged that the position was rather more complicated than this, and went on to claim that the community corrections movement had actually resulted in an undesirable *extension* of the state's social control apparatus. This was attributed to 'a strong conservative backlash against anything smacking of leniency towards crime and criminals' (Scull, 1984: 175), which he saw as the product of 'the accelerating volume of crime over the past quarter century' (Scull, 1984: 177).

Even with these revisions, however, Scull's decarceration thesis is still defective. For example, no attempt is made to examine the relationship between the crime rate and the rate of imprisonment,[119] or to explain how the ideological factors favouring stronger control measures come to outweigh the economic imperatives favouring decarceration. Another major issue which the thesis fails to address fully is the debate about recent 'alternatives to custody' and how they relate to the 'extension of social control' argument. For an attempt to confront these issues we turn now to a rival thesis which has been put forward by two very influential theorists of social control, Stanley Cohen and Thomas Mathiesen.

### Cohen and Mathiesen: the 'dispersal of discipline' thesis

In a series of works, especially his 1979 article 'The Punitive City' and his 1985 book *Visions of Social Control*, Stanley Cohen has painted a nightmarish vision of the city of the future as being increasingly subjected to a sophisticated social control network. Unlike Scull, who initially described the community corrections movement as a reversal of the original 'great transformation', Cohen has always considered it to be simply a continuation of the same 'disciplinary' project, albeit on a much more ambitious scale. Whereas the first transformation had the effect of concentrating the social control energies of the state on highly selected populations of deviants *within* specially designated institutions like the prison and the asylum, he points out that this is no longer the case. Instead, recent penal developments associated with the community corrections movement demonstrate that the state is now spreading its tentacles of control ever more deeply into the tissues of society by significantly widening the reach and the scope of its social control apparatus. Cohen describes the key features of this second transformation in a memorable series of metaphors.[120] They include:

- *Widening the net*   This concept refers to the process whereby community programmes tend to 'capture' many who would not formerly have been 'at risk', as when a cautioning scheme is used not only as an alternative to prosecution but also for those who would otherwise have been informally dealt with. The end result is to 'increase rather than decrease the total *number* who get into the system in the first place' (1979: 347, italics in original).
- *Thinning the mesh*   Not only are more brought into the system, but the *amount of intervention* to which offenders are subject is also much greater if they are referred to one of the newer more 'intensive' community orders than would have been the case if a more traditional alternative to custody such as a fine, ordinary probation or conditional discharge had been used instead.
- *Blurring*   As a result of these and other developments – notably the current proposal for 'seamless sentences' (see above) – there is a blurring of formerly rigid distinctions between institutional and non-institutional forms of control, or even between what is or is not regarded as punishment. Ultimately, Cohen foresees a day when 'it will be impossible to determine who exactly is enmeshed in the social control system' (1979: 346).
- *Penetration*   The combined effect of these tendencies is that the whole (considerably enlarged) system of social control is now extending more and

more deeply into the *informal* networks of society. Even more important, though, is the fact that these measures actually *augment* the existing prison system. They do not displace it; on the contrary, they enable the prison to reach out into the community. And so, as Downes has put it, '[w]e end up with the worst of both worlds: an unreconstructed *ancien régime pénal* and a new-style carceral society' (1988: 60).

Cohen sees the whole of the community corrections movement as 'merely an extension of the overall pattern established in the nineteenth century' (1979: 359), whereby the mode of control founded on *discipline* is dispersed out of the big institutions in which it originated, and into the rest of society. ('Discipline' is the concept developed by Foucault (1977) to characterize the attempt to transform the 'soul' of the offender – see Chapter 3). Cohen cites (1979: 347, 357) the community service order as just one obvious example of a form of punishment which penetrates deeply into the informal social networks of civil society by requiring offenders to undertake socially useful work in the community. Moreover, the fact that the community service order is often used in place of less intrusive penalties such as the fine is seen as evidence of its 'mesh-thinning' tendencies.

This 'dispersal of discipline' thesis has been taken a stage further by the Norwegian criminologist, Thomas Mathiesen (1983). In a prediction which echoes the concerns voiced by Cohen, he too foresees that 'the control system as a totality may *expand rather than shrink*' as a result of recent proposals to strengthen society's social control mechanisms by, among other things, developing 'crime care in the community'. But whereas Cohen's main concern is with crime control strategies that are individualistic in the sense that they still aim at 'a disciplining of the law-breakers "one by one"' (1983: 132), Mathiesen discerns in certain other recent developments the emergence of a new and complementary strategy that could 'move fully away from individualism, and focus on *control of whole groups and categories*' (1983: 139) by means of general surveillance. Mathiesen gives the following examples of the kind of social control techniques he has in mind:

> TV cameras on subway stations and in supermarkets, the development of advanced computer techniques in intelligence and surveillance, a general strengthening of the police, a general strengthening of the large privately-run security companies, as well as a whole range of other types of surveillance of whole categories of people – all of this is something we have begun to get, and have begun to get used to. (1983: 139)

Mathiesen believes that these new societal or collective forms of control will increasingly impinge on the everyday lives of groups and categories of people and that, as such, they represent a break with individualism as the archetypal form of social control.[121] Nevertheless, he still characterizes them as 'disciplinary' measures and so they too are seen as extensions of the original carceral project, in which more efficient disciplinary social control measures are dispersed into the wider society. The difference for Mathiesen is that the new techniques he describes involve 'a change *from open to hidden discipline* . . . The new control out there in society is either completely outside the individual's range of vision, or at least quite a bit less visible than the control forms of pure individual liberalism' (1983: 139).

While closed circuit television cameras of the kind mentioned by Mathiesen undoubtedly extend the range of surveillance, their impact is still partial and limited since they depend on the capacity and attentiveness of operatives who monitor the screens to identify and respond to incidents justifying a call to the police or security officials. They can also, of course, be used retrospectively after an incident has occurred in order to obtain evidence and help to identify an offender. As such, these relatively passive technologies at best represent a quantitative increase in the capacity of social control agencies to detect law-breaking whether by individuals or groups of individuals. However, recent technological developments hold out the prospect of a qualitative change in the nature of social control by combining video equipment with sophisticated computer software which allows images to be converted into numerical data and analysed by means of complex algorithms (see Norris, 1995). This makes it possible, for example, for vehicle number plates to be read automatically or facial features to be checked against a database of known offenders. Linked to an intruder alarm system the use of algorithmic surveillance could detect the breach of a perimeter offence by a human intruder, activate and direct cameras to the site of the breach and alert police and security personnel. More controversially, such a system could be programmed to monitor selected public spaces; for example to detect the presence of groups of people during certain hours of the day or night, or to monitor crowds for signs of disorder, relaying such information automatically to police control rooms.

Although Mathiesen's somewhat gloomy assessment of recent develop-ments in social control may be in keeping with the spirit of the times – and while its Orwellian overtones fit the concerns of social control theorists speculating on the future – it is not without its critics. David Garland (1995: 3), for example, has reminded us that, viewed sociologically, surveillance is and always has been an essential element of social control and, quite apart from being an inescapable adjunct of modernity, does have benevolent as well as repressive potential. Moreover, while technologies of the kind we have referred to above could be used to increase *detection* rates, there is no necessary connection between this and any increase (or indeed reduction) in the level of *penalties* for offenders once they are caught.[122] (This is not, however, to belittle the important issues concerning civil liberties and privacy which undoubtedly do exist regarding the access to and use of the information which is gathered by way of these new technologies.)

More generally, Tony Bottoms (1983) has questioned the validity of the 'dispersal of discipline thesis', while finding much to commend in Cohen's and Mathiesen's analysis of specific control mechanisms. The central thrust of Bottoms' critique is that many of the new community control measures that are described by Cohen and Mathiesen are not in fact *disciplinary* measures – at least not in the sense in which Foucault used the term.

Bottoms argues persuasively (1983: 182) that Foucault's notion of discipline contains two key elements: one is *surveillance*, and the other involves the *'mechanics of a training'* which aims to produce an obedient subject by repeatedly working on the offender's 'soul'. This, according to Foucault, was the fundamental objective of the original carceral project which emerged from the first great transformation of punishment. But if this is the case then Mathiesen is mistaken to characterize the recent move towards a more collective form of social control as a dispersal of *discipline*. For the techniques he describes depend almost exclusively on the technique of surveillance alone, making use of advanced technological developments and improved methods of policing rather than any 'mechanics of a training'.

Of the more individualistic forms of control, the community service order is cited by both Cohen and Mathiesen as evidence of their contention that punishment is beginning to penetrate ever more deeply into the informal networks of society, and again this is depicted as an extension of *discipline*. Bottoms agrees that it appears to conform to some of the tendencies described by Cohen – mesh-thinning and community penetration in particular – but again he is doubtful whether this alone is sufficient to warrant the term 'discipline'. For although work can be, and indeed has been, used for disciplinary purposes ever since the birth of the carceral system, Bottoms argues that there are other aspects of the community service order, such as the element of reparation which it involves, that make it less congruent with the dispersal of discipline thesis, at least when the sentence was first introduced.[123]

A much more serious charge against the 'dispersal of discipline' thesis in Bottoms' eyes is its neglect of certain other features of contemporary penal systems that are not at all consistent with the 'dispersal of discipline' thesis and which therefore cast some doubt on its universal applicability. Chief among these 'neglected features' of contemporary penal systems is the dramatic post-war growth in the use of the fine, particularly in the period up to 1980. This is important for two reasons: first, because the fine is manifestly *not* a disciplinary penalty in Foucault's sense of the word; and, second, because (as we have seen in Table 5.1 above) it is the fine – rather than any of the more disciplinary penalties available to the courts (such as probation) – that has displaced imprisonment most significantly since the war, despite the substantial decline in its usage since the mid-1970s.

This is not at all what one would expect of an emerging 'carceral society'. Rather, it chimes in with Bottoms' more general observation in 1983 that until then it was the *'penalties not involving continuing supervision by a penal agent'* (Bottoms, 1983: 169) – that is, such non-disciplinary measures as the fine, and the suspended sentence – that appeared on balance to have flourished since the war, at the expense of arguably more disciplinary measures such as imprisonment and probation (see Table 5.1). Finally, Bottoms noted that the recent growth of concern for victims within the criminal justice system is another development which cannot be explained by the dispersal of discipline thesis.

For all these reasons Bottoms concluded that the 'dispersal of discipline' thesis is not a particularly helpful way of characterizing recent penal developments. What was needed instead, he believed, was a thesis that could account for the relative *decline* in the significance of disciplinary punishments within the total apparatus of social control. With this aim in mind he tentatively advanced a third thesis which we call the *'juridical revival'* thesis.

*Bottoms' 'juridical revival' thesis*

In developing his rival theory, Bottoms reminds us (1983: 176) that at the time of the original 'great transformation' there was a third model of punishment besides the traditional or *corporal* model and the now overwhelmingly dominant *carceral* model which displaced it. This third model, which Bottoms calls the *juridical* system of punishment, was proposed by the classical reformers such as Beccaria (see Chapter 2) but ultimately exerted much less influence on forms of punishment at the time than did the disciplinary ideas of reformers like Bentham. Bottoms suggests (1983: 195), that the reason for this was because the social control techniques that were available at that time were largely ineffective in maintaining order. However, circumstances change, and the essence of Bottoms' thesis is that we may now be heading towards a second 'great transformation' – not from the concentration of discipline in the prison to the dispersal of discipline throughout society, as Cohen and Mathiesen have argued – but from a carceral to a juridical system of punishment. The effect of this is seen as *diminishing* rather than increasing the role of punishment as a method of social control.

Unlike the carceral project which, as we have seen, was based on reforming offenders through discipline, the juridical project aimed at 'requalifying individuals as subjects' (Bottoms, 1980a: 21).[124] This 'requalification' was to be achieved through the application of a standard set of penalties that were intended to be fixed in duration and proportionate to the seriousness of the offence. Once the punishment was completed the offender would be re-admitted to society as a full member with undiminished rights of citizenship. Most importantly, the preventive 'message' which the punishment was intended to represent was to be transmitted by the simple symbolic fact of punishment itself. Accordingly, there was no need for specific social control agencies designed to 'mould' offenders into obedient subjects (1983: 176).

In the light of this analysis Bottoms concluded that many of the modern penal developments to which he has drawn attention are more accurately characterized as embodying juridical rather than carceral tendencies. This is particularly true of the fine, which Bottoms correctly suggests is more of a classical than a disciplinary punishment (1983: 178), but there are other pointers in the same direction. These include the general increase in penalties not involving supervision by a penal agent, the increase in compensation payments by the courts, and also the recent growth of interest in the principle of reparation.

As for the reasons underlying these developments, Bottoms suggests (1983: 196) that the key to the debate lies in a more detailed appreciation of the nature of the transition from early to late capitalism than is to be found in any of the previous accounts. One strand in his proposed explanation is based on certain changes in the nature of law and social control that have occurred during this period: changes that have been characterized by Kamenka and Tay (1975) as a shift towards a 'bureaucratic–administrative' social and legal order in advanced capitalist societies (see Chapter 3). A key feature of this development is a shift in the locus of social control from the formal punishment system to other bureaucratic agencies, both public and private.[125] Another aspect is the increased reliance on non-disciplinary forms of social control, based on a variety of techniques such as increased surveillance, negotiation and formal warnings.

## CONCLUSION: THE FUTURE OF PUNISHMENT?

We have now examined three of the most important contributions to the current debate about the nature of our contemporary social control system. Even at the time he wrote there was little evidence to support Scull's 'decarceration' thesis, except at the level of official rhetoric, though even that has now ended. However, the 1991 reforms did offer some support for both the other theories ('dispersal of discipline' and 'juridical revival'), suggesting a possible bifurcatory approach in relation to different groups of offenders (see Cavadino and Dignan, 1992: 197). Thus, at the time it seemed possible that the introduction of unit fines might herald a reinvigoration of this 'juridical-style' penalty, particularly for less serious but impoverished offenders who might previously have been imprisoned instead. Many developments in the treatment of younger offenders around that time were also more consistent with a 'juridical' rather than a 'disciplinary' approach.[126] However, other features of the 'just deserts' package suggested a strengthening of the disciplinary and control elements associated with community penalties such as probation and the community service order, as did the introduction of the 'combination order'.

In the light of the counter-reforms which began in 1993 there is now little immediate prospect of a resurgence in 'juridical' penalties for any group of offenders. Indeed, the most recent statistics show a continuing increase in the proportionate use of supervisory community sentences (especially probation), and also custodial sentences, at the expense of non-supervisory penalties. The first of these tendencies is more consistent with the 'dispersal of discipline' thesis. Moreover, further government support for electronic monitoring (both as a means of enforcing curfew orders and also as a form of pre-release mechanism; see Chapter 8) and the recent revival of interest in the idea of intermittent custody seem likely to 'blur' still further the distinction between institutional and non-institutional forms of social control (as suggested by Cohen). On the other hand, the recent (and continuing) upsurge in the use of custody represents a clear change, and at the very least a partial reverse in the direction of penal policy back towards custody and away from community punishments, at least for the time being.

Realistically, albeit reluctantly, we have to acknowledge that the recent track record strongly suggests that substantial decarceration is unlikely to occur in England and Wales at least in the foreseeable future. If it ever does occur it will almost certainly not be brought about either as a result of a mere 'strategy of encouragement', nor from a revival of the old 'rehabilitative ideal', nor in response to pressures from 'just deserts' reformists, despite the best endeavours of some, and occasional undoubted successes in some other countries.[127] Any significant change in the direction of penal policy of the kind we are advocating will require a much more prescriptive structuring of sentencing discretion (see

Chapter 4) and/or a vigorous and well-supported application of systems management techniques (see Chapter 9). But neither of these is likely to come about without a radical change in the penal ideologies of sentencers, the public, other criminal justice practitioners and policy-makers and (above all) government politicians. Could this happen?

In spite of the somewhat gloomy short-term prognosis, we believe and hope that the longer-term future of penality remains open. We do not believe that there is any inexorable tendency at work in the evolution of penal policy, whether in the direction of increased use of custody, net-widening or an intensification of social control. In spite of the many recent policy failures that we have recounted we remain convinced that diversion and decarceration are desirable and achievable goals. We are fortified in this conviction by the fact that genuine decarceration has occurred in other jurisdictions such as the Netherlands (Downes, 1988) and Ontario, Canada (McMahon, 1992) in the recent past. Indeed, it happened in England and Wales early in the twentieth century, when the prison population was halved between the years 1908 and 1923 (Rutherford, 1986: 123–131). A substantial decarceration also occurred with young offenders in England and Wales in the 1980s, as we shall recount in Chapter 9.

Moreover, we are reasonably hopeful that strategies could be devised to ensure that decarceration can be attained without widening the criminal justice net – or thinning its mesh – to an unacceptable extent. Several pieces of recent research (see, for example, Bottoms, 1995b: 10–11) confirm that it is possible for relatively intensive non-custodial penalties to be accurately 'targeted' so that they do not serve to 'thin the mesh' or 'up-tariff' offenders (see Chapter 9). McMahon (1992) also found that decarceration in Ontario was not accompanied by any general net-widening, except in the near-inevitable sense that if a supervisory sentence is used as a substitute for a short prison term then the offender is likely to stay 'within the net' for longer. The experience of the Kettering Adult Reparation Board (Dignan, 1991) was that the introduction of a reparation scheme may have had some 'net-widening' and 'mesh-thinning' effects with a small proportion of offenders (although a higher proportion were diverted from prosecution altogether); however, we would regard these particular effects as acceptable, since one result was that victims were benefited by the reparation carried out as a result.

While it may be possible to envisage decarcerative strategies, and even to identify ones that have been successful either elsewhere or in the past, this is no guarantee that they are likely to happen in England and Wales in the near future. For example, some of the genuine decarceration documented by McMahon in Ontario happened because there was a strong prevailing belief in the rehabilitative ideal which is unlikely to return, at least in its previous form. Nevertheless, we believe that there are grounds for believing, cautiously, that moves towards decarceration could occur in the not-too-distant future. The reasons for our cautious optimism are based on a reading of the penality debate that differs in several key respects from the three accounts we have been considering.

In the first place we are not convinced that the term 'carceral' is the best way of describing the original penal transformation that took place during the late eighteenth and early nineteenth centuries. For in reality the displacement of corporal and capital punishment during this period was accomplished by a variety of practices (including transportation for a time), in addition to the various non-custodial penalties that have subsequently been developed alongside the carceral system. In our view the change in the nature of penality that accompanied the original 'great transformation', and also those that have taken place thereafter, are more accurately characterized according to the social functions they perform (or are intended to perform), as opposed to the precise institutional form they may take at any given time.[128]

In the early days of imprisonment, one of the main social functions it was intended to perform was to 'transform'[129] offenders into obedient subjects by subjecting them to the disciplinary techniques to which Foucault (and later Bottoms) refer. Subsequently other non-custodial penalties – notably probation – have been developed with similar 'transformatory' objectives in mind. Although the collapse of the rehabilitative ideal cast doubt on their transformatory potential, existing penal measures such as imprisonment and probation were not abandoned, though they were displaced to some extent by the introduction and expansion of alternative penal measures such as the fine, suspended sentence, community service and others. Following the collapse of the rehabilitative ideal, the justification for all penal measures came to rest on rather different philosophical foundations (see Chapter 2) which, in turn, were founded on the rather different social functions that punishment can perform.

We will examine the various social functions that are associated with the use of imprisonment in Chapter 6. Here, we wish to emphasize that the various non-custodial penalties that have been introduced alongside imprisonment itself are likewise intended to perform a range of different social functions. One function involves the application of some form of unpleasantness or deprivation on offenders, though the 'commodity' of which the offender is deprived may take a number of different forms: 'liberty' in the case of imprisonment, 'time' in the case of community service and 'money' in the case of fines. One of the most distinctive aspects of the 1991 reforms was their attempt to 'rank' these different penal currencies as part of a comprehensive tariff covering the full range of offences from the most to the least serious.[130] However, 'deprivation' is not a feature of all penalties. Some, such as the conditional discharge and the suspended sentence, are principally admonitory in the way they operate. Finally, it is worth noting that some non-custodial penalties may also be intended to perform preventive or incapacitative functions. For example, disqualification is intended to stop motoring offenders from driving, attendance centre orders may be used to keep football hooligans away from matches, and curfews backed by electronic monitoring are intended to prevent offenders being 'at large' at times when they are thought most likely to offend.

Most contributors to the 'nature of penality' debate have tended to gloss over these differences in the social functions performed by different forms of punishment and the way in which the importance that is attached to them has waxed and waned over time. They have also overlooked one feature which is shared by virtually all the conventional forms of punishment we have been considering up till now: that they rely almost exclusively on the application of 'external' as opposed to 'internal' sanctions and, as such, are directed primarily *against* an offender.[131]

During the last few years, however, two rather different sets of penal responses have emerged which could, conceivably, contain the seeds of a distinctly different kind of penality. One set of responses seeks to engage offenders in a variety of processes that require them to reflect on the harm they have caused to others and encourages them to try to make amends for what they have done. Some of these processes involve some form of dialogue between victims and offenders (for example mediation, family group or community conferencing or circle sentencing) and are associated with an approach that has come to be known as restorative justice.[132] Others involve the use of cognitive behavioural techniques[133] that do not necessarily require the participation of a victim. One feature that both sets of processes have in common is that they rely on the use of *internal sanctions* which operate on the basis of an offender's conscience rather than the application of external sanctions of the kind that characterize most conventional forms of punishment.

A second set of penal responses seeks to identify and address the *causes* of a person's offending behaviour with a view to reducing the likelihood that the person will reoffend in the future. Several aspects of the New Labour government's youth justice reform programme which was introduced in the Crime and Disorder Act 1998 (see Chapter 9) typify this approach. They include the use of parenting orders in cases where a young person's offending behaviour is felt to be attributable to poor or inappropriate parenting skills, and also action plan orders, which can be used to try to tackle school attendance problems in cases where offending is felt to be attributable to truanting, and the use of mentors in cases where a young person is felt to have inappropriate peer-group relationships. Some restorative justice approaches (notably family group conferencing) also encourage young offenders and their families to devise 'action plans' that will deliver appropriate reparation for victims and at the same time seek to address factors that are felt to have precipitated an offence.

We are inclined to believe that the best chance of achieving significant diversion and decarceration in the future could rest on the development of restorative and reintegrative techniques of the kind we have just described. At the very least, a comprehensive strategy which aimed, wherever possible, to combine appropriate reparation for victims with the reintegration of offenders back into the community would offer a coherent and humane basis for moving away from the prevailing obsession with imprisonment as a response to crime. We are encouraged by the rapid growth of interest in such techniques on the part of penal policy-makers in very many penal jurisdictions around the world and consider that they offer the best prospect for the development of a 'replacement penal discourse'[134] that could challenge and change the basic assumptions that inform the current debate about punishment and the form it should take. We shall return to these issues, and to our own vision for a just and humane (and predominantly non-custodial) penal system in our final chapter.

## NOTES

1 This approach was initially favoured by the Conservative governments of the 1980s and 1990s, but has by no means been abandoned by New Labour. As we shall see in Chapter 6, it has increasingly come to be associated with the policy of prison privatization.

2 See also Cavadino et al.(1999: ch. 3).

3 The right-wing American criminologist, James Q. Wilson (1975: 180), was one of the first to try to 'calibrate' the severity of punishment by linking it to the degree of restriction it imposes on an offender's liberty. See also Cavadino et al. (1999: 107).

4 Despite attempts by some academic commentators – notably Sparks (1971) – to establish such a scale by invoking the analogy of a 'penological ladder', this did not meet with general approval among either judges (Ashworth et al. 1984: 28–30) or magistrates (Tarling, 1979: 9).

5 S. 79(2)(a) Powers of Criminal Courts (Sentencing) Act 2000 (hereafter abbreviated to PCC(S)A 2000).

6 S. 35(1) PCC(S)A 2000.

7 In the case of adult offenders. A range of other sentences are also available to the courts, including disqualification from driving, confiscation and exclusion orders. The reparation order, which is only available in respect of young offenders, is dealt with in Chapter 9.

8 It will be noted that the way offences are grouped together for the purpose of Table 5.1 is different from the way they are ranked within the current sentencing framework. The reason for this will become apparent when we refer back to this table in the penultimate section of this chapter.

9 S. 12, PCC(S)A 2000.

10 The table is based on Table 8.1 in Bottoms, 1983: 167 and Table 1 in Bottoms, 1980a: 6, updated in the light of the relevant volumes of the Criminal Statistics for England and Wales for 1989 (Home Office, 1990c), 1994 (Home Office, 1995b) and 1999 (Home Office, 2000a).

11 In magistrates' courts the proportionate use of discharges (most of which were conditional) fell back from the peak of 26 per cent, which was reached in 1991, to 21 per cent in 1999. The corresponding figures for the Crown Court were 5 per cent and 3 per cent respectively (Ayres et al., 2000: paras. 29 and 35). Their proportionate usage in the youth courts can also be expected to decline following the introduction of the reparation order, see Chapter 9.

12 The power was contained in the Criminal Justice Administration Act, 1914. The normal maximum repayment period which was established by case-law before the 1991 reforms was twelve months (*R. v. Knight* (1980) 2 Cr App Rep (S) 82). However in some exceptional cases much longer periods have been approved, as in *R. v. Olliver and Olliver* (1989) 11 Cr App R (S) 10.

13 The same Act also extended the power to allow fines to by paid by instalments to the higher courts for the first time.

14 See Crow (1996) who has kindly given permission for Figure 5.2 to be used here. See also Crow et al. (1994b).

15 A useful phrase which was coined by Ashworth (1983: 277).

16 However, in one important respect the unit fine system could be said to be out of step with the notion of 'just deserts'. Since it takes individual circumstances into account when calculating the quantum of punishment, it incorporates an element of 'offender-based' proportionality as opposed to the principle of 'offence-based' deserts which generally underlay the 1991 Act; although because it aimed at achieving 'equality of impact' it could be said to be in line with the general philosophy of 'just deserts' (Cavadino et al., 1999: 161).

17  In another survey of just over 100 people working in various parts of the criminal justice system in South Yorkshire only 27 per cent of all respondents disagreed with unit fines in principle, and only 14 per cent of magistrates did so (Crow et al., 1994b).

18  A notable and highly dubious *cause célèbre* was a case involving a man who appeared to have been fined £1200 for dropping a crisp packet in the street. However, the real reason for imposing the maximum £100 per unit was because he had failed to disclose his income to the court and, on appeal, his fine was reduced to £48 once he agreed to divulge his means. Whatever one might think of the merits of this particular strategy of fine enforcement, it clearly has little bearing on the principle of the unit fine and yet cases like this were instrumental in hastening its demise.

19  See also Crow (1996), who reported similar trends in respect of a more local study covering four magistrates' courts.

20  S. 128(1) PCC(S)A 2000.

21  However, there is nothing to stop the court from proceeding on whatever information it has.

22  S. 126 PCC(S)A 2000.

23  S. 128(4) PCC(S)A 2000.

24  These relate to those on low incomes – around £100 per week – those on average incomes – around £250 p.w. and those on high incomes – around £600 p.w.

25  This was confirmed by Home Office minister David Maclean when the 1993 Bill was before the House of Commons (Gibson et al., 1994: 167).

26  Charman et al. (1996). See also Flood-Page and Mackie (1998: 50ff) who also found wide disparities among magistrates' courts.

27  S. 82 (5) Magistrates' Courts Act 1980 and s. 139 PCC(S)A 2000.

28  See also Softley (1978); NACRO (1981); Moxon (1983); Casale and Hillsman (1986); Crow and Simon (1987).

29  Calculated from Home Office (1995b: Table 6).

30  See Walker and Wall (1997) and Pantazis and Gordon (1997).

31  *R. v. Oldham Justices and another, ex parte Cawley and Others* [1995] QB 1.

32  It is questionable how fair or effective this particular method of enforcement may be since deductions from the official level of income support are likely to aggravate any existing financial problems, which may well have been responsible for the offence being committed in the first place.

33  In line with recommendations contained in a consultative paper (Home Office, 1996c).

34  The power to do so was already on the statute book, but the relevant section of the Criminal Justice Act 1972 had never been brought into force.

35  Section 37, in force from 1 January 1998. Now s. 59 of the Powers of Criminal Courts (Sentencing) Act 2000.

36  On the history and development of reparation, see Schafer (1960); Jacob (1977); Harding (1982) and Wright (1991).

37  Though the otherwise comprehensive 1991 sentencing framework curiously made no reference whatever to the issue of victim compensation, nor to the related principle of reparation.

38  Though somewhat illogically, they are not precluded from fining the offender at the same time (PCC(S)A 2000, section 130(12)).

39  The legal framework relating to compensation orders is set out in sections 130–4 of the PCC(S)A 2000. Additional guidance for magistrates on the use of compensation is contained in Home Office Circular 53/1993 (Home Office, 1993a).

40  This was also reflected in the decision to publish a Victim's Charter (Home Office, 1990d) in February 1990, which purported to set out the rights and entitlements of

victims of crime, though it contained no new remedies. The Victim's Charter was revised in 1996 and is currently being reviewed (Home Office, 2001). For an attempt to clarify the distinction between reparation and various other victim-based measures see Dignan and Cavadino (1996).

41  Figures taken from the relevant volumes of the Criminal Statistics for England and Wales (Home Office 2000a). See also Flood-Page and Mackie (1998: 16–7).

42  A similar trend has also been experienced in Scotland (Hamilton and Wisniewski, 1996: 11).

43  Even though the legislation makes it clear that compensation should be considered even in the absence of any application on the part of the victim, the Court of Appeal has advised sentencers against 'simply plucking a figure from the air' (*R. v. Oliver* (1989) 11 Cr App R (S) 10. See also Moxon et al. (1992).

44  In its policy document 'Criminal Justice: The Way Ahead', the government indicated that it is considering the possibility of establishing a 'Victims Fund' that would ensure earlier payment of compensation for victims (Home Office, 2001: para. 3.118). However, there was no suggestion that this would be linked with the system of fines in the way that we have proposed.

45  The first scheme of this kind was established in Kitchener, Ontario, during the 1970s. Similar ones were subsequently established elsewhere in North America, where they were originally known as Victim Offender Reconciliation Programs or VORPs, and also beyond. See Peachey (1989) and Wright (1991) for the early history of this approach in North America.

46  In 1993 it was renamed the 'Northamptonshire Diversion Unit'.

47  See, for example, Morris et al. (1993); McElrea (1994); and, for an overview of these and other related developments, Dignan and Cavadino (1996); Dignan with Lowey (2000).

48  For example, while the precedence of compensation over the fine was established in the Criminal Justice Act 1982, established case law requires that when a custodial sentence is imposed the victim's need for compensation is subordinated to the need for punishment.

49  For further discussion of the relationship between restorative and retributive theories of justice and how they might be reconciled, see Zedner (1994) and Cavadino and Dignan (1997b).

50  See Cavadino et al. (1999: ch. 4) for a more thematic account of the history and recent development of community punishments in general.

51  A Green Paper published in 1995 (Home Office, 1995d) proposed to subsume all existing orders within a new generic 'community sentence', the precise components of which were to be stipulated by individual sentencers. However, the adoption of a 'pick and mix' approach raised fears that it might shorten the tariff, thereby increasing prison numbers still further (Ashworth et al., 1995; Howard League, 1995; Penal Affairs Consortium, 1995c). As the response was also unenthusiastic even among sentencers themselves, the proposals were never adopted.

52  As we shall see, the Criminal Justice and Court Services Act 2000 creates two new additional community orders: exclusion orders and drug abstinence orders.

53  S. 35(1) PCC(S)A 2000.

54  S. 38 Crime (Sentences) Act 1997. The value of the 'safeguard' of requiring consent was often rendered nugatory in practice by the court's power to impose a custodial sentence where consent was withheld. It remains to be seen whether the removal of consent in relation to community service can be reconciled with the prohibition on the use of 'forced labour' under the European Convention on Human Rights.

55  In section 8. But see now section 41 PCC(S)A 2000.

56  See Schedule 2, PCC(S)A 2000 for further details.

57  This upper limit (and the one relating to 'specified activities') does not apply to those convicted of a sexual offence.

58  These requirements provide the legal framework for 'intensive probation' programmes (see below).

59  Rutherford notes (1986: 153) that spending on the service increased by 70 per cent in real terms between 1970 and 1980 while the number of probation officers was also 60 per cent higher than a decade earlier. Numbers peaked at 7,776 in 1994, and declined to 7,171 in 1997 (Sheriff, 1998; Cavadino et al., 1999: 100).

60  See also Pease (1999: 4).

61  The Criminal Justice Act 1967 changed the name of the service to the Probation and After-Care Service to reflect its new responsibilities, though it was changed back again by the Criminal Justice Act 1982.

62  Under the Children and Young Persons Act 1969 (see Chapter 9), which replaced probation with the juvenile supervision order. Supervision under these orders could be carried out by either probation officers or social workers.

63  It is important not to exaggerate the deterioration in relations between magistrates and the probation service, however. A pilot study undertaken by the Home Office in 1993–4 showed that 88 per cent of magistrates questioned were very or fairly satisfied with the work of the probation service, 90 per cent felt they had a very good or fairly good working relationship with the service, and just over three quarters were very satisfied or quite satisfied with the availability of staff to appear in court (May, 1997).

64  This hallowed phrase was incorporated into Schedule 3(8), Powers of Criminal Courts Act 1973; interestingly the full account of their duties contained in the schedule also made reference to the duty of 'supervising' their probationers, but the traditional formulation of the duty frequently omits this reference.

65  Various labels have been coined for this strategy including 'corporatism' (Pratt, 1989) and 'expedient managerialism' (Rutherford, 1993). Others (see for example Christie, 1993) have analysed such developments in a much broader political context, and we will return to the continuing debate about the changing nature of social control and forms of state regulation in the second part of this chapter.

66  These are described more fully in Cavadino et al. (1999: ch. 4).

67  Similar developments in relation to the Prison Service are discussed in Chapter 6.

68  Including community service, subject to certain restrictions, in the shape of the combination order (see below).

69  The approach that was endorsed in the National Standards had been developed during the early 1990s by a number of 'intensive probation' schemes (see Mair et al., 1994) that focused specifically on higher tariff offenders. They were, for a time, envisaged as the leading alternative to custody prior to the advent of the combination order (see below).

70  SI 1995 No. 2622. The House of Lords at one stage in 1995 rejected these proposals, which were also criticized by three former Home Secretaries (*The Guardian*, 7 April 1995) and unsuccessfully challenged in the High Court (in February 1996).

71  Michael Howard's proposals serve as a reminder that militarism has been just as potent an influence on Conservative penal thinking in the past as managerialism. For further examples, see our discussion in Chapter 9 of initiatives such as the 'short sharp shock' and 'boot camps'.

72  They included, for example, a major cross-departmental review of the entire criminal justice system, which instituted a working group on the effectiveness of dealing with offending behaviour, resulting in the 1998 report *Reducing Offending* (Goldblatt and Lewis, 1998), discussed in more detail in Chapter 11.

73  See for example Nellis (1997).

74 Led by a National Director with a full range of operational responsibilities, and serviced by a headquarters staff located within the Home Office.

75 This is underlined by the new funding arrangements whereby the new Service is to be funded entirely by central Government, which has hitherto been responsible for providing 80 per cent of funds, the remainder coming from the relevant local authorities.

76 Unnecessarily in our view. Other community orders that come in for the same treatment are the community service order, which is renamed as the community punishment order and the combination order, which is renamed as the community punishment and rehabilitation order (section 44 and 45 respectively). We mostly refer to all these orders under the titles by which they were originally known, and by which we suspect they will continue to be better known for some time to come.

77 See, for example, McWilliams (1987, 1992) and, more recently, Nellis (1995: 24).

78 For example, 'The Government is also committed to providing more effective and tougher community punishments' (HC Deb. 2 March 1998, col. 690).

79 It can only be imposed for an 'imprisonable' offence, but this includes many relatively minor offences for which custodial penalties are rarely imposed in practice.

80 Section 12, but see now PCC(S)A 2000, section 37. For an overview of electronic monitoring see Whitfield (1997). Originally the curfew order was only available for offenders aged 16 or over, but section 43 of the Crime (Sentences) Act 1997 (brought into force as from February 2001) made it available for offenders of all ages from 10 upwards.

81 In section 13 of the 1991 Act, but see now PCC(S)A 2000, section 38. Initially the offender's consent was required before electronic monitoring could be imposed, but the consent requirement for this and other community orders was abolished by the Crime (Sentences) Act 1997.

82 In which the villain attached an electronic bracelet to Spiderman in order to track his movements. A New Mexico judge who read the story approached computer companies and a monitoring device was devised, based on technical developments patented during the late 1960s by a Harvard professor, Dr Ralph Schwitzgebel (NACRO, 1988).

83 More recent American assessments of the practice are much less sanguine than earlier ones (Whitfield, 1995: 19) and some have attributed the expansion of tagging to 'technofallacies' – defined as 'a naive belief in the superiority of technology, and a completely unrealistic expectation of what it might achieve'. The number of American offenders who are tagged is said to have declined sharply and now probably accounts for less than 1 per cent of the supervised offender population.

84 Programmes also exist in parts of Canada, Australia and New Zealand (Penal Affairs Consortium, 1995e).

85 Of the 50 defendants who were monitored more than half (29) either violated their curfew (18) or were charged with a new offence (11) (Mair and Nee, 1990: 44). Very high levels of technical malfunction were also reported: no fewer than 159 instances in respect of only 50 'taggings'.

86 Electronic monitoring is also now used as part of the 'home detention curfew' scheme for monitoring certain offenders who are released early from custodial sentences. See Chapter 8, below.

87 See Mortimer and Mair (1997); Mortimer and May (1998); and Mortimer et al. (1999).

88 Mortimer and May (1998) estimate that a *three month* curfew order would cost more than the *annual* cost of a community service order, and only slightly less than a *twelve month* probation order. However, the annual cost of a curfew order would still be just under one-third the average cost of twelve months in prison. See also Cavadino et al. (1999: 127, n. 65).

89 Jack Straw has spoken of tagging as 'the future of community punishment', and has suggested that it 'may in future be used to monitor offenders wherever they are in the community' (Home Office, 1997b).

90 Such unintended consequences are quite common when 'tough' alternatives to custody are adopted. See for example the history of the suspended sentence, below.

91 Sections 61–4. But see now PCC(S)A 2000 sections 52–8.

92 This aspect of the order resembles the somewhat similar American 'drug courts'. See Bean (1996).

93 The Act also provides for the compulsory testing of offenders for drugs at various points of the criminal justice process: for example after being charged with a relevant offence; after conviction of a relevant offence in connection with a community sentence containing a drug testing requirement; and after release from prison on licence.

94 The possible shift towards a more generic approach was foreshadowed in a 1995 Green Paper (Home Office, 1995d), but received an unenthusiastic response and was quietly shelved. See note 51 above.

95 A second audit, in April 2000, found that only 62 per cent of those who failed to turn up for a supervision meeting or community service session were breached.

96 Section 53(5), which amends Schedule 3 of the PCC(S)A 2000.

97 Section 62. Benefit entitlement is reduced by 40 per cent of the single adult rate, which is equivalent to a reduction of £20.88 on the full entitlement of £94.70 at April 2000 rates. Joint claimants will also be affected, but only in respect of the 'offending' party. Other benefit entitlements such as Housing Benefit will not be affected.

98 See, for example, Brody (1976); Maltz (1984) and Lloyd et al. (1994: 3–10).

99 See, for example, Lloyd et al. (1994), who compared the actual reconviction rate with the predicted rate for imprisonment, probation and community service. See also Mair (1997) for further discussion.

100 McIvor (1992) has also shown that offenders whose experience of community service is rewarding and worthwhile tend to have lower reconviction rates than those who find it unrewarding.

101 See, for example, Goldblatt and Lewis (1998: 104); Vennard et al. (1997: 3); Andrews et al. (1990: 384); and Lipsey (1992: 138).

102 Although by no means all. It should not be forgotten (as we pointed out in Chapter 2) that prisons are highly criminogenic environments, in which a variety of offences – notably assaults, drug offences and many property offences – are routinely committed, often with relative impunity.

103 Technically, the power to suspend a sentence is not a separate sentence but a variant of imprisonment. The Criminal Justice Act 1991 abolished a little-used measure known as the partly suspended sentence (see Dignan, 1984).

104 This is a remarkably similar result to the effect of the introduction of community service, as we have seen.

105 In *R. v. O'Keefe* [1969] 2 QB 29.

106 Originally in section 22(2) of the Powers of Criminal Courts Act 1973; but see now section 118(4)(a) PCC(S)A 2000.

107 See now section 119(2) PCC(S)A 2000. Consequently, whereas 71 per cent of offenders who were in breach of a suspended sentence in 1988 were dealt with by means of an immediate custodial sentence, this was true of just 22 per cent of those who had been conditionally discharged. The automatic activation of the suspended sentence on breach, and its effect on the prison population, was described by Bottoms as a 'kick-back' effect (Bottoms, 1980b: 6).

108 *R. v. Ithell* (1969) 53 Cr App R 210.

109 Powers of Criminal Courts Act 1973 section 22 , as substituted by Criminal Justice Act 1991 section 5(1). But see now PCC(S)A 2000 section 118 (4)(b).

110 'The Criminal Justice Act 1991 potentially marks the end of what has been called our carceral society, i.e., an over reliance on and therefore an overuse of imprisonment as a means of dealing with offenders' (Mathieson, 1992: 148).

111 Custody rates also increased in 1999 for summary motoring and non-motoring offences (Ayres, 2000).

112 Some of these concerns were subsequently echoed in relation to the policy of 'care in the community' for psychiatric patients which was pursued in the 1980s, following incidents such as the stabbing of Jonathon Zito by Christopher Clunis in December 1992 (see Ritchie, 1994).

113 In England during the period 1956–78, spending on the prison system increased at a rate two and a half times as great as for public expenditure generally (Rutherford, 1986: 90; Shaw, 1980). During the period 1980–1990 spending on public order showed a threefold increase compared with a two or two-and-a-half-fold increase on other public services such as education, health and social services (Central Statistical Office, 1991: Table 9.4).

114 McMahon's more recent (1992) and very careful analysis of post-war penal trends in the Canadian province of Ontario provides another telling exception to Scull's thesis (see also Cavadino, 1994c). She demonstrates that decarceration also occurred in Ontario in the 1960s and early 1970s, at least in the sense that admissions to prison and numbers in prison declined relative to the total population of Ontario during this period. In contrast to Scull's economistic explanation for the decline, both McMahon and Downes (1988) attribute the decarceration that appears to have taken place during this period to the influence of the then prevailing ideology of rehabilitation.

115 The Dutch experience also fails to conform to predictions based on Scull's fiscal crisis theory in relation to the mentally ill, for whom institutional care has survived to a much greater extent than in either England or the United States.

116 Moreover, this decline took place against a background of steadily rising conviction and recorded crime rates (Rutherford, 1986: 129).

117 A Marxist, or post-Marxist, might see this gap between the 'rhetoric' (or ideological message conveyed by the 'discourse' of the penal system) and its material reality as significant. See Chapter 3 for a more detailed discussion of the idea that the penal system may form part of a state's 'Ideological State Apparatus'.

118 McMahon (1992) points out that in Ontario there was a period during the late 1970s when decarcerative rhetoric was at its height, and numerous new community programmes labelled as 'alternatives to custody' were being developed but prison populations remained largely stable. However this was preceded in the case of Ontario, as we have seen, by a period of real, albeit limited, decarceration.

119 Even though it is evidently not a constant one, since at other times the prison population has fallen in spite of a rising crime rate (see for example n. 116 above).

120 The uncritical use of such metaphors to suggest an inexorable expansion in the numbers of people subject to penal control together with an intensification of that control has been criticized by McMahon (1992: 32) on two main grounds: first for contributing to a 'new orthodoxy' that is not fully supported by the empirical data; and second for fostering a nihilistic attitude to the prospects for penal reform. Once it becomes accepted that well-meaning attempts to provide alternatives to custody will inevitably result only in wider and stronger 'nets' of social control, it is but a short step to concluding that any penal reform projects are doomed to failure.

121 Others have discerned in such developments the emergence of a 'new penology' (Feeley and Simon, 1992) in which the adoption of a 'managerialist' perspective is

increasingly harnessed to the task of regulating levels of deviance by targeting categories and sub-populations rather than individual deviants. Also perhaps relevant here are developments such as the Criminal Justice and Public Order Act 1984, Part V of which conferred wide powers on the police to take action against groups such as squatters, new age travellers, road protesters, participants in raves and hunt saboteurs.

122 Indeed, it can plausibly be argued that an increased probability of detection could enable punishments to be made more lenient, since as we saw in Chapter 2 deterrence is far more likely to be achieved by increasing the perceived risk of detection than by severer penalties.

123 Bottoms was writing before the introduction of uniform standards, the introduction of a compulsory manual labour element and the renaming of community service as 'community punishment' (see above). He did anticipate that the measure 'could yet be developed in a more disciplinary form' (1983: 180), and he might reach a different conclusion today in the light of these more recent developments.

124 But see Chapter 2, note 17.

125 For example government departments, local authorities, television licensing authority, private security firms etc.

126 The same might also be said of the attempt by the Criminal Justice Act 1991 to grade penalties according to desert criteria.

127 See for example, von Hirsch (1993: 91–4).

128 As we shall see in Chapter 6, a somewhat similar analytical–explanatory framework was originally devised by Thomas Mathiesen (1974, 1990) specifically in connection with the rise and continued existence of imprisonment as one of the dominant forms of punishment in late capitalist societies.

129 As opposed to changing the way in which offenders are punished, which involves a rather different kind of 'transformation'. The latter refers to changes at the level of institutional practice rather than changes in the character or behaviour of individual offenders, which is the sense in which we are using the term at this point.

130 We have explained elsewhere (Cavadino et al., 1999: 121) why we believe this attempt was ultimately doomed to failure since its principal effect was simply to confirm the status of imprisonment as setting the 'gold standard' with regard to punishment, compared with which all other measures are likely to be dismissed as 'base metal counterfeits'.

131 There have been exceptions, such as probation (at least in its early 'police court missionary' phase), and also the 'silent' penitentiary system. What is distinctive about the responses we are about to describe is their reliance on a form of normative or moralizing discourse with an offender. (This makes them fit well with Anthony Duff's 'communicative theory of punishment' which we mentioned in Chapter 2.) This kind of approach can also be deployed within a custodial setting (see Chapter 6).

132 See Marshall (1999) and Dignan and Lowey (2000) for a fuller account of the various restorative justice processes and techniques.

133 As the name suggests, these techniques are based on a synthesis of methods drawn from behavioural and cognitive psychology (Hollin, 1990; Meichenbaum, 1977) and include anger management programmes and also training in moral reasoning.

134 See Ashworth (1997); Cavadino et al. (1999: 31); and Dignan (forthcoming).

# 6
# Prisons and the Penal Crisis

Of all the punishments inflicted within the English penal system, imprisonment is both the most important and the most problematic in terms of its impact on the rest of the system. Other penalties may be imposed with greater frequency,[1] but imprisonment can still justifiably be described as the *dominant* method of punishment within the English penal system.

This is not just because it is the severest penalty available. In part it is because the courts have traditionally been prepared to invoke this supposed 'sanction of last resort' as a routine penalty for a wide range of not-so-serious, non-violent property offences.[2] The dominance of imprisonment within our penal tradition has been further reinforced by a tendency to conceptualize all non-custodial penalties as 'alternatives to imprisonment' rather than as appropriate sanctions in their own right. Although the 1991 Criminal Justice Act sought to discourage both these tendencies – by encouraging the greater use of 'community penalties' – its impact was subsequently severely undermined by the Major government's reversal of decades of well-founded scepticism when Michael Howard proclaimed in 1993 that 'prison works'. As we have seen, imprisonment has also been used as the standard 'default sanction' – for example for persistent offenders for whom previous non-custodial options are perceived to have failed; or when an offender is in breach of a non-custodial measure such as probation, or community service. Indeed, until recently it was also used as the standard default sanction in the case of fine defaulters, even though the original offence may not have been serious enough to warrant imprisonment.

Yet custody is by far the most expensive of all penal measures: in the financial year 1997–8 the estimated monthly cost of keeping a person in prison was £2,070,[3] which is approximately 11 times the cost of a one-month's probation supervision (£183) and 15 times as expensive as a month's community service supervision (Home Office, 1999: 73). In 1997–8 £1,740 million was spent on the prison service, compared with £500 million spent on probation. This contribution to the 'crisis of penological resources' (see Chapter 1) is just one reason why the problems of imprisonment are so acute that they must form a central part of any account of the current penal crisis. In this chapter we will briefly consider why imprisonment should have assumed this dominant rôle within the penal system before returning to the crises within the prison system.

## THE FUNCTIONS AND AIMS OF IMPRISONMENT

### *The social functions of imprisonment*

Historically, the birth of the modern prison was part of a much broader movement in which 'institutions' of various kinds came to be adopted as the solution to a wide range of social problems. The start of this 'great confinement' (Foucault, 1967: ch. 2) can be traced back to the 1600s, though the replacement of physical suffering by imprisonment as the dominant form of punishment (a process that Foucault described as the 'great transformation') did not take place until the end of the eighteenth and beginning of the nineteenth centuries. This coincided with the emergence of industrial capitalism as the dominant mode of production in all the large European countries.

In Chapter 3 we discussed some of the sociological explanations which have been put forward for the rise of the prison.[4] An interesting radical explanation for the *continued existence* of the prison has been put forward by Norwegian penologist Thomas Mathiesen (1974, 1990, 2000). Mathiesen suggests that the reason why imprisonment remains the dominant mode of punishment has to do with the important social functions which it performs within advanced capitalist societies. The first of these he terms 'the expurgatory function'. Those who are both unproductive and disruptive of the normal processes of production are liable to find themselves being 'siphoned off' and 'contained' in prison where they can do least damage.

The second he calls 'the power-draining function', since those who are contained in this way are not only prevented from interfering with the normal processes of production but are also denied the opportunity to exercise responsibility, since the institution in which they are contained is designed to function on the basis of minimal practical contributions from the prisoners themselves. A third, 'symbolic' function refers to the stigmatizing effect of imprisonment, which enables those on the outside to distance themselves, in terms of their own moral self-perceptions, from those who have been publicly labelled in this way.

This is closely related to a fourth function, the 'diverting function' of imprisonment. Here Mathiesen draws attention to the fact that the commission of socially harmful acts is by no means the prerogative of one particular section of society. Rather, he suggests that 'socially dangerous acts are increasingly being committed by individuals and classes with power in society' (1974: 78). But because the ultimate sanction of imprisonment tends to be reserved for a highly selected group of offenders, drawn mainly from the lower working class, concern in the media and in the population at large tends to focus on the fairly narrow band of offences which such offenders are most likely to commit (for example personal violence, and relatively petty property offences). This has the effect of diverting public attention away from much more serious forms of social harm such as those resulting from major acts of pollution, or the deliberate compromise of safety standards in the pursuit of profit. Those who are responsible for these harms are not seen as appropriate subjects for the ultimate sanction of imprisonment, since they are not only powerful indi- viduals in their own right, but are also engaged in the process of production themselves. Finally, Mathiesen has recently identified (1990: 138) a fifth social function of imprisonment, which he calls the 'action function'. Because prison has the highest profile of any sanction in common use in our kind of society, it plays an important part in reassuring people that 'something is being done' about the problem of law and order, and the social threats which they are persuaded to take most seriously.[5]

Perhaps, however, imprisonment is not so functional to modern capitalism as Mathiesen suggests, for there is also a heavy price to be paid, not only in terms of resources and human suffering, but also in managing the increasing tensions that are associated with the steadily worsening penal crisis – as we shall see.

### Official aims of imprisonment

At an official level, a rather different set of ideas – or ideologies – has sought over the years to justify (or *legitimate*) the English prison system. The fact that these ideologies have largely failed to convince even those working within the Prison Service is largely to blame for the crisis of legitimacy in which it now finds itself.

Changing ideas about the official aims of imprisonment at the time were summarized in the Report of the Committee of Inquiry into the United Kingdom Prison Services which reported in 1979 under the Chairmanship of Lord Justice May (1979). In the early nineteenth century, the chief official aims of imprisonment were the imposition of deterrent and retributive justice on offenders, while not ruling out the possibility of reform and a return to society. By the turn of the century, the twin imperatives of deterrence and reformation had been adopted as official policy, and the subsequent ascendancy of the 'treatment model' was soon enshrined in the prison rules themselves.[6] By 1964 the following classic formulation had been given pride of place as Prison Rule Number 1: 'The purpose of the training and treatment of convicted prisoners shall be to encourage and assist them to lead a good and useful life.'[7]

The ascendancy of the treatment ethic was soon to be undermined by the collapse of the rehabilitative ideal in the 1970s, however (see Chapters 1 and 2). This served to emphasize the already glaring gap between the official rhetoric about what the system was supposed to be achieving and the sad reality that constituted the daily routine in the vast majority of penal establishments at a time of rapidly deteriorating conditions. The May Committee formally acknowledged that 'the rhetoric of "treatment and training" had had its day and should be replaced' (May, 1979: para. 4.27). But the task of devising an acceptable alternative formulation that would fill the 'moral vacuum' created by the demise of the treatment model proved beyond it.

The problem confronting the Committee stemmed from its conviction that no alternative philosophy commanding wide public support had taken the place of the treatment model. Consequently, any attempt to devise a new statement of purpose would be susceptible to the criticism that it lacked a coherent philosophical foundation. At the same time it warned (para. 4.28) that 'the absence of real objectives can in the end lead only to the brutalization of all the participants'. The May Committee put forward the notion of 'positive custody'[8] in the hope of grafting onto the Prison Service's basic custodial

functions an ethic that would inspire the development of hopeful and pur-
posive regimes; but this was swiftly condemned by critics (King and Morgan,
1980: 28) as vague, meaningless, and no less rhetorical a statement than the
discredited notion of treatment and training it was intended to replace. A rival
formulation preferred by some academic commentators (including King
and Morgan, 1980; see also McConville, 1975) was the notion of 'humane
containment', though there was no consensus over the content of this concept,[9]
and it in turn was criticized by May (ironically) for lacking idealism.

In 1988 the Prison Department adopted a 'Statement of Purpose' which read
as follows:

> Her Majesty's Prison Service serves the public by keeping in custody those
> committed by the courts. Our duty is to look after them with humanity and to help
> them to lead law-abiding and useful lives in custody and on release.

This Statement of Purpose has since been revised, and the official rôle of the
Prison Service[10] is currently expressed in Home Office Aim 4, which refers to
the: 'Effective execution of the sentence of the courts so as to reduce re-
offending and protect the public'. In support of this general aim, the Prison
Service has the following two more specific objectives:

1   To protect the public by holding those committed by the courts in a safe,
    decent and healthy environment;
2   To reduce crime by providing constructive regimes which address
    offending behaviour, improve educational and work skills and promote
    law-abiding behaviour in custody and after release.

In addition, the Prison Service has, with the agreement of ministers, set out
thirteen Key Performance Indicators (KPIs) which identify a number of targets
and provide a set of self-imposed measures by which its performance can be
measured.[11]

However, the most coherent and comprehensive recent attempt to articulate
a set of aspirations for the Prison Service was contained in Lord Justice Woolf's
magisterial report (Woolf and Tumim, 1991) on the Strangeways prison riot
and related disturbances in April 1990. Commenting specifically on the Prison
Service's 1988 Statement of Purpose, Woolf argued, first, that it is not enough
for prisoners to be treated with humanity, since one of the primary objectives
of the Prison Service ought to be that they should also be treated with justice;
and he called for the Prison Rules to be redrafted to reflect this requirement
(Woolf and Tumim, 1991: para. 10.23). Second, he urged that, consistent with
their responsibilities to uphold law and order, prisons should do more to
minimize the prospect of prisoners reoffending after their release (para. 10.24).
To this end he advocated, on the one hand, a programme of measures designed
to improve the conditions in which they are held; and, on the other hand,
encouragement for prisoners to take responsibility both for their offence and
also for what happens to them in prison. Third, when speaking of the need for
security he made clear that this encompasses far more than a preoccupation
with physical containment (para. 10.39).[12]

Finally, Woolf made it clear that in his view the attainment of the Prison Service's Statement of Purpose required an appropriate balance to be struck between the three elements – of security, control and justice – and made no attempt to hide his strong feeling that for too long the requirements of justice had been neglected by an over-zealous concentration on the other two concerns. Getting the balance right, he suggested, would provide a 'challenging, constructive and worthwhile rôle for the prison service' (para. 43). By carefully reworking and synthesizing the bare bones contained in the existing Statement of Purpose in this way, Woolf was widely credited[13] with skilfully constructing the kind of broad consensus that had eluded May and others in support of a liberal programme to tackle some of the prison system's most endemic and intractable problems.

Although Woolf's proposals for a new prison ethos met with an overwhelmingly positive reception from prison reformers and (at least initially) government ministers alike, there were also a few dissenting voices (Shaw, 1992a; Sim, 1994b). Sim (1994b) in particular delivered a wide-ranging and trenchant critique, complaining *inter alia* that Woolf's reformist rhetoric did nothing to challenge (and indeed could help to legitimize) the maintenance of social order within prisons through repression.[14] He was critical also of Woolf's implicit support for a highly conventional (and in Sim's view defective) notion of accountability which fails to acknowledge the centralization of state power and concomitant marginalization of democratic accountability during the 1980s.

Ten years after the publication of the Woolf Report, some of its proposals have been accepted and implemented as we shall see. However, several other crucial recommendations have not been adopted and, in some cases, are not even on the Prison Service's agenda even though the factors they address were felt to have directly contributed to the riots.[15] The most important of these is the need to fundamentally reassess the priority that is still given throughout the prison system to security considerations at the expense of other pressing concerns. This will be a recurrent theme in the rest of this chapter.

In the previous edition of this book we expressed the hope that the moral vacuum that was identified by May might come to be replaced by an alternative moral philosophy, backed by an adequately enforced 'human rights' approach (which we alluded to in Chapter 2). We also suggested that this would require the adoption of a comprehensive set of enforceable rights for prisoners that would help to secure the minimum standards required to preserve their dignity, humanity and individuality while in prison. Since then the Human Rights Act 1998 has been brought into force (on 2 October 2000), the effect of which is to incorporate the European Convention on Human Rights into English law (see the Introduction). The Act is a major constitutional reform that sets out for the first time the fundamental rights and freedoms that all UK citizens – including prisoners – are entitled to under English law. The Human Rights Act is likely to have important repercussions for the Prison Service, and in the course of this chapter we will assess the extent to which it might help to encourage the adoption of a commitment to the human rights of prison inmates on the part of the Prison Service and also penal policy-makers.[16] However, our starting point lies with the different crises we identified in Chapter 1, and specifically the effect they have had on the prison system and the way the authorities have responded to them.

## THE PRISON SYSTEM AND ITS CRISES

The problems that beset the English prison system can be described in terms of a set of interlocking crises – over security, numbers and overcrowding, conditions and régimes, secrecy and the control of information, management at all levels, the maintenance of order and control and the lack of effective grievance procedures. Many of these individual crises are related to a *general crisis of resources*, which has intensified as the prison population grew to record levels during the mid–late 1990s, while the Prison Service was required during much of this period to absorb drastic Treasury-inspired budget cuts. All the individual 'crises' have contributed to a deep-seated *crisis of legitimacy* within prisons. In recent years there has been an air of almost permanent crisis-management throughout the Prison Service, which has continually frustrated attempts at longer-term policy-making and policy-implementation designed to tackle the underlying causes of the crisis. Prominent among the short-term preoccupations that have done so much to shape – and damage – prison policy over the years have been concerns over prison security which are apt, periodically, to erupt into full-blown 'crises of containment'.

### Crises of containment

The first major crisis of containment in the post-war English penal system occurred in the mid-1960s. Until then, security considerations had been low on the prison authorities' agenda. However, this was already beginning to change as a result of changes in the composition of the prison population, due mainly to an increased willingness on the part of judges to pass very long terms of imprisonment for offences which they regarded as particularly serious. Growing official concern over security was brought to a head by a succession of highly publicized escapes including two of the Great Train Robbers (Charlie Wilson in 1964, and Ronnie Biggs in 1965) and the spy George Blake in October 1966 – all of whom were serving unprecedentedly long sentences. But this was only the most visible tip of a growing iceberg as the escape rate had been steadily increasing ever since the turn of the century (Thomas and Pooley, 1980: 32). With the appointment of Lord Mountbatten to inquire into prison security in 1966, the crisis of containment moved to the top of the political agenda. The responses adopted in the wake of Mountbatten's report did much to shape the prison system of today, with continuing repercussions for the contemporary penal crisis.

The Mountbatten Report (Home Office, 1966) identified a number of weaknesses, both in the physical security of prisons and in the way they were administered. One recommendation which was immediately adopted was that convicted prisoners should be categorized according to their security risk on reception into prison, and that their security category should determine the type of institution to which they are ultimately allocated. As a result of this change, all other aims (including those of training and treatment, preparation for release and the maintenance of internal control) were subordinated at a stroke to the requirements of security. Under Mountbatten's four-level classification system:

> Category A consists of 'those whose escape would be highly dangerous to the public or the police or to the security of the state'.[17] Such inmates are invariably housed in 'maximum security' conditions.

> In Category B are 'those prisoners for whom the very highest conditions of security are not necessary, but for whom escape must be made very difficult'.[18] Such inmates are likely to be housed in 'closed' but not necessarily 'maximum security' conditions.

> Category C comprises 'prisoners who cannot be trusted in open conditions, but who do not have the ability or resources to make a determined escape bid'.

> In Category D are 'those who can reasonably be entrusted to serve their sentences in open conditions' where there is little physical security.[19]

In terms of physical security, Mountbatten believed that existing prisons were sadly deficient, and so he proposed that one new, 'escape-proof' top-security prison should be built on the Isle of Wight to house *all* maximum security prisoners (those in Category A) in 'as liberal and constructive a régime as possible'. This 'concentration policy', as it was dubbed, would have allowed lower security conditions to prevail throughout the rest of the prison system, but ultimately it was rejected, at least partly because of fears that *control* would be difficult in such a 'fortress prison', since its population would consist almost exclusively of 'no-hopers'. It was also feared that the régime would inevitably become repressive, despite Mountbatten's hopes for a liberal approach. In the end a compromise policy was adopted, which is still in operation, along the lines suggested by the later Radzinowicz Report (Advisory Council on the Penal System, 1968). This sought to dilute the anticipated control problem by spreading the high security-risk prisoners among a small number of prisons and subjecting them to the same régime as the lower-security (Category B) inmates with whom they would be housed. Although this strategy came to be known as the 'dispersal policy', this is something of a misnomer as it entails a considerable degree of concentration within a few high security establishments – currently five 'dispersal prisons' proper plus five others with high security arrangements.[20] It also involved a drastic (and expensive) upgrading of the security arrangements in these prisons. However its most pervasive, and in many respects most detrimental, effect has been to influence the nature of the entire prison estate,[21] which is now divided into several different types of penal establishments, each of which is reserved for a different category of inmate. This has not only distorted the amount of money that is spent on the different types of prisons, but has also rendered them much less flexible in the way they are used, particularly during periods of overcrowding (see below).

In addition to the high-security prison estate there are also eleven Category B training prisons for male prisoners.[22] They tend to have a secure perimeter and relatively high levels of staffing, though the degree of security and also the type of régime on offer vary considerably. There are currently 33 Category C prisons, which tend to have lower levels of staff supervision and less secure perimeters, though once again there is considerable variation between establishments. One of the largest sectors of the prison estate consists of around 40 local prisons, many of which are extremely old and poorly resourced. There are also ten 'open' prisons with minimal perimeter security for prisoners who can be trusted not to abscond. Since the introduction of home detention curfew in January 1999 (see Chapter 8), however, open prisons are under-occupied. Five are currently under review, in spite of a previous assessment that the open prison estate was a precious commodity that was not being utilized as effectively as it could be.[23] Finally, a small number of prisons have been designated 'resettlement prisons', of which the three best known are Blantyre House and Kirklevington (Category C) and Latchmere House (open) (Flynn, 1996). They were established following a recommendation by the Prison Service's Control Review Committee (Home Office, 1984a) that long-term prisoners needed a period of preparation for life outside prior to being released.

Despite the occasional notable exception, the dispersal policy has largely succeeded in tackling the external security problem. During the 25 years following the Mountbatten Report, the number of Category A prisoners escaping averaged less than one per year,[24] though no fewer than 16 Category A prisoners escaped during the early 1990s.[25] Overall, however, the total number of escapes has fallen by 89 per cent since 1992–3, despite a near 50 per cent increase in the average prison population over the same period.[26] But the costs, financial and otherwise, have been considerable. Within the dispersal prisons themselves, the arrangements designed for a small number of Category A prisoners[27] have resulted in a much more restrictive and custodial régime for the majority of prisoners who did not present a security risk. King and Morgan (1980: 74) have described how, following the introduction of dispersal prisons, security considerations permeated inwards from external defences[28] to focus on internal buildings and even the régime itself. As a result, surveillance was increased by the installation of closed-circuit television, freedom of movement and time spent on association were drastically curtailed, and communal dining was phased out in favour of solitary meals provided in cells. Although the effects have been experienced most intensely within the dispersal prisons themselves, the rest of the prison system has not been immune from the growing security syndrome. Perimeter security has been strengthened throughout the closed prison system even if the level of paranoia has not been quite so acute. And all establishments have been affected indirectly, first by the considerable diversion of resources required to upgrade security at the dispersal prisons;[29] and second, as we shall see, by a policy of avoiding overcrowding and under-manning within the dispersal system, thus concentrating these problems in other prisons.

The problems associated with paying excessive regard to security at the expense of other considerations were recognized by Lord Justice Woolf who, while acknowledging the need for a reasonable and effective degree of security for those who need it, spoke also of the need to maintain the proper balance between security, control and justice even for these prisoners. In particular he warned (Woolf and Tumim, 1991: para. 9.40) that excessive security and control would be counter-productive since they would foster genuine grievances and a sense of oppression with which other inmates would be likely to sympathize. Unfortunately, these warnings went unheeded almost from the outset. The Woolf Report was published in February 1991; by the summer, security concerns were once again in the ascendancy following the escape of two IRA suspects from Brixton Prison. In the ensuing White Paper, *Custody, Care and Justice* (Home Office, 1991b) the government's sense of priorities was starkly reflected in the adoption (in effect) of a two-speed approach on implementing the Woolf proposals. In the fast lane was, most conspicuously, a package of measures to improve security and control including the introduction of annual security audits and the installation of X-ray machines and metal detectors in the entrances to maximum security prisons. These were to be given first claim on the Prison Service's budget and were accompanied by the introduction (in the Prison Security Act 1992) of a new offence of prison mutiny, and increased penalties for those convicted of assisting prison escapers. In the slow lane – to be implemented only over a timescale of 20 to 25 years, and then only out of existing resources – were many of the reforms to which Woolf had attached particular importance (see below).

Then, almost exactly thirty years after its emergence as a paramount policy concern, the crisis of containment was back at the top of the political agenda during the mid-1990s following yet another series of highly embarrassing security lapses. The first of these involved a short-lived escape by a number of armed prisoners from the Special Security Unit at the new dispersal prison at Whitemoor in September 1994, which was followed by the discovery of Semtex explosives and detonators at the prison. The government's embarrassment was heightened still further by allegations that prison staff were sent on errands by prisoners and that the Home Secretary had ignored warnings relating to security at the jail from the Chairman of the Board of Visitors. An inquiry set up to investigate the incident (Woodcock, 1994: para. 9.3) spoke of 'a disaster waiting to happen' in which 'so many things were wrong, so many procedures and policies totally ignored and with such regularity that the escape could have taken place on any day of any week with the same chance of success'.

The Whitemoor breakout was followed in January 1995 by the escape of three life sentence prisoners from Parkhurst dispersal prison. Although the prisoners were soon to be recaptured, the political fallout from the episode proved impossible to contain. The immediate response by the Director General of the Prison Service, Derek Lewis, was to remove the governor amid allegations that he was being made a scapegoat for policy failings at a higher level. Even more spectacular was the sacking by the Home Secretary of the Director General himself – which took place shortly after the Conservative Party Conference in October 1995 – in response to the publication of Sir John Learmont's (1995) highly critical report into the Parkhurst breakout.

Like his predecessor Lord Mountbatten, Learmont called for a new system of prisoners' classification, this time to be based on six separate security categories. The sense of penological *déjà vu* was heightened by a reopening of the 'concentration versus dispersal' policy debate (Penal Affairs Consortium, 1995h). Learmont doubted whether dispersal prisons could meet the requirements of the next century even after upgrading, and recommended a single new high security prison (a so-called 'super-max' prison) for the estimated 200 or so prisoners who would be assigned to his proposed new categories 1 ('exceptional security risk' inmates) or 2 ('high security risk' inmates).[30] The parallels with Mountbatten did not stop there, for Learmont also favoured a 'purposeful training régime', at least for the high security prison, offering a wide range of facilities.

The real impact of the Learmont Report however, lay in a profound change in administrative philosophy which was immediately reflected in the everyday experiences of prison inmates throughout the system rather than the adoption of these more grandiose policy prescriptions. The Conservative government at the time and senior prison administrators blamed the Whitemoor and Parkhurst security lapses on an overly permissive régime in which effective power and control lay with inmates rather than prison staff, and were determined to return power unequivocally to staff and prison management by adopting a 'decent but austere' prison régime. Policy changes included an increase in internal and perimeter security, restrictions on temporary release, the introduction of dedicated search teams, mandatory drug testing, restrictions on personal possessions,[31] the introduction of a new 'sticks and carrots' régime of incentives and earned privileges (see below) and the replacement of prison phone cards with a new Personal Identification Number (PIN) system (Creighton and King, 2000: 136). The PIN system restricts calls to pre-approved numbers and automatically deducts amounts from each inmate's credited account (thereby eliminating the need for cards and also a source of racketeering within prisons). The consequences for prisoners were immediate and profound since they emerged with fewer privileges, less personal property and were subject to far more frequent and thorough searches than before (Liebling, 2001).

In January 1999, the Home Secretary announced that the government had decided not to proceed with Learmont's recommendation for a single 'super-max' high-security prison (nor for a separate special 'control' prison), 'in the light of significant improvements to security in the Category A estate'.[32] Indeed, no fewer than 118 out of Learmont's 127 recommendations had been implemented in full by this stage, which clearly illustrated the continuing overwhelming influence of security on prison policy at the expense of justice and humanity. Inmates who are identified as constituting an 'exceptional escape risk' are currently held in two Special Security Units,[33] which are effectively prisons within a prison. Within the SSU they are held in 'small group isolation' in conditions that were described as 'cramped' and 'claustrophobic' by a former Chief Medical Officer; and are denied many of the basic rights to which other prisoners are entitled including access to library, gymnasium and chapel. They are also subjected to 'closed' visits in which the inmate sits behind a glass barrier and communicates via a telephone or grille and, despite such intensive security, are also subjected to strip-searches before and after every visit, supplemented by occasional even more intimate (and humiliating) 'squat' searches. Human rights organizations have complained that such conditions constitute cruel, inhuman or degrading treatment,[34] and the government's own inquiry, carried out in 1996, concluded that conditions in the SSUs could lead to mental illness.[35] The unremitting emphasis on security at the expense of humanity in the Learmont Report was roundly condemned by the former Chief Inspector of Prisons Judge Stephen Tumim, who described it as 'the road to the concentration camp' (*The Guardian*, 28 October 1995).

### The prison numbers crisis and overcrowding

Compared with the periodic and often highly spectacular crises of containment we described above, the ongoing prison numbers crisis – and the related problem of overcrowding – may appear less dramatic, but is just as insidious in terms of its impact both on the development of prison policy and also on the lives of inmates. Prison overcrowding is predominantly a post-war phenomenon and follows a sustained period of surplus capacity between 1908 and 1938, during which period the average daily prison population was halved from 22,000 to 11,000 and some 25 prisons were closed (Rutherford, 1986: 130–1). The period since the war has been one of almost relentless expansion, however,[36] and even though periodic attempts have been made to expand the size of the prison estate, for most of the time these have been insufficient to stave off serious overcrowding in the system.

Traditionally, the degree of prison overcrowding is measured with reference to a figure termed the 'certified normal accommodation' or 'CNA' (Morgan, 1995). This is the number of prisoners for whom government-appointed inspectors certify that each prison has adequate space (though it may include single and double cells plus dormitory accommodation). However, these figures never give the full picture. For one thing, the certified normal accommodation is a notional figure only. Not all accommodation that is supposedly available will actually be usable, because at any one time some of it[37] will be out of commission during refurbishment (either routine, or in response to damage inflicted during prison disturbances), and also because of the need for some spare capacity to accommodate receptions and transfers. Moreover, inmates are not spread evenly throughout the prison system since, as we have seen, there are many different types of prison institution, and corresponding restrictions on the types of inmates for whom each category of prison is deemed suitable. Consequently, the prison system as a whole is extremely inflexible with regard to the use that can be made of accommodation that is theoretically available. It is thus possible (and commonplace) for there to be substantial surplus capacity in some parts of the system, and gross overcrowding in others. This inflexibility is further aggravated by a clear policy to protect certain parts of the system (notably high-security prisons) from the worst effects of overcrowding, with the result that the problem is almost exclusively associated with local prisons and remand centres.

The system as a whole is said to be overcrowded when the total number of inmates exceeds the number of places that are notionally available throughout the entire prison estate,[38] but even when the prison system as a whole is not technically overcrowded (as was the case in 1945, and briefly again in 1992), individual institutions may still suffer from severe overcrowding. During the period 1946 to 1986, the prison population approximately trebled, while the CNA barely doubled in size (Home Office, 1986). Faced with a steadily deteriorating problem of prison overcrowding, the government responded in 1982 by embarking on the biggest prison building programme since the mid-Victorian era. It involved the construction of 21 new prisons, containing an additional 11,285 new prison places, at a capital cost of £1.2 billion (Barclay, 1995: 10).[39] Partly as a result of the new accommodation, and partly because of reductions in the prison population in 1989 and 1990, the capacity of the prison system was technically in surplus by late 1990 for the first time in nearly forty years. In 1993 the CNA exceeded the prison population by 2,050.

Influenced by these trends and by Home Office projections based upon them, Lord Justice Woolf optimistically predicted that prison overcrowding could become a 'thing of the past' (Woolf and Tumim, 1991: para. 1.189). Consequently, the Woolf Report of February 1991 recommended the adoption of a new Prison Rule setting a maximum level of occupancy for each prison, corresponding to its CNA (Woolf and Tumim, 1991: para. 11.141). Ultimately, no prison would be allowed to exceed its certified capacity by more than 3 per cent for longer than seven days in any three month period. In exceptional circumstances, such as a riot or major disturbance, however, Woolf proposed that the Home Secretary should have the power to authorize temporary dispensations provided that Parliament was notified. If long-term equilibrium could not be maintained in this way, Woolf suggested that it would be preferable for the Home Secretary to make use of his discretionary powers to release prisoners early (see Chapter 8) rather than allow the system to become seriously overcrowded once more. This proposal was rejected outright by the government.

Woolf was in any event being hopelessly optimistic, as were the Home Office projections on which he based his recommendations. Even at those times when CNA exceeded population, the problem of overcrowding persisted since there were still insufficient prison places of the right categories and in the right locations. And after 1993 – the year of the government's 'law and order counter-reformation' – the positive trends went into reverse. By 1999 half the prisons in England and Wales were once again overcrowded, and over 12,000 people (just under one in five) were held two to a cell designed for one in 1999–2000 (Cullen and Minchin, 2000a: 4).[40] On 29 October 1999, there were 66,016 prisoners in England and Wales. This was just 3,800 below the system's 'operational capacity', which is the number of inmates that can be accommodated even allowing for the overcrowding (Prison Reform Trust, 1999b). The Prison Service has advised the Home Office that once the population rises to within 1000 of operational capacity, there is a strong likelihood that surplus inmates will need to be accommodated in police cells as the system itself would no longer be able to cope (HM Prison Service, 1999a). Following the drastic increase in the size of the prison population over the last few years, the prospects for an early end to the crisis of overcrowding (and the air of crisis management with which it is associated) have evaporated, to the evident dismay of those (such as prison governors) who have to cope with the consequences.[41]

The effects of overcrowding, and its impact on penal policy, are manifested in various ways. Most obviously, prison overcrowding has an adverse effect on living conditions (see next section), but it also results in restricted régimes since there is neither the space, the facilities nor the resources to provide inmates with a full range of training, work and educational opportunities when there are too many prisoners to cope with. Relations between staff and inmates can also be adversely affected in such circumstances. Moreover, overcrowding frequently results in the postponement of long-overdue and badly needed refurbishment programmes, thereby perpetuating squalor and dilapidation.[42] Another consequence of overcrowding is the need to transfer prisoners around the system in the quest for available accommodation. This is not only highly disruptive to prisoners and their families but also contributes to the sense of bitterness and hostility which Woolf identified as a factor increasing the likelihood of reoffending on release (Woolf and Tumim, 1991: para. 10.27). Finally, the increase in tension and frustration caused by overcrowding is widely believed to aggravate the crisis of control by increasing the risk of disturbances, such as the riot at Strangeways in 1990.

### The crisis of conditions

The present crisis of conditions comprises several elements which individually and collectively help to influence the quality of life of those living and working in the English penal system: first, the sheer wretchedness of the physical accommodation in which the great majority of prisoners are housed; second, the impoverished and repressive nature of the régimes to which most of them are routinely subjected; and third, the nature of the social relationships that exist between inmates themselves, between inmates and staff, and between inmates and outsiders, including ordinary members of the community.

In very general terms, the trend since the Woolf Report is that there have been some improvements in physical conditions, though the scope for further improvement is severely restricted by the continuing population pressure. There were some very significant deteriorations in prison régimes during the mid-1990s, as the Prison Service struggled to cope with a rapidly expanding prison population during a period of financial stringency and an officially endorsed policy of austerity towards inmates. Since 1997 there has been a significant investment in the development of more constructive prison régimes, with the aim of reducing the stubbornly high reconviction rates that are associated with the use of imprisonment. However, much of the emphasis has been on the introduction of specific high-profile treatment programmes in individual prisons rather than securing improvements in prison régimes as a whole. In other respects – particularly with regard to the kind of relationships that exist in prison – there have been some more hopeful indications. The Prison Service's Director General, Martin Narey, has at least acknowledged the need to address some of the chronic problems associated with the more overt forms of prison officer brutality towards inmates, and the corrupting legacy of institutional racism. However, progress overall has been patchy to date, and it would be true to say that the crisis of conditions is still as intractable as ever. It is likely to remain so unless and until the fundamental problem of grossly excessive prison numbers is finally resolved.

One disturbing barometer of the scale of the continuing crisis of conditions is the rate of suicides by prisoners, which doubled during the 1970s, and doubled again in the 1980s (Shaw, 1992a: 162). In 1999 there were a record 91 self-inflicted deaths in prison (Cullen and Minchin, 2000a).[43] Moreover, the rate of increase in prison suicides is far higher than might be expected from the rise in the prison population. In 1988 the suicide rate was 25 per 100,000 receptions into prison custody. By 1994 this had almost doubled to 49 per 100,000 receptions. But in 1999 the suicide rate was more than 67 per 100,000 receptions.[44] Compared with the general population, prisoners are between two and seven times more likely to kill themselves (Howard League, 1996). Even allowing for their generally adverse psychiatric profile (see Chapter 1), this is unacceptably high. Suicides are disproportionately high among young prisoners, remand inmates, mentally disordered prisoners and those beginning very long sentences (Prison Reform Trust, 1997b). Prison suicides are believed to result from an interaction between a number of factors.[45] They include a pre-custodial history of vulnerability, such as anxiety or depression; background stress factors, such as bullying; and situational triggers, such as changes of location or missed visits (see below). Compared with the general population, prison inmates who commit suicide are far *less* likely to have had a history of psychiatric illness or treatment (Liebling, 1997). The problem of prison suicides has long been recognized (HM Chief Inspector of Prisons, 1990a), and a programme of suicide prevention measures was introduced in 1994. While the strategy may have been well conceived, however, the Chief Inspector of Prisons has blamed the continuing unacceptably high levels of prison suicides on a lack of commitment and defective implementation on the part of staff and senior management (HM Chief Inspector of Prisons, 1999a).[46]

The accommodation in which prisoners are held is obviously a key element in the quality of life they experience. For many years the state of that accommodation in some parts of the prison system has become a byword for squalor, as reports by the Chief Inspector of Prisons have repeatedly testified.[47] As Lord Justice Woolf (Woolf and Tumim, 1991: para. 10.19) observed, justice itself is compromised if prisoners are held in conditions that are 'inhumane or degrading, or are otherwise wholly inappropriate'. Perhaps the nadir for the Prison Service was a finding by the European Committee for the Prevention of Torture and Inhuman or Degrading Treatment and Punishment (1991) that a number of features found in three English local prisons[48] – including the overcrowding, lack of integral sanitation and inadequate régime activities – were indeed inhuman and degrading.

For many years inmates' lack of access to toilet facilities symbolized the decrepit condition of much of the contemporary prison estate. The ending of the practice of 'slopping out' was not officially proclaimed until April 1996, though even this proved premature, as reports by the Chief Inspector of Prisons confirmed that the practice persisted in some prisons (including Exeter and Portland) until at least the turn of the century. Moreover, the method mostly used to provide toilet facilities is far from ideal, since it involves a conversion of the middle cell of each block of three into two cubicles, each serving an adjoining cell. Not only does this consign many prisoners to 'sleeping in the toilet' since they lack adequate screening (Shaw, 1992a: 169;

HM Chief Inspector of Prisons, 2000a) but the decommissioning of cells for this purpose further exacerbated the prison overcrowding problem while the work was taking place.

As with so many other aspects of prison life, it is in the local prisons that the provision of facilities and constructive activities are particularly deplorable. They are the most overcrowded, holding on average 26 per cent more inmates than they are resourced to do (HM Chief Inspector of Prisons, 1999b). Yet these same institutions house many prisoners on remand who are awaiting trial and who have not been found guilty of any offence.[49] Logically, those still presumed innocent might expect better treatment than those proved guilty. But as the government's own Chief Inspector (2000a) has pointed out, despite all the evidence and repeated criticism, the reality continues to defy this logic. This depressing state of affairs is reflected in the appallingly high suicide rate among remand prisoners. In recent years remand prisoners have accounted for over half of all prison suicides, even though they comprise less than one fifth of the total prison population. And up to two thirds of all suicides have occurred in local prisons.

Deplorable as the physical conditions in most English prisons undoubtedly are, their effects on the inmates who have to endure them may be less damaging than the restrictive and repressive daily régimes to which many of them are routinely subjected.[50] Prison régimes are restrictive in many respects, but one of the most obvious of these is the serious lack of suitably constructive and purposeful activities for inmates to engage in. Basic guidelines for prison régimes are set out in the European Standard Minimum Rules 1973, revised in 1987.[51] Rule 71(3) states that 'sufficient work of a useful nature, or, if appropriate, other purposeful activities, should be provided to keep prisoners actively employed for a normal working day'. However, these rules have no legal force in England, where there are no enforceable minimum standards relating to prison work, or indeed to conditions generally.[52] Prison Rule 31(1) places an upper limit on the number of hours which a convicted prisoner may be required to work each day (ten hours), but a much more serious problem is the lack of suitable work or other constructive activity. Indeed, since the 1970s opportunities for work and other purposeful activities in prison have actually decreased. Whereas in 1972–3 the average working week for prison workshops was 28 hours, by 1988–9 this had been reduced to 21 hours (NACRO, 1990; see also King and McDermott, 1989: 119; McDermott and King, 1989) following a decision in 1986 to close 54 workshops on cost grounds. By 1999–2000 the Prison Service's key performance indicator (KPI) *target* figure for the total average time to be engaged in purposeful activity was only 24 hours per week (HM Prison Service, 2000), but it failed to meet even this modest target. On average prisoners spent just 23.2 hours a week on such activities during 1999–2000, which is just ten minutes per day more than it was a decade ago. Once again the position tends to be far worse in local prisons. The lowest figure recorded was just over eleven hours a week (less than two hours per day) at Brixton Prison (Prison Reform Trust, 2000d).[53]

Even the definition of purposeful activity is highly questionable since it includes wing cleaning, maintenance and orderly work. Indeed, much of the work that has traditionally been provided in prison is dull, repetitive and demeaning. Far from equipping prisoners with useful skills which might improve their prospects for employment on release, it seems only to reflect a narrow work ethic that approves of hard manual labour as an instrument of punishment in its own right. More than a quarter of a century ago, even the government's own Control Review Committee (Home Office, 1984a: para. 95) censured the Prison Department for continuing to operate an industry-based system of the traditional kind. In its place they called for a diversification of facilities – including education, vocational training or therapy, in addition to work – in response to the individual's own needs and abilities. In 1994 the Chief Inspector of Prisons' Annual Report called for an urgent review of the wages paid in prison workshops and for trial schemes to be introduced which would allow prisoners to be employed by outside companies for realistic wages in return for a full working week. Little has changed with regard to the provision of work and remuneration for inmates over the intervening years.

Likewise, the provision of education and training opportunities in prison remains poor, with regard to both quality and quantity, despite some recent attempts to reverse decades of neglect. In 1998 the government announced an unprecedented investment in prisoner education as part of the Comprehensive Spending Review.[54] This followed more than a decade of chronic under-funding for prison education, however, during which the education budget in prisons was reduced from 3.55 per cent of the total Prison Service budget in 1984–5 to 2.94 per cent by 1993–4. Moreover, educational services that had hitherto been provided free of charge by local authorities and colleges were 'contracted out' during the same period, as part of the Conservative government's prison privatization programme (see Chapter 7). This was heavily criticized for its effect on the morale of service providers (Prison Reform Trust, 1994), quite apart from the disruption it caused for prison inmates. The renewed emphasis on the provision of basic education following the comprehensive spending review seems likely to result in improved levels of prisoner literacy and numeracy. However, it is unlikely to address some of the more fundamental failings of the prison education system that have been highlighted in numerous inspection reports compiled by the Chief Inspector of Prisons.[55]

One failing relates to the absence of any systematic educational needs assessment at the time an inmate enters prison. A second shortcoming which adversely affects the quality of educational facilities relates to the continual disruption of planned educational programmes, either as a result of inmates being moved to other establishments before completing a course, or because of alleged shortages of security staff for the purposes of supervision. A third problem relates to the narrowness of the core curriculum that is provided by the Prison Service. Unfortunately, the recent emphasis by the government on basic competency in literacy and numeracy, however laudable, could exacerbate this problem by diverting resources that might otherwise be devoted to more creative subjects such as art and music. In spite of the greatly increased spending on prison education since 1998, Minister of Prisons Paul Boateng had to concede that by October 1999 most prisons had no more money in real terms than they had in 1995–6.[56] This means that the drastic cuts imposed under the previous government in 1996–7 have not yet been restored.

One final problem that was identified by the Chief Inspector of Prisons in his 1998–9 Annual Report relates to the often grotesque disparities in the amount of money for educational courses that is made available per prisoner per year both within and between different types of prison.[57]

The quality of prison régimes more generally is also liable to be adversely affected by staffing problems either routinely, as a result of demands imposed by security measures, or exceptionally, as a result of industrial action on the part of prison staff. Either may result in the cancellation of work, education programmes, visits or other leisure activities. Inmates are known to attach considerable importance to such activities, and to visits in particular (Wozniak and McAllister, 1991), and even the *threat* of reductions in the quality of the régime provided has been linked with prison riots and disturbances (Home Office, 1987; and see below). But at least as important as the levels of service that are provided is the way inmates are personally treated in the institution and, in particular, the nature of the relationships between staff and inmates. This affects not only the quality of life for all who live and work in prison, but also the potential for maintaining order, and is an issue that we will return to in discussing the crises of control and legitimacy.

Another aspect of prison conditions that significantly affects the quality of life for inmates relates to their relative vulnerability at the hands of their fellow inmates, and the susceptibility of some prisoners in particular to assaults and intimidation. One of the Prison Service's thirteen key performance indicators for 1999–2000 was to ensure that the number of assaults on prisoners, staff and others expressed as a percentage of the average prison population is lower than 9 per cent. In fact there were 6,431 recorded assaults in 1999–2000, which yields an assault rate of just under ten per cent – greater than the KPI target. And yet the only assaults that are counted for the purpose of this measure are those[58] that result in proven adjudications. At best this is likely to provide a very partial indication of the true extent of violence in prisons.[59] The actual extent of prison violence is likely to be very much higher than this. In one survey covering two adult male prisons and two male young offender institutions in 1994–5 victimization of inmates was found to be pervasive (O'Donnell and Edgar, 1996, 1998). No fewer than 46 per cent of young offenders and 30 per cent of adult offenders reported that they had either been assaulted, robbed or threatened with violence in the preceding *month*, though most reported that they felt safe most of the time in spite of this very high level of victimization.

The most deleterious impact on prison conditions, however, has been the continuing preoccupation with security, which has been with us since the adoption of the dispersal system. A study published shortly before the Strangeways riot (King and McDermott, 1989) portrayed a marked deterioration in the quality of prison régimes across a range of different types of prisons over a period of twenty years, and a further study (McDermot and King, 1989) showed that a package of measures known as Fresh Start had failed to reverse the decline in standards.

Lord Woolf believed that unacceptable prison conditions had played a part in precipitating the Strangeways riots, and many of his recommendations were intended to halt and reverse the steady decline in standards. In the ensuing

White Paper on prisons – *Custody, Care and Justice* (Home Office, 1991b) – the government adopted a classical 'cherry-picking' response to the recommendations, despite Woolf's insistence (1991: para. 1.168) that they should be treated as an integrated package. Some, such as the introduction of integral sanitation and a package of measures to enable prisoners to maintain better links with the outside world (by extending the use of phone cards, improving visiting and home leave entitlements) were adopted with relative alacrity, though some of these latter improvements proved relatively short-lived, as we have seen.

Some of Woolf's other recommendations met with a much more lukewarm response. This was certainly true of his proposal that the prison service should adopt a national system of accredited standards. Although these would be 'aspirational' in the first instance, he recommended that they would ultimately be incorporated into the Prison Rules which would render them enforceable by the legal procedure of judicial review. The Prison Service's preferred use of self-imposed targets set out annually in its key performance indicators falls a long way short of Woolf's recommendation since, as we have seen, the targets are modest, restrictively defined and, crucially, are unenforceable. As such, they represent not so much a commitment to the kind of minimum standards called for by Woolf, as an example of the extension of private sector 'managerialism' to the running of public sector prisons.

Woolf had also recommended that prisoners should be given a 'compact' or 'contract' setting out the basic entitlement that they could normally expect to receive and, in return, the responsibilities expected of them. This was one of the measures Woolf considered necessary in the interests of justice and resulted from his conclusion that grievances over the inconsistent provision of facilities in different prisons had helped to fuel the riots. Although the Prison Service briefly toyed with the idea of 'model prison compacts' which were introduced on a piecemeal basis in a number of prisons (HM Prison Service, 1995), this approach was swiftly reversed in the aftermath of the Woodcock enquiry into the prison escapes from Whitemoor (Woodcock, 1994). Henceforth, prisoners' allowances were to be redefined as privileges which had to be earned rather than expectations to which they were entitled, as Woolf had recommended, and the Prison Rules were swiftly amended[60] to allow for the introduction of a scheme of 'Incentives and Earned Privileges' (see below).

Prisoners who had signed compacts that ostensibly entitled them to certain allowances as of right, challenged the new incentives régime on the ground that it unlawfully denied them their legitimate expectations. However, the Court of Appeal rejected this argument, ruling that the only legitimate expectation to which they were entitled was to benefit from any lawful policy that was promulgated from time to time by the Secretary of State.[61] The effect of this ruling was to render prisoners acutely vulnerable to adverse changes in the quality of their living conditions and their ability to maintain contact with the outside world. This vulnerability was ruthlessly exploited by Michael Howard's 'austerity drive' during the 'law and order counter reformation' that commenced in 1993 and continued until the change of government in 1997.[62] The entire episode provides a telling illustration of the way in which security considerations that are prompted by the actions of a handful of high-risk prisoners consistently ride roughshod over the requirement of justice for all inmates, which is precisely the malady that Woolf had perceptively diagnosed.

One of Woolf's most radical proposals with regard to prison conditions was to convert most of the prison estate into a system of '*community prisons*' which would be situated, where possible, close to the main centres of population, and which would enable the majority of prisoners to be detained close to where they live. This would make it very much easier for most prisoners irrespective of their security classification to maintain close links with family and community, and thus assist in the process of reintegration on release. It would also have the advantage of reducing or even eliminating altogether the practice of regularly transferring inmates, often at short notice and frequently to distant parts of the country, which Woolf identified as another major source of grievance (see below) during the period preceding the Strangeways riots. The biggest drawback is that such a drastic reconfiguration of the prison estate could not be achieved without the injection of substantial resources and, probably, a significant reduction in the size of the prison population. Not surprisingly, perhaps, this was one proposal for which the government and prison authorities showed little or no enthusiasm, and ten years after the Woolf Report was published over a third of the prison population (and half of all women prisoners) were imprisoned more than 50 miles from their committal court town, while over one sixth of the prison population were detained more than 100 miles away from home.[63]

During the decade following the Woolf Report, his radical agenda for reform was almost entirely eclipsed by the twin shadows cast by the heightened concerns over security and drastic budget restrictions. Although the shadows are no longer quite as dark and oppressive as they were during Michael Howard's era of 'decent austerity', Woolf's proposed 'new dawn' for prisons still seems as distant as ever. And yet the case for redressing the balance by injecting a greater measure of justice into the way the prison system operates remains as compelling as it was in the aftermath of Strangeways. Drastic action to improve both the physical conditions and quality of prison régimes is not only justified (and long overdue) on humanitarian grounds, but would also be likely to elicit a more positive attitude on the part of prisoners. It could even have a beneficial effect on the problem of control within the prisons, as we will argue below.[64] Indeed, the need to improve the quality of prison régimes will require a programme of reform that in some respects looks beyond the agenda set by Lord Woolf, who had surprisingly little to say about the need to improve prisoner–staff relationships. This in our view is one of the most important issues that will need to be addressed if the crucial crisis of legitimacy is to be effectively tackled. (We will have more to say about this towards the end of this chapter.)

### The crisis of control

Prison riots are the most visible and spectacular symbols of a more pervasive crisis of control within the prison system. At a more mundane level the problem of disruptive behaviour poses a predictable – but equally intractable – problem for prison authorities. Having briefly examined prison riots and the competing explanations of their causes in Chapter 1, we are more concerned in this section with the issue of day-to-day control and the responses that have been developed for dealing with disruptive inmates. It is important to differentiate at the outset between the formal disciplinary system, which is used to deal with offences against prison discipline, and the informal disciplinary system, which affords a wide range of strategies for dealing with disruptive behaviour. As we shall see, both of these control systems have all too often proved counter-productive in practice, and have diverted attention away from the need to improve the quality of the régimes themselves, the most important aspect of which is the state of relations between staff and inmates. In this section we are chiefly concerned with the range of informal disciplinary measures that are available to the prison authorities, and the problems that are associated with the way they have been used. We will return to the formal disciplinary system when discussing the crisis of legitimacy.

The three principal informal methods of exerting control over inmates who are perceived to be disruptive involve the use of physical force or restraint, transfer and segregation. In the past, punishment or repression based on the use of physical force was the standard response for those who resisted 'good order and discipline' in prisons. Flogging and birching fell into disuse after 1962, and corporal punishment was formally abolished in 1967 (Thomas, 1972: 201). However, the tradition of exercising control by force lives on in a variety of ways. The use of force is authorized under Rule 47 of the 1999 Prison Rules, which prescribe that force should not be used unnecessarily, and then only as much as is necessary. Where it is necessary, only approved 'control and restraint' (C and R) techniques are supposed to be used 'unless this is impractical'. Although the C and R Manuals that have been issued by the Prison Service are classified, the techniques are said to be based on the martial art known as Aikido (Leech, 1995: 264). Other less sophisticated forms of physical restraint are also used routinely, such as bodybelts,[65] ratchet hand-cuffs, ankle straps, staves and batons. In addition to these 'approved' methods of force and physical restraint, prison staff are frequently alleged and have sometimes been proved to resort unofficially to unapproved and unlawful methods, including deliberate assaults or the use of excessive force in restraining an inmate.[66]

When the dispersal system was adopted, it was erroneously assumed that the problem of control was just another aspect of the security problem, and that the most disruptive prisoners were likely to be the high-security ones and *vice versa* (King and Elliott, 1977; King and Morgan, 1980; King, 1985; Adams, 1994: 181).[67] Not only was this assumption soon to be disproved, but it also became apparent that the relatively relaxed régimes and undifferentiated interior space associated with the dispersal prisons posed enormous control problems within their high-security perimeters. When, almost from the outset, the dispersal prisons began to experience serious control problems, prison authorities resorted to a combination of physical force, segregation and reallocation, none of which were conspicuously successful in averting or even quelling disorder.

One of the earliest official responses to the prison riots of the 1970s was to set up a special clandestine 'in-house' riot squad of specially trained prison staff (known as the 'MUFTI' – 'Minimum Use of Force Tactical Intervention' – squad). This was used to break up a protest demonstration at Wormwood Scrubs in August 1979, but it was only after information began to reach the media about the scale of the injuries it had inflicted that the Home Office was grudgingly forced to concede its existence (Thomas and Pooley, 1980: 136; Adams, 1994: 180). After initial denials that any of the prisoners had been injured, it later emerged that no fewer than 54 had sustained injuries as a result of assaults by the staff, and that similar squads had previously been used to deal with disturbances at Gartree in 1978, and at Hull and Styal in 1979. The paramilitary approach was taken a stage further in Scotland where a hostage-taking incident at Peterhead prison in 1986 resulted in the SAS (Special Air Services) being brought in to undertake the first armed intervention in a British prison dispute (Scraton et al., 1991: 24). Although this brought about the release of the hostage concerned, another was seized almost immediately at Perth prison, suggesting that the only long-term outcome of this particular intervention was a further escalation in the depressing retaliatory spiral of violence.

Apart from the use of physical force, one of the commonest options adopted by the authorities when confronted with disruptive prisoners is the physical segregation of those responsible.[68] Under Rule 45 of the 1999 Prison Rules, a prison governor has the power to order the 'removal from association' of a prisoner where this appears desirable 'for the maintenance of good order and discipline'.[69] Prisoners segregated in this way are held in virtual isolation, being shut in their cells in the punishment block for 23 hours per day, which means they are deprived of virtually all opportunities for work, education and recreation (Creighton and King, 2000: 117).[70] In spite of these severe deprivations,[71] removal from association is categorized as an administrative procedure rather than a disciplinary sanction, though its use can often make matters worse by fuelling discontent among prisoners, as we shall see.[72] Attempts to challenge the legality of the segregation procedure have proved unsuccessful in the past,[73] and it is by no means certain that a renewed challenge under Article 3 of the European Convention on Human Rights would succeed unless the conditions were wholly exceptional (see below).

Segregation is often combined with another administrative process – the temporary transfer procedure – which is used to reallocate difficult or disruptive prisoners from their original prison to the segregation block of a local prison. Although intended to provide a temporary (one month's) 'cooling off' respite before returning to the original prison, the governor there may apply to the Prison Service to have the inmate transferred to another establishment. At the time of the Strangeways riot a large number of inmates who were alleged to be especially disruptive were shunted from one prison to another every few months. The procedure was known by a variety of nicknames including the 'magic roundabout' or 'merry-go-round', and gave rise to a Prison Service joke about British Rail (as the then-nationalized railway system was known) being another penal establishment.

For a long time temporary transfers – sometimes as many as 100,000 each year – were authorized under Home Office Circular Instruction 10/74 (otherwise known as 'Rule Ten-Seventy-Four' or, in prison jargon, the 'Ghost Train'). Following recommendations contained in the Woolf Report a new procedure for managing persistently disruptive inmates was introduced.[74] This still authorized the use of transfers in the interests of 'good order and discipline', but only as a last resort, and subject to a régime of safeguards that are now incorporated into Instructions to Governors 28/93. The most important safeguard is that such decisions must be taken on reasoned grounds, which should be communicated to the inmate within 24 hours of the transfer or segregation.[75]

The revised procedure for dealing with disruptive inmates took the form of a five-stage programme in which prison governors are advised to adopt a graduated response in which they should consider and reject each of the following options before moving on to the next:

i)   segregation at the 'parent' prison;
ii)  temporary transfer to a local prison (see above);
iii) reallocation by prison service headquarters to another suitable prison;
iv)  transfer to a special unit or (after 1998) a Close Supervision Centre (see below); and
v)   centrally managed regular transfers over an indefinite period to either local or training prisons.

The latter is now known as the 'Continuous Assessment Scheme', and is intended as the measure of last resort for inmates who really cannot be dealt with in any other way. Under the revised procedure segregation in a settled location (stage iv) is intended to largely take the place of the widely discredited temporary transfer system.

The use of specially adapted and designated segregation units as a means of dealing with particularly disruptive prisoners who could not be controlled within the relatively liberal and constructive régime of the standard dispersal prison has a long and not very honourable or successful history. It began in 1974 with the introduction of a special 'control unit' at Wakefield,[76] following widespread prison disturbances in 1972. Within the control unit, both the physical conditions and the régime were intentionally spartan, to act as a disincentive, and any amelioration had to be 'earned' by satisfactory behaviour over a prolonged period. Following the controversy surrounding its use,[77] the operation of the control units was suspended in 1975, and in 1983 the government's own Control Review Committee accepted that this particular response to the problem of disorder within the prison system represented a blind alley for the Prison Service (Home Office, 1984a: para. 52).

In its place, the Committee recommended the creation of a new system of small sized 'Special Units' (see Bottomley and Hay, 1991) which offered a variety of different non-punitive régimes as a way of coping with seriously disruptive prisoners. Within these units, the need for tight security was counterbalanced by a liberal and humane régime in which the emphasis was on the resocialization of violently disruptive and aggressive prisoners who have often proved extremely difficult to handle in the normal prison environment. Three such Special Units were operational at any one time,[78] but despite some evidence of success in coping with the disruptive behaviour of some of the most intractable prisoners in the prison system (Boag, 1988, 1989; Bottomley, 1990; Martin, 1991; Cooke, 1989), the Special Units themselves fell victim to the more repressive penal climate that accompanied the security clamp-down of the mid 1990s.

In July 1995, the Prison Service established a project[79] to investigate the feasibility of introducing a new 'Strict Régime' unit, which in 1998 resulted in the creation of a radically different system of 'Closed Supervision Centres' (CSCs) based at Woodhill and Durham prisons. Their operating philosophy owed far more to the discredited and unsuccessful Control Unit initiative of the 1970s than the rather more enlightened (and penologically better informed) approach that had been pioneered in the Special Units they replaced. In a depressing illustration of the tendency for English penal history to repeat itself, and particularly its mistakes, the Closed Supervision Centres were founded on the notion of a 'progressive' or 'staged' system that incorporated a crude and mechanistic 'stick and carrot' approach to eliciting good behaviour. The 'stick' consisted of a restricted régime offering no association, compulsory prison issue clothing and 'basic' or minimal privileges.[80] The 'carrots' on offer consisted of a graded series of 'earned privileges' that were intended to operate as a reward for compliant behaviour. Thus, prisoners were expected to graduate initially to a so-called 'structured' régime providing some opportunity for participating in association, constructive activities and behaviour programmes and thence to an 'intervention' unit, in which privileges would reach the 'standard' level on offer in the rest of the high security estate.

Unfortunately (but all too predictably in the light of the Woolf Report) the early experience of the CSC system exposed a number of extremely serious operational failings, which served to expose basic flaws in the assumptions on which it rested. A thorough evaluation of the system found that out of 51 prisoners housed during its first 28 months of operation, only twelve inmates 'progressed' from it and, of these, only four managed to settle on normal location without any recurrence of their disruptive behaviour (Clare and Bottomley, 2001: 103). Although 30 prisoners were thought to show reduced levels of disruptive behaviour within the CSC compared with outside, six showed an increased level of assaultive behaviour. Moreover, a group of eight prisoners 'refused to co-operate with the system from the outset and embarked upon a persistent campaign of confrontation and challenge, involving dirty protests, violence and/or threats of violence against staff, as well as litigation against the system'. Noting that for several of these prisoners their behaviour had deteriorated dramatically following their transfer to the CSC, the report authors noted laconically that 'it would be unwise to claim that the overall effect of CSCs on these prisoners had been anything other than very negative'. Liebling (2001: 156) suggested that several of these inmates became more violent (and more disturbed) than they had been at any stage during their prison careers. Her interviews with this group of inmates revealed a perceived lack of legitimacy with regard to every aspect of the system's operation which 'gave every excuse they needed to vent all the anger, frustration and hatred they could muster against its staff' (2001: 159).[81]

A similar though somewhat less extreme 'sticks and carrots' régime known as the Incentives and Earned Privileges (IEP) scheme[82] was also introduced to the rest of the prison system in July 1995, as part of the post-Learmont security clamp-down. A Home Office funded evaluation of this scheme (Liebling et al., 1999) found that there had been no significant overall improvements to prisoner behaviour in the five establishments studied. Significantly, however, there were reductions (from relatively high levels) in favourable inmate perceptions of staff fairness, relations with staff, régime fairness, consistency of treatment and progress in prison.[83] Paradoxically, negative feelings such as these among inmates are known[84] to be highly detrimental to the maintenance of order in prisons, which was supposed to be the main aim of the IEP system itself. Thus, it appeared that perceptions of unfairness on the part of inmates offset and outweighed any beneficial effects of the new system. None of this should have come as any surprise in the wake of the Woolf Report. As it is, the entire episode serves to highlight the chronic inability of English penal policy-makers to learn from either the depressingly long litany of well-documented policy failures or the much shorter (and often unsung) paean of more constructive interventions.[85]

As for Woolf himself, his main strategy for tackling the control problem (as we shall see below) was to attend to the genuine sense of grievance that he accepted was primarily to blame for most of the disturbances. However, he did also accept the need for some improvements in the security and control apparatus to deal with the much smaller number of disruptive and difficult prisoners who would undoubtedly remain.[86] In order to tackle this residual control problem, Woolf's proposed solution was heavily influenced by recent American thinking on the prison design. Instead of the large-scale, relatively inflexible, open access wings of conventional prison design, he favoured the use of a rather different model that is often referred to as a '*new generation prison*', which is based on a collection of small, self-contained decentralized units (Ditchfield, 1990: 84–7). The first such prison – Woodhill, near Milton Keynes – was opened in July 1992. The theory is that within such a system, a variety of régimes may be offered to cater for the specific requirements of different groups of prisoners under the one roof. Being smaller, such designs are said to offer better standards of surveillance and control and also better inter-personal relations between staff and inmates. However, Andrew Rutherford (1985: 408), one of the few British observers to have examined the new generation prisons in operation in America, has cautioned that they should not be seen as a panacea for all the existing system's ills. While there are undoubtedly some very successful new generation prisons in operation (including Oak Park Heights in Minnesota which was visited by the Woolf inquiry team), there are also some not-so-successful ones that can be just as repressive and brutal as those they are designed to replace (see also Scraton et al., 1991: 138). Rutherford's conclusion – that the key to success lies in the management approach that is adopted and the way prisoners are treated rather than in prison architecture – chimes in well with Woolf's general approach.

As for the rest of the prison estate, Woolf advocated a fundamental restructuring of existing prison buildings to incorporate at least some elements of the 'new generation' design. One of the most radical proposals advocated a reorganization of the existing prison estate into a series of small prison units, each housing no more than 400 inmates. Where necessary, Woolf suggested that this could be achieved by housing two or more self-contained prison units on the same site and within the same perimeter walls. Within each of these prison units the available accommodation would be further sub-divided into a series of smaller living units, each housing no more than 50 to 70 prisoners. This would enable a greater variety of specialized régimes to be offered throughout the prison system, in an attempt to combat the deficiencies of the present control system which, as we have seen, relies to an excessive extent on the ineffective strategies of segregation and transfer.

One sadly neglected response to the control problem in prisons is the need to develop an appropriate strategy to improve the generally very poor state of staff–inmate relations. The importance of putting this relationship onto a more positive footing was recognized in 1984 by the Control Review Committee which was at pains to stress that: 'At the end of the day, nothing else that we can say will be as important as the general proposition that relations between staff and prisoners are at the heart of the whole prison system and that control and security flow from getting that relationship right' (Home Office, 1984a: para. 16). We will have more to say on the subject in relation to the crisis of legitimacy. But perhaps one reason for the continuing neglect of this issue (including, as we have seen, by Woolf) – is to do with a rather different crisis in which prison officers themselves are a central part of the problem. This is the continuing crisis of authority, which we will discuss next.

### The crisis of authority

The 'crisis of authority' (as it was christened by Fitzgerald and Sim, 1982) – or the prison staff crisis – has a number of related components.[87] At one level it can be seen as a classic industrial relations problem, in which changes in the aims and style of prison management are resisted by staff who have become increasingly willing to deploy their own countervailing power through trade union activities. At one time this included regular recourse to strike action and other forms of 'working to rule'. An attempt by the Conservative government to resolve the problem in 1994 by withdrawing the right to take strike action[88] caused considerable resentment on the part of the Prison Officers' Association, and if anything worsened the industrial relations climate.[89] In a Home Office commissioned report on 'Modernising the Management of the Prison Service' (Laming, 2000) 'industrial relations' were singled out as one of the most significant blocks to effective performance by the service, and the relationship between management and trade unions was said to be 'reminiscent of some parts of the motor industry in the 1960s'.[90] Clearly there is still no obvious solution in sight to the continuing problem of prison staff unrest.

However, there is much more to the crisis of authority than an industrial relations problem, intractable as that may be. For it also encompasses first, some very profound changes in both the philosophy and organizational form of prison management itself; and secondly, some equally fundamental changes in the state of relations between prison officers and other prison personnel including inmates, governors, and other types of prison staff. These have created what in Chapter 1 we characterized as one aspect of the penal system's crisis of legitimacy – the system's lack of legitimacy with penal staff. It is on these elements of the 'crisis of authority' that we shall concentrate in this section.

The changing style of prison management during the post-war era has been characterized (Ditchfield, 1990: 147–52) as a shift in the source of authority from a highly personalized form of power to a 'bureaucratic-lawful' model (Barak-Galanz, 1981),[91] in which authority is increasingly derived from a more bureaucratic system of general rules and regulations.[92] In the immediate post-war period, changes in management style were partly induced by changes in the nature of the prison régime, including those associated with the rehabilitative ideal. The latter not only required a much higher level of social interaction among inmates than had previously been allowed, but also called into question the traditional rôle of ordinary prison officers, with its almost exclusive emphasis on custody and discipline. Although the custodial function was still pre-eminent, uniformed staff increasingly resented the growing numbers of specialist and professionally trained welfare staff such as probation officers, educational workers and prison psychologists, who were brought into prisons in growing numbers for the purpose of treatment and training.

These professional personnel were resented, not only because their qualifications entitled them to better pay and conditions of service than ordinary prison officers, but also because they were considered to be usurping a rôle to which prison officers also aspired, however unsuited to it they might be by way of temperament, training or ideology. Growing tension between the various categories of prison workers was reflected in the findings of a survey into the attitudes of Scottish prison officers, many more of whom expressed concern about relations with social workers, psychologists and psychiatrists in particular (28 per cent, 27 per cent and 43 per cent respectively) than they did about relations with prisoners (Wozniak and McAllister, 1991). The survey also showed a high level of concern about relations with prison governors, who were blamed, among other things, for giving in to prisoners and failing to offer staff sufficient support.

Much of the resentment expressed by prison officers stems from a feeling that they are undervalued for the necessary, and increasingly dangerous,[93] work they are expected to do. Moreover, as Fitzgerald and Sim point out (1982: 123), they are also concerned that their job itself is under attack. In addition to the vociferous (and increasingly violent) protests of prisoners, and the alleged insensitivity on the part of the authorities towards their own concerns must now be added the threat of privatization (see Chapter 7). This has already resulted in the loss of certain former functions, such as court escort duties, which used to provide welcome relief to an otherwise tedious routine, and is increasingly seen as a threat to the jobs and livelihood of many prison officers. Another major source of prison staff resentment is over the issue of prisoners' rights and conditions, efforts to improve which are likely to be equated with attempts to subvert their own legitimate authority. Such attitudes are linked to the widely-shared perception that society cares more about prisoners than about prison staff.[94] Thus, while prison officers are on the whole strongly supportive of moves to improve prison standards and régimes (Prison Officers' Association, 1990), they were less keen on the idea of a Prisons Ombudsman, and are strongly opposed to prisoners having legal representation at grievance procedures (according to a survey of Scottish prison officers by Wozniak and McAllister, 1991). In keeping with these authoritarian attitudes, a majority of staff seem to want a tightening of prison régimes and a return to greater discipline.

Woolf acknowledged that any substantial change in the way prisoners are treated would require a major contribution from prison officers and considered that the best way of ensuring this, given the poor state of Prison Service morale, would be through improved in-service training. Among the benefits which he anticipated were improvements in staff self-esteem, reductions in racial discrimination and improved relations with inmates as increased skills enabled staff to offer training and advice. While such recommendations represented a step in the right direction, Woolf had surprisingly little to say about the basic rôle, attitudes and cultural values of the prison staff themselves, despite the critical importance of these to the nature of prison régimes. All too often in the past, attempts by governors and others to liberalize the prison system have been obstructed and frustrated by the actions and prejudices of basic grade officers fearful of losing their 'authority' and control.

Ironically, the clearest assessment of the need for a fundamental cultural change on the part of all staff working in the prison system has come from the present Director General of the Prison Service, Martin Narey. In a speech[95] whose bitter eloquence was born out of personal knowledge, he complained of a 'litany of failure and moral neglect', of the 'very immorality of our treatment of some prisoners and the degradation of some establishments', and he admitted that for too long the Prison Service 'used to tolerate inhumanity'. With equal frankness, he also appeared to acknowledge the monumental scale of the task and strength of cultural resistance from within the service by threatening to leave his post unless he received the support he required in order to push through the radical changes he believed were needed. Here indeed is a crisis of authority of epic proportions, in which even the Director General of the prison service finds it necessary to challenge so publicly the stubbornly recalcitrant elements within that service.

Another key component in the continuing 'crisis of authority' is the organizational crisis within the Prison Service, which was cruelly exposed by the Strangeways riot of April 1990, and about which Lord Woolf unsurprisingly had rather more to say. At that time the Prison Service formed an integral part (the Prison Department) of the Home Office and was characterized by a 'top down' structure with a very high level of central control (Prison Reform Trust, 1991). This caused particular problems at the time of the riots for the Strangeways governor, who was required throughout to consult his superiors within the Prison Department, many of whom had no operational experience. The performance of Director General Christopher Train drew particularly heavy criticism from both the media and politicians (Shaw, 1992a: 166), though the organizational problems confronting the Prison Service had long been recognized. Woolf himself spoke scathingly of the gulf that existed between Home Office ministers, Prison Headquarters staff and those working in the service itself, and of the deep 'dissension, division and distrust' that existed at all levels of the service (Woolf and Tumim, 1991: paras 12.1–12.4). His primary concern was the need for 'clear and visible leadership' of the service by someone recruited internally. Although he had no specific recommendations regarding the organizational structure of the service, he did stress the desirability of a much less directive, 'hands-off' approach by ministers which would leave the Director General free to manage and be publicly answerable for the performance of the service.

The issue of organizational reform for the Prison Service was already on the political agenda at the time of the Woolf inquiry, however, following a recommendation by the Government Efficiency Unit[96] to give a wide range of government bodies a more independent '*agency status*' to carry out many of the executive functions of government 'within a policy and resources framework set by a department' (Home Office, 1988c: para. 19). Although the government's initial response to the idea of extending agency status to the Prison Service was non-committal (Home Office, 1989) the proposal gained fresh momentum in the wake of a review of Prison Service management which was set up under the direction of Sir Raymond Lygo following the escape of two IRA suspects from Brixton prison in the summer of 1991. The Lygo Report (1991) strongly recommended the conferment of agency status on the Prison Service and this time the government accepted the proposal.

The Prison Service became an executive agency in April 1993. In theory, the aim of agency status is to allow the Prison Service to operate at arm's length from central government under the direction of a chief executive (or Director General). 'Operational' matters are the responsibility of the Director General, who works to a policy and resources framework set by the Home Secretary. Meanwhile, much responsibility and authority for implementing policy is devolved from headquarters to individual governors. In practice, however, the new management structure does not seem to have given the Prison Service greater freedom from political interference in the day-to-day running of prisons, to say the least. Following his appointment as Home Secretary, Michael Howard appeared determined to maintain an active involvement across a wide range of issues. Thus he let it be known that he was opposed to the installation of in-cell television, vetoed on political grounds the three candidates shortlisted for the first post of Prisons Ombudsman, and called for a crackdown on prison régimes involving restrictions on home leave, reduced standards of comfort and tougher disciplinary penalties.

In strict constitutional terms, under the doctrine of ministerial responsibility the Home Secretary remains accountable to Parliament for the performance of the Prison Service even after its 'devolution', although critics of the restructuring feared that it would result in a loss of public accountability. These fears appeared to be confirmed in the aftermath of the most recent 'crisis of containment', involving the Parkhurst and Whitemoor breakouts in 1994 and 1995. The Woodcock Report (1994) into the Whitemoor incident spoke of confusion surrounding the respective rôles of ministers, headquarters and individual prison governors, identifying a particular difficulty in relation to the distinction between 'operational' and 'policy' matters, leading to confusion as to where responsibility ultimately rests. This confusion over their respective rôles and responsibilities further intensified after Derek Lewis was sacked by Mr Howard in October 1995 following the publication of the Learmont Report (1995), and responded by issuing a writ against Mr Howard alleging repeated interference in operational matters in support of a claim for damages for wrongful dismissal (*The Guardian*, 19 October 1995). In March 1996, the High Court ruled in favour of his claim (*The Guardian*, 30 March 1996).

Since the General Election of 1997 the Prison Service has experienced further organizational reform. Agency status was confirmed in 1999 (HM Prison Service, 1999b) following a quinquennial review. A new area structure was adopted in April 2000, which is based on the same geographical and operational boundaries as other criminal justice agencies such as the police and probation.[97] The Chief Inspector of Prisons (1999b) has suggested that the adoption of co-terminous boundaries across the entire criminal justice system could finally pave the way towards the adoption of Lord Woolf's concept of community clusters of prisons, wherein each region would contain sufficient numbers and types of prison places to satisfy the needs of the prisoner population within that area.[98] The respective rôles and responsibilities of the Home Secretary and the Director General of the Prison Service have been redefined and clarified (HM Prison Service, 1999b) following the constitutional confusion that was exposed during the political fall-out that accompanied the Whitemoor and Parkhurst escapes in the mid-1990s. The Home Secretary retains responsibility for determining the strategic direction for the prison service, but is now assisted by a designated Minister for Prisons, who chairs a Prison Service Strategy Board comprising the Director General and other executive directors of the Prison Service, and non-executive directors who are appointed by the Home Secretary. However, this falls a long way short of the much more radical constitutional reform which the former Director General of the Prison Service, Derek Lewis (1996), has called for. In his view, nothing short of statutory separation of the Prison Service from the Home Office is required, which would entail the appointment of an independent board with statutory authority and powers to appoint and remove the senior prisons management. In the absence of such a reform he believes that ministers continue to wield authority without responsibility, while the Prison Service has responsibility without authority.

Meanwhile, the latest in a very long line of official reports on the management of the Prison Service (Laming, 2000) reiterates *inter alia* the need for 'strong leadership' and a degree of stability; improvements in training and personnel practices; and the adoption of a more transparent and much less cumbersome decision-making process and more effective mechanisms of accountability. Similar recommendations have been repeatedly made over the years.[99] Whatever the intrinsic merits of agency status in other respects, it has signally failed so far to resolve (or even ameliorate) the continuing organizational crisis within the Prison Service, which forms part of the wider crisis of authority.

Even judged against the more modest yardstick of improving political and operational accountability, on present evidence the verdict is also decisively negative despite the changes that have taken place since 1997. In this, as in other spheres, the doctrine of ministerial responsibility in its present state remains a deeply flawed mechanism for securing the accountability of those whose actions and policies contribute to or exacerbate the continuing crises within the prison system. Fortunately, as we shall see in the sections to come, other forms of accountability exist. While these are not an adequate substitute for genuine political accountability, some modest gains have nevertheless been achieved by a variety of watchdog agencies, foremost among which has been the Inspectorate of Prisons.

### The crisis of visibility

For most of the twentieth century the world of the prisons was a closed one, screened from public view under a cloak of protective legislation that was originally designed to safeguard national security. Indeed, so impenetrable was the prison system to public gaze until fairly recently, that of the ten major prison disturbances that took place in English dispersal prisons between October 1969 and May 1993, only two (at Hull in 1976 and at Wormwood Scrubs in 1979) were the subject of officially published reports (Ditchfield, 1990: 5). The inhibiting effect of the Official Secrets Act on those working within the prison system was tellingly (and, naturally enough, anonymously) described in 1975 by two assistant governors in the following terms:

> This all-pervasive Act not only inhibits disclosures of injustices which inevitably occur in any system but also prevents open dialogue between those within and outside the Prison Service wishing to improve the quality of training in our prisons and borstals. The ruling that prison officers should not express a view publicly leads to frustration, sterility and inertia. (cited in Briggs, 1975: 22)

The effect of prison secrecy on prisoners themselves has often been to deny them access to even the most basic information relating to their detention (see Plotnikoff, 1986: 18; Loucks, 1993: 1).[100] However, an added problem relates to the complexity and impenetrability of the relevant information even where it is available. Part of the problem stems from the fact that the main piece of primary legislation – the Prison Act 1952[101] – was conceived as an enabling Act, and was intended to confer as much discretion as possible on the Home Secretary (Livingstone and Owen, 1999: 5). Much of the regulatory framework governing prison life is thus contained in the Prison Rules, which are in the form of delegated legislation drawn up and amended by the Home Secretary. Even these Prison Rules provide only an outline framework and, like the Prison Act itself, are designed to maximize the discretion conferred on the prison authorities. The Rules are, in turn, supplemented by Standing Orders (which cover all aspects of prison life) and Prison Service Orders and Instructions (formerly Advice and Instructions to Governors and, before that, Circular Instructions), none of which have the force of law (Creighton and King, 2000: 13–14). Taken as a whole, the legal framework for regulating the prison system has been established not with a view to articulating the rights and entitlements of prisoners but to service the administrative requirements of the prison authorities[102] including the need for flexibility and the desire for protection from both scrutiny and challenge.

Prison reformers have long complained about restrictions on the control of information in prisons, including administrative regulations and instructions governing prisons. Traditionally, many of these were not available to the public, to prisoners, or even their lawyers (Loucks, 1993: 1). Fortunately, the often obsessive climate of secrecy in the past has now given way to a more enlightened attitude on the part of both the Prison Service and the Home Office, at least with regard to the dissemination of basic information about prison life. One milestone was the agreement in 1990 to publish jointly with the Prison Reform Trust a Prisoners' Information Pack which tells prisoners what they are entitled to in language they can understand.[103] Another was the decision in 1999 to allow access to the families concerned to the inquest reports relating to all deaths in custody (HM Prison Service, 2000).

Another product of the traditional climate of secrecy that pervaded the Prison Service was the policy of rigorously censoring prisoners' correspondence, which for many years effectively denied prisoners the opportunity of communicating their grievances to the outside world. As we pointed out in Chapter 1, this explains the popularity of certain forms of prison disorder, such as rooftop demonstrations and hostage-taking, since these are ways of opening up a channel of communication with the outside world that in normal circumstances would not exist. Although the routine censorship of all prison correspondence is no longer practised (following a recommendation in the Woolf Report) except in high-security prisons, some restrictions still remain including a right to prevent correspondence in the interests of good order and discipline.[104] Moreover, oral access to the media is still subject to some restrictions since unauthorized telephone calls to the media continue to be treated as disciplinary offences. The House of Lords decided in 1999 that the blanket ban on oral communication between prisoners who believed they were the victims of a miscarriage of justice and a campaigning journalist was a violation of the prisoner's fundamental rights.[105] However, the key issue in this case was not simply a prisoner's freedom of expression, but the right of access to justice, in respect of which campaigning journalists can often play a critical rôle. It does not necessarily follow from this case, therefore, that the Human Rights Act will result in greater general rights of access on the part of prisoners to the media.

It is not only prisoners who are adversely affected by the restrictions imposed on the flow of information. Prison officers have also been denied access in the past to many of the regulations to which governor grades are entitled. Such attitudes can have serious repercussions, as the Chief Inspector of Prisons' (1984) report on prison suicides acknowledged. This revealed that staff at all levels were unfamiliar with the relevant regulations on such fundamental matters as suicide prevention. Another consequence of the obsessive concern with secrecy in the past is the labyrinthine complexity of the regulations themselves, which we described above.

Much of the credit for the lifting of the veil of secrecy surrounding life in prison in recent years lies with the official Prisons Inspectorate,[106] whose reports have made public a great deal of (often highly damning) information about prison conditions. Although they have also been criticized by some (Morgan, 1985; Laming, 2000: 22) for relying too heavily on subjective impressions as opposed to more objective, transparent and measurable criteria, it would be difficult to underestimate the impact they have had on both political and public opinion.[107] Some credit is also due to the top echelons of the Prison Service itself, who as we have seen are also far less likely now than they were in the past to connive at the culture of secrecy that is still practised by many in the service. Commendable as these improvements undoubtedly are, however, much remains to be done to open up the prison system to outside scrutiny, which is the best antidote to inertia and complacency. A freedom of information charter with suitable limited provision for genuine security considerations would be much more consistent with the commitment to a rights-based Prison Service which we would wish to see.

## The crisis of legitimacy

We argued in Chapter 1 that prisons' lack of legitimacy *for their inmates* – what Woolf called prisoners' sense of injustice – is a key factor in the genesis of prison disorders, and that this crisis of legitimacy is in turn primarily the result of a real lack of justice within the prison system. Woolf's similar analysis led to his central finding that the stability of the prison system depends on the right 'balance' being struck between justice, security and control (Woolf and Tumim, 1991: para. 1.148).

Prisoners' sense of injustice appears to stem not only from a general dissatisfaction with the conditions and regimes that are to be found in most of England's prisons, but also from four specific grievances, which are closely related to each other. First there are allegations of physical mistreatment and outright brutality on the part of some staff. A second source of complaint relates to the allegedly arbitrary and oppressive way in which power is exercised over prisoners even without violence. Third, there is resentment about the perceived unfairness of the internal disciplinary system within prisons. And fourth, these grievances are compounded by the absence of effective and independent mechanisms for securing redress for them. We shall discuss these in turn before outlining our general conclusions on how the crisis of legitimacy within the prisons should be tackled.

PHYSICAL VIOLENCE BY STAFF    The fairly constant stream of past allegations (Boyle, 1977: 174; Scraton et al., 1991: 19)[108] that prison officers frequently physically mistreat prisoners, especially those inmates whom they perceive to be 'trouble-makers', has recently received incontrovertible official confirmation from two authoritative sources. In 1996 the Chief Inspector of Prisons expressed anxiety about the illegal use of force against inmates in the segregation unit at Wormwood Scrubs, and on 6 September 2000 three prison officers had the dubious distinction of becoming the first in modern English penal history to be imprisoned for acts of brutality against prisoners.[109] Between 1 January and 30 June 1999, a total of 44 prison officers (including those at Wormwood Scrubs) were suspended in prisons in England and Wales for a variety of alleged assaults against prisoners. Prior to these revelations, the normally impenetrable shroud of prison secrecy ensured that official confirmation of flagrant brutality on the part of prison officers was exceedingly rare. And even where the veil of secrecy was occasionally pierced, those responsible were unlikely to be made fully accountable, or even identified. For example, following a disturbance at Hull Prison in 1976 several prison officers were ultimately convicted of conspiring to assault and beat prisoners but escaped prison sentences. And in 1992 an inquest jury returned a verdict of unlawful killing on Barry Prosser, an inmate at Winson Green Prison, who was kicked to death by the staff who were being paid to look after him (Coggan and Walker, 1982). So powerful was the conspiracy of silence, however, that no one was convicted for his killing.

Allegations of physical brutality have also frequently featured in the grievances that prisoners engaged in disturbances ask to be publicized. Two examples occurred at Perth (in Scotland) in 1987 and Strangeways in 1990. Although the Woolf Report made no comment on the authenticity of the complaints made by the Strangeways prisoners, it did acknowledge (para. 9.25) that the Prison Service had failed to persuade many prisoners that they had been treated fairly. Even if they are effective in the short run, attempts to maintain control in prisons by extreme physical force seriously damage the legitimacy of the prison régime and ultimately may well prove counter-productive even in control terms.

ARBITRARY AND OPPRESSIVE EXERCISE OF POWER    As we saw earlier in this chapter, the two main methods of dealing with disruptive prisoners (apart from physical force) are based on segregation and transfer. These have given rise to complaints because of the arbitrary and oppressive way in which they are said to be used. Instead of investigating the grievances that may have provoked a disturbance, the stock response for many years has been to isolate 'trouble-makers' by subjecting them to solitary confinement under Rule 45.

The transfer procedure has similarly aroused resentment for the same kind of reasons. As a strategy for dealing with disruptive inmates, it may have seriously backfired in the past. For, as the Woolf inquiry discovered, 'a transfer against the wishes of a prisoner is one of the most resented actions which the Prison Service can take . . . Such transfers can appear to the inmate to be unjust, and, in the way they are effected, may leave deep scars of resentment' (para. 9.34). Many of the prisoners who were actively involved in the disturbances in Strangeways and elsewhere were known to have been transferred there recently from other establishments. Moreover, social stability within prisons seems to be influenced by the presence or absence of a settled and predictable environment (see Bottoms et al., 1990; Sparks and Bottoms, 1995), in which case frequent and sudden moves for prisoners could have disruptive consequences, quite apart from any specific grievances to which they might give rise.

Until recently, as we have seen, dissatisfaction about transfers was further compounded by the fact that no reasons were given for them and prisoners had no right to contest transfer decisions. Following the Woolf Report the position has improved somewhat as reasons now have to be recorded by the governor on the inmate's record, and inmates should be told the reasons 'as far as is practicable' and 'as soon as possible', although there is no hearing and no right of appeal.[110] Moreover, prisoners still have no right to be informed of the reasons *before* their transfer. The House of Lords has now ruled that all decisions taken in pursuance of the Prison Rules are susceptible to challenge by means of judicial review.[111] However, so long as administrative measures are used to secure disciplinary or security objectives, prisoners are likely to continue to harbour grievances about the absence of further procedural safeguards in the form of hearings and rights of appeal.

THE PRISON DISCIPLINARY SYSTEM    The disciplinary procedures to which prisoners are subject can substantially increase their period of captivity or worsen its conditions, and yet they lack many of the safeguards that are normally associated with judicial processes. Consequently, the prison disciplinary system is generally perceived by prisoners as operating in an arbitrary and unjust manner and has long been a focus for discontent on the part of inmates.

Before 1992 there was a two-tier system for adjudicating alleged disciplinary offences in which responsibility rested either with the prison governor or the prison Board of Visitors, depending on the seriousness of the offence. Prison governors were responsible for carrying out a preliminary investigation into all cases, and also for dealing with the least serious of these (constituting the vast majority). More serious cases were adjudicated by the prison's Board of Visitors. Although supposedly independent of the prison system,[112] members of the Board are appointed by the Home Office and mainly comprise local dignitaries, most of whom are lay magistrates (and therefore partly responsible for sentencing offenders to prison in the first place). The considerable disciplinary powers that were available to both tiers were not matched by the kind of judicial safeguards that are available to those on trial for ordinary criminal offences, and consequently were viewed with deep suspicion and resentment by the prisoners themselves (see Maguire et al., 1985; Prior, 1985: Appendix 11).

As part of its attempt to improve the standard of justice within prisons, the Woolf Report recommended that Boards of Visitors should no longer be involved in the adjudication of disciplinary proceedings, and that there should be a clear differentiation between disciplinary and criminal proceedings. Under the new system, which is closely based on Woolf's proposals, governors can refer to the police conduct which also constitutes an offence under the criminal law (such as assault or possession of drugs), but relatively minor disciplinary offences (whether criminal offences or not) are dealt with by a governor or deputy governor.

The full catalogue of offences against prison discipline is set out in Rule 51 of the 1999 Prison Rules.[113] While some of these also constitute an offence against the ordinary criminal law (for example assault and theft), many fall a long way short of such conduct and are acts that at worst might be considered anti-social. Examples include the use of abusive or indecent language, showing disrespect or being idle or careless at work. However, one of the most vague and contentious of all the rules that clearly lacked the specificity required by the rule of law has now been dropped. This was the so-called 'catch-all' provision contained in the pre-1999 version of the Prison Rules, which forbade 'offending in any way against good order and discipline' (see Loucks, 1995).

A variety of disciplinary penalties is available to the governor, whose powers were substantially increased on more than one occasion by Home Secretary Michael Howard. Since April 1995,[114] these powers include the issuing of a caution, forfeiture of privileges (for up to 42 days), exclusion from associated work or activities (21 days), stoppage of earnings (42 days), cellular confinement (for up to 14 days), and the award of additional days (formerly known as loss of remission, 42 days).

There were 104,000 proven offences against prison discipline in 1999, which yields a rate of 161 offences per 100 prisoners (Home Office, 2000b).[115] The commonest offences were disobeying lawful orders, unauthorized drug use and possessing unauthorized articles (Home Office, 2000b). The most frequently imposed punishments were additional days, followed by forfeiture of privileges and stoppage or reduction of earnings. The average prison population in 1999 was 1,150 higher than it would otherwise have been as a result of the additional days added to sentences.

In many respects the current prison disciplinary system falls far short of the normal judicial safeguards that would conventionally be associated with the imposition of such significant deprivations of liberty, and would appear highly vulnerable to a successful challenge under the Human Rights Act (Quinn, 1993, 1995; Prison Reform Trust, 2000c). Article 6 of the European Convention on Human Rights guarantees the right to a fair and public hearing by an independent tribunal established by law to anyone who is charged with a criminal offence or faces a determination of their civil rights. It seems highly improbable that the current system of hearings before a prison governor would be construed as compatible with the Convention. The governor is far from independent in the eyes of prisoners, the hearings are not in public, and entitlement to legal representation is dependent on the governor's discretion instead of being available as of right.[116]

Another major complaint about the prison disciplinary system used to be that it lacked any appeal to an outside body. The only appeal procedure involved an internal application to Prison Service Headquarters for determination by an Area Manager, but the success rate for such actions was less than 10 per cent (Livingstone and Owen, 1993: 203). However, in 1994, a Prisons Ombudsman was appointed following a recommendation to that effect by Woolf (see below). The Prisons Ombudsman is available as a final avenue of appeal against disciplinary findings, but only after all internal appeal procedures have been exhausted. Moreover, the Ombudsman is heavily dependent on information provided by prison staff in reaching a decision. It is probably still too early to say whether this new procedure will ultimately prove successful in assuaging concerns on the part of inmates about the fairness of the prison disciplinary system or whether it will merely raise their expectations only to disappoint them again.

GRIEVANCE PROCEDURES   Prisoners with grievances can always complain through the official channels and procedures. Before 1990 there was a complex and cumbersome internal grievance procedure which – like the prison disciplinary procedure – evoked precious little confidence in those it was intended to assist. This was again largely because it lacked any provision for independent review, and reserved the sole power to remedy grievances to the governors and the Home Secretary. Moreover, some of the Prison Rules seemed to have been designed to intimidate and deter prisoners who might have a legitimate grievance from pursuing it. For example, before 1989 it was an offence against the Prison Rules to make a 'false and malicious' allegation against a prison officer, which meant that complainants ran the risk of committing a disciplinary offence unless they could be certain of proving the allegation.

Following widespread concern over the perceived inadequacies of the grievance procedure, the system was reviewed by the Chief Inspector of Prisons (HM Chief Inspector of Prisons, 1987), leading to a reform of the system in September 1990. However, the new procedure was only marginally less cumbersome than the old (Woolf and Tumim, 1991: paras 14.321–14.325) and still lacked an independent element. Prisoners had a number of avenues of complaint – to the prison governor, to the Board of Visitors,[117] to the Prison Service area manager, to the Home Secretary, to a Member of Parliament, and to the courts via an action for judicial review – but none of these could be said to be effective in protecting prisoners from injustice and ill-treatment. Those procedures which were internal to the Prison Service were perceived by prisoners as unfair and ineffective, while those which involved recourse to outside bodies such as the courts were expensive, time-consuming, and severely limited in their scope.

Woolf recommended that, as a matter of good practice, reasons should be given to prisoners for any decisions that might adversely affect them to any material extent. He anticipated that this might forestall a number of complaints under the grievance procedure by reducing the sense of injustice to which such decisions often give rise; and also improve the quality of decision-making by deterring arbitrary decisions. Woolf also agreed that an independent element in the complaints procedure was not just an 'optional extra' and recommended the appointment of what he called an independent 'Complaints Adjudicator' who would both act as the final avenue of appeal in disciplinary matters, and also 'recommend, advise and conciliate' at the final stage of the grievance procedure (para. 14.349).

The government accepted the broad thrust of the Woolf proposals on this issue, and in October 1994 – after a delay of nearly two years[118] – the first Prisons Ombudsman (Admiral Sir Peter Woodhead) was appointed. (The current Ombudsman is Stephen Shaw, formerly the Director of the Prison Reform Trust, appointed in 1999.) His main responsibility is to investigate complaints about prisoners' treatment in both public and privately-run prisons including disciplinary decisions, but excluding complaints about convictions, sentence lengths and release dates. All internal procedures have to be exhausted before a complaint can be made to the Ombudsman. His powers are limited to making recommendations and do not extend to the award of compensation, although he may recommend an *ex gratia* payment. The present Ombudsman has a staff of eighteen,[119] which represents a 50 per cent increase in resources since 1994, though the workload is also substantially greater than had originally been forecast and concerns over under-resourcing have still not been fully allayed (Prisons Ombudsman, 2000.)

The early years of the Prisons Ombudsman were marred by a series of serious and damaging disputes over his initial appointment and terms of reference. In May 1996 these were drastically curtailed by Michael Howard, who barred him from investigating ministerial decisions affecting prisoners (*The Guardian*, 9 May 1996). The effect of the public wrangling which preceded this decision called into question the independence of the Prisons Ombudsman, but after a vigorous campaign by the first incumbent, Sir Peter Woodhead, the Ombudsman's terms of reference were restored and have subsequently been extended.[120] Relations with both the Home Office and Prison Service are now said to be on a much more even keel (Prisons Ombudsman, 2000).

Each year the Prisons Ombudsman receives around 2,000 complaints, most of which relate to adjudications and the handling of prisoners' property and cash. But because over two thirds are ineligible, the number of completed investigations is only around 500. Of these, the Prisons Ombudsman upholds the complaint and recommends a remedy in around one third of these cases, though even where a complaint is not upheld, a recommendation may still be made if the investigation discloses a problem affecting other prisoners apart from the unsuccessful complainant. Consequently, approximately one half of all investigations result in a recommendation being made. The great majority of recommendations are accepted by the Prison Service, which represents a considerable improvement on the early years, during which the Ombudsman reported that as many as 18 per cent of recommendations had been rejected, apparently for no good reason (Prisons Ombudsman, 1995).

The advent of the Prisons Ombudsman should, at least, rectify one outstanding defect that has long been associated with the prison system's complaints procedures: the absence of any independent oversight. However, the system does suffer from a number of weaknesses that may serve to increase rather than alleviate prisoners' feelings of injustice. One is the stipulation that all internal complaints procedures have to be satisfied before a complaint becomes eligible, which accounted for half of all the complaints that were received in 1999–2000. A second, related problem is that of delay in dealing with the complaints internally, which means that many complaints relate to events that are more than a year old. A third problem is that some prisons are suspected of placing barriers in the way of prisoners who wish to make a complaint.[121]

There are also some more general factors which may limit the effectiveness of grievance procedures such as the Ombudsman, however formally fair. One is the closed nature of prisons. If an action that is complained of is 'invisible', taking place behind closed doors, it may be impossible for a prisoner to establish that it has in fact occurred. Second, a successful complaint is only likely if it can be shown that a rule has been broken, or that specific entitlements have been denied. In other words, grievance procedures are of limited value where the rules themselves are defective or lack the full force of law: hence the importance of properly enforceable minimum standards and safeguards covering all aspects of prison life. Third, most forms of grievance procedures share some of the limitations associated with the more formal processes of litigation on which they tend to be modelled. The most important of these has to do with the 'all-or-nothing' character of the remedy, thereby eliminating the possibility of a compromise outcome based on a finding that a complainant may have some justifiable grounds for feeling aggrieved even where the rules have been properly observed (Vagg, 1991: 153). (Consequently it may be that alternative approaches to conflict resolution such as mediation, or even collective negotiations, could have rather more to contribute within prisons just as they do outside.) And finally, a further limitation with grievance procedures generally is their relatively narrow focus (Vagg, 1991: 152), since they are primarily intended to deal with individual complaints rather than collective issues affecting groups of prisoners or even the inmate population as a whole. And yet many of the issues about which prisoners feel most aggrieved (for example regarding prison conditions and facilities, or the attitude or behaviour of members of staff) affect them collectively and not just as individuals.[122]

Although the improvements of recent years are to be welcomed, there is a danger that altering the prison system's grievance procedures without attending sufficiently to conditions, régimes and standards, and perhaps above all to the nature and quality of the relationships between prison officers and inmates, will merely raise expectations which cannot be fulfilled (Cavadino, 1994a; Sim, 1994b), leading to a perception that only lip service is being paid to considerations of fairness and justice. The net effect on the crisis of legitimacy could be small, and could even be negative.

### Conclusion: how to tackle the crisis of legitimacy

A recurring theme throughout the Woolf Report is that the attainment of justice is an essential prerequisite if security and control are to be maintained in future. Put simply, intolerable conditions, hostile staff, needlessly harsh régimes and unfair procedures will increase prisoners' sense of injustice and exacerbate problems of security and control. Conversely, better and fairer prisons are far more likely to receive some degree of endorsement (or 'legitimation') from them, with benefits for security and control.

There is mounting research evidence that this is indeed the case, and that the best way to create legitimacy with inmates is to treat prisoners justly, respecting their dignity and their rights. Fairer and better régimes are not only more popular with prisoners, they also encourage them to behave better (Cooke, 1989, 1991; Bottoms et al., 1990: 91; Sparks and Bottoms, 1995). Experience from elsewhere in Western Europe in the recent past reinforces this conclusion. For example, West Germany suffered from riots and other serious prison problems up to the mid-1970s, but these problems have been much diminished following reforms which gave prisoners new legal rights and increased entitlements to home leave. The Netherlands' penal system, which also places greater emphasis on prisoners' rights, likewise has fewer problems of disorder (Downes, 1988; but cf. van Swaaningen and de Jonge, 1995).

However, this is by no means simply a question of giving prisoners *formal* rights and *formally* fair procedures, important though these are. There is always likely to be a significant gap between the provision of formal justice 'in the books' and substantive justice in practice, and this gap will almost inevitably be increased in an institution like the prison which lacks visibility and legitimacy, where prisoners are relatively powerless and where relationships between different groups of inhabitants are in a poor state. Lip-service justice, however formally impressive on paper, will never deliver legitimacy. We need to create an atmosphere and ethos in which prisoners' rights are genuinely and effectively respected, and where they in return afford legitimacy to the institution and behave accordingly.

How is this to be achieved? In our view the conventional approach to regulating life within prisons suffers from many of the same defects as the approach that is typically adopted outside the prison walls: namely, that there is a disproportionate emphasis on *material* rewards and punishments. Liebling (2001: 159) has astutely pointed out that this 'rational choice' model – which is based on a rather crude form of instrumental reasoning – is singularly inappropriate for a group of emotionally unstable and often brutalized individuals. Many prison inmates who pose the greatest 'control' problems have very little control over their own behaviour and most are probably habituated to high levels of material deprivation. Very many inmates suffer from chronic under-socialization, and exceptionally low levels of self-esteem. And yet almost all prisoners have a highly developed sense of fair and unfair treatment and, whatever their perceptions of their own esteem, are acutely aware when they are not accorded the respect to which they feel they are entitled. Not surprisingly, these often highly charged perceptions on the part of prisoners are shaped above all by their personal dealings and relationships with prison staff. When staff act 'unfairly' or unnecessarily punitively, this is likely to reinforce inmates' intuitive perception that they themselves are the unjustly wronged victims of a cruel and vindictive system.

Although it might seem counter-intuitive, an approach that is based on a moralistic rather than an instrumentalist form of reasoning – in which prisoners are treated fairly and with respect by staff who seek to constantly engage and interact with them as fellow human beings – may be more likely to succeed than the more instrumentalist approaches that have so manifestly failed in the past.[123] The approach we favour is best described as a 'relational' one in the sense that the fostering of constructive and respectful social relationships between staff and inmates should be accorded the highest priority.[124] For relationships not only provide the context in which prisoners' perceptions of the way they are being treated are fostered, but also afford the only context in which any kind of constructive dialogue, emotional engagement and behavioural or attitudinal change is likely to be possible.[125] This kind of approach is all too rare within the English prison system. Moreover, as we have seen, most recent attempts at reform have also sadly neglected the state of relations between staff and inmates. Nevertheless, the very few successful initiatives that have been developed in British prisons in recent years have all been founded on a 'relational' approach of the kind we have just outlined.

The best-known of these was the pioneering régime that evolved at the Special Unit which was set up in Barlinnie Prison in 1973 to house some of Scotland's most violent and disruptive prisoners. The régime that evolved at Barlinnie afforded considerable scope for prisoners to plan their own daily routines, and also to participate with others in the day-to-day running of the community (Whatmore, 1987). Despite problems over the years – many of them political difficulties due to resentment of the unit from elsewhere in the Scottish prison system – it appears to have been remarkably successful in reducing the overall level of assaultive and disruptive behaviour on the part of its inmates (Cooke, 1989: 133), quite apart from the part it played in the rehabilitation of Jimmy Boyle, its most notable success story (see Boyle, 1977).[126]

The unit's régime had a number of distinctive features which contributed to its success. They included a relatively high staff–prisoner ratio; an ethos encouraging much less authoritarian relationships between staff and inmates; a regular 'community meeting' that acted as a forum for the redress of grievances, release of tensions and the assertion of non-confrontational group norms; certain privileges not normally available in penal establishments; and last but not least, regular and frequent visiting arrangements enabling contact to be maintained with family and friends. However, in spite of its international acclaim as one of the very few success stories within the British prison system, the Barlinnie Special Unit closed in March 1995 (Bowden, 1995). The ending of this liberal Scottish experiment[127] marked a partial return to the failed policies of the past, and a revival of more austere isolation and control units including the recommissioning of the notorious 'cage' cells at Inverness for prisoners who are considered to be particularly recalcitrant.

Exceptional though it was, the Barlinnie unit was not a unique outpost of enlightenment in Britain. Grendon Underwood Prison is also run on the lines of a therapeutic community for prisoners with personality disorders,[128] many of whom are among the most difficult and dangerous in the prison system. Selection for Grendon is unique since prisoners must first have been recommended by a medical officer and are then interviewed by Grendon staff to see if they will fit in (Leech and Cheney, 1999: 298). No one is compelled to go there, and inmates are free to return to the general prison system at any time, or they may be returned without consent if they fail to comply with the exacting requirements expected of them. While at Grendon, prisoners are expected to take part in a group therapy process, which teaches them about responsibility and the effect their actions have on other people. They are called to account for their behaviour (by fellow inmates rather than staff), and have to explain their conduct to the community as a whole. Like Barlinnie, Grendon has achieved some notable success stories, including a prisoner who graduated from the strip cells of Dartmoor to Grendon, from which he emerged with 'a different (and far more successful) outlook on life', and ultimately went on to produce the highly acclaimed *Prisons Handbook* (Leech and Cheney, 1999: 102). Nor was Mark Leech's experience unique. A seven year reconviction study showed significant reductions in levels of re-imprisonment and violent offences for those who stayed at Grendon for more than eighteen months after controlling for risk and mode of leaving Grendon (Taylor, 2000).[129] In spite (or possibly because) of its unique nature within the prison system as a whole, Grendon prison has been engaged in a long-term battle of survival within the prison system, and for a long time was denied both adequate resources and appropriate support from Prison Service Headquarters (HM Chief Inspector of Prisons, 1998).[130]

A third 'beacon of enlightenment' within the British penal system in recent years has been Blantyre House, a Category C prison that provides a resettlement function for longer-term prisoners within a relatively open régime. The prison is almost unique in that it enables prisoners to develop and pursue 'personal career plans', which are negotiated with management (Leech and Cheney, 1999: 40). Prisoners are encouraged to grow in self-reliance and self-respect, chiefly through their relations with staff, with each other and with people from the outside community. Indeed, they are expected to work in the community rather than in the prison workshops. Security systems have a very low profile, but violence, alcohol and drugs are not acceptable and result in instant transfer. Moreover, the reconviction rate at Blantyre is just 8 per cent after two years, compared with a rate of 57 per cent for those who left all other prisons in 1996 (Cullen and Minchin, 2000a).

However, Blantyre House has also endured fraught relationships with senior management within the Prison Service for a number of years,[131] and had previously been threatened with closure. Then, on 5 May 2000 both the governor and deputy governor of the prison were abruptly removed from their posts and replaced, just hours before a heavy-handed and badly botched raid on the prison was carried out by 84 prison officers in full riot gear accompanied by 'sniffer dogs'. A devastating report on the raid by the House of Commons Home Affairs Select Committee (2000) condemned the raid. It was also highly critical of the attempts made by the Prison Service to mislead the Committee itself, the media and also the public as to the purpose of the raid and the significance of what was found. One clue to the real motive that lay behind the raid lay in press reports suggesting that the Director General of the Prison Service believed that the former governor 'had allowed the balance to slip between progressive methods . . . and the need for security'.[132] Once again, the Blantyre House fiasco serves as an unwelcome reminder of the Prison Service's enduring capacity to snatch failure from the jaws of success, and its chronic inability to learn even from its own all-too-rare successes, let alone its much more numerous failures.

To give credit where it is due, significant moves have been made in the last few years[133] to try to improve conditions and arrangements for prison inmates. But in conclusion, if we are to create legitimacy within prisons we need to alter régime methods, atmospheres, attitudes and relationships as well as the formal entitlements of prisoners. And one additional, inescapable issue is that of resources. For example, one vital factor in the success of the Barlinnie Special Unit was its high staff/inmate ratio, which facilitated positive relationships while also maintaining necessary levels of security and control. More generally, it will be impossible to give prisoners effective entitlements to decent conditions without the material resources required. Consequently there can be little chance of successfully implementing reforms in anything more than small pockets within the prison system while an acute crisis of penal resources prevails. At present this crisis is set to worsen further as the prison population continues to soar. This trend needs to be forcibly reversed if we are ever to progress towards the goal of just and legitimate confinement, rather than travel (in Judge Tumim's words) along the road to the penal concentration camp.

## NOTES

1　In 1999, just under 80,000 of the 341,700 people sentenced for indictable offences were given custodial sentences (23.4 per cent of the total), compared with 97,700 (28.6 per cent) who were given community sentences, 92,100 (27 per cent) who were fined and 58,900 (17.2 per cent) who were discharged (Ayres, 2000).

2　Although the proportion of people in prison who have been convicted of more serious crimes (those involving violence, sex and robbery) had been increasing in recent years, the trend appears to have reversed following the 1993 law and order 'counter-reformation'. Around 54 per cent of the male sentenced population and 72 per cent of the female sentenced population who were held in prison on 30 June 1999 had been convicted of offences other than those involving violence, sex and robbery (calculated from Cullen and Minchin, 2000a: Table 1).

3　The cost of imprisonment itself varies according to the type of institution. In 1999 the average annual cost of a prison place was £22,649, though this ranged from £14,505 in the case of an open prison to £34,383 for a maximum security 'dispersal' prison (Prison Reform Trust, 2000a).

4　See also Matthews (1999).

5　This function of imprisonment was perhaps particularly evident during Conservative Party conferences during the 1980s and 1990s, when the announcement of prison building programmes, increased sentences of imprisonment and restrictions on parole provided successive Tory Home Secretaries with an opportunity to court popularity. But of course a similar analysis can also be applied to announcements of new 'tough' measures by governments of any political stamp.

6　The Prison Rules form part of the regulatory framework for the treatment of prisoners in England and Wales. They have the status of delegated legislation and are issued by the Secretary of State in the form of Statutory Instruments made under the Prison Act 1952. The first set of Prison Rules was issued in 1964 though they have been regularly updated since then and have subsequently been replaced by a new set of rules issued in 1999 (SI 1999/728; for text see also Creighton and King, 2000: App. 2 and Leech and Cheney, 1999, 2001).

7　The formulation still appears in the Prison Rules 1999, though it has been relegated to Rule Number 3.

8　As defined by the May Committee (May, 1979: para. 4.26) this would require the authorities to:

a)　create an environment which can assist [prisoners] to respond and contribute to society as positively as possible;

b)　preserve and promote their self respect;

c)　minimize, to the degree of security necessary in each particular case, the harmful effects of their removal from normal life;

d)　prepare them for and assist them on discharge.

9　Fitzgerald and Sim (1980: 82–3) dismiss 'humane containment' as mere 'zoo-keeping'.

10　See HM Prisons Corporate Information page on the Prison Service website at www.hmprisonservice.gov.uk/corporate/dynpage.asp?Page=26

11　See HM Prison Service (2000). We will deal with these indicators and the extent to which they have been achieved in the sections that follow. However, well-founded doubts have been raised concerning both the reliability of the KPI performance data, and even the validity of the indicators themselves, since others might advocate different goals for the Prison Service (Prison Reform Trust, 2000d).

12 Woolf referred approvingly (para. 10.39) to the concept of 'dynamic security', which is the idea that there is a close link between the nature of a prison régime – and the way the Prison Service discharges its various rôles – and the risk of disruptive behaviour by prisoners. See also Dunbar (1985).

13 See, for example, Player and Jenkins (1994: 11–14); Harding and Koffman (1995: 245).

14 He was particularly critical of Woolf's support of modern 'paramilitarist' techniques of 'Control and Restraint'. See below.

15 See Levenson (2000) and Prison Reform Trust (2000b) for a summary of the main Woolf proposals and an assessment of the progress to date in implementing them.

16 See also Prison Reform Trust (2000c); Arnott and Creighton (2000: 35–6).

17 Category A status is the only one that can apply to all types of prisoners, whether male, female, juvenile, sentenced or remand. Following a helicopter escape from Gartree in 1988, Category A prisoners are now assigned to one of three further sub-categories: 'standard risk', 'high risk' or 'exceptional risk'. The category to which an inmate is assigned can make a considerable difference to the type and location of penal establishment in which they are likely to be held, and also the kind of régime to which they are subjected. See Creighton and King (2000: 58) for details.

18 Unsentenced prisoners are automatically assigned to the B category, unless provisionally placed in Category A. Sentenced male prisoners are first held in an observation, classification and allocation unit of a local prison or remand centre before being assigned to a category and allocated to an appropriate institution.

19 All prisoners who are held in open prisons have to be in Category D, though these constitute less than 10 per cent of the total prison population. In addition, prisoners who either have escaped, or have attempted to, or who are believed to be planning to escape may be placed on a supplementary 'Escape' or 'E List', which will also affect the kind of prison in which they may be held (Fitzgerald and Sim, 1982: 46; Adams, 1994: 151; Creighton and King, 2000: 55).

20 The five dispersal prisons, used to house long-term convicted adult male prisoners, are Full Sutton, Frankland, Long Lartin, Wakefield and Whitemoor. Another four prisons (Belmarsh, Doncaster, Durham and Woodhill) are principally local prisons. Of the latter, the first pair provide maximum security remand facilities, while the latter pair contain close supervision centres which we will discuss further below. In addition, Durham (a male local prison) contains a high-security wing for female prisoners.

21 At the turn of the century there were 137 prisons in England and Wales (Chapman and Niven, 2000).

22 The female prison estate currently comprises five closed prisons, four local prisons, three open prisons and one remand centre plus four female wings in male establishments. Offenders aged from 15 to 20 have until now mostly been housed in young offender institutions (YOIs), consisting of 15 closed and two open YOIs; there are also so far three secure training centres for persistent offenders aged 12 to 14. Young offenders under the age of 18 sentenced to Detention and Training Orders will in future be sent to a completely separate system of custodial institutions, while 18–20 year-olds will in future be housed in adult prisons, following the dismantling of the YOI system. (See Chapter 9.)

23 Prison Service Security Group (1996); Prison Reform Trust (1999a).

24 Figures cited in a speech by the then Home Secretary, Kenneth Baker, to the Prison Reform Trust on 18 July 1991.

25 Parliamentary Answer by Baroness Blatch on 13 July 1995.

26 HM Prison Service (2000). Nevertheless, the Prison Service failed to meet its KPI target for the number of escapes for 1999–2000, since the 30 escapes from prisons

and 8 from prison service escorts produced an escape rate of 0.059 per cent of the average prison population against a target of 0.05 per cent.

27  In February 1997 there were approximately 900 Category A prisoners, which is roughly 1.5 per cent of the total prison population.

28  These include double security fences, barbed wire, geophonic alarms, high-mast flood-lighting, perimeter defence forces, dog patrols, VHF radio systems, emergency control rooms and radio links with local police stations.

29  HM Chief Inspector of Prisons (1997a) expressed concern that the Prison Service was divided into two distinct parts: 'the "haves" of the dispersal estate . . . and the "have nots" (all the other establishments), who have neither the same resources, nor the same dedicated functional direction and management'.

30  Learmont also proposed establishing a single new 'control' prison for particularly disruptive prisoners (see below).

31  Achieved by a policy of 'volumetric control' which largely restricted the number of possessions an inmate could keep in prison to what could be contained within a box of a standard size.

32  In answer to a Parliamentary Question by Ms Ryan on 26 January 1999.

33  Whitemoor SSU holds convicted exceptional risk Category A prisoners, and a High Security Unit at Belmarsh holds remand prisoners who have provisionally been categorized as either high or exceptional security risks, plus a small number of convicted exceptional risk prisoners who are on temporary transfer.

34  Amnesty International (1997).

35  Acheson, D. (1996: para. 4.6). The report was not published, but its main conclusions are reported in Creighton and King (2000: 44).

36  Table 1.1 in Chapter 1 details the increase in the total prison population between 1975 and the present day.

37  A margin of at least 5 per cent is said to be needed to cater for accommodation that is temporarily out of commission (Morgan, 1995: 101).

38  A rather more objective measure of defining overcrowding would relate it to the amount of cell space that is available for each inmate. The European Committee for the Prevention of Torture, Inhuman or Degrading Treatment and Punishment has stipulated that cells of $4m^2$ and smaller are unacceptable, irrespective of their use (CPT, 1993: para. 81; Evans and Morgan, 1997: 674), and that at least $9m^2$ would be required for two-person cells. During a visit to Armley Prison in Leeds in 1990, the CPT considered it 'outrageous' that up to three inmates were held in cells of just $8.6\ m^2$ (CPT, 1991).

39  The prison building programme did not stop there, and in the decade since 1987 the CNA rose from 41,990 to 56,330 (Home Office, 1999: 54), and a further 22 prisons either opened or reopened during the last decade of the twentieth century (Prison Reform Trust, 1999b).

40  This was equivalent to 19 per cent of the average prison population, and means that the prison service failed to meet its KPI target for 1999–2000 of no more than 18 per cent of prisoners held in such overcrowded conditions.

41  Brendan O'Friel, chairman of the Prison Governor's Association, spoke in unusually apocalyptic terms when addressing the Association's annual confer- ence in 1994 (Penal Affairs Consortium, 1995a: 4): 'Overcrowded prisons are unhealthy places, far more likely to turn out embittered, hardened and contaminated individuals. . . . I appeal in the strongest possible terms to those in the rest of the criminal justice system to recognize that if the rise in the prison population continues, the whole criminal justice system could be plunged into chaos.'

42  Alternatively, it may result in inappropriate alternative accommodation being

pressed into service. In the past this has included police cells, converted boats and former military camps.

43 In 2000 the number of prison suicides fell slightly (for the first time since 1995) to 82. The rate per 100,000 also fell from a record 140 in 1999 to 127.

44 See Prison Reform Trust (1997b) for suicide rates in 1988 and 1994. The most recent rate is calculated from figures reported in Cullen and Minchin (2000a).

45 See in particular Liebling (1992, 1997); Liebling and Kraup (1993); and Crighton and Towl (1997).

46 Unaccountably, reducing the number of prison suicides does not feature in the Prison Service's list of Key Performance Indicators, which may provide further evidence of a lack of commitment, and certainly indicates a curious ordering of priorities. However, the Director General of the Prison Service instructed all prison governors to make the prevention of prisoner suicides their highest personal priority for 2001. HM (*Prison Service On-line News Service*, 3 January 2001).

47 See for example Her Majesty's Chief Inspector of Prisons report for 1998–9, where the Chief Inspector referred to three of the most critical inspection reports that he had been obliged to publish, concerning unacceptable treatment of and conditions for prisoners at HMYOI Feltham, HMP Wormwood Scrubs and HMP Wandsworth.

48 Brixton, Wandsworth and Leeds.

49 Though 75 per cent of the local prison population comprises sentenced prisoners, including those serving short, medium, long and even life sentences (HM Chief Inspector of Prisons, 1999b).

50 As with prison conditions, it is impossible to generalize about English prison régimes since many operate constructive programmes that are delivered by committed and well-trained staff, while others are unrelentingly impoverished. Again, it tends to be the local prisons that suffer the worst forms of deprivation in terms of constructive activities, work or educational opportunities or even simply time spent out of the cell.

51 Available on-line at: www.penlex.org.uk/pages/europrul.html

52 A set of Operating Standards covering accommodation, basic necessities and facilities was published in 1994. However, the Standards were not intended to be legally enforceable. The document itself never had a high profile, and appears to have been almost totally eclipsed by the more recent adoption of 'key performance indicators' (see below).

53 Brixton Prison has an unenviable reputation. It was publicly branded by Prisons Minister Paul Boateng in 1999 as the first 'failing' prison in the country and was given a year to improve or face the threat of privatization. Following a snap inspection carried out eight months later, the Chief Inspector of Prisons, Sir David Ramsbotham complained that conditions had deteriorated since his previous visit, and included practices which were 'totally unacceptable in any jail' (*The Guardian*, 31 January 2001).

54 In total an extra £76 million was committed to improvements in education, treatment and counselling facilities and the development of more constructive prison régimes.

55 See in particular HM Chief Inspector of Prisons (1999b).

56 Answer to Parliamentary question on 26 October 1999.

57 Among the starkest disparities, within local prisons the sums range from £189 at Birmingham Prison to £755 at Hull; and within Category B and C prisons from £304 at Featherstone to £1,340 at Blantyre House.

58 Including attempted assault, incitement and assisting another person in an assault.

59 Even on this restricted definition, the average assault rate was remarkably high in certain types of institutions, such as remand centres, where it was 33.5 per cent.

60  See now Prison Rules 1999, Rule 8. They authorize differentials in the amount of money individual prisoners are allowed to earn or spend, the amount of time they are allowed to spend out of cells or in association with others, and the number and frequency of visits to which they are entitled.

61  *R. v. Secretary of State for the Home Department, ex parte Hargreaves* [1997] 1 All ER 397.

62  The changes included restrictions on home leave and temporary release. Prisoners also experienced reductions in their time out of cell, access to educational classes and other facilities in the wake of the security clampdown that followed the Whitemoor and Parkhurst incidents.

63  *Hansard*, 23 March 2000 and *Hansard*, 6 July 2000; also reported in Prison Reform Trust (2000c) and *The Guardian* 29 January 2001.

64  This appears to have been the case in France, for example, where a single improvement – the introduction of colour televisions in cells – has been credited with transforming both the attitudes of prisoners (by increasing their willingness to work, in order to pay for the hire of the sets) and also the problem of disorder (by helping to counter boredom and reduce the level of antagonism between inmates) (HM Chief Inspector of Prisons, 1990b). In England and Wales limited access to in-cell television is now available to certain prisoners as part of the Incentives and Earned Privileges Scheme (see below), which represents a modest relaxation of the restrictions imposed during Michael Howard's era of austerity.

65  Bodybelts were used 95 times in 1995, and fewer than 80 times in 1999 according to prison figures (Home Office, 2000b). The Prison Reform Trust has campaigned against this 'medieval method of restraint', which it describes as inhuman and degrading, as well as dangerous to prisoners. Research has been commissioned by the Prison Service, but not so far published, to help determine whether it should be retained as an authorized method of restraint (Prison Reform Trust, 2000a: 20). Conceivably the use of the bodybelt could be successfully challenged under Article 3 of the European Convention on Human Rights and the Human Rights Act, which might explain why its use is being reconsidered by the Prison Service.

66  Between 1 January and 30 June 1999, a total of 44 prison officers (including 26 at one prison: Wormwood Scrubs) were suspended in prisons in England and Wales for a variety of alleged assaults against prisoners: Penal Lexicon on-line database: www.penlex.org.uk/pages/suspend.html. On 6 September 2000 three prison officers at Wormwood Scrubs became the first prison officers in modern British penal history to be jailed for acts of brutality following a vicious assault against a prison inmate (*Independent*, 7 September 2000).

67  Even Category C prisons experience control problems. See Marshall (1997) for a study of the methods used to deal with these.

68  Restraints – the commonest form of which consists of confinement to a special cell – were used on 1,865 male prisoners and 91 female prisoners in 1999 (Home Office, 2000b).

69  Rule 45 also authorizes the removal of a prisoner from association where this appears desirable 'in his own interests', and is usually used for the protection of vulnerable inmates such as child or sex offenders with their agreement.

70  The period of segregation can last up to three days initially, but is then renewable for up to a month (and at monthly intervals thereafter) provided this is authorized by a member of the Board of Visitors or a representative of the Home Secretary. Requests are only exceptionally refused and can be renewed without limit. The effect is little different from indefinite solitary confinement.

71  The 'special cells' (also known as 'strip cells') in which violent or refractory prisoners may be temporarily housed are often totally unfurnished. In addition, certain designated special cells, which are essentially a cell within a cell, have double doors, opaque windows and dim lighting.

72 Reasons have to be given for the segregation, but may do little to allay a prisoner's sense of grievance since they may simply state that the inmate's behaviour posed a threat to the smooth running of the establishment.

73 For example in the conjoined appeals of *R. v. Deputy Governor of Parkhurst Prison, ex parte Hague; Weldon v. Home Office* [1992] 1 AC 58.

74 This is known as the Management Strategy for Disruptive Prisoners, and is set out in Instructions to Governors 28/93.

75 Although this represents an improvement on the old procedure, it still only provides a partial safeguard against abuse. The new transfer procedure was itself criticized by the Prison Ombudsman in 1995 after the death of an inmate who had been moved from one segregation block to another 21 times within a two year period (*The Guardian*, 24 March 1995).

76 The control unit was modelled on austere segregation units known as punishment 'cages' at Peterhead and Inverness in Scotland, which are vividly described in Boyle (1977). A second control unit was planned but never used (Liebling, 2001: 128).

77 The unit was bitterly opposed by inmates, and was the subject of an unsuccessful legal challenge, since the courts somewhat surprisingly declined to accept that the conditions in the control unit amounted to 'cruel and unusual punishment'; *Williams v. Home Office* (No. 2) [1981] 1 All ER 1211. The court's questionable insistence that conditions would need to be both cruel and unusual would no longer prevail under the new legal order brought into play by the Human Rights Act.

78 Liebling (2001: 133). The units were based at Parkhurst (opened in 1985), Lincoln (opened in 1987), Hull (opened in 1988) and Woodhill (which replaced Lincoln in 1993). The Units housed around 22 prisoners in 1996, but a roughly equal number of inmates were deemed too disruptive even for these units and remained on indefinite 'Continuous Assessment Scheme' or 'merry-go-round' status (see above).

79 This culminated in the Spurr Report (HM Prison Service, 1996) which was not published, though its contents and assumptions are discussed perceptively and in detail in Liebling (2001).

80 In the post-Learmont era the list of privileges to which an inmate was entitled was very limited indeed, as the following account illustrates. 'Prisoners were unlocked with an SO and 5 officers. They were entitled to one hour's exercise, which was taken in pairs, in separate yards. They were searched before and after, with their hands above their heads. They had few visits, which took place in closed conditions (except legal visits). They were fed through hatches. They had no access to education; and limited access to the library. They could send and receive letters (Liebling, 2001: 139).

81 The system was also severely criticized by HM Chief Inspector of Prisons (1999c) during a thematic review of the CSC system. He complained that the majority of prisoners who failed to progress were consigned to varying degrees of restriction 'with a significant proportion experiencing open-ended, long-term segregation in conditions that equate with punishment'. He was also concerned about the differential effect that such conditions might have on the mental health of different types of violent and disruptive prisoners. See also critical commentaries by Stephen Shaw (1998; 1999) before he became the Prisons Ombudsman.

82 The four main privileges are: access to private cash above the normal set amounts; extra or improved visits; eligibility to participate in enhanced earning schemes; and, for certain groups of prisoners, earned community visits.

83 Unsurprisingly, perhaps, the introduction of the new scheme in 1995 sparked off a protest by prisoners at Full Sutton Prison, which was only quelled with the aid of a prison officer 'riot squad' together with police and other emergency services (*The Guardian*, 16 November 1995).

84  See in particular Sparks and Bottoms (1995) and Sparks et al. (1996).

85  See also Sparks (2001: 166) on the history of penal politics and the 'repetition compulsion'.

86  Estimates vary as to the number of seriously and intractably disruptive inmates. HM Chief Inspector of Prisons (1999c: 2) has expressed concern in this context over the treatment of 1400 inmates who are allegedly dangerous and suffering from severe personality disorders. However, Liebling (2001) has suggested that the really difficult prisoners number no more than 40 (1.1 per cent) of the 3,500 who are housed in the high security estate, which represents 0.08 of the total prison population.

87  These include a crisis of resources, an industrial relations crisis, an organizational or managerial crisis and a crisis of prison officers' 'authority' (see Fitzgerald and Sim, 1982: 11–5). Just as in the wider penal crisis of which they comprise a central element, these crises contribute to a growing crisis of legitimacy within the Prison Service itself.

88  Criminal Justice and Public Order Act 1994, section 127.

89  In January 1999 (unlawful) industrial action over pay was reported in two thirds of prisons which only ceased when the Home Office obtained an injunction in the courts (Prison Reform Trust, 1999c: 3).

90  In April 2000 there were said to be 230 outstanding disputes over management intentions to change working practices alone (Laming, 2000: 16), some of which were over three years old.

91  Cf. Kamenka and Tay (1975); see also the section on the Weberian sociological tradition in Chapter 3.

92  This distinction closely resembles Max Weber's (1968; see also Chapter 3) three-fold typology of traditional, charismatic and 'legal' authority.

93  In the survey of staff and prisoners' attitudes in Scottish prisons carried out by Wozniak and McAllister (1991), a majority of officers (60 per cent) expressed fears about their personal safety, and 48 per cent claimed to have been assaulted by a prisoner.

94  No less than 84 per cent of staff who were questioned in a 1983 attitude survey expressed such a view (see Home Office, 1985b: 57).

95  Narey (2001). The speech is worth reading in full for its frank assessment of the need for a root-and-branch change in the nature of Prison Service culture.

96  This was part of the government's '*Next Steps*' initiative, which proclaimed as its main aims the improvement of efficiency in government and the delivery of better quality services to the public.

97  This attempt to modernize the various criminal justice agencies and the way they are governed is another example of '*systemic managerialism*' which we referred to in Chapter 5.

98  With the exception of high-security prisoners, who would continue to be accommodated in the much smaller number of dispersal or high security prisons.

99  Further evidence, perhaps, of the apparent absence of any institutional learning capacity that appears to characterize not only the Prison Service but the penal policy-making process more generally. Unless a cognitive learning process can be developed for the penal system as a whole it seems to be destined to continue repudiating the positive lessons of the past while unknowingly repeating past policy failures. See also Sparks (2001).

100  For the current position, see Loucks (2000: 2).

101  The 1952 Act has been repeatedly condemned as anachronistic by penal reform groups (see for example, Prison Reform Trust, 1996a). As it was a consolidation measure, many of its main sections date back almost unaltered to the nineteenth

century. It thus takes no account of important subsequent national developments such as the introduction of the Prisons Ombudsman and the adoption of agency status, nor of equally important international developments such as the Council of Europe's European Prison Rules, to say nothing of the incorporation of the European Convention on Human Rights in the Human Rights Act 1998. In short, a wholesale revision of existing prison law is long overdue. This does not mean that it is likely to happen because, cynical but true, successive governments are aware that such reforms win few votes.

102  But not those responsible for implementing the instructions. Lord Woolf referred to the 'confetti of instructions' emanating from Headquarters, while Learmont spoke of a 'blizzard of paperwork'. The Laming report (2000) reiterated the criticism, albeit using more prosaic language.

103  A number of publications are now available including booklets on Lifers, Women Prisoners and Female Young Offenders, Male Prisoners and Young Offenders and Visiting and Contact arrangements. All can be accessed electronically via the Prison Service web-site: www.hmprisonservice.gov.uk/life/dynpage.asp?Page=140. See also Leech and Cheney (2001).

104  In addition, all mail in all penal establishments remains liable to be opened out of sight of the prisoner and scanned for illicit enclosures before it is returned to the intended recipient.

105  *R. v. Secretary of State for the Home Department, ex parte Simms and Another* [1999] 3 All ER 400–25. In response to this defeat, the Prison Service indicated that it would draw up new procedures requiring prisoners and journalists to undertake that they would only discuss matters relating to a possible miscarriage of justice (Leech and Cheney, 1999: 258).

106  Ironically, the culture of secrecy has proved far more resilient among many Boards of Visitors, over half of which failed to publish their annual reports in spite of their official 'prisons watchdog' rôle (see below), and despite repeated encouragement from the Home Office to do so (Prison Reform Trust, 1999c).

107  Possibly for that reason, the Chief Inspector of Prisons appears fated – at least in the current era – to suffer a somewhat strained relationship with the Home Secretary of the day. Reports that Jack Straw was minded not to renew Sir David Ramsbotham's tenure (a fate which previously befell Judge Stephen Tumim when Michael Howard was Home Secretary) despite the latter's publicly expressed willingness to continue in post appeared to confirm a tendency for Home Secretaries to 'shoot the messenger' who bears uncomfortable tidings rather than heeding and acting on the message that is delivered.

108  See for example the allegations of violence at issue in the case of *Weldon v Home Office* [1992] 1 AC 58.

109  *Independent*, 7 September 2000. One officer was acquitted but a further 23 officers who were suspended over the allegations of brutality have yet to stand trial.

110  And see also note 72, above, which is likely to apply to reasons given for transfers as well as to segregation.

111  *R. v. Deputy Governor of Parkhurst Prison ex parte Hague* [1992] 1 AC 58. This case also decided that the administrative procedures for transfer and segregation that had been operated by the Prison Service for more than ten years were unlawful.

112  One previous unsatisfactory aspect of the Board of Visitor system was that their involvement in prison disciplinary proceedings caused them to be identified with the prison establishment. It also required them to perform a dual rôle, and one that was at odds with their other important function, which is to act as a 'watchdog', and as one channel for prisoners' complaints.

113  See Leech and Cheney (1999: 374); King and Creighton (2000: 335). Also available electronically at: www.hmprisonservice.gov.uk/filestore/15_308.pdf

114  The new limits represented an across-the-board rise of 50 per cent in the maximum level of virtually all governors' disciplinary powers.

115  Both figures are slightly down compared with 1998.

116  Although the previously established policy of denying legal representation to those facing disciplinary proceedings was called into question by the European Court of Human Rights in *Campbell and Fell v UK* (1982) 5 EHRR 207, the House of Lords has since refused to uphold a general right of representation in *Hone and McCantan v Board of Visitors, Maze Prison* [1988] 1 All ER 381.

117  One of the primary responsibilities of Boards of Visitors (Prison Rule 77(4) is to draw attention to any abuse of prisoners, but the way many Boards have discharged this responsibility has been severely criticized by the Chief Inspector or Prisons, Prisons Ombudsman and others (Prison Reform Trust, 1998a).

118  The delay was largely due to the fact that Home Secretary Michael Howard vetoed the three nominees originally shortlisted for the post, apparently thinking that they were all too liberal.

119  Personal communication.

120  The Ombudsman's remit will in future also encompass those on community penalties and those who are subject to supervision on licence (Prisons Ombudsman, 2000: 3).

121  The Ombudsman has referred to at least one prison in which it is necessary to 'apply for a form for a form for a form', and has lamented the under-representation of complaints from younger prisoners and women prisoners, pointing out that not a single complaint has been received from at least two young offender institutions since the Prisons Ombudsman was established in 1994 (Prisons Ombudsman, 2000).

122  There is no intrinsic reason why this should be the case. Other jurisdictions, notably the United States, have developed procedures such as the 'class action' which enables similar cases to be dealt with as a single action with implications for all the members of the class in question. Courts in the United States have also been prepared to adopt a more activist approach in relation to complaints about prison life, in which they are prepared to consider complaints about, for example, prison conditions and their effects in the aggregate, and not just the impact of a grievance on an individual (Vagg, 1991: 153).

123  Liebling (2001: 160) reaches very similar conclusions with regard to the most difficult and intractable group of prisoners who are housed in the close supervision centres we discussed above. We believe that the same also holds true of the great majority of prison inmates throughout the entire system.

124  This type of approach has much in common with the restorative justice approach that we have described elsewhere. The Relationships Foundation has developed a 'Relational Audit' to assess the quality of relationships within prisons. To date audits have been conducted in one Scottish prison in 1994 (Scottish Prison Service, 1994) and one London prison (Prison Reform Trust, 1997c).

125  The approach has much in common with the kind of '*social crime prevention*' techniques (see Tremblay and Craig, 1995; Hope, 1995; Tonry and Farrington, 1995) that have been developed for use in schools; for example via personal and social education programmes.

126  See also the evaluation of a comparable unit at Shotts Prison in Scotland, which was likewise based on the adoption of a similar therapeutic model (Bottomley, et al., 1994).

127  The somewhat similar unit at Shotts Prison also merged with the rest of Shotts

Prison in April 2000, as part of a 'rationalization' of the Scottish prison estate (Scottish Prison Service, 2000). Another relatively enlightened outpost within the English prison system, Parkhurst C wing, was also closed after it fell victim to the security clampdown following the 1995 prison breakouts.

128 Or, more precisely, five separate therapeutic communities within the one prison.

129 These findings, using a 'control group' methodology, broadly replicated those of an earlier four-year reconviction study at the same prison (Marshall, 1997). See also Genders and Player (1995).

130 There are signs that Grendon's 'pariah' status within the rest of the Prison Service may finally be coming to an end, since a special therapeutic unit is also planned for a new (private) prison for Category B and C prisoners in Staffordshire.

131 The former governor admitted that 'bullying' by his Area Manager was one way of describing their relationship (House of Commons Home Affairs Select Committee, 2000).

132 Penal Lexicon 'What's New Page', 26 July 2000.

133 Most of which (apart from the introduction of the Prisons Ombudsman and the ending of 'slopping out') have been instituted by the New Labour government in the period after 1997. However, even under New Labour, the implementation of the full Woolf agenda of reforms seems as remote as ever.

# 7

# Prison Privatization: Panacea or Pandora's Box?

In the late 1980s and early 1990s the seemingly relentless rise in prison numbers had the initial effect of tempering the Conservative government's instinctive law and order preferences with a much more pragmatic approach (see Chapter 11). One of the clearest manifestations of this was its continuing support for bifurcatory measures designed to restrict the use of custody for less serious offenders while advocating the full force of the law to be directed against 'the real villains'. Both the promotion of alternatives to imprisonment, which we dealt with in Chapter 5, and the alterations to early release procedures which are dealt with in Chapter 8, illustrate the influence of pragmatic considerations on the shaping of penal policy during this period. Around the same time, however, a new option began to take shape which not only chimed in perfectly with the government's ideological predilections but appeared to offer a practical solution to many of the problems confronting the penal system. They included the need to greatly increase prison capacity, and also improve its standards; the need for more flexible and accommodating working practices on the part of prison and probation staff and the need for greater accountability from those responsible for running prison services. The claim that all this could be achieved at substantially reduced costs simply by encouraging greater private sector involvement in the delivery of penal policy came increasingly to be seen by some[1] as a 'quick-fix' solution to many of the penal system's most pressing problems.

Unfortunately, the claims advanced on behalf of 'technical fixes' (Sparks, 1994) rarely withstand closer scrutiny and, as we shall see, this is also the case with prison privatization. Not only is the policy unlikely to deliver the more extravagant benefits proclaimed by its supporters, but it also raises some very serious ethical, political and practical issues of its own that have not yet been adequately addressed by penal policy-makers. In the sections that follow, we will begin by discussing the meaning of privatization and the various forms it can take. We will then briefly sketch its recent resurgence in England and Wales and the factors that have contributed to it. Our primary aim, however, will be to assess (in the light of the evidence that is currently available) the extent to which prison privatization is likely to offer a solution to the interconnecting crises we described in Chapters 1 and 6.

## MEANING AND FORMS OF PRIVATIZATION

Privatization involves 'the systematic transfer of government functions and programs into the private sector' (Adam Smith Institute, n.d.: 17–18).[2] The first candidates for privatization comprised previously nationalized industries that were involved in the manufacture of goods,[3] followed by some of the former public utilities (telecommunications, gas, electricity and water) that are responsible for providing major public services. It was not long before some on the right began calling for an extension of the policy into the social sphere, including the delivery of punishment (Adam Smith Institute, 1984; Young, 1987) and other aspects of the criminal justice system including certain police functions and even some court services.

Private sector involvement in the penal system may take a variety of forms. In the case of prisons, it could in theory extend to selling off the entire prison system as a going concern, which was the approach adopted for many of the other formerly state-owned monopolies (Shaw, 1989: 56). In practice, however, the government has so far opted for a more limited form of private sector involvement, comprising the 'contracting out'[4] of specific functions to private operators in relation to individual institutions. There are at least five distinct sets of functions relating to the activities of the prison service that could in principle be contracted out in this way.

First there are the various *ancillary* services which do not form part of the 'core function': activities such as catering, education, health care, prison workshops and farms, and also prison escort services. A great many prison ancillary services have now been contracted out both in the United Kingdom and elsewhere. A second function involves the *design and construction* work for new prisons, rather than relying on in-house services as in the past. A third relates to the *financing* of new prisons – by raising money through investments, private loans or the stock market – as an alternative to directly using taxpayers' money. This has become increasingly common in the United States, where voters' demands for more punitive sentences have not always been matched by a willingness to pay for these out of current revenue (Shichor, 1995: 142–6). Fourth, the most controversial form of contracting out to date involves the *management and operation* of all or part of an entire institution. We describe the extent to which this has happened to date in England and Wales in the next section. In all the above options, the involvement of the private sector is limited to the *delivery of services* while the government retains responsibility for allocating the contract, monitoring its performance and also determining prison policy at least at a strategic level (and, of course, ultimately footing the bill through contractual payments to the private firms). In theory at least, a fifth option might be to contract out some of these functions as well.[5]

Finally, a useful distinction is sometimes drawn regarding the 'depth of penetration' by the private sector into the 'prisons market'. This refers to the kind of institutions that may be considered suitable for privatization. These vary considerably from so-called 'shallow-end' institutions – which are those housing relatively low security-risk inmates such as juveniles, remand prisoners and those in open prisons at one extreme – to those which operate at the 'deep-end', catering in the main for high-risk or even maximum-security adult prisoners at the other. As we shall see in the next section, the tendency has been for privatization to involve mainly shallow-end institutions, at least initially, though in England and Wales both the pace and 'depth' of its immersion have increased rapidly after a somewhat hesitant start.

## A BRIEF HISTORY OF PRISON PRIVATIZATION

Privately run prisons are not just a recent phenomenon. From the Middle Ages to the nineteenth century, the running of English prisons was frequently entrusted to private jail keepers, who received no official payment but were expected to charge fees from their captive 'customers' for the services they provided (Pugh, 1968). These included the provision of food, bedding and fuel, but fees were also charged for admission and discharge (Porter, 1990: 67), and were adjusted according to rank and ability to pay (McConville, 1981: 9). Jeremy Bentham's Panopticon prison proposal (see Chapter 2) was also envisaged as a privately run profit-making concern, and one of the reasons for its failure to secure Parliamentary approval was a fear that it would rely too heavily on the exploitation of prison labour (Ryan and Ward, 1989a: 62a). The capacity for exploitation and extortion on the part of private jail keepers eventually became a target for penal reformers and contributed to the abolition of the fee system in 1815 (McConville, 1981: 247–8).

By this stage, however, private sector involvement in the penal system was beginning to assume a rather different form as a result of the rapid growth of penal transportation after 1788 (Shaw, 1966; Hughes, 1987; and James et al., 1997: 10–11). Convict ships were operated by private contractors, but were regulated by highly detailed specifications set out in contracts drawn up by the British government. Responsibility for monitoring performance and enforcing the terms of the contract was entrusted to government-employed 'surgeon-superintendents' and naval agents, who accompanied each consignment of convicts.

The early history of prison privatization clearly foreshadows a number of more recent types of joint venture between governments and private enterprise in the operation of the penal system. Moreover, some (for example, Shichor, 1995: 43) have argued that the historical experience illuminates a number of potential defects relating to the policy of prison privatization that it would be unwise to ignore. They include, first, the potential for exploitation and mistreatment of inmates by contractors; second, a lack of effective external oversight; and third, the possibility of corruption between government officials, official inspectors, prison staff members and private contractors. As we shall see, the brief recent history of contracting out in England and Wales confirms the wisdom of taking at least some of these warnings very seriously in assessing whether privatization is capable of addressing any of the prison system's current problems. It also provides an instructive, if not particularly edifying, insight into the way that a major shift in penal policy, which has radical implications for the entire prison system, has been formulated and implemented.

Strictly speaking, the recent antecedents of prison privatization in England and Wales can be traced back to 1970 when the government entered into a contract with the private security firm, Securicor Ltd, to operate detention centres at the four principal airports for the purpose of holding the growing number of suspected illegal immigrants.[6] This novel arrangement, which extended to the provision of associated escort services, excited little interest at the time, even though by 1988 nearly half of all detained immigrants were said to be held in these and a small number of other private facilities (Joint Council for the Welfare of Immigrants, 1988: 13, quoting Green, 1989). The next tentative step towards prison privatization appears to have been unrelated to this development. However, it too, was prompted by pragmatic rather than ideological concerns, in response to growing alarm over the use of police cells as temporary accommodation for remand prisoners, for whom no room could be found in the chronically overcrowded prisons of the late 1980s. One temporary expedient which the Home Office resorted to in May 1988 involved the use of the Alma Dettingen military barracks near Camberley. Although the prisoners were guarded by military police and troops, the catering service was contracted out to a small company in Surrey in what has been described as 'virtually the first breach in the state monopoly of imprisonment since "nationalization" of the county gaols and recidivist prisons in the late 1870s' (Shaw, 1992b).

The contracting out of prisons themselves was first advocated in England and Wales in a pamphlet published by the Adam Smith Institute (a right-wing think-tank) in 1984 but was not taken seriously in either government circles or the Home Office at the time. Indeed, Home Secretary Douglas Hurd informed the House of Commons on 16 July 1987 that: 'I do not think there is a case, and I do not believe that the House would accept a case, for auctioning or privatizing the prisons or handing over the business of keeping prisoners safe to anyone other than government servants' (HC Deb. 16 July 1987, vol. 119, col. 1299).[7] By this stage, however, the cause of prison privatization had been taken up by a small number of Conservative back bench MPs and peers who began to promote it with almost evangelical zeal, backed by tireless and ultimately highly effective lobbying by the would-be providers of private prisons themselves. The result was a policy U-turn, the scale and speed of which was only exceeded by the government's contemporaneous law and order 'counter-reformation' (see Chapter 4, above).

One important precursor of this policy shift was a report by the House of Commons Home Affairs Select Committee (1987) which called for private firms to be allowed to tender for the construction and management of custodial institutions, and particularly those in the remand sector 'because it is there that the most overcrowding in the prison system is concentrated'. Their three-page report followed a brief visit by the Committee to visit a number of private prisons in the United States, which 'profoundly impressed' the Conservative members of the Committee.[8] Shortly afterwards, its chairman, Sir Edward Gardner, was recruited to serve as chairman of Contract Prisons, a company founded 'to exploit the new opportunities' (Windlesham, 1993: 288), following his retirement from Parliament at the 1987 General Election. His new appointment set in motion a 'revolving door' through which other senior Conservative politicians[9] together with growing numbers of senior staff formerly employed by the prison service, senior civil servants and even members of the prison inspectorate (see below) were to pass as the momentum towards privatization gathered strength. Thus, a powerful combination of personal self-interest and corporate self-aggrandizement has been another important factor in the recent resurgence of prison privatization, reinforced by a close overlap between the political and commercial interests associated with senior members of the Conservative Party (Windlesham, 1993: 288–9).

The report by the Home Affairs Committee was followed by a much more ideologically partisan report by Peter Young (1987), of the Adam Smith Institute, who advocated prison privatization partly as a means of breaking the 'monopolistic provision' of imprisonment by the state but also, more specifically, to counter trade union influence on prison policy. As we shall see, such ideological considerations have proved crucial on more than one occasion in the campaign to promote the policy. The first real signs of a change in the government's attitude towards privatization came with the publication of a Green Paper in the autumn of 1988 (Home Office, 1988d). This specifically proposed the contracting out of court and escort duties that had hitherto been carried out by police and prison officers, and also recommended an experiment to assess the scope for greater involvement by the private sector in the management of remand prisons. The latter recommendation was partly in response to a dramatic increase in the size of the remand population over the previous decade.[10] Moreover, this sector of the prison estate was felt to raise fewer operational difficulties or issues of principle than those sectors responsible for holding sentenced prisoners. Management consultants were appointed to make detailed recommendations, and a legislative opportunity presented itself in the shape of the Criminal Justice Bill which was being drafted to implement the government's 1991 reform programme.

By this stage, however, the largely pragmatic considerations favouring the introduction of contracting out in relation to remand prisons had become much less compelling following a fall in the overall remand population. Since the proposal was not expected to produce substantial savings, Home Secretary David Waddington's initial inclination was against the inclusion of a power to contract out certain remand prisons (Windlesham, 1993: 297). Before dropping it, however, he sought confirmation from Prime Minister Margaret Thatcher who insisted that the move towards privatization should go ahead.[11] Even so, the original wording of the Bill made it clear that, apart from court escort services,[12] the power to contract out was to be limited first, to remand centres; and second, only to those established after the implementation of the Act. Existing remand centres and prisons housing sentenced prisoners were not initially covered by the Bill. In the end, however, these restrictions were overturned by a 'sub-plot . . . to which at least one Home Office junior minister was sympathetic, and which only came to light as the Bill progressed' (Windlesham, 1993: 420). This involved a back bench Conservative MP tabling an amendment extending the power to contract out any type of prison, whether holding remand or sentenced prisoners, and whether new or existing.

Although this went far beyond official government policy at the time, the substance of the amendment was retained in section 84 of the 1991 Criminal

Justice Act,[13] with the connivance of junior Home Office Minister Angela Rumbold. Nevertheless she assured the House that '[i]f, and only if, the contracted remand centre proves a success might we move towards privatization of other parts of the prison service' (HC Deb. vol. 186, col. 720, 7 Feb. 1991). This assurance counted for little, however, for even before the first remand centre to be contracted out – Wolds Prison – had taken its first inmates in April 1992, Home Secretary Kenneth Baker unexpectedly announced in December 1991 a second candidate for contracting out. This was to be another new prison at Blakenhurst, which would cater for both remand *and* sentenced prisoners.[14] As Lord Windlesham (himself a supporter of contracting out, at least in respect of remand centres) has pointed out (1993: 426): 'To claim that the tendering exercise had been a success in showing how much the private sector had to offer fell well short of fulfilling the undertaking to evaluate the actual experience of private sector management in practice.'[15]

Not long after this there was another even more significant extension to the contracting out policy when it was announced that the management of the existing prison at Strangeways, rebuilt after the 1990 riot, would also be contracted out, though in the event the tender was won by the in-house Prison Service bid.[16] The third private prison – Buckley Hall, near Rochdale – had previously been mothballed but was recommissioned and put out to tender. The next three private prisons (at Fazakerley, Bridgend and Salford) were the first 'DCMF' prisons – designed, constructed, managed and financed by the private sector – which is the model that has subsequently been adopted for all new private prisons. Under these contracts, the private contractors arrange finance to meet the capital costs and only start to receive payments when the first places become available. Thereafter, the Prison Service pays a set fee for each available place over a 25-year period.

In September 1993 Home Secretary Michael Howard announced that the government was planning for about 10 per cent of the prisons in England and Wales (12 prisons in total) to be contracted out during the 'initial phase' of the process, with the aim of creating a sufficiently large private sector to be able to provide sustained competition (HM Prison Service, 1993).[17] At that time it was envisaged that up to seven existing prisons would be contracted out, and a 'market-testing' programme to identify suitable candidates was launched, involving over 20 prisons. However, in October 1994 the Prison Officers Association (POA) successfully complained to the Central Arbitration Committee that they had not been properly consulted about the market testing exercise. The initial result was to seriously delay the whole process, which was later abandoned by Michael Howard, who was said to have been advised that he would be exceeding his powers if he were to grant leases to private companies in respect of properties that he did not own (Nathan, 1996d).

Another setback to government plans to contract out existing prisons was caused by uncertainty surrounding the effect of European Union laws designed to protect the jobs and conditions of workers affected by take-overs and mergers. Under the European Commission's Acquired Rights Directive[18] contractors are obliged to maintain existing jobs and conditions in respect of any contracts they win. Assuming this applies to the contracting out of existing prisons and ancillary services such as court escorts,[19] it would seriously undermine their profitability since this largely depends on contractors being able to reduce the size of both the workforce and the wage bill.[20]

In other respects, however, prison privatization proceeded at an even faster pace under the Conservative government. Thus, by May 1997 the process of contracting out had been extended to include all prison-court escort services, and a wide range of other ancillary services, such as education and some catering services. Of even greater significance was the launch of the Private Finance Initiative in November 1992, the aim of which was to prevent any new public expenditure from being agreed by the Treasury unless the use of private finance has first been considered. In May 1995 the Prison Service appointed a firm of management consultants to find out how much further privatization could be extended under this initiative. The report concluded that the scope was considerable, and recommended that private finance could be used *inter alia* for: major refurbishment projects involving whole prisons,[21] projects for the replacement or refurbishment of individual ancillary service functions (such as catering, prison industry workshops, health care, non-core administration and so on), self contained projects such as new CCTV systems, IT or communication projects. This paved the way for 'Project Quantum', which was launched in July 1996 with a view to privatizing 1200 administrative jobs within the prison service involving finance, personnel and inmate record systems (*The Guardian*, 30 July 1996). The project aimed to save £50 million per annum and reduce the Prison Service's administrative budget by 30 per cent.

Thus, within a remarkably short space of time, prison privatization in England and Wales had progressed from being a seemingly outlandish proposal to a fiercely competitive and seemingly well-entrenched multi-million pound market. For a brief period immediately following the 1997 General Election, the longer term future of prison privatization in England and Wales seemed more doubtful since the victorious Labour party had pledged repeatedly and unequivocally while in opposition, to take private prisons back into public ownership.[22] However, this 'principled opposition' began to melt away within days of the election victory. One week later Jack Straw, the new Labour Home Secretary, announced that he would be prepared to sign contracts that were already in the pipeline if this proved to be the only way of providing new accommodation quickly. Just over one year later he confirmed[23] that a complete *volte face* had taken place when he announced that, in the wake of two internal (and therefore secret) Prison Service reviews, all new prisons in England and Wales would be privately built and run. The reviews were said to have concluded, first, that the option of using private finance to build new prisons while retaining the management function within the public sector was not affordable and did not offer value for money; and second, that the immediate transfer of private prisons back to the public sector could not be justified for the same reasons.

The only consolation offered to the public sector was a commitment to allow the Prison Service to tender for private management contracts when these expired,[24] and over the next four years it successfully tendered for three contracts in the face of competition from the private sector.[25] These individual set-backs for the private sector did not in any way signal a weakening in the Labour government's new-found enthusiasm for the policy of prison privatization as a whole, however. By the end of January 2001 nine prisons were being managed by the private sector (though two of these were due to revert to public sector management), five of which were also designed, constructed and financed by the private sector.[26] A further four 'DCMF' prisons were either in the pipeline or at the planning stage. Moreover, in July 1999 the prisons minister, Paul Boateng had announced that Brixton prison was to be market tested with a view to privatizing it after it was publicly denigrated as a 'failing' prison, and he subsequently indicated that other prisons felt to be failing in terms of régime quality and costs would follow suit (Prison Reform Trust, 2001: 2).[27] Then in December 2001 the Director General of the Prison Service announced plans to sell off to developers a number of the 37 English prisons which are no longer fit for modern use and replace them with larger and more modern facilities. Consequently, the policy of encouraging private sector involvement in the design, construction, financing and operation of prisons in England and Wales now appears unassailable, at least for the foreseeable future.[28]

In this section we have identified some of the main forces that have helped to shape the fast-moving policy developments. In the following sections we will examine the claims that have been advanced on behalf of the policy, and assess the extent to which it is likely to provide lasting solutions to the many pressing problems confronting the prison system which we discussed in Chapter 6.

## PANACEA OR PANDORA'S BOX?

The main philosophical justification for prison privatization derives from the *laissez-faire* free-market economic theories championed by right-wing governments in the 1980s and 1990s. Various economic 'nostrums' are invoked by 'true believers' to support the case for privatizing areas of public provision. (See particularly, in relation to prison privatization, Young, 1987; Hutto, 1990; and Logan, 1990.) They include a reliance on 'free competition' through the market-place as the best spur to efficiency and quality of service, and also as the most effective scourge of restrictive practices and vested (trade union) interest; a split between the producers and purchasers of public services and a rhetorical belief in 'rolling back the frontiers of the state', at least to the extent of reducing its 'social rôle and responsibilities' (Kamerman and Kahn, 1989: 256).[29] To put it crudely, the seductive appeal of prison privatization is that it offers more (prison capacity) and better (quality of service) for less money. On the face of it, however, one of the strongest arguments deployed by supporters of prison privatization is the lamentable and all-too-obvious failings associated with the publicly-run prison service which we documented in Chapter 6. Before examining the specific claims advanced on behalf of prison privatization, we wish to comment on the theoretical foundations underpinning the programme.

First, whatever sentimental attachment some might feel towards a mythical bygone era in which a free and unregulated market supposedly delivered the best of all possible outcomes in response to the laws of supply and demand, such a model is singularly inappropriate today, whether in relation to the provision of social services in general or the practice of punishment in particular. For whatever the position might have been in the past, today there is no such thing as an unregulated market. Instead, the size of the custodial 'market' itself, the nature of the services to be supplied, and also the terms in which this is to happen, including even (to some extent) the identities of the 'players' are all determined by the state, which is quite at liberty to forbid public sector institutions from submitting a bid should it choose to do so. Indeed, this is precisely what happened with both the Wolds and Blakenhurst prison tenders. Moreover, the government has it in its power to alter the balance of advantage between the public and private sectors[30], for example by starving the one of the resources it might need to implement the Woolf reforms across the board, while ensuring that the other is given the opportunity to develop a limited number of 'show-case' institutions, intended to show off the private sector in the best light.[31]

Governments are not the only ones who are capable of 'rigging the market', however. For, as Sutherland (1956: 90) pointed out, 'big business does not like competition, and makes careful arrangements to reduce it and eliminate it'. This is most easily done where there are relatively few powerful corporations, the 'entry price' is high, and opportunities for reallocating the contract are limited, all of which applies to the privatized prisons market. Despite an increase in the number of companies aspiring to join the 'corrections–commercial complex'[32] (Lilly and Knepper, 1990, 1992), the market itself is dominated by a small handful of multinational corporations or conglomerates for whom various mechanisms might be available to limit competition. One is that of price-fixing; another is the taking over of rivals.[33] One danger is that once a government comes to depend on a small number of private companies, it may be 'held to ransom' and have little choice but to pay the higher prices charged to increase profitability. The risk would appear to be even greater where private operators are licensed not only to operate a particular institution but also to build, own and run it, as is now to be the case with all future tenders in England and Wales.

Second, the classical free market model in which the laws of supply and demand ensure responsiveness by the producer to the needs of the purchaser is difficult to apply in the context of prison privatization (Shichor, 1995: 71–3). For instead of the traditional dyadic relationships linking vendor and purchaser or even provider and client, with prison privatization there are three parties to the relationship – the third being the state, which provides the money. At the very least this is likely to distort the 'normal' operation of supply and demand mechanisms. Thus, the inmates for whom the contractor's services are ostensibly provided are not free to shop around or 'take it or leave it' (Palumbo, 1986), and are therefore much more dependent on the contractor than would normally be the case, particularly given their political, economic and social impotence (Geis, 1987). Conversely, the service providers are much less dependent on the 'consumers' of their services for their economic success than they are on their primary customer or paying client, the government. Consequently, inmates may have even less control over their fate in a privatized prison system than in one provided directly by the state itself. At the very least there may well be a conflict of interest between the needs and desires of the parties to this triadic relationship, which underlines the importance of not accepting at face value the free-market rhetoric that is usually used in support of prison privatization.

Third, while the deplorable state of the publicly run prison system has to be acknowledged, it may be as well to remember that the principal reason why it came into being in the first place was because of the excesses and short-comings associated with an earlier era of private provision. It may well be that, as Sparks (1994: 26) has argued, all prison systems by their very nature suffer from legitimacy deficits even at the best of times. But then the crucial question raised by prison privatization is not whether it is capable of 'delivering more for less' – though we will also consider whether this is indeed the case – but whether, in the light of the available evidence, it is likely to alleviate or aggravate the crisis of legitimacy, as well as the other pressing problems confronting the English prison system.

### The crisis of resources

On the face of it, prison privatization might be expected to alleviate the crisis of resources in a variety of ways, the main one being a reduction in operating costs as a result of increased competition. Because the use of custody is a labour-intensive practice, the most obvious way to reduce costs would be to take on fewer staff, for example by investing instead in advanced technology such as electronic surveillance systems. Savings could also be made by reducing the level of training for new or existing staff, paying staff less and providing fewer fringe benefits, possibly in conjunction with a derecognition of traditional trade unions. There is evidence that all of these strategies have been pursued in the practice of prison privatization in England and Wales. As we shall see, however, there is little conclusive evidence that private prisons do offer a decisive cost advantage over public ones, and some evidence that even where financial savings are made there may be other damaging 'costs' to the prison system.

The Conservative governments that introduced prison privatization repeatedly claimed that privately-run prisons were cheaper than those in the public sector, and often cited a 15 to 25 per cent cost advantage in favour of the former, compared with their nearest public sector counterparts.[34] Unfortunately, such claims have never been accompanied by the necessary information which would enable reliable cost comparisons to be made. Indeed, one of the main problems bedevilling any serious attempts to compare public and private sector prison costs has been the additional screen of secrecy surrounding the latter as a result of collusive action between government and contractors to deny access to 'financially sensitive' information on the grounds of 'commercial confidentiality' (see below). In the absence of a rigorous, independently conducted comparison of costs, or even the production of sufficiently detailed and reliable data to support them, claims of this kind would at best seem to be premature, and may be positively misleading.[35] Moreover, they are contradicted by conclusions based on several authoritative studies including a number of published comparative evaluations in the US, which has a much longer experience with privatized prison institutions (see Shichor, 1995, chs 6 and 9 for details).

The United States General Accounting Office (1991, 1996) has now undertaken a number of thorough, wide-ranging reviews of the evidence obtained from a variety of empirical studies. These have consistently concluded that private prisons cannot be shown to have a clear advantage over public ones, and that no clear-cut recommendation in their favour can therefore be made. These findings are also supported by other more recent meta-analytical studies (Abt Associates, 1998; Pratt and Maahs, 1999). This cautious line was also echoed by the United Kingdom's National Audit Office report (1994) on Wolds Prison (and the manner in which the contract was awarded). It reported that the Home Office had not expected to make any financial savings from the private sector operation of Wolds prison, and concluded that 'there are difficulties in comparing performance and results and costs with those of Prison Service prisons, if indeed that is a fair basis of comparison'.

The difficulties referred to in the report are well known (see McDonald, 1989; Shichor, 1995) and include the need to ensure that like is being compared with like.[36] Another problem is that the accountancy rules (for example in relation to 'depreciation costs', and also the way capital expenditure is dealt with) may be different for the two sectors (McDonald, 1994: 41). Moreover, the expenditure figures quoted by private prison operators may frequently underrepresent the true costs by omitting ancillary costs such as the market testing and contracting processes themselves. Nor are they likely to acknowledge the costs of various 'hidden benefits' that may continue to be provided by the public sector, such as the cost of utilities, repair of vandalism, and also public support services that might be required in the event of a major disturbance or other difficulties (Shichor, 1995: 140). There is also a risk that private contractors may be tempted to put in unrealistically low bids at the outset, to establish a presence in the market,[37] after which they will seek to recoup lost profits once the government has come to depend (politically or economically) on their services.[38]

What does seem clear is that private prison contractors have sought to reduce operating costs using most of the strategies that we outlined at the beginning of the section, but often these attempts appear to have given rise to additional problems. Thus, staffing levels are reported[39] to be far lower at contracted-out prisons, which have 16 per cent fewer staff per prisoner than those in prisons operated by the public sector. However, several privately operated prisons that rely heavily on the use of controversial high-technology security and control systems have encountered serious operational difficulties. Both Doncaster and Blakenhurst, for example, were subsequently authorized to appoint large numbers of additional staff (Nathan, 1995b: 15), which may be seen as a tacit admission that the original staffing levels had been set much too low.[40] Consequently, the scope for savings is also likely to be correspondingly smaller than was originally envisaged.

Pay and conditions at privately-run prisons also compare unfavourably with the public sector. For example, salaries are 14 per cent lower,[41] and staff deliver 10 per cent more hours on average, as a result of a longer working week, shorter planned time off and lower levels of absence through sickness.

High levels of staff turnover – of around 30 per cent[42] – have also been experienced at contracted out prisons,[43] raising questions about the fitness of some of the staff who have been appointed.

Despite the vigorous cost-cutting strategies deployed by private prison operators, the publicly available evidence suggests that the overall savings to the prison service are nowhere near as great as has been claimed by politicians and private sector advocates. Moreover, the difference in operating costs between the two sectors has diminished quite substantially over the last few years. For several years the Home Office has attempted to compare the operating costs of four privately operated prisons[44] with a number of public sector prisons that are claimed to be broadly comparable, using methodology developed by Coopers and Lybrand (1995). The methodology itself is far from rigorous and is not in any way based on 'like for like' comparisons, so the comparisons need to be treated with considerable caution. For example, the selection of comparators does not take full account of differences in prison age, design and composition, all of which are likely to have a significant bearing on operating costs. Also, the cost measures that are used are themselves highly sensitive to the levels of occupancy in the prisons under comparison.[45]

Three measures are used to compare the operational costs of the two sectors: cost per prisoner; cost per 'baseline CNA place' (the total number of places that the prison is certified to offer); and cost per 'in-use CNA place' (after excluding places that are temporarily out of use because of refurbishment etc.). In comparing the two sectors it is important to note first, that overcrowding will tend to reduce the cost per prisoner measure; and second, that if the prison attracts extra funding for accommodating additional prisoners over and above the CNA (as will normally be the case with privately contracted prisons) this will have the effect of increasing the cost per baseline CNA place. However, the latter can also present a misleading picture unless any cells that are temporarily out of commission are also taken into account (as in the cost per in-use CNA place).[46] Arguably, therefore, the latter measure provides the least misleading and least biased of the three indicators.

Successive reviews (Woodbridge, 1999; Park, 2000) have tended to portray privately operated prisons in a flattering light on the 'cost per prisoner' measure, which in recent years has fluctuated between 11 and 15 per cent.[47] (This is the measure that tends to be highlighted by government supporters and privatization advocates.) On the other two measures, however, the differences between the two sectors have tended to converge in recent years, and in the two most recent surveys the private sector showed little or no saving relative to the public sector prisons selected as comparators.[48] The disparity between the measures is largely explained by the fact that the private sector prisons tend on average to be much more severely overcrowded than their public sector comparators.[49] (Why this should be so is unclear and raises some interesting questions in view of the additional costs to the public purse that are involved.) The convergence between the measures appears to reflect a significant reduction in operating costs in public sector prisons over the last few years. The economic arguments in favour of private sector prison management in England and Wales are therefore far from conclusive and, if anything, appear to be significantly weakening over time.

Turning briefly to some of the ancillary services that have been contracted out, here too the 'promise' that has been held out by advocates of privatization has frequently not been matched by its performance. One of the most striking illustrations of the gap between the two relates to the privatization on 1 November 1997 of the industrial functions of Coldingley prison. This was established in the late 1960s as the first industrial training prison, but at the time it was privatized the industrial facilities were losing around £250,000 per year. Less than one year after privatization, however, the company concerned[50] had incurred losses estimated at £472,200 despite paying the 200 inmates at the prison only £7 per day to make road signs, clothes and engineering equipment (*The Guardian*, 29 January 1999).

On 1 February 1999 the scheme ignominiously became the first prison privatization project to revert to Prison Service control, when the five-year contract was rescinded, and the staff once again became public sector employees. An internal audit report[51] was scathing, accusing the management at Coldingley of showing 'a total disregard for many of the fundamental tenets of government accounting and Prison Service financial policy' (Prison Reform Trust, 1999e). The audit recommended that the company should be pursued for the recovery of hundreds of thousands of pounds, though it is not clear whether it was penalized for breaching the terms of the agreement. However, the Director General of the Prison Service did launch an inquiry into whether disciplinary and/or criminal proceedings should be taken in respect of senior management within the service.

Nor was this an isolated example. For example, Chief Prisons Inspector Judge Tumim's otherwise glowing first report on the (public sector) Woodhill prison at Milton Keynes after its opening was marred only by criticism levelled at the high cost of the private catering contract, which was estimated to be 'far higher than that of employing prison officer caterers assisted by inmates' (Nathan, 1994c: 15). Moreover, plans to contract out the prison escort service for the remaining area in England and Wales received an embarrassing setback in December 1994 when all four private sector bids were found to be higher than the existing costs of providing the service (Nathan, 1995a: 16).

Finally, another major sphere in which it is claimed that private sector involvement can help to alleviate the crisis of resources (apart from its possible impact on operating costs) is in respect of prison building and the way this is financed. However, the rôle of the private finance initiative (PFI), which has been supported by both Conservative and Labour governments since its introduction in 1992, is one of the most controversial aspects of the prison privatization policy in England and Wales. The National Audit Office (1997) anticipated that the first two PFI contracts (to build, maintain and operate for 25 years new prisons at Bridgend and Fazakerley) would yield a number of benefits. They included a quicker construction period,[52] more innovative forms of design and operational methods, and a transfer to the private sector of major constructional, maintenance and operational risks. These were expected to yield aggregate savings of 10 per cent when compared with building prisons using public finance and then contracting them out to the private sector.

Others, however, have been far more critical about the policy, and have voiced deep scepticism with regard to any benefits that might accrue to the national interest (as opposed to private shareholders). Critics include even the *Economist* (28 January 1995), which described the initiative as a 'sham', and 'a boon only for politicians and those businessmen keen to profit from the public purse'. The economic arguments in support of the policy seem far from convincing since the state can always borrow money far more cheaply than private institutions because, unlike them, there is no danger of the state going bankrupt or reneging on its debts. However, it will be expected to pay a considerably higher return on the money that is borrowed on its behalf by those private institutions,[53] even though the element of 'risk' they assume is in reality largely illusory (since the government would almost certainly be obliged to step in and underwrite the contract if anything went seriously wrong with the performance of the contract).

In spite of the negligible real risks to the private sector, the consortium that was awarded the PFI contract for Fazakerley prison succeeded in refinancing the project in November 1999, four years into the contract. The effects of this deal were spectacularly good for the consortium's shareholders, since their profits were expected to increase by 61 per cent,[54] and the timetable for repayment of their investments was brought forward (Comptroller and Auditor General, 2000). However, it is much less easy to see whether any commensurate benefit would be likely to accrue to the public sector; or, as the National Audit Office report rather more cryptically put it, 'substantial refinancing gains to the private sector may threaten the perceived value for money of the project'.

The other principal justification that is used in support of PFI is that capital expenditure which is incurred by the private sector does not count against the public sector borrowing requirement,[55] which successive governments over the last quarter of a century have been at pains to reduce, in pursuit of a tight fiscal policy. However, the argument that PFI is needed to ensure that the Treasury meets its (self-imposed) public debt target[56] is unsustainable since it has been calculated that even if all PFI expenditure had been raised in the traditional way, by government borrowing, the Treasury's 'sustainable investment' rule could comfortably have been met.[57] Despite the 'sleight of hand' produced by the Treasury's somewhat arcane accounting rules, the public sector will ultimately still have to pay for the assets and services being provided by the private sector. It will also have to pay for the needlessly inflated debt repayments, plus the sufficiently attractive profit margins that are deemed to be necessary in order to attract private investment in the first place.[58] 'Efficiency savings' on a truly massive (and, on current evidence, improbable) scale are likely to be required if the public sector really is to benefit from the PFI initiative in the long run. A more likely outcome is that any marginal fiscal advantages which may appear to accrue in the short term will be gained at the expense of future tax-payers. They are likely to find that a growing proportion of public revenue needs to be devoted to the servicing of the PFI debts that were incurred by previous generations of politicians who were taken in by the temptation to commit themselves to additional public expenditure while postponing the day of (financial) reckoning.

One of the biggest objections to the PFI programme thus relates to the 25-year duration of the contract since this will effectively bind successor governments to the policy throughout the period, whatever their views about prison privatization and regardless of subsequent changes in demand for facilities of the type being provided. Indeed, critics of the policy (Shichor, 1995: 158) argue that privatization is likely to greatly *increase* the expansionary pressures on penal policy, because powerful multinational firms will wish to maintain high levels of incarceration and are likely to lobby governments energetically in support of this aim. A more serious and immediate threat (Sparks, 1994: 25) is that private investment may have removed the economic and political constraints on expanding the use of custody, which until very recently have given governments a strong incentive to encourage sentencers to treat prison places as a scarce resource. Indeed, the government's 1993 'law and order counter-reformation' may in part have reflected a conscious decision to exploit the opportunity thus created in an attempt to build its way out of the prison numbers crisis, by providing more prison places, instead of continuing to preach restraint within the context of a new sentencing framework.

A sobering example of what can happen when an expansionist policy is given free rein is provided by recent penal trends in the United States in general (Shichor, 1995: 10), and the state of California in particular (Bronstein, 1993–4: 8). In 1971, the US incarceration rate of 96 per 100,000 was approximately the same as the present rate in the United Kingdom. Following an unprecedented increase in imprisonment between 1980 and 1990, however, the number of prisoners in state and federal institutions grew by 134 per cent, and the incarceration rate per 100,000 increased from 139 in 1980 to 292 a decade later. In California the number of adult prisoners increased from 22,600 in 1980 to nearly 110,000 by 1993, an increase of almost 500 per cent over 13 years. During that period almost 14 billion dollars was spent on new prison construction, while state funding for the public school and higher education systems was drastically reduced. In spite of such massive expenditure, prisons were even more overcrowded by the end of the period than they were at the beginning (60 per cent compared with 50 per cent); and crime had also gone up dramatically during this period. The American experience contains a serious warning for advocates of privatization in Britain and elsewhere. For although privatization may expand the spatial capacity of an overloaded public prison system, it also expands the punitive capacity of the state and, such is the demand for custody, it is most unlikely to alleviate the resurgent problem of prison overcrowding (see below).

With regard to the crisis of resources it would thus be fair to say that attempts by private prison contractors to drive down operating costs have not yet provided convincing proof that the private sector is able to achieve significant cost savings compared with the public sector. They have also demonstrated that the strategy of cost reduction has created additional problems of its own, some of which we will consider more fully in the sections that follow.

### The crisis of containment

At first it seemed unlikely that 'security issues' would pose much of a problem for contracted out prisons since it was originally intended that they would only house remand prisoners, and indeed the regime at Wolds prison was initially designed specifically with this group of prisoners in mind.[59] However, problems were experienced from very early on in delivering such a régime since, notwithstanding their *legal status*, the social *reality* in practice was that the vast majority of inmates were not only factually guilty of the offences for which they were facing trial (or sentence), but many also had previous experience *as prisoners* (James and Bottomley, 1998: 226).[60] The problems experienced by this dissonance between legal status and social reality posed a number of early control problems, and resulted in some early modifications to the régime at Wolds (see below), but a combination of external factors was to have an even greater impact. They included the massive contemporaneous increase in prison numbers, the associated policy decision to alter the status of Wolds to enable it to take sentenced as well as remand inmates, the rapid extension in the scope of prison privatization and the security clampdown following the Whitemoor and Parkhurst escapes. The sudden expansion of private sector involvement to include sentenced prisoners also put paid to the idea that Wolds was a test-bed for developing a new approach for dealing with remand inmates, and inevitably influenced the design of the next series of privately managed prisons, with regard to both their physical and dynamic aspects.

Once the policy of prison privatization was extended to cover sentenced prisoners the first of the contracted out prisons were initially intended to house mainly relatively low security risk inmates. However, they were by no means confined exclusively to 'shallow-end' institutions (see above), and by the end of 2002, privately managed prisons will encompass a wide range of prison types, including local and training prisons, one designated exclusively for female inmates (Ashford to the south west of London), one designated exclusively for young offenders (Ashfield, near Bristol) and one containing a 'Grendon-style' therapeutic community (see Chapter 6) (Dovegate in Staffordshire). The only major category that is missing consists of high-security or dispersal prisons, though Doncaster prison started to become a Category A local prison during 1997–8, and had achieved full category A status by 1998–9 (Park, 2000: 5). The Learmont Report, which was set up in the wake of the crisis of containment in the mid-1990s felt it would be inappropriate 'for the foreseeable future' for privatization to be extended to parts of the prison estate including the dispersal or high-security sector. Learmont also felt it would be inappropriate for his proposed maximum security and control prisons (see Chapter 6) to be privately run. However, the House of Commons Home Affairs Committee (1997) has subsequently adopted a somewhat softer line. It suggested that 'while no absolute bar should be placed on the management of high risk prisons by private companies, progress toward this should follow a cautious, step-by-step approach'. Given the rate at which the policy has been extended across the rest of the prison estate, such a move cannot be ruled out in future, even though the need for very high levels of staff and security would presumably diminish still further the scope for significant savings.

Although containment is now much less of an issue for the Prison Service in general than it was in the wake of the high profile escapes of the mid-1990s the private sector has had its share of security problems, albeit of a less dramatic nature. The problems have been most acute at Buckley Hall, which experienced an unusually high number of prisoners absconding from leave during 1994 and 1995 (Nathan, 1996a). In October 1995 the Home Office controller[61] expressed concern to Group 4 who were responsible for operating the prison (Nathan, 1996b). Further escapes took place during 1996, including one which was recorded by a television crew who happened to be filming at the prison at the time.[62] Group 4 was warned (but was not subjected to a financial penalty), and agreed to upgrade security at its own expense.[63]

### The prison numbers crisis and the problem of overcrowding

We have already explained that, far from being a solution to the prison numbers crisis, the policy of prison privatization is likely to make it very much worse by removing the fiscal and political constraints that formerly acted as an effective brake on rampant prison expansionism.

When the first privately operated prison, Wolds, came into operation in April 1992, prison numbers (including both remand and sentenced prisoners) had been falling. Indeed, with roughly as many cells available as there were prisoners the problem of prison overcrowding was no longer so acute as to necessitate the new capacity provided by private prisons. As we have seen, the principal impetus behind the programme at that time was ideological rather than operational. For a short time Wolds was intended to operate as an experimental show-case to pilot a prison régime designed specifically for remand prisoners[64] (James and Bottomley, 1998: 225). By mid-1994, however, the prison population was once again growing rapidly and was already breaking new records. This was one of the main reasons that lay behind the decision to fully 'incorporate' Wolds into the public-sector prison system, and also to open it up to sentenced as well as remand inmates,[65] since it could then help to alleviate the increasingly chronic overcrowding problems in the rest of the system. The effect on Wolds was dramatic. Its CNA was increased, and the number of single cells was reduced, which exposed Wolds for the first time to the 'scourge' of overcrowding from which it had initially been protected. The change was noted in the third annual report of the Wolds Board of Visitors (1995), which drew attention to 15 per cent overcrowding, and which necessitated some prisoners to be housed three to a cell, resulting in an inevitable deterioration in standards (see below).

As for the other privately operated prisons that came on stream after Wolds, provision for a degree of overcrowding was incorporated into their operating contracts from the outset. Consequently, they have been no less immune to the problem of overcrowding than the rest of the system, in spite of the additional charges that are liable to be incurred when additional prisoners are admitted in excess of CNA. Indeed, each of the four privately operated prisons that have featured in the Home Office's annual review of comparative costs and performance was substantially more overcrowded in 1998–9 than any of the public sector prisons selected as comparators.[66] Another new private prison, Altcourse at Fazakerly, which is a DCMF prison that opened in December 1997 with a CNA of 600, had an average of 416 inmates sharing cells in 1998–9 (Nathan, 2000a). It is clear that privately operated prisons are no less liable to overcrowding than their public sector counterparts. In many cases they appear to be even more susceptible, though it is not at all clear why this should be so in view of the additional cost to the public purse.

### The crisis of conditions

In Chapter 6 we analysed the crisis of conditions within the English prison system in terms of the following three elements: physical conditions and facilities; régimes and activities; and the nature of the various sets of social relationships that exist within a prison setting.[67] Supporters of prison privatization claim that it is capable of delivering not only cheaper, but also better quality conditions and services than publicly-run prisons. In this section we will assess these claims in respect of the same three elements in the light of the available evidence. In doing so we will draw on two principal sources. One is the evaluation of Wolds prison (James et al., 1997), which was also the first, and is to date the most thorough attempt to compare privately operated prisons with comparable ones in the public sector.[68] The second is the annual Home Office review exercise (Woodbridge, 1999; Park, 2000), which also compares four privately operated prisons with a range of public sector 'comparators', not just in terms of their comparative costs but also in terms of a variety of other key performance indicators. The latter include the number of hours unlocked on weekdays, time spent on purposeful activities, number of accredited courses available and rate of assaults. Finally, we will also examine the incidence of suicides in privately operated prisons, since as we suggested in Chapter 6, this is one barometer of the scale of the continuing crisis of conditions within Britain's prison system.

PHYSICAL CONDITIONS   In terms of their physical conditions, there is undoubtedly a huge contrast between privately operated prisons and the older public sector prisons housing similar categories of inmates. However, there is much less to choose between the conditions and facilities in the newer prisons across the public–private sector divide, which provides a far more valid comparison. James et al. (1997: 135) reported that *all* the new prisons in their survey provided markedly superior conditions and facilities than those experienced elsewhere in the prison system. In general, they suggest that the balance sheet allows few simple conclusions to be reached about the advantages or disadvantages associated with private sector as opposed to public sector prison management. Prisoners at Wolds appeared to rate the physical conditions at Wolds somewhat more highly than did those at Woodhill, particularly regarding the food. However, the overcrowding at Wolds is known to have resulted in a deterioration in the standards available compared with when the prison first opened (James and Bottomley, 1998: 230). The same may well be true of other privately operated prisons, several of which, as we have seen, now experience considerably higher levels of overcrowding than many other broadly comparable public sector prisons, or indeed Wolds itself.

RÉGIMES AND ACTIVITIES   One distinctive feature of contracted-out prisons, at least in the early days, was that their operating contracts contained some very detailed specifications relating to their régimes and the way these were to be delivered. In many cases these compared very favourably with their public sector counterparts, notably with regard to the amount of time prisoners spend out of their cells. In Wolds prison, for example, Group 4 was initially required to provide 15 hours out of cell for all inmates, which was unprecedented – at least in respect of untried inmates, who normally experience the worst conditions in the whole prison estate. Over time, however, these early differentials have decreased markedly. This is partly a result of the adoption of 'key performance indicators' across the prison service, which has obliged the public sector prisons to considerably 'raise their game'. However, it may also reflect a gradual erosion of standards in privately operated prisons like Wolds since their inception. Thus in 1998–9, Wolds was only providing an average 11.7 hours per day out of cells (Park, 2000: 19), and two of the other contracted-out prisons in the Home Office comparative review were providing less than this. Indeed Doncaster's 10.3 hours not only fell well short of its 12 hours target, but was also fractionally lower than one of its public sector comparators.

In many respects, however, time spent out of cell is a rather questionable measure of the quality of a prison régime since much depends on the way that time is used. Judge Tumim's remarks about Wolds following a prison inspection are instructive in this respect, since his praise for the amount of out of cell time was heavily qualified by the critical remarks he made about the atmosphere of 'corrupting lethargy', and the widespread drug abuse (HM Chief Inspector of Prisons, 1993c). Although free to spend up to 14 hours a day out of their cells, only one quarter chose to do so, and the educational facilities that were available were not being used.

The number of hours per week spent on purposeful activity, and the form this takes may provide a better guide to the quality of a prison's régime. Once again the balance of advantage does not consistently favour the privately managed sector. In the 1998–9 comparative review Wolds prison managed to provide 29.1 hours per week of purposeful activity for its inmates, which was the highest for any of the prisons in the review. It also provided more hours of education and work or workshop activities than any of its comparators. However, privately-managed Doncaster only managed 17 hours of purposeful activities (less than one of its public sector comparators), over half of which was spent doing domestic work because there is no workshop provision. Moreover, there were no accredited courses for prisoners to follow at Doncaster whereas all three of its public sector comparators offered a minimum of 24 courses (Park, 2000: 15). And while privately-managed Blakenhurst performed marginally better than its public sector comparators on purposeful activities it, too, was outperformed by one of the latter with regard to time spent on education and training and time spent in work or workshops.[69]

SOCIAL DYNAMICS    Finally, as we stressed in Chapter 6, prison conditions and the general quality of life in prison are significantly influenced by the state of relations between staff and inmates. These, in turn, are likely to be influenced by the calibre of staff recruited, the ratio of staff to inmates, and also the quality of training and preparation of the staff. Critics of privatization (for example, Shichor, 1995: 190) point out that all of these factors are likely to be adversely affected by attempts to reduce costs, which may result in the recruitment of lower quality staff, high turnover, inadequate training and preparation and low staff morale. An additional danger is that there may be too few staff to deliver meaningful services, including the provision of constructive activities, or even to provide adequate levels of security or protection for groups of vulnerable inmates. On the other hand, the government confidently anticipated that staff–inmate relationships in private sector prisons would be improved by virtue of the fact that most private custody officers would be newly recruited from very different walks of life. Consequently, they would not be socialized into the stereotypical prison officer culture associated with most public sector prisons.

Strenuous attempts were initially made at Wolds prison to develop a distinctive ethos that was derived from the US-inspired concept of 'direct supervision'. Under the Wolds version, a single Unit Supervisor exercised responsibility for a living unit of 50 inmates (James et al., 1997: 69). A key aspect of this approach was the assumption that effective control was more likely to be achieved on the basis of constructive relationships between inmates and staff than by coercion. We will examine this particular claim more fully in the following section. In terms of its impact on staff–prisoner relations it does appear to have been largely effective, since both staff and inmates identified the quality of these relationships as being one of the most important aspects of the prison (James et al., 1997: 85). Many contrasted the respect shown to them by staff at Wolds with their much less constructive experiences at public sector prisons.

However, there was also clear evidence of similar or even greater innovations in prison management style in some of the recently opened *public sector* prisons, notably Woodhill and Highdown. Thus, Woodhill in particular exhibited a similar emphasis on the value of staff–inmate relations and their centrality to the quality of the prison régime. Staff at Woodhill were particularly proud of their positive relationships with inmates, and a small majority of inmates also felt that the prison was better than others they had experienced. Although inmates at Wolds rated their staff even more highly than those at Woodhill, the latter's achievement was in some respects even more remarkable since it was a far larger and more complex prison, performing a much wider range of functions than Wolds.[70]

Relations with other inmates also have a very direct impact on the quality of life in prison, and here the balance of advantage tends to reside fairly consistently with public sector prisons. In the Home Office's comparative review all four contracted-out prisons were out-performed by most of their public sector comparators,[71] and in some cases the differences were decisive. For example, the 19 per cent assault rate at contracted-out Blakenhurst was roughly three times as high as its two public sector comparators. Likewise, Doncaster's assault rate of nearly 20 per cent was far worse than any of its three public sector comparators, and was more than four times as high as public sector Home House (Park, 2000: 15).

One final and even more sombre index of the quality of prison régimes relates to the rate of suicides. Between April 1992, when the first commercially managed prison opened, and the end of 1998, 21 suicides were recorded in these establishments. In 1998 alone ten of the 83 prison suicides recorded for that year took place in commercially managed prisons, which is a far higher rate than would be expected on the basis of the number of prisoners housed there.[72] The evidence we have reviewed so far presents a somewhat chequered picture. It would be difficult to conclude from this that prison privatization offers an easy solution to the long-running crisis of conditions and, in some respects at least, it may even aggravate it. This also seems to be the case with regard to the crisis of control, to which we now turn.

### The crisis of control

Virtually all privately-managed prisons have experienced serious control problems, at least during the initial period after opening. In most cases the problems appear to have been more severe, and more intractable, than would normally be expected in the case of a comparable newly-commissioned public sector prison. The first privately-managed prison, Wolds, provides a good illustration but is by no means unique. Nor is it the worst example. Although, as we have seen, the system of 'direct supervision' at Wolds largely succeeded in generating constructive relationships between staff and inmates, it was judged to be far less successful in terms of controlling, let alone reducing, the disruptive behaviour of some prisoners (James et al., 1997: 70). One problem stemmed from the adoption of a 'free flow' model, whereby prisoners could not only choose whether or not to participate in the various activities on offer, but could also visit living units other than their own at will. This diluted the effectiveness of the 'direct supervision' concept, and provided an opportunity for some prisoners to steal from cells in other living units, and also to bully or 'tax'[73] weaker inmates. The control problems provoked a wide-ranging review of the concept of 'direct supervision' and the overall management of the prison régime (James and Bottomley, 1998: 228). This was followed by the appointment of a new director and, ultimately, a partial reversal to a more traditional style of control closer to the kind of régimes found in public sector prisons.[74]

Other contracted-out prisons have experienced even more serious control problems, however. At Blakenhurst, for example, the managing consortium (United Kingdom Detention Services) became the first private prison contractor to be fined[75] (£41,166.90) under the terms of its contract with the Prison Service after it lost control of the prison during a disturbance on 24 February 1994 (Nathan, 1994b: 13). Doubts have also been voiced about the level of training given to Blakenhurst staff, particularly following the disclosure that on six occasions in its first fifteen months of operation the prison's operators notified the Prison Service of behaviour calling into question the fitness of individual employees.[76] Poor training and inexperience on the part of Blakenhurst prison's staff and managers were also criticized by the Chief Inspector of Prisons and may have been a factor contributing to a loss of control in February 1994, resulting in £30,000 worth of damage (HM Chief Inspector of Prisons, 1995). Indeed, between its opening in May 1993 and 30 March 1994 there were seven acts of concerted indiscipline in the prison. Moreover, the Board of Visitors' first report criticized the use of the segregation unit and the practice of segregation under Rule 43 (see Chapter 6) as further punishment for more troublesome prisoners, and complained more specifically about the length of time certain prisoners were housed in the segregation unit.

The position at Doncaster has also given rise to serious concern since it opened in June 1994. Nicknamed 'Doncatraz' because of its location,[77] it was once described as 'probably the most unstable in the country' (Shaw, 1994). Between 1 September 1994 and 30 June 1995 a total of 403 incidents were reported including eleven acts of concerted indiscipline, nine fires and one barricade. Bullying was also reported to be rife at the prison, and a letter from a prisoner (*The Guardian*, 24 August 1994; Prison Reform Trust, 1996b) claimed that the prison was 'understaffed, inefficient, chaotic and dangerous'. The Home Office's response to Doncaster's mounting problems was to take the unprecedented step of appointing a second 'controller' to monitor the contractor's performance over a two week period, while the company[78] drafted in – at public expense – 20 extra managers and staff to run the prison.

While the control problems at Doncaster have become legendary, they are by no means unique. For example Parc prison, in South Wales, which is one of the first DCMF prisons to be built and operated under the Private Finance Initiative (see above) experienced two suicides, eight mini-riots and two officers taken hostage even before its official opening in July 1998 (*The Guardian*, 29 July 1998).[79] A second DCMF prison, Forest Bank at Salford, also experienced a riot involving 30 prisoners shortly after it was opened in July 2000 (*The Guardian*, 1 August 2000). Some of the control problems that have been experienced in privately operated prisons may be attributable to a lack of experience on the part of recently recruited and inadequately trained staff. But even after making appropriate allowance for 'teething problems' the record of private prisons in England is a sobering one, and raises serious doubts about their ability to maintain order and freedom from fear for personal safety on the part of staff and inmates alike.

## The crisis of authority

As we mentioned in Chapter 6, the 'crisis of authority' stems in part from feelings of resentment and alienation on the part of prison officers that their rôle, and even their jobs may be under attack. One particularly potent threat to their livelihoods is the policy of privatization itself, and in particular the process of market testing, which has been recently revived. This has undoubtedly contributed to a serious loss of morale – and increased industrial unrest – on the part of prison staff at all levels within *publicly*-run prisons. Indeed, an inquiry into disturbances at Everthorpe prison in January 1995, which was conducted by a Prison Service area manager, concluded that heightened concern and a loss of morale caused by the prison's inclusion among those to be market tested and hence possibly privatized was one of the contributory causes since a substantial proportion of management time in the period immediately prior to the incidents had been devoted towards the establishment's response to this process (Nathan, 1995a: 15). More recently, the accelerating pace of the prison privatization programme has provoked an upsurge of industrial unrest in the prison system in protest at the resumption of market testing (*The Guardian*, 2 and 3 August 2000). In this sense it is fair to say that prison privatization has almost certainly exacerbated the already deteriorating crisis of authority which we discussed in Chapter 6. And in general it is hard to see how privatization could ameliorate the deep 'dissension, division and distrust' at (and between) all levels of the Prison Service which Woolf identified (see Chapter 6).

Another factor that may have adversely affected the morale of private prison staff relates to the attitude of the private prison sector towards trade unions. Staff at Blakenhurst prison, for example, were initially not allowed to join a trade union, but were encouraged by the prison operators (United Kingdom Detention Services) to participate in an alternative staff consultation forum instead. However, this drew adverse comment in Judge Stephen Tumim's first report on the prison (HM Chief Inspector of Prisons, 1995), which described the forum as inconsistent and ineffective. Since then the prison has agreed to recognize the Prison Service Union (PSU), though this is not affiliated to the TUC, and is considered to be more moderate than the rival and longer-established Prison Officers' Association to which the majority of public sector prison officers belong (Prison Reform Trust, 2000f).

Another aspect of the crisis of authority relates to the ongoing debate about the adequacy of existing arrangements for ensuring accountability on the part of those who wield considerable power (including, on occasion, the use of deadly force) over the lives of vulnerable prison inmates (Ryan, 1994). The onset of prison privatization has given fresh impetus to this debate because of the potential threat to prisoners' civil liberties and well-being when the power to which they are subject is conferred on private corporations. Thus, critics of privatization (for example, Ryan and Ward, 1989b) have warned of the danger that disciplinary powers could be abused by private prison operators, particularly where their exercise might result in a prisoner's release being delayed by the imposition of 'additional days' (for which the operator could expect to receive payment).

In an attempt to allay such concerns the Criminal Justice Act 1991 placed the exercise of such powers under external control. Thus, while a private prison has a 'director' who has broadly the same duties and functions as the governor in a state prison, these do not extend to the conduct of disciplinary hearings or the imposition of any disciplinary award. Moreover, the director has no power to segregate a prisoner temporarily (under Rule 45), nor any power to order cellular confinement or to apply any restraints to a prisoner. All of these powers are exercised instead by a 'controller', who is appointed by the Home Secretary, and whose other duties are to keep under review and report to the Home Secretary on the running of the relevant prison by the director, and to investigate and report on any allegations made against 'prisoner custody officers' (i.e. prison officers) in the performance of their duties. In the event of a major prison disturbance the Home Secretary has the power to appoint a (public sector) prison governor who would assume the powers of both controller or director where the Home Secretary believes that the latter has lost, or is in danger of losing control of the prison or part of it.[80] The Learmont report (see Chapter 6) was also critical of the fact that private prisons did not fit into the normal organizational structure of the Prison Service.

The division of functions within each of the privatized prisons themselves between the director, representing the company's interest, and the controller, representing the interests of the state has also been a source of friction. Clarification of the controller's rôle as the Home Office's representative on-site – especially in terms of monitoring performance – was called for by the Chief Inspector of Prisons in 1994 (HM Chief Inspector of Prisons, 1994). And critics (for example, Ryan, 1994) have called into question the controller's effectiveness as a safeguard, citing the ever-present risk of such monitors being 'captured' by the local management when they operate permanently on-site. For all these reasons it would appear that privatization has very little to offer as a possible solution to the crisis of authority, and has probably had a destabilizing effect overall.

### The crisis of visibility

Prisons are closed institutions. Prisoners are vulnerable to abuse of power and yet have few enforceable rights. They are also relatively powerless to draw attention to their grievances. In circumstances such as these, openness is an essential precondition of accountability and, as we saw in Chapter 6, some important steps have been made in recent years to open up the prison system to outside scrutiny, though it would be premature at this stage to speak of an era of penal *glasnost*. An important issue raised by the policy of prison privatization relates to the strength of private firms' commitment to the requirement of openness, partly because of fears that the rights and well-being of prisoners may be sacrificed in the interests of private profit (McDonald, 1994: 42); and partly because activities in the private sector have traditionally enjoyed a degree of protective immunity from scrutiny on the part of state officials and other individuals compared with public sector activities (Starr, 1989: 92). The history of the privatization programme has done little so far to dispel these fears.

Right from the outset the Home Office refused to publish any of the final contracts for private prisons on the grounds of 'commercial confidentiality' (even though the concept does not operate in the United States, and indeed is 'wholly alien to the theory of perfect competition' (Nathan, 1993b: 13)). In response to criticism from the Prison Reform Trust concessions were made in 1993, which resulted in staffing details being published in the Prison Service Annual Report, which enabled some cost comparisons to be made,[81] though information relating to implied profit levels and also to penalty clauses continued to be withheld. In the end these restrictions were partially circumvented by the Prison Reform Trust which managed to obtain documents relating to Doncaster and Blakenhurst by requesting copies from the Securities and Exchange Commission in the United States (Nathan, 1994c: 11). A policy of non-disclosure still applies to the Home Office controller's reports (Prison Reform Trust, 1993) though Chief Inspector of Prisons Judge Tumim's first report on Blakenhurst (HM Chief Inspector of Prisons, 1995) made the surprising criticism that not even the controller had a current copy of the contract, which, as the report laconically observed, limited his ability to monitor compliance with it.

Finally, although the veil of secrecy has been partially lifted with regard to some aspects of the management of public sector prisons, the cloak of commercial confidentiality is still used to suppress disclosures that are deemed to be 'sensitive' with regard to the contracted-out sector. For example, the threat of legal action by Premier Prison Services Ltd in 2000 resulted in the destruction of copies of a report by Scotland's Chief Inspector of Prisons in which he disclosed that staffing levels at Kilmarnock Prison were between 30 and 50 per cent lower than in prisons run by the Scottish Prison Service (Nathan, 2000b: 14). This paranoid attitude towards the disclosure of information that is clearly in the public interest is indefensible in a democracy, particularly when the private corporations involved stand to benefit so handsomely from public largesse. It also demonstrates that prison privatization is unlikely to even ameliorate, let alone resolve, the continuing crisis of visibility.

## The crisis of legitimacy

Supporters of prison privatization (for example, Logan, 1990; McDonald, 1994) are apt to deny that it poses any special legitimation problems. They do so by emphasizing a sharp distinction between the *allocation* of punishment – which most of them would accept remains a function of the state and, as such, is properly discharged by public agencies such as the courts – and the *delivery* of punishment which they consider may properly be delegated, subject to appropriate safeguards, to any agency, public or private. As Sparks (1994: 22) points out, *how* that punishment is delivered, by whom, and on what terms, is then presented as a purely technical issue to be resolved by considering the comparative costs, quality and efficiency of the various contenders.

Critics of the policy (for example, Ryan and Ward, 1989a; Shichor, 1995) are more likely to argue against it on ethical and moral grounds, and frequently invoke the proposition that, as the state has a monopoly on the use of coercive force, punishment is properly a matter for the state alone. Radzinowicz (1988) articulated this objection in the following terms:

> . . . in a democracy grounded on the rule of law and public accountability the enforcement of penal legislation, which includes prisoners deprived of their liberty while awaiting trial, should be the undiluted responsibility of the State. It is one thing for private companies to provide services for the prison system but it is altogether a different matter for bodies whose motivation is primarily commercial to have coercive powers over prisoners.

Whatever its intrinsic merits, this objection is unlikely to persuade supporters of privatization, most of whom are in any event ideologically committed to 'rolling back the frontiers of the state'. Moreover, it has to be conceded that people's views regarding the 'proper rôle of the state' have changed in the past, and are liable to change again over time. Nevertheless we would argue that prison privatization does raise a number of special legitimation problems of its own that are not so easily dismissed.

The first is that any delegation of coercive power carries with it the very real danger that this will be used 'to further private rather than public interests' (Lawrence, 1986: 662). The most obvious of these 'private ends' is the pursuit of profit and the extension of corporate hegemony, but it extends also to the promotion of personal self-interest,[82] and even the pursuit of private vendettas. While it is true that public sector prisons are susceptible to a variety of abusive practices (including the use of unauthorized violence, neglect, waste and ineptitude), they are not prone to the potential additional problems of corporate or personal greed that private prisons are (Shichor, 1995: 179). The brief history of prison privatization in England and Wales to date provides plenty of ammunition for critics in these respects.

One of the clearest examples of the enhanced opportunities which the policy of prison privatization provides for the promotion of personal self-interest is afforded by the 'revolving door syndrome' connecting politicians and public servants to jobs with private security firms. For many people the decision by an individual to seek better career prospects within the new privatized prisons might not be thought to raise any ethical issues. Often this will be the case. However, a different view might be taken where the individual concerned has been employed in a sensitive public post, with access to inside knowledge or contacts that would be useful to prospective commercial rivals. The more senior the post, the greater the likelihood that this will be the case. The possibility of the new employer gaining an unfair advantage in this way is particularly great where those who are recruited had responsibility for regulating or inspecting the agency in question. By 14 July 1994, 33 senior ex-Prison Service employees (including 21 governors, 2 inspectors of prisons, one regional director and two deputy regional directors) had been 'poached' by six of the private companies competing to secure prison contracts (see Nathan, 1994d: 17 for details).

Ethical issues of a more serious kind are raised where an individual who is recruited by a private prison operator was previously part of the policy-making or decision-making process which benefited either that particular contractor or private prison operators in general. At the very least, such transfers may give rise to allegations of 'sleaze' on the part of those involved since they convey the impression of rewards being extended in return for past favours. Shichor's (1995: 127) opinion is that, although such activities cannot be classified as outright bribes, the difference may be only one of degree. Accusations of this kind, and the suspicions on which they are based, may be expected to undermine the legitimacy of an institution if they gain widespread currency.

As we have seen, politicians who were involved in the policy-making process have benefited subsequently by being offered positions within private prison firms, and the same has also been true of senior civil servants.[83] Particular concern was expressed at Group 4's recruitment in 1992 of a member of the tender evaluation panel within the Home Office's Remands Contracts Unit nine months after the contract to run Wolds prison had been awarded to Group 4. A Civil Service enquiry found no impropriety in the move (Nathan, 1993a: 13), though the House of Commons Public Accounts Committee expressed 'particular interest' in both the fact and timing of the departure during an investigation into the cost of running the Wolds prison in February 1995 (Nathan, 1995a: 15). Further questions were raised about the allocation of the contract to Group 4 when it was learned, first, that the successful tender (for which the Prison Service was not allowed to bid) was £2 million more than that submitted by two rival firms (Nathan, 1994c: 14); and second, that Group 4 was to be paid £5.9 million a year to run Wolds instead of the £4.4 million estimated at the time the contract was awarded.[84] The Committee expressed concern that a full explanation was not available as to why the lower bids had not been accepted, and recommended that 'to avoid any question of impropriety, detailed reasons should always be recorded whenever a contract is not awarded to a tenderer who submits the lowest bid, and who is judged capable of meeting the key performance criteria'. The Committee also made clear that it looked to 'the Prison Service to take a firm line with contractors, and to invoke the penalty clause whenever deficiencies persist beyond a reasonable time and no action is being taken to resolve them'. Similar concerns were expressed by the National Audit Office (1994)[85] and the Chief Inspector of Prisons (HM Chief Inspector of Prisons, 1993c), who was also critical of the lack of effective monitoring of the financial arrangements between Group 4 and the Prison Service, and concluded that it was 'impossible to determine' whether they were providing value for money.

The risk that the coercive power of the state might be abused in the pursuit of private interests was highlighted by an incident of a rather different kind at Blakenhurst Prison where in May 1994 a UKDS custody officer was jailed for 18 months after plotting to arrange the beating up of two prisoners whom he suspected of putting drugs in his coffee (Nathan, 1995b: 13). He was alleged to have offered to disguise two prisoners and leave their cell doors unlocked in order to facilitate a night-time revenge attack against the pair he suspected, but the plan was foiled when details of the scheme were leaked. The officer was then said to have attempted to bribe the intended attackers – by offering one of them 28 days off a three year sentence, and the other a move to an open prison – so that the matter could be dealt with internally by the prison. They refused to go along with this, and went on hunger strike to ensure that the police and Home Office mounted an investigation. They also alleged that Blakenhurst staff were given £50 'backhanders' to keep silent about a riot in February 1994, though this was denied by UKDS who informed the court that the payments were made to staff in recognition of the way they handled the riot. Whatever the explanation for these particular payments might be, the fact that private firms have a lot at stake – including the possibility of a substantial fine, or reduced prospects in future tender applications – increases the risk that people might be tempted, possibly in response to pressure or induce-ments, to be 'economical with the truth'.

Another incident that raised concerns about the illegitimate use of coercion, this time by private prison staff themselves, relates to the death of Alston Manning, who was a black prisoner at Blakenhurst prison. In March 1998 a coroner's jury returned a unanimous verdict that Manning was unlawfully killed by staff in December 1995 while he was being restrained during a fruitless search for drugs (Prison Reform Trust, 1998a:13; 1998b: 16). Seven prison custody officers were suspended pending criminal investigations, and two of the most senior staff involved in the incident claimed to be ignorant of Home Office guidance warning of the dangers involved in the restraint technique they were using.

Some supporters of prison privatization (for example, McDonald, 1994: 42) are prepared to concede that concerns about prisoners' rights and welfare being sacrificed in the pursuit of profit are genuine and need to be taken seriously. However, they are also at pains to emphasize the safeguards which can be built into the system and which, they argue, reduce the likelihood of a return to the abuses associated with nineteenth century private prisons. Among the safeguards mentioned by McDonald are the following: procedures for protecting prisoners' rights which can be written into the contract, so that failure to uphold them can be termed a violation of the contract; putting full-time government monitors into private facilities; establishing independent ombudsmen and grievance procedures. So how effective have these arrangements proved since private prisons were introduced?

In the first place, it must be very doubtful whether any of these safeguards would be capable of preventing the possible abuses we outlined above, caused by firms or individuals pursuing their own private ends at the expense of the public interest. Second, while it is certainly the case that the régime standards specified in the contracts are superior in certain respects to those provided in many state prisons, it may be questioned whether this really demonstrates the inherent superiority of contracting-out, or whether it is simply the result of a political decision to find the money for improvements in one very limited sector of the prison system while withholding it from those parts where the need is greatest. If the latter is the case, it can only fuel the crisis of legitimacy. For as we saw in Chapter 6, prisoners' sense of fair play is likely to be particularly inflamed by what they see as inconsistent and arbitrary treatment at the hands of the authorities which results in their being treated less favourably than other prisoners. As prisoners are hardly in a position to exercise a 'consumer choice' in the matter, it may be suspected that those who are assigned to the inferior conditions of most public sector prisons are less likely to be persuaded of the innate superiority of private provision than to reflect bitterly on the unfairness of the way they are being treated. But in any event, how strong are the safeguards afforded by the specifications laid down in the contract? Prisoners themselves are not parties to the contracts, and therefore have no enforceable rights against either the private prison operator or the Prison Service in the event of a breach. In that respect the remedies that are available to prisoners in private prisons are certainly no better than those held in public sector institutions (Livingstone and Owen, 1999: 31–2).

Third, the placing of full-time government controllers into each of the private prisons has not been conspicuously successful so far in avoiding the many embarrassing scandals we have recounted.[86] Some of the reasons for this include: a failure to specify performance indicators in the contract against which the performance of the group can be specifically measured; a failure to even provide the controller in at least one instance with a current copy of the contract; and a lack of clarity as to the rôle of the controller with regard to his duty to monitor the contract (HM Chief Inspector of Prisons, 1994).

Fourth, there have also been complaints, by the Board of Visitors at Blakenhurst, over the ineffective and inefficient grievance/complaints procedures at the prison (Nathan, 1994b: 13). Even more disturbing is the first report of the work of the Prisons Ombudsman (1995), whose remit also extends to the privately-run prisons. In it he commented (para. 6.7) that 'one area of particular difficulty centred around complaints from contracted-out prisons', since not one of the 31 complaints from Blakenhurst, Doncaster and Wolds was eligible for investigation. The reason was that none had been through the requests/complaints system. As the Ombudsman drily observed, 'either the contracted-out prisons are extremely successful in resolving formal complaints which come to them, or there is considerable confusion about the respective responsibilities of the Director and Controller in the requests/complaints system in contracted-out gaols'.

Faced with these shortcomings, we are forced to conclude that the institutional procedures which have been introduced as part of the privatization process are inadequate to safeguard against even the special legitimation problems to which the policy is particularly vulnerable, let alone the wider crisis of legitimacy we examined in Chapter 6. At best the privatization process is a damaging distraction from the need to embark on a programme of fundamental reform directed at the whole of the prison system – indeed, the whole penal system. At worst, its potentially destructive impact on both the prison numbers crisis and the crisis of legitimacy could render such a programme of reform unattainable. Privatization as an ideology and as a practice is not only unlikely to provide a remedy for the malaise affecting the prison system; it could easily become a major part of the problem.

## NOTES

1  Particularly by those on the right wing of the Conservative party, but not exclusively so. Among the academic criminologists to have advocated privatization, see in particular McConville and Williams (1985) and Taylor and Pease (1989).

2  We use the terms 'private sector' and 'privatization' to refer to the commercial (profit-making) sector, as distinct from the 'voluntary sector' (charities etc.) and the 'informal sector' of active but unpaid citizens. Voluntary organizations run 'intermediate treatment' and other non-custodial projects, and the voluntary sector was invited to bid for the government's secure training centres for 12 to 15 year olds, an invitation it declined. Within the criminal justice system as a whole certain activities have also been transferred to what has been described as the informal sector, as in the case of 'neighbourhood watch' (see Mawby, 1989; Nellis, 1989).

3  Rolls-Royce, British Steel, British Shipbuilding, British Leyland and British Aerospace were among the first government-owned concerns to be privatized.

4  Technically, the government does not regard this as 'privatization', which may result in misleading answers being given to parliamentary questions on the subject unless they are very carefully phrased (Nathan, 1995a: 18).

5  This has not yet happened anywhere, as far as we are aware. However, Nathan (1994c: 16) reported that in 1994 the Department of Justice in the Australian state of Victoria was planning to privatize the contracting-out process itself, by appointing consultants Coopers and Lybrand to oversee the bidding process relating to three new prisons which were to be financed, designed, built and operated by private firms.

6　See McDonald (1994), citing Green (1989) and Rutherford (1990). Interestingly, an increase in the number of illegal immigrants during the 1970s, combined with a lack of funding for new facilities to house them, has also been linked to the development of privatization in the corrections sphere in the United States (Windlesham, 1993: 281).

7　Mr Hurd did, however, accept the need to consider how private sector skills and knowledge might be used to supervise and accelerate the delivery of the prison-building programme, in response to concerns expressed by the Comptroller and Auditor General and also the House of Commons Public Accounts Committee that the government's ambitious and costly prison-building target might fall short of its target of matching available places with the total prison population by the end of the decade (Windlesham, 1993: 279).

8　According to a press statement issued by Sir John Wheeler MP on 31 October 1986.

9　Most notable of whom was Conservative Party Chairman Sir Norman Fowler, who was a non-executive director of Group 4 until he resigned in September 1993 following an outcry over his dual role. In addition, Sir John Wheeler MP, who succeeded Sir Edward Gardner as Chairman of the Home Affairs Committee was a former Chairman of the British Security Industries Association, many of whose members have bid for contracts.

10　In the ten year period between 1979 and 1988, the remand population increased by 76 per cent from 6,629 to 11,667, compared with a much more modest rate of increase (18 per cent) in the overall size of the prison population (James and Bottomley, 1998: 223).

11　The episode sheds interesting light on Mrs Thatcher's approach to criminal justice policy, which appears not to have been particularly interventionist at this time, though this did not stop her from giving free rein to her ideological instincts in response to a specific enquiry, without reference to Cabinet Committee or even other Home Office ministers (Windlesham, 1993: 298).

12　The first contract for these was awarded to Group 4 Securitas with effect from 5 April 1993.

13　The legislative scope for prison privatization has since been extended still further by section 96 of the Criminal Justice and Public Order Act 1994, which allows for the contracting out of *parts* of public sector prisons. Moreover, section 99 authorizes the contracting out of any functions or activities at state-run prisons, which raises the prospect of private sector prison staff being brought in to undertake duties in prisons that have not themselves (yet) been privatized.

14　N.B. Wolds Prison was itself recategorized as a prison catering for both remand and sentenced prisoners in 1995.

15　In the event, the evaluation of Wolds prison (by Professor Keith Bottomley of Hull University) which was supposed to have been successfully completed before any other parts of the prison service were privatized, did not appear until April 1996, and then only in summary form (Bottomley et al., 1996).

16　For a time this placed HMP Strangeways in a somewhat anomalous position since the terms on which it was managed by the Prison Service closely resembled the model adopted for private corporations. This included the incorporation of a 'Service Level Agreement' between the Governor and the Prison Service, and also the appointment of a 'Compliance Manager', with a role akin to that of the 'controller' in contracted-out institutions (see note 61 below). However, the Prison Service has subsequently proposed the introduction of similar 'Service Delivery Agreements' for all prisons, with a view to encouraging the adoption of concepts such as financial efficiency and contract compliance, which are associated with the private sector (Jago and Thompson, 1999: 231).

17  In 1998 it was predicted that this 'target' would be achieved by March 2002, by which time the certified normal accommodation of the prison service as a whole was forecast to be 67,700, 6,600 of which (9.7 per cent) were expected to be managed by the private sector (Hansard, 17 July 1998, as reported by Nathan, 1998c: 15).

18  Directive (77/187), which was implemented in the UK in 1981 by the Transfer of Undertakings (Protection of Employment) Regulations (TUPE) (Crabbe, 1993: 34–5).

19  The High Court ruled in 1993 (*Kenny v. South Manchester College* (1993) IRLR: 265) that Prison Service education lecturers' pay and conditions should remain as they were before the service was put out to tender (Nathan, 1993c: 14). Moreover the government was forced to concede (after taking legal advice) that existing staff contracts and conditions of employment at Strangeways would be honoured even if a private operator were to secure the contract (Nathan, 1993a: 12).

20  Subsequently, the Labour government has altered the term of the Private Finance Initiative (see below) to ensure that it complies with the Directive (*The Guardian*, 14 March 2000).

21  In which the contractor would first refurbish (and/or extend) and then take over and manage its entire operation.

22  Both John Prescott (who was to become Deputy Prime Minister) and Jack Straw (who was to become Home Secretary) had reiterated the party's clearly stated opposition to the policy of prison privatization in speeches to the annual conference of the Prison Officers' Association (in 1994 and 1996 respectively). See Prison Reform Trust (1998b: 1).

23  In a speech delivered, ironically, at another annual conference of the Prison Officers' Association on 18 May 1998 (Prison Reform Trust, 1998b: 1).

24  The Prison Service had not been allowed to bid for the Wolds and Blakenhurst tenders.

25  The first of these – Buckley Hall – had previously been managed by Group 4 since it reopened in 1994. In October 1999 it became the first privately operated prison to revert to public sector control. Then in January 2001 the Prison Service was named as preferred bidder to take over the management of Blakenhurst prison from United Kingdom Detention Services (UKDS). The third successful public sector bid was to continue running Strangeways prison when its contract came up for renewal, also in January 2001.

26  They were Parc, Altcourse, Lowdham Grange, Ashfield and Forest Bank.

27  It remains to be seen whether any private concern will show any serious interest in taking on such a challenge, let alone succeed with it. A far better solution in our view for failing prisons of this kind would be to close them.

28  In marked contrast to the position in other jurisdictions such as New Zealand and the Australian state of Victoria, which appear to have concluded that prison privatization is a 'failed experiment' (Cavadino and Dignan, forthcoming).

29  It has often been observed that the attitude of the new right towards the rôle of the state is not entirely consistent, however, and that the conservative agenda in relation to crime control has been to extend the reach of the law and extend the power of the state to enforce it while cutting back on its responsibilities for health, welfare and other social programmes (Shichor, 1995: 59).

30  As, arguably, happened in both the educational and health services under the post-1979 Conservative governments.

31  Similar criticisms have been voiced against certain privately-run correctional institutions in the United States, particularly the Silverdale Detention Centre in Tennessee, which is operated by 'market leaders' Corrections Corporation of America, and which has been described as 'the most researched correctional facility in the United States' (Shichor, 1995: 177).

32 Various terms have been coined to express the same idea including 'criminal justice–industrial complex' (Quinney, 1977; Maghan, 1991; Shichor, 1995) and 'correctional industrial complex' (Bronstein, 1993/4).

33 For example, the US 'market leaders' Corrections Corporation of America was reported to have acquired one of its major US competitors, Concept Inc., which was described at the time as the third largest company in the corrections industry (Nathan, 1995b: 19).

34 The cross-party House of Commons Home Affairs Committee (1997) was far more cautious in its report on the management of the prison service in England and Wales. Although it concluded that privately managed prisons had, at least in their early years, delivered savings to the Prison Service it felt that it was premature to be specific about the extent of such savings. Moreover, it acknowledged that it was arguable that similar results could have been achieved within the public sector if the Prison Service had been managed more efficiently.

35 Since they may not, in fact, be comparing 'like with like'. For example, a Group 4 Factsheet contrasted a projected operating cost of £279 per prisoner place for Buckley Hall with an average cost for state managed prisons of £357 (Nathan, 1995a: 16). However, the latter average was almost certainly based on all prison categories including the extremely high-cost dispersal prisons, and also older prisons whose operating costs may also be expected to be greater. In February 1996 an unpublished consultants' report was said to show virtually no cost difference between state and private sector prisons, though the figures were later 'corrected' by the Prison Service (*The Guardian*, 19 February 1996).

36 A frequently-voiced criticism of prison privatization (for example, Ryan and Ward, 1989a) is that it may involve the 'creaming off' of the most profitable shallow-end institutions, which would give a misleading impression of private sector efficiency, effectiveness and, possibly, humanity while leaving a hard-core of intractable offenders to be dealt with in the resources-starved public sector.

37 A practice referred to as 'lowballing' in the United States (Shichor, 1995: 160).

38 There was a substantial 'cost-overrun' at Wolds prison, where the estimated costs increased from £21.5m over 5 years to more than £28m The additional costs (which related to bigger than expected expenditure on external visits and a failure to allow for utility costs) were made good at the taxpayer's expense. Similar, though even larger, overruns have been experienced by the prison building and refurbishment programme, amounting to £79m for the 21 prisons involved (Nathan, 1994c).

39 The comparisons that follow were reported in a restricted circulation report (Prison Service Planning Group, 1997, cited by Nathan, 1998a: 15).

40 Staff at Blakenhurst also expressed concern about staffing levels to Chief Inspector of Prisons Judge Stephen Tumim (HM Chief Inspector of Prisons, 1995) following a serious disturbance in February 1994, and similar concerns have been voiced in relation to Doncaster (*The Guardian*, 1 February 1995 and 8 September 1995).

41 At Blakenhurst prison starting salaries were reported to have been cut from £13,500 per year when the prison first opened, to £12,500. Staff at several private prisons are reported to have no meal breaks. See Prison Reform Trust (2000f, p. 24 of online version).

42 Figures cited by Mr. Phil Hornsby, general secretary of the Prison Service Union (PSU). See Prison Reform Trust (2000f, p. 24 of online version).

43 For example, at Doncaster prison of the 629 staff recruited between June 1994 and 1 November 1995, no fewer than 127 (one in five) had resigned, while twelve had been dismissed (Nathan, 1995d: 16). At Blakenhurst 42 of the prison's 308 staff resigned between May 1993 and July 1994 (HC Deb. 13 July 1994, cited in Nathan, 1994c: 15), which is almost one in seven.

44 For latest studies see Woodbridge (1999) and Park (2000). The four privately-operated prisons are Blakenhurst, Buckley Hall, Doncaster and Wolds. None of these are DCMF prisons since the DCMF arrangements only came into operation during the 1998–9 financial year.

45 Critics who argued for years that the methodology on which the comparative costs have been calculated was flawed were tacitly vindicated in 2001, when Coopers and Lybrand were asked by the prison service to devise a new methodology after the Prison Service had spent years defending the validity of its original approach (Prison Reform Trust, 2001: 2).

46 This is less likely to affect the privately managed prisons, which tend to be much newer than many of their public sector comparators. Thus, the latter are likely to be disadvantaged unless differences in available accommodation are taken into account.

47 In 1998–9 it was 13 per cent (Park, 2000: 4).

48 Indeed, in 1997–8 the cost per baseline CNA measure revealed a 2 per cent advantage in favour of the public sector prisons (Park, 2000: 4).

49 In 1998–9 the extent to which the four privately operated prisons were overcrowded averaged 21.5 per cent, whereas for the public sector comparators the average was only 6.2 per cent (figures calculated from table shown in Park, 2000: 32).

50 Wackenhut (UK) Ltd, which already had contracts for the management of prison escort services and an immigration detention centre, and which claimed extensive experience overseas.

51 The fact that this report was not published illustrates the point that the doctrine of commercial confidentiality can easily lead to the squandering of public money being covered up.

52 Although proponents of privatization have claimed that the private sector can design, plan and build a prison inside a year, compared with around seven years for the public sector, the actual reduction is much more modest, partly because of the inevitable delays incurred at the planning stage. In July 1994 the National Audit Office reported that the average time taken to build a prison had fallen from seven to only four years (Nathan, 1994c: 18).

53 PFI schemes require interest payments some 5 per cent above the rate the Treasury would pay if it borrowed directly. This means for every £1 billion of PFI contracts there is an extra cost to the public sector of £50 million per year.

54 From £17.5 million at the time the contract was awarded to £28.2 million,

55 In jargon parlance, it has the effect of appearing to move capital spending 'off-balance sheet'.

56 The Treasury has adopted a 'sustainable investment' rule which requires that the net ratio of public debt to national income should be below 40 per cent of GDP over the economic cycle.

57 Robinson (2000) has calculated that even if the £11bn of PFI capital expenditure incurred during 1999–2002 had been replaced by normal public sector capital spending, the net debt:GDP ratio would still have fallen to 36.4 per cent by the end of the current Parliamentary term.

58 It is estimated that in 2004–5 the government will be spending £3.6bn per year simply servicing the PFI contracts (which also relate to new roads, hospitals etc. as well as prisons) (Robinson, 2000).

59 One of the key concepts influencing the design of the prison environment was that of 'normalization', which was intended to reflect the legally innocent status of the intended population (James and Bottomley, 1998: 225).

60 As many as 84 per cent had been in prison before, including one fifth for whom this was at least the sixth occasion on which they had been in prison.

61 'Controllers' are appointed by the Home Secretary *inter alia* to monitor the running of a private prison. Their other responsibilities – to investigate and report on allegations made against private prison staff, and to administer certain disciplinary functions – are described in more detail below.

62 Between December 1994, when the prison opened, and July 1996 the proportion of inmates who failed to return on time after home leave was just under 5 per cent, which compares with an average of 0.4 per cent for all male Category C prisons (Hansard, 9 July 1996, as cited in Nathan, 1996c: 16).

63 Since then, Buckley Hall has become the first privately managed prison to revert to public sector management (see above).

64 This was also in line with Woolf's recommendation that 'remand prisoners should be held in prisons which . . . [are] entirely separate from prisons for sentenced prisoners' (Woolf and Tumim, 1991: para. 11.80).

65 The latter decision was also prompted in part by the operational problems that had been encountered when dealing with the exclusively remand population in the period immediately after opening (James and Bottomley, 1998: 230).

66 Doncaster's population was 138 per cent of its in-use CNA, enough to place it in the top ten most overcrowded prisons in England and Wales in 1999 (Prison Reform Trust, 1999b). The equivalent figures for the other prisons were Blakenhurst 128 per cent; Wolds 111 per cent and Buckley Hall 109 per cent (Park, 2000: 32). In marked contrast, several of the comparator prisons were under-occupied. At Wellingborough, for example only 89 per cent of its in-use accommodation was occupied.

67 We will not consider the performance of private sector providers of ancillary services and facilities, though we did briefly examine this in the previous edition of this book (Cavadino and Dignan, 1997a: 166).

68 The comparative aspect of the Wolds evaluation comprised two elements. One involved a reasonably detailed comparison with Woodhill prison near Milton Keynes. Although not directly comparable, since Woodhill is a much larger multi function prison, it was at least a relatively recently commissioned public sector prison. The second element comprised a briefer study of privately operated Blakenhurst and three other new public sector local prisons: Belmarsh, Bullingdon and Highdown.

69 The number of accredited courses at Blakenhurst (20) also compared very unfavourably with the 51 on offer at Bullingdon and 91 at Elmley, its two public sector comparators (Park, 2000: 8).

70 Conversely, inmates at Blakenhurst were more critical of the staff there, and somewhat surprisingly extolled the virtues of public sector POA staff. This was cited by James et al. (1997: 135) as a graphic warning against over-simplistic generalizations about the nature of staff–inmate relations in the two sectors.

71 The only exception was Wolds, which had a higher rate of assaults as a percentage of the population than two of its public sector comparators, but a slightly lower rate than a third (Park, 2000: 19).

72 As we have seen, the proportion of prisoners housed in private sector accommodation is not due to reach 10 per cent until the end of March 2002. See above, n. 17.

73 Extorting money or goods by means of threats.

74 This development represented a very different kind of 'normalization' than was intended by the management team who were first awarded the contract (see n. 59 above).

75 Between February 1994 and February 1999 a total of 13 fines were imposed on private prison contractors, totalling £565,000 (Leech and Cheney, 1999: 229).

76 HC Deb. 13 July 1994, cited in Nathan (1994c: 15). Four officers were dismissed, a fifth was suspended and a sixth resigned.

77 The prison is situated on an island between two rivers on the site of a former power station, with access via a newly erected bridge.

78 Premier Prison Services Ltd, which is jointly owned by the American Wackenhut Corporation and the British firm Serco (Nathan, 1995c: 13).

79 During its first year of operation, Parc was fined a total of over £360,000 for failing to meet performance standards on four separate occasions. This is the worst record of any privately operated prison to date.

80 This 'contingency' rôle for the public sector, and the resources required to discharge it if necessary, represents another 'hidden cost' that needs to be taken into account when comparing public and private sector prison costs.

81 And see Woodbridge (1999) and Park (2000).

82 For example a former director of the Corrections Corporation of America was imprisoned following the payment of bribes to a Kentucky corrections chief in order to secure a lucrative private prison contract (Nathan, 1996b: 16).

83 In 1997 the Chief Inspector of Prisons team leader left the Prisons Inspectorate to work for Group 4 shortly after writing a highly favourable report on Buckley Hall – run by none other than Group 4 (Nathan, 1999: 13). Nevertheless the group lost the Buckley Hall contract when it was retendered in October 1999.

84 The additional costs were to pay for vandalism at the prison (£100,000), maintenance (£500,000), utility costs (£250,000) and an extra £40,000 a year to cover an underestimate on the cost of transporting prisoners on outside visits.

85 The NAO also expressed concern that there were 'no performance indicators in the contract against which the performance of the group can be specifically measured'.

86 In 1997 the House of Commons Home Affairs Committee (1997) suggested that there might be benefits to the management of a contracted out prison in transferring the adjudication functions from the Home Office controller to the prison director, though the Committee did not consider the time was right to recommend such a step to be taken. Were such a step to be taken, it would open up new possibilities for abuses of the kind that the controller was originally intended to prevent.

# 8

# Early Release: the Penal System's Safety Valve

Over the last few decades, one of the main government responses to the growing prison population and the resulting resources crisis has been the development of administrative mechanisms to release prisoners before the end of their sentences. It has also been one of the most effective, given the failure of both judicial initiatives (see Chapter 4) and legislation (based on the 'strategy of encouragement'; see Chapters 4 and 5) to provide significant or lasting solutions to the problem. From the government's point of view, the main advantage of early release (especially those forms that occur by executive discretion, for example parole) is that it operates independently of the courts' decisions on sentence, and bypasses judicial discretion.[1] Consequently, it has been used on numerous occasions as an effective safety valve when the upward pressure on prison numbers has threatened to overwhelm the system. As with any system of crisis management, however, the demands of administrative convenience have resulted in frequent pragmatic alterations of policy. These have rendered the system vulnerable to criticism from penal reformers and sentencers alike and, in the case of parole, have contributed to cynicism and bitterness on the part of many prisoners.

The whole concept of early release is difficult to justify from a variety of value positions, and in principle many would prefer a system where 'what you get is what you serve' – in other words, the sentence pronounced by the judge denotes the exact length of time to be spent in prison. This is variously known as 'real time sentencing', 'honesty in sentencing' and 'truth in sentencing'. Those who favour a 'Strategy A' approach to criminal justice tend to dislike early release because it lets prisoners off with a lesser punishment than the 'law and order' mentality deems to be appropriate (whether for reasons of desert, deterrence or incapacitation). It is also thought to make a mockery of the sentence pronounced on the offender in court. The traditional, 'classicist' legal view which informs the 'justice model' has a different objection. It holds that early release offends against due process and the rule of law, because it means that the amount of punishment undergone for the crime is not determined by a judge following a hearing in open court. The latter procedure would ensure that offenders had the full rights of natural justice, to hear all the evidence, present evidence, argue their case, have the decision justified by reasons and have rights of appeal; but instead the length of their punishment is determined by a discretionary administrative process which may be both secretive and unaccountable. It may also lead to unfair disproportionality, with offences of similar seriousness eventually receiving very different punishments (or *vice versa*).

Such arguments tend to appeal to judges, whose power to determine offenders' punishments is infringed by early release, and who have consequently often opposed and obstructed proposals to increase early release. Objections founded on 'natural justice' grounds also resonate with prisoners, who may feel that the vital question of when they will be released is governed by a cruelly opaque and arbitrary process.[2] Most supporters of 'Strategy C' are also repelled by the defects in due process and proportionality that are associated with early release procedures. On the other hand they also believe that prison terms should be humanely short, at least for inmates who pose no serious threat to the safety of the public. Consequently, they insist that early release should as far as possible be automatic; but where it is discretionary, the discretion should be exercised within procedures which maximize due process and natural justice. Ideally, decisions to grant or withhold parole should be made by a court, or at least by procedures which mimic court procedures as far as possible, with judicial-style hearings, reasons for decisions, rights to legal representation and appeal, and so on. As we shall see, such arguments have wielded influence over the years, and there has been something of a trend recently towards the '*judicialization*' of parole.[3]

On the other hand, support for a highly discretionary early release system comes from two quarters. The first of these is the traditional positivist 'individualized treatment model' (see Chapter 2), according to which it is only right that experts should make administrative decisions about when release occurs, since they are in the best position to judge when the offender is fit to be released. However, even though modern-day advocates of rehabilitation for offenders may still favour retaining early release, they tend to agree with other proponents of Strategy C that discretion should be limited by considerations of due process and fairness. The strongest support for discretionary early release comes from Strategy B – such a system is ideal for the practical, managerial task of regulating the size of the prison population both flexibly and cheaply. But such a strategy runs into the highly practical problem of legitimacy since principled opposition to the system makes it difficult to implement with long-term political success. An even bigger weakness with a penal management strategy dependent on early release is its failure to address the real cause of prison overcrowding, which, as we have seen, stems from the sentencing powers and practices of the courts – the real 'crux of the crisis'. As the Carlisle Committee pointedly said in 1988: 'Expediting the release of prisoners while doing nothing to stem the flow of admissions is like bailing water from a boat without repairing the gaping hole in its bottom' (1988: para. 236). Consequently, as experience has repeatedly shown, such a strategy can do no more than temporarily contain the crisis.

Various administrative mechanisms exist which allow the early release of prisoners (see also Sparks, 1998: 8–9). For example, the Home Secretary has a discretionary power under section 36 of the Criminal Justice Act 1991 to release any prisoner on licence on compassionate grounds in exceptional circumstances.[4] There is also a further power – although it has never been used – under section 32 of the Criminal Justice Act 1982 to let out defined categories of offenders up to six months early. But the most important of these mechanisms are *automatic* early release, traditionally known as *remission*, and *discretionary* early release, traditionally known as *parole*. These have recently been augmented by *home detention curfew*, a scheme which commenced in January 1999. This allows short-term prisoners to be released early subject to a home curfew enforced by electronic monitoring. We will begin with brief historical accounts[5] of the development of remission and parole, proceed to consider the system of early release introduced by the Criminal Justice Act 1991, discuss subsequent developments and finally draw our conclusions about the possible future of early release.

## REMISSION: THE ORIGINAL SAFETY VALVE

The practice of early release from a sentence was originally devised in the eighteenth century, in response to the administrative difficulties experienced by the authorities in operating the penal system of the day. One of the earliest systems was introduced for offenders who were sentenced to transportation and consisted of a 'ticket of leave' which was issued as a reward for good conduct. A similar scheme was extended to ordinary sentences of imprisonment under the Prison Act 1898. However, remission of sentence was still not something to which prisoners were entitled as of right. Instead it had to be earned under an elaborate system of 'marks' which were awarded for 'industry and good conduct'. Because of this, the award of remission was originally seen as a potent instrument for controlling the behaviour of prison inmates. Indeed, many recent accounts of the system have continued to emphasize this traditional role (see for example, Cross, 1971: 87; Fitzgerald and Sim, 1982: 101; Stanley and Baginsky, 1984: 98).

More recently, however, it would be more accurate to say that the primary function of remission has been to control the size of the prison population in response to the worsening problem of prison overcrowding. In theory remission was still a reward for good behaviour while in prison, but in practice remission of a set fraction of a prison sentence became automatic unless some or all of it was lost for breaches of prison rules or discipline. Various changes were introduced to the system of remission between 1940 and 1992, all of which were intended to reduce pressure on prison numbers and had little to do with the more effective maintenance of prison discipline. For example, in 1940 the remission period was extended from one sixth to one third of a prison sentence, and in August 1987 it was further increased to one half for sentences of twelve months or less.[6]

This system of remission (and the word itself) was abolished by the Criminal Justice Act 1991. But as we shall see, prisoners are still normally released automatically before the end of their nominal sentence, even if they have not already been 'paroled'. Their release date can still be delayed if they misbehave in prison, as up to 42 'additional days' (the new name for 'loss of remission') may be awarded by the prison governor for offences against prison discipline.

## OLD-STYLE PAROLE, 1967–1992

When it was first introduced in 1967, parole differed from remission in four important respects. First, release on parole 'licence' was considered to be a privilege rather than an entitlement, and hence was in theory a discretionary gift in the hands of the administrative authorities – unlike remission, which for all practical purposes had by now become an entitlement that could only be forfeited for bad behaviour. Second, parole, if awarded, took effect at an earlier stage, since prisoners normally became eligible to be considered for parole during the middle third of their sentences. Third, a parolee was subject to compulsory supervision by a probation officer until the normal date of remission was reached. And fourth, parolees could be recalled to prison at any stage during their parole. This could either occur as a result of a court order following a conviction for a further offence, or as a result of a decision by the Home Secretary (in reality by the Parole Unit at the Home Office), which did not require either a further offence or even a breach of the terms of the licence.

### 1967–1972: *from principle to pragmatism*

Although it had been foreshadowed by the eighteenth-century 'ticket of leave' system, parole itself made rather a belated appearance on the English penal scene. It was not until the Criminal Justice Act 1967 that the then Labour Government introduced parole to England and Wales, with the first prisoners receiving parole in 1968. By then it had long been established in a number of other jurisdictions, most notably the US. Opinions differ as to the exact nature of the impetus which brought parole into being, for it has been described both as a manifestation of the then prevailing 'rehabilitative ideal' (Morgan, 1983: 137) and also as a product of 'penological pragmatism' (Bottomley, 1984: 25). This should not come as a surprise, for a good many penal developments in this country have had ambiguous rationales.[7] In fact it would be true to say that *both* strands – ideological and practical – contributed to the origins and subsequent development of parole, though the weight of their respective contributions has altered over the years. The general trend may be described as a shift from principle to pragmatism.

Foremost among the ideological considerations that helped to promote and also to shape the original system of parole was the optimistic belief in the possibility of rehabilitating offenders through punishment, which was shared by penal reformers and politicians in the 1960s,[8] and also by some key penal policy-makers at the Home Office. One of the clearest expressions of this 'rehabilitative optimism' was contained in the White Paper which announced the government's intention to introduce a system of parole, and which boldly asserted that, '[a] considerable number of long-term prisoners reach a recognizable peak in their training at which they may respond to generous treatment, but after which, if kept in prison, they may go downhill' (Home Office, 1965: para. 5).

Claims such as these were unsupported by any empirical evidence. It was never adequately explained why such a 'peak response', even if it were to exist, should manifest itself only during the middle third of an offender's sentence, which was the original period of eligibility for parole. However, the rehabilitative ideal involved far more than this rather quirky belief in the theory of 'peak response'. Another important feature of parole which chimed in with the positivistic philosophy of treatment was the element of compulsory supervision of the offender by a probation officer after release. A third link between parole and positivism is one that has grown in importance as the original 'peak response' idea became discredited. This is the reliance on developing scientific methods for predicting the risk of future reoffending as the basis for determining whether it is safe to parole an offender or not.

So the introduction of parole clearly owed a great deal to the ideology of rehabilitative optimism. Indeed, at first, parole was not particularly well designed for the more practical task of reducing prison numbers. Two features in particular limited its utility for this purpose. The first of these concerned the decision-making structure. The government had originally envisaged an explicitly administrative procedure which would have vested considerable discretion in the Home Secretary. However, parliamentary opposition resulted in a compromise which led to the adoption of a cumbersome three-tier ('tripartite') decision-making process – comprising *Local Review Committees* (LRCs), a statutory *Parole Board* and the *Home Secretary* – which was specifically designed to limit the number of applicants being granted parole. The first stage in the process consisted of an assessment by a Local Review Committee (LRC) which was attached to each prison and which acted as a filter to reduce the number of cases to be considered by the Parole Board. The Parole Board is an independent body[9] with responsibility for making final recommendations on parole applications to the Home Secretary; its membership includes judges, psychiatrists, probation officers and criminologists. The Home Secretary was not bound to grant parole when recommended to do so by the Board, and so could 'veto' an individual's parole, but was unable to parole a prisoner without a positive decision by the Board. So long as this balance of power remained intact, it would be relatively difficult for governments to use parole as a means of reducing the prison population.

A second feature which limited the usefulness of parole in this respect during its early years was the adoption of a restrictive eligibility threshold: prisoners could not be even considered for parole until they had served twelve months or one third of the sentence, whichever was longer. The effect of this was to restrict parole to prisoners serving more than eighteen months, most of whom would normally be housed in the comparatively less overcrowded conditions of a closed training prison. Consequently, parole was not likely to significantly reduce numbers in the local prisons which were subject to the most severe overcrowding.

Given these very cautious beginnings it is hardly surprising that the initial parole rate was exceedingly modest. In 1969, the system's first full year of operation, just over a quarter of those eligible were paroled. But things were about to change.

### 1972–1991: expansion, pragmatism and bifurcation

Two developments conspired to change the face of parole from the early 1970s onwards. The first was the collapse of rehabilitative optimism (see Chapter 2), which seriously undermined the main rationale that had originally led to the introduction of parole. But parole survived – indeed, the numbers of prisoners paroled expanded dramatically – because it was seen as too useful a 'safety valve' for the practical purpose of reducing the numbers of people in prison. As a result, the development of the parole system over the next two decades was shaped much more by pragmatic considerations than by the ideological concerns that had brought it into being.

Many of the changes to parole during the period 1972–81 represented a shift in the balance of power between Home Office and Parole Board in favour of the former. This was of vital importance if parole was to be used as a practical instrument of executive policy. Thus in 1972 the Home Secretary was given the power to determine certain categories of prisoner who might then be released by him *without* reference to the Parole Board, provided they had received a unanimously favourable recommendation from the LRC. And in 1975 the Home Secretary, Roy Jenkins, explicitly encouraged both the Parole Board and LRCs to grant parole much more readily, especially to relatively minor property offenders. As a result of these changes, by 1981 parole was being granted at more than twice the rate it had been a decade earlier – in 55 per cent of cases considered compared with 27 per cent in 1969. But even this was not sufficient to abate the prison numbers crisis.

In 1981 news broke of a more radical Home Office proposal to release short-term prisoners[10] automatically after one third of their sentences. Once again, the main justification for such a move was the prospect of a reduction in the prison population (by up to 7,000) rather than any principled commitment to the concept of early release. But this time, the government faced revolt: it was reaching the limits to which a policy of ever-increasing administrative pragmatism could be taken without incurring severe problems of legitimacy. The proposal was dropped, partly as a result of strong opposition from the judiciary, who regarded it as an unacceptable interference with the length of sentence passed by the court, but partly also due to Home Secretary William Whitelaw's hostile reception at the 1981 Conservative Party Conference for law and order policies which were perceived as being too soft. However, the substance of the proposal for automatic release was eventually to resurface – albeit in slightly different guise – following the more comprehensive review of parole undertaken by Lord Carlisle in 1987–8 (see below).

Following this setback the government adopted an alternative approach. In July 1984, Home Secretary Leon Brittan introduced a strongly *'bifurcatory'* package of measures (see Chapter 1), increasing eligibility for parole for shorter-term prisoners while simultaneously reducing it for certain categories of more serious offender. At the lower end, the threshold of eligibility for parole was reduced from twelve to six months, and a speeded-up procedure was introduced which effectively obliged LRCs to operate a presumption in favour of parole for short-term prisoners. But at the same time, it was announced that those serving life imprisonment for certain types of murder would not normally be released for at least twenty years; and those serving five years or more for offences of violence or drug-trafficking were warned that they would be unlikely to be paroled until a few months before their remission date. In this way the Home Secretary hoped to secure much-needed relief for the problem of prison overcrowding while appeasing the influential 'law-and-order' factions within the Conservative party (Maguire, 1992: 185). The new 'twin-track' policy did have the desired effect of increasing the overall rate of early release (with 11,886 prisoners receiving parole in 1984 compared with 5,346 in 1983). But the changes also contributed to a growing sense of unease about the way the entire parole process was operating.

### Pressure for reform: the legacy of pragmatism

After two decades of almost continuous modification, the scope and importance of the parole system had changed beyond recognition. Between 1969 and 1989, the number of prisoners eligible for parole more than tripled, from 7,264 to 24,445; the percentage of prisoners who opted out by refusing to be considered for parole more than halved (from 6.7 per cent to 2.8 per cent); the overall *percentage* of parole applications granted more than doubled (from 27 to 58 per cent), and the *number* of parole applications that were actually granted went up more than sevenfold (from 1,833 to 13,751).

Equally noteworthy, however, was the marked *decline* in the parole rate for long-term prisoners following the introduction of Mr Brittan's restrictions on parole: whereas in 1983 33.5 per cent of prisoners serving more than five years whose cases were considered received parole, this figure slumped to 19.6 per cent in 1984. By contrast, the equivalent 1984 figure for prisoners serving less than two years was 76.4 per cent. So short-term prisoners were much more likely to be granted parole than those serving longer sentences, and the difference between the two types of prisoner had widened considerably. In other words, parole was serving to *increase the differentials* between different offenders' sentences.[11]

This bifurcatory tendency had two predictable consequences. One was to contribute to the relentless build-up in the long-term prison population which virtually wiped out the gains that had been secured by extending parole to short-term prisoners (Carlisle, 1988: para. 38). The second consequence was to generate unrest about parole within prisons, exacerbating the already serious crisis of legitimacy. The policy of bifurcation was widely seen as unfair, repressive and discriminatory, and in the case of long-term prisoners it was seen as removing any incentive to behave well in prison. It seems likely that at least two serious prison disturbances in Scotland (at Peterhead in 1986 and Perth in 1987) were directly linked with these changes in parole, which also applied to Scotland (Scraton et al., 1991: 25, 104).

Another fiercely criticized aspect of the parole system – which had caused widespread resentment among prisoners from the very beginning – concerned the decision-making process itself, and its failure to comply with even the most elementary requirements of natural justice and due process. This was epitomized in the refusal to give reasons where parole was not granted, and in the generally secret nature of the whole parole exercise. Prisoners were excluded from the deliberations of the LRC and the Parole Board, and were not allowed to be represented at them, although it was standard practice for prisoners to be interviewed by a Local Review Committee member. Consequently, there was no way of challenging any of the evidence on which the parole decision was based, even though much of it was said to be subjective and anecdotal (Cohen and Taylor, 1978: 90). Finally, there was no right of appeal against a refusal of parole, nor any effective way to review or question the decision-making process. This lack of fairness and natural justice was all of a piece with the generally pragmatic nature of parole policies over the years – political and administrative expediency ruled at the expense of principle and justice.

The way the system had developed also led to the curious anomaly that compulsory supervision was only imposed on offenders who had been granted parole. Those who were refused parole were eventually released without supervision, even though they were likely to be 'worse risks', and arguably in *greater* need of supervision on release. There were also several other practical weaknesses associated with the parole process, many of which had been exacerbated by the pragmatically inspired reforms of the 1970s and 1980s. One was the sheer volume of cases to be dealt with, which had two rather unfortunate consequences. In the case of longer-term inmates it tended to result in serious delays in the processing of applications,[12] causing resentment, and further increasing the magnifying effect on sentencing differentials mentioned earlier. Conversely, in the case of shorter-sentenced prisoners the procedure was excessively hurried – partly because there was insufficient time to process the applications thoroughly; and partly because the documentation was frequently inadequate. The result was a high success rate of prisoners' applications on the basis of minimal scrutiny, thereby fuelling criticism by judges that there had been a clandestine revival of the 'semi-automatic' parole policy which they had seen off in 1981.

There was thus a compelling case for a thorough overhaul of the whole system of early release, to which was added potent pressure, notably from the judiciary. In 1987 the government announced a comprehensive review of parole under the chairmanship of Lord Carlisle. The Carlisle report (published in November 1988) was the first major independent review of the parole system since its inception. However, it too bore the hallmarks of yet another exercise in penological pragmatism. The Carlisle Committee was hamstrung by its restricted terms of reference, which forbade it from inquiring into the sentencing process – although it was this very process which had largely necessitated the development of the early release 'safety valves' in the first place. Hence the Committee's complaint, which we quoted earlier, that its brief was 'like bailing water from a boat without repairing the gaping hole in its bottom' (1988: para. 236). These terms of reference appear to have been dictated more by a concern to defuse the growing judicial hostility towards the quick parole procedure for short-term prisoners than by any willingness to get to grips with the fundamentals of the system.

In terms of its general philosophical approach, the Carlisle Committee expressed strong support for two key principles.[13] These were, first, the idea of *parsimony* in the use of custody, and secondly, the notion of *'real time custodial sentencing'* (Carlisle, 1988: paras 210, 217 and 232), in which 'what you get is what you serve' (also known as 'honesty in sentencing', or 'truth in sentencing'). But, being unable to recommend that the lengths of the sentences passed by judges should be significantly reduced across the board, the Committee inevitably found that these two principles clashed with each other.

So it reluctantly accepted the continuing need for early release mechanisms, which would inevitably mean that time spent in custody ('what you serve') would be appreciably less than the sentence pronounced by the judge ('what you get'). But in order to restore at least some meaning to the full sentence passed, it recommended a rather uneasy compromise. This was a modified version of Mr Brittan's twin-track approach in which both the restrictive and the more liberal elements of Mr Brittan's package were significantly watered down. Most of the Carlisle Committee recommendations were subsequently incorporated in the Criminal Justice Act 1991, whose provisions for early release from custody are still in force today, although they have since been supplemented by the introduction of 'home detention curfew'.

### EARLY RELEASE FOLLOWING THE CRIMINAL JUSTICE ACT 1991

The Criminal Justice Act 1991 replaced the previously distinct concepts of remission and parole with a new framework. The system applies differently to four categories of offender: those sentenced to less than 12 months; those sentenced to 12 months or more but less than four years; those sentenced to determinate sentences of four years or more; and those sentenced to life.[14] Figure 8.1 sets out the new system in diagrammatic form.

(i)   *Those sentenced to imprisonment for less than 12 months* are normally released automatically after serving one half of their sentence. This is known as '*Automatic Unconditional Release*'. However, the term 'unconditional' is something of a misnomer. It is true that release for this category of prisoners does not involve compulsory *supervision* or other conditions such as residence requirements. However, the unexpired portion of the sentence is held in suspense, and may be reactivated by a court if the offender is reconvicted of an offence committed before the end of the original term (or 'sentence expiry date'). This was a major departure from previous practice, reflecting the Carlisle Committee's desire to restore some meaning to the whole term originally imposed by the court. It is still possible for prisoners to 'lose remission' for misbehaviour in prison, although the terminology has changed: the commission of a disciplinary offence may be punished by a postponement of the date for Automatic Unconditional Release (known as the 'award of additional days').

(ii)   *Those sentenced to 12 months or more but less than four years* are also released from custody automatically after serving one-half of their sentence – again, subject to any 'additional days' awarded for misconduct in prison. This is known as '*Automatic Conditional Release*' – 'conditional' because when first released these prisoners are 'on licence', meaning that they undergo a compulsory period of supervision which normally lasts until three quarters of the original term has elapsed,[15] after which their release becomes 'unconditional'. Other conditions, such as conditions of residence, can also be imposed on their release. Failure to comply with the conditions of a licence is punishable by either a fine or recall to prison. But

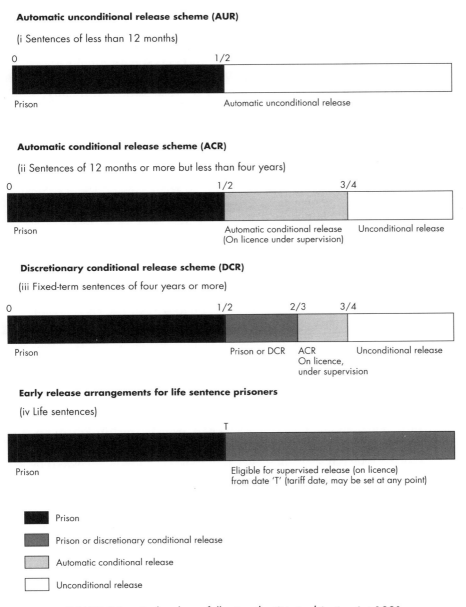

**Automatic unconditional release scheme (AUR)**

(i Sentences of less than 12 months)

Prison

Automatic unconditional release

**Automatic conditional release scheme (ACR)**

(ii Sentences of 12 months or more but less than four years)

Prison

Automatic conditional release
(On licence under supervision)

Unconditional release

**Discretionary conditional release scheme (DCR)**

(iii Fixed-term sentences of four years or more)

Prison

Prison or DCR

ACR
On licence,
under supervision

Unconditional release

**Early release arrangements for life sentence prisoners**

(iv Life sentences)

Prison

Eligible for supervised release (on licence)
from date 'T' (tariff date, may be set at any point)

- Prison
- Prison or discretionary conditional release
- Automatic conditional release
- Unconditional release

FIGURE 8.1    *Early release following the Criminal Justice Act 1991*

additionally, the Home Secretary can recall any prisoner on licence back to prison, even if there has been no breach of the licence terms or reconviction.[16] And, as with automatic unconditional release, any released prisoners who reoffend before their final sentence expiry dates can be made to serve the remainder of their sentences.

(iii) *Those who receive sentences of four years or more (other than life) are eligible to apply for 'Discretionary Conditional Release' after serving one half of* their sentence. Even if their applications are unsuccessful, they are normally released after serving two thirds (subject to delays for misbehaviour in prison). It is the Parole Board which decides whether to release prisoners in this category – and the process is still informally known as 'parole' – with the Home Secretary having a veto over the release of those serving 15 years or more. Prisoners are released on licence initially, which lasts until three quarters of the original term has elapsed.[17] Again, the court has the power to reactivate the unexpired portion of their sentences if they reoffend; and again the Home Secretary has the power to recall to prison even if there has been no reconviction or breach of licence conditions.

(iv) *Those sentenced to life imprisonment* can be released either by the Parole Board or by the Home Secretary on the recommendation of the Parole Board.[18] The prisoner does not become eligible to be considered for release until the 'tariff' period (explained later in this chapter) has expired; this 'tariff' can be of any length. Release is always 'on licence', which lasts for the rest of the offender's life. Consequently, lifers remain liable to recall (whether or not there has been a breach of any of the conditions imposed in the licence) or to revocation by a court if the lifer is convicted of a subsequent offence.

### Discretionary release: decision-making procedure

The original tripartite structure of Local Review Committees, Parole Board and Home Secretary was ended by the 1991 Act, which abolished the Local Review Committees. The Carlisle Committee (1988: para. 313) would have gone further by removing the Home Secretary from the picture and giving the final say on all discretionary release decisions to the Parole Board rather than the Home Secretary. Instead, however, the Home Secretary's veto was retained in respect of those serving sentences of seven years or more; in 1998 this was amended to those serving fifteen years or more.

As regards the provision of due process and natural justice in the decision-making process, the 1991 Act itself was a disappointment. With the exception of discretionary life sentence prisoners (see below) it gave prisoners few additional rights, reflecting instead a preference for more flexible administrative measures. However, the government did accept the need for greater openness and certain procedural improvements were introduced in 1992. Applicants now have the right to be interviewed by a member of the Parole Board, and the report of this interview is disclosed to the prisoner, as is the dossier of reports on which the Parole Board's decision is made. The Parole Board (sitting in panels of three) still sits in private to decide whether to grant parole, but has to give reasons for its decisions. While these do represent some moves in the direction of 'judicialization' of the process, it is still far from a comprehensive due process package: for example, there is no right to an oral hearing, and no right of appeal from the Parole Board's decision.

Another change to the system in the early 1990s concerned the *criteria* which the Parole Board are required to take into account when assessing applications for release. One of the main criticisms that had been directed against the old system of parole (for example, Hood, 1974b: 8; Ashworth, 1983: 368) was that it amounted to a form of 'executive resentencing' since the criteria included not only factors relating to the risk of future offending, but also those relating to the seriousness of the offence. Since the seriousness of the offence is typically one of the main factors influencing the length of the original sentence, this meant that any mitigating or aggravating factors would be given 'double weighting', first, at the time of sentence, and then when considering parole. The Carlisle Committee's response to such criticisms was to recommend that in future the parole decision should simply be based upon an evaluation of the risk of the prisoner committing a serious offence while on parole, balanced against the benefit to both the prisoner and the public of an early release under supervision (Carlisle, 1988: para. 321). The 1991 Act allowed the Home Secretary to set criteria for the Parole Board to apply, and the 'release directions' which were subsequently issued (in 1992, revised in 1996) did indeed focus *primarily* on the risk of future reoffending. This does not fully eliminate the problem of 'double weighting', as factors increasing risk include past offending and the seriousness of the current offence, both of which will have largely determined the sentence originally passed. (Indeed, the directions specifically instruct the Board to take into account 'the nature and circumstances of the original offence'.) Perhaps more importantly, the criteria are framed in such a way as to make any risk that may be thought to exist bear almost paramount importance, since the Board is directed to 'take into account that safeguarding the public may often outweigh the benefits to the offender of early release'. Fears expressed at the time of their introduction that these criteria would lead to a steep decline in the overall rate of parole have been borne out. In the year 1999–2000 41 per cent of prisoners considered for parole were granted it, compared with 53 per cent in 1991 (and 62 per cent in 1984). Of all prisoners eligible for parole whose cases were reviewed between 1992 and 1995, about 70 per cent were paroled at some point in their sentence; under the DCR scheme this figure has dropped by a third to 48 per cent (Hood and Shute, 2000: x).

Doubtless part of the reason for this is that the 'risk of reoffending' criterion (which is not restricted merely to the risk of committing *serious* or violent offences), demands a prediction which is difficult for Parole Board members to make accurately, in circumstances which conspire to encourage them to 'play safe' and hence to overestimate the actual risks involved in release. Hood and Shute (2000: 46–8) have found that Parole Board members do in fact systematically overestimate risks of reoffending when compared with validated statistical methods of making the same prediction. As a result, although half of a sample of prisoners being considered for parole had a low statistical risk of reconviction for a serious offence while on licence, only half of these low-risk prisoners were actually paroled by the Board (Hood and Shute, 2000: ch. 4 and 77–8). The cautious nature of the Parole Board's decision-making is evidenced by the very low rate of reoffending among those offenders it does deem safe enough to release: fewer than 4 per cent of parolees (and under 3 per cent of 'lifer' licensees) were recalled to prison for further offending in 1997–8.

There are also concerns about some of the other criteria that have to be taken into account when assessing applications for release. These include 'whether the prisoner has shown by his attitude and behaviour in custody that he is willing to address his offending behaviour . . . and has made positive effort and progress in doing so'. Clearly such a criterion is both vague and subjective, leaving the prisoner's liberty largely at the mercy of the possibly arbitrary assessments and reports of Prison Service staff and the interpretations put on them by Parole Board panel members. There is also a specific problem concerning those prisoners who continue to deny that they were ever guilty of the offence for which they were convicted. Although there is no blanket Parole Board policy against granting parole to 'offence deniers' (which would be unlawful),[19] denial is often a potent factor working against a prisoner since it is seen as an indication of poor attitude and unwillingness to address one's offending behaviour (Hood and Shute, 2000: 29–30). This, of course, places genuinely innocent prisoners in a cruel 'Catch-22' dilemma – should they continue to honestly deny the offence and jeopardize their parole chances, or lie and admit the offence, crushing their chances of ever having their miscarriage of justice righted? Given the number of such miscarriages which have come to light in recent years and the likelihood that many more have not, there is no saying how many people, wrongly in prison to start with, have been kept in because they honestly assert their innocence.[20]

The discretionary release of *lifers* (see Padfield, 1983; NACRO, 1995b) – whether sentenced to 'life imprisonment' as the *mandatory* sentence for murder, or as a *discretionary* sentence that is available for a number of other serious offences – is governed by special procedures.[21] The controversial (and exceedingly complicated) nature of these procedures is a matter of particular concern in view of the rapid growth in the number of lifers in England and Wales. On 31 March 2000 there were 4,469 such prisoners representing around 7 per cent of the total prison population compared with only 140 in 1957 (representing 3 per cent).[22] One source of complication stems from the fact that the two categories of lifers – 'mandatory' and 'discretionary' lifers – are governed by very different rules.

Both categories of life sentence prisoner have a '*tariff*' period set for them.[23] This tariff is the *minimum* amount of time they must spend in prison in order to satisfy the requirements of retribution and deterrence.[24] Once a lifer has served the tariff period, the release decision is based on an assessment of the risk involved in releasing that person into the community.

In the case of *mandatory lifers* all the most important decisions relating to release are the responsibility of the Parole Board and the Home Secretary. The Home Secretary (or more likely in practice a junior Home Office minister) sets the all-important 'tariff'. He is required to consult the trial judge and the Lord Chief Justice before doing so, but is not bound by their views. In effect, therefore, he has the power to lengthen the period which in the judges' opinion ought to be served by mandatory life sentence prisoners – a politician overruling a judicial decision about how long an offender should spend in prison. Home Secretaries have made frequent use of this power,[25] but no less a person than the Lord Chief Justice Lord Woolf has predicted that it could soon be removed now that the Human Rights Act 1998 requires courts as far as possible to interpret English law in accordance with the European Convention on Human Rights (*The Guardian*, 13 October 2000).[26]

In 1988 Home Secretary Douglas Hurd imposed the first 'whole life tariff', creating a category of prisoners who are never to be released. Since then, whole life tariffs have been imposed on thirty mandatory lifers, of whom the best known is 'Moors murderer' Myra Hindley. Such a policy creates a category of prisoners who almost literally have 'nothing to lose', and might therefore be less amenable to control. More fundamentally, however, it is contrary to the requirements of natural justice to place the fate of individuals entirely in the hands of elected politicians whose decisions may be influenced by considerations of electoral advantage. This practice of imposing whole life tariffs was upheld as lawful by the House of Lords in March 2000 when it was challenged in the courts by Myra Hindley herself.[27] As we write, Hindley is pursuing a further challenge to the European Court of Human Rights.

The final decision on the release of a mandatory lifer is also the responsibility of the Home Secretary. Although he may only order the release on the recommendation of the Parole Board, he is not obliged to accept their recommendation even though the tariff period has expired and the Parole Board has decided that the prisoner is not dangerous.[28] Nor does the Home Secretary's decision need to be based on risk assessment alone. The published 'release directions' state that 'the Home Secretary is also concerned with the wider political implications, including the effect on public confidence in the life sentence system which release may have, i.e., how the public would be likely to respond to the lifer being released at that juncture'. (Again, it remains to be seen whether and how long this arrangement may survive the Human Rights Act.)

Mandatory lifers have secured a few procedural concessions in recent years. Since December 1992 they have been given reasons for decisions reached about their release dates and access to reports on their cases prepared by the Parole Board. A House of Lords ruling in 1993 further decided that they were entitled to be told of the judicial recommendation as to the 'tariff' they should serve; to be given the opportunity to make representations as to the tariff period; and to be informed of the Home Secretary's decision as to the 'tariff' together with reasons for any departure by him from the judicial view.[29] However, the Home Secretary retains a wide discretion to fix their tariff periods and determine the final release date, and the whole procedure remains far from the 'judicialized' ideal.

*Discretionary lifers* on the other hand are now subject to a much more judicialized procedure, following successful court challenges in 1988 and 1990 to the previous system which treated them in the same way as mandatory lifers. The discretionary lifer system also now applies to two categories of 'lifer' where the sentence is not passed at the judge's discretion: first, 'mandatory' life sentences for lesser offences than murder passed under the 'two strikes and you're out' provisions of the Crime (Sentences) Act 1997 (see Chapter 4); and second, people who are found guilty of murder when under the age of eighteen.[30]

It is now the trial judge who sets the 'tariff' period for a discretionary lifer when passing sentence. After the tariff has elapsed the Parole Board alone is responsible for deciding whether or not the prisoner is released on licence, based on the perceived risk to the public. The Home Secretary's contentious involvement in these essentially judicial decisions is thus greatly reduced[31] for this particular category of lifer. The Parole Board follows a more judicial procedure in such cases, setting up 'Discretionary Lifer Panels'[32] which hold oral hearings to decide whether to grant parole. Prisoners are entitled to attend hearings; to be legally represented; to apply for others to attend; to hear and question the evidence of other parties; to call authorized witnesses; to make pre-hearing representations; and, normally, to see reports on themselves which are submitted by the Board. Despite some remaining flaws – notably the absence of any right of appeal from Parole Board decisions – the procedural safeguards that have been adopted with respect to discretionary lifers set a standard against which to measure those applying to other categories of inmate. As we have seen, those for mandatory lifers in particular fall far short of an acceptable level of fairness at present. Even with the fairer procedure now applying to discretionary lifers, however, there has been a general trend to parole fewer prisoners: in 1993 Discretionary Lifer Panel hearings resulted in release in 20 per cent of cases; by 1998–9, this had declined to 9 per cent (Padfield and Liebling, 2000).

### The impact of the 1991 reforms

The Carlisle Committee was given an impossible challenge: to render the system of early release more palatable to the judiciary while avoiding an unacceptable increase in prison numbers. The Committee itself was fully aware that this could probably not be achieved without addressing the sentencing process itself, yet it was precluded from doing this by the unrealistically narrow terms of reference it was given. Even if the overall strategy of the 1991 'just deserts' reform package had not been abandoned, the consequence of the shift towards 'real-time sentencing' would have been to increase the prison population. For the early release provisions of the 1991 Act were intended to ensure that the great majority of short-sentence prisoners would serve a larger proportion of their sentence in custody (not becoming eligible for release until they had served half their sentences instead of one third). In the case of more serious offenders serving longer sentences, the new provisions were always likely to ensure that they served even more time in prison – especially given the 'safety first' attitude that the Parole Board seems to take, as we saw above. Furthermore, under the new provisions prisoners who are released early remain 'at risk', and if they reoffend may find themselves having to serve the unexpired portion of their original prison sentence. Hood and Shute (1996: 86) estimate that the new system has added about 1,000 prisoners to the total prison population. If this inflation of the prison population were to be avoided, sentencers would have to reduce the levels of their sentences to compensate. Consequently, the Carlisle Committee recommended 'a thorough reassessment of present sentencing levels' and 'a determined attempt on the part of the Government and the judiciary to secure a corresponding reduction in sentencing at all levels' (1988: para. 295).

This did not happen. The 1991 Act contained no provisions instructing sentencers to scale down general sentencing levels. In 1992 the Lord Chief

Justice[33] urged sentencers to take into account the effect of the new arrangements for early release and the actual period likely to be served in custody as a result. If this had any effect at all it was only very temporary, for since then there has been a sharp *increase* rather than a reduction in the overall level of sentencing,[34] despite the fact that most prisoners now have to serve a larger proportion of their sentences in custody than before. The Carlisle Committee warned in 1988 that should changes to early release lead to an increase in prison numbers 'the case for a root and branch review of sentencing law and practice would become irresistible' (para. 298). But, as we saw in Chapter 4, the current review of sentencing practice seems likely to move in a very different direction from that envisaged by Carlisle.

### 1995–7: threatened near-abolition

We saw previously that the Strategy A, 'law and order' mindset regards almost any early release as abhorrent because it lets criminals off too easily. It was only logical, then, that the Conservative government's wholehearted adoption of Strategy A between 1993 and 1997 placed the whole system of early release in jeopardy. Home Secretary Michael Howard informed Conservative Party conference in October 1995 that he intended 'to get honesty back into sentencing'. Prisoners would lose any prospect of early release whatsoever, with the sole exception that 'model prisoners should get a little time off for good behaviour'. This proposal found its way into the Crime (Sentences) Act 1997, passed shortly before the 1997 General Election, which provided that prisoners sentenced to up to three years could earn a maximum discount of one sixth of their prison terms. Longer-term prisoners could similarly not be paroled until the five sixths point of their sentences.

This scheme represented a reckless disregard for practical ('Strategy B') considerations regarding the numbers of people in prison. For it was calculated (Penal Affairs Consortium, 1995c) that these changes to early release would have increased the prison population by 24,000.[35] To accommodate so many extra prisoners without increasing prison overcrowding would have required 41 new prisons the size of Dartmoor. But these drastic proposals were never implemented. Although the Act was passed, the relevant sections were never brought into force, and were eventually repealed by the incoming Labour government's Crime and Disorder Act 1998.[36] This Act took the system of early release in a very different direction.

### Home detention curfew: early release goes electronic

Whereas Michael Howard had sought to reduce early release (with the inevitable result of further increasing the prison population), New Labour's Home Secretary Jack Straw took a small but pioneering step towards letting some prisoners out even earlier. Section 99 of the Crime and Disorder Act 1998 introduced 'home detention curfew' (HDC), a scheme which started operating on 28 January 1999. It allows prisoners serving sentences of three months or over but less than four years to be considered for release up to 60 days earlier than would normally occur (under Automatic Unconditional Release or Automatic Conditional Release). Release is on licence, and the conditions include a home curfew for at least 9 hours per day, enforced by electronic monitoring (or 'tagging'), as described in Chapter 5. The decision as to whether a prisoner is released on HDC is a discretionary one, with the discretion resting formally with the Home Secretary but in practice with the prison governor (not the Parole Board). The governor's decision is taken on the basis of a risk assessment carried out by prison and probation staff. This is not a scheme designed to maximize natural justice, but a flexible, administrative arrange-ment intended to achieve the (Strategy B) practical, managerial goals of reducing prison numbers and hopefully achieving a smooth and safe transition from custody to freedom for many prisoners.

Home detention curfew was originally expected to reduce the prison population by around 4,000, but in the event the reduction achieved in the first year of operation was only about half this amount. This was because only 31 per cent of eligible prisoners were granted release by governors, compared with an expected rate of around 50 per cent.[37] It seems clear that this was because governors were being deliberately and decidedly cautious when assessing the risk of prisoners either reoffending or failing to comply with their release conditions (at least in the scheme's early days). One result of this caution was a very high successful completion rate for HDC in 1999 of 95 per cent. It remains to be seen whether either the government or prison governors may take a less cautious attitude as the scheme progresses.

### The seamless sentence?

The government's review of the entire framework of sentencing carried out in 2000 and 2001 (Halliday, 2001: see chs 4 and 5) could have major implications for the current system of early release. It seems certain to lead to harsher sentences for persistent offenders and more flexible 'seamless' sentences mixing periods in custody with supervision in the community. Extensions in the use of electronic monitoring and other methods of more intensive community supervision following release are also on the agenda.

One particular development which seems definitely on the way goes under the name of 'Custody Plus'. This will be a new type of sentence to replace short prison sentences of up to 12 months. Currently, as we have seen, those who are released from sentences of this length receive 'Automatic Unconditional Release' and therefore are not subject to any compulsory supervision (although they are at risk of returning to serve the rest of their sentence if they reoffend). The policy document *Criminal Justice: The Way Ahead* (Home Office, 2001: 43) stated as a general principle 'that every offender released from prison who needs it should have follow-up support or supervision'. The new 'Custody Plus' sentence would consist of a fixed period in prison, followed by a further period under an enforced programme in the community (similar to the detention and training order for young offenders: see Chapter 9), with provision for return to custody for breach of the supervision conditions. It is not clear whether this would in itself lead to greater or fewer numbers in prison, but Jack Straw indicated that he would expect some persistent offenders to receive 'Custody Plus' sentences who presently receive non-custodial sentences (*The Guardian*, 22 January 2001).

For longer-term prisoners, it seems that in future all offenders will be supervised right up to the end of their sentences' (Home Office, 2001: 47; Halliday, 2001). And legislation has already been introduced to allow for electronic monitoring to be incorporated into any release licence (not only the new home detention curfew system).[38] Early release seems likely to take on a very different appearance in the near future. The chances are that it will form part of a new system under which increasing numbers of offenders will spend a greater length of time in prison, while also being subject to more and more intensive (and intrusive) supervision and surveillance on their release.

## CONCLUSION: EARLY RELEASE EVALUATED

Should we release prisoners early at all? Or is 'real time sentencing' preferable, safer and fairer?

Broadly speaking, three arguments are put forward for releasing prisoners early, and in our opinion all of them provide valid reasons for retaining an early release system of some kind. First, early release is advocated as a way of dealing with deficiencies elsewhere in the criminal justice system. These include the shortcomings of the criminal appeals system; the disparities in sentence lengths that are an inevitable outcome of unfettered judicial discretion; and most cogently of all the over-use of custody by sentencers and the excessive length of many custodial sentences. Ideally, all these problems would be best tackled at source; nevertheless it would probably be politically impractical in the foreseeable future to engineer the massive reduction in overall sentence lengths which would be required to compensate for a complete abolition of early release. So even if progressive moves in the direction of 'real time sentencing' might be generally desirable in the long run, there is a strong pragmatic case for retaining some kind of early release, at least for the time being, in the interests of humanity and of limiting prison numbers in a manner which is both practical and publicly acceptable. In this respect, although we remain somewhat sceptical about the real benefits of electronic monitoring of offenders (see Chapter 5 and Cavadino et al., 1999: 19–20, 210), it might be worth accepting in the context of rendering early release more palatable to the public.

A second argument for early release stems from the remarkable fact that parole is one of the few penal measures for which there seems to be some clear evidence that it does actually 'work' in the sense of reducing reoffending rates for those who receive it. Research has shown (Nuttall et al., 1977; Ward, 1987; Carlisle, 1988: para 48; Hann et al., 1991) that reconviction rates are significantly lower for those who are released on parole than for those who have been refused it. For example, one study (Nuttall et al., 1977) found that 8 per cent of paroled prisoners were reconvicted within 6 months of release compared with 29 per cent of non-parolees. It is true that 'better risk' offenders do tend to be selected for discretionary parole to start with; but even taking account of risk factors, parolees still seem to do better (Hann et al., 1991: 68–73). It is possible that parolees' better results may be due partly to the *deleterious* consequences of the 'knock-back' received by prisoners who are refused discretionary parole (Hann et al., 1991: 73–4). However, probably the likeliest explanation is that the combination of supervision and the threat of being returned to prison does serve to reduce the rate of reoffending after release.[39] And it seems at least intuitively likely that a degree of support and supervision from the probation service in the months following release from prison could well be of genuine assistance to many prisoners who would otherwise be left completely to their own devices as soon as they find themselves outside the prison walls. If this is the case, it argues for a system of *automatic* early release (with compulsory supervision) so that as many prisoners as possible receive its benefits, rather than a discretionary system, especially one which denies potential parolees many of the normal rights of natural justice.[40]

A third argument – and one that, conversely, argues for *discretionary* early release, at least in certain cases – is that a parole system enables the length of a prison sentence to be modified in the light of developments after the time it is passed. Perhaps most importantly, parole allows an offender to be released when (and not until) the degree of risk to the public is thought to have diminished to an acceptable level. And indeed, even the most radical penal reformers (for example 'abolitionists' – see Sim, 1992: 296) envisage some continuing need for at least a few exceptionally dangerous offenders to be detained on an indeterminate basis for purposes of incapacitation. (This is also true of our own futuristic vision for the penal system which we outline in our final chapter.) So long as this is the case, there will obviously have to be some means for determining when they are sufficiently safe to be released. However, the existing system of discretionary early release (even as reformed in recent years) is a poor method of doing this. It should be replaced by a judicial system of review in which all the relevant evidence could be thoroughly and openly assessed while effectively safeguarding the interests of the applicant – bearing in mind all the difficulties associated with the assessment of dangerousness and the well-established tendency for dangerousness to be officially 'over-predicted' (Bottoms, 1977; Monahan, 1981; Cavadino, 1989: 99–100). There should be a full judicial hearing with a right to publicly funded legal representation and an unrestricted right of appeal, and certainly no political veto on releases. Decisions should also, as far as possible, be based not on the impressions, guesses and hunches even of experienced experts, since these are known to be inaccurate and to give rise to the risk of unconscious prejudices swaying release decisions. They ought instead to be based on a precise set of overt criteria which have an established and valid bearing on the genuine likelihood of the prisoner posing a serious risk if released.

So in our opinion, a morally defensible penal system would include provision for early release, although the existing system would require a significant overhaul. And this would need to form part of a more comprehensive reform package, which would also have to include measures to reduce levels of custodial sentencing. On the other hand, to abolish early release without at the same time addressing the need for reform of sentencing – which remains the crux of the crisis – would be to court disaster on a truly epic scale.

## NOTES

1  The threat of judicial opposition remains, however, and has been instrumental on more than one occasion in shaping the development of early release mechanisms.

2  For these reasons Brian Stratton, writing of his experiences in prison (1973: 44), claimed that 'parole and the people running it are to blame for much of the tension in prisons today'.

3  An important factor in this 'judicialization' has been the growing impact of the European Convention on Human Rights on the reform of English law, even before the implementation of the Human Rights Act 1998.

4  This power was used by Home Secretary Jack Straw in August 2000 to release the gangland murderer Reggie Kray a few weeks before his death from cancer.

5  A more detailed historical account of the first 25 years of parole is contained in Cavadino and Dignan (1992: ch. 6).

6  This was at a time when a more liberal and pragmatic penal policy was being put together under Home Secretary Douglas Hurd (see Chapter 11). The immediate effect of this increase in remission was a reduction in the prison population by approximately 3,500; at the same time Lord Carlisle's wide-ranging review of early release was announced (see below).

7  See in particular the history of the suspended sentence as described by Bottoms (1981); and also that of the community service order as described by Pease (1985).

8  Windlesham (1993: 106) points out that throughout the 1960s and 1970s the part played by party political ideology in shaping penal reforms such as the parole system was very much less significant than in the period since 1980 and that, 'in the consensual politics of the day' such reforms were less likely to be shaped by party political objectives than by 'the surrounding world of penal thought'. Conservative politicians as well as those in the ruling Labour Party were likely to believe in the possibility of rehabilitating offenders by measures such as parole.

9  This independent status was formalized in 1996, when the Parole Board became an Executive Non-Departmental Public Body.

10  Those serving between six months and three years. After release at the one-third stage, offenders would have been supervised in the community during the second third of the sentence. This proposal emanated from an internal review of parole (Home Office, 1981b).

11  This is not an inevitable result of parole, for it has not had the same effect in other jurisdictions such as Canada (Polvi and Pease, 1991: 225).

12  Indeed, in 1988 and 1989, delays in processing applications had grown so long that in many cases prisoners' parole dates had passed before they were informed of the decision.

13  These two principles had also influenced the Canadian Sentencing Commission's (1987) report on sentencing and parole.

14  The statutory rules are contained in Part II of the Criminal Justice Act 1991; the rules relating to life sentence prisoners are now to be found in the Crime (Sentences) Act 1997, ss. 28–34. The new arrangements for non-lifers apply only to prisoners sentenced after 1 October 1992. The old arrangements continue to apply in most respects to those sentenced before then, though as time goes on they constitute a steadily diminishing proportion of the total prison population.

15  The courts have the power to pass 'extended sentences' on sex offenders. The effect is to lengthen the period during which the offender remains on licence, under supervision and 'at risk', for up to an extra ten years. (This power to pass extended sentences also apples to violent offenders who are sentenced to four years or more.

For violent offenders the maximum extra supervision period is five years.) Prisoners who are recalled during this period are eligible to be considered by the Parole Board for re-release on licence and may have their cases considered on an annual basis (Crime and Disorder Act 1998, ss. 58–60).

16 This may be done on the recommendation of the Parole Board, but the Home Secretary can also act without the Board's recommendation if this appears 'expedient in the public interest' (Criminal Justice Act 1991, s. 39(2)). Recalled prisoners are entitled to a Parole Board hearing after their recall. This recall power was extended to short-term as well as long-term prisoners from 1 January 1999, by section 103 of the Crime and Disorder Act 1998.

17 Again, for sex offenders and violent offenders given 'extended sentences' the licence may last until the very end of the sentence; see n. 15 above.

18 Whether the Home Secretary is involved in the release decision depends on whether the prisoner is a 'mandatory' or 'discretionary' lifer: see below.

19 *R. v. Secretary of State for the Home Department ex parte Zulfikar* (*The Times*, 26 July 1995). In *R. v. Parole Board ex p. Oyston* ([2000] Legal Action, June 2000, p. 15) the Court of Appeal ruled that the Parole Board had erred by assuming that the risk of reoffending could only be reduced by formal offending behaviour work. The applicant had been unable to participate in this activity because of his persistent denial of guilt.

20 Harold Williams may have been one of these innocent victims. In August 2000 his murder conviction was referred to the Court of Appeal as a possible miscarriage of justice by the Criminal Cases Review Commission. He was convicted in 1977, and would have been paroled in 1988 had he admitted his guilt. In October 2000, Williams died in prison.

21 As we saw in Chapter 4, the Crime (Sentences) Act 1997 makes life imprisonment a 'semi-mandatory' sentence for those convicted for a second time of any of a number of relatively serious crimes. The procedures for the release of these lifers are the same as for 'discretionary' lifers.

22 (*Prison Report* No. 51, June 2000, p. 9); Penal Affairs Consortium (1994). Looked at in a European context, the figures are even more startling. A survey by the Quaker Council for European Affairs (McGeorge, 1990) estimated that the number of lifers in England, Wales and Scotland (3,054) greatly exceeded the combined figure for all other countries in Western Europe (2,688).

23 A judge imposing a mandatory life sentence for murder may also recommend a minimum term that should actually be served. This may or not may not be the same as the 'tariff' which is set later. For practical purposes, however, the tariff is of greater importance.

24 In 1996 Lord Chief Justice Bingham advised judges that the standard starting point for the tariff should be 14 years (*The Guardian*, 28 July 2000).

25 According to figures produced by the House of Lords Select Committee on Murder and Life Imprisonment (Nathan Committee, 1989), between April and September 1988 only 32 per cent of judges' recommendations were accepted by Home Office ministers; 60 per cent of tariffs were increased and only 8 per cent were reduced.

26 In February 2001 the High Court held that the Home Secretary's power to fix and increase tariffs was not incompatible with the European Convention on Human Rights, but the judges indicated that they only reached their decision because of binding House of Lords precedents and that an appeal might well succeed. (*R. v. Secretary of State for the Home Department ex parte Anderson and Taylor*, LTL 26/3/01.)

27 *R. v. Secretary of State for the Home Department ex parte Hindley* [2000] 2 WLR 730.

28 In recent years Home Secretaries have been rejecting a higher proportion of cases than in the early 1980s in spite of the fact that the Parole Board has reduced the

proportion of recommendations for release made over the same period (see McGeorge, 1995: 7). As a result, the probability of a life sentence prisoner being released after review dropped from 1 in 3 to 1 in 5 during the 13 years between 1980 and 1992. Moreover, the actual time served by mandatory lifers increased by 50 per cent over a ten-year period (*The Guardian*, 30 June 1995).

29 *R. v. Secretary of State for the Home Department, ex parte Doody* [1993] 3 WLR 154.

30 These young offenders receive the mandatory indeterminate sentence of 'detention during Her Majesty's Pleasure' (Powers of Criminal Courts (Sentencing) Act 2000, s. 90) . The power of the Home Secretary to set the 'tariff' period in such cases was successfully challenged in the European Court of Human Rights by the youths who murdered James Bulger (see Chapter 9) in the case of *V. and T. v. United Kingdom* (2000) 30 EHRR 121; while his power to make the final decision as to release was similarly held to be a breach of human rights in *Hussain v. United Kingdom* (1996) 22 EHRR 1.

31 But not eliminated, since the Home Secretary retains the power to issue general directions to the Board, and can thereby influence the way it exercises its discretion. Moreover, he retains the right to revoke the licence of any long-term or life sentence prisoner without a recommendation by the Board if this appears expedient to him in the public interest.

32 Consisting of a High Court Judge (who chairs the panel), a psychiatrist or probation officer, and a layperson or probation officer.

33 In a *Practice Direction* (*Crime: Sentencing*) [1992] 1 WLR 948.

34 Between 1992 and 1999, sentences of immediate custody rose as a proportion of Crown Court sentences from 44 per cent to 63 per cent, the highest level since 1968. The 'custody rate' at magistrates' courts also increased from 5 to 12.5 per cent over the same period. The average *length* of a custodial sentence passed in a magistrates' court was 2.8 months in both these years, but in the Crown Court increased from 20.8 to 24.1 months (Mattinson, 1998; White et al., 1999; Ayres, 2000).

35 That is, unless at the same time courts reduced the lengths of the sentences they passed to compensate. The Crime (Sentences) Act 1997 did contain a section instructing courts to do so, but experience – such as with the Lord Chief Justice's Practice Direction of 1992 – suggests this would have had little effect.

36 The Labour Government took a different approach to 'honesty in sentencing', deciding that it would be sufficiently 'honest' if judges when pronouncing sentence gave a full explanation of what the sentence meant in terms of time to be served in prison and eligibility for early release rather than merely stating the nominal length of the sentence. (This has been called 'transparency in sentencing'.) Effect was given to this by a Practice Direction issued to courts by the Lord Chief Justice (*Practice Direction* (*Custodial Sentences: Explanation*) (1998) 1 Cr App R 397).

37 From 28 January to 30 November 1999, 45,000 prisoners were eligible for HDC, of whom almost 14,000 were released (Dodgson and Mortimer, 1999).

38 Criminal Justice and Court Services Act 2000, s. 62.

39 This would be consistent with the finding that certain supervisory non-custodial sentences appear able to exert a 'holding effect' on supervisees and at least delay reoffending while the supervision lasts: see Ashworth, (1983: 32); Raynor (1988: 111).

40 A contrary view would be taken by anyone who believed that it is the 'demonstration of trust' placed in the prisoner (Hann et al., 1991: 73) which generates the beneficial effect, and that this demonstration would be lost in automatic early release. We find this implausible.

# 9

# Young Offenders: Systems Management or System Disaster?

There is a curious ambivalence in what Durkheim (see Chapter 3) would have called our 'collective sentiments' about young offenders. On the one hand, the image of the 'young thug' is a perennial focus for fear, hatred and periodic 'moral panics' (Pearson, 1983; Cohen, 1980), and this sometimes leads to particularly punitive measures being devised for young offenders. Examples include the 'short, sharp shock' detention centre in 1980 and the 'boot camp' in the 1990s. On the other hand, our attitudes towards 'children in trouble' can also be infected with the sentimentality evoked by children generally in our culture, which can lead to less punitive measures being countenanced for them. Perhaps because of this ambivalence, the history of the penal treatment of young offenders has been especially chequered and contradictory.

Experience in England and Wales in the last few decades shows this particularly well. An Act of Parliament (the Children and Young Persons Act 1969) which was intended to create a radically new and more lenient system for dealing with juvenile offenders led paradoxically to a massive increase in the incarceration of young people in the 1970s. In the 1980s, despite an apparently discouraging political climate, developments in juvenile justice were hailed as highly successful in reducing the custody rate for young people and as showing the way forward for more general reform of the criminal justice system. But these approaches to youthful offending were in turn to fall out of favour with the government in the 1990s as the pendulum swung against the young offender once more. Currently, the trend towards harsher treatment for youthful offenders is still under way; but at the same time there are some developments pointing in a more humane direction.

## YOUNG PEOPLE AND CRIME

There hardly seems to have been a time, at least since the early nineteenth century, when the criminal activity of young people has not been a cause of major public concern. We seem to be repeatedly told, not least by the media, that crime among young people is a serious and ever-worsening problem, often in contrast to a previous golden age (typically located 20 years in the past) when youth posed no great threat to public order and safety. If we check the historical record, however, we find that at the time of the supposed golden age people were saying exactly the same things (Pearson, 1983).

It is true that adolescents do appear to commit a disproportionate number of crimes compared with their elders. In 1999, 41 per cent of people found guilty of or cautioned[1] for an indictable offence in England and Wales were under 21. For every 100 people aged under 21 in 1999, there were 3 convictions and cautions for indictable offences, compared with 0.8 per 100 for adults. The peak age for committing a detected offence was 18 for boys and 15 for girls in 1999. But little of this was serious crime, especially for offenders under 18, whose commonest detected crime is shoplifting.[2] The vast majority of really serious crime is committed by adults.

As the above figures suggest, offending by young people is in the great majority of cases a transient phenomenon of adolescence. Research studies (see for example, Belson, 1975; West, 1982; Graham and Bowling, 1995) suggest that most young people commit at least some minor offences, which in the main go undetected, while even the ones who are repeatedly caught offending in their teens typically 'grow out of crime' as they progress to adulthood (Osborn and West, 1980; Rutherford, 1992: ch. 2; Flood-Page et al., 2000: 18–19). To complete this comparatively unthreatening picture of young people's crime, the official statistics suggest that – far from a youth crime wave being upon us – offending by young people has been *decreasing* in recent years. The number of people under 21 who were found guilty of or cautioned for an indictable offence in 1999 was down by 33 per cent on the figure for 1985, and 13 per cent less than in 1992. This is only partly because there are now fewer young people in the population; even in relation to their numbers, convictions and cautions have gone down from 3.8 per 100 under-21s in 1985 to 3.0 in 1999.[3]

And yet young people continue to contribute substantially to the 'numbers crisis' in the custodial system. On 31 May 2000 young offenders accounted for 17 per cent of the 'prison population' (which includes custodial institutions for young offenders).[4] (Hardly any other Western European countries lock up as many young people proportionately (Goldson and Peters, 2000), despite research results suggesting that young English people commit fewer offences than their counterparts in other Western European countries.)[5] The way we deal with young offenders also has ramifications for the penal system's 'crisis of legitimacy'. For example, conditions and regimes at young offender institutions such as those at Portland and Feltham have been the subject of particular concern and criticism recently. In 1999 the Chief Inspector of Prisons described conditions at Feltham as 'unacceptable in a civilised country'; in March 2000 he was similarly scathing about Portland, describing conditions there as a 'moral outrage' (HM Chief Inspector of Prisons, 1999d, 2000c). Serious allegations about brutal staff behaviour in Portland over many years began to emerge in 1999, and in August 2000 four staff members were suspended as police commenced investigations. The most disturbing single recent incident concerning young offenders was the racist murder of Zahid Mubarek by another inmate in 2000, which led to an internal inquiry concluding that Feltham was 'institutionally racist' (*The Guardian*, 22 January 2001).

In general, young offenders represent a crucial facet of the penal crisis. For while, on the one hand, concern about young offenders has played an important part in fuelling the ideology of law and order and thereby worsening the crisis, recent experience of dealing with young offenders successfully has also indicated some ways in which the crisis could be defused if the right lessons could be learned and applied.

## YOUNG OFFENDERS: THE LEGAL FRAMEWORK

*Children under ten* (the 'age of criminal responsibility') cannot be prosecuted for offences at all.[6] However, children below (and indeed above) this age can be made the subject of *civil* care and supervision orders under the Children Act 1989 if the child's interests are felt to require it. If certain criteria are met, a child can be placed in secure accommodation within the system of local authority care (see further Cavadino, 1994b).

'*Juvenile*' offenders – between their tenth and eighteenth birthdays – form a particular legal category. The *youth justice system* which deals with offenders between these ages is summarized in diagram form in Figure 9.1, which differs in certain respects from the equivalent scheme for adults shown in Figure I.1 in the Introduction.

One difference between juvenile and adult offenders relates to what for adults is known as the 'cautioning' of offenders by the police as an alternative to prosecution. A new system for offenders under 18 was introduced by the Crime and Disorder Act 1998.[7] Young offenders who admit their guilt to the police may now receive either an official '*reprimand*' or a more serious '*warning*' (also known as a '*final warning*'). Normally an offender can receive only one reprimand and one warning before being prosecuted.[8] Offenders who are *warned* are referred to the local youth offending team (YOT), who should assess their suitability for a 'rehabilitation programme' (also known as 'change programmes') and where appropriate implement the programme. These rehabilitation programmes may include a variety of training and other measures and activities, including getting offenders to apologize to victims and perform reparation for either individual victims or the community.[9] Reprimands, warnings and any failure by an offender to agree to or cooperate with a rehabilitation programme can be cited in court in future should the young person offend again.

The rules as to remand in custody prior to trial also differ for young suspects (under the age of 17). If not left at liberty or conditionally free on bail, young offenders may be remanded to live in local authority accommodation, which may be secure accommodation if certain criteria are met. The practice of sending female suspects in this age range to custody prior to trial was ended in the 1980s, and as long ago as 1991 the government pledged to do the same for males under 17. However, it is still possible for boys of 15 or 16 to be remanded into custody; indeed the numbers have increased in recent years.[10]

If prosecuted, offenders under 18 are normally tried in the *youth court*, a specialized version of the magistrates' court. (Until 1992, this court was known as the 'juvenile court', and dealt only with offenders who had not reached the age of 17.) Youth court magistrates are drawn from a special panel of local magistrates who have particular experience or interest in work with young people, and the court's proceedings are not open to the public.

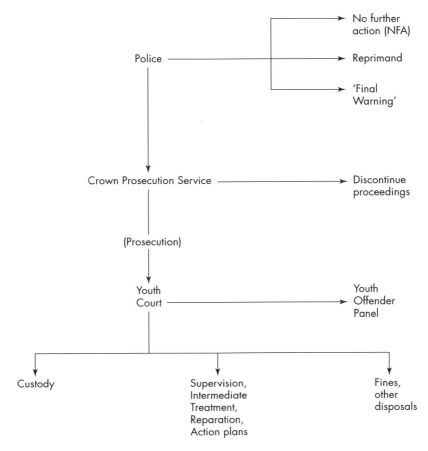

FIGURE 9.1   *The youth justice system*

Although, as we shall see, youth courts have the power to impose some punitive sentences including custodial ones, it always has a statutory duty 'to have regard to the welfare of the child' in making its decisions (Children and Young Persons Act 1933, s. 44(1)). And in general, youth is officially seen as a mitigating factor in sentencing. Although there may well be occasions when sentencers come down particularly hard on young offenders, it is more often the case that a young offender will receive a less harsh sentence than an adult who has committed a similar crime (see for example Flood-Page and Mackie, 1998: 123–4).

Young people under 18 cannot be sentenced to adult prisons, but from the age of 12 upwards they may receive a *detention and training order* ('DTO') for a period of between four and 24 months.[11] (For offenders aged 12 to 14, this sentence is only available for 'persistent offenders', a term not defined in the legislation.) The first half of a DTO is served in custody, which currently normally takes the form of a *young offender institution* for those aged 15 to 17, or a *secure training centre* for those who are under 15. The second half of the sentence is served under supervision in the community. For certain particularly serious offences, offenders aged 10 to 17 can be sentenced to long-term detention.[12] Young people under 18 can be made the subject of *supervision orders* (the equivalent of 'community rehabilitation orders', previously called 'probation orders' for older offenders),[13] under which they are supervised by probation officers, social workers, or youth justice workers from the local 'youth offending team' or 'YOT' (see below). These supervision orders may contain special conditions, including 'intermediate treatment requirements', which will feature later in this chapter, and requirements to make reparation either to the victim of the offence or the community at large. Another special sentence for young offenders (including 'young adults' aged 18 to 20) is the *attendance centre* order. This requires the offender to attend a centre, typically run by the police on Saturday afternoons, to engage in PE and other activities. Other disposals, such as fines, curfews with electronic monitoring and community punishment orders (previously known as community service orders), are also available. Fines may be imposed on the offender's parents, who may also be 'bound over' so that they are legally obliged to take proper control over their children and ensure that they comply with any community sentences imposed on them. Finally, a whole raft of new orders for young offenders was introduced by the Crime and Disorder Act 1998, including *action plan orders* and *reparation orders*.[14]

Another recent innovation – first introduced on a 'pilot' or experimental basis in some areas in June 2000 – is the *youth offender panel* (YOP).[15] When a young offender is prosecuted for the first time and pleads guilty, the youth court will normally[16] sentence the offender by making a 'referral order' referring the offender to a youth offender panel.[17] The YOP then agrees a 'youth offender contract' with the young offender, containing a 'programme of behaviour the aim of which is the prevention of re-offending by the offender'.[18] If a contract cannot be agreed or is breached, the young offender will be returned to court to be sentenced for the offence.

Every local authority area has a multi-agency *youth offending team* (or 'YOT'), containing representatives from the police, probation service, local authority social services, the local health and education services and others, whose role is to co-ordinate and provide youth justice services in the area according to a 'youth justice plan' formulated by the local authority in consultation with other agencies.[19] There is also a national Youth Justice Board which monitors the operation of the youth justice system, advises YOTs, other local agencies and the Home Secretary about the running of youth justice, and has a developing responsibility for custodial and other secure facilities (now known collectively as the 'juvenile secure estate') for young people under 18. YOTs, youth justice plans and the Youth Justice Board were all introduced by the Crime and Disorder Act 1998 (sections 29–32).

'*Young adult*' offenders – between their eighteenth and twenty-first birthdays – fall into a different category from those under 18. Young adults receive 'old-style' cautions rather than reprimands and warnings, and are not tried in the youth court but in the normal magistrates' and Crown courts. At present, young adults can receive the custodial sentence *detention in a young offender institution*[20] instead of an adult sentence of imprisonment. However, this special sentence is soon to be abolished[21] with the result that this age range will be able to receive almost exactly the same range of sentences as adults over 21.


## SYSTEM DISASTER: JUVENILE JUSTICE, 1969–1982

The recent history of 'juvenile justice' or 'youth justice'[22] has been particularly complex and paradoxical. One thread which runs strongly throughout this history, as indeed it does through adult penology (see Chapter 2), is the ideological contest which has been waged over the years between different philosophies or 'models' of what the system should be attempting to achieve. On the one hand is the 'positivistic' approach which holds that young offenders should be helped rather than punished, often known in the juvenile context as the 'welfare model'.[23] Opposing positivism are more traditional, punishment-oriented (or 'classicist') approaches. One of these is the 'justice model' which, like its adult counterpart, seeks to reduce official discretion in the system; to ensure that like cases are treated alike according to the offenders' 'just deserts'; and to ensure that suspects' rights of 'due process' are upheld (Morris et al., 1980; Taylor et al., 1979). Another punishment-oriented approach is, again, the potent ideology of 'law and order' which leads to a punitive 'Strategy A' approach (see Chapters 1 and 2). A third approach which is becoming increasingly influential in the youth justice sphere is the 'restorative justice' approach which advocates a more participatory decision-making process, in which offenders, victims and other interested parties collectively seek to resolve an offence (see also Chapters 5 and 11).

Since the nineteenth century, there has been special, more positivistic provision for young offenders in the criminal justice system (Muncie, 1984: ch. 2; Morris and Giller, 1987: ch. 1), and there was a long-term, seemingly inexorable trend towards a welfare approach which reached a high point in 1969 with the passing of the Children and Young Persons Act (CYPA). The Labour government of 1964 to 1970 proposed a radical reform of juvenile justice with the intention of engineering a significant shift towards a much more positivistic system in which the young person's welfare would be the prime consideration.[24] Had everything gone as originally intended, the CYPA would have meant that no child under the age of 14 could have been prosecuted for any offence other than homicide. Instead, children in trouble with the law or in any other kind of need would be dealt with by means of civil care proceedings. Even above the age of 14, the Act envisaged the phasing out of criminal proceedings for all but the most serious of juvenile offenders, and even these (if prosecuted) could not have been sentenced to punitive custody but could only be placed in care.

But this never came to pass, for in 1970 an incoming Conservative government decided that the CYPA should only be partially implemented. Some welfare disposals were introduced, but the minimum age for prosecutions remained at 10, and the juvenile court remained essentially a 'junior criminal court' with the power to impose custodial sentences, rather than the welfare tribunal which the CYPA had intended. Even in its heavily modified form the Act immediately attracted strong criticisms, notably from magistrates, court clerks and the police. The result was a series of measures (notably in the Criminal Law Act 1977) which increased the powers of juvenile court magistrates to specify what should happen to young offenders they sentenced and to enforce the court orders they made. All this was despite the fact that the governing party from 1974 to 1979 was the same Labour Party which had introduced the CYPA in the first place. By this time the 'rehabilitative ideal' had collapsed and there was a noticeable shift across the political spectrum towards a Strategy A 'law and order' attitude, part of a phenomenon Stuart Hall (1979) called 'the Great Moving Right Show'. The radical reform which the CYPA was supposed to usher in had been completely abandoned.

Ironically, however, despite many loud claims to the effect that the CYPA had led to an unconscionable softness in the juvenile justice system, all the objective evidence in the 1970s was that young offenders were actually getting a much harsher deal. Although the intention of the CYPA was that juveniles who offended should be helped rather than punished and that they should be dealt with in the community rather than sent to custody, the actual result was, spectacularly, the reverse. There was a distinct decline in the use of community-based disposals for juvenile offenders coupled with a massive rise in the use of custody, from 3,000 custodial sentences in 1970 to over 7,000 in 1978. The most telling figures are for males between the ages of 14 and 16 inclusive. Only 6 per cent of sentenced offenders in this category were sent to detention centre or borstal in 1970 (the last year before the CYPA came into force). By 1978 the proportion had doubled to 12 per cent.[25] The new, half-implemented system was proving a disaster for young offenders.

The swing towards Strategy A gathered further momentum in 1979 with the election of a Conservative government under Margaret Thatcher. Law and order – and in particular, measures to deal with 'young criminals' – had formed a major plank in the Conservative platform in the general election campaign. A White Paper, *Young Offenders* (Home Office et al., 1980) and the subsequent Criminal Justice Act of 1982 brought about the changes to the framework of custodial sentences for young people which we discuss in the following section and also further increased the powers of magistrates to insert specific requirements into young offenders' supervision orders. But as we shall see, the Criminal Justice Act 1982 was not an unremittingly punitive statute, and other approaches also made some impact.

## SHORT SHARP SHOCKS AND BEYOND: CUSTODY FOR YOUNG OFFENDERS, 1979–1992

Prior to the Criminal Justice Act of 1982, the custodial sentences available for offenders under 21 were imprisonment (for young adults), long term detention for juveniles who committed serious offences, detention centre orders, and borstal training. Borstals and detention centres were custodial institutions which catered for both juveniles and young adults. 'Borstal training' was a semi-indeterminate sentence for offenders aged 15 or more which lasted for a minimum of six months and a maximum of two years. The detention centre (DC) sentence was shorter (three to six months) available for boys[26] from the age of 14 upwards. Detention centres had been created by the Criminal Justice Act 1948; their original rationale had been to provide young offenders with a 'short, sharp shock' as a deterrent, and consequently their regimes were less concerned with reformative treatment than borstals, and were more brisk and militaristic. Over the years, however, many DCs were modified to incorporate aspects of positive training and came to resemble short-term borstals. However, in 1979 the Conservative Party revived the idea of the 'short, sharp shock' DC, and gave it great prominence in their election manifesto (Conservative Party, 1979: 19–20).

The 'short, sharp shock' was first introduced on an experimental basis in 1980 in two DCs and extended to two more in 1981. The new regimes involved a brisker pace in carrying out tasks, hard physical work, more physical education, fewer privileges and an increased number of parades, inspections and drills. As well as becoming 'sharper' in the experimental centres, the DC sentence also became shorter: its minimum and maximum lengths were reduced to 21 days and four months respectively by the Criminal Justice Act 1982. The same Act also abolished the sentence of imprisonment for under-21s and transformed the borstal sentence into a new order for 'youth custody' (YC). Unlike borstal, this was a determinate sentence whose length was fixed by the sentencing court (albeit with possibilities of early release, like adult imprisonment), with a minimum of four months one day.

Of these changes, only the most publicized one (tougher regimes in DCs) could fairly be said to be the product of law and order ideology. The new DC sentence was after all shorter; while the new determinate youth custody sentence can be seen as influenced by 'justice model' thinking more than anything. The 1982 Act also introduced 'gatekeeping' criteria – the forerunners of those contained in the Criminal Justice Act 1991 (see Chapter 4) – which needed to be met before a court could pass a custodial sentence upon a young offender.

Perhaps the most predictable result of these changes concerned the new DC regimes. To few people's surprise, monitoring found that the modified regimes appeared to be no more effective than the previous ones at deterring either the DC inmates themselves or the youth population in their catchment areas (Home Office, 1984b). However, the government's response to the failure of its 'experiment' was not to abandon it but, remarkably, to extend the tougher regime to all DCs. Less foreseen was the effect on sentencing patterns of the 1982 Act. Although there was no noticeable proportionate increase or decrease in custodial sentences, there was a dramatic shift in the relative use of DC and borstal/youth custody sentences.[27] Magistrates seemed keen to use their power (newly granted under the 1982 Act) to send young offenders to 'borstal', while being much less tempted by the supposed attractions of the 'short, sharp shock' DC sentence. The result was that detention centres emptied while youth custody centres bulged at the seams. The government responded pragmatically by deciding to abolish the separate DC sentence. The Criminal Justice Act of 1988 created a new generic sentence of 'detention in a young offender institution' (YOI). DCs and youth custody centres all became YOIs; courts now decided on the length of the sentence but the Prison Service decided which institution the offender went to. The creation of the YOI sentence was an interesting (and rare) example of the Thatcher government removing a sentencing option from the magistrates – perhaps an indication of the way that shortages of penal resources can act as a potent determinant of policy under the right circumstances.

## SYSTEMS MANAGEMENT WITH YOUNG OFFENDERS

Paradoxically, although the 1980s witnessed the enthusiastic espousal of 'law and order' rhetoric by the government, it was also the decade of what has been called 'the successful revolution' (Jones, 1989) in juvenile justice. New methods, collectively known as *'systems management'*, transformed the scene and (its adherents claimed) succeeded in reducing the rates of juvenile custody, juvenile prosecution and even juvenile crime. Not the least of systems management's successes was that it gained the interest and support of the government for its aims and methods in the 1980s, although it was to lose it again in the 1990s.

The most influential pioneers of systems management in juvenile justice were a group of academics (all of them experienced former practitioners), often referred to simply as 'Lancaster' because of their original association with Lancaster University's Centre of Youth, Crime and Community. The 'Lancaster' group and its offshoots[28] engaged in research on juvenile justice, published influential works (most notably *Out of Care* by Thorpe et al., 1980), did consultancy work to advise juvenile justice practitioners as to how to implement systems management in their local areas, and generally promoted the approach. The Lancaster approach is essentially a 'minimum intervention' approach when it comes to young offenders themselves (although advocating strenuous intervention in the youth justice *system*). Young people, as we have seen, usually grow out of their offending phase. In the meantime, while the problems they pose have to be managed, harsh punishment (and especially custody) is not only unnecessary and inhumane but likely to be counter-productive in 'labelling' them as criminals and setting them off on a criminal career.

The systems management approach starts with 'systems *analysis'*. This means analysing what really happens in the criminal justice system: looking at the ways in which all the different agencies interact and interconnect to form the entire system. It also means determining how and why suspects and defendants pass through the various stages of the criminal process, commencing with the police investigation and possibly culminating in a custodial sentence or other court disposal. Chapter 4 of this book is largely an exercise in 'systems analysis' of the national criminal justice system; however, the Lancaster approach stresses the need to apply systems analysis to the youth justice system *in a particular local area*. Accurate systems analysis facilitates effective systems *intervention*: the system can be modified in ways which the analysis suggests will achieve specific desired results, such as a decrease in the numbers of young people ending up in custody. In this way, Lancaster-style systems analysis seeks to employ the kind of *managerialist* techniques associated with the 'Strategy B' approach to criminal justice, but with the ultimate aim of achieving *humanitarian* ('Strategy C') goals.

Systems management techniques include *decarceration, diversion from court and from custody, gatekeeping, targeting, inter-agency co-operation*, and *monitoring*: concepts whose meaning should become clear during the following discussion.

As we saw in Chapter 5, *decarceration* is a word which can be used to refer to the general movement to reduce or abolish custodial and institutional methods of dealing with offenders and other deviants. In this sense the entire thrust of Lancaster systems management is decarcerative, and a significant recent English example of successful partial decarceration. Thorpe et al. (1980: 34) use the word in a more limited sense, to mean essentially the closure of custodial and residential institutions – as happened, famously and almost literally overnight, in Massachusetts in 1972 (Rutherford, 1992: ch. 4). This can form one part of a systems management strategy, on the basis that people cannot be placed in institutions that do not exist, and the fewer institutional places are available, the more pressure there will be on the system to find less oppressive alternatives. *Diversion*, on the other hand, refers to earlier stages in the process, where decisions can be made to remove young people from the route to custody through the system and divert them along other routes, including removing them from the criminal justice system entirely.

The diagram of the youth justice process given previously in Figure 9.1 illustrates the various possible routes for diversion at different stages. Diversion from the route to custody occurs when offenders and suspects are processed in the directions indicated by the arrows on the right-hand side of the diagram. The first opportunity for diversion occurs when the police can opt to reprimand or warn an offender instead of proceeding towards a possible prosecution. Thus the police can act as '*gatekeepers*' to the youth justice system if they choose to reprimand and warn rather than prosecute. Diversion could also occur at the Crown Prosecution Service stage, as the CPS has the final say over whether a prosecution proceeds to court or is discontinued (for example, because evidence is insufficient or the offence is only trivial). The CPS could in theory also refer a case back to the police with a recommendation for a reprimand or warning. So far, however, the CPS has not played a major role in gatekeeping and diverting juvenile offenders from court (see Gelsthorpe and Giller, 1990).

The advocates of systems management in the 1980s and 1990s vigorously exploited a novel diversionary and gatekeeping mechanism that was originally set up in anticipation of the full implementation of the Children and Young Persons Act 1969. As we have seen, this envisaged that children who had committed offences would normally only be dealt with by means of civil care proceedings, and only then if they could be said to be in need of 'care and control'. Many police force areas set up formal mechanisms to enable them to consult closely with local authority social service departments to operate this new system (Bottoms, 2001). These gatekeeping arrangements – which came to be known variously as 'cautioning panels', 'juvenile liaison bureaux' or something similar – formed an extra stage in the route towards court for most young offenders. Over time, they evolved in many areas into multi-agency panels, comprising members of the police, probation, social and educational services, which would deliberate as to whether a young offender had to be prosecuted or whether the police should be recommended to administer a caution instead. Another possibility in some places was a 'caution plus' – in effect, the forerunner of the 'final warning' – whereby a caution was combined with some additional action or intervention.

Cautioning panels are currently dying out. This is partly because the new statutory framework for reprimands and warnings leaves much less room for discretion in deciding whether the police should initiate prosecution, but also because of the contemporary emphasis by government on speeding up the flow of young offenders through the criminal justice system – a flow which this extra stage inevitably slowed up. Nevertheless, the cautioning panel was of great historical importance[29] in many ways – for example, in pioneering gatekeeping, diversion and the inter-agency approach involved in getting different bodies to co-operate in setting up the panel and making it work. In addition – as we shall see – they demonstrated that systems management can have a significant successful impact on what happens to young offenders in a local area.

The introduction of youth offender panels (YOPs) creates a new avenue for diversion, for offenders who are taken to court for the first time, plead guilty and have not committed offences which are not serious enough to attract a custodial sentence. If the offender is not diverted from court by alternatives to prosecution, he or she can be diverted *out of court* by being referred to the YOP. The YOP then works out a 'youth offender contract' with the young person, which can contain a wide range of requirements about the offender's behaviour and participation in various activities. These can include reparation to the victim of the crime or to the community, or training programmes aimed at addressing the young person's offending behaviour. One notable feature of the legislation introducing YOPs is that it normally *requires* the court to refer offenders in the prescribed category to the YOP, thus imposing fairly strict 'gatekeeping' rules on the court.[30]

For offenders who have not (on this occasion) been diverted *from court* by reprimand or warning, or diverted *out of court* by referral to a YOP, diversion *from custody* is still possible if the court can be persuaded to pass a suitable non-custodial sentence instead. Here the *pre-sentence report* (or 'PSR': see Chapter 4) can play an important role. These reports (provided by probation officers or, in the case of many juveniles, by social workers or YOT members) discuss the current offence and the young person's offending behaviour, supply the court with information on the offender's social background, and also advise the court as to how the offender could be dealt with in the community. The agencies providing PSRs can do much to improve the diversionary effectiveness of reports by accurately *targeting* offenders who are genuinely at risk of being sent to custody and suggesting credible alternative non-custodial sentences.

It is worth stressing the need for accurate 'targeting' of these more intensive sentences in systems management thinking. If not well targeted, these sentences might be passed, not instead of custody, but instead of a less drastic penalty such as a fine. This means that offenders are *'up-tariffed'* – given sentences further 'up the tariff' of available disposals than they might have received. This, in turn, will increase their chances of being sent to custody if they reoffend subsequently, as courts have a tendency to move offenders further up the 'tariff' with each successive offence, reasoning that all the less intrusive measures have been tried unsuccessfully. (In other words, the courts tend in practice to employ a largely 'offender-based' rather than an 'offence-based' tariff: see Chapter 4.) Indeed, this 'up-tariffing' phenomenon formed an important part of Lancaster's analysis of what had caused the system disaster of juvenile justice in the 1970s. New welfare-based measures had been applied to young people without serious records of offending by well-meaning practitioners, with the unintended result that if the young people subsequently came before the courts they would be propelled more readily into custody because they were seen as already high up the tariff.

For a long time, *intermediate treatment* ('IT') was foremost among diversionary non-custodial penalties for juvenile offenders. Under the influence of systems management thinking, the 1980s saw the development of many 'intensive IT' programmes, designed and reserved for 'high tariff' or 'heavy end' juvenile offenders thought to be at risk of custody. Whether based on group work or one-to-one sessions between offenders and youth justice workers, such programmes are typically detailed in a 'specified activities order' laid down by the court as part of a supervision order. One of their explicit aims is to confront young offenders with the negative consequences of their anti-social actions, for themselves and those around them, and to explore how to avoid further involvement in offending. (Such programmes are often termed 'cognitive behavioural' training, since they aim to change behaviour by working on the young offender's perceptions and attitudes.) Intensive IT programmes are presented to the courts by IT workers and report writers as viable alternatives to custody, one recurring theme being that they are 'not a soft option' since they force offenders to take a hard look at their offending behaviour and its consequences. IT received significant support and funding from the government in the 1980s, as indeed did the systems management approach in general up until the Conservatives' momentous swing in the direction of 'law and order' ideology in 1993.

Since their introduction in 2000 (and earlier in some places),[31] *reparation orders* and *action plan orders* also provide opportunities to divert from custody and to keep young offenders 'down the tariff' of youth court disposals below the level when the court may feel that custody is the only remaining untried option. The court makes these orders on the advice of a 'specific sentence report', a type of pre-sentence report made by a probation officer, social worker or YOT member specifically dealing with the offender's suitability for this order and the requirements to be included in it. Both types of order can last for three months, and are carried out under the supervision of a probation officer, social worker or YOT member. Reparation orders require the young offender to make reparation to the victim of the offence or a person otherwise affected by it, or to the community at large. They were envisaged as relatively low-tariff interventions (at 'Level 1' – see Chapter 5) and were intended to largely supplant the conditional discharge. But the potential of the reparation order for diverting offenders off the route to custody is – at least in theory – increased by a statutory rule that the court should give reasons for *not* making a reparation order where it has the power to do so.[32]

Action plan orders require the offenders to comply with plans which are intended to address their offending behaviour. Again these plans may include elements of reparation and restorative justice. Other elements may include the kind of programme pioneered in the 1980s under the aegis of 'intermediate treatment' (which still exists as a separate sentencing option, and in some places is still used more than the new orders), aimed at confronting the young offenders' criminal behaviour and getting them to discuss and think about whether it is right or sensible to carry on offending, and how to avoid committing crimes in future. Unlike reparation orders, action plan orders are 'community sentences' ('Level 2') and are intended to provide short but structured interventions for young offenders who may have committed a relatively serious offence that requires a somewhat higher-tariff disposal.

Typically, initiatives to apply systems management to the local youth justice system came from social workers dealing with young offenders within local authority social services departments or voluntary agencies (Rutherford, 1992: ch. 1). However, *inter-agency co-operation* is needed to make systems management a success – not only at points in the system where agencies most obviously work together (such as in a cautioning panel or YOT), but wherever the activities of the agencies intersect. All the local agencies may be able to agree in principle on the common objectives of decreasing prosecution and custody for young offenders and on a broad strategy to achieve this. Often, local youth justice workers have taken a leading role in fostering communication between agencies – for example, trying to ensure that the youth court magistrates understand the work of the local youth justice services and have confidence in their community programmes as viable alternatives to custody.

The final component of systems management is continuing *monitoring* of the modified system to ensure that diversion is being achieved. Even systems managers' actions are capable of having unintended counterproductive consequences, so the system must be constantly watched (and if necessary re-modified) to guard against this.

On the pragmatic level, systems management could claim a substantial degree of success in the 1980s and early 1990s. In 1992, 82 per cent of known indictable offenders under 17 were cautioned compared with 49 per cent in 1980.[33] The cautioning of young offenders received the stamp of government approval, in the 1980 White Paper *Young Offenders* (Home Office et al., 1980: para. 38), and in government guidelines for the police and CPS on decisions to caution or prosecute (Home Office, 1985a, 1990b; Director of Public Prosecutions, 1986). As for diversion from *custody*, the most relevant statistic is the percentage of custodial sentences imposed on prosecuted male offenders aged between 14 and 16. This declined from a peak of 12 per cent in the years 1979 to 1985 to 7 per cent in 1990 (before increasing again to 9 per cent in 1992). Thanks partly to demographic change and partly to diversion from court, this meant a decrease in absolute numbers from 7,700 boys sentenced to custody in 1981 to 1,400 per year in 1990–92.[34] Prosecution and custody rates are by no means constant across England and Wales, and there is plenty of evidence that systems management had a notable effect in those areas where it was most determinedly implemented. Areas such as Northampton (which pioneered systems management for juveniles) achieved particularly high cautioning rates (Bowden and Stevens, 1986). Some localities became 'custody-free zones' for juveniles under 17. And in places boasting intensive IT schemes, custody rates proved to be significantly lower than elsewhere (NACRO Juvenile Crime Section, 1987).

Central government interest in systems management in juvenile justice was, at one stage, sufficiently strong that it was seen as something of a model for improving the criminal justice system as a whole. Prior to 1993, the government increasingly favoured the diversion of less serious offenders of all ages from court and from custody[35] as part of its bifurcatory strategy, and extended the application of custody criteria to adults in the Criminal Justice Act 1991. The inter-agency liaison and monitoring that forms an important element of systems management also found favour. A central recommendation of the Woolf Report (Woolf and Tumim, 1991), happily accepted by the government in 1991, was for the creation of a national inter-agency Criminal Justice Consultative Council (plus similar local bodies) 'to promote better understanding, co-operation and co-ordination in the administration of the criminal justice system' by, *inter alia*, 'considering . . . information about the operation of the system' (Home Office, 1991b: para. 1.10). Again, part of the rationale for converting the 'juvenile court' into the 'youth court' and bringing 17 year olds within its remit was to apply the systems management approach to offenders of that age in the hope that greater diversion from court and from custody would be the result.

The achievements of systems management were impressive in a decade in which law and order ideology was on the rise. Moreover, the approach could plausibly claim that it even succeeded in reducing the amount of crime committed by young people by preventing them from being labelled as serious criminals. The government accepted in its 1980 White Paper that 'juvenile offenders who can be diverted from the criminal justice system at an early stage in their offending are less likely to re-offend than those who become involved in judicial proceedings' (Home Office et al., 1980: para. 38), and this belief is widely shared although as yet the empirical evidence is tenuous.[36] Some researchers have also claimed that intensive IT schemes lead to a lesser rate of reoffending than do custody[37] and even that successful systems management can help reduce the overall juvenile crime rate in the locality (Bowden and Stevens, 1986).

The most serious political problem for systems management is that it is necessarily anathema to proponents of 'law and order ideology' because it seeks to limit punishment rather than intensify it, and it was this which induced the Conservative government to switch from favouring systems management in the 1980s to attacking it in the 1990s. However, it has also been subjected to criticism from a variety of other theoretical and political perspectives. On the one hand, diversion from court incurs the traditional, classicistic objection that decisions about detected offenders should be taken by a court of law, not by out-of-court discretion. On the other hand, adherents of the 'welfare model' have questioned the systems management doctrine that intensive IT provision should be 'targeted' and rigorously reserved for young people at risk of custody, arguing that the potential benefits of IT provision should be available to all who need it.

John Pitts (1986a, 1988) criticized Lancaster-style systems analysis and management on theoretical and political grounds from a radical perspective.

He described Lancaster's analysis of juvenile justice as the 'collusion and cock-up' thesis (that excessive incarceration of children is essentially caused by benign but bungling practitioners), and complained that this 'ignores government and the role of the state in elaborating both an ideology and an apparatus of social control' (Pitts, 1988: 24). He further objected to the non-confrontationist stance of systems management and the willingness of its proponents to work within the government's agenda, fearing that this would inevitably result in the co-option of practitioners into the government's 'law and order' strategy.

In line with the 'radical pluralist' account which we sketched in Chapter 3, we would agree that systems analysis neglects the political and ideological dimensions and for this reason cannot provide a *complete* theory of the penal system. But it is a useful, if inevitably partial, analytical tool which has the significant virtue of facilitating practical and politically realistic techniques for ameliorating the penal system, even in the absence of more general progress in the politics of penality – although systems management could surely be much more effective if the political and ideological tide were to turn firmly against 'law and order' and Strategy A. Moreover, Pitts' criticism rests on an overly conspiratorial and monolithic concept of government and the state. We do not doubt that governments can have an interest in fostering law and order ideology, but they are usually also concerned to defuse the penal crisis. From this perspective, the fact that the Conservative government viewed systems management favourably in the 1980s can be seen as a positive feature of those times, and the government's abandonment of it in the 1990s, which we discuss in the next section, was a step in the wrong direction.

### SHORT, SHARP SHOCKS REVISITED (1993–1997)

As we said at the beginning of this chapter, there seems to be a constant public perception of a severely worsening crime wave among young people. Periodically, this perception reaches the level of what Stan Cohen famously christened a 'moral panic' (Cohen, 1980), such as 'the demonization of young offenders' (Graef, 1995) which has been seen in recent years. One starting point for this was in 1991, when riots in Oxford, Cardiff and North Shields focused media and public attention on the phenomenon of youths 'joyriding' and 'hotting' other people's cars. In the following years stories appeared about individual youngsters (sometimes given nicknames such as 'Ratboy', 'Spider-boy' and even 'Boomerang Boy') who were said to be responsible for mini-crime waves in particular localities. An image was created of inadequate official responses to juvenile crime and in particular to these persistent young offenders, who are supposedly repeatedly given bail whereupon they offend again ('bail bandits'), or who are sent on safari holidays instead of being punished.[38]

A number of factors gave rise to this moral panic, including of course genuine concern about the commission of crime by young people, as well as government eagerness to foster and exploit the ideology of law and order (see Chapter 11). The flames were also fanned by a public debate inspired by an inquiry into juvenile crime by the House of Commons Home Affairs Select Committee (1993) in 1992–3, which led to a variety of interest groups (notably police organizations) making highly publicized claims about the supposed extent of juvenile crime and about persistent young offenders in particular. The temperature was already rising when boiling point was reached in February 1993 with the shocking murder of two-year-old James Bulger by two ten-year-old boys in Liverpool. As well as being highly atypical, the Bulger case was also, strictly speaking, irrelevant to most of the issues under debate, since offenders aged ten and upwards can be detained for life for murder, as indeed were the culprits in this case. However, it added to an atmosphere of 'demonization' in which John Major's Conservative government saw fit to tilt policy decisively in the direction of Strategy A.

In concrete terms, this led to three separate developments in policy regarding young offenders around this time. The first related to the *cautioning* of young offenders. Until 1993, government policy had been to encourage the greater use of cautioning (for adults as well as for young offenders), but this policy was sharply reversed with the introduction of new guidance issued to the police and CPS in 1994. According to this guidance, for offenders of any age, a second caution should only be considered 'where the subsequent offence is trivial; or where there has been a sufficient lapse of time since the first caution to suggest that it had some effect' (Home Office, 1994f: para. 8). Cautions were never to be used for the most serious offences such as attempted murder and rape, and only exceptionally for other indictable-only offences, whatever the offender's age or previous record (para. 5). The presumption contained in previous guidance (Home Office, 1985a, 1990b; Director of Public Prosecutions, 1986) in favour of cautioning juvenile offenders was deleted. This new policy had a significant and measurable effect on the rate of cautioning for offenders generally, especially those under 18. For example, whereas in 1992 59 per cent of known male offenders aged 15 to 17 were cautioned rather than prosecuted, by 1999 this had been reduced to 45 per cent (Home Office, 2000a: Table 5.3).

The second main policy innovation was the introduction of a new custodial penalty for persistent offenders who would otherwise be too young to be sentenced to custody, known as a '*secure training order*'.[39] This was intended to close a supposed gap in the law concerning offenders who were below the normal age for custodial sentences (which was then 15) and who had not committed a sufficiently grave offence rendering them liable to long-term detention, but whose persistent (albeit relatively petty) offending made them 'a menace to the community' in the words of Home Secretary Kenneth Clarke (HC Deb. 2 March 1993). It was a matter of controversy how many of these persistent young offenders existed, whether the existing law really was incapable of dealing with them, and whether custody was a suitable response to the problem (see Cavadino, 1994b; Cavadino and Dignan, 1997a: 263–5; Cavadino et al., 1999: 184–7). Nevertheless, the secure training order was introduced for 12- to 14-year-old persistent offenders, with the first half of the order being served in one of five new '*secure training centres*', each housing 40 offenders, to be built and run by the private sector, and the second half to be served under supervision in the community. The first of these secure training centres, at Medway in Kent, suffered severe problems following its opening in April 1998. A crisis inspection in late 1998 found that virtually all the staff were unqualified and unused to working with young people; that they were using excessive and sometimes dangerous physical restraint on the inmates; that there had been a great deal of disorder including a riot in June 1998, and that 30 per cent of the staff including two senior managers had resigned in its first six months. Moreover, two thirds of its inmates had reoffended even before the end of their post-release supervision (*Prison Report* No. 46, February 1999: 15–16; Hagell et al., 2000). Two further STCs (Hassockfield and Rainsbrook) have also opened more recently.

The third main innovation for young offenders in this period was the so-called '*boot camp*', or 'high intensity training' (Cavadino and Dignan, 1997a: 265–6). The term 'boot camp' was an American import, but in essence, the idea was merely yet another revival of the militaristic 'short, sharp shock' detention centre which had proved such a conspicuous failure in the early 1980s. The first English institution to be called a 'boot camp' opened in June 1996 at Thorn Cross Young Offender Institution in Cheshire, catering for 60 'young adult' offenders aged from 18 to 20. The Thorn Cross regime is in fact less tough, less militaristic and more constructive than a typical American boot camp, including basic education and personal skills training and has acquired a good reputation.[40] No longer is it generally referred to as a 'boot camp'. Somewhat different was the 'boot camp' at Colchester, where young offenders sentenced to detention in a young offender institution were placed in the Ministry of Defence's military corrective training centre along with military offenders. However, this arrangement only lasted from February 1997 to March 1998 when it was ended by New Labour Home Secretary Jack Straw on the grounds that it did not represent 'value for money', costing as it did around twice per inmate as a normal young offender institution (HC Deb. 22 January 1998).

### NO MORE EXCUSES: NEW LABOUR AND YOUNG OFFENDERS

Just as the Conservatives came to power in 1979 promising new measures to deal with young offenders, so too did New Labour in 1997. One of Labour's five 'key pledges' in its 1997 Election Manifesto (Labour Party, 1997) was a specific promise to halve the time taken to bring persistent young offenders to court from 142 days to 71 days. In pursuance of this aim, the government in 1997 issued national guidance to courts and set up various local pilot projects experimenting with methods of 'fast tracking' the prosecution of young recidivists. (By the third quarter of 2000, the average time from arrest to sentence had been reduced to 95 days, though the pledge itself seemed unlikely to be met before 2002.)

But this was merely one of a wide array of innovations in the treatment of young offenders pursued by New Labour in its first few years in power. A White Paper entitled *No More Excuses* (Home Office, 1997c) trailed a number of measures which were included in the Crime and Disorder Act 1998. Labour's first term in government also saw the Youth Justice and Criminal Evidence Act 1999, which introduced youth offender panels, and a variety of other (non-statutory) developments in the youth justice system. Many of these are still being introduced or in their early days as we write.[41] New Labour's new provisions for youth justice and youth offending included the following:

*General*
- A new statutory 'principal aim' for the entire youth justice system: to prevent offending by children and young persons.[42]
- A statutory duty on local authorities and the police to formulate crime and disorder reduction strategies and to produce annual 'youth justice plans' in their localities after consulting with citizens and other relevant organizations.[43]
- A national *Youth Justice Board* to monitor the operation of the youth justice system, fund new initiatives, promote good practice and advise the Home Secretary on the operation of the youth justice system and the setting of national standards.[44]
- A statutory duty for local authorities to provide comprehensive youth justice services linked to the introduction of new multi-agency *youth offending teams* in each local authority area (see above).
- Provision for local authorities to introduce local *child curfews* banning children under ten from streets and other public places at night unless supervised by a responsible adult.[45] (This provision, which so far has never been used, was extended to children under the age of 16 by the government's Criminal Justice and Police Act 2001.)

*The pre-court process*
- The replacement of cautions for offenders under 18 with the new system of '*reprimands*' and '*warnings*' (see above; see also Dignan, 1999). This differs from Michael Howard's 1994 cautioning guidelines (which remain in force for offenders over 18) in more than just the names of the measures. A diversionary alternative to prosecution may be used twice per offender rather than normally once, but the second time it is a 'final warning' which involves more than just a telling-off, and the rule forbidding repeated warnings is written into statute rather than just guidance.
- '*Fast tracking*' of the prosecution of persistent young offenders (see above).

*The court process*
- Referral of offenders who are prosecuted for the first time to *youth offender panels* (see above).
- A package of initiatives aimed at '*opening up the youth court*', by encouraging greater communication between youth court magistrates and young offenders and their families and making the court more open to victims and the general public (Allen et al., 2000; Home Office and Lord Chancellor's Department, 2001).
- Abolition of the legal doctrine of *doli incapax*, the presumption that children aged 10 to 13 are incapable of committing a crime unless they can be shown to appreciate the difference between right and wrong.[46]

*Sentences for young offenders*

- *Child safety orders* which magistrates' courts can impose on children under ten who have committed acts for which they could have been prosecuted if over that age[47] or if the child is thought to be at risk of committing such acts. These orders place the child under the supervision of a social worker or youth justice worker and require the child to comply with specific requirements made by the court.
- Powers for courts to impose *parenting orders* on the parents of children who commit offences or act anti-socially or who are put under child safety orders.[48] Parents are required to attend counselling and guidance sessions and comply with other conditions.
- *Reparation orders* requiring young offenders to make reparation to the victim of the offence or the community at large (see above; see also Dignan, 1999; Holdaway et al., 2001).
- *Action plan orders* requiring young offenders to comply with programmes to address their offending behaviour (see above; see also Dignan, 1999; Holdaway et al., 2001).
- New community-based 'Intensive Supervision and Surveillance Programmes' (ISSPs), to be attached to supervision orders, community rehabilitation (probation) orders or bail supervision packages, or to form part of post-custodial supervision for those given detention and training orders (see below). These commenced in selected areas in April 2001, and are intended to be 'targeted' on persistent offenders who have been charged or warned at least four times within a 12-month period. They will involve intensive monitoring of the young offender's movements and whereabouts by means such as electronic monitoring and telephone monitoring using voice verification technology, as well as other measures intended to address the young person's offending behaviour and encourage the performance of reparation (Home Office, 2001).
- Replacement of the custodial sentences 'detention in a young offender institution' and 'secure training order' by the new *detention and training order* for offenders aged 10–17.[49] This sentence is available for young offenders aged 15–17, and to those aged 12–14 as long as they are 'persistent offenders'. Eventually the Act envisages offenders as young as ten being detained under these orders provided they are 'persistent' and the court thinks that custody is necessary to protect the public from the child.
- Abolition of the 'detention in a young offender institution' sentence for young adults aged 18–20, making this age group liable to sentences of adult imprisonment.[50]

This flurry of proposals, initiatives and legislation represents a mixture of Strategies A, B and C. Strategy A is quite well represented, for example in the 'finality' of the final warning (where previously further cautioning might have been an option)[51] and in curfew orders, not to mention the White Paper's title *No More Excuses* and much of the government's rhetoric. One particular strain of Strategy A which is well in evidence here is the notion – highly fashionable and proving very attractive to politicians in recent years – of *'zero tolerance'* (Cavadino et al., 1999: 28–30). This is the idea that even petty and first-time offending should be met with (in Jack Straw's words)[52] 'tough, early inter-vention' in order to 'nip it in the bud'. Indeed, when introducing the Crime and Disorder Act 1998 into Parliament as a Bill, Mr Straw said that it was 'about implementing a zero tolerance strategy'. On the other hand, measures such as the final warning, reparation and action plan orders and youth offender panels also contain a welcome element of reparation and restorative justice, which is redolent of Strategy C. And there is in addition a great deal of managerial Strategy B in the mix, with measures to routinize and 'systematize' the entire youth justice system; to overhaul the culture of youth justice by introducing youth offending teams; to ensure standard good practice nationally by means of the Youth Justice Board; and to make the prosecution process more speedy and efficient.

Managerialism, combined with a laudable desire to protect offenders in the younger age ranges, is also in evidence in the government's policy towards custody for young offenders. In 1997 a 'Thematic Review' by Chief Inspector of Prisons Sir David Ramsbotham recommended that children under 18 should be dealt with separately from those of 18 and over, and that the Prison Service should lose all responsibility for them (HM Chief Inspector of Prisons, 1997b). The government has been moving steadily in this direction in a process of review and reform which is still continuing. The detention and training order for under-18s came into force in April 2000, at which time the Youth Justice Board assumed responsibility for the commissioning of places and for regime standards in the 'juvenile secure estate' (custody and local authority secure accommodation for those under 18). It remains to be seen exactly what shape custody and secure accommodation for those under 18 takes in the future and whether significant improvements can be achieved over the lamentably poor conditions, regimes and training programmes uncovered by the Chief Inspector in his 1997 Thematic Review and in many inspections of individual institutions before and since. Even if things do improve for those under 18 who find themselves in custody, there is a danger that this may be at the expense of 'young adults' aged 18 to 20, who, as we have seen, will in future be given adult sentences of imprisonment and serve them in adult prisons.[53]

But of equal importance to the way young people are treated when in custody is the prior question of how many young offenders find their way into custody in the first place. And here, as with adult offenders, the trend in the early 2000s is still significantly upwards. The numbers of people under 21 in custody under sentence rose from 5,319 in 1994 to 8,344 in 1999.[54] And, again as with adults, this is driven by court sentencing decisions. In 1994, 17,200 people under 21 received custodial sentences; in 1999 the figure was 25,600, an increase of 49 per cent.[55] This trend could worsen: there is a danger that if conditions were to improve for young people in custody, and sentencers came to feel that the overall experience was more likely to be 'constructive', they could become even less inhibited about the imposition of custodial sentences for young offenders than they have in the past. It should be borne in mind that, although there is evidence that some kinds of intervention – such as 'cognitive behavioural' training to try to alter young offenders' attitude towards crime – may well work to some extent to reduce young people's offending, they are much more likely to work if the young person is not locked up in custody (McGuire, 1995; Vennard et al., 1997; Andrews et al., 1990: 382; Lipsey, 1992: 138). It remains true that 'prison doesn't work' to reform either young or adult offenders. Yet the government is, in effect, adopting the view that taking steps to reduce the numbers of young people in custody, or even to stop a continued rise, is not a priority.[56]

We think it should be. Essentially there are two opposing views about young offenders: the 'zero tolerance' view (Strategy A) and the Strategy C approach which combines an inclination to 'minimum intervention' with a preference for restorative and rehabilitative measures where intervention occurs. Jack Straw believes that young offenders do not simply grow out of crime – although in general it seems that they do (Cavadino et al., 1999: 182–4; Flood-Page et al., 2000: 18–19) – and that tough early intervention is needed to nip offending in the bud. Even if some of this 'tough early intervention' takes positive forms such as reparation or programmes to confront offending behaviour, the tougher you get and the earlier you get tough, the greater the likelihood that young offenders will suffer the adverse effects of stigmatizing 'labelling' and accelerate 'up the tariff' into overcrowded and damaging custodial institutions before they have a chance to grow out of crime. Take, for example, the new Intensive Supervision and Surveillance Programmes for persistent young offenders. While it does make sense for rehabilitative efforts to be concentrated on persistent offenders and for these efforts to take place in the community rather than in custody, there are dangers of such a scheme backfiring if great care is not taken, including careful targeting, gatekeeping and monitoring of the usage and effects of such schemes (à la systems management). Otherwise these intensive and demanding (and easy to breach) schemes could be imposed on young people who would otherwise have received less intense, less stigmatizing treatment. This might actually have been more effective (or less damaging), and might have created less risk of catapulting the offender into custody when the enormous demands of the programme prove too much for a messed-up young person to comply with. At the moment more young people are already being thrust up the tariff into custody, and the situation could well worsen in the near future. Indeed, we could have another system disaster on our hands, as in the 1970s when juvenile custody rates were simply allowed to rise without being checked.

The government's current approach borrows a great deal from the pioneering work done by the proponents of systems management from the 1980s onwards, for example in its emphasis on system-wide thinking and co-ordination and co-operation between agencies. We think the government should borrow more from systems management, adopting its humanitarian (Strategy C) goals and its minimum-intervention bias[57] as well as its managerial (Strategy B) techniques – while simultaneously increasing the emphasis on restorative justice and other constructive approaches – if the problem of youth crime and young offenders is to be successfully and humanely managed in future.

## NOTES

1 For some offenders under 18 in 1999, 'cautions' includes 'reprimands' and 'warnings' – explained later in this chapter and in the Introduction – which were first introduced in some areas at the end of September 1998.

2 In 1999, male offenders under 18 were mainly found guilty or cautioned for theft and handling stolen goods (46 per cent) and burglary (14 per cent), compared with figures of 34 per cent and 6 per cent for males over 21. (These figures and those in the text are taken or calculated from Home Office, 2000a: ch. 5 and Ayres, 2000.)

3 Despite the sceptical belief in some quarters that these statistics must be unfounded since 'common sense' tells us that youth crime *must* be an increasing problem, careful official research suggests not: see Cavadino et al. (1999: 181); Collier (1996).

4 Calculated from Cullen and Minchin (2000b: Table B).

5 A recent international self-report study found that 44 per cent of young people in England and Wales admitted to delinquent behaviour in the previous year compared with between 57 and 72 per cent in Portugal, Spain, the Netherlands and Switzerland (Junger-Tas et al., 1994).

6 The minimum age for prosecution varies widely between different countries; for example, it is 8 in Scotland, 15 in Sweden and normally 18 in Belgium. The British minimum ages are very low compared with most of Western Europe.

7 Crime and Disorder Act 1998, ss. 65–6. In the past, cautions had to be administered in a police station. The procedure for young offenders has now been made more flexible, to encourage different styles of delivery that are more in keeping with a restorative justice approach (Home Office and Youth Justice Board, 2001).

8 There is an exception: if the offender was previously warned more than two years ago and the police regard the current offence as 'not so serious as to require a charge to be brought', then a second warning may be given (Crime and Disorder Act 1998, s. 65).

9 Although 'change programmes' were envisaged as standard components of a final warning, they were in practice assessed as being appropriate for less than half of all warned offenders during the original two-year pilot of the reparation and warning scheme (Holdaway et al., 2001: 77).

10 Between April and November 2000, 1,068 unconvicted boys under 17 were remanded to custody, compared with 440 in 1992; only about 30 per cent of these are charged with serious violent or sexual offences (*The Guardian*, 2 January 2001).

11 Powers of Criminal Courts (Sentencing) Act 2000, s. 100.

12 Powers of Criminal Courts (Sentencing) Act 2000, ss. 90 and 91.

13 Powers of Criminal Courts (Sentencing) Act 2000, s.63. It is also possible for offenders aged 16 or 17 ('near adults') to receive probation orders.

14 Powers of Criminal Courts (Sentencing) Act 2000, ss. 69 and 73.

15 Powers of Criminal Courts (Sentencing) Act 2000, ss. 16–32.

16 A referral order must be made for such offenders unless the court decides to pass a custodial sentence, absolute discharge or a hospital order detaining the offender in a hospital under the Mental Health Act 1983 (Powers of Criminal Courts (Sentencing) Act 2000, ss. 16–17).

17 Comprising at least one member of the local youth offending team (see below), plus two other people selected from a panel that is recruited from the local community.

18 Powers of Criminal Courts (Sentencing) Act 2000, s. 23.

19 The composition, powers and functioning of youth offending teams are described more fully in Holdaway et al. (2001).

20 Powers of Criminal Courts (Sentencing) Act 2000, s. 96.

21 Criminal Justice and Court Services Act 2000, s. 61.

22 Since the Criminal Justice Act 1991 replaced the 'juvenile court' with the 'youth court' the phrase 'youth justice' has largely superseded the older usage 'juvenile justice'. However, the term 'juvenile' is still useful to refer (since 1992) to the age range 10 to 17 inclusive.

23 A distinction is sometimes made between two positivist models: the pseudo-medical 'treatment model', and the 'welfare' or 'social welfare' model which sees social work intervention with the children and their families as the primary method of providing them with help (Rutherford, 1992: ch. 2).

24 This was the time when the 'rehabilitative ideal' dominated penal thinking in both England and Scotland. The Social Work (Scotland) Act 1968 also adopted a positivistic welfare-based approach as part of an equally radical reform of the juvenile justice system in Scotland. This system has prevailed largely intact in Scotland (and similar systems also exist in the Scandinavian countries) despite the discrediting of the rehabilitative ideal in the adult sphere during the 1970s (Martin and Murray, 1982; Pratt, 1986; Bottoms, 2001).

25 Figures abstracted and calculated from Home Office (1981a: Table 7.7).

26 There was only ever one detention centre for girls, Moor Court, which opened in 1962 but was closed in 1969.

27 Whereas 69 boys had been sentenced to borstal for every 100 sent to DC in 1982, in 1986 the corresponding figure was 168. (Calculated from Home Office, 1988b: Tables 7.8 and 7.10.)

28 Some members of the Lancaster group were later associated with Social Information Systems (SIS), a private consultancy organization, which advised local social services authorities and other bodies on how to implement systems management techniques.

29 The same might also be said of 'caution plus' initiatives. Although they were few in number they pioneered the combination of diversion linked with a more interventionist approach towards young offenders that assumed greater significance in the reforms introduced by the New Labour government (see below).

30 But only in respect of those who plead guilty, an important limitation. Another distinctive feature of the referral order is that it makes no provision for legal representation at the panel. The gatekeeping rules would fail to operate if lawyers were to advise defendants that their rights were unlikely to be adequately safeguarded if they attended a panel, and that they should therefore plead not guilty.

31 These orders were 'piloted' in selected areas from the end of September 1998 onwards. See Holdaway et al. (2001) for results of the pilot evaluation. Action plan and reparation orders are made under the Powers of Criminal Courts (Sentencing) Act 2000, ss. 69 and 73 (originally ss. 69 and 67 of the Crime and Disorder Act 1998).

32 Powers of Criminal Courts (Sentencing) Act 2000, s. 73(8).

33 Calculated from Home Office (1990c and 1993b: Table 5.22.)

34 Home Office (1990c and 1993b: Tables 7.8–7.9). The percentage figures are better than they look, given the increase in cautioning which diverted from the courts many young people, most of whom would presumably have received non-custodial sentences. Custodial sentences as a proportion of all males aged 14 to 16 who were *found guilty* or *cautioned* decreased impressively from 8 per cent in 1981 to 2 per cent in the years 1990 to 1992. (Calculated from Home Office, 1990c and 1993b: Tables 5.22 and 7.8.)

35 In 1988 the government applauded a halving in the number of juvenile offenders held in custody during the six-year period 1981–7 (Home Office, 1988a: para. 2.21).

36 One encouraging finding is that 83 per cent of offenders cautioned in 1988 were not convicted of an offence in the following two years: 87 per cent of cautioned

offenders under 14, 78 per cent of those aged 14 to 16, and 75 per cent of those aged 17 to 20 were not convicted within this time. Young adults cautioned for theft or violence were slightly less likely to be reconvicted than if they had been convicted in court (Home Office, 1994a). However, other research has been equivocal over whether cautioning young offenders is demonstrably better than prosecution (Farrington and Bennett, 1981; Mott, 1983). There are some raw research figures suggesting that cautioning is generally more effective than prosecution for first- or second-time offenders, equally effective following the third offence but less effective thereafter (Audit Commission, 1996: 9), but this remains unproven.

37  However, the most rigorous study to date of the effectiveness of IT compared with custody only found some slight evidence suggesting that certain forms of intensive IT have a modest advantage over custody (Bottoms, 1995b: 21–2).

38  The 'safari' issue achieved prominence when a children's therapy centre took a 17-year-old offender who was in local authority care on a trip to Africa as part of a rehabilitation programme in late 1993. This led to a directive from the Department of Health to social services departments in February 1994 forbidding overseas trips for offenders in care; similar provisions were also inserted into the 1995 National Standards for the Supervision of Offenders in the Community (Home Office et al., 1995: 20, 28).

39  Introduced by the Criminal Justice and Public Order Act 1994, ss. 1–15. The sentence is now incorporated into the detention and training order (Powers of Criminal Courts (Sentencing) Act 2000, s. 100.

40  Indeed, an evaluation for the Home Office found that Thorn Cross' positive regime was significantly better than other custodial institutions for young offenders in terms of reconvictions of its inmates after release (Farrington et al., 2000).

41  The youth justice reforms contained in the Crime and Disorder Act 1998 were initially introduced in selected areas as pilot schemes, and the results of the national evaluation of the pilots have now been published (Holdaway et al., 2001). The referral order is also being piloted, and the first interim report was published in January 2001 (Newburn et al., 2001).

42  Crime and Disorder Act 1998, s. 37.

43  Crime and Disorder Act 1998, ss. 38 and 40.

44  Crime and Disorder Act 1998, s. 41.

45  Crime and Disorder Act 1998, s. 14.

46  Crime and Disorder Act 1998, s. 34.

47  Crime and Disorder Act 1998, s. 11, which also allows for a child safety order where the child breaks a local curfew or acts in an 'anti-social' manner likely to cause 'harassment, alarm or distress' to others. Only two such orders were imposed during the piloting of youth justice reforms contained in the Crime and Disorder Act 1998 (Holdaway et al., 2001: 108).

48  Crime and Disorder Act 1998, s. 8.

49  Crime and Disorder Act 1998, ss.73–9.

50  Criminal Justice and Court Services Act 2000, s. 61.

51  Not that this seems to have been very common under the pre-existing system of juvenile cautioning: Evans (1994: 69) found that young offenders were usually prosecuted after their second caution, and that the proportion receiving three or more cautions was less than 4 per cent.

52  Home Office Press Release, 16 March 2000.

53  Criminal Justice and Court Services Act 2000, s. 61.

54  Calculated from Cullen and Minchin (2000b: Table 1). At the same time the number of boys aged 15 and 16 remanded to custody increased even more dramatically: see above, n. 10.

55 Calculated from Home Office (2000a: Table 7.13). The increase is not accounted for by an increase in young people coming before the courts: the proportion of those sentenced for indictable offences who were sentenced to custody increased from 0.3 to 2.8 per cent for under-14s, from 13 to 15 per cent for those aged 15–17, and from 18 to 23 per cent for those aged 18 to 20.

56 In early 2001 it was announced that 400 new custodial places would be provided for young offenders (Home Office, 2001). The official position is that this will not mean more young people being held in custody, but more suitable provision for them, separate from prisons for older offenders (*The Guardian*, 22 March 2001).

57 Our own view is that minimum intervention is appropriate provided it does not prejudice the needs and interests of victims. There may be a balance to be struck here, as for instance if minimum intervention with offenders meant that victims were deprived of their right to reparation. However, there are ways of achieving a satisfactory balance, including providing flexible ways of encouraging reparation outside the mainstream criminal justice system.

# 10

# Bias in the Criminal Justice System

We referred in Chapter 2 to the basic principle of justice which states that like cases should be treated alike. If two people have committed crimes of similar gravity, then justice demands that they should normally be equally liable to punishment, unless there is some important *relevant* difference between the two cases or some other strong justification for departing from equal treatment. We have already seen in Chapter 4 how the arrangements for sentencing in England and Wales fail to ensure even rough equality of treatment for similar offenders – on the contrary, the wide and relatively unguided discretion granted to sentencers ensures that there are enormous disparities, geographical and otherwise. Such disparities can, and doubtless often do, operate in a more or less arbitrary manner, so that the punishment an offender suffers bears little relation either to the offence or to the characteristics of the offender, being more a result of factors such as the local sentencing culture or the whims of the particular sentencers. In this chapter, however, we concentrate on *biases* within the criminal justice system – injustices which are related to certain characteristics of the offender. We consider three such characteristics: social class, race and gender.

As we shall see, these biases do not only – or indeed, primarily – occur at the sentencing stage, or even within the *penal* system, as opposed to the wider *criminal justice* system. Bias can operate at any or every stage of the criminal process, stages which include investigation and charge by the police, prosecution decisions by the Crown Prosecution Service, bail decisions, court verdicts and sentencing decisions (see Figure I.1 in the Introduction). Further possibilities for bias arise after sentence, in official decisions concerning *inter alia* allocation to different prisons and early release. The penal system cannot be viewed in isolation when considering the issue of bias. Suppose, for example, that the sentencing practices of the courts were unbiased, but the prior actions of the police ensured that members of an oppressed group were prosecuted to an unfair extent. In that case the sentencing system viewed on its own would seem fair, but would have the effect of reproducing the bias created in a previous stage of the process. Consequently, this chapter deals with the entire criminal justice system.

At any stage, bias can occur for a variety of reasons. It often results, not from deliberate discrimination, but from unconscious prejudices and stereotypes (fixed preconceptions that some kinds of people are more criminal than others) and even as an unintended consequence of *prima facie* reasonable attitudes, practices and decisions. But whatever the causes, such biases add weight to radical critiques which claim that the penal system functions to reinforce the position of powerful sections of society over the less powerful. They also – yet again – suggest that the penal system's crisis of legitimacy may be largely self-inflicted: the system is perceived as unjust because it really is unjust.

The issue of bias in the criminal justice system has received a measure of official recognition. One result has been section 95 of the Criminal Justice Act 1991, which requires the Home Secretary every year 'to publish such information as he considers expedient for the purpose of . . . facilitating the performance by [persons engaged in the administration of criminal justice] of their duty to avoid discriminating against any persons on the ground of race or sex or any other improper ground', a provision which has led to the issuing of several publications (for example Home Office, 2000e, 2000f) containing the results of research and monitoring. To some extent this has helped in the identification of biases within the system. But so far there is little sign that it has brought about any diminution in the actual occurrence of bias.

## CLASS

Although the regular official series of criminal and penal statistics do not provide data on social class or occupation, it is clear that the penal system's subjects are overwhelmingly working class, and that unskilled and unemployed people are particularly over-represented in the penal population. The 1991 National Prison Survey found that 6 per cent of prisoners aged 17 or over had never had a job. Of the rest, 82 per cent had had manual occupations (compared with 56 per cent of the general population), and 41 per cent were unskilled (compared with 19 per cent generally). Just prior to imprisonment, one third of prisoners were unemployed (Walmsley et al., 1992: 10–11, 21). Similarly, Harris and Webb (1987: 115–16) found that almost all of a sample of 971 boys on supervision orders were working-class, and fewer than 8 per cent had a parent in a 'white-collar' job. Several surveys of defendants in criminal courts have yielded similar results. One found that only 5 per cent of defendants in Sheffield in 1971 and 1972 (excluding motoring cases) were from social classes I and II, compared with 35 per cent of the general population (Bottoms and McClean, 1976: 75); while a recent study of four magistrates' courts in the North of England in 1993 found that between 75 and 91 per cent of defendants sampled were unemployed (Crow et al., 1995: 46; cf. Crow and Simon, 1987).

This does not in itself demonstrate that there is a class bias operating in the criminal justice system to produce these results, for they could occur without bias if a similar proportion of *crimes* were committed by members of the working class. But 'self-report' research studies (in which respondents are asked in confidence what offences they have committed) suggest that this is not the case. It seems that there is *some* greater tendency for people from lower socio-economic groups to commit offences, or at least the kind of offences which tend to be dealt with by means of the normal criminal justice system. (This is not perhaps surprising when – just to mention the most obvious line of explanation – the vast majority of recorded crime is against property, which is exactly what poorer people lack.) But the class differential in commission of crimes as measured by self-report studies is much smaller than the class differential in officially processed offenders (see, for example Rutter and Giller, 1983: 132–7; Hood and Sparks, 1970: ch. 2). Gold's (1966: 44) American findings were fairly typical: 'About five times more lowest than highest status boys appear in the official records; if records were complete and unselective we estimate that the ratio should be closer to 1.5:1.' Somehow, between the commission of offences and the official responses of prosecution and punishment, the difference between the classes gets vastly magnified.

Such magnification could occur for a variety of reasons, not all of them necessarily connected with bias. Perhaps some misdeeds of middle-class offenders are relatively invisible and hence unlikely to come to official notice. This is probably true of embezzlement and tax dodging compared to burglary and robbery, for example. But there could also be biases operating at the various stages of the criminal process which ensure that middle-class offenders are dealt with more leniently. At many of these stages, there is as yet little research evidence to confirm or deny the existence of class bias in the system. But there are some straws in the wind.

A classic study in the United States in the 1960s by Piliavin and Briar (1964) indicates one way in which unintended class bias could occur at the police stage. The authors found that police officers who came across juveniles committing offences were expected to exercise discretion as to whether to arrest or reprimand the juvenile. The result was that, for nearly all minor violators and for some serious delinquents, it was the police's *assessment of the youth's character* which was the prime determinant of the officers' decisions. Officers decided whether the young person was basically law-abiding and 'salvageable', or an incorrigible 'punk', and made their decisions accordingly. This assessment of 'character' was, however, based on the very limited information available to the officers, notably 'cues' such as the youths' race, dress and – most importantly – their *demeanour*. Those who failed to show the police what was considered to be sufficient respect received negative character assessments and harsher treatment. Since attitudes towards the police vary across socio-economic groups,[1] such a criterion is extremely likely to result in effective class discrimination. It could also be that a 'rougher' demeanour not intended to convey disrespect could be misinterpreted, again to the disadvantage of the suspect from the lower socio-economic group.

Such a bias could occur at a very early stage in the criminal process, before the police have even discovered or decided that an offence has been committed. When police officers encounter members of the public they often have to decide – perhaps instantly – whether this person is a potential criminal or not. There is usually little to go on in making this decision except by using stereotypical 'cues' which mark people as either 'rough' or 'respectable', yet a snap decision of this kind may condition the entire ensuing interaction (Cain, 1971: 81–4; Bottomley, 1973: ch. 2). This suggests that the police may be much less likely to suspect or investigate middle-class people – or, probably equally importantly, people who give the impression of belonging to the stably employed 'respectable working class'. And indeed studies have found that unemployed[2] people are significantly more likely to be stopped on foot by the police than those who have a job (Skogan, 1990: 28–9, 61; Smith, 1983: 101). As a result, the police will be likely to detect or recognize a higher proportion of offences committed by those in lower socio-economic groups.

Subsequent to detection of an offence comes the decision whether or not to prosecute or caution. In England, Bennett (1979) found that middle-class juvenile offenders in London were more likely than their working-class counterparts to be cautioned instead of being prosecuted for minor offences. There could be several factors influencing the police decision which have the effect of creating a class bias. Farrington and Bennett (1981) demonstrated that a juvenile's perceived 'bad attitude' is a potent determining factor of the police decision in London as well as in the US; other studies have found that the offenders' *parents'* perceived attitudes are influential (Bennett, 1979; Fisher and Mawby, 1982; Gold, 1966). And Landau and Nathan (1983), again in London, found that the police were more inclined to prosecute 'latch-key children', a practice likely to work against low-income families.

It is also the case that, at the investigation and prosecution stages, typically middle-class offences can be dealt with in a radically different manner from 'ordinary crime', often by agencies other than the police. For example, breaches of factory health and safety regulations, including those which threaten or cause serious accidents,[3] are policed by an agency (the Health and Safety Executive) which prefers to warn rather than prosecute. Carson (1971) found that in the 1960s the HSE's predecessor, the Inspectorate of Factories, prosecuted a mere 1.5 per cent of detected offences. However, when a firm was detected offending three or more times the rate of prosecution increased – to 3.5 per cent! Even disregarding cases where the Inspectorate took no formal action at all, this made an overall 'cautioning rate' of 98 per cent. This later declined to 84 per cent by 1991–2 (calculated from Health and Safety Executive, 1992) – but it still puts the police's cautioning rate of 33 per cent[4] in the shade. (See Sanders, 1985; Sanders and Young, 2000: 365–8.) Similarly, the Inland Revenue very rarely prosecutes tax fraud offenders, although the Department of Social Security is much more likely to prosecute those people (from lower socio-economic groups) who defraud the benefits system (NACRO, 1986a: ch. 10; Cook, 1989: ch. 7).

There is a distinct lack of studies at the sentencing stage which directly compare the sentences received by working-class and middle-class offenders *for the same offences*,[5] although it is (for example) highly plausible that sentencers might perceive a middle-class offender as less incorrigible and therefore deserving of a lesser sentence. Again, sentencers (themselves overwhelmingly middle-class) might well feel that a middle-class offender has already suffered enough through the disgrace of conviction, and sentence leniently as a result. Or richer defendants may be able to afford better lawyers who are more adept at representing their clients' circumstances as mitigating their culpability. There is plenty of anecdotal evidence of apparent leniency towards middle-class offenders, especially those convicted of typical 'white collar' offences: the £3 million fraudsters in the 1960s whose prison sentences were a fraction of those imposed on the £2 million Great Train Robbers (Morris, 1980: 92); the non-custodial sentences passed on insider dealer Geoffrey Collier in 1987 and (following a much-questioned plea-bargain agreement) fraudulent trader

Roger Levitt in 1993; and the halving of 'Guinness trial' defendant Ernest Saunders' sentence to 2½ years by the Court of Appeal in 1991 following evidence that he was suffering from pre-senile dementia (which went into remission after his release).

Research does seem to have confirmed that the courts are often much more punitive towards the relatively poor people who fraudulently draw too much social security than towards the relatively well-off people who defraud the Inland Revenue of what may be much greater sums (Cook, 1989: 160–5).[6] Again, this is not the result of intentional class bias, but the effect of the prevailing (Marxists might say 'bourgeois') ideology which holds that the latter method of defrauding the public purse is less reprehensible than the former.

Unemployed people can, again, get a particularly raw deal at the sentencing stage. Traditionally, the fact that an offender has a job and a steady work record has been regarded as counting in his or her favour, whereas unemployment has been seen as reflecting negatively on the offender's character. Again, sentencers may sometimes decide to pass non-custodial sentences on employed offenders so that they do not lose their jobs although they would imprison a similar but unemployed offender. (An analogous effect can occur when the court decides whether to grant bail or remand in custody.) Finally, unemployment can restrict the sentencing options the court perceives itself as having. In particular, the court may be reluctant to impose a fine or other financial penalty on an unemployed offender, because the sum imposed would seem (to the relatively affluent sentencer) ridiculously small if related to the offender's means, or because it is felt that the offender could not or will not pay up. Research studies have confirmed that unemployed offenders are significantly less likely to be fined than those who are employed. Although some of the unemployed who might otherwise have been fined are given discharges or probation orders, others receive custodial sentences (Softley, 1978; Crow et al., 1989).

Following a sentence of imprisonment, white-collar offenders are much more likely to be allocated to open prisons, where the conditions and regime may be distinctly preferable (Jones et al., 1977: especially 66–70). This fact was highlighted in August 1990 when three businessmen found guilty of dishonesty offences involving millions of pounds in the 'Guinness affair' were transferred instantly from the slum conditions of Brixton Prison to the relatively salubrious Ford Open Prison. It is also possible that white-collar offenders get parole more easily (Levi, 1989: 102–5); certainly this was suggested by the experience of jockey Lester Piggott, who in 1988 was paroled at the earliest opportunity from his (relatively speaking, hardly draconian) three-year prison sentence imposed for evading over £3 million in taxes.

None of this will come as any surprise to Marxists, who as we saw in Chapter 3, view the penal system as an instrument of class power. The particular injustices suffered by the unemployed can be explained by a sophisticated Marxism which sees the role of the criminal justice system (and the historic role of the police in particular) as the imposition of order on the 'rough' rather than 'respectable' sections of the working class (for example, Cohen, 1981). (It can also be maintained that the roles of criminal justice agencies have recently been shifting towards a greater emphasis on controlling an emerging 'underclass' of the impoverished and permanently unemployed – a perception by no means confined to Marxists.) However, traditional Marxism has more difficulty in providing explanations for the injustices we now proceed to investigate: those concerning race and gender.

## RACE

According to official estimates, around 7 per cent of the population is of non-white ethnic origin. Yet in 1999 18 per cent of male prisoners and 25 per cent of female prisoners were non-white.[7] The most dramatic discrepancy concerns 'black' (or 'Afro-Caribbean') people,[8] who account for around 2 per cent of people aged 10 and over in England and Wales, but comprised 12 per cent of the male and 19 per cent of the female prison population in 1999. It has been estimated that at this rate nearly one in ten young black men will have received a custodial sentence before their 21st birthday, double the proportion of their white peers (*New Law Journal*, 30 March 1990; *The Guardian*, 27 February 1989). Why do such disproportionately large numbers of black people find their way into custody?

One obvious hypothesis would be that black people are more likely to commit offences than white people. Since racial discrimination (conscious and unconscious, direct and indirect) results in black people being dispropor-tionately disadvantaged in terms of unemployment and homelessness, this would not be surprising. However, there is no real evidence that this is the case. When it has been claimed – notoriously, by the Metropolitan Police in 1982 and again by Metropolitan Police Commissioner Paul Condon in 1995 – that black people are disproportionately involved in crime, the statistics produced to back up these claims have been rightly criticized as unreliable and misleading (Smith, 1982; Crow, 1987: 305). A recent Home Office research study (Graham and Bowling, 1995) found that young Afro-Caribbeans had very similar rates of offending to white youths (see similarly Flood-Page et al., 2000: 20).

However, it is clear from a plethora of research studies that Afro-Caribbean people are disproportionately the object of police attention and suspicion. For example, a national study using British Crime Survey data from 1996 found that 23 per cent of black respondents had been stopped by the police during the previous year compared with 16 per cent of whites and 15 per cent of Asians (Bucke, 1997).[9] Black people are also more likely to be stopped several times in a year, and to be searched by the police following a stop. Overall, black people are, according to official figures, five times more likely to be searched by the police on the streets than white people.[10]

These results are presumably not unrelated to what the Policy Studies Institute found when invited to survey the work of the police in London in the early 1980s, that 'racialist language and racial prejudice were prominent and pervasive [in the Metropolitan Police] and that many individual officers and also whole groups were preoccupied with ethnic differences'. (Ninety-eight per cent of police officers are white: Home Office, 2000e: 62.) Although this racism did not usually manifest itself on the street, the PSI specifically noted that 'one criterion that police officers use for stopping people (especially in areas of *low* ethnic concentration) is that they are black' (Smith and Gray, 1983: 109–10). It seems that many police officers hold inaccurate, stereotyped views of black people, automatically placing them in the 'rough' (potentially criminal) category, especially when they are seen in areas where they 'don't belong'.[11] Research has found instances of police officers acting on the basis of stereotypes such as 'the assumption that West Indians running or carrying a bag are up to no good' (Southgate and Ekblom, 1986: 11).

The issue of police racism, and of their use of stop and search powers in particular, came to the fore in Lord Scarman's inquiry into the Brixton riots of 1981 (Scarman, 1986) and again on the publication of the Policy Studies Institute research on the Metropolitan Police in 1983. But little seemed to have changed by the time the Macpherson Report was published in February 1999. This was the report of an official inquiry into the case of Stephen Lawrence, a black student who was murdered by a gang of white youths at a south-east London bus stop in April 1993. Macpherson concluded that the bungled police investigation into the murder, as a result of which none of the murderers was brought to justice, was affected by the *'institutional racism'* evident in the Metropolitan Police.[12] This institutional racism, Macpherson thought, was for the most part unintentional and unconscious, but the police were nevertheless infected by 'processes, attitudes and behaviour which amount to discrimination through unwitting prejudice, ignorance, thoughtlessness, and racist stereotyping which disadvantage minority ethnic people' (Macpherson, 1999: 6.34). Macpherson identified stop and search practices as a particular cause of ill-feeling between the police and the black community, and said: 'we are clear that the perception and experience of the minority communities that discrimination is a major element in the stop and search problem is correct' (para. 45.8).

More recently there has been a backlash against the Macpherson Report from some quarters, with claims that the police, especially in London, have become afraid to use their stop and search powers (on black people in particular) and that street crime has risen as a result. The then Conservative Leader of the Opposition, William Hague, complained in December 2000 that 'the way in which the Macpherson Report has been used to brand every officer and every branch of the force as racist, has contributed directly to a collapse of police morale and recruitment and has led to a crisis on our streets' (*The Guardian*, 15 December 2000). Such claims are of dubious validity. Although recorded stops and searches did decline significantly following the report's publication, there was a *smaller* decrease in searches of black people than of white suspects.[13] And while street robbery (unlike crime generally) was on the rise at this time, it seems unlikely that a reduced number of stops and searches was a cause of this, since stops and searches rarely produce evidence of robberies and there is no reason to believe that people are deterred from committing robberies by the prospect of being searched. There is now official ethnic monitoring of stops and searches (following a Macpherson recommendation), and senior police officers in London currently claim to be moving towards a more 'targeted' and 'intelligence-led' use of stop and search (O'Connor, 2000). Whether any of this will result in any long-term improvement in police practices remains to be seen.

Black people are also *arrested* more often than their numbers in the general population would lead one to expect – four times as often as white people in 1998–9 (Home Office, 2000e: 19). Some of this difference may be explained by the fact that many arrests result from stops, which as we have just seen happen more often to black people (Willis, 1983: 18–19). It is also the case that black people are arrested particularly often for offences 'in which there is considerable scope for selective perception of potential or actual offenders' (Stevens and Willis, 1979: 41).[14] Phillips and Brown (1998: 44–5) found that the evidence against arrested black and Asian suspects was less often sufficient to charge them than in cases of arrested white suspects.

There is also evidence that race can make a difference to the police's decision whether to *caution* offenders or proceed to prosecution. The overall 'cautioning rate' (percentage of known offenders who are cautioned rather than prosecuted) for notifiable offences in 1999–2000 was 16 per cent for whites, 15 per cent for Asians and 11 per cent for black people (Home Office, 2000e: 20). Landau and Nathan (1983) found in London that white juveniles were significantly more likely to be cautioned than their black counterparts. A white juvenile with previous convictions was over four times more likely to be cautioned than a similar black youth.[15] Some other studies have found that black defendants are more likely to have been brought to court for offences which caused no loss, damage or injury (Stevens and Willis, 1979: 37; Crow and Cove, 1984), raising the possibility that similar white offenders might not have been prosecuted. This could, however, be partly due to the actions of victims rather than the police: perhaps similar offences by white people might have gone unreported to the police in the first place (see Shah and Pease, 1992).

Interestingly, research has found that ethnic minority defendants (both black and Asian) are more likely to have the prosecutions against them dropped after being charged by the police, that black defendants are more likely to plead not guilty, and that black and Asian defendants who plead not guilty are more likely to be acquitted in court (Home Office, 2000e: 37; Phillips and Brown, 1998). This suggests that the police may often charge ethnic minority suspects on the basis of a lesser amount of solid evidence than they might require in the case of a white suspect.

Black defendants are more likely than whites to be *committed for Crown Court trial*, according to a number of studies (Fitzgerald, 1993: 19–21; Home Office, 2000e: 38) – and, as we saw in Chapter 4, defendants who are tried in the Crown Court are likely to receive harsher sentences than those tried by magistrates. The higher committal rate seems to be partly the result of black defendants more often electing to be tried at the Crown Court, but it is at least as often due to magistrates declining jurisdiction. Moreover, black Crown Court defendants are *remanded in custody*, instead of being granted bail, more often than whites: one study found 26 per cent of sentenced black defendants had been remanded in custody compared with 20 per cent of whites and 18 per cent of Asians (Hood, 1992: 146–7). The fact that black defendants who are remanded in custody are much more likely than their white counterparts to be acquitted or not proceeded against (Fitzgerald, 1993: 22) suggests that black people are often wrongly denied bail.

There is good evidence that race can also play an important part in *sentencing*. Several studies in the United States indicate that black defendants tend to receive more severe sentences (including more custodial sentences and more death sentences; see, for example, Spohn et al., 1981–2; Baldus et al., 1986, 1989), but the evidence from the US is not entirely consistent (Pruitt and Wilson, 1983). Nor is it consistent in England, with several studies (for example, McConville and Baldwin, 1982; Crow and Cove, 1984; Moxon, 1988: 59) having found no evidence of racial bias in sentencing, but a variety of others (see, for example, NACRO, 1986b: ch. 3; Walker, 1988; Hudson, 1989) finding that black defendants are more likely to receive custodial sentences than are comparable white defendants.

The largest and most rigorous study of this question – Roger Hood's *Race and Sentencing* (1992) – provides the best evidence to date of a race effect in sentencing. Hood carefully examined sentencing at five Crown Courts in the West Midlands in 1989, and found that 57 per cent of black male defendants were sentenced to custody compared with 48 per cent of the white men; for women the figures were 29 per cent and 23 per cent. Taking into account all other relevant variables such as the offence charged and the offender's previous record, black men were 5 per cent more likely than white men to be sent to prison (Hood, 1992: 75–9; 163).[16] At one court (Dudley Crown Court), black defendants were 23 per cent more likely to receive custody. Adult black and Asian males also received longer average sentences of imprisonment, and were particularly likely to receive sentences of over three years.

Several studies have found that, although black offenders are to be found disproportionately in prisons, they are *under*-represented in other sectors of the penal system. Notably, black offenders have been found to receive proportionately fewer probation orders; and there have also been claims that young black offenders have been under-represented on intermediate treatment programmes (Taylor, 1981; NACRO, 1986b: ch. 4; Moxon, 1988; Pitts, 1986b: 133). These phenomena could well be related: for some reason black offenders are deemed unsuitable for non-custodial supervisory sentences and as a result find their way into custody relatively quickly. This raises questions not only about sentencers, but also about the role of the probation officers and youth justice workers who assess offenders' suitability for these disposals and relay their assessments to the courts in pre-sentence reports (PSRs). Some studies have indeed suggested that PSRs serve to disadvantage black defendants. For example, de la Motta (1984) found that reports on young black defendants in Nottingham were three times as likely as those on whites to make no recommendation as to sentence – usually interpreted by the sentencing court to amount to a veiled recommendation for custody. It has been suggested that 'probation officers may well make fewer recommendations for supervision in the community because they lack the confidence to carry this out successfully' (NACRO, 1986b: 16). (Ninety-one per cent of probation staff are white: Home Office, 2000e: 64.) However, other studies have found no such differences between recommendations in reports on black and white defendants (Mair, 1986; Moxon, 1988; Hood, 1992: 150–60) – but still fewer black defendants received probation orders than whites. One factor seems to be that PSRs are prepared less often on black defendants (for example Hood, 1992: 150–1;

Flood-Page and Mackie, 1998: 117), which is partly (but only partly) because reports are usually prepared in advance only on defendants pleading guilty, and black defendants are more likely to plead not guilty.[17] The 1994 change in the law allowing courts to dispense with PSRs before sentencing adults to custody (see Chapter 4) could have made matters worse for black defendants.

The overall situation may have altered in recent years. A study of sentencing in the mid-1990s found no difference in custody rates between black and white defendants whether or not other factors were taken into account, although Asian men received more custodial sentences than would have been expected on this basis (Flood-Page and Mackie, 1998: 115–20). Currently, it seems that black offenders are slightly more likely to receive community sentences than white offenders, but not less likely to receive custody (instead they receive fewer discharges) (Home Office, 2000e: 38). Concerns remain about both sentencing and the quality of treatment ethnic minority offenders receive from the probation service. A recent thematic inspection (HM Inspectorate of Probation, 2000) revealed that the quality of pre-sentence reports on white offenders was significantly higher than those prepared for offenders from ethnic minorities. The quality of supervision given to African and Afro-Caribbean probationers also raised significant concerns with regard to risk assessments, the level of contact received and enforcement practice.

Bias against black people in the criminal justice system does not by any means cease at the point of sentence. Black prisoners are less likely than whites to be allocated to open prisons (NACRO, 1986b: 20). Elaine Genders and Elaine Player (1989) have provided substantial evidence of racial discrimination within prisons, finding for example that the best jobs were regularly allocated to white prisoners. Again, inaccurate racial stereotypes (this time held by prison officers) had a lot to answer for. Prison officers (97 per cent of whom are white: Home Office, 2000e: 64) believed that Afro-Caribbean prisoners were arrogant, lazy and anti-authority, had 'chips on their shoulders' and tended to stick together. Although these stereotypes were demonstrably false, they led prison staff to perceive black prisoners as unsuitable for the most desirable jobs.

Genders and Player's findings were perfectly exemplified by the case of John Alexander. Southampton County Court found in May 1987 that the Home Office had unlawfully discriminated against Mr Alexander, a black prisoner whose application to work in the prison at Parkhurst was refused on the basis of an assessment report which stated that 'he displays the usual traits associated with his ethnic background, being arrogant, suspicious of staff, anti-authority, devious and possessing a very large chip on his shoulder'. The Prison Service has had a formal race relations policy since 1983 and has made repeated statements in recent years opposing any discrimination or display of prejudice by prison staff or by prisoners against each other, but racism is of course not so easily eradicated. This was reflected in the findings of the 1991 National Prison Survey (Walmsley et al., 1992: 38) that only 29 per cent of black Caribbean prisoners felt that prison officers treated them well, compared with 43 per cent of white prisoners. Another study (Burnett and Farrell, 1994) found that nearly half of black prisoners reported having been racially victimized by prison staff and over half thought they had been discriminated against over access to facilities and activities.

Even more disturbing was the murder of Zahid Mubarek in March 2000 by a rabidly racist fellow inmate in Feltham Young Offender Institution. The Prison Service inquiry into this incident was reported to have found that Feltham was imbued with institutional racism, with ethnic minority staff and inmates being subjected to overt racist abuse from prison officers (*The Guardian*, 22 January 2001). The incident also led to the Prison Service inviting the Commission for Racial Equality to carry out a formal inquiry into racism in prisons. Already, in March 2000, prisons minister Paul Boateng had ordered an inquiry into racism among prison officers in Full Sutton Prison near York. The Prison Service Director General Martin Narey has reported receiving hate mail following his own admissions that institutional racism and indeed 'pockets of malicious racism' exist within the Prison Service (*The Guardian*, 14 February 2001). It seems clear that racism and racial discrimination remain a potent and undeniable reality in English prisons.

There is a little evidence about the relationship between race and the *parole* decision. A Home Office (1994e) study of parole recommendations in 1990 found that the proportions of ethnic minority prisoners recommended for parole were lower than those of white prisoners, but the differences tended to vanish when other factors such as type of offence and length of sentence were taken into account. When the figures were 'normalized' to allow for these factors, 60 per cent of white prisoners who were considered were recommended for parole compared with 56 per cent of those of West Indian or Guyanese ethnic origin. More recent figures for the granting of parole and home detention curfew show little difference between eligible black and white prisoners. Asian prisoners are more likely to be granted early release, probably because they generally represent a lesser risk of reconviction and are less likely to commit offences in prison (Home Office, 2000e: 42).

To sum up: it may not be true to say that there is bias working consistently against black people throughout the entire criminal justice system. Nevertheless, it seems that a black person who comes into contact with the criminal justice system has a good chance of being seriously disadvantaged compared with a white person, and may be particularly likely to end up in prison. There may be some cause for hope, if not optimism, in the fact that the race issue in criminal justice has become increasingly recognized as one of the most pressing issues in criminal justice, having been stressed as such by the national Criminal Justice Consultative Council (1994), by the Lord Chief Justice Lord Taylor in 1995, and repeatedly by Jack Straw during his time as Home Secretary, especially since the Macpherson Report in 1999. Steps have been taken, for example, to ensure that sentencers receive racial awareness training and that ethnic monitoring is introduced and improved throughout the criminal justice system. The legal duty not to discriminate on grounds of race has been extended to the police by the Race Relations (Amendment) Act 2000, and all public bodies are to be put under a legal duty to positively promote good race relations and equality of opportunity (*The Guardian*, 21 February 2001). Race is clearly now seen as a potential source of serious illegitimacy – and rightly, since studies have repeatedly shown not only that black people have considerably less confidence in criminal justice than white people (see, for example, Dholakia and Sumner, 1993: 34–5; Skogan, 1990: 55), but also that large proportions of white as well as black people believe that justice is biased against black people (for example, Smellie and Crow, 1991: 20; Flood-Page et al., 2000: 54). There is no reason to doubt the genuine concern of many people within the criminal justice system about the issue of racial discrimination, but it is also too early to say whether such concern will lead to any real improvement.

**GENDER**

Within the criminal justice system, the dimension of gender differs in one crucial respect from those of class and race: in this case, members of the oppressed group (women) are distinctly *under*-represented in the criminal statistics. Women and girls accounted for a mere 5 per cent of the prison population in 1999,[18] despite comprising just over half of the general population. (Nevertheless, there are currently more women prisoners than ever before – 3,250 in 1999 – and in recent years their numbers have been rising even faster than men's.) Women are also under-represented at previous stages of the criminal justice system, though to lesser extents. In 1999, 16 per cent of those found guilty of indictable offences and 17 per cent of those found guilty or cautioned were female,[19] while only 15 per cent of those arrested in 1999–2000 were female (Home Office, 2000f: 9).

Again the question arises as to whether this difference is due to a real difference in offending behaviour between the two sections of the population (in this case, males and females). With very rare exceptions,[20] commentators agree that females do, in fact, commit fewer offences than do males, although the difference may be much smaller than the official figures suggest. Moreover, female offenders generally commit less serious offences than their male counterparts, and have committed fewer offences previously: the typical detected female offender is 'a young girl, a first offender charged with shoplifting' (Heidensohn, 1985: 11). Explanations for this state of affairs vary. Positivistic explanations exist which claim that differing male and female biologies are the cause: girls may not literally be made out of sugar and spice and all things nice, but their hormones lead them to be more law-abiding. More plausible in our opinion are theories which emphasize the different social experiences of males and females. Girls are socialized to be more passive and conformist than boys, and throughout their lives girls and women may find themselves subject to greater informal social controls; they may also have less opportunity to commit certain types of crime (see, for example, Smart, 1976: 66–70; Heidensohn, 1985: ch. 9).

Whatever the explanation, if we accept that women and girls do in fact commit fewer (and generally less serious) offences than men and boys, then the bare statistics say nothing about whether there is any bias operating in the criminal justice system either in favour of women or against them. Perhaps there would be even fewer women in prison if they were treated the same as comparable male offenders; or perhaps there would be more. There have traditionally been two rival schools of thought on this issue, one holding that female offenders are dealt with more leniently than males and one asserting the reverse.

The first view – the 'chivalry theory' – claims that chivalry leads police and sentencers (who are predominantly male)[21] to afford women less harsh treatment. It is easy to point to incidents which appear to bear this out. Our personal favourite is a case reported in the *Daily Mirror* in January 1978: '*Judge frees "inhuman" mum*. A mother who flogged her eight-year-old son with a belt, gave him cold baths and forced him to stand naked for hours at night . . . was saved from prison *because she has another child to care for*' (cited by Heidensohn, 1985: 51; our italics). Were the chivalry theory to be correct, this would not of course mean that there is no sexist bias in the criminal justice system, but that the sexism takes the form of a condescending 'chivalry' which may benefit some female offenders but is hardly likely to advance the general cause of female social equality. (It is, however, the kind of view often propounded by anti-feminists of the 'women should stop moaning because they get the better deal as things are' ilk.)

The opposing view, put forward in particular by feminist commentators, has been termed the 'evil woman' theory (Nagel and Hagan, 1983). It asserts that women who offend will receive *harsher* treatment from the criminal justice system. This is because women who commit crimes are seen as 'doubly deviant': they have offended not only against the law, but also against deeply ingrained social norms about how women should be, so they are perceived as being particularly depraved. Rebellious anti-social behaviour on the part of a young man may be reprehensible, but it is less disturbing because such behaviour is after all masculine – 'boys will be boys'. Similar conduct on the part of a young woman is far more unsettling because it is unfeminine. Moreover, there is a tendency for female criminality to be 'sexualized' in a way that male offending is not. Female offenders are assumed to be sexually deviant, or their sexuality is regarded as associated with their offending, assumptions which are not made with male offenders. The result is that women's crimes evoke an especially punitive response. This punitiveness may be overt, or it may be disguised as paternalistic concern for the woman's welfare. The woman's disturbing deviance may be rationalized away as 'sickness', leading to a positivistic 'treatment' measure which could be more intrusive than the sentence a male offender would receive for a similar offence. (See generally Heidensohn, 1985: ch. 3.)

These theories can be tested against the evidence that exists concerning the different stages of the criminal process. At the first stages of initial contact between the police and possible female suspects, one clearly established fact is that the police stop and search men much more often than women (in fact about twice as often).[22] A national survey of boys and girls aged 14 and 15, carried out by Home Office researchers in 1983 (Riley and Shaw, 1985; Riley, 1986) casts some light on the phenomenon. Boys were more than twice as likely to have been stopped by the police than girls of the same age (29 per cent compared with 13 per cent in the preceding twelve months). Boys were more likely to be stopped if they and their friends were delinquent, but this was not true for girls. Girls were more likely to be stopped if their lifestyles were 'unfeminine' – if they went around in mixed-sex groups, were relatively more involved with drugs and alcohol, spent more time with their friends and were subject to less parental supervision. These findings do not show that the police treat girls worse than boys, but they do lend some support to the feminist claim that females are dealt with by criminal justice agencies according to different criteria from those applied to males, criteria related to traditional female gender-roles, with the result that their femininity is being policed as much as their offending. This is a theme which will recur as we progress through the criminal process.

Moving on to the decision whether to *arrest* a suspect, while there is little directly relevant British research evidence, a study of drug arrests in Chicago between 1942 and 1970 found 'a tendency not to arrest females as often as males if they behaved in expected, stereotypic ways. During drugs raids females often cried, claimed to have been led astray by men, or expressed concern about the fate of their children. These behaviors usually were successful' (de Fleur, 1975: 101). However, females who were more aggressive and hostile were arrested more often than those who behaved in more traditionally feminine ways.

There is no doubt that detected female offenders are *cautioned* much more often than males. In 1999, 48 per cent of females found guilty of or cautioned for an indictable offence received a caution, compared with 30 per cent of males (Ayres, 2000: Table 4). Claims have been made that such figures show chivalry operating in women's favour (Walker, 1968: 299–300), and also that they show the reverse (Smart, 1976: 137–8).[23] It is of course necessary to take into account the type of offences involved and the offenders' previous records in deciding whether any bias goes into the creation of the statistical difference between the sexes. Ideally, one should also allow for other variables which may affect the decision whether to caution or prosecute, such as social class and race. Landau and Nathan's (1983) study of juvenile cautioning in London found that, when such other variables were controlled for, the sex of the offender made no significant difference to the decision of the police (see also Landau, 1981). (However, Loraine Gelsthorpe (1989: 106) found evidence that girls were more likely than boys to be cautioned for offences of similar seriousness.) Again, although girls are not overall dealt with more harshly than boys, it may be that they are judged by different, gender-role-related criteria. It has been suggested that the police again act more leniently towards female offenders who act in stereotypically feminine ways, such as showing remorse by crying or apologizing (Gelsthorpe, 1985: 3; 1989: 105).[24]

Women are *remanded in custody* less often than men, apparently because they are less likely to have breached bail in the past or to be of no fixed abode (Flood-Page and Mackie, 1998: 121). When women are remanded in custody, they are less likely than remanded males to be subsequently sentenced to custody by the court (35 per cent of female and 47 per cent of male remandees in 1999 – Home Office, 2000f: 15). This could mean that some women are being remanded in custody when comparable male offenders are not;[25] certainly it means that many women offenders are being sent to prison before trial although their actual offence is subsequently not deemed serious enough to warrant deprivation of liberty. Forty-eight per cent of women who are remanded in custody are charged with theft or fraud rather than more serious or violent offences (Home Office, 2000f: 15).

The 'chivalry' and 'evil woman' theories have both been put forward in respect of *sentencing*. The bare statistics show, as one would expect, that women and girls sentenced for indictable offences on the whole receive less severe sentences than males. In 1999, 13.5 per cent of females' sentences were custodial compared with 25 per cent of males' (Ayres, 2000: Table 11). Sentencing patterns differ in some other respects as well: women are much more likely than males to receive probation orders, and less likely to be fined or ordered to perform community service.[26] Do these figures indicate bias – and if so, in what direction?

Pat Carlen (1983) argues that sexist bias enters into the sentencing decision to the disadvantage of women who offend against the norms of femininity. From her interviews with sheriffs (Scottish judges) she concludes that when sentencers are 'faced with a sentencing dilemma in a case where the offender is female, they mainly decide their sentence on the basis of their assessment of the woman as mother' (Carlen, 1983: 63). All the sheriffs she interviewed said (chivalrously) that they particularly hated sending women to prison. Nevertheless, they admitted that they sometimes imprisoned women in circumstances when they would have fined a man, because women were normally financially dependent on their husbands and often could not afford to pay a fine appropriate to the offence. They would be particularly inclined to send a woman to prison if her children were in care. Carlen quotes sheriffs as commenting: 'If she's a good mother we don't want to take her away. If she's not a good mother it doesn't really matter', and 'One often finds out, when inquiries are made, that the women have left their husbands and their children are already in care. In those cases it may seem a very good idea to send them to prison for three months to sort themselves out' (Carlen, 1983: 67).

Carlen's claim that sentencers make their decisions in this manner receives some support from surveys of women in prison, a disproportionate number of whom seem to have unconventional family backgrounds. Of Carlen's own sample of 20 Scottish women prisoners only one was currently married and living with her husband (Carlen, 1983: 38). In another Scottish sample, 65 per cent of the women prisoners had children under 18, but only half of these had been looking after them immediately prior to being imprisoned (Dobash et al., 1986: 193). In England, Genders and Player found that half of their sample of women prisoners over the age of 30 had a non-conventional background; fewer than half of those with dependent children lived within a 'traditional nuclear family setting' (in which they included living with a long-term cohabitee) (Genders and Player, 1986: 360). The findings of the 1991 National Prison Survey (Walmsley et al., 1992: 17) differed only slightly from this: 49 per cent of female prisoners of 18 or over had been living with a spouse or partner prior to their imprisonment, and nearly a half of those with dependent children were unmarried. Further support for Carlen's thesis comes from a study of magistrates' sentencing in Cambridge by Farrington and Morris. They found that women who were divorced or separated or had a 'deviant family back-ground' were more likely to receive a relatively severe sentence, but these factors made no difference to the kind of sentences which male offenders received (Farrington and Morris, 1983: 244–5). (In the United States, Nagel (1981) made similar findings.)

Overall, Farrington and Morris found that the sentences received by female defendants at the Cambridge City Magistrates' Court were not significantly heavier or lighter than those passed on men when the relevant factors of offence type and offender's previous record were controlled for. In combination with their findings about the effects of 'deviant family backgrounds', this suggests the possibility that there could be sexist biases in sentencing operating *in both directions* (and, in this study, cancelling each other out). Women who are married and looking after their children may be the beneficiaries of chivalry and receive a lighter sentence than a man, but women who are less acceptably feminine – who are perceived as 'evil women' because they are not good wives and mothers[27] – may be treated more harshly.

However, the same cancelling out of biases was not apparent in two studies of Crown Court sentencing practice (Moxon, 1988; Hood, 1992: ch. 11); chivalry seemed to predominate. (Nagel (1981) has also found this to be true in the US.) After allowing for factors such as offence and criminal record, women were significantly less likely than men to receive a custodial sentence. For example, Moxon (1988: 54) found that male first offenders charged with theft or fraud were almost twice as likely to receive unsuspended custody as were comparable women. Similarly, Hedderman and Hough (1994) found that in 1992 female first offenders were only half as likely to receive a sentence of immediate imprisonment than were male first offenders, and the pattern was similar for specific offences such as theft and for offenders with one, two or three previous convictions. Flood-Page and Mackie (1998: 121–3) found much the same picture emerging in the mid-1990s. Dowds and Hedderman (1997) found a more mixed picture when they examined a large sample of male and female adult offenders sentenced in 1991 for shoplifting, violence and drugs offences. Taking other factors into account, female shoplifters were less likely than comparable males to receive a prison sentence. Men and women were equally likely to be imprisoned for their first conviction for violence or a repeat drug offence – but women were less likely to receive custody for a *first drug* conviction or *repeated violent* offence.

It is not entirely clear how or whether these findings can be reconciled with those of Farrington and Morris. But it is noticeable that Farrington and Morris divided sentences into two categories, 'relatively lenient' and 'relatively severe', the latter including probation, community service and suspended sentences, whereas the other studies divided sentences into unsuspended custody and non-custodial sentences. Farrington and Morris's finding could therefore be explained by the known tendency for courts to sentence women disproportionately to probation, while the other studies suggest that – as Carlen's sheriffs claimed – courts may often be fairly loath to sentence women (especially mothers) to *custody*.

It is often claimed (for example Mawby, 1977; Fitzgerald and Sim, 1979: 81) that women must be sentenced more harshly because a greater proportion of women who receive prison sentences have no previous convictions compared with imprisoned men: this was true of 38 per cent of women serving prison sentences in 1991 but only 10 per cent of male prisoners (Walmsley et al., 1992:

64). (Similarly, a much smaller proportion of female than male prisoners have been found guilty of a violent offence.)[28] This argument looks convincing at first sight, but it is fallacious. For these kinds of percentages are just what we should expect to find given that the great bulk of the female offender population consists of people with no or few previous convictions, and the figures are perfectly compatible with women receiving sentences which are similar to, or more lenient than, those passed on comparable male offenders (Walker, 1981). The correct comparison – of how female and male offenders with similar records are actually dealt with at the sentencing stage – was the comparison made by the studies we mentioned in the previous two paragraphs.

There seems to be a particular reluctance on the part of sentencing courts to impose fines on women. This could be partly – though probably not entirely – due to sentencers taking into account the fact that women are less likely to have their own income and more likely to have childcare responsibilities (Dowds and Hedderman, 1997; Gelsthorpe and Loucks, 1997). The result of this seems to be that (like unemployed offenders, whom courts are also reluctant to fine) a woman may end up receiving a less severe sentence than a male offender (such as a discharge rather than a fine) but may also sometimes receive a more intrusive sentence such as probation.

The preponderance of research evidence, however, suggests that women who offend are not on the whole sentenced more severely than comparable males, and that they sometimes receive more lenient sentences, including escaping custody where a male would not. What is not known, however, is to what extent this could be accounted for by arguably relevant differences in the situations of male and female offenders, such as childcare responsibilities. Perhaps a woman with a child to look after does not deserve to escape imprisonment any more than an otherwise comparable male offender without such a responsibility, but does the child deserve to lose its mother? It may well be that such considerations – perhaps rightly – account for the differences between men and women as regards whether they receive custodial sentences. The possibility also remains that some women – perhaps those who are perceived as especially deviant because of their lifestyles or their particular crimes – come off worse than comparable male offenders because of their gender. As Chris Tchaikovsky of the organization Women in Prison has aptly put it: 'Judges tell me all the time that they never send women to prison. The truth is that the woman in the neat white blouse who is sorry and depressed is acceptable, but the girl in the leather jacket with the Mohican haircut and the drug problem is treated very badly' (*The Guardian*, 9 February 1994).

Much attention has been focused in recent years on the position of women who kill their violent male partners. The best-known example is Sara Thornton, whose murder conviction was quashed and a retrial ordered by the Court of Appeal in December 1995. It is argued that the legal defence of 'provocation' (which can reduce a charge of murder to manslaughter, with consequent possibilities of a lesser sentence than the mandatory life imprisonment sentence for murder) serves to prejudice women in comparison with men, because it requires a sudden loss of self-control. Men may be more able to avail themselves of this defence because they are more likely to kill women using methods such as strangulation which they can claim resulted from a sudden burst of anger, whereas women's methods of killing their partner may look more premeditated. Moreover, the law has been slow to recognize the effects of 'cumulative provocation' consisting of recurrent violence over a long period (Nicolson and Sanghvi, 1995). These arguments may well be correct, despite the fact that women seem to succeed in pleading provocation in a higher proportion of domestic homicides than do men (Hedderman and Hough, 1994). For it seems very likely that women in such cases are typically subjected to much higher degrees of provocation (and especially of violence) from their partners than the men are. The law of provocation was significantly reinterpreted by the Court of Appeal in the 1990s,[29] giving greater recognition to 'cumulative provocation' but still requiring 'loss of self control' to establish the provocation defence. It cannot of course be assumed that homicide – one of the rarest of offences – provides a typical picture of the way the legal and penal systems deal routinely with the great bulk of non-violent female offending.

If courts do indeed have a *general* tendency to be relatively lenient with female offenders, especially as regards custody, it could be a leniency bought by exploiting stereotyped notions about women and their crimes, at the price of reinforcing these stereotypes. Defence lawyers' pleas in mitigation and pre-sentence reports might encourage leniency by playing on the positivistic idea that women who offend are sick, or 'mad rather than bad', or by portraying the woman as weak, and led astray by a dominant man. In arguing that the women cannot help their actions, lawyers and probation officers could be helping to perpetuate the sexist ideology which holds that women are in general weaker, less rational than men and more driven by their emotions. Mary Eaton (1986) makes the wider claim that mitigation pleas and pre-sentence reports reinforce prevailing ideologies about women's rightful roles within the family by stressing either the normality of the woman's domestic behaviour (and therefore her essential goodness) or else its abnormality (as either a cause or a symptom of the pathology that has led her to offend).

It is doubtless the perception of women who offend as 'mad rather than bad' and in need of help (perhaps combined in some cases with reluctance to impose a fine) which leads to the tendency for female offenders to receive more probation and supervision orders than males.[30] Such paternalism could have the effect of 'up-tariffing' (see Chapter 9) some female offenders with comparatively trivial offending records, leading to an increased danger of a more severe sentence if they re-offend subsequently.

When women are sentenced to custody, how does their treatment compare to that of men? At first sight it might seem that they are treated better, since penal establishments for females are on the whole (superficially at least, and with some notable exceptions) physically less unpleasant places than those for males. But in some respects women prisoners are worse off. For example, because women comprise such a small percentage of the prison population (only 17 out of the 130-plus penal institutions in England and Wales accommodate females) this means that women are often held at enormous distances from their homes, in remote locations, making visiting a particular problem. Again, it is probably the case that, for a variety of social and psychological reasons, women find the experience of imprisonment much more traumatic than men do (Heidensohn, 1985: 75–9), leading to a higher incidence of flare-ups and self-mutilation in women's prisons.[31]

It can be argued that women prisoners *should* be treated differently from men because their circumstances and needs are different. Most of them have children under 16, of whom only a quarter are being cared for by the child's father or a spouse or partner;[32] they are more likely to be dependent on opiate drugs, and nearly half report having been physically and/or sexually abused (HM Chief Inspector of Prisons, 1997c). And indeed women prisoners are treated differently from men – but whether these differences are appropriate to their needs is another question. Traditionally, the training of female prisoners is directed towards equipping them to perform the work they are thought most likely to do when they are released, namely housework. The general picture has not changed much: the work that women do in prison is still dominated by domestic-type tasks such as cleaning, sewing and cooking, which also figure prominently in the training provided for female prisoners, along with training for traditionally female jobs such as typing, catering and hairdressing (Hamlyn and Lewis, 2000: chs. 4 and 5). Genders and Player, who studied female youth custody centres (now called young offender institutions), found this stereotyping of women's work to be combined with psychological rehabilitation theory:

> an important part of the treatment and training of young women serving youth custody relates to the building of self-confidence and self-esteem, the lack of which is deemed responsible for much of the attention- and approval-seeking which causes many girls to come into conflict with the law. The skills which are taught in youth custody centres, however, continue to permit success mainly within the boundaries of stereotypical female roles. The concentration upon personal hygiene and appearance, through training in beauty care and hairdressing, and the development of domestic skills, such as cleaning, cooking and household budgeting, makes clear those areas in which delinquent young women are expected to develop feelings of self-worth. (Genders and Player, 1986: 368)

The positivistic 'mad not bad' stereotype of female offenders has had a particular influence on prison regimes for women. An official Home Office publication of 1977 stated that 'most of the women in prison wish to conform with society but for various reasons are unable to do so. For example, many are in need of medical or psychiatric treatment' (Home Office, 1977a: 101). Even if female prisoners are more likely to be mentally ill than male prisoners are, this would only mean that a larger *minority* of female prisoners are in need of psychiatric treatment[33] (Morris, 1987: 124–5; Heidensohn, 1985: 73–5). It seems likely that female prisoners are *treated* as mentally ill to an excessive extent; certainly they seem to be prescribed psychotropic medication to a much greater extent than male prisoners (Morris, 1987: 124). This is not to deny that a great deal of mental *distress* is suffered by female prisoners: as we said before, women prisoners probably do suffer from imprisonment to a greater extent than men do.

In 1968 – roughly at the zenith of the 'rehabilitative ideal' – it was announced that Holloway (by far the largest women's penal establishment in England) was to be redesigned and rebuilt as, in essence, a secure psychiatric hospital.

The new design turned out to be disastrous, and in 1981 the prison was given a 'modified brief' by the Home Office, abandoning the notion that all its inmates should be treated according to a medical model. This did not prevent the rebuilt Holloway from suffering severe problems, including overcrowding and low staff morale, compounded by a public scandal which blew up in 1984 about the prisoners' living conditions. Ironically, the most damning publicity was directed at the psychiatric unit (known to inmates as 'the Muppet House'), in which there were three suicides and several outbreaks of self-mutilation. The scandal resulted in a Home Office inquiry, following which the prison improved significantly (HM Chief Inspector of Prisons, 1992). Subsequently, however, conditions deteriorated again, provoking an unprecedented walkout by Chief Inspector of Prisons Sir David Ramsbotham in December 1995 after inspectors had reportedly found squalid conditions and a heavy-handed, over-zealous security regime in place at Holloway. This was again followed by an apparent improvement in conditions, at least for the time being, but Holloway's problems seem to recur on a regular basis.

In recent years, female prisoners seem to have suffered at least as much as male inmates from the 'security first' atmosphere engendered by the Woodcock (1994) and Learmont (1995) reports into prison security, despite the fact that women generally pose much less of a threat to security. One manifestation of this was a policy introduced in April 1995 that women prisoners (including those in advanced stages of pregnancy) should be handcuffed or chained when being treated in hospitals outside prisons. The outcry which followed a TV news report of a prisoner chained to a prison officer hours before and after giving birth led to a modification of the policy in January 1996, but only to exempt women arriving at hospital to give birth (and most of those attending ante-natal checks) from being cuffed or chained while in the hospital.

Overall, though, it appears that female offenders do not in general receive harsher treatment than their opposite numbers of the opposite sex; and sometimes they may receive more lenient treatment, perhaps especially as regards the decision to impose custodial sentences. However, it also seems very likely that *some* women are effectively punished for deviating from conventional feminine norms, and that the system tends to react to female offenders in a manner which is, one way or another, imbued with sexism. To use Althusser's terminology, the penal system can be seen both as part of the 'Repressive State Apparatus' imposing punitive sanctions on deviant women and as an 'Ideological State Apparatus' communicating and reproducing the sexist ideology which structures patriarchal society (Eaton, 1986: 88–9; above, Chapter 3). Or, as a Durkheimian might put it, our social culture is still permeated with sexism, which is bound to find expression in our punitive practices.

Currently women offenders are being punished increasingly harshly for their deviance. Indeed, the female prison population has recently been growing much more rapidly than the numbers of male prisoners. Between 1993 and 1999 the male prison population rose by a massive 43 per cent, but the numbers of female prisoners more than doubled, from 1,560 to 3,250. This disproportionate rise is probably not because women are now being sentenced more harshly than men, but because the increase in sentence severity since 1993 has in particular meant that a great many more relatively petty offenders have been sent to prison, or sent there for longer. And since, as we have seen, most female offenders are relatively petty criminals, this shift has affected women disproportionately.

We should stress in conclusion that, although we accept the possibility that women offenders sometimes escape custody where men would not, we are emphatically *not* advocating that more women should be sent to prison. On the contrary, since women in prison are predominantly relatively petty, non-violent offenders with few previous convictions, a large proportion of them could probably be decarcerated or diverted from custody with comparatively little difficulty, if there were the political will to do so. Nancy Seear and Elaine Player, reporting on women in the penal system for the Howard League for Penal Reform, were surprised to find near-unanimous agreement from prison governors, prison officers, educationalists and ex-offenders that very many women in prison should not be there at all (Seear and Player, 1986: 12), and proposed a plausible programme for reducing the female prison population to tiny proportions (see also Carlen, 1990). In a penal system which was generally fair and did not exercise the massive 'overkill' of punishment we exposed in Chapter 2, this could be achieved without any need to exercise 'chivalry'. But at present, of course, the trend is very much in the opposite direction.

## NOTES

1   The Policy Studies Institute (Smith, 1983: 247) found that Londoners in the professional and managerial occupational groups were more critical of the police than others; but it also seemed that unemployed people were significantly more likely to be critical of the police than people in employment. Similarly, results from the national British Crime Survey (Skogan, 1990: 13–14) have shown people who are unemployed, less educated or living in the inner city to be less happy with the police than others.

2   It does not, however, seem to be the case that *employed working class* people are stopped more often than middle class people. In fact, if stops in cars are included, professionals and higher earners are more likely to be stopped, because they are more likely to drive cars (Skogan, 1990: 28–9; 61).

3   For evidence that deaths at work which are caused by managers' culpable carelessness are dealt with very differently from other deaths caused by fault, see Bergman (1991). In May 2000 the government announced its intention to introduce a new offence of 'corporate killing' for which *companies* could be prosecuted (Sanders and Young, 2000: 368–71), but this would not affect the criminal liability of the individual managers who might be at fault.

4   This figure is for 1999 (Ayres, 2000).

5   For an article attempting the tricky task of comparing the treatment of white collar and other offenders, see Levi (1989). See also Nelken (1997).

6   Disparity can also be detected in Court of Appeal decisions about the appropriate sentences for these offences, although the gap has narrowed to some extent in recent years. Two fairly typical cases are *R. v. Hayes* (1981) 3 Cr App Rep (S) 205 (nine months' imprisonment for conspiracy to defraud the Inland Revenue of £19,424)

and *R. v. Adams* (1985) 7 Cr App Rep (S) 411 (two years' custody for defrauding social security of £7,000).

7   45 per cent of non-white people in English prisons are not of UK nationality, indicating that drug couriers account for some of the racial disparity, especially among females (75 per cent of foreign female prisoners are serving sentences for drugs offences). But only for some of it. When non-UK nationals are excluded from the figures, 14 per cent of male and 15 per cent of female prisoners are of ethnic minority origin (Home Office, 2000e: ch. 7).

8   In this book, we use the term 'black' to refer to people of African or Caribbean ethnic origin only. This chapter concentrates on the most obvious and most disturbing statistical differences between the races in the criminal justice system, which are between 'white' people on the one hand and 'black' people on the other. Comparisons between whites and people of 'Asian' (Indian, Pakistani or Bangladeshi) ethnic origin often yield very different results. For example, the preponderance of research suggests that Asian people are *under*-represented in both recorded and unrecorded offending (e.g. Stevens and Willis, 1979: 2; Graham and Bowling, 1995) and are stopped by the police less often than Afro-Caribbeans and either less often or about as often as whites (Smith, 1983: 95; Skogan, 1990: 28). Hood (1992: 75–9) found that, unlike black defendants, Asian Crown Court defendants were slightly less likely than whites to be sentenced to custody. Genders and Player (1989) found that, within prisons, Asians were regarded stereotypically by staff as 'model prisoners', in stark contrast to Afro-Caribbeans.

9   See also Flood-Page et al. (2000: 49–50); Skogan (1990: 27–9; 1994: 25–6, 73); Willis (1983: 14).

10  Home Office (2000e: 8) These figures may not be as bad as they seem when different social, demographic and lifestyle characteristics of different ethnic groups are taken into account. The average black person may be more likely to be found on the city streets than the average white person, and the racial differences in stop and search rates sometimes disappear when these factors are controlled for (MVA and Miller, 2000). Nevertheless it seems unlikely that a ratio as great as 5 to 1 can be satisfactorily explained away entirely in this way.

11  'Demeanour' could also be important here. Either stereotyping by the police, or the fact that black people tend to be more critical of the police than whites (Field, 1984: ch. 7; Flood-Page et al., 2000: 54; Mirrlees-Black, 2001; Sims and Myhill, 2001), or both, could lead to the police perceiving black people as having a bad attitude towards them and discriminating against them as a result.

12  Evidence of institutional racism on the part of the Crown Prosecution Service was also reported by an independent inquiry into allegations of racial discrimination against CPS staff (*The Guardian*, 11 May 2000).

13  In the year 1999–2000 recorded stops and searches fell by 41 per cent in London and 14 per cent on average elsewhere, but searches of black people fell by only 35 and 10 per cent respectively (Home Office, 2000e: 7–8).

14  This was particularly noticeable for the (now abolished) offence of 'sus', or 'being a suspected person loitering with intent'. Black people were 15 times more likely than whites to be arrested for this offence, a figure which led Home Office researchers to wonder politely 'whether some of the difference may be accounted for by the possibility that the suspicions of policemen bear disproportionately on blacks' (Stevens and Willis, 1979: 33).

15  See also Commission for Racial Equality (1992). A study in London by Farrington and Bennett (1981) found that race made no significant difference to cautioning rates; but it is possible that their lumping together of blacks and Asians affected their results.

16   This difference was not statistically significant at the .05 level conventionally used
     by statisticians, and in theory there is a 7 per cent chance that it could be attributable
     to chance. However, in the light of other evidence about the effects of race in
     criminal justice and the fact that the difference is in the 'expected' direction, Hood
     (1992: 80–1; 1995) is doubtless justified in taking it as evidence of a genuine 'race
     effect' in sentencing.

17   Since it appears that more black than white defendants are *acquitted*, or have their
     cases dismissed by the court for lack of evidence (Walker, 1988; Phillips and Brown,
     1998; Home Office, 2000e: 37), it may be that black defendants deny guilt more
     often simply because black people are more often wrongly arrested and wrongly
     prosecuted.

18   Calculated from Cullen and Minchin (2000a).

19   Calculated from Ayres (2000), Table 4.

20   One outstanding (and notoriously sexist) exception was Otto Pollak (1961), who
     claimed that women are responsible for vast amounts of crime which go undetected
     because of women's more deceitful nature and because chivalrous men do not want
     to see women prosecuted or punished (see Heidensohn, 1985: 118–21).

21   83 per cent of police officers are male, as are around 90 per cent of Crown Court
     judges and 51 per cent of magistrates (Home Office, 2000f: ch. 10). Some research
     suggests that women magistrates deal more severely with female defendants
     (Farrington and Morris, 1983: 245), which may fit in with the 'chivalry theory'. On
     the other hand, it could mean that 'good', law-abiding women tend to come down
     harder on 'evil', law-breaking women than men do.

22   The 1988 British Crime Survey found that 20 per cent of males and 10 per cent of
     females had been stopped in the previous 14 months, while the 1992 BCS found
     figures of 28 and 16 per cent over a 12 month period (Skogan, 1990: 28; 1994: 73).
     See also Flood-Page et al. (2000: 48–9).

23   Walker's claim was based on unrefined statistics which took no account of the
     seriousness of the offence or the offender's previous record; on the other hand,
     Smart's claim was based on a statistical fallacy which Walker later refuted (Walker,
     1981: 380–1).

24   However, it is not clear that the police are acting in a *directly* sexist manner at this
     point. Gelsthorpe suggests that boys who showed remorse (which they did less
     often than girls) were also more likely to be cautioned.

25   It is possible that many sentencers pass a non-custodial sentence rather than a short
     prison sentence on a woman who has been remanded in custody, reasoning that
     she has already had 'a taste of custody'. If so, the fact that women's prison sentences
     are on average much shorter than men's (because their offences are less serious)
     could explain the gender difference pointed out in the text.

26   In 1999, 22 per cent of females sentenced for indictable offences were placed on
     probation or supervision orders, 7 per cent given community service orders and 21
     per cent fined. The corresponding figures for male offenders were 13, 9 and 28 per
     cent (Ayres, 2000: Table 8).

27   The case of Susan Jones is of interest. Mrs Jones' four-year prison sentence for
     robbing seven building societies was quashed by the Court of Appeal in July 1991
     and a probation order with a condition of psychiatric treatment was substituted.
     The trial judge had referred to her 'wicked crimes', but the Court of Appeal judges
     stated that she was '*not a wicked woman*' and had only robbed because she had
     become desperate about her family's debts and was concerned about her twin
     children but 'did not want to worry her husband' (*The Guardian*, 30 July 1991).

28   On 30 June 1999, only 25 per cent of female sentenced prisoners were in prison for
     violent or sexual offences including robbery, compared with 44 per cent of male
     prisoners (calculated from Cullen and Minchin, 2000a: Table 1).

29  In the cases of *R. v. Ahluwalia* [1992] 4 All ER 889 and *R. v. Humphries* [1995] 4 All
    ER 1008.

30  See above, n. 26.

31  Women prisoners are punished for offences against prison discipline much more
    often than men: in 1999 there were 213 offences per 100 female prisoners compared
    with 158 per 100 males (Home Office, 2000f: 32). Part of the reason for this seems
    to be that, although the governing Prison Rules do not vary, there are generally
    more unnecessary restrictions placed on women prisoners and the rules are more
    rigorously enforced against them (NACRO, 1992; Morris, 1987: 121–4).

32  There are four mother and baby units within women's prisons (in Holloway,
    Askham Grange, Styal and New Hall prisons) with places for 72 women and their
    babies, who can only stay with their mothers up to the age of 18 months. The Prison
    Service is currently considering expanding the places available and allowing
    children up to the age of four. It is a controversial question whether this is the right
    approach to the needs of mothers and their children, as opposed to ensuring that
    as few mothers as possible are in prison in the first place.

33  Studies such as Gunn et al. (1991) have only found a very small percentage of
    women prisoners suffering from psychoses such as schizophrenia, although rather
    more with neurotic disorders and depression. It is only possible to conclude that *a
    majority* of female prisoners are mentally disordered by including categories such
    as drug dependency and 'personality disorder'. The latter is not a treatable illness
    but essentially a judgement that the individual has an unusual personality, for
    example by reason of anti-social behaviour. Not surprisingly, many prisoners (both
    male and female) can be diagnosed in this manner.

# 11

# Solving the Crisis?

Throughout this book we have seen how wide, deep and persistent the penal crisis is. It pervades every area and aspect of the penal system, manifesting itself in both a running malaise and periodic dramatic eruptions. There are, of course, those who deny that there is any present or impending crisis, and from time to time it is claimed that the problems of the penal system are now on their way to being solved. For example, Home Secretary Jack Straw told Parliament in 1998 that 'there is no danger of the prison population getting out of control' (HC Deb., 2 March 1998, col. 690). More recently he announced that prison numbers might well continue to rise, but that this had been 'factored into our spending plans' (*The Guardian*, 1 February 2001). In our opinion, however – and there is plenty of evidence for this throughout the preceding chapters – the penal crisis remains real and significant, and a solution looks as far away as ever.

In this final chapter we trace the recent history of strategies to solve the penal crisis and assess the likely (and in our view grim) future for the penal system if current policies are continued. We go on to expound our own ideas of the kind of medium- and long-term programmes which should be adopted to tackle the crisis, and discuss the prospects of this type of approach being adopted by government.

## RESPONSES TO THE CRISIS, 1970–2001

### From positivism to 'law and order': 1970–1987

In the heyday of the 'rehabilitative ideal' in the 1960s, penal strategies on the whole moved fairly straightforwardly in a single, seemingly progressive direction. New penal measures (such as parole) were introduced for avowedly rehabilitative purposes, with the double advantage that they were not only ideologically attractive but also promised to reduce the prison population and hence ease the penal system's resource problems. In the 1970s, however, both the ideological and resource difficulties heightened as the legitimating ideology of the rehabilitative ideal collapsed and the penal population threatened to spiral out of control.

The response to this by both Conservative and Labour governments in the 1970s was predominantly pragmatic. Efforts were made to restrain the prison population by exhorting sentencers to use custody less extensively and for shorter periods, while providing them with a greater variety of non-custodial penalties to use as alternatives (the 'strategy of encouragement': see Chapter 5). At the same time, an increasing number of prisoners were released before the ends of their sentences (see Chapter 8). The discrediting of rehabilitation led to a shift towards 'law and order ideology' (Hall, 1979), and Tony Bottoms made his first perceptive sighting of the trend towards 'bifurcation' in penal policy (Bottoms, 1977). The overall strategy for the prison population was to attempt to achieve a 'standstill'. As Rutherford says, this 'amounted to an effort to hold the line on prison population size but did not include a concerted strategy to effect substantial reductions . . . By the end of the 1970s standstill policy was near to collapse' (Rutherford, 1986: 56).

It was at this stage – in 1979 – that the Conservative government of Margaret Thatcher came to power. The Conservative Party has usually portrayed itself as being 'tougher on crime' than its Labour opponents, and until recently has more often than not been rewarded by general public approval for this stance. However, 'law and order' had never been such a prominent election campaign theme as it was in 1979, when the Conservatives committed themselves to increasing the resources of the criminal justice system (especially the police), to introducing the 'short sharp shock' detention centre (see Chapter 9), and to increasing the sentencing powers of the courts. Although Home Secretary William Whitelaw tried to inject an element of liberal pragmatism by introducing earlier automatic parole for short-term prisoners, this proposal was defeated by the combined opposition of the judges and the 1981 Conservative Party Conference (see Chapter 8). In March 1982, Mr Whitelaw effectively announced the end of the 'standstill policy' by telling Parliament: 'We are determined to ensure that there will be room in the prison system for every person whom the judges and magistrates decide should go there, and we will continue to do whatever is necessary for that purpose' (HC Deb. 25 March 1982; Rutherford, 1986: 56–7). This heralded the birth of the most extensive programme of prison building this century (see Chapter 6).

This did not, however, mean that the Thatcher government's penal policies in the early 1980s were entirely determined by law and order ideology. One material factor was that, since the process of building prisons is a slow one, the continuing rise in the prison population was bound to outstrip the provision of new places for some time. (For example, although 3,500 new places were provided in the system between 1980 and 1987, the prison population rose by over 5,800 over the same period.) So pragmatic considerations still encouraged the government to make some attempt to *limit the rise* in the prison population by continuing to encourage diversion from court and custody and shorter sentences for many 'run-of-the-mill' offenders. Thus, for example, the same White Paper that introduced the 'short sharp shock' detention centre also approved the practice of cautioning juvenile offenders, an approval later extended to older less serious offenders by Home Office Circulars and the 1986 Code for Crown Prosecutors (Home Office et al., 1980: para. 38; Home Office, 1985a, 1990b; Director of Public Prosecutions, 1986). The Government also lent support to the use of alternatives to custody such as community service orders (see Chapter 5), and intermediate treatment for juvenile offenders (see Chapter 9), and supported attempts by the Lord Chief Justice to reduce the length of custodial sentences for non-violent petty offenders.

But these measures were to apply only to supposedly 'less serious offenders'. Bifurcation was not only alive and well but taking on a new lease of life, with less harsh measures still being advocated for petty offenders while the full force of 'law and order' rhetoric and treatment was focused on the more serious 'violent criminals and thugs' (as the 1979 Conservative Manifesto called them). Indeed, William Whitelaw's immediate successor as Home Secretary, Leon Brittan, will probably be best remembered in the penal context for his classically bifurcatory alterations to the parole system (see Chapter 8), which he announced to the Conservative Party Conference in a speech full of equally classical 'law and order' rhetoric (Scraton et al., 1991: 134–7).

Overall, it could hardly be claimed that the penal strategy of the early 1980s proved an outstanding success. The prison population continued to rise throughout the 1980s (from 42,220 in 1979 to a peak of 49,949 in 1988, with a record leap of 3,000 in the year of 1985), while outbreaks of riots and disorder within prisons continued to be a regular occurrence. The 'short, sharp shock' had proved a disappointment, recorded crime had risen in every calendar year of the decade except for a one per cent drop in 1983 (Home Office, 1990c: Table 2.1), and Britain's inner cities were hit by serious rioting in the summers of 1981 and 1985. The magazine *Punch* once memorably observed that Mrs Thatcher's bark might be dogmatic but her bite was pragmatic, and so it proved now. In the second half of the 1980s, the Conservative government altered course.

### 'Just deserts' and the Woolf Report: 1987–1992

A profound change in the government's approach to criminal justice took place following the Conservative victory in the general election of 1987. The shift occurred first under Douglas Hurd,[1] who was Home Secretary from 1985 to 1989, but the new policies continued to be pursued under his successors David Waddington (1989 to 1990) and Kenneth Baker (1990 to 1992). One highly significant moment was a meeting of Home Office ministers and civil servants at Leeds Castle in Kent in September 1987, two months after the prison population had reached a then record high of 50,979. When presented with statistical projections of an increase in the prison population to over 60,000 in the foreseeable future, possibly reaching 70,000 by the year 2000, ministers resolved that this should not be allowed to happen (Windlesham, 1993: 237–9).

The resulting new 'Hurd approach' represented a shift towards eclectic pragmatism – a predominantly managerial, 'Strategy B' approach, although it also contained some elements of Strategy C, and retained echoes of Strategy A rhetoric and policies towards more serious offenders. It meant that the volume of 'law and order' rhetoric emanating from government was significantly toned down, and was combined with other themes and approaches to crime and punishment such as privatization, crime prevention and a new emphasis on the role of the 'community' in schemes such as neighbourhood watch (Reiner and Cross, 1991). Prominent in this new pragmatic mix was the theme of managerialism (see Chapter 1), which included a continued favouring of the systems management approach to criminal justice (see

Chapter 9), and in particular the expanded use of cautioning for adult offenders as well as juveniles. Above all, there was the 'just deserts' package of reforms contained in the Criminal Justice Act of 1991.

The 1991 Act was preceded by a Green Paper (*Punishment, Custody and the Community*) in 1988 and a White Paper (*Crime, Justice and Protecting the Public*) in 1990 (Home Office, 1988a, 1990a), described by a Home Office minister as aiming 'to change the way we think about criminals and punishments'.[2] The Green Paper stated bluntly that 'imprisonment is not the most effective punishment for most crime. Custody should be reserved for very serious offences, especially when the offender is violent and a continuing risk to the public' (Home Office, 1988a: para. 1.8). Both Green and White Papers contained a procession of negative statements about imprisonment, exemplified by the White Paper's famous phrase that prison 'can be an expensive way of making bad people worse' (Home Office, 1990a: para. 2.7), and advocated dealing with many more offenders than hitherto by means of community penalties rather than custody. However, this was still a *bifurcatory* policy, for while less serious offenders were to be diverted from custody, at the same time violent and sexual offenders were to be treated more harshly (Home Office (1990a: paras 2.15, 3.12–3.13). Moreover, this was what we call *punitive bifurcation* – meaning that it was punitive not only towards the more serious offenders, but also towards the less serious. True, the intention was to deal with them in the community rather than in custody; but the influence of 'law and order' ideology lingered on in the insistence that the non-custodial measures were to be 'tough' and punitive in nature, rather than being primarily intended to rehabilitate offenders or to make them perform reparation for victims.

Philosophically, this 'just deserts' package was heavily influenced by the 'justice model' (see Chapter 2). The Green and White Papers emphasized that offenders should be regarded as individually responsible for their actions and needed to be made to face up to their responsibilities (see, for example, Home Office, 1988a: paras 1.1–1.3), and as we saw in Chapter 4 the new legislative framework for sentencing contained in the 1991 Act was based on the 'just deserts' notion of proportionality between the seriousness of the offence and the severity of the sentence. But this was heavily qualified by the bifurcatory exceptions for violent and sexual offenders, who were liable to get *more* than their just deserts. Nevertheless, the 'just deserts' package represented an attempt to tackle not only the material crisis of resources (by reducing the prison population) but also the general ideological crisis of legitimacy by putting forward 'just deserts' as a legitimating ideology for punishment.

Another strand of the government's strategy around this time was its response to the Woolf Report on the 1990 disturbances in Strangeways and other prisons (Woolf and Tumim, 1991). As we saw in Chapters 1 and 6, Woolf implicitly diagnosed the major cause of prison disorder as being a lack of justice in prisons leading to a crisis of legitimacy, and produced a set of recommendations aimed at improving conditions and regimes within prisons and alleviating prisoners' sense of injustice, with particular emphasis on improving grievance and disciplinary procedures. The government generally accepted the Woolf Report and implemented a number of its recommen-dations (see Chapter 6), including a programme to abolish 'slopping out', some relaxations of restrictions on prisoners' contact with their families and the outside world, and the creation of the Prisons Ombudsman. Until the autumn of 1992, the government held to this strategy based upon the Criminal Justice Act 1991, acceptance of the Woolf Report and a generally managerial approach to criminal justice. There were even suggestions around this time that the era of law and order ideology as a potent force in criminal justice policy was coming to an end (Reiner and Cross, 1991; Cavadino, 1994a).

This more liberal and pragmatic strategy for criminal justice started showing some signs of success. In the first months following the implementation of the Criminal Justice Act 1991 in October 1992, sentencing became less harsh,[3] and the prison population fell from 45,835 in September to 40,606 in December 1992.[4] But it was not to last.

### Law and order reinvigorated: 1993–1997

The extraordinary U-turn of the Conservative government under John Major on criminal justice policy – the 'law and order counter-reformation' – is difficult to explain without reference to the general political situation and party political electoral calculations. The change occurred when the government had slipped into deep trouble with the politically disastrous devaluation of the pound on 'Black Wednesday' on 16 September 1992. Thereafter the Conservatives seemed to make a deliberate strategic decision to attempt to regain popularity by 'playing the law and order card' which had served them well in the past. October 1992 saw the implementation of the Criminal Justice Act 1991, followed rapidly by a backlash from sections of the media and the judiciary against its perceived 'softness'. Instead of defending the policy package which had been put together over five years by successive Conservative Home Secretaries, the government increasingly came to assume the remarkable role of critic of its own policies and legislation. Key components of its strategy – the attempt to reduce the prison population by means of the 1991 legislation, the positive response to the Woolf Report, and the encouragement of systems management – were all abandoned between 1993 and 1995.

In February 1993, at a time of public horror over the murder of two-year-old James Bulger by two ten-year-old boys in Liverpool, John Major said: 'I would like the public to have a crusade against crime and change from being forgiving of crime to being considerate of the victim. Society needs to condemn a little more and understand a little less' (*Mail on Sunday*, 21 February 1993). Home Secretary Kenneth Clarke announced the creation of secure training centres for persistent young offenders at around the same time (see Chapter 9). In May, Mr Clarke announced that two significant provisions of the Criminal Justice Act 1991 – the unit fines system (see Chapter 5) and the original section 29 which had restricted the ability of courts to take previous convictions into account when sentencing offenders (see Chapter 4) – were to be summarily repealed (which was achieved by the Criminal Justice Act 1993).

In May 1993 the office of Home Secretary passed to Michael Howard, a right-winger with a profound attachment to the rhetoric and ideology of law and order, who was put in charge of implementing the government's 'crusade against crime' along 'Strategy A' lines. At the Conservative Party conference of October 1993, he announced a 27-point programme to toughen up the criminal justice system (including, for example restrictions on the granting of bail and the use of cautions). Mr Howard proclaimed that *'prison works'* (see Chapter 2) and said of his package of proposals: 'This may mean that more people will go to prison. I do not flinch from that. We shall no longer judge the success of our system of justice by a fall in the prison population.' The Hurd approach was being rapidly jettisoned, with the abandonment of attempts to limit the prison population, and a retreat from 'just deserts'. A retreat from Woolf's strategy for prisons was also evident in Mr Howard's speech. Conditions in prisons should, Mr Howard said, be 'decent but austere', a remark which was later given substance by increased disciplinary powers for prison governors, a 40 per cent reduction in prisoners' home leave and a new national 'incentive scheme' under which prisoners have to earn 'privileges' by good behaviour (see Chapter 6). Subsequently, the government moved even further in the direction of Strategy A, introducing legislation to provide for mandatory 'two or three strikes and you're out' sentences for certain categories of repeat offenders (see Chapter 4) and proposing massive cutbacks to the system of early release (see Chapter 8).

The results of this atmosphere of law and order were as one would expect. Sentencers responded to the encouragement to make more punitive decisions from early 1993 onwards. The prison population rose immediately from its low point of 40,600 in December 1992 and by 1995 was breaking all previous records. By 1997 the daily average prison population was 61,114 – a spectacular 51 per cent above the December 1992 figure.

But the Conservatives failed to reap the reward in terms of popularity with the electorate which they must have hoped for. Although the Conservatives had always (according to opinion polls) been seen as having the best policies on crime, usually by a very wide margin, the Labour Party took a lead on this issue for the first time in 1993 and maintained it thereafter. The demise of the Conservatives' advantage in this area was doubtless assisted by factors such as the embarrassment caused by developments such as privatization (see Chapter 7) and the Whitemoor and Parkhurst escapes in 1994 and 1995 (see Chapter 6). But it was also facilitated by the efforts of Tony Blair – first as Shadow Home Secretary from 1992 to 1994 and thereafter as Labour leader – to alter Labour's public image from being 'soft on crime' to being – in Mr Blair's constantly reiterated slogan – 'tough on crime and tough on the causes of crime' (Blair, 1993; Labour Party, 1997). Although the phrase 'tough on the causes of crime' indicated that the Labour Party was still concerned with what it saw as the social roots of crime such as unemployment, the whole slogan (and Labour's general rhetoric from 1992 onwards) was clearly calculated to appeal to populist sentiments by fostering the impression that Labour wanted to deal severely with offenders. By the time of the General Election in May 1997 the two main parties were bidding against each other for who could sound 'toughest' on law and order.

### *'Tough on crime, tough on the causes of crime': New Labour, 1997 onwards*

The General Election of May 1997 resulted in a landslide victory for Tony Blair's 'New Labour' party. For all their recurrent use of the word 'tough', it would have been difficult for Labour to incline more towards Strategy A than Michael Howard had. And indeed the approach of Labour Home Secretary Jack Straw proved to be a mixture of Strategies A, B and C. Soon after taking office, Mr Straw declared that he had 'no interest in chanting a simplistic mantra that prison works'.[5] Yet Strategy A rhetoric lived on in talk of 'toughness' and 'zero tolerance' (see Cavadino et al., 1999: 28–30): the title of Mr Straw's 1997 White Paper on young offenders (*No More Excuses*, Home Office, 1997c) was typical.

Overtly, the New Labour strategy is one of rational, evidence-based crime control: finding out 'what works' to combat crime and then firmly implementing effective policies. Thus, for example, in February 2001 the government published a policy document billed as a '10-year crime plan' to reduce crime and modernize the criminal justice system. It contained a wide variety of measures (introduced, planned or under consideration), that were presented as 'a comprehensive, evidence-based programme to reduce crime, targeting both crime and its causes' (Home Office, 2001: 9). A managerial, Strategy B approach, then. And there is much about the government's approach that is indeed both sensible and welcome, including an increased emphasis on funding and implementing measures which have been shown to be effective in preventing the commission of crimes in the first place. But the clear subtext is a determination not to give the Conservatives political ammunition on law and order issues by appearing to be 'soft on crime'. This is, of course, a considerable constraint on the kind of policies that can be pursued, since it means they can never stray too far away from a 'Strategy A' agenda. Even though the evidence as to 'what works' shows that prison doesn't work, the government feels it has to act as if the reverse were true. The overall effect is not all that far removed from the combination of Strategies A and B we have termed *'punitive managerialism'* (Cavadino et al., 1999: 54). Elements of Strategy C – such as 'restorative justice'-type measures like reparation orders for young offenders – have their place in the overall approach, but a very limited one. Such measures are for the most part justified by the government on the basis that they are *effective* ways of reducing crime (and perhaps in some instances helpful to victims), rather than that they are humane or needed to give effect to the rights of offenders.

This kind of mixed strategy is almost a new kind of 'bifurcation', with government policy going in more than one direction at once. On the one hand, for example, some prisoners may now have access to television in their cells and the opportunity to be released on home detention curfew. On the other hand, there has so far been no serious attempt to limit the numbers going to prison in the first place, or the lengths of their sentences. Indeed, measures such as the implementation of 'two and three strikes and you're out' sentences and tougher enforcement of community penalties have been deliberately aimed at putting more people into prison. On the one hand, some more positive measures have been introduced for young offenders (such as reparation and action plan orders and referral to the youth offender panel). On the other hand, the numbers of young offenders going into custody are being allowed to rise, and this seems likely to accelerate as persistent offenders (half of whom are under 21) are increasingly targeted for tough punishment.

There was a moment in the summer of 1998 when it seemed that the New Labour government might be moving decisively away from the Strategy A policies of its predecessor. Jack Straw had set up a Cross Departmental Review of the Criminal Justice System which commissioned a report from the Home Office Research and Statistics Directorate on how offending could be effectively dealt with. The resulting report, *Reducing Offending* (Goldblatt and Lewis, 1998) was summarized in a newspaper headline as 'Prison doesn't work' (*The Guardian*, 22 July 1998; see Cavadino et al., 1999: 213–15). This was a slight distortion. What the report actually said was that 'the cost-effectiveness of imprisonment in terms of crime control cannot be assessed with any degree of reliability' and pointed out that targeted anti-burglary crime prevention methods were likely to be ten times more cost-effective than locking up burglars (Goldblatt and Lewis, 1998: 94, 98, 135). Its overall tone was sceptical about the effectiveness of punitive measures such as custody, and it stressed the need to develop, research and implement effective ways of both preventing crime before it happens and reforming offenders when it does. In retrospect, Jack Straw's enthusiastic welcome for the report looks less like an endorsement of its implicit anti-custodial bias, and more like an attempt to use it politically as supposed evidential backing for his own policies. However, these remain wedded to the use of custody and other 'tough' measures which in fact find little support in *Reducing Offending*.

As the General Election of June 2001 approached, the tenor of both the rhetoric and most of the actual policies became more punitive. By now the Conservative Party (now led by William Hague) had left far behind its initial post-1997 approach of making very little noise over law and order (Cavadino et al., 1999: 215–16) and reverted to its usual strategy of labelling the Labour Party as 'soft on crime' and promising even tougher policies (Conservative Party, 1999, 2000). These included more 'two or three strikes and you're out' sentences, a tenfold increase in the number of young offenders held in secure training centres (*The Guardian*, 16 September 1999), a revival of Michael Howard's plan to provide 'honesty in sentencing' by drastically reducing opportunities for early release (see Chapter 8), and an increased number of criminals in prison generally.[6] While Labour's own policies were by no means identical to these – and hardly needed to be, given their overwhelming lead in the opinion polls – it was still 'toughness' that was emphasized along with the rationalistic emphasis on 'what works'. In all likelihood this resulted from a combination of electoral calculation and the personal inclinations of key politicians including Tony Blair and Jack Straw.

One aspect of the government's strategy which has emerged ever more strongly as time has passed is a *concentration on the persistent offender*, with recidivists being singled out for particularly tough measures. This marks a departure from the previous policy (dating from the 'Hurd era' and its policy of 'punitive bifurcation'), whereby it was only *serious* (and dangerous) violent and sexual offenders who were singled out in this way, with petty persistent offenders being largely left to receive what might be termed (relatively) petty persistent punishment, commensurate with the 'just deserts' for their latest offence. Although the tough approach to serious and allegedly dangerous offenders is of course still in place, the new emphasis is on new measures for petty persistent offenders, with no regard to just deserts. Thus, in 2000 the government instigated a review of the sentencing framework aimed at overthrowing the 'just deserts' structure introduced by the Criminal Justice Act 1991 and introducing a progressive 'offender-based tariff' with harsher and harsher punishments the more an individual persists in reoffending (Halliday, 2001; and see Chapter 4). Similarly, highly intrusive measures – including both custody and intensive supervision in the community – are either in place or on their way for young repeat offenders (see Chapter 9). On the one hand, this concentration on persistence is defended (*à la* Strategy B) as being based on evidence about what is likely to be effective in reducing crime. It is claimed that there are 100,000 offenders who are responsible for half of all crime[7] and that special measures targeted on them can be effective in significantly reducing crime rates. On the other hand, such a tough approach towards a bunch of unpopular social nuisances has obvious 'Strategy A' appeal. The approach conspicuous by its absence is of course Strategy C, whose advocates would tend to regard such disproportionately intrusive responses to petty crimes – even a succession of petty crimes – as an infringement of human rights.

There is also plenty of reason to doubt the likely effectiveness of such an approach even from a Strategy B point of view. It should be borne in mind that out of this year's 100,000 most persistent offenders, as many as 20,000 will drop out of this Premier League of offending next year (Home Office, 2001: 116) so our efforts on them may well be wasted. Again, 50,000 of them are under 21, and even the most persistent young offenders usually grow out of offending, or at least out of persistent offending (Hagell and Newburn, 1994). Moreover, the history of penology is littered with failed attempts to tackle the problem of persistent offenders by introducing new sentences (see, for example, Ashworth, 2000: 160–2). It is true enough that it makes sense on the basis of research to target *reformative* measures on recidivists – preferably in the community – if we want them to have the maximum effect in terms of crime reduction. But trusting to custody as an effective treatment for recidivism looks like folly. Furthermore, it seems all too likely that any new measures for persistent offenders will, in practice, be targeted only vaguely at those who are judged to be 'persistent' with no particular criterion for deciding who qualifies for this description.[8] The result could well be a very large number of 'persistent' offenders sent to custody to no good long-term effect. Indeed, Jack Straw has explicitly stated that prison numbers may well have to rise to accommodate persistent offenders who would not have been sent to prison under the present arrangements (*The Guardian*, 1 February 2001).

This is just one manifestation of the government's general apparent indifference to what is happening to the prison population, which (apart from a temporary slight dip brought about by the introduction of home detention curfew in 1999) continues on its upwards trend to heights not even attained under Michael Howard. (Mr Howard bequeathed Labour a daily average prison population of 61,114 in 1997; in 1999 the figure was 64,770, with a further rise to up to 80,300 projected by 2007: White and Cullen, 2000.) In the summer of 1997, the new Labour government took a deliberate decision to commit extra resources to prisons and to reverse the party's policy on private prisons in preference to taking action to cut the size of the prison population, moves which were explicitly defended in terms of the government's need not to seem 'soft on crime' (Cavadino et al., 1999: 53). The 'ten-year crime plan' published in February 2001 (Home Office, 2001) contained provision for an extra 2,660 prison places, which on the basis of present trends and past experience looks likely to prove an inadequate response. Inadequate both in terms of the material crisis of penal resources, and in terms of the legitimacy of locking up such a large slice of the population, with all the attendant problems of the crisis of legitimacy we have seen throughout this book. The whole approach to the use of imprisonment contrasts starkly and cruelly with that of the 'Hurd era', when it was possible for a Green Paper to state: 'Custody should be reserved for very serious offences, especially when the offender is violent and a continuing risk to the public' (Home Office, 1988a: para. 1.8). At present, despite the promiscuous mixture of philosophies and approaches contained in the government's penal policy, the general trend is still towards greater and harsher punishment, and more and more use of imprisonment. The more enlightened aspects of current policy are bound to be outweighed in the long run by this overarching and accelerating harshness. So, if the immediate future for the penal system looks none too healthy, the long-term prospects threaten to be even worse. Unless, that is, a new and different approach is taken to the penal system and the penal crisis.

## HOW TO SOLVE THE CRISIS

### Approaches to the penal crisis

In the Introduction, we briefly set out what we term three broad 'Strategies' for criminal justice: the highly punitive Strategy A, the managerial Strategy B and the humanitarian, rights-based Strategy C.[9] Government penal strategies in recent years have combined elements of all three approaches, but it is fair to say that the first two have tended to dominate. Strategy A rhetoric and ideology reached its zenith under Michael Howard; as we have seen, New Labour's approach is more mixed but has much more of Strategies A and B than C in the mixture. Strategies A and B have both failed to solve the penal crisis to date, and indeed the effects of Strategy A – under Michael Howard in particular, but with enduring resonance since his departure in 1997 – have exacerbated the crisis to an unprecedented degree. As we have argued more fully elsewhere (Cavadino et al., 1999: ch. 2), Strategy A is both ineffective and inefficient in controlling crime, while its immorality (in punishing too much) inevitably creates crises of legitimacy. Strategy B, on the other hand, is morally empty and hence equally incapable of providing legitimacy to punishment, unless its managerial techniques are wedded to – and placed in the service of – a valid moral ideology based on human rights. So, although the difficulties involved are immense, we are firmly of the opinion that only an approach based on Strategy C has any chance of providing a real, long-term solution to the crisis. For only a systematic strategy of affording a consistent respect for human rights can effectively create the legitimacy whose lack is the key to the crisis. And on a more practical note, only a principled drive to avoid unnecessary human suffering by restricting incarceration to cases where it is genuinely necessary is likely to limit the numbers in prison to suitably manageable and affordable levels. We proceed to discuss what such a strategy would entail, and what chance it might have of being deployed in the foreseeable future.

### Measures to solve the crisis

The penal crisis is a pressing political and moral problem which requires drastic action. It cannot await a detailed blueprint for radical reform. On the other hand, it is also a deep-seated, long-running problem which requires the wholesale reform of the system along principled lines. If the crisis is to be solved, we need an evolutionary approach, combining short-term measures and medium- and long-term reform in the context of a coherent overall strategy.

Any such strategy needs to commence from the recognition of the unpopular truth that *the penal system can do very little to control crime*. As we saw in Chapter 2, alleged reductive mechanisms such as deterrence, incapacitation, denunciation and reform can at best only have very limited effects in reducing the amount of crime. No doubt the ways in which we treat offenders could be made more effective than they currently are, and we would certainly favour attempts to pursue rehabilitation and investigate 'what works' to reform offenders. But even if such efforts were highly successful, they could still have little effect on overall crime rates given the fact that only two offences in every hundred committed result in a conviction, with another one in a hundred attracting a police caution (Home Office, 1999a: 29). Consequently it is foolish, as well as inhumane, to look to punitive policies to solve the problems of crime. Crime levels have much more to do with social factors (such as the fragmentation of communities and the lack of legitimate opportunities for young people) and economic trends (see, for example, Field, 1990) than with punishment. Consequently, they would be better tackled by concentrating on the social causes of crime and on crime prevention strategies (see Pease, 1997) than by looking to punishment for a solution.

The only really plausible theory put forward in recent years linking national crime rates with punishment methods – John Braithwaite's theory of 'reintegrative shaming' (see Chapter 2) – provides a prescription not for greater punitiveness but for much *less* harsh levels of punishment than we currently indulge in, together with a shift towards a different approach. Such an approach fits well with our preference for a much greater employment of reparation and other 'restorative justice' measures among our responses to crime (Dignan, 1994). (We shall expand on our own vision for a much more restorative approach to crime later in this chapter.) If we are right about this, then it follows that, despite what adherents of law and order ideology usually claim, the interests of victims and potential victims of crime do not demand harsh punishment for offenders. On the contrary, a less punitive strategy could not only be more beneficial to the public generally (and considerably less expensive), but could also be more victim-friendly, while running little risk of creating more victims. Indeed, the strategy we advocate could well be said to fit the New Labour motto of being 'tough on crime and tough on the causes of crime'. It is tough in the sense of being hard-headed about implementing an effective (and cost-effective) system of responding to crime, whereas to be excessively tough *on criminals* may be hard-*hearted* (which holds attraction for some people), but in terms of effectiveness and cost it is actually soft-*headed* (see further Cavadino et al., 1999: 53–5).

The most urgent priority in tackling the penal crisis is the pressing need to defuse the prison numbers crisis as quickly as possible. In the short term, there is much to be said for implementing emergency measures to reduce prison numbers and relieve the pressure on the prison system. This could be achieved relatively easily simply by using the Home Secretary's existing powers (under section 32 of the Criminal Justice Act 1982) to order that whole categories of prisoners should be released a few months early. (Such 'amnesties' are common in some other countries such as France.) In the slightly longer term, it would be perfectly possible to instruct prison governors to use their powers of temporary release and home leave as soon as a prison became full to ensure that no prison exceeded its Certified Normal Accommodation (Crook, 1991), or even to place non-violent offenders on a waiting list to enter prison, as used to occur in the Netherlands. A variety of other measures – such as a determined expansion of bail information schemes (see Chapter 4) – could also make significant inroads into the numbers of people in prison. Above all, perhaps, government could assist the numbers crisis by ceasing to encourage harsher court decisions with law and order rhetoric.

But numbers are only part of the problem. If we are right in identifying the crisis of legitimacy as the key to the crisis, and in our further claim that the widespread sense of injustice surrounding the penal system is mainly due to the fact that it really is deeply unjust, then the inference is clear. The Woolf Report was entirely correct to suggest that, more than anything, the penal system needs a massive injection of genuine justice. We would go further and submit that in the long term – but as soon as is humanly possible – *the penal system needs to be reconstructed around the principle of respect for human rights*. We are fortified in this (Strategy C) conclusion by the evidence we cited in Chapter 6, from both British research (Bottoms et al., 1990: 91; Sparks and Bottoms, 1995; Cooke 1989, 1991) and from experience elsewhere in Western Europe demonstrating that, while it may not be easy to create genuine improvements in justice, there are nevertheless hopeful signs that when these are achieved they do indeed foster legitimacy.

Adopting a human rights approach in the present penal situation means recognizing that it is morally and practically imperative both to provide those resources which will improve conditions for penal subjects from their present state and increasingly to deny those resources (notably places within prisons) which worsen them. It also requires a consistent and principled approach to the question of *prisoners' rights*. If human beings have fundamental rights (such as the equal right to maximum positive freedom we proposed in Chapter 2), then it follows that prisoners have a great many more specific rights – that is, strong moral entitlements which should be guaranteed by law and which they do not automatically lose by virtue of having transgressed the law.[10] These include rights to certain decent minimum standards of living conditions, the right to fair and independent channels for pursuing grievances against others who infringe their rights, the right to equally fair disciplinary procedures before their liberties are further infringed, and so on. It is therefore vital that more than lip service should be paid to the Woolf Report by ensuring that a minimum code of standards for prison conditions becomes legally enforceable as soon as possible and that prisoners should as far as possible come to feel that they can get a genuinely fair hearing in disciplinary and grievance procedures. As we indicated in Chapter 6, both they and we have little such confidence at present (although it remains to be seen how much effect developments such as the introduction of the Prisons Ombudsman may have in the long term).

Vital as they undoubtedly are, however, neither better physical conditions nor improved grievance and discipline procedures are sufficient in themselves. One of the most important rights that prisoners should have (although one which was, uncharacteristically, somewhat neglected by Woolf) is the preservation of as much autonomy and personal responsibility as is compatible with their inevitable loss of liberty. This is of central importance both in providing constructive and successful prison regimes, and in securing legitimacy for the prison system as a whole by those who are most directly and immediately affected by it. If we are to make a reality of this right to inmate autonomy, there are important implications for prison regimes and, crucially, for the relationship between staff and inmates. As we saw in Chapter 6, staff–prisoner relationships within the English penal system generally leave much to be desired, although a great deal could still be learned from positive examples such as Grendon Underwood, Blantyre House and the (now closed) Barlinnie Special Unit in Scotland.

The Woolf Report was primarily concerned with issues of justice for prisoners within the context of a prison sentence. Equally important for a human rights approach is the justice of imprisonment itself, which leads to the issue of *the justice of sentencing* – and indeed, the justice of other decisions made within the criminal justice system. This can be divided into two further questions, the first relating to consistency (or fairness between different offenders), and the second relating to the general severity of punishment and in particular the extent to which it takes the form of incarceration. We saw in Chapter 4 that there is much inconsistency in sentencing, and in Chapter 10 that some sections of the population can rightly claim that they are the subject of bias at various stages of the criminal and penal process. We also noted in Chapter 2 that it is a principle of justice that like cases should be treated alike, and that there is something to be said for trying to achieve at least a rough proportionality between severity of punishment and gravity of offence. These considerations lead us to support the 'guidelines' approach to sentencing discussed in Chapter 4, with guidelines being issued to courts to bring about both a greater measure of consistency and a more suitable degree of proportionality in sentencing. We would prefer a Sentencing Council as proposed by Ashworth (1995a: 343–51) which had the power to issue its own sentencing guidelines to courts, although a satisfactory guideline system could also be achieved in the context of the Sentencing Advisory Panel created by the Crime and Disorder Act 1998, given a sufficiently strong lead from the government and senior judiciary.

However, inconsistency is not the worst possible evil of a penal system. There would be little to recommend a system which was perfectly consistent but appallingly vicious, and indeed it could be said from recent experience in the United States that over-emphasizing consistency (especially in an ideological climate of 'law and order') can have just this kind of result (Hudson, 1987; but see von Hirsch, 1993: ch. 10). From a human rights point of view, the worst fault of our penal system is not inconsistency but excess of punishment: every single day that an individual is imprisoned unnecessarily represents not only a shamefully extravagant waste of resources but, more importantly, a grave infringement of human rights. For this reason, it is important that the system of sentencing guidelines should be explicitly and strongly geared to reducing general levels of punishment as well as to pursuing consistency. (Although it is early days, there seems little chance that the new system involving the Sentencing Advisory Panel, or any system that might replace it in the near future, will have this kind of orientation, given the government's current attitude to general levels of punishment.)

A similar approach, involving guidelines aimed at not only consistency but also reduction of punishment by the encouragement of cautions and other methods of diversion, should also be applied to the decision whether to prosecute alleged offenders – as indeed was increasingly the strategy of central government prior to the advent of Michael Howard (see Chapter 9). The role of the Crown Prosecution Service could well prove to be just as crucial as that of the courts if a substantial reduction of the prison population were to be secured and sustained. This has certainly been the experience elsewhere in Europe, for example, in the Netherlands (Downes, 1988), and more recently in West Germany (Feest, 1988; Graham, 1988).

In the short-to-medium term, therefore, we would advocate the following specific measures – explained and canvassed in the preceding chapters – for tackling the penal crisis. (Although some of these measures would require immediate input of resources, the resulting reduction in the prison population would soon bring about considerable overall savings.) We favour:

- Emergency steps to reduce the prison population by means of executive powers;
- Reform of discretionary early release to make the procedures fairer and remove the Home Secretary's remaining powers to veto release;
- Enforceable ceilings on the numbers in individual prisons;
- Implementation of Woolf's scheme for 'community prisons';
- A legally enforceable code of minimum standards for prison conditions together with a short and rigid timetable for implementation and the allocation of sufficient resources to make this possible;
- General implementation within prisons of the humanistic approach which proved so successful at the Barlinnie Special Unit and at Blantyre House;

- An expansion of home leave and visiting rights for prisoners;
- Extension of the remit and resources of the Prisons Ombudsman to enable prisoners to take their grievances directly to him;
- Immediate abandonment of such misguided initiatives as mandatory and minimum sentences, new custodial sentences for petty persistent offenders, and an end to further privatization in the prison system with the ultimate aim of abandoning the policy altogether;
- Giving the Sentencing Advisory Panel and Court of Appeal an explicit remit to produce comprehensive guidelines aimed at achieving both consistency in sentencing and a reduction in the use of custody;
- Retention of the 'just deserts' sentencing framework introduced by the Criminal Justice Act 1991, and its strengthening by abolition of disproportionately long incapacitatory sentences and clarification of its 'offence-based' tariff with only a small degree of 'progression' for more persistent offenders;
- Restoration of the requirement for mandatory pre-sentence reports before the passing of custodial and community sentences;
- Reintroduction of unit fines;
- A rapid expansion of bail information schemes and the provision of many more bail hostel places;
- Encouragement and application of 'systems management' techniques to the criminal justice system, including:
  - new guidelines to encourage higher rates of cautioning; and
  - the expansion of schemes aimed at diverting offenders from prosecution and from custody.

On the last of these points, while we favour continuing efforts to combine diversion and the rehabilitation of offenders[11] we would particularly advocate diversionary schemes which involve a 'restorative justice' approach, with offenders performing *reparation* for victims and the community and attempts being made to bring about the 'reintegrative shaming' of the offender. This would be an *inclusive* approach, aiming to keep offenders within the mainstream community (or bring them back in) rather than *excluding* them by punitive measures such as custody or other types of stigmatizing punishment.[12] We have explained in Chapter 2 why we think the restorative approach is appropriate within a system based upon human rights (and see also Cavadino and Dignan, 1997b; Dignan, forthcoming). Indeed, as we have outlined elsewhere (Dignan, 1994; Dignan and Cavadino, 1996; Cavadino and Dignan, 1997b) they could point the way forward to a radically different and radically more just penal system in which reparative and restorative measures constituted the normal response to offending, with punitive measures being very much the exception.

It is possible to envisage a perfectly workable future criminal justice system which made minimal use of imprisonment.[13] Most offences could be dealt with by a local mediation service (or youth offending team for juvenile offenders; YOTs already do some work similar to this). A suitable 'restorative package' could be agreed between the offender and the victim[14] and arranged by the local mediation service, with the Crown Prosecution Service certifying that the overall package was an appropriate resolution of the case, bearing in mind the public interest and maintaining at least a rough proportionality between the seriousness of the offence and the severity of the sanction. However, a more serious case could still go to court if no suitable agreement was reached, if mediation was inappropriate, if either party refused mediation or if the alleged offender denied guilt.

The most serious crimes would normally still go to court in any event. But even in cases which reached court, the usual outcome would be that the offender would be ordered to make reparation either to the victim or to the community generally, perhaps combined with some measures aimed at the reformation of the offender. Many existing forms of non-custodial punishment (for example the fine, community service and even probation) could readily be reformulated to serve restorative justice rather than purely retributive or reformative ends (see Cavadino et al., 1999; Dignan, forthcoming). Thus, even in cases for which informal diversionary restorative justice processes are inappropriate, inapplicable or inadequate by themselves, it is possible to envisage a range of court-imposed punishments that could be adapted to promote restorative justice outcomes. There is potential, in other words, for restorative justice to change the terms of reference by which the punishment of offenders is debated and, in so doing, to furnish a kind of 'replacement discourse' (Ashworth, 1997: 14–15) that would seek the reintegration and inclusion of offenders rather than their punitive exclusion. Custody would only be used where this was necessary to incapacitate genuinely dangerous offenders from committing serious offences (or perhaps, very exceptionally, as a 'last resort' sanction for failing to comply with court orders when all other sanctions had failed). Even then, the custodial regime would be geared towards respecting the prisoner's rights, encouraging reparative work, facilitating the voluntary rehabilitation of the offender, and securing the earliest possible release from custody. Even within a prison setting there is a strong argument for replacing the cruder forms of instrumental reasoning based on sanctions and incentives that have proved so ineffective and even counterproductive in the past (Liebling, 2001) with a 'relational' approach that draws on restorative justice insights. This would involve the use of normative or 'moralistic' forms of reasoning with offenders of the kind that have been deployed in Barlinnie, Grendon Underwood and Blantyre House (see Chapter 6; Dignan, forthcoming).

### The prospects

This kind of model for a penal system seems a long way from where we are now, and it will probably strike many readers as incredible that it could ever be implemented successfully, or that public opinion would ever allow it to be. For it is usually assumed that public opinion is irredeemably wedded to the punitive attitude of 'law and order' and will not tolerate much of a shift in the direction of leniency. But there is a great deal of evidence that the British public, although apparently at present more punitive than most other populations outside the US (van Dijk and Mayhew, 1992: 46; Mayhew, 1994: 5), is by no means as closed-minded as is often supposed. It appears, for example, that although most people when asked say they think sentences should be tougher than they are, this is because they underestimate the harshness of the sentences that courts typically pass at present (Hough and Roberts, 1998; Mattinson and Mirrlees-Black, 2000). Compensation and community service find great favour as alternatives to custody for non-violent offenders (see, for example, Hough and Mayhew, 1985: ch. 6; van Dijk and Mayhew, 1992: 46), while many victims of crime express support for compensation and other restorative measures (see, for example, Mattinson and Mirrlees-Black, 2000: ch. 6). Only 18 per cent of people agree that it is right to 'build more prisons and pay for them by raising taxes or cutting spending in other areas' (Hough and Roberts, 1998: 35). These findings suggest that what the public really wants to see is an *adequate* response to crime, but they do not necessarily demand a punitive one, let alone an inhumane one. Nor do they wish vast quantities of public money to be spent on keeping offenders locked up.

Moreover – while accepting that public opinion would hardly take kindly to the immediate introduction of a model such as the one we have sketched – it is also the case that governments can often succeed with measures which go against the current state of public opinion. A classic example is the abolition of capital punishment in 1965: even today opinion polls regularly demonstrate that substantial majorities of the public would like to see capital punishment restored, yet this is perhaps the least of the penal system's legitimacy problems. Progressive measures can be 'acceptable' in the sense that the public will put up with them even if they are not what the public will tell opinion pollsters they want. We are not naive enough to believe that the utopia of a just and minimalist penal system can be rapidly achieved, but there is no reason why moves in that direction could not be pursued and given every encouragement by an enlightened government.

A more important obstacle to progressive reforms than generalized 'public opinion' might well be the opposition of certain occupational groups within the criminal justice system with vested interests in retaining the status quo, perhaps most notably the prison officers and the judiciary. Most criminal justice agencies contain only a small minority of individuals who already espouse a human rights approach – Rutherford (1993: 7) found that such people constituted 'a rather small and distinct minority' among the upper echelons of the criminal justice system. In the past the judiciary in particular has made its political weight felt to destructive effect in the penal realm, for example in helping to scupper proposed reforms of the parole system in 1981 (see Chapter 8) and in enfeebling the Criminal Justice Act 1991 (see Chapter 4). Joanna Shapland (1988) has perceptively suggested that one of the reasons for this kind of resistance stems from the tendency towards stasis that results from the existence of a largely decentralized collection of relatively autonomous agencies which she likens to feudal 'fiefdoms', each jealously guarding its own independence and methods of working.[15] In such circumstances she suggests that change is difficult, since the 'fiefs' are hard either to persuade or coerce successfully. However, a strategy for change is possible if it combines a measure of both coercion (via legislation imposing some legally enforceable duties on the fiefs) and persuasion following 'Round Table' consultation and negotiation with the fiefdoms.

Nor is it necessarily the case that the interests of the 'fiefdoms' invariably lead them to favour illiberal policies. For example, judicial criticisms of government penal policy have by no means all been one way in recent years. The judiciary tend to favour arrangements which maximize their own power and oppose those which *confine* their discretion or negate their decisions: hence their hostility to mandatory and minimum sentences and to the Home Secretary's role in the early release process (see Chapter 8). On the other hand, they are less concerned about the *structuring* of their discretion by means of guidelines, and some senior members of the judiciary – notably Lord Woolf, who became Lord Chief Justice in June 2000 – strongly favour a reduction in prison numbers.[16] In the circumstances, the chances would be good for a 'Round Table' agreement between government and judiciary for a guideline system aimed at reducing the use of custody from its present level. Currently, it may well be that it is the government, not the judges, which poses the greater barrier to such a development. Similarly, it should be borne in mind that prison officers actively support some progressive reforms, such as the introduction of minimum standards for physical conditions within prisons, for the very good reason that they perceive such measures to be in their own best interests as well as the prisoners'. They tend, however, to oppose measures which would improve standards of justice for prisoners in potential disputes with prison officers, such as giving prisoners the right to legal representation in disciplinary hearings (see Wozniak and McAllister, 1991). But – given that governments have in recent years had little compunction about confronting prison officers over pay, conditions, trade union rights and privatization – it is hard to see why they could not be brought onside by a committed government using a shrewd combination of reason and power. Persuasive techniques could include, for example, the provision of appropriate financial and career incentives for co-operation with the government's strategy.

There is also the possibility – to return to the feudal metaphor – of change being forced by revolt among the peasants. So far peasants' revolts – in the shape of prison riots – have been contained, albeit with difficulty. But they would potentially strengthen the hand of a government which had the will to use its power to bring about change from above. Is this likely to happen?

The immediate political situation is clearly not encouraging for the kind of penal programme we should wish to see. We would like to see a concerted drive to reduce the prison population; the government is happy to see, and to some extent encourage, further increases. We would like to retain the Criminal Justice Act 1991 and strengthen the 'just deserts' orientation of its sentencing framework; the government is intent on repealing it and ensuring that persistent offenders get decidedly more than their just deserts. We want a major reorientation of penality towards restorative justice; there have been some tentative steps in this direction for young offenders but little as yet in the adult sphere.[17] Above all we wish to see a demotion of 'toughness' towards criminals as the benchmark of policy and the hallmark of political rhetoric, while the government (and even more so the main political opposition party) are more than ever wedded to both.

Nevertheless, the prospects for penal improvement are not all hopeless. It has usually proved to be the case in Britain that 'law and order ideology' can only prevail in penal policy for a limited time before its effects in exacerbating the crisis brings government into a rude collision with very concrete material realities. In a highly competitive political situation, long-term penal and financial consequences can be ignored by political parties for the sake of hoped-for electoral advantage. And individual politicians with instincts which lead them to favour 'tough' rhetoric and policies – in the case of New Labour, instincts which have grown following many years of frustrating opposition seen as the result of being 'out of touch' with the electorate – can also play their part. But will such a situation endure forever? We have seen occasions (such as at Leeds Castle in 1987) when fiscal and other pragmatic considerations have overridden powerful ideological pressures to pursue punitive policies. Perhaps the best hope for the penal system is that this will happen again soon.

There is a Chinese word for 'crisis' which literally translates into English as 'danger-opportunity'. The penal crisis is indeed a situation of great danger, but if the danger is recognized it could provide the opportunity and incentive for making bold and far-sighted moves in a progressive direction. In the long run, we have to make a choice between a morally and financially bankrupt, permanently crisis-ridden and inexorably deteriorating penal system and one worthy of a modern and civilized society. We said at the end of Chapter 1 that we need to change people's minds about punishment. There is a long way to go, and the way looks much longer than it did a decade ago, but the task is not impossible. We saw in Chapter 2 that ideas about punishment have changed radically in the past when the times were right. Perhaps – just perhaps – the time for another change is not quite as far off as it now seems.

## NOTES

1  Other important players in the story as well as Mr Hurd included John Patten, a Home Office minister from 1987 to 1992, and David Faulkner, the Deputy Under-Secretary of State in the Home Office.

2  John Patten MP, addressing the Association of Chief Officers of Probation on 15 September 1988.

3  The proportion of custodial sentences passed on indictable offenders dropped from 16 per cent in the period January–September 1992 to 12 per cent in the last quarter of 1992 (Home Office, 1993b: para. 7.11).

4  These are 'actual' figures. Using 'seasonally adjusted' figures which allow for the usual drop in the prison population at the end of the year, the population still declined very significantly from 45,400 to 42,300 (Home Office, 1994d: Tables 1.2 and 1.3).

5  Quoted in *Prison Report* No. 41, Winter 1997, p. 3.

6  'I think that it may be necessary to have more people in prison, in order to deal with the law and order situation in this country.' William Hague MP, quoted in *The Guardian*, 28 December 2000.

7  'Tackling Persistent Offenders is Key to Improving Effectiveness in the Criminal Justice System', Home Office Press Release, 31 January 2001; Home Office (2001: Annex B).

8  As is the case for young offenders aged from 12 to 14, who may receive a detention and training order if the court simply decides they are 'persistent' (Powers of Criminal Courts (Sentencing) Act 2000, s. 100).

9  See further Cavadino et al. (1999), especially ch. 2. This typology of criminal justice strategies is not exhaustive. It is also possible, for example, to hold to a Marxist or an 'abolitionist' approach (see, for example, Sim, 1994a). We will concentrate on Strategies A, B and C because although, for example, abolitionists have at times achieved real success campaigning on various issues (see Sim, 1992), their views are unlikely to be adopted wholesale by anyone close to governmental power in the foreseeable future.

10  This has been cogently argued by Genevra Richardson (1985: 23–4), who concludes that 'whatever view of imprisonment prevails . . . imprisonment justifies only that degree of interference required to achieve separation from the rest of the community: all remaining rights should be safeguarded.'

11  For example, in the shape of 'change programmes' attached to warnings for young offenders, action plan orders and other training programmes based in the community.

12  For the concepts of 'inclusion' and 'exclusion' and their relationship to different versions of 'communitarian' philosophy, see Cavadino et al. (1999: 48–50).

13  Cf. Blom-Cooper (1988: ch. 3). Such a vision has some affinities with the 'abolitionist' position of critics such as Joe Sim (1992, 1994a), who does not in fact call for the total abolition of confinement but merely of the institution of prison as we know it.

14  Provided the victim is willing to take part. Not all crimes have identifiable individual victims, of course (although mediation can work very well when the victim is a corporate entity such as a business, even a large one: see Dignan, 1991). However, in 'victimless' cases, or those in which the victim is unwilling, an appropriate body representing the whole community – possibly the Crown Prosecution Service – could take on the role of the victim in the process, seeking to ensure that adequate reparation is made to the general public. Restorative packages could also include measures aimed at reforming offenders, for example by confronting their offending behaviour, treatment for drug addiction, etc.

15  We explained in Chapter 3 how these 'fiefdoms' fit into our general 'radical pluralist' analysis of penality.

16  Indeed – in what the press called a 'clash' with Jack Straw, Lord Woolf has been outspoken in calling overcrowding 'the AIDS virus of the prison system' and advocating a decrease both in the prison population and in the volume of 'tough talk' from politicians on law and order (*The Guardian*, 28 December 2000 and 1 February 2001).

17  Though at the time of writing the government was preparing to fund and rigorously evaluate a major series of experimental restorative justice initiatives aimed at adult offenders including those who have committed more serious offences such as those involving violence.

# A Self-study Guide to Electronic Sources Available on the Internet

We have tried to describe the English penal system as it was in April 2001. However, the pace of change is so fast (and appears to be increasing) that events will inevitably have moved on by the time this book appears in print. Fortunately, there is now a growing number of electronic websites that make it very much easier to follow events and keep pace with the latest penal developments as they occur. We have included references to electronic sources, where available, in the bibliography, but for convenience we present a selection of some of the more useful websites below, together with brief annotations that will hopefully make it easier for readers to keep themselves up to date until the next edition appears. They should also enable readers to consult the original sources if they wish to investigate topics in greater depth than we have been able to cover in the book. It is always possible, of course, that some of these website addresses may change or be discontinued.

## 1. Legislation

www.hmso.gov.uk/acts.htm
Provides access to Acts of the United Kingdom Parliament and also explanatory notes which summarize their main provisions.

www.parliament.the-stationery-office.co.uk/pa/pabills.htm
Provides access to the titles and full text of Bills that are currently before Parliament.

www.legislation.hmso.gov.uk/stat.htm
Provides access to the full text of recent (and also draft) statutory instruments.

## 2. Official Parliamentary reports on penal matters

www.parliament.the-stationery-office.co.uk/pa/cm/cmhaff.htm
Contains reports published by the House of Commons Home Affairs Committee.

## 3. Information produced by the Home Office

www.homeoffice.gov.uk
The Home Office's home page. Provides access to a wide range of information about the criminal justice system and government policies, including current and past official press releases on legislation and other government initiatives.

www.homeoffice.gov.uk/rds/index.htm
Provides access to a variety of publications produced by the Research and
Statistics Directorate. The most important of these are listed below:
Home Office Statistical Bulletins
Home Office Research Studies
Research Findings
Miscellaneous publications including Occasional Papers produced by the
Home Office.

www.homeoffice.gov.uk/rds/digest41.html
Provides access to Digest 4, which contains information on the Criminal Justice
System in England and Wales.

www.official-documents.co.uk/document/cm50/5001/5001-00.htm
Contains the latest Criminal Statistics for England and Wales

www.homeoffice.gov.uk/rds/pdfs/probation99.pdf
Contains the latest Probation Statistics for England and Wales

www.homeoffice.gov.uk/rds/prisons1.html
Contains monthly briefings on the prison population.
A Command Paper, 'Prison Statistics, England and Wales' is published
annually which contains more extensive tables and commentary on the prison
population. Extracts from this publication are also available electronically on
this site.

### 4. Other official publications relating the criminal justice system

www.criminal-justice-system.gov.uk/stratplan.htm
Contains Criminal Justice System strategic plan for 1999–2000 to 2001–2002.

www.criminal-justice-system.gov.uk/strategy_targets/busplan.htm
Contains CJS Business Plan 2000–2001.

### 5. Major penal agencies and organizations

*Prison Service website*
www.hmprisonservice.gov.uk/
Contains some statistics (e.g. relating to staffing levels, and also a daily prison
population briefing) plus news (which includes an archive service), copy of the
Prison Rules, Prison Orders and Corporate Information. The latter includes
the Annual Report, Framework Document, Business Plan and information
relating to privately managed prisons (see Contracts and Competitions
Group).

*Scottish Prison Service*
www.sps.gov.uk/
Contains annual reports, research, publications and statistics relating to the
Scottish prison service.

*HM Chief Inspector of Prisons*
www.homeoffice.gov.uk/hmipris/hmipris.htm
Contains information about the inspectorate, the inspection programme, and a full list of inspection reports (including thematic reports) published on the website.

*Prisons Ombudsman*
www.homeoffice.gov.uk/prisons/prisomb.htm
Provides access to annual reports.

*Parole Board website*
www.paroleboard.gov.uk/
Contains annual report and other publications plus news section and press releases.

*HM Inspectorate of Probation*
www.homeoffice.gov.uk/hmiprob/hmiprob.htm
Contains references to a variety of publications relating to the probation service, plus details of inspection reports.

*Sentencing Advisory Panel*
www.sentencing-advisory-panel.gov.uk/info.htm
Contains annual reports and advice to the Court of Appeal.

*Youth Justice Board*
www.youth-justice-board.gov.uk/index.cfm
Contains information about the Board's policies, aims and responsibilities, guidance manuals and information relating to Youth Offending Teams.

## 6. Penal Reform Organizations

*Penal Lexicon*
www.penlex.org.uk/pages/index.html
Provides access to a wide range of publications from a variety of official and penal reform organizations. The latter include the Penal Affairs Consortium and Prison Reform Trust. Also contains links to official documents e.g. relevant UK legislation, Prison Rules 1999, European Prison Rules, some recent UK case law, reports from the Prisons Ombudsman, HM Chief Inspector of Prisons, Boards of Prison Visitors etc. and links to other British and overseas sites. One of its most useful features is a 'What's New' section, which is updated every few days, and is linked to an archive dating back to July 1995. Also provides access to Prison Privatization Report International for news of privately managed prisons in the UK and abroad.

*Other penal reform organisations*
www.howardleague.org/
www.nacro.org.uk/
www.prisonreformtrust.org.uk/main.html

### 7. Law Reform Organisations and ongoing reviews

*The Law Commission*
www.open.gov.uk/lawcomm/

*Criminal Courts Review by Lord Justice Auld*
www.criminal-courts-review.org.uk/index.htm

### 8. Other relevant government departments referred to in the text

*Lord Chancellor's Department*
www.open.gov.uk/lcd/
Contains links to Human Rights legislation and regulations, Judicial Statistics, Judicial Studies Board, Justices' Clerks' Society and Magistrates' Association.

# References

Abt Associates (1998) *Private Prisons in the United States: An Assessment of Current Practice*. Cambridge, MA: Abt Associates Inc.

Acheson, D. (1996) *Review on the Effects on Health in the Special Secure Units at Full Sutton, Whitemoor and Belmarsh Prisons*. (Unpublished).

Adam Smith Institute (1984) *Justice Policy*. London: ASI Research.

Adam Smith Institute (n.d.) *Privatizing America*. Washington DC: Adam Smith Institute.

Adams, R. (1994) *Prison Riots in Britain and the USA*. Basingstoke: Macmillan.

Advisory Council on the Penal System (1968) (chaired by Sir Leon Radzinowicz), *The Regime for Long-term Prisoners in Conditions of Maximum Security*. London: HMSO.

Advisory Council on the Penal System (1970) *Non-custodial and Semi-custodial Penalties*. London: HMSO.

Advisory Council on the Penal System (1977) *The Length of Prison Sentences*. London: HMSO.

Advisory Council on the Treatment of Offenders (1952 and 1957) *Alternatives to Short Terms of Imprisonment*. London: HMSO.

Allen, C., Crow, I. and Cavadino, M. (2000) *Evaluation of the Youth Court Demonstration Project*. Home Office Research Study No. 214. London: Home Office.

Althusser, L. (1969) *For Marx*. London: Allen Lane.

Althusser, L. (1971) *Lenin and Philosophy and Other Essays*. New York and London: Monthly Review Press.

American Friends Service Committee (1971) *Struggle for Justice*. New York: Hill and Wang.

Amnesty International (1997) *Special Security Units: Cruel, Inhuman or Degrading Treatment*. London: Amnesty International. Also available on-line at: www.oil.ca/amnesty/ailib/aipub/1997/EUR/44500697.htm

Andrews, D. A., Zinger, I., Hodge, R.D., Bonta, J., Gendreau, P. and Cullen, F.T. (1990) 'Does Correctional Treatment Work? A Clinically Relevant and Psychologically Informed Meta-Analysis', *Criminology*, 28: 369–429.

Arnott, H. and Creighton, S. (2000) 'Implications for Prisoners of the Human Rights Act', *Legal Action*, September 2000.

Ashworth, A. (1983) *Sentencing and Penal Policy*. London: Weidenfeld & Nicolson.

Ashworth, A. (1984) *Sentencing in the Crown Court*. Occasional Paper No 10. Oxford: Oxford Centre for Criminological Research.

Ashworth, A. (1987) 'Devising Sentencing Guidance for England' in K. Pease and M. Wasik (eds), *Sentencing Reform: Guidance or Guidelines?*, pp. 81–104. Manchester: Manchester University Press.

Ashworth, A. (1990) 'The White Paper on Criminal Justice Policy and Sentencing', *Criminal Law Review*, 217–24.

Ashworth, A. (1995a) *Sentencing and Criminal Justice* (2nd edn). London: Butterworths.

Ashworth, A. (1995b) 'Reflections on the Role of the Sentencing Scholar' in C. Clarkson and R. Morgan (eds) *The Politics of Sentencing Reform*, pp. 251–65. Oxford: Oxford University Press.

Ashworth, A. (1997) 'Sentenced by the Media?', *Criminal Justice Matters*, 29: 14–15.

Ashworth, A. (1998) *The Criminal Process: An Evaluative Study.* Oxford: Oxford University Press.

Ashworth, A. (2000) *Sentencing and Criminal Justice* (3rd edn). London: Butterworths.

Ashworth, A. and Gibson, B. (1994) 'The Criminal Justice Act 1993: Altering the Sentencing Framework', [1994] *Criminal Law Review*, 101–9.

Ashworth, A. and Hough, M. (1996) 'Sentencing and the Climate of Opinion', [1996] *Criminal Law Review*, 776–86.

Ashworth, A., Genders, E., Mansfield, G., Peay, J. and Player, E. (1984) *Sentencing in the Crown Court*, Occasional Paper No. 10. Oxford: Oxford Centre for Criminological Research.

Ashworth, A., von Hirsch, A., Bottoms, A. and Wasik, A. (1995) 'Bespoke Tailoring Won't Suit Community Sentences', *New Law Journal*, 145: 970–2.

Audit Commission (1996) *Misspent Youth: Young People and Crime.* London: Audit Commission.

Audit Commission (1998) *Misspent Youth '98: the Challenge for Youth Justice.* London: Audit Commission.

Auld, Lord Justice (2000a) *Criminal Courts Review – Progress Report No. 1; May 2000.* Also available on-line at: www.criminal-courts-review.org.uk/index.htm

Auld, Lord Justice (2000b) *Criminal Courts Review – Progress Report No. 3; 6 October 2000.*

Ayres, M. with colleagues (2000) *Cautions, Court Proceedings and Sentencing England and Wales*, Home Office Statistical Bulletin 19/00. London: Home Office.

Baldus, D., Pulaski, C. and Woodworth, G. (1986) 'Arbitrariness and Discrimination in the Administration of the Death Penalty: A Challenge to State Supreme Courts', *Stetson Law Review*, 15: 133–261.

Baldus, D.C., Woodworth, G.W. and Pulaski, C.A. Jr. (1989) *Equal Justice and the Death Penalty: A Legal and Empirical Analysis*, Boston: NorthEastern University Press.

Baldwin, J. (1976) 'Social Composition of the Magistracy', *British Journal of Criminology*, 16: 171–4.

Barak-Galanz, I.L. (1981) 'Towards a Conceptual Schema of Prison Management Styles', *The Prison Journal*, 61(2): Autumn–Winter.

Barclay, G. (1995) *The Criminal Justice System in England and Wales.* London: Home Office.

Barclay, G.C. and Tavares, C. (2000) *International Comparisons of Criminal Justice Statistics 1998.* Home Office Statistical Bulletin 04/00. London: Home Office.

Barclay, G.C., Tavares, C. and Prout, A. (eds) (1995) *Digest 3: Information on the Criminal Justice System in England and Wales.* London: Home Office Research and Statistics Department.

Baumer, T.L. and Mendelsohn, R.I. (1992) 'Electronically Monitored Home Confinement: Does it Work?' in J.M. Byrne et al. (eds), *Smart Sentencing: The Emergence of Intermediate Sanctions*, pp. 54–67. London: Sage Publications.

Baxter, R. and Nuttall, C. (1975) 'Severe Sentences: No Deterrent to Crime?', *New Society*, 2 January: 11–13.

Bean, P. (1981) *Punishment: A Philosophical and Criminological Inquiry.* Oxford: Martin Robertson.

Bean, P. (1996) 'America's Drug Courts: A New Development in Criminal Justice', [1996] *Criminal Law Review*, 718–21.

Beccaria, C. (1963) *On Crimes and Punishments.* Indianapolis: Bobbs-Merrill.

Belson, W.A. (1975) *Juvenile Theft: The Causal Factors.* London: Harper & Row.

Bennett, T. (1979) 'The Social Distribution of Criminal Labels', *British Journal of Criminology*, 19: 134–45.

Bennett, T. and Wright, R. (1984) *Burglars on Burglary.* Aldershot: Gower.

Bentham, J. (1970) *An Introduction to the Principles of Morals and Legislation*. London: Methuen.

Bergman, D. (1991) *Deaths at Work: Accidents or Corporate Crime?* London: Workers' Educational Association.

Beyleveld, D. (1980) *A Bibliography on General Deterrence Research*. Westmead: Saxon House.

Blair, T. (1993) 'Why Crime is a Socialist Issue', *New Statesman and Society*, 29 January 1993: 27–8.

Boag, D. (1988) 'The Special Unit at Lincoln Prison: Descriptive Account of the First Six Months', unpublished report to the Home Office.

Boag, D. (1989) 'The Lincoln Special Unit: 30 November 1987 to 25 July 1988: the Second Descriptive Account', unpublished report to the Home Office.

Blom-Cooper, L. (1988) *The Penalty of Imprisonment*. London: Prison Reform Trust.

Bottomley, A.K. (1970) *Prison Before Trial* (Occasional Papers on Social Administration, No. 39). London: Bell.

Bottomley, A.K. (1973) *Decisions in the Penal Process*. London: Martin Robertson.

Bottomley, A.K. (1980) 'The "Justice Model" in America and Britain: Development and Analysis', in A.E. Bottoms and R.H. Preston (eds), *The Coming Penal Crisis: A Criminological and Theological Explanation*, pp. 25–52. Edinburgh: Scottish Academic Press.

Bottomley, A.K. (1984) 'Dilemmas of Parole in a Penal Crisis', *Howard Journal of Criminal Justice*, 23: 24–40.

Bottomley, A.K. (1990) 'Lincoln Special Unit', unpublished report to the Home Office.

Bottomley, A.K. and Hay, W. (eds) (1991) *Special Units for Difficult Prisoners*. Hull: University of Hull Press.

Bottomley, A.K. and Pease, K. (1986) *Crime and Punishment: Interpreting the Data*. Milton Keynes: Open University Press.

Bottomley, A.K., James, A., Clare, E. and Liebling, A. (1996) *Wolds Remand Prison: An Evaluation*. Home Office Research Findings No. 32. London: HMSO.

Bottomley, A.K., Liebling, A. and Sparks, R. (1994) *An Evaluation of Barlinnie and Shotts Units*. Scottish Prison Service Occasional Papers No. 7. Edinburgh: Scottish Prison Service.

Bottoms, A.E. (1977) 'Reflections on the Renaissance of Dangerousness', *Howard Journal of Criminal Justice*, 16: 70–96.

Bottoms, A.E. (1980a) 'An Introduction to "The Coming Crisis" ', in A.E. Bottoms and R.H. Preston (eds), *The Coming Penal Crisis: A Criminological and Theological Explanation*, pp. 1–24. Edinburgh: Scottish Academic Press.

Bottoms, A.E. (1980b) *The Suspended Sentence after Ten Years: A Review and Reassessment*. Leeds: University of Leeds Centre for Social Work and Applied Social Studies (Occasional Paper No. 2).

Bottoms, A.E. (1981) 'The Suspended Sentence', *British Journal of Criminology*, 21: 1–26.

Bottoms, A.E. (1983) 'Neglected Features of Contemporary Penal Systems', in D. Garland and P. Young (eds), *The Power to Punish: Contemporary Penality and Social Analysis*, pp. 166–202. London: Heinemann.

Bottoms, A.E. (1987) 'Limiting Prison Use: Experience in England and Wales', *Howard Journal of Criminal Justice*, 26: 177–202.

Bottoms, A.E. (1995a) 'The Philosophy and Politics of Punishment and Sentencing', in C. Clarkson and R. Morgan (eds), *The Politics of Sentencing Reform*, pp. 17–49. Oxford: Clarendon Press.

Bottoms, A.E. (1995b) *Intensive Community Supervision for Young Offenders: Outcomes, Process and Cost*. Cambridge: Institute of Criminology.

Bottoms, A.E. (2001) 'The Divergent Developments of Juvenile Justice Policy and Practice in England and Scotland' in P. Rosenheim, F. Zimring and D. Tanenhaus (eds) *The Juvenile Court at 100*. Chicago: University of Chicago Press.

Bottoms, A.E. and Brownsword, R. (1983) 'Dangerousness and Rights', in J.W. Hinton (ed.), *Dangerousness: Problems of Assessment and Prediction*. London: George Allen and Unwin.

Bottoms, A.E. and McClean, J.D. (1976) *Defendants in the Criminal Process*. London: Routledge and Kegan Paul.

Bottoms, A.E. and McWilliams, W. (1979) 'A Non-Treatment Paradigm for Probation Practice', *British Journal of Social Work*, 9: 159–202.

Bottoms, A.E. and Preston, R.H. (eds) (1980) *The Coming Penal Crisis: A Criminological and Theological Exploration*. Edinburgh: Scottish Academic Press.

Bottoms, A.E. and Stevenson, S. (1992) ' "What Went Wrong?": Criminal Justice Policy in England and Wales, 1945–70', in D. Downes (ed.), *Unravelling Criminal Justice*, pp. 1–45. Basingstoke: Macmillan Press.

Bottoms, A.E., Hay, W. and Sparks, J.R. (1990) 'Situational and Social Approaches to the Prevention of Disorder in Long-term Prisons', *The Prison Journal* (Journal of the Pennsylvania Prison Society), 70: 83–95.

Bowden, J. (1995) 'Barlinnie Special Unit: the end of an Experiment', *Prison Report*, 30: 24–5.

Bowden, J. and Stevens, M. (1986) 'Justice for Juveniles – A Corporate Strategy in Northampton', *Justice of the Peace*, 150: 326–9, 345–7.

Boyle, J. (1977) *A Sense of Freedom*. London: Pan Books.

Braithwaite, J. (1989) *Crime, Shame and Reintegration*. Cambridge: Cambridge University Press.

Briggs, D. (1975) *In Place of Prison*. London: Temple Smith.

Brody, S.R. (1976) *The Effectiveness of Sentencing*, Home Office Research Study No. 35. London: HMSO.

Brody, S.R. and Tarling, R. (1980) *Taking Offenders out of Circulation*, Home Office Research Study No. 64. London: HMSO.

Bronstein, A.J. (1993–4) 'More Prison Less Crime?', *Criminal Justice Matters*, 14: 8–9.

Brown, D. (1998) *Offending on Bail and Police Use of Conditional Bail*, Home Office Research Findings No. 72. London: Home Office Research and Statistics Directorate.

Bucke, T. (1997) *Ethnicity and Contacts with the Police: Findings from the British Crime Survey*. Home Office Research Findings No. 59. London: Home Office.

Burnett, R. and Farrell, G. (1994) *Reported and Unreported Racial Incidents in Prison*, University of Oxford Centre for Criminological Research Occasional Paper No. 14.

Burney, E. (1979) *JP, Magistrate, Court and Community*. London: Hutchinson.

Burnside, J. and Baker, N. (eds) (1994) *Relational Justice: Repairing the Breach*. Winchester: Waterside Press.

Burton, M. (1983) 'Understanding Mental Health Services: Theory and Practice', *Critical Social Policy*, 3: 54–74.

Byrne, J.M., Lurigio, A.J., Petersilia, J. (1992) *Smart Sentencing: The Emergence of Intermediate Sanctions*. London: Sage Publications.

Cain, M. (1971) 'On the Beat: Interactions and Relations in Rural and Urban Police Forces', in S. Cohen (ed.), *Images of Deviance*. Harmondsworth: Penguin.

Campbell, S. and Harrington, V. (2000) *Youth Crime: Findings from the 1998–99 Youth Lifestyles Survey*, Home Office Research Findings No. 126. London: Home Office.

Canadian Sentencing Commission (1987) *Sentencing Reform: A Canadian Approach*. Report of the Canadian Sentencing Commission, Canada: Ministry of Supply and Services.

Carlen, P. (1983) *Women's Imprisonment: A Study in Social Control*. London: Routledge and Kegan Paul.

Carlen, P. (1990) *Alternatives to Women's Imprisonment*. Milton Keynes: Open University Press.

Carlen, P. and Cook, D. (eds) (1989) *Paying for Crime*. Milton Keynes: Open University Press.

Carlisle, M. (1988) *The Parole System in England and Wales: Report of the Review Committee*, Cm 532. London: HMSO.

Carson, W.G. (1971) 'White Collar Crime and the Enforcement of Factory Legislation', in W.G. Carson and P. Wiles (eds), *Crime and Delinquency in Britain*, pp 192–206. London: Martin Robertson.

Casale, S. and Hillsman, S. (1986) *The Enforcement of Fines as Criminal Sanctions: The English Experience and its Relevance to American Practice*. London and New York: Vera Institute.

Cavadino, M. (1983) 'An Examination and Evaluation of English Mental Health Law'. Unpublished PhD thesis, University of Sheffield.

Cavadino, M. (1989) *Mental Health Law in Context: Doctors' Orders?* Aldershot: Dartmouth.

Cavadino, M. (1992) 'Theorising the Penal Crisis', in K. Bottomley, D. Farrington, T. Fowles, R. Reiner and S. Walklate (eds), *Criminal Justice: Theory and Practice*, pp. 1–22. London: British Society of Criminology.

Cavadino, M. (1994a) 'The UK Penal Crisis: Where Next?', in A. Duff, S. Marshall, R.E. Dobash and R.P. Dobash (eds), *Penal Theory and Penal Practice: Tradition and Innovation in Criminal Justice*, pp. 42–56. Manchester: Manchester University Press.

Cavadino, M. (1994b) 'Persistent Young Offenders', *Journal of Child Law*, 6: 2–7.

Cavadino, M. (1994c) Review of M.W. McMahon, *The Persistent Prison? Rethinking Decarceration and Penal Reform*, in *Social and Legal Studies*, 3: 554–5.

Cavadino, M. (1997a) 'A Vindication of the Rights of Psychiatric Patients', *Journal of Law and Society*, 24: 235–51.

Cavadino, M. (1997b) *The Law of Gravity: Offence Seriousness and Criminal Justice*. Sheffield: Joint Unit for Social Services Research.

Cavadino, M. (1997c) 'Pre-Sentence Reports: The Effects of Legislation and National Standards', *British Journal of Criminology*, 37: 529–48.

Cavadino, M. and Dignan, J. (1992) *The Penal System: An Introduction*, London: Sage Publications.

Cavadino, M. and Dignan, J. (1997a) *The Penal System: An Introduction* (2nd edn), London: Sage Publications.

Cavadino, M. and Dignan, J. (1997b) 'Reparation, Retribution and Rights', *International Review of Victimology*, 4: 233–53.

Cavadino, M. and Dignan, J. (with others) (forthcoming) *Penal Systems: A Comparative Approach*. London: Sage Publications.

Cavadino, P. and Gibson, B. (1993) *Bail: The Law, Best Practice and the Debate*. Winchester: Waterside Press.

Cavadino, M., Crow, I. and Dignan, J. (1999) *Criminal Justice 2000*. Winchester: Waterside Press.

Central Statistical Office (1991) *The CSO Blue Book*, 1991 edition. UK National Accounts, D. Ruffles (ed.), London: HMSO.

Chapman, B. and Niven, S. (2000) *A Guide to the Criminal Justice System in England and Wales*. London: Research Development and Statistics Directorate, Home Office.

Chapman, L. (1978) *Your Disobedient Servant*. London: Chatto and Windus.

Charles, N., Whittaker, C. and Ball, C. (1997) *Sentencing Without a Pre-Sentence Report*. Home Office Research Findings No. 47. London: Home Office Research and Statistics Directorate.

Charman, E., Gibson, B., Honess, T. and Morgan, R. (1996) *Imposition of Fines Following the Criminal Justice Act 1993*. Home Office Research Findings No. 34. London: Home Office Research and Statistics Directorate.

Cheetham, J. (1998) 'Crime, Probation and Social Work: Enduring Rights and Wrongs', in D. Faulkner and A. Gibbs (eds), *New Politics, New Probation?* Oxford: University of Oxford Centre for Criminological Research.

Christiansen, K.O. (1975) 'On General Prevention from an Empirical Viewpoint', in National Swedish Council for Crime Prevention, *General Deterrence: A Conference on Current Research and Standpoints, June 2–4, 1975*. Stockholm: National Swedish Council for Crime Prevention, pp. 60–74.

Christie, N. (1978) 'Conflicts as Property', *British Journal of Criminology*, 17: 1–15.

Christie, N. (1993) *Crime Control as Industry*. London: Routledge.

Clare, E. and Bottomley, K. (eds) (2001) *Evaluation of Close Supervision Centres*, Home Office Research Study No. 136. London: Home Office Research, Development and Statistics Directorate.

Clarkson, C. and Morgan, R. (eds) *The Politics of Sentencing Reform*, Oxford: Oxford University Press.

Coggan, G. and Walker, M. (1982) *Frightened for My Life*. London: Fontana.

Cohen, P. (1981) 'Policing the Working Class City', in M. Fitzgerald, G. McLennan and J. Pawson (eds), *Crime and Society: Readings in History and Theory*, pp. 116–33. London: Routledge and Kegan Paul.

Cohen, S. (1979) 'The Punitive City: Notes on the Dispersal of Social Control', *Contemporary Crises*. 3: 339–63.

Cohen, S. (1980) *Folk Devils and Moral Panics: The Creation of the Mods and Rockers*. Oxford: Martin Robertson.

Cohen, S. (1985) *Visions of Social Control*. Cambridge: Polity Press.

Cohen, S. and Taylor, L. (1978) *Prison Secrets*. London: National Council for Civil Liberties/Radical Alternatives to Prison.

Collier, P. (1996) *Police Disposals of Notifiable Offences Cleared Up, Following Arrest or Report by Age, Gender and Offence*, Home Office Statistical Findings 2/96. London: Home Office.

Collier, P. and Tarling, R. (1987) 'International Comparison of Prison Populations', *Home Office Research Bulletin*, 23: 48–54.

Commission for Racial Equality (1992) *Juvenile Cautioning – Ethnic Monitoring in Practice*. London: Commission for Racial Equality.

Committee for the Prevention of Torture (1991) *Report to the United Kingdom Government on the visit to United Kingdom carried out by the CPT from 29 July 1990 to 10 August 1990*. Council of Europe, CPT/INF series. Also available on-line at: www.cpt.coe.int

Committee for the Prevention of Torture (1993) *Report to the Finnish Government on the visit to Finland carried out by the CPT from 10 to 20 May 1992*. Council of Europe, CPT/INF series. Also available on-line at: www.cpt.coe.int

Comptroller and Auditor General (2000) *The Refinancing of the Fazakerley PFI Prison Contract*, Report by the Comptroller and Auditor General, HC 584, Session 1999–2000. Also available on-line at: www.nao.gov.uk/publications/nao_reports/9900584.pdf

Conservative Party (1979) *Conservative Manifesto 1979*. London: Conservative Party.

Conservative Party (1999) *The Common Sense Revolution*. London: Conservative Party.

Conservative Party (2000) *Believing in Britain*. London: Conservative Party.

Cook, D. (1989) *Rich Law, Poor Law: Differential Response to Tax and Supplementary Benefit Fraud*. Milton Keynes: Open University Press.

Cooke, D.J. (1989) 'Containing Violent Prisoners: An Analysis of the Barlinnie Special Unit', *British Journal of Criminology*, 29: 129–43.

Cooke, D.J. (1991) 'Violence in Prisons: The Influence of Regime Factors', *Howard Journal of Criminal Justice*, 30: 95–109.

Coopers and Lybrand (1995) *Review of Comparative Costs and Performance of Privately and Publicly Operated Prisons 1994–5*.

Crabbe, T. (1993) 'Private Profits in the Public Sector', *International Union Rights* (Journal of the International Centre for Trade Union Rights), 1 (4): 34–5.

Creighton, S. and King, V. (2000) *Prisoners and the Law* (2nd edn). London: Butterworths.

Crighton, D. and Towl, G. (1997) 'Self-inflicted deaths in England and Wales: an analysis of the data for 1988–90 and 1994–5', in Suicide and Self-Injury in Prisons, *Issues in Criminological and Legal Psychology*, 28.

Criminal Justice Consultative Council (1994) *Race and the Criminal Justice System*. London: Criminal Justice Consultative Council.

Crook, F. (1991) 'Shut the Door and Let Them Out', *The Guardian*, 4 September.

Cross, Sir R. (1971) *Punishment, Prisons and the Public*. London: Stevens.

Crow, I. (1987) 'Black People and Criminal Justice in the UK', *Howard Journal of Criminal Justice*, 26: 303–14.

Crow, I. (1996) 'Le Choix des Peines et les Récent Changements Legislatifs en Grande-Bretagne', *Déviance et Société*, 20: 3–16.

Crow, I. and Cove, J. (1984) 'Ethnic Minorities and the Courts', [1984] *Criminal Law Review*, 413–17.

Crow, I. and Simon, F. (1987) *Unemployment and Magistrates' Courts*. London: NACRO.

Crow, I., Cavadino, M., Dignan, J., Johnston, V. and Walker, M. (1995) *The Impact of the Criminal Justice Act 1991 in Four Areas in the North of England*. Sheffield: University of Sheffield.

Crow, I., Celnick, A., Palmer, C. and Wiles, P. (1994a) *Attitudes to Criminal Justice: the Results of the South Yorkshire Study*. Sheffield: University of Sheffield.

Crow, I., Johnston, V., Dignan, J., Cavadino, M. and Walker, M. (1994b) 'Magistrates' Views of the Criminal Justice Act 1991', *Justice of the Peace*, 158: 37–40.

Crow, I., Richardson, P., Riddington, C. and Simon, F. (1989) *Unemployment, Crime and Offenders*. London: Routledge.

Cullen and Minchin (2000a) *The Prison Population in 1999: A Statistical Review*, Home Office Research Findings No. 118. London: Home Office Research and Statistics Directorate.

Cullen, C. and Minchin, M. (2000b) *Prison Population Brief England and Wales; May 2000*. London: Home Office.

Dahl, R.A. (1961) *Who Governs?* New Haven: Yale University Press.

Dahl, R.A. (1985) *A Preface to Economic Democracy*. Cambridge: Polity Press.

Darbyshire, P. (1999) 'A Comment on the Powers of Magistrates' Clerks', [1999] *Criminal Law Review*, 377–86.

Davies, C. (1971) 'Pre-trial Imprisonment: A Liverpool Study', *British Journal of Criminology*, 11: 32–48.

Davis, G., Boucherat, J. and Watson, D. (1988) 'Reparation in the Service of Diversion: The Subordination of a Good Idea', *Howard Journal of Criminal Justice*, 27: 127–262.

Davis, G., Boucherat, J. and Watson, D. (1989) 'Pre-court Decision-making in Juvenile Justice', *British Journal of Criminology*, 29: 219–35.

Davis, K.C. (1969) *Discretionary Justice: A Preliminary Inquiry*. London: University of Illinois Press.

Dholakia, N. and Sumner, M. (1993) 'Research, Policy and Racial Justice', in D. Cook and B. Hudson (eds), *Racism and Criminology*, pp. 28–44. London: Sage Publications.

Dignan, J. (1984) 'The Sword of Damocles and the Clang of the Prison Gates: Prospects on the Inception of the Partly Suspended Sentence', *Howard Journal of Criminal Justice*, 23: 183–200.

Dignan, J. (1991) *Repairing the Damage: An Evaluation of an Experimental Adult Reparation Scheme in Kettering, Northamptonshire*. Sheffield: University of Sheffield, Centre for Criminological and Legal Research.

Dignan, J. (1992) 'Repairing the Damage: Can Reparation be Made to Work in the Service of Diversion?' *British Journal of Criminology*, 32: 453–72.

Dignan, J. (1994) 'Reintegration through Reparation: A Way Forward for Restorative Justice?', in A. Duff, S. Marshall, R.E. Dobash and R.P. Dobash (eds), *Penal Theory and Penal Practice: Tradition and Innovation in Criminal Justice*, pp. 231–44. Manchester: Manchester University Press.

Dignan, J. (1999) 'The Crime and Disorder Act and the Prospects for Restorative Justice', [1999] *Criminal Law Review*, 48–60.

Dignan, J. (forthcoming) 'Towards a Systemic Model of Restorative Justice: Extending the Boundaries while Acknowledging the Need for Constraints' in A.E. Bottoms, J. Roberts and A. von Hirsch (eds), *Restorative Justice and Criminal Justice: Theory and Conflict*. Oxford: Hart Publishing.

Dignan, J. (with K. Lowey) (2000) *Restorative Justice Options for Northern Ireland*. Belfast: Criminal Justice Review Commission/Northern Ireland Office.

Dignan, J. and Cavadino, M. (1996) 'Towards a Framework for Conceptualising and Evaluating Models of Criminal Justice from a Victim's Perspective', *International Review of Victimology*, 4: 153–82.

Dignan, J. and Wynne, A. (1997) 'A Microcosm of the Local Community?', *British Journal of Criminology*, 37: 184–97.

van Dijk, J.J.M. and Mayhew, P. (1992) *Criminal Victimization in the Industrialized World: Key Findings of the 1989 and 1992 International Crime Surveys*. The Hague: Directorate for Crime Prevention, Ministry of Justice.

Director of Public Prosecutions (1986) 'Code for Crown Prosecutors', *Law Society Gazette*, 23 July.

Ditchfield, J. (1976) *Police Cautioning in England and Wales*. Home Office Research Study No. 37. London: HMSO.

Ditchfield, J. (1990) *Control in Prisons: A Review of the Literature*. Home Office Research Study No. 118. London: HMSO.

Dobash, R.P., Dobash, R.E. and Gutteridge, S. (1986) *The Imprisonment of Women*. Oxford: Basil Blackwell.

Dodgson, K. and Mortimer, E. (1999) *Home Detention Curfew – The First Year of Operation*. Home Office Research Findings No. 110. London: Home Office.

Dowds, L. and Hedderman, C. (1997) 'The Sentencing of Men and Women', in C. Hedderman and L. Gelsthorpe (eds), *Understanding the Sentencing of Women*, pp. 7–22. Home Office Research Study No. 170. London: Home Office.

Downes, D. (1988) *Contrasts in Tolerance: Post-War Penal Policy in The Netherlands and England and Wales*. Oxford: Oxford University Press.

Duff, R.A. (1986) *Trials and Punishments*. Cambridge: Cambridge University Press.

Dunbar, I. (1985) *A Sense of Direction*. London: Home Office.

Durkheim, É. (1960) *The Division of Labor in Society*. Glencoe: Free Press.

Durkheim, É. (1973) 'Two Laws of Penal Evolution', *Economy and Society*, 2: 285–308.

Dworkin, R. (1978) *Taking Rights Seriously* (new impression). London: Gerald Duckworth.

East, R. and Doherty, M. (1984) 'The Practical Operation of Bail', *Legal Action*, March 1984, 12–13.

Eaton, M. (1986) *Justice for Women? Family, Court and Social Control*. Milton Keynes: Open University Press.

Elkins, M., Gray, C. and Hidkyar, B. (2000) *Prison Population Brief: England and Wales; July 2000*, Research Development Statistics. London: Home Office.

Elliott, R., Airs, J. and Webb, S. (1999) *Community Penalties for Fine Default and Persistent Petty Offending*, Home Office Research Findings No. 98. London: Home Office Research and Statistics Directorate.

Evans, R. (1994) 'Cautioning: Counting the Cost of Retrenchment', *Criminal Law Review*, 566–75.

Evans, M. and Morgan, R. (1997) 'The European Convention for the Prevention of Torture: 1992–1997', *International and Comparative Law Quarterly*, 46: 665–75.

Farrington, D.P. and Bennett, T. (1981) 'Police Cautioning of Juveniles in London', *British Journal of Criminology*, 21: 123–35.

Farrington, D., Hancock, G., Livingston, M., Painter, K. and Towl, G. (2000) *Evaluation of Intensive Regimes for Young Offenders*, Home Office Research Findings No. 121. London: Home Office.

Farrington, D.P. and Morris, A.M. (1983) 'Sex, Sentencing and Reconviction', *British Journal of Criminology*, 23: 229–48.

Faulkner, D. and Gibbs, A. (eds), *New Politics, New Probation?* Oxford: University of Oxford Centre for Criminological Research.

Feeley, M.M. and Simon, J. (1992) 'The New Penology: Emerging Strategy of Corrections and its Implications', *Criminology*, 30 (4): 449–74.

Feeney, F. (1985) 'Interdependence as a Working Concept', in D. Moxon (ed.), *Managing Criminal Justice: A Collection of Papers*, pp. 8–17. London: HMSO.

Feest, J. (1988) *Reducing the Prison Population: Lessons from the West German Experience?* London: NACRO.

Field, S. (1984) *The Attitudes of Ethnic Minorities*, Home Office Research Study No. 80. London: HMSO.

Field, S. (1990) *Trends in Crime and their Interpretation: A Study of Recorded Crime in Post War England and Wales*, Home Office Research Study No. 119. London: HMSO.

Fisher, C.J. and Mawby, R.L. (1982) 'Juvenile Delinquency and Police Discretion in an Inner City Area', *British Journal of Criminology*, 22: 63–75.

Fitzgerald, M. (1993) *Ethnic Minorities and the Criminal Justice System*. The Royal Commission on Criminal Justice, Research Study No. 20. London: HMSO.

Fitzgerald, M. and Sim, J. (1979) *British Prisons* (1st edn). Oxford: Basil Blackwell.

Fitzgerald, M. and Sim, J. (1980) 'Legitimating the Prison Crisis: A Critical Review of the May Report', *Howard Journal of Criminal Justice*, 19: 73–84.

Fitzgerald, M. and Sim, J. (1982) *British Prisons* (2nd edn). Oxford: Basil Blackwell.

Fitzmaurice, C. and Pease, K. (1982) 'Prison Sentences and Population: A Comparison of some European Countries', *Justice of the Peace*, 148: 575–9.

Fitzmaurice, C.T. and Pease, K. (1986) *The Psychology of Judicial Sentencing*. Manchester: Manchester University Press.

de Fleur, L.B. (1975) 'Bias Influences on Drug Arrest Records: Implications for Deviance Research', *American Sociological Review*, 40: 88–103.

Flood-Page, C. and Mackie, A. (1998) *Sentencing Practice: An Examination of Decisions in Magistrates' Courts and the Crown Court in the md-1990s*. Home Office Research Study No. 180. London: Home Office.

Flood-Page, C., Campbell, S., Harrington, V. and Miller, J. (2000) *Youth Crime: Findings from the 1998–99 Youth Lifestyles Survey*. Home Office Research Study No. 209. London: Home Office.

Flynn, N. (1995) 'Germany's Crime Backlash', *Prison Report* 30, Spring 1995: 8–9.

Flynn, N. (1996) 'Who's Afraid of Resettlement Prisons?', *Prison Report* 35 (Summer): 4–5.

Foucault, M. (1967) *Madness and Civilization*. London: Tavistock.

Foucault, M. (1977) *Discipline and Punish: The Birth of the Prison*. London: Allen Lane.

Foucault, M. (1980) 'Prison Talk', in C. Gordon (ed.), *Michel Foucault: Power/Knowledge, Selected Interviews and Other Writings 1972–1977*. Brighton: Harvester Press.

Fox, L.W. (1934) *The Modern English Prison*. London: Routledge and Kegan Paul.

Garland, D. (1985) *Punishment and Welfare: A History of Penal Strategies*. Aldershot: Gower.

Garland, D. (1990a) 'Frameworks of Inquiry in the Sociology of Punishment', *British Journal of Sociology*, 41: 1–15.

Garland, D. (1990b) *Punishment and Modern Society: A Study in Social Theory*. Oxford: Clarendon Press.

Garland, D. (1995) 'Panopticon Days: Surveillance and Society', *Criminal Justice Matters*, 20: 3–4.

Garland, D. and Young, P. (eds) (1983a) *The Power to Punish: Contemporary Penality and Social Analysis*. London: Heinemann.

Garland, D. and Young, P. (1983b) 'Towards a Social Analysis of Penality', in D. Garland and P. Young (eds), *The Power to Punish: Contemporary Penality and Social Analysis*, pp. 1–36. London: Heinemann.

Geis, G. (1987) 'The Privatization of Prisons: Panacea or Placebo?', in B.J. Carroll, R.W. Conant and T.A. Easton (eds), *Private Means, Public Ends: Private Business in Social Service Delivery*, pp. 76–97. New York: Praeger.

Gelsthorpe, L. (1985) 'Girls and Juvenile Justice', *Youth and Policy*, 11: 1–5.

Gelsthorpe, L. (1989) *Sexism and the Female Offender: An Organizational Analysis*. Aldershot: Gower.

Gelsthorpe, L. and Giller, H. (1990) 'More Justice for Juveniles: Does More Mean Better?', [1990] *Criminal Law Review*, 153–64.

Gelsthorpe, L. and Loucks, N. (1997) 'Magistrates' Explanations of Sentencing Decisions', in C. Hedderman and L. Gelsthorpe (eds), *Understanding the Sentencing of Women*. Home Office Research Study No. 170, pp. 23–53. London: Home Office.

Gelsthorpe, L. and Raynor, P. (1995) 'Quality and Effectiveness in Probation Officers' Reports', *British Journal of Criminology*, 35: 188–200.

Genders, E. and Player, E. (1986) 'Women's Imprisonment: The Effects of Youth Custody', *British Journal of Criminology*, 26: 357–71.

Genders, E. and Player, E. (1989) *Race Relations in Prisons*. Oxford: Clarendon Press.

Genders, E. and Player, E. (1995) *Grendon: A Study of a Therapeutic Prison*. London: Clarendon Press.

Gendreau, P. and Ross, R.R. (1987) 'Revivification of Rehabilitation: Evidence from the 1980s', *Justice Quarterly*, 4: 349–407.

Gewirth, A. (1978) *Reason and Morality*, Chicago: University of Chicago Press.

Gibson, B. (1987) 'Why Bournemouth?', *Justice of the Peace*, 151: 520–1.

Gibson, B. (1990a) *Unit Fines*. Winchester: Waterside Press.

Gibson, B. (1990b) 'Unit Fines', *The Magistrate*, 46: 60–1.

Gibson, B., Cavadino, P., Rutherford, A., Ashworth, A. and Harding, J. (1994) *Criminal Justice in Transition*. Winchester: Waterside Press.

Giddens, A. (1989) *Sociology*. Cambridge: Polity Press.

Gill, M. (2000) *Commercial Robbery*. London: Blackstone Press.

Gold, M. (1966) 'Undetected Delinquent Activity', *Journal of Research in Crime and Delinquency*, 3: 27–46.

Goldblatt, P. and Lewis, C. (eds) (1998) *Reducing Offending: an Assessment of Research Evidence on Ways of Dealing with Offending Behaviour*. Home Office Research Study No. 187. London: HMSO.

Goldson, B. and Peters, E. (2000) *Tough Justice – Responding to Children in Trouble*. London: The Children's Society.

Gould, C. (1988) *Rethinking Democracy*. Cambridge: Cambridge University Press.

Gowers, E. (1953) *Report of the Royal Commission on Capital Punishment*, Cmd 8932. London: HMSO.

Graef, R. (1995) 'The Demonisation of Young Offenders: The New Enemy Within'. Paper presented at the British Criminology Conference, University of Loughborough, 20 July 1995.

Graham, J. (1988) 'The Declining Prison Population in the Federal Republic of Germany', *Home Office Research and Planning Unit Research Bulletin*, 24: 47–52.

Graham, J. and Bowling, B. (1995) *Young People and Crime*. Home Office Research Study No. 145. London: HMSO.

Gramsci, A. (1971) *Selections from the Prison Notebooks of Antonio Gramsci* (eds Q. Hoare and G. Nowell-Smith). London: Lawrence and Wishart.

Green, P. (1989) 'Private Sector Involvement in the Immigrant Detention Centres'. London: Howard League for Penal Reform.

Griffith, J.A.G. (1997) *The Politics of the Judiciary* (5th edn). London: Fontana.

Grindrod, H. and Black, G. (1989) *Suicides at Leeds Prison: An Enquiry into the Deaths of Five Teenagers during 1988–9*. The Howard League for Penal Reform.

Gunn, J., Maden, T. and Swinton, M. (1991) *Mentally Disordered Prisoners*. London: Home Office.

Habermas, J. (1976) *Legitimation Crisis*. London: Heinemann.

Hagell, A. and Newburn, T. (1994) *Persistent Young Offenders*. London: Policy Studies Institute.

Hagell, A., Hazel, N. and Shaw, C. (2000) *Evaluation of Medway Secure Training Centre*. London: Home Office.

Hall, S. (1979) 'The Great Moving Right Show', *Marxism Today*, 23: 14–20.

Hall, S. (1980) *Drifting into a Law and Order Society*. London: Cobden Trust.

Hall, S., Clarke, J., Critcher, C., Jefferson, T. and Roberts, B. (1978) *Policing the Crisis*. London: Macmillan.

Halliday, J. (2001) *Making Punishments Work: Report of a Review of the Sentencing Framework for England and Wales*. London: Home Office Communication Directorate.

Hamilton, J. and Wisniewski, M. (1996) *The Use of the Compensation Order in Scotland*. Edinburgh: The Scottish Central Research Unit.

Hamlyn, B. and Lewis, D. (2000) *Women Prisoners: A Survey of Their Work and Training Experiences in Custody and on Release*. Home Office Research Study No. 208. London: Home Office.

Hann, R., Harman, R. and Pease, K. (1991) 'Does Parole Reduce the Risk of Reconviction?', *Howard Journal of Criminal Justice*, 30: 66–75.

Harding, C. and Koffman, L. (1995) *Sentencing and the Penal System: Text and Materials* (2nd edn). London: Sweet and Maxwell.

Harding, J. (1982) *Victims and Offenders: Needs and Responsibilities*. London: Bedford Square Press/NCVO.

Harris, R.J. (1977) 'The Probation Officer as Social Worker', *British Journal of Social Work*, 7: 433–42.

Harris, R. and Webb, D. (1987) *Welfare, Power and Juvenile Justice*. London: Tavistock.

Hart, H.L.A. (1968) *Punishment and Responsibility*. Oxford: Oxford University Press.

Haxby, D. (1978) *Probation: A Changing Service*. London: Constable.

Health and Safety Executive (1992) *Annual Report, 1991–2*. London: Health and Safety Executive.

Hedderman, C. and Gelsthorpe, L. (eds) (1997) *Understanding the Sentencing of Women*, Home Office Research Study No. 170. London: Home Office.

Hedderman, C. and Hough, M. (1994) *Does the Criminal Justice System Treat Men and Women Differently?* Home Office Research and Statistics Department Research Findings No. 10. London: Home Office.

Hedderman, C. and Moxon, D. (1992) *Magistrates' Court or Crown Court? Mode of Trial Decisions and Sentencing*, Home Office Research Study No. 125. London: HMSO.

Hedderman, C. and Moxon, D. (1994) 'Mode of Trial Decisions and Sentencing Differences Between Courts', *Howard Journal of Criminal Justice*, 33: 97–108.

Heidensohn, F. (1985) *Women and Crime*. Basingstoke: Macmillan.

Hennessy, J. (1987) *Report of an Inquiry by Her Majesty's Chief Inspector of Prisons for England and Wales into the Disturbances in Prison Service Establishments in England between 29 April–2 May 1986*. London: HMSO.

Hinton, J.W. (ed.) (n.d.) *Dangerousness: Problems of Assessment and Prediction*. London: George Allen and Unwin.

von Hirsch, A. (1976) *Doing Justice: The Choice of Punishments* (Report of the Committee for the Study of Incarceration). New York: Hill and Wang.

von Hirsch, A. (1986) *Past or Future Crimes: Deservedness and Dangerousness in the Sentencing of Criminals*. Manchester: Manchester University Press.

von Hirsch, A. (1987) 'Guidance by Numbers or by Words? Numerical versus Narrative Guidelines for Sentencers', in K. Pease and M. Wasik (eds), *Sentencing Reform: Guidance or Guidelines?*, pp. 46–69. Manchester: Manchester University Press.

von Hirsch, A. (1993) *Censure and Sanctions*. Oxford: Clarendon Press.

von Hirsch, A. (1998) 'Proportionate Sentences: a Desert Perspective' in A. von Hirsch and A. Ashworth (eds), *Principled Sentencing: Readings on Theory and Policy* (2nd edn), Oxford: Hart Publishing.

von Hirsch, A., Bottoms, A.E., Burney, E. and Wikström, P.-O. (1999) *Criminal Deterrence and Sentence Severity: An Analysis of Recent Research*. Oxford: Hart Publishing.

HM Chief Inspector of Prisons (1984) *Suicides in Prison*. London: HMSO.

HM Chief Inspector of Prisons (1987) *A Review of Prisoners' Complaints*. London: HMSO.

HM Chief Inspector of Prisons (1990a) *Report of a Review by Her Majesty's Chief Inspector of Prisons for England and Wales of Suicide and Self-harm in Prison Service Establishments in England and Wales*. London: HMSO.

HM Chief Inspector of Prisons (1990b) *Report of HM Chief Inspector of Prisons, 1989*. HC 598. London: HMSO.

HM Chief Inspector of Prisons (1992) *HM Prison Holloway: Report by HM Chief Inspector of Prisons*. London: Home Office.

HM Chief Inspector of Prisons (1993a) *Doing Time or Using Time: Report of a Review by Her Majesty's Chief Inspector of Prisons for England and Wales of Regimes of Prison Service Establishments in England and Wales*, Cm 2128. London: HMSO.

HM Chief Inspector of Prisons (1993b) *Report on HM Prison Blantyre House*. London: HMSO.

HM Chief Inspector of Prisons (1993c) *Report on Wolds Remand Prison*. London: HMSO.

HM Chief Inspector of Prisons (1994) *Report of HM Chief Inspector of Prisons, April 1993–March 1994*. London: HMSO.

HM Chief Inspector of Prisons (1995) *HM Prison, Blakenhurst: A Report by HM Chief Inspector of Prisons*. London: Home Office.

HM Chief Inspector of Prisons (1997a) *HM Prison Whitemoor: Report of an Unannounced Short Inspection, 19 June 1997*. London: HMSO.

HM Chief Inspector of Prisons for England and Wales (1997b) *Young Prisoners: A Thematic Review by HM Chief Inspector of Prisons for England and Wales*. London: Home Office.

HM Chief Inspector of Prisons for England and Wales (1997c) *Women in Prison: A Thematic Review by HM Chief Inspector of Prisons*. London: Home Office.

HM Chief Inspector of Prisons (1998) *Report on HM Prisons Grendon and Springhill, February 1998*. London: Home Office. Also available on-line at: www.penlex.org.uk/pages/cigrend.html

HM Chief Inspector of Prisons (1999a) *Suicide is Everyone's Concern: A Thematic Review by Her Majesty's Chief Inspector of Prisons*. London: Home Office. Also available on-line at: www.penlex.org.uk/pages/cisuic03.html#8

HM Chief Inspector of Prisons (1999b) *1998–9 Annual Report of Chief Inspector of Prisons.* London: Home Office.

HM Chief Inspector of Prisons (1999c) *Inspection of Close Supervision Centres: A Thematic Inspection by Her Majesty's Chief Inspector of Prisons.* London: Home Office. Also available on-line at: www.penlex.org.uk/pages/cicsc00.html#8

HM Chief Inspector of Prisons (1999d) *HMYOI and Remand Centre Feltham, Report of an Unannounced Full Inspection 30 November–4 December 1998.* London: Home Office.

HM Chief Inspector of Prisons (2000a) *Unjust Deserts: A Thematic Review by Her Majesty's Chief Inspector of Prisons of the Treatment and Conditions of Unsentenced Prisoners in England and Wales.* London: Home Office. Also available on-line at: www.penlex.org.uk/pages/ciunj01.html

HM Chief Inspector of Prisons (2000b) *Report on HM Prison Blantyre House.* London: Home Office.

HM Chief Inspector of Prisons (2000c) *Inspection Report on a Full Announced Inspection of HMYOI Portland 24 October–3 November 1999.* London: Home Office.

HM Inspectorate of Probation (2000) *Towards Race Equality.* Thematic Inspection Report. London: Home Office. Also available on-line at: www.homeoffice.gov.uk/newindexs/index_probation.htm

HM Prison Service (1993) 'Michael Howard Unveils Plans for More Private Sector Involvement in the Prison Service', News Release, 2 September 1993.

HM Prison Service (1995) *Prison Service Annual Report and Accounts April 1993–March 1994*, HC185. London: HMSO.

HM Prison Service (1996) *Management of Disruptive Prisoners: CRC Review Project Final Report* (The Spurr Report). HM Prison Service: Unpublished Report.

HM Prison Service (1999a) *Prison Population Brief*, July 1999.

HM Prison Service (1999b) *Framework Document.* London: The Stationery Office. Also available on-line at: www.hmprisonservice.gov.uk/filestore/33_38.pdf

HM Prison Service (1999c) *Annual Report and Accounts April 1998–March 1999.* London: The Stationery Office.

HM Prison Service (2000) *HM Prison Service Annual Report and Accounts April 1999–March 2000*, Cm 622. London: The Stationery Office. Also available on-line at www.hmprisonservice.gov.uk/corporate/dynpage.asp?Page=26

HM Prison Service (2001) *On-Line News.* See www.hmprisonservice.gov.uk/news/

Hogg, R. (1979) 'Imprisonment and Society under early British Capitalism' in T. Platt and P. Takagi (eds), *Punishment and Penal Discipline: Essays on the Prison and the Prisoners' Movement.* Berkeley, CA: Crime and Social Justice Associates.

Holdaway, S., Davidson, N., Dignan, J., Hammersley, R., Hine, J. and Marsh, P. (2001) *New Strategies to Address Youth Offending: the National Evaluation of Pilot Youth Offending Teams.* RDS Occasional Paper No. 69. London: Home Office Research, Development and Statistics Directorate. Also available on-line at www.homeoffice.gov.uk/rds/index.html

Hollin, C.R. (1990) *Cognitive-Behavioural Interventions with Young Offenders*, Elmsford: Pergamon Press.

Home Office (1956) *Report of the Commissioners of Prisons, 1955.* London: HMSO.

Home Office (1965) *The Adult Offender*, Cmnd 2852. London: HMSO.

Home Office (1966) *Report of the Inquiry into Prison Escapes and Security by Admiral of the Fleet, the Earl Mountbatten of Burma*, Cmnd 3175. London: HMSO.

Home Office (1977a) *Prisons and the Prisoner: The Work of the Prison Service in England and Wales.* London: HMSO.

Home Office (1977b) *Prison Statistics, 1976*, Cmnd 6884. London: HMSO.

Home Office (1980) *Criminal Statistics, England and Wales 1979*, Cmnd 8098. London: HMSO.

Home Office (1981a) *Criminal Statistics, England and Wales 1980,* Cmnd 8668. London: HMSO.

Home Office (1981b) *Review of Parole in England and Wales.* London: HMSO.

Home Office (1984a) *Managing the Long Term Prison System: The Report of the Control Review Committee.* London: HMSO.

Home Office (1984b) *Tougher Regimes in Detention Centres: Report of an Evaluation by the Young Offender Psychology Unit.* London: HMSO.

Home Office (1984c) *Statement of National Objectives and Priorities for the Probation Service.* London: Home Office.

Home Office (1985a) *The Cautioning of Offenders,* Home Office Circular 14/1985. London: Home Office.

Home Office (1985b) *Staff Attitudes in the Prison Service.* London: HMSO.

Home Office (1985c) *Criminal Statistics, England and Wales 1984,* Cmnd 9621. London: HMSO.

Home Office (1986) *Prison Statistics, England and Wales 1985,* Cmnd 9903. London: HMSO.

Home Office (1987) *Report of an Inquiry by HM Chief Inspector of Prisons for England and Wales into the Disturbances in Prison Service Establishments in England Between 29 April–2 May, 1986.* London: HMSO.

Home Office (1988a) *Punishment, Custody and the Community,* Cm 424. London: HMSO.

Home Office (1988b) *Criminal Statistics, England and Wales 1987,* Cm 498. London: HMSO.

Home Office (1988c) *Improving Management in Government: the Next Steps,* Government Efficiency Unit. London: HMSO.

Home Office (1988d) *Private Sector Involvement in the Remand System,* Cm 434. London: HMSO.

Home Office (1989) *HM Prison Service – Review of Organization and Location above Management Level.* London: HMSO.

Home Office (1990a) *Crime, Justice and Protecting the Public: The Government's Proposals for Legislation,* Cm 965. London: HMSO.

Home Office (1990b) *The Cautioning of Offenders,* Home Office Circular 59/1990.

Home Office (1990c) *Criminal Statistics, England and Wales 1989,* Cm 1322. London: HMSO.

Home Office (1990d) *Victim's Charter: A Statement of the Rights of Victims of Crime.* London: HMSO.

Home Office (1990e) *Supervision and Punishment in the Community,* Cmnd 966. London: HMSO.

Home Office (1991a) *The Prison Population in 1990,* Home Office Statistical Bulletin 9/91. London: Home Office.

Home Office (1991b) *Custody, Care and Justice: The Way Ahead for the Prison Service in England and Wales,* Cm 1647. London: HMSO.

Home Office (1992) *Costs of the Criminal Justice System: Volume 1. The Crown Court.* London: HMSO.

Home Office (1993a) *Compensation in the Criminal Courts,* Home Office Circular 53/1993. London: HMSO.

Home Office (1993b) *Criminal Statistics, England and Wales 1992,* Cm 2410. London: HMSO.

Home Office (1994a) *The Criminal Histories of Those Cautioned in 1985, 1988 and 1991,* Home Office Statistical Bulletin 8/94. London: Home Office.

Home Office (1994b) *Cautions, Court Proceedings and Sentencing, England and Wales, 1993,* Home Office Statistical Bulletin 19/94. London: Home Office.

Home Office (1994c) *Monitoring of the Criminal Justice Acts 1991 and 1993 – Results from a Special Data Collection Exercise*, Home Office Statistical Bulletin 20/94, London: Home Office.

Home Office (1994d) *Prison Statistics, England and Wales 1992*, Cm 2581. London: HMSO.

Home Office (1994e) *Parole Recommendations and Ethnic Origin, England and Wales 1990*. Home Office Statistical Bulletin 2/94. London: Home Office.

Home Office (1994f) *The Cautioning of Offenders*, Home Office Circular 18/1994. London: Home Office.

Home Office (1995a) *The Prison Population in 1994*, Home Office Statistical Bulletin 8/95. London: Home Office.

Home Office (1995b) *Criminal Statistics, England and Wales 1994*, Cm 3010. London: HMSO.

Home Office (1995c) *Mode of Trial: A Consultation Document*. London: HMSO.

Home Office (1995d) *Strengthening Punishment in the Community: A Consultation Document*, Cm 2780. London: HMSO.

Home Office (1995e) *Review of Probation Officer Recruitment and Qualifying Training*. London: Home Office.

Home Office (1996a) *Prison Statistics, England and Wales 1994*, Cm 3087. London: HMSO.

Home Office (1996b) *The Prison Population in 1995*, Home Office Statistical Bulletin 14/96. London: Home Office.

Home Office (1996c) *Alternative Penalties for Fine Defaulters and Low Level Offenders*. London: Home Office.

Home Office (1997a) *New Millennium – New Training for Probation Officer Recruits*. Home Office Press Release 185/97, 29 July 1997.

Home Office (1997b) *Electronic Monitoring – the Future of Community Punishment*, Home Office Press Release, 12 November 1997.

Home Office (1997c) *No More Excuses – A New Approach to Tackling Youth Crime in England and Wales*, Cm 3809. London: The Stationery Office.

Home Office (1998a) *Delivering an Enhanced Level of Community Supervision: Report of a Thematic Inspection on the Work of Approved Probation and Bail Hostels*. HM Inspectorate of Probation. Also available on-line at: www.homeoffice.gov.uk/hmiprob/delcsl.htm

Home Office (1998b) *Prisons–Probation Review: Final Report*. London: HMSO.

Home Office (1998c) *Joining Forces to Protect the Public*. London: HMSO.

Home Office (1999) *Digest 4: Information on the Criminal Justice System in England and Wales*. London: Home Office Research and Statistics Department.

Home Office (2000a) *Criminal Statistics, England and Wales 1999*, Cm 4649. London: The Stationery Office.

Home Office (2000b) *Prison Statistics, 1999*, Cm 4805. London: The Stationery Office.

Home Office (2000c) 'Criminal Justice (Mode of Trial) Bill Briefing Note'. London: Home Office.

Home Office (2000d) *Home Secretary Announces Sentencing Framework Review*, Home Office Press Release 129/00, 16 May 2000.

Home Office (2000e) *Statistics on Race and the Criminal Justice System 2000*. London: Home Office.

Home Office (2000f) *Statistics on Women and the Criminal Justice System 2000*. London: Home Office.

Home Office (2000g) *The Final Warning Scheme: Guidance for Youth Offending Teams*. London: Home Office. Also available on-line at: www.homeoffice.gov.uk/cdact/yotguide.htm

Home Office (2001) *Criminal Justice: The Way Ahead*, Cm 5074. London: The Stationery Office.

Home Office, Department of Health and Welsh Office (1992) *National Standards for the Supervision of Offenders in the Community*. London: Home Office.

Home Office, Department of Health and Welsh Office (1995) *National Standards for the Supervision of Offenders in the Community*. London: Home Office.

Home Office, Department of Health and Welsh Office (2000) *National Standards for the Supervision of Offenders in the Community*. London: Home Office.

Home Office and Lord Chancellor's Department (2001) *The Youth Court 2001: The Changing Culture of the Youth Court – Good Practice Guide*. London: Home Office.

Home Office, Welsh Office and Department of Health and Social Security (1980) *Young Offenders*, Cmnd 8045. London: HMSO.

Home Office and Youth Justice Board (2001) *Final Warning Scheme: Further Guidance for the Police and Youth Offending Teams*. Home Office and Youth Justice Board, January 2001. Also available on-line at: www.homeoffice.gov.uk

Hood, R. (1962) *Sentencing in Magistrates' Courts*. London: Stevens.

Hood, R. (1972) *Sentencing the Motoring Offender*. London: Heinemann.

Hood, R. (1974a) 'Some Fundamental Dilemmas of the English Parole System and a Suggestion for an Alternative Structure', in D.A. Thomas (ed.), *Parole: Its Implications for the Criminal Justice and Penal Systems*, pp. 1–17. Cambridge: Institute of Criminology.

Hood, R. (1974b) 'Tolerance and the Tariff', in J. Baldwin and A.K. Bottomley (eds), *Criminal Justice: Selected Readings* (1978), pp. 296–307. London: Martin Robertson.

Hood, R. (1992) *Race and Sentencing: A Study in the Crown Court* (in collaboration with G. Cordovil). Oxford: Clarendon Press.

Hood, R. (1995) 'Race and Sentencing: A Reply', [1995] *Criminal Law Review*, 272–9.

Hood, R. and Shute, S. (1996) 'Parole Criteria, Parole Decisions and the Prison Population: Evaluating the Impact of the Criminal Justice Act 1991', [1996] *Criminal Law Review*, 77–87.

Hood, R. and Shute, S. (2000) *The Parole System at Work: A Study of Risk Based Decision-making*, Home Office Research Study No. 202. London: Home Office.

Hood, R. and Sparks, R. (1970) *Key Issues in Criminology*. London: Weidenfeld & Nicolson.

Hope, T. (1995) 'Community Crime Prevention' in M. Tonry and D.P. Farrington (eds), *Building a Safer Society: Strategic Approaches to Crime Prevention*. Chicago: University of Chicago Press.

Hough, M. and Mayhew, P. (1985) *Taking Account of Crime: Key Findings from the 1984 British Crime Survey*, Home Office Research Study No. 85. London: HMSO.

Hough, M. and Roberts, J. (1998) *Attitudes to Punishment: Findings from the British Crime Survey*, Home Office Research Study No. 179. London: Home Office.

House of Commons Home Affairs Select Committee (1987) *Contract Provision of Prisons* (Fourth Report, Session 1986/7, HC291). London: HMSO.

House of Commons Home Affairs Select Committee (1993) *Sixth Report: Juvenile Offenders*. London: HMSO.

House of Commons Home Affairs Committee (1995) *Judicial Appointments*. London: HMSO.

House of Commons Home Affairs Committee (1997) *The Management of the Prison Service (Public and Private), Volume 1, 19 March 1997* (Second Report, Session 1996/7, HC 57-1). London: HMSO.

House of Commons Home Affairs Committee (2000) *Fourth Report. Blantyre House Prison*. Session 1999–2000. London: Stationery Office. The whole report is also available online at: www.parliament.the-stationery-office.co.uk/pa/cm199900/cmselect/cmhaff/904/90403.htm

Howard League (1993) *The Dynamics of Justice*. London: Howard League.

Howard League (1995) 'No Merits in a Single Community Sentence', *Criminal Justice*, 13 (3): 12.

Howard League (1996) 'Suicide and Self-Injury in Prison'. *Fact Sheet 19*. London: Howard League.

Hucklesby, A. (1994) 'The Use and Abuse of Conditional Bail', *Howard Journal of Criminal Justice*, 33: 258–70.

Hucklesby (1997) 'Court Culture: An Explanation of Variations in the Use of Bail in Magistrates' Courts', *Howard Journal of Criminal Justice*, 36: 129.

Hudson, B. (1984) 'The Rising Use of Imprisonment: The Impact of "Decarceration" Policies', *Critical Social Policy*, 11: 46–59.

Hudson, B. (1987) *Justice Through Punishment: A Critique of the 'Justice Model' of Corrections*. London: Macmillan Education.

Hudson, B. (1989) 'Discrimination and Disparity: The Influence of Race on Sentencing', *New Community*, 16: 23–34.

Hudson, J. and Galaway, B. (eds) (1977) *Restitution in Criminal Justice*. Lexington: D.C. Heath.

Hughes, R. (1987) *The Fatal Shore: A History of Transportation of Convicts to Australia, 1187–1868*, London: Collins Harvill.

Humphrey, C. (1991) 'Calling in the Experts: the Financial Management Initiative, Private Sector Management Consultants and the Probation Service', *Howard Journal of Criminal Justice*, 30: 1–18.

Humphry, D. and May, D. (1977) 'Why the Prisons Could Explode', *Sunday Times*, 23 January.

Hurd, D. (2000) 'Prison and the Coming Election', *Prison Report* No. 51 (June).

Hutto, T.D. (1990) 'The Privatization of Prisons' in J.W. Murphy and J.E. Dison (eds), *Are Prisons any Better? Twenty Years of Correctional Reform*, pp. 111–27. Newbury Park, CA: Sage Publications.

Ignatieff, M. (1978) *A Just Measure of Pain: The Penitentiary in the Industrial Revolution 1750–1850*. New York: Columbia University Press.

Ignatieff, M. (1981) 'State, Civil Society, and Total Institution: A Critique of Recent Social Histories of Punishment', in M. Tonry and N. Morris (eds), *Crime and Justice*, vol. 3. Chicago: University of Chicago Press.

International Bar Association (1990) 'Sentencing Questionnaire' (2nd edn). Unpublished; presented at the 23rd biennial conference of the International Bar Association, 19–23 September.

Jacob, B. (1977) 'The Concept of Restitution: An Historical Overview', in J. Hudson and B. Galaway (eds), *Restitution in Criminal Justice*, pp. 45–62. Lexington: D.C. Heath.

Jago, R. and Thompson, E. (1999) 'Privatisation of Prisons', in M. Leech and D. Cheney, *The Prisons Handbook 2000* (4th edn), pp. 229–31. Winchester: Waterside Press.

James, A.L. (1995) 'Probation Values for the 1990s – and Beyond?', *Howard Journal of Criminal Justice*, 34: 326–43.

James, A. and Bottomley, K. (1998) 'Prison Privatisation and the Remand Population: Principle versus Pragmatism?', *Howard Journal of Criminal Justice*, 37: 223–33.

James, A.L., Bottomley, A.K., Liebling, A. and Clare, E. (1997) *Privatizing Prisons: Rhetoric and Reality*. London: Sage Publications.

Joint Council for the Welfare of Immigrants (1988) *Annual Report 1988*. London: Joint Council for the Welfare of Immigrants.

Jones, D. (1989) 'The Successful Revolution', *Community Care*, 30 March: i–ii.

Jones, H., Cornes, P. and Stackford, R. (1977) *Open Prisons*. London: Routledge and Kegan Paul.

Jones, P. (1985) 'Remand Decisions at Magistrates' Courts' in D. Moxon (ed.), *Managing Criminal Justice: A Collection of Papers*, pp. 106–17. London: HMSO.

Judicial Studies Board (2000) *Annual Report, 1999–2000*. London: Judicial Studies Board. [Can also be accessed via the Lord Chancellor's Department web page.]

Junger-Tas, J., Terlouw, G.-J. and Klein, M.W. (1994) *Delinquent Behaviour Among Young People in the Western World: First Results of the International Self-Report Delinquency Study*. Amsterdam: Kugler.

Justices' Clerks' Society (1982) 'A Case for Summary Trial: Proposals for a Redistribution of Criminal Business'. Unpublished.

Kamenka, E. and Tay, A.E.-S. (1975) 'Beyond Bourgeois Individualism: The Contemporary Crisis in Law and Legal Ideology', in E. Kamenka and R.S. Neale (eds), *Feudalism, Capitalism and Beyond*. pp. 126–44. London: Edward Arnold.

Kamerman, S.B. and Kahn, A.J. (eds) (1989) *Privatization and the Welfare State*, Princeton, NJ: Princeton University Press.

Kellner, P. and Crowther-Hunt, N. (1980) *The Civil Servants: An Inquiry into Britain's Ruling Class*. London: Macdonald Futura.

Kershaw, C. (1999) *Reconviction of Offenders Sentenced or Released from Prison in 1994*. Home Office Research Findings No. 90. London: Home Office.

Kershaw, C., Budd, T., Kinshott, G., Mattinson, J., Mayhew, P. and Myhill, A. (2000) *The 2000 British Crime Survey England and Wales*. Home Office Statistical Bulletin 18/00. London: Home Office.

van Kesteren, J., Mayhew, P. and Nieuwbeerta, P. (2001) *Criminal Victimisation in Seventeen Industrialised Countries: Key Findings from the 2000 International Crime Victims Survey*. The Hague: WODC.

King, R.D. (1985) 'Control in Prison', in M. Maguire, J. Vagg and R. Morgan (eds), *Accountability and Prisons: Opening up a Closed World*. London: Tavistock.

King, R.D. and Elliott, K.W. (1977) *Albany: Birth of a Prison – End of an Era*. London: Routledge and Kegan Paul.

King, R.D. and McDermott, K. (1989) 'British Prisons 1970–1987: The Ever-Deepening Crisis', *British Journal of Criminology*, 29: 107–28.

King, R.D. and Morgan, R. (1980) *The Future of the Prison System*. Farnborough, Hants: Gower.

Kuhn, T.S. (1962) *The Structure of Scientific Revolutions*. Chicago: University of Chicago Press.

Labour Party (1997) *New Labour: Because Britain Deserves Better* (General Election Manifesto). London: Labour Party.

Lacey, N. (1988) *State Punishment: Political Principles and Community Values*. London: Routledge.

Laming of Tewin, Lord (2000) *Modernising the Management of the Prison Service: An Independent Report by the Targeted Performance Initiative Working Group*, London: HM Prison Service. Also available on-line at: www.hmprisonservice.gov.uk/filestore/263_281.pdf

Landau, S.F. (1981) 'Juveniles and the Police: Who is Charged Immediately and Who is Referred to the Juvenile Bureau?', *British Journal of Criminology*, 21: 27–46.

Landau, S.F. and Nathan, G. (1983) 'Selecting Delinquents for Cautioning in the London Metropolitan Area', *British Journal of Criminology*, 23: 128–49.

Lane, Lord (1993) *Report of the Committee on the Penalty for Homicide*. London: Prison Reform Trust.

Law Commission (1994) *Binding Over*, Cm 2439. London: HMSO.

Law Commission (1999) *Bail and the Human Rights Act 1998*. Consultation Paper no. 157. London: Law Commission. Text is also available at www.open.gov.uk/lawcomm/

Lawrence, D.M. (1986) 'Private Exercise of Governmental Power', *Indiana Law Journal*, 61: 647–95.

Learmont, J. (1995) *Review of Prison Service Security in England and Wales and the Escape from Parkhurst Prison on Tuesday 3rd January 1995*, Cm 3020. London: HMSO.

Leech, M. (1995) *The Prisoners' Handbook*, Oxford: Oxford University Press.

Leech, M. and Cheney, D. (1999) *The Prisons Handbook 2000* (4th edn). Winchester: Waterside Press.

Leech, M. and Cheney, D. (2001) *The Prisons Handbook 2001*, (5th edn). Winchester: Waterside Press.

Levenson, J. (2000) 'Still afraid of the Woolf Report?', *Prison Report*, 51 (Summer): 18–19. London: Prison Reform Trust.

Levi, M. (1989) 'Fraudulent Justice? Sentencing the Business Criminal' in P. Carlen and D. Cook (eds), *Paying for Crime*, pp. 86–108. Milton Keynes: Open University Press.

Levi, M. (1997) 'Violent Crime' in M. Maguire, R. Morgan and R. Reiner (eds), *The Oxford Handbook of Criminology* (2nd edn), pp. 841–89. Oxford: Clarendon Press.

Lewis, D. (1996) 'Prisons: the case for constitutional reform', *Prison Report*, 35 (Summer): 10–11. London: Prison Reform Trust.

Lewis, D. (1997) *Hidden Agendas: Politics, Law and Disorder*. London: Hamish Hamilton.

Lewis, H. and Mair, G. (1989) *Bail and Probation Work, ii. The Use of London Probation Hostels for Bailees*, Home Office Research and Planning Unit Paper 50. London: HMSO.

Liebling, A. (1992) *Suicides in Prison*. London: Routledge.

Liebling, A. (1997) 'Risk and Prison Suicide', in H. Kemshall and J. Pritchard (eds), *Good Practice in Risk Assessment and Risk Management*. London: Jessica Kingsley.

Liebling, A. (2001) 'Policy and practice in the management of disruptive prisoners: incentives and earned privileges, the Spurr Report and Close Supervision Centres', in E. Clare and K. Bottomley (eds), *Evaluation of Close Supervision Centres*, Home Office Research Study No. 136. London: Home Office Research, Development and Statistics Directorate.

Liebling, A. and Kraup, H. (1993) *Suicide Attempts and Self-Injury in Male Prisons*. Cambridge: Institute of Criminology.

Liebling, A., Muir, G., Rose, G. and Bottoms, A. (1999) *Incentives and Earned Privileges for Prisoners – An Evaluation*. Home Office Research Findings No. 87. London: Home Office Research and Statistics Directorate.

Lilly, J.R. (1990) 'Tagging Reviewed', *Howard Journal of Criminal Justice*, 29: 229–45.

Lilly, J.R. and Knepper, P. (1990) 'The corrections–industrial complex', *Prison Service Journal*, 87: 43–52.

Lilly, J.R. and Knepper, P. (1992) 'An International Perspective on the Privatization of Corrections', *Howard Journal of Criminal Justice*, 31: 174–91.

Lipsey, M.W. (1992) 'The Effect of Treatment on Juvenile Delinquents: Results from Meta-Analysis', in Friedrich Lösel, Doris Bender and Thomas Bliesener (eds), *Psychology and Law: International Perspectives*, pp. 131–43. Berlin: Walter de Gruyter.

Lipton, D., Martinson, R. and Wilks, J. (1975) *Effectiveness of Treatment Evaluation Studies*. New York: Praeger.

Livingstone, S. and Owen, T. (1993) *Prison Law: Text and Materials*. Oxford: Oxford University Press.

Livingstone, S. and Owen, T. (1999) *Prison Law*. Oxford: Oxford University Press.

Lloyd, C. (1992) *Bail Information Schemes: Practice and Effects*, Home Office Research and Planning Unit Paper No. 69. London: HMSO.

Lloyd, C., Mair, G. and Hough, M. (1994) *Explaining Reconviction Rates: A Critical Analysis*, Home Office Research Study No. 136. London: HMSO.

Logan, C. (1990) *Private Prisons: Cons and Pros*. Oxford: Oxford University Press.

Lombroso, C. (1876) *L'Uomo Delinquente*. Milan: Hoepli.

Lord Chancellor's Department (1999) *Judicial Statistics 1998*. London: HMSO.

Lord Chancellor's Department (2000) *Judicial Statistics 1999*. London: HMSO.

Lösel, F., Bender, D. and Bliesener, T. (eds) (1992) *Psychology and Law: International Perspectives.* Berlin: Walter de Gruyter.

Loucks, N. (1993) *Prison Rules: A Working Guide, New edn.* London: Prison Reform Trust.

Loucks, N. (1995) *Anything Goes: The Use of the 'Catch-all' Disciplinary Rule in Prison Service Establishments.* London: Prison Reform Trust.

Loucks, N. (2000) *Prison Rules: A Working Guide, Millennium edn.* London: Prison Reform Trust.

Lukes, S. (1975) *Émile Durkheim: His Life and Work.* Harmondsworth: Penguin.

Lygo, R. (1991) *Management of the Prison Service: A Report.* London: Home Office.

Lynn, J. and Jay, A. (eds) (1981) *Yes Minister: The Diaries of a Cabinet Minister by the Rt. Hon. James Hacker MP.* London: British Broadcasting Corporation.

McConville, M. and Baldwin, J. (1982) 'The Influence of Race on Sentencing in England', [1982] *Criminal Law Review*, 652–8.

McConville, S. (1975) 'Future Prospects of Imprisonment in Britain' in S. McConville (ed.), *The Use of Imprisonment*, pp. 107–25. London: Routledge and Kegan Paul.

McConville, S. (1981) *A History of English Prison Administration Volume 1, 1760–1877.* London: Routledge and Kegan Paul.

McConville, S. and Williams, J.E. (1985) *Crime and Punishment: A Radical Rethink*, London: Tawney Society.

McDermott, K. and King, R. (1989) 'A Fresh Start: The Enhancement of Prison Regimes', *Howard Journal of Criminal Justice*, 28: 161–76.

McDonald, D.C. (ed.) (1989) 'The Cost of Corrections: in Search of the Bottom Line', *Research in Corrections*, 2: 1–25.

McDonald, D.C. (ed.) (1990) *Private Prisons and the Public Interest.* New Brunswick, NJ: Rutgers University Press.

McDonald, D.C. (1994) 'Public Imprisonment by Private Means: the Re-emergence of Private Prisons in the United States, the United Kingdom and Australia', *British Journal of Criminology*, 34: 29–48.

McElrea, F.W. (1994) 'Justice in the Community: The New Zealand Experience', in Burnside and Baker (eds) (1994) *Relational Justice: Repairing the Breach.* Winchester: Waterside Press.

McGeorge, N. (1990) *A Fair Deal for Lifers.* London: Quaker Peace and Service.

McGeorge, N. (1995) 'Lifer Imprisonment', *Criminal Justice*, 13 (2): 6–7.

McGuire, J. (ed.) (1995) *What Works: Reducing Re-offending – Guidelines from Research and Practice.* London: Wiley.

McGuire, J. and Priestley, P. (1995) 'Reviewing "What Works": Past, Present and Future' in J. McGuire (ed.), *What Works: Reducing Re-offending*, pp. 3–34. Chichester: Wiley.

McIvor, G. (1992) *Sentenced to Serve.* Aldershot: Avebury.

McLennan, G. (1989) *Marxism, Pluralism and Beyond.* Cambridge: Polity Press.

McMahon, M.W. (1992) *The Persistent Prison? Rethinking Decarceration and Penal Reform.* Toronto: University of Toronto Press.

Macnamara, D.E.J. and Kelly, R.J. (eds) (1991) *Perspectives on Deviance: Dominance, Degradation and Denigration.* Cincinnati, OH: Anderson.

Macpherson, W. (1999) *The Stephen Lawrence Inquiry: Report of an Inquiry by Sir William Macpherson*, Cm 4262–I. London: The Stationery Office.

MacRae, D.G. (1974) *Weber.* Glasgow: Fontana/Collins.

McWilliams, W. (1981) 'The Probation Officer at Court: From Friend to Acquaintance', *Howard Journal of Criminal Justice*, 20: 97–116.

McWilliams, W. (1987) 'Probation, Pragmatism and Policy', *Howard Journal of Criminal Justice*, 26: 97–121.

McWilliams, W. (1992) 'The Rise and Development of Management Thought in the

English Probation Service' in R. Statham and P. Whitehead (eds), *Managing the Probation Service: Issues for the 1990s*. Harlow: Longman.

Maghan, J. (1991) 'Privatization of Corrections: Anticipating the Unanticipated' in D.E.J. Macnamara and R.J. Kelly (eds), *Perspectives on Deviance: Dominance, Degradation and Denigration*, pp. 135–91. Cincinnati, OH: Anderson.

Magistrates' Association (1989) *Sentencing Guide for Criminal Offences (Other than Road Traffic) and Compensation Table*. London: Magistrates' Association.

Magistrates' Association (1997) *Sentencing Guidelines*. London: Magistrates' Association. [See also Watkins et al., 1998, Appendix C; 2000.]

Maguire, M. (1992) 'Parole' in E. Stockdale and S. Casale (eds), *Criminal Jusitice Under Stress*, pp. 179–207. London: Blackstone.

Maguire, M. (with T. Bennett) (1982) *Burglary in a Dwelling: The Offence, the Offender and the Victim*. London: Heinemann.

Maguire, M. and Pointing, J. (eds) (1988) *Victims of Crime: a New Deal*. Milton Keynes and Philadelphia: Open University Press.

Maguire, M., Morgan, R. and Reiner, R. (eds) (1994) *The Oxford Handbook of Criminology* (1st edn). Oxford: Clarendon Press.

Maguire, M., Morgan, R. and Reiner, R. (eds) (1997) *The Oxford Handbook of Criminology* (2nd edn). Oxford: Clarendon Press.

Maguire, M., Vagg J. and Morgan R. (eds) (1985) *Accountability and Prisons: Opening up a Closed World*. London: Tavistock.

Mair, G. (1986) 'Ethnic Minorities, Probation and the Magistrates' Courts', *British Journal of Criminology*, 26: 147–55.

Mair, G. (1988) *Bail and Probation Work: The ILPS Temporary Bail Action Project*, Home Office Research and Planning Unit Paper No. 46. London: HMSO.

Mair, G. (1997) 'Community Penalties and the Probation Service' in M. Maguire, R. Morgan and R. Reiner (eds), *The Oxford Handbook of Criminology* (2nd edn), pp. 1195–1232. Oxford: Oxford University Press.

Mair, G. and Lloyd, C. (1996) 'Policy and Progress in the Development of Bail Schemes in England and Wales', in F. Paterson (ed.), *Understanding Bail in Britain*. London: The Scottish Office Central Research Unit.

Mair, G. and Nee, C. (1990) *Electronic Monitoring: The Trials and their Results*, Home Office Research Study No. 120. London: HMSO.

Mair, G ., Lloyd, C., Nee, C. and Sibbitt, R. (1994) *Intensive Probation in England and Wales: an Evaluation*, Home Office Research Study No. 133. London: HMSO.

Maltz, M. (1984) *Recidivism*, London: Academic Press.

Marshall, S. (1997) *A Reconviction Study of HMP Grendon Therapeutic Community*. Home Office Research Findings No. 53. London: Home Office Research and Statistics Directorate.

Marshall, S. (1997) *Control in Category C Prisons*, Home Office Research Findings No. 54. London: Home Office Research and Statistics Directorate.

Marshall, T.F. (1985) *Alternatives to Criminal Courts: the Potential for Non-judicial Settlement*. Aldershot: Gower.

Marshall, T.F. (1999) *Restorative Justice: An Overview*. London: Home Office Research Development and Statistics Directorate.

Marshall, T.F. and Merry, S. (1990) *Crime and Accountability: Victim/Offender Mediation in Practice*. London: HMSO.

Martin, F.M. and Murray, K. (eds) (1982) *The Scottish Juvenile Justice System*. Edinburgh: Scottish Academic Press.

Martin, J.P. (1991) 'Parkhurst Special Unit: Some Aspects of Management' in R. Walmsley (ed.), *Managing Difficult Prisoners: the Parkhurst Special Unit*, Home Office Research Study No. 122. London: HMSO.

Martinson, R. (1974) 'What Works? – Questions and Answers about Prison Reform', *The Public Interest*, 35 (Spring): 22–54.

Martinson, R. (1979) 'New Findings, New Views: A Note of Caution Regarding Sentencing Reform', *Hofstra Law Review*, 7: 243–58.

Marx, K. (1977) *Selected Writings* (ed. D. McLellan). Oxford: Oxford University Press.

Mathiesen, T. (1974) *The Politics of Abolition: Essays in Political Action Theory*. Oxford: Martin Robertson.

Mathiesen, T. (1980) 'The Future of Control Systems – the case of Norway', *International Journal of the Sociology of Law*, 8: 149–64. [Also in D. Garland and P. Young (eds) (1983) *The Power to Punish: Contemporary Penality and Social Analysis*, pp. 130–45. London: Heinemann.]

Mathiesen, T. (1983) 'The Future of Control Systems – the Case of Norway' in D. Garland, and P. Young (eds), *The Power to Punish: Contemporary Penalty and Social Analysis*, pp. 130–45. London: Heinemann. (First published in *International Journal of the Sociology of Law* (1980), 8: 149–64.)

Mathiesen, T. (1990) *Prison on Trial*. London: Sage Publications.

Mathiesen, T. (2000) *Prison on Trial*. Winchester: Waterside Press.

Mathieson, D. (1992) 'The Probation Service', in E. Stockdale and S. Casale (eds), *Criminal Justice under Stress*, pp. 142–59. London: Blackstone.

Mattinson, J. and colleagues (1998) *Cautions, Court Proceedings and Sentencing England and Wales 1997*, Home Office Statistical Bulletin 18/98. London: Home Office.

Mattinson, J. and Mirrlees-Black, C. (2000) *Attitudes to Crime and Criminal Justice: Findings from the 1998 British Crime Survey*. Home Office Research Study No. 200. London: Home Office.

Matthews, R. (1979) 'Decarceration and the Fiscal Crisis' in B. Fine et al. (eds), *Capitalism and the Rule of Law: From Deviancy Theory to Marxism*, pp. 100–17. London: Hutchinson.

Matthews, R. (ed.) (1989) *Privatizing Criminal Justice*. London: Sage Publications.

Matthews, R. (1999) *Doing Time: An Introduction to the Sociology of Imprisonment*. Basingstoke: Macmillan.

Mawby, R. (1977) 'Sexual Discrimination and the Law', *Probation Journal*, 24: 38–43.

Mawby, R.I. (1989) 'The Voluntary Sector's Role in a Mixed Economy of Criminal Justice', in R. Matthews (ed.), *Privatising Criminal Justice*, pp. 135–54. London: Sage Publications.

May, C. (1997) *Magistrates' Views of the Probation Service*. Home Office Statistical Bulletin 48/97. London: Home Office.

May, J. (1979) *Committee of Inquiry into the United Kingdom Prison Services: Report*, Cmnd 7673. London: HMSO.

Mayhew, P. (1994) *Findings from the International Crime Survey*. Home Office Research Findings No. 8. London: Home Office.

Mayhew, P. and White, P. (1997) *The 1996 International Crime Victimisation Survey*. Home Office Research Findings No. 57. London: Home Office.

Meichenbaum, D. (1977) *Cognitive-Bahavior Modification: An Integrative Approach*, New York: Plenum.

Merton, R.K. (1968) *Social Theory and Social Structure* (enlarged edn). New York: Free Press.

Mirrlees-Black, C. (2001) *Confidence in the Criminal Justice System: Findings from the 2000 British Crime Survey*. Home Office Research Findings No. 137. London: Home Office.

Mirrlees-Black, C., Budd, T., Partridge, S. and Mayhew, P. (1998) *The British Crime Survey England and Wales*. Home Office Statistical Bulletin 21/98. London: Home Office.

Monahan, J. (1981) *Predicting Violent Behavior: An Assessment of Clinical Techniques*. London: Sage.

Morgan, N. (1983) 'The Shaping of Parole in England and Wales', [1983] *Criminal Law Review*, 137–51.

Morgan, P. (1992) *Offending While on Bail: a Survey of Recent Studies*, Home Office Research and Planning Unit Paper No. 65. London: HMSO.

Morgan, P. and Henderson, P. (1998) *Remand Decisions and Offending on Bail: Evaluation of the Bail Process Project.* Home Office Research Study No. 184. London: HMSO.

Morgan, R. (1985) 'Her Majesty's Inspectorate of Prisons' in M. Maguire, J. Vagg and R. Morgan (eds), *Accountability and Prisons: Opening up a Closed World.* London: Tavistock.

Morgan, R. (1995) 'Prison' in M. Walker (ed.), *Interpreting Crime Statistics*, pp. 91–110. Oxford: Clarendon Press.

Morgan, R. and Jones, S. (1992) 'Bail or Jail?' in E. Stockdale and S. Casale (eds), *Criminal Justice under Stress*, pp. 34–63. London: Blackstone.

Morris, A. (1987) *Women, Crime and Criminal Justice.* Oxford: Basil Blackwell.

Morris, A. and Giller, H. (1987) *Understanding Juvenile Justice.* London: Croom Helm.

Morris, A., Giller, H., Szwed, E. and Geach, H. (1980) *Justice for Children.* London: Macmillan.

Morris, A., Maxwell, G.M., and Robertson, J.P. (1993) 'Giving Victims a Voice: A New Zealand Experiment', *Howard Journal of Criminal Justice*, 32: 304–21.

Morris, N. (1974) *The Future of Imprisonment.* London: University of Chicago Press.

Morris, T. (1980) 'Penology and the Crimes of the Powerful' in A.E. Bottoms and R.H. Preston (eds), *The Coming Penal Crisis: A Criminological and Theological Exploration.* Edinburgh: Scottish Academic Press.

Morris, T. (1989) *Crime and Criminal Justice Since 1945.* Oxford: Basil Blackwell.

Mortimer, E. and Mair, G. (1997) *Curfew Orders with Electronic Monitoring: the First Twelve Months.* Home Office Research Findings No. 51. London: Home Office Research and Statistics Directorate.

Mortimer, E. and May, C. (1998) *Electronic Monitoring of Curfew Orders: the Second Year of the Trials.* Home Office Research Findings No. 66. London: Home Office Research and Statistics Directorate.

Mortimer, E., Pereira, E. and Walter, I. (1999) *Making the Tag Fit: Further Analysis from the First Two Years of the Trials of Curfew Orders. Curfew Orders with Electronic Monitoring: the First Twelve Months.* Home Office Research Findings No. 105. London: Home Office Research and Statistics Directorate.

Mott, J. (1983) 'Police Decisions for Dealing with Juvenile Offenders', *British Journal of Criminology*, 23: 249–62.

de la Motta, K. (1984) 'Blacks in the Criminal Justice System'. Unpublished MSc thesis, Aston University.

Moxon, D. (1983) 'Fine Default, Unemployment and the Use of Imprisonment', *Home Office Research Bulletin*, 16: 38–41.

Moxon, D. (1988) *Sentencing Practice in the Crown Court*, Home Office Research Study No. 103. London: HMSO.

Moxon, D. and Whittaker, C. (1996) *Imprisonment for Fine Default*, Home Office Research Findings No. 35. London: Home Office Research and Statistics Directorate.

Moxon, D., Corkery, J.M. and Hedderman, C. (1992) *Developments in the Use of Compensation Orders in Magistrates' Courts Since October 1988*, Home Office Research Study No. 126. London: HMSO.

Moxon, D., Sutton, M. and Hedderman, C. (1990) *Unit Fines: Experiments in Four Courts*, Research and Planning Unit Paper 59. London: HMSO.

Muncie, J. (1984) *'The Trouble with Kids Today': Youth and Crime in Post-War Britain.* London: Hutchinson.

Muncie, J. (1990) 'A Prisoner in My Own Home: The Politics and Practice of Electronic Monitoring', *Probation Journal*, 37: 72–7.

Murphy, J. (1979) *Retribution, Justice and Therapy: Essays in the Philosophy of Law*. London: D. Reidel Publishing.

Murphy, J. (1992) *Retribution Reconsidered*. Dordrecht: Kluwer Academic Publishers.

MVA and Miller, J. (2000) *Profiling Populations Available for Stops and Searches*. Police Research Series Paper 131. London: Home Office.

NACRO (1981) *Fine Default: Report of a NACRO Working Party*. London: NACRO.

NACRO (1986a) *Enforcement of the Law Relating to Social Security: Report of a NACRO Working Party*. London: NACRO.

NACRO (1986b) *Black People and the Criminal Justice System*. London: NACRO.

NACRO (1988) 'The Electronic Monitoring of Offenders', Briefing Paper. London: NACRO.

NACRO (1990) 'Work in Prisons', Briefing Paper. London: NACRO.

NACRO (1991) 'Prison Overcrowding: Some Facts and Figures', Briefing Paper. London: NACRO.

NACRO (1992) 'Offences against Discipline in Women's Prisons', Briefing Paper. London: NACRO.

NACRO (1993) 'Remands in Custody: Some Facts and Figures', Briefing Paper. London: NACRO.

NACRO (1995a) 'The Cost of Penal Measures', Briefing Paper. London: NACRO.

NACRO (1995b) 'Life Sentence Prisoners', Briefing Paper. London: NACRO.

NACRO (1998a) 'Bail Support', Briefing Paper. London: NACRO.

NACRO (1998b) *Contrasting Judgements: Report on Two International Sentencing Seminars*. London: NACRO.

NACRO Juvenile Crime Section (1987) *Diverting Juveniles from Custody: Findings from the Fourth Census of Projects funded under the DHSS Intermediate Treatment Initiative*. London: NACRO.

Nagel, I. (1981) 'Sex Differences in the Processing of Criminal Defendants' in A. Morris and L. Gelsthorpe (eds), *Women and Crime*, pp. 104–24. Cambridge: Institute of Criminology.

Nagel, I.H. and Hagan, J. (1983) 'Gender and Crime: Offence Patterns and Criminal Court Sanctions' in M. Tonry and N. Morris (eds), *Crime and Justice*, vol. 4, pp. 91–144. Chicago: University of Chicago Press.

Narey, M. (1997) *Review of Delay in the Criminal Justice System*. London: HMSO.

Narey, M. (2001) Speech to the Prison Service Conference, 5 February 2001. Also available on-line at www.hmprisonservice.gov.uk/news/newstext.asp/201

Nathan, H.L., Baron Nathan of Churt (Chairman) (1989) *Report of the Select Committee on Murder and Life Imprisonment*, HL Paper 78, Session 1988/9, vol. 1.

Nathan, S. (1993a) 'Privatisation Factfile 1', *Prison Report*, 22: 12–14.

Nathan, S. (1993b) 'Privatisation Factfile 2', *Prison Report*, 22: 12–13.

Nathan, S. (1993c) 'Privatisation Factfile 3', *Prison Report*, 24: 11–18.

Nathan, S. (1994a) 'Privatisation Factfile 5', *Prison Report*, 26: 13–16.

Nathan, S. (1994b) 'Privatisation Factfile 6', *Prison Report*, 27: 13–16.

Nathan, S. (1994c) 'Privatisation Factfile 7', *Prison Report*, 28: 11–18.

Nathan, S. (1994d) 'Privatisation Factfile 8', *Prison Report*, 29: 13–20.

Nathan, S. (1995a) 'Privatisation Factfile 9', *Prison Report*, 30: 13–20.

Nathan, S. (1995b) 'Privatisation Factfile 10', *Prison Report*, 31: 13–20.

Nathan, S. (1995c) 'Privatisation Factfile 11', *Prison Report*, 32: 11–18.

Nathan, S. (1995d) 'Privatisation Factfile 12', *Prison Report*, 33: 13–20.

Nathan, S. (1996a) 'Privatisation Factfile 13', *Prison Report*, 34: 13–20.

Nathan, S. (1996b) 'Privatisation Factfile 14', *Prison Report*, 35: 13–16.

Nathan, S. (1996c) 'Privatisation Factfile 15', *Prison Report*, 36: 13–16.

Nathan, S. (1996d) 'Privatisation Factfile 16', *Prison Report*, 37: 13–16.

Nathan, S. (1998a) 'Privatisation Factfile 21', *Prison Report*, 42: 13–16.

Nathan, S. (1998b) 'Privatisation Factfile 22', *Prison Report*, 43: 13–16.

Nathan, S. (1998c) 'Privatisation Factfile 23', *Prison Report*, 44: 15–18.

Nathan, S. (1999) 'Privatisation Factfile 28', *Prison Report*, 44: 13–16.

Nathan, S. (2000a) 'Privatisation Factfile 30', *Prison Report*, 51: 13–16.

Nathan, S. (2000b) 'Privatisation Factfile 32', *Prison Report*, 53: 13–16.

National Audit Office (1994) *Wolds Remand Prison: A Report by the Comptroller and Auditor General.* London: HMSO.

National Audit Office (1997) *The PFI Contracts for Bridgend and Fazakerley Prisons*, Report by the Comptroller and Auditor General HC 253 1997/8; and Press Notice, 31 October 1997.

Nelken, D. (1997) 'White Collar Crime' in M. Maguire, R. Morgan and R. Reiner (eds), *The Oxford Handbook of Criminology* (2nd edn), pp. 891–924. Oxford: Clarendon Press.

Nellis, M. (1989) 'Juvenile Justice and the Voluntary Sector' in R. Matthews (ed.), *Privatizing Criminal Justice.* London: Sage Publications.

Nellis, M. (1991) 'The Electronic Monitoring of Offenders in England and Wales: Recent Developments and Future Prospects', *British Journal of Criminology*, 31: 165–85.

Nellis, M. (1995) 'Probation Values for the 1990s', *Howard Journal of Criminal Justice*, 34: 19–44.

Nellis, M. (1997) 'Time for Reflection', *The Guardian (Society)*, 1 October.

Nellis, M. (1998) 'Community Justice: A New Name for the Probation Service', *Justice of the Peace*, 162: 319–20.

Newburn, T., Masters, G., Earle, R., Goldie, S., Crawford, A., Sharpe, K., Netten, A., Hale, C., Uglow, S. and Saunders, R. (2001) *The Introduction of Referral Orders into the Youth Justice System.* First interim report. RDS Occasional Paper No. 70. Also available on-line at: www.homeoffice.gov.uk/rds/index.html

Nicolson, D. and Sanghvi, R. (1995) 'More Justice for Battered Women', *New Law Journal*, 28 July: 1122–4.

Norris, C. (1995) 'Video Charts: Algorithmic Surveillance', *Criminal Justice Matters*, 20: 7–8.

Norris, C. and Armstrong, G. (1999) *The Maximum Surveillance Society: The Rise of CCTV.* Oxford: Berg.

Nuttall, C.P. et al. (1977) *Parole in England and Wales*, Home Office Research Study No. 38. London: HMSO.

Oatham, E. and Simon, F. (1972) 'Are Suspended Sentences Working?', *New Society*, 21: 233.

O'Connor, D. (2000) 'Stop and Think', *The Guardian (Society)*, 19 January.

O'Donnell, I. and Edgar, K. (1996) *Victimisation in Prisons*, Home Office Research Findings No. 37. London: Home Office Research and Statistics Directorate.

O'Donnell, I. and Edgar, K. (1998) 'Routine Victimisation in Prisons', *Howard Journal of Criminal Justice*, 37: 266–79.

Osborn, S.G. and West, D.J. (1980) 'Do Young Delinquents Really Reform?', *Journal of Adolescence*, 3: 99–114.

Padfield, N.M. (1993) 'Parole and the Life Sentence Prisoner', *Howard Journal of Criminal Justice*, 32: 87–98.

Padfield, N.M. (1995) *Text and Materials on the Criminal Justice Process.* London: Butterworths.

Padfield, N. and Liebling, A., with Arnold, H. (2000) *Discretionary Lifer Panels – An Exploration of Decision-making*, Home Office Research Findings No. 132. London: Home Office.

Palmer, T. (1975) 'Martinson Revisited', *Journal for Research in Crime and Delinquency*, 12: 133–52.

Palumbo, D.J. (1986) 'Privatization and Corrections Policy', *Policy Studies Review*, 5: 598–605.

Pantazis, C. and Gordon, D. (1997) 'Television Licence Evasion and the Criminalization of Female Poverty', *Howard Journal of Criminal Justice*, 36: 170–86.

Park, I. (2000) *Review of Comparative Costs and Performance of Privately and Publicly Operated Prisons, 1998–9*, Home Office Statistical Bulletin 6/00. London: Home Office.

Parker, H., Sumner, M. and Jarvis, G. (1989) *Unmasking the Magistrates: The 'Custody or Not' Decision in Sentencing Young Offenders*. Milton Keynes: Open University Press.

Parsons, T. (1937) *The Structure of Social Action*. New York: McGraw-Hill.

Parsons, T. (1951) *The Social System*. New York: Free Press.

Paternoster, R., Saltzman, L.E., Waldo, G.P. and Chiricos, T.G. (1983) 'Perceived Risk and Social Control: Do Sanctions Really Deter?', *Law and Society Review*, 17: 457–79.

Paterson, F. (1996) *Understanding Bail in Britain*. London: The Scottish Office Central Research Unit.

Peachey, D.E. (1989) 'The Kitchener Experiment in Mediation and Criminal Justice: Victims, Offenders and Community' in M. Wright and B. Galaway (eds), *Mediation and Criminal Justice: Victims, Offenders and the Community*. London: Sage Publications.

Pearson, G. (1983) *Hooligan: A History of Respectable Fears*. London: Macmillan.

Pease, K. (1980) 'Community Service and Prison: Are they Alternatives?' in K. Pease and W. McWilliams (eds), *Community Service by Order*. Edinburgh: Scottish Academic Press.

Pease, K. (1985) 'Community Service Orders' in N. Morris and M. Tonry (eds), *Criminal Justice: An Annual Review of Research*, vol. 6, pp. 51–94. Chicago: University of Chicago Press.

Pease, K. (1992) 'Punitiveness and Prison Populations: An International Comparison', *Justice of the Peace*, 156: 405–8.

Pease, K. (1994) 'Cross-national Imprisonment Rates: Limitations of Method and Possible Conclusions', *British Journal of Criminology*, 34, Special Issue: 116–30.

Pease, K. (1997) 'Crime Prevention' in M. Maguire, R. Morgan and R. Reiner (eds), *The Oxford Handbook of Criminology* (2nd edn), pp. 659–703; 963–95. Oxford: Clarendon Press.

Pease, K. (1999) 'The Probation Career of Al Truism', *Howard Journal of Criminal Justice*, 38: 2–15.

Pease, K. and Wasik, M. (1987) *Sentencing Reform: Guidance or Guidelines?* Manchester: Manchester University Press.

Pease, K., Billingham, S. and Earnshaw, I. (1977) *Community Service Assessed in 1976*, Home Office Research Study No. 39. London: HMSO.

Penal Affairs Consortium (1994) *The Mandatory Life Sentence*. London: Penal Affairs Consortium.

Penal Affairs Consortium (1995a) *Prison Overcrowding*. London: Penal Affairs Consortium.

Penal Affairs Consortium (1995b) *'Boot Camps' for Young Offenders*. London: Penal Affairs Consortium.

Penal Affairs Consortium (1995c) *Sentencing and Early Release: The Home Secretary's Proposals*. London: Penal Affairs Consortium.

Penal Affairs Consortium (1995d) *The Imprisonment of Fine Defaulters*. London: Penal Affairs Consortium.

Penal Affairs Consortium (1995e) *The Electronic Monitoring of Offenders*. London: Penal Affairs Consortium.

Penal Affairs Consortium (1995f) *The Case for Mandatory Pre-Sentence Reports*. London: Penal Affairs Consortium.

Penal Affairs Consortium (1995g) *The Case for a Sentencing Council*. London: Penal Affairs Consortium.

Penal Affairs Consortium (1995h) *The 'Supermax' Option*. London: Penal Affairs Consortium.

Penal Affairs Consortium (1999) *The Prison System: Regime and Population Trends*. London: Penal Affairs Consortium.

Penal Affairs Consortium (2000) *A Joint Manifesto for Penal Reform 2000*. London: Penal Affairs Consortium.

Phillips, C. and Brown, D. (1998) *Entry into the Criminal Justice System: A Survey of Police Arrests and Their Outcomes*, Home Office Research Study No. 185. London: Home Office.

Piliavin, I. and Briar, S. (1964) 'Police Encounters with Juveniles', *American Journal of Sociology*, 70: 206–14.

Pitts, J. (1986a) 'Thinking about Intermediate Treatment', *Youth and Policy*, 17: 1–8.

Pitts, J. (1986b) 'Black Young People and Juvenile Crime: Some Unanswered Questions' in R. Matthews and J. Young (eds), *Confronting Crime*, pp. 118–44. London: Sage Publications.

Pitts, J. (1988) *The Politics of Juvenile Crime*. London: Sage Publications.

Player, E. and Jenkins, M. (eds) (1994) *Prisons after Woolf*. London: Routledge.

Plotnikoff, J. (1986) *Prison Rules: A Working Guide*. London: Prison Reform Trust.

Pollak, O. (1961) *The Criminality of Women*. New York: A.S. Barnes.

Polvi, N. and Pease, K. (1991) 'Parole and its Problems: a Canadian–English Comparison', *Howard Journal of Criminal Justice*, 30: 218–30.

Porter, R.G. (1990) 'The Privatization of Prisons in the United States: a Policy that Britain should not Emulate', *Howard Journal of Criminal Justice*, 29: 65–81.

Pratt, J. (1986) 'A Comparative Analysis of Two Different Systems of Juvenile Justice: Some Implications for England and Wales', *Howard Journal of Criminal Justice*, 25: 33–51.

Pratt, J. (1989) 'Corporatism: The Third Model of Juvenile Justice', *British Journal of Criminology*, 29: 236–54.

Pratt, T.C. and Maahs, J. (1999) 'Are Private Prisons More Cost Effective than Public Prisons? A Meta Analysis of Evaluation Research Studies', *Crime and Delinquency*, 45 (3): 358–71.

Prior, P.J. (1985) *Report of the Committee on the Prison Disciplinary System*, Cmnd 9641-I. London: HMSO.

Prison Officers' Association (1990) *Prison Regimes: the View of the Prison Officers' Association*. London: POA.

Prison Reform Trust, (1991) *Management and Structure of the Prison Service: Woolf Briefing Paper No. 2*. London: Prison Reform Trust.

Prison Reform Trust (1993) *Wolds Remand Prison – Contracting-out: A First Year Report*. London: Prison Reform Trust.

Prison Reform Trust (1994) *The Future of the Prison Education Service*. London: Prison Reform Trust.

Prison Reform Trust (1996a) 'Act of Immunity'. *Prison Report*, 36 (Autumn): 3. London: Prison Reform Trust.

Prison Reform Trust (1996b) *The Doncatraz File*. London: Prison Reform Trust. Also available on-line at: www.penlex.org.uk/pages/dc5.html

Prison Reform Trust (1997a) *Sentencing: A Geographical Lottery*. London: Prison Reform Trust.

Prison Reform Trust (1997b) *The Rising Toll of Prison Suicides*. London: Prison Reform Trust. Also available on-line at: www.penlex.org.uk/pages/prtsuic.html

Prison Reform Trust (1997c) 'Key Relationships', *Prison Report*, 40 (Autumn): 22. London: Prison Reform Trust.

Prison Reform Trust (1998a) 'Boards of Visitors: Whistle-blowers or Governors' Patsies?, *Prison Report*, 44 (Summer): 6–7. London: Prison Reform Trust.

Prison Reform Trust (1998b) *Prison Privatization Report International*, Volume 21. London: Prison Reform Trust.

Prison Reform Trust (1999a) 'On Closing Open Prisons', *Prison Report*, 49 (November): 3. London: Prison Reform Trust.

Prison Reform Trust (1999b) *A System Under Pressure: the Effects of Prison Overcrowding.* London: Prison Reform Trust. Also available on-line at: www.penlex.org.uk/pages/prt.html

Prison Reform Trust (1999c) *Prison Report*, 46 (February): 3. London: Prison Reform Trust.

Prison Reform Trust (1999d) 'Publish or be Damned', *Prison Report*, 46 (February): 9. London: Prison Reform Trust.

Prison Reform Trust (1999e) *Prison Privatization Report International*, Volume 27. London: Prison Reform Trust.

Prison Reform Trust (2000a) *Prison Report*, 50 (March): 12. London: Prison Reform Trust.

Prison Reform Trust (2000b) *Strangeways: Ten Years On – The Continuing Implications of the Strangeways Riot*, London: Prison Reform Trust. Also available on-line at: www.penlex.org.uk/pages/prt.html

Prison Reform Trust (2000c) *A Hard Act to Follow? Prisons and the Human Rights Act.* London: Prison Reform Trust. Also available on-line at www.penlex.org.uk/pages/prt.html

Prison Reform Trust (2000d) *The Prisons League Table 1999–2000: Performance Against Key Performance Indicators.* London: Prison Reform Trust. Also available on-line at www.penlex.org.uk/pages/prt.html

Prison Reform Trust (2000e) 'Below the Belt', *Prison Report*, 53 (December): 20. London: Prison Reform Trust.

Prison Reform Trust (2000f) *Prison Privatization Report International*, Volume 37. London: Prison Reform Trust. Also available on-line at: www.penlex.org.uk/pages/prtpre37.html

Prison Reform Trust (2001) *Prison Privatization Report International*, Volume 38. London: Prison Reform Trust.

Prison Service Planning Group (1997) *Contracted Prisons: Cost and Staffing Comparison 1995–6.* (Internal report; restricted circulation). Prison Service Planning Group.

Prison Service Security Group (1996) *Open Prisons Review.*

Prisons Ombudsman (1995) *Prisons Ombudsman: A Six Month Review.* London: Prisons Ombudsman.

Prisons Ombudsman (2000) *Prisons Ombudsman: Annual Report 1999–2000.* London: Prisons Ombudsman. Also available on-line at: www.penlex.org.uk/pages/oms2000.html#2

Pruitt, C.R. and Wilson, J.Q. (1983) 'A Longitudinal Study of the Effect of Race on Sentencing', *Law and Society Review*, 17: 613–35.

Pugh, R.B. (1968) *Imprisonment in Medieval England*, Cambridge: Cambridge University Press.

Quinn, P.M. (1993) 'Adjudications in Prison: Custody, Care and a Little Less Justice', *Howard Journal of Criminal Justice'*, 32: 191–202.

Quinn, P.M. (1995) 'Adjudications in Prison: Custody, Care and a Little Less Justice', in Leech, M. (ed.), *The Prisoners' Handbook 1995.* Oxford: Oxford University Press, pp. 320–7.

Quinney, R. (1977) *Class, State and Crime: on the Theory and Practice of Criminal Justice.* New York: David McKay.

Radzinowicz, L. (1988) Letter to *The Times*, 22 September.

Radzinowicz, L. and Hood, R. (1978) 'A Dangerous Direction for Sentencing Reform', [1978] *Criminal Law Review*, 713–24.

Raine, J.W. (1989) *Local Justice – Ideals and Realities*. Edinburgh: Clark.

Raynor, P. (1988) *Probation as an Alternative to Custody: A Case Study*. Aldershot: Avebury.

Raynor, P. (1993) *Social Work, Justice and Control*. Oxford: Basil Blackwell.

Reed, J. and Lyne, M. (2000) 'Inpatient Care of Mentally Ill Prisoners: Results of a Year's Programme of Semistructured Inspections', *British Medical Journal*, 320: 1031–4.

Reiner, R. and Cross, M. (1991) 'Introduction: Beyond Law and Order – Crime and Criminology into the 1990s' in R. Reiner and M. Cross (eds), *Beyond Law and Order: Criminal Justice Policy and Politics into the 1990s*, pp. 1–17. Basingstoke: Macmillan.

Richardson, G. (1985) 'The Case for Prisoners' Rights' in M. Maguire, J. Vagg and R. Morgan (eds), *Accountability and Prisons: Opening Up a Closed World*. London: Tavistock Publications.

Riley, D. (1986) 'Sex Differences in Teenage Crime: The Role of Lifestyle', *Home Office Research Bulletin*, 20: 34–8.

Riley, D. and Shaw, M. (1985) *Parental Supervision and Juvenile Delinquency*, Home Office Research Study No. 83. London: HMSO.

Riley, D. and Vennard, J. (1988) *Triable Either Way Cases: Crown Court or Magistrates' Courts*, Home Office Research Study No. 98. London, HMSO.

Ritchie, J.H. (1994) *Report of the Inquiry into the Care and Treatment of Christopher Clunis*. London: HMSO.

Robinson, P. (2000) 'Capital Gains', *The Guardian*, 14 March 2000.

Ross, R.R., Fabiano, E.A. and Ewles, C.D. (1988) 'Reasoning and Rehabilitation', *International Journal of Offender Therapy and Comparative Criminology*, 32: 29–35.

Rothman, D. J. (1971) *The Discovery of the Asylum*. Boston and Toronto: Little, Brown.

Royal Commission on Criminal Justice (1993) *Report*, Cm 2263. London: HMSO.

Ruggles-Brise, E. (1921) *The English Prison System*. London: Macmillan.

Rumgay, J. (1989) 'Talking Tough: Empty Threats in Probation Practice', *Howard Journal of Criminal Justice*, 28: 177–86.

Rusche, G. and Kirchheimer, O. (1939) *Punishment and Social Structure*. New York: Columbia University Press.

Russell, N. and Morgan, R. (2001) *Sentencing of Domestic Burglary*. Sentencing Advisory Panel Research Report 1. London: Sentencing Advisory Panel.

Rutherford, A. (1985) 'The New Generation of Prisons', *New Society*, 20 September, 73: 408–10.

Rutherford, A. (1986) *Prisons and the Process of Justice*. Oxford: Oxford University Press.

Rutherford, A. (1988) 'The English Penal Crisis: Paradox and Possibilities', [1988] *Current Legal Problems*, 93–113.

Rutherford, A. (1990) 'British Penal Policy and the Idea of Prison Privatization' in D.C. McDonald (ed.), *Private Prisons and the Public Interest*, pp. 42–65. New Brunswick, NJ: Rutgers University Press.

Rutherford, A. (1992) *Growing out of Crime: The New Era*. Winchester: Waterside Press.

Rutherford, A. (1993) *Criminal Justice and the Pusuit of Decency*. Oxford: Oxford University Press.

Rutter, M. and Giller, H. (1983) *Juvenile Delinquency: Trends and Perspectives*. Harmondsworth: Penguin.

Ryan, M. (1978) *The Acceptable Pressure Group*. Farnborough: Saxon House.

Ryan, M. (1993) Review of first edition of M. Cavadino and J. Dignan, *The Penal System: An Introduction*, in *International Journal of the Sociology of Law*, 21: 399–401.

Ryan, M. (1994) 'Some Arguments against the Use of Private Prisons' in C. Martin (ed.), *Contracts to Punish: Private or Public?* Report of a Conference organised by the Institute for the Study and Treatment of Delinquency, held in Manchester on 24 November 1994.

Ryan, M. and Ward, T. (1989a) *Privatization and the Penal System: the American Experience and the Debate in Britain*. Milton Keynes: Open University.

Ryan, M. and Ward, T. (1989b) 'Privatization and Penal Politics' in R. Matthews (ed.), *Privatizing Criminal Justice*, pp. 53–73. London: Sage Publications.

Sabol, W.J. (1990) 'Imprisonment, Fines and Diverting Offenders from Custody: Implications of Sentencing Discretion for Penal Policy', *Howard Journal of Criminal Justice*, 29: 25–41.

Sanders, A. (1985) 'Class Bias in Prosecutions', *Howard Journal of Criminal Justice*, 24: 176–97.

Sanders, A. (2001) *Community Justice: Modernising the Magistracy in England and Wales*. London: Institute for Public Policy Research Criminal Justice Forum.

Sanders, A. and Young, R. (2000) *Criminal Justice* (2nd edn). London: Butterworths.

Scarman, L. (1986) *The Scarman Report*. Harmondsworth: Penguin.

Schafer, S. (1960) *Restitution to the Victims of Crime*. London: Stevens and Sons.

Scottish Prison Service (1994) *Relational Audits in the Scottish Prison System, a Report by Cate Brett et al., The Relationships Foundation*. Edinburgh: Scottish Prison Service. Also available on-line at: www.sps.gov.uk/research/rational%20Audits%2000P.htm

Scottish Prison Service (2000) *The Scottish Prison Service Annual Report and Accounts 1999–2000*. Edinburgh: Scottish Prison Service. Also available on-line at: www.sps. gov.uk/Annual%20report%202000/sps0-00.htm

Scraton, P., Sim, J. and Skidmore, P. (1991) *Prisons Under Protest*. Milton Keynes: Open University Press.

Scull, A. (1977) *Decarceration: Community Treatment and the Deviant – A Radical View* (1st edn). Englewood Cliffs, NJ: Prentice-Hall.

Scull, A. (1983) 'Community Corrections: Panacea, Progress or Pretence?' in D. Garland, and P. Young (eds), *The Power to Punish: Contemporary Penalty and Social Analysis*, pp. 146–65. London: Heinemann.

Scull, A. (1984) *Decarceration: Community Treatment and the Deviant – A Radical View* (2nd edn). Cambridge: Polity Press.

Seago, P., Walker, C. and Wall, D. (2000) 'The Development of the Professional Magistracy in England and Wales', [2000] *Criminal Law Review*, 631–51.

Seear, N. and Player, E. (1986) *Women in the Penal System*. London: Howard League for Penal Reform.

Sentencing Advisory Panel (2000) *First Annual Report*. London: Sentencing Advisory Panel. Also available on-line at www.sentencing-advisory-panel.gov.uk/info.htm

Sentencing Advisory Panel (2001) *Sentencing Guidelines for Domestic Burglary: Consultation Paper*. London: Sentencing Advisory Panel.

Shah, R. and Pease, K. (1992) 'Crime, Race and Reporting to the Police', *Howard Journal of Criminal Justice*, 31: 192–9.

Shapland, J. (1984) 'The Victim, the Criminal Justice System and Compensation', *British Journal of Criminology*, 24: 131–49.

Shapland, J. (1988) 'Fiefs and Peasants: Accomplishing Change for Victims in the Criminal Justice System' in M. Maguire and J. Pointing (eds), *Victims of Crime: A New Deal*, pp. 187–94. Milton Keynes and Philadelphia: Open University Press.

Shapland, J., Willmore, J. and Duff, P. (1985) *Victims in the Criminal Justice System*. Aldershot: Gower. (Cambridge Studies in Criminology, 53.)

Shaw, A. (1966) *Convicts and the Colonies*. London: Faber.

Shaw, R. and Haines, K. (eds) (1989) *The Criminal Justice System: A Central Role for the Probation Service*. Cambridge: University of Cambridge, Institute of Criminology.

Shaw, S. (1980) *Paying the Penalty: an Analysis of the Cost of Penal Sanctions*. London: NACRO.

Shaw, S. (1989) 'A Bull Market for Prisons' in P. Carter, T. Jeffs, and M. Smith (eds), *Social Work and Social Welfare Yearbook 1*. Milton Keynes: Open University Press.

Shaw, S. (1992a) 'Prisons' in E. Stockdale and S. Casale (eds) *Criminal Justice Under Stress*, pp. 160–78. London: Blackstone

Shaw, S. (1992b) 'The Short History of Prison Privatization', *Prison Service Journal*, 87: 30–2.

Shaw, S. (1994) 'The Privatization of Prisons'. Talk given by Stephen Shaw at a meeting of the British Society of Criminology, North of England branch, at the University of Leeds, 23 November 1994.

Shaw, S. (1998) 'Desolation Row', *Prison Report*, 44 (Summer): 10–11. London: Prison Reform Trust.

Shaw, S. (1999) 'Desolation Row Revisited', *Prison Report*, 47 (May): 8–9. London: Prison Reform Trust.

Shelbourn, C. (1978) 'State Compensation for Detention', [1978] *Criminal Law Review*, 22–30.

Sheridan, A. (1980) *Michel Foucault: The Will to Truth*. London: Tavistock.

Sheriff, P. (1998) *Summary Probation Statistics England and Wales 1997*, Home Office Statistical Bulletin 12/98. London: Home Office.

Shichor, D. (1995) *Prisons for Profit: Private Prisons/Public Concerns*. Thousand Oaks, CA: Sage Publications.

Sim, J. (1990) *Medical Power in Prisons*. Milton Keynes: Open University Press.

Sim, J. (1992) ' "When You Ain't Got Nothing You Got Nothing to Lose": The Peterhead Rebellion, the State and the Case for Prison Abolition' in K. Bottomley, T. Fowles and R. Reiner (eds), *Criminal Justice: Theory and Practice,* pp. 273–300. London: British Society of Criminology.

Sim, J. (1994a) 'The Abolitionist Approach: a British Perspective' in A. Duff, S. Marshall, R.E. Dobash and R.P. Dobash (eds), *Penal Theory and Penal Practice: Tradition and Innovation in Criminal Justice*, pp. 263–84. Manchester: Manchester University Press.

Sim, J. (1994b) 'Reforming the Penal Wasteland' in E. Player and M. Jenkins (eds), *Prison after Woolf*, pp. 31–45. London: Routledge.

Simon, F. and Weatheritt, M. (1974) *The Use of Bail and Custody by London Magistrates' Courts Before and After the Criminal Justice Act, 1967*, Home Office Research Study No. 20. London: HMSO.

Sims, L. and Myhill, A. (2001) *Policing and the Public: Findings from the 2000 British Crime Survey*, Home Office Research Findings No. 136. London: Home Office.

Singleton, N., Mettzer, H. and Gatward, R. (1998) *Psychiatric Morbidity Among Prisoners in England and Wales: The Report of a Survey Carried Out in 1997*. London: The Stationery Office.

Skogan, W.G. (1990) *The Police and Public in England and Wales: A British Crime Survey Report*, Home Office Research Study No. 117. London: HMSO.

Skogan, W.G. (1994) *Contacts Between Police and Public: Findings from the 1992 British Crime Survey*, Home Office Research Study No. 134. London: HMSO.

Smart, C. (1976) *Women, Crime and Criminology: A Feminist Critique*. London: Routledge and Kegan Paul.

Smellie, E. and Crow, I. (1991) *Black People's Experience of Criminal Justice*. London: NACRO.

Smith, D.J. (1983) *Police and People in London I: A Survey of Londoners*. London: Policy Studies Institute.

Smith, D.J. (1994) 'Race, Crime and Criminal Justice' in M. Maguire, R. Morgan and R. Reiner (eds), *The Oxford Handbook of Criminology* (1st edn), pp. 1041–1117. Oxford: Clarendon Press.

Smith, D.J. and Gray, J. (1983) *Police and People in London IV: The Police in Action*. London: Policy Studies Institute.

Smith, S. (1982) *Race and Crime Statistics*. London: Board for Social Responsibility, Church of England.

Softley, P. (1978) *Fines in Magistrates' Courts*, Home Office Research Study No. 46. London: HMSO.

Southgate, P. and Ekblom, P. (1986) *Police–Public Encounters*, Home Office Research Study No. 90. London: HMSO.

Sparks, C. (1998) 'Freed by the Stroke of a Pen', *Prison Report*, 43 (June): 8–9.

Sparks, J.R. and Bottoms, A.E. (1995) 'Legitimacy and Order in Prisons', *British Journal of Sociology*, 46: 45–62.

Sparks, J.R. and Bottoms, A.E. and Hay, W. (1996) *Prisons and the Problem of Order*, Oxford: Clarendon Press.

Sparks, R.F. (1971) 'The Use of Suspended Sentences', *Criminal Law Review*, 384–401.

Sparks, R. (1994) 'Can Prisons Be Legitimate? Penal Politics, Privatization, and the Timeliness of an Old Idea', *British Journal of Criminology*, 34, Special Issue: 14–28.

Sparks, R. (2001) 'The Special Handling of Difficult Prisoners in Comparative Context: a Note on Research Resources and Research Needs', in E. Clare and K. Bottomley (eds), *Evaluation of Close Supervision Centres*, Home Office Research Study No. 136. London: Home Office Research, Development and Statistics Directorate.

Spohn, C., Gruhl, J. and Welch, S. (1981–2) 'The Effect of Race on Sentencing: A Re-examination of an Unsettled Question', *Law and Society Review*, 16: 71–88.

Stanley, S. and Baginsky, M. (1984) *Alternatives to Imprisonment*. London: Peter Owen.

Starr, P. (1989) 'The Meaning of Privatization' in S.B. Kamerman and A.J. Kahn (eds), *Privatization and the Welfare State*, pp. 15–48. Princeton NJ: Princeton, University Press.

Stern, V. (1993) *Bricks of Shame: Britain's Prisons* (2nd edn). London: Penguin.

Stevens, P. and Willis, C.F. (1979) *Race, Crime and Arrests*, Home Office Research Study No. 58. London: HMSO.

Stockdale, E. and Casale, S. (eds) (1992) *Criminal Justice under Stress*. London: Blackstone.

Stolzenberg, L. and D'Alessio, S.J. (1997) ' "Three Strikes and You're Out". The Impact of California's New Mandatory Sentencing Law on Serious Crime Rates', *Crime and Delinquency*, 43: 457–69.

Stone, C. (1988) *Bail Information for the Crown Prosecution Service*. London: Vera Institute of Justice.

Stratton, B. (1973) *Who Guards the Guards?* London: North London Group of PROP (Preservation of the Rights of Prisoners).

Streatfeild, Mr Justice (1961) *Report of the Interdepartmental Committee on the Business of the Criminal Courts*, Cmnd 1289. London: HMSO.

Sutherland, E.H. (1956) 'Crime of Corporations' in A. Cohen, A. Lindesmith and K. Schuessler (eds), *The Sutherland Papers*, pp. 78–96. Bloomington, IN: Indiana University Press.

van Swaaningen, R. and de Jonge, G. (1995) 'The Dutch Prison System and Penal Policy' in V. Ruggiero, M. Ryan and J. Sim (eds), *Western European Penal Systems: A Critical Anatomy*. London: Sage Publications.

Tarling, R. (1979) *Sentencing Practice in the Magistrates' Court*, Home Office Research Study No. 56. London: HMSO.

Tarling, R. (1993) *Analysing Offending: Data, Models and Interpretations*. London: HMSO.

Tarling, R. and Weatheritt, M. (1979) *Sentencing Practice in Magistrates' Courts*, Home Office Research Study No. 56. London: HMSO.

Tarling, R., Moxon, D. and Jones, P. (1985) 'Sentencing of Adults and Juveniles in Magistrates' Courts', in D. Moxon (ed.), *Managing Criminal Justice*. London: HMSO.

Taylor, I., Walton, P. and Young, J. (1973) *The New Criminology: For a Social Theory of Deviance*. London: Routledge and Kegan Paul.

Taylor, L., Lacey, R. and Bracken, D. (1979) *In Whose Best Interests? The Unjust Treatment of Children in Courts and Institutions*. London: Cobden Trust/MIND.

Taylor, M. and Pease, K. (1989) 'Private Prisons and Penal Purpose' in R. Matthews (ed.), *Privatizing Criminal Justice*, pp. 178–94. London: Sage Publications.

Taylor, P. (1993) 'Judges and Sentencing', *Journal of the Law Society of Scotland*, 129–31.

Taylor, R. (2000) *A Seven-Year Reconviction Study of HMP Grendon Therapeutic Community*, Home Office Research Findings No. 115. London: Home Office Research and Statistics Directorate.

Taylor, W. (1981) *Probation and After-Care in a Multi-Racial Society*. London: Commission for Racial Equality.

Thomas, D.A. (1979) *Principles of Sentencing: The Sentencing Policies of the Court of Appeal Criminal Division* (2nd edn). London: Heinemann.

Thomas, D. A. (1983) 'Sentencing Discretion and Appellate Review' in J. Shapland (ed.), *Decision-making in the Legal System*, Issues in Criminological and Legal Psychology, Occasional Paper No. 5. Leicester: Division of Criminology and Legal Psychology, the British Psychological Society.

Thomas, D.A. (1995) 'Sentencing Reform: England and Wales' in C. Clarkson and R. Morgan, (eds) *The Politics of Sentencing Reform*, pp. 125–47. Oxford: Oxford University Press.

Thomas, D.A. (2000) *Sentencing Referencer*. London: Sweet and Maxwell.

Thomas, J.E. (1972) *The English Prison Officer Since 1850*. London: Routledge and Kegan Paul.

Thomas, J.E. and Pooley, R. (1980) *The Exploding Prison: Prison Riots and the Case of Hull*. London: Junction Books.

Thompson, E.P. (1977) *Whigs and Hunters: The Origin of the Black Act*. Harmondsworth: Penguin.

Thompson, E.P. (1978) *The Poverty of Theory and Other Essays*. London: Merlin Press.

Thorpe, D.H., Smith, D., Green, C.J. and Paley, J.G. (1980) *Out of Care: The Community Support of Juvenile Offenders*. London: George Allen and Unwin.

Tonry, M. and Farrington, D.P. (eds) (1995) *Building a Safer Society: Strategic Approaches to Crime Prevention*. Chicago: University of Chicago Press.

Törnudd, P. (1993) *Fifteen Years of Decreasing Prisoner Rates in Finland*. Helsinki: National Research Institute of Legal Policy.

Travis, A. (1993) 'Ministers' Tough Rhetoric to Blame for Overcrowding, Say Prison Reformers', *The Guardian*, 8 September.

Travis, A. (2001) 'Jails Chief Threatens to Resign', *The Guardian*, 6 January.

Tremblay, R.E. and Craig, W.M. (1995) 'Developmental Crime Prevention' in M. Tonry and D.P. Farrington (eds), *Building a Safer Society: Strategic Approaches to Crime Prevention*, pp. 151–234. Chicago: University of Chicago Press.

Turnbull, P., McSweeney, T. and Hough, M. (2000a) *Drug Treatment and Testing Orders – The 18-month evaluation*, Home Office Research Findings No. 128. London: Home Office Research and Statistics Directorate.

Turnbull, P., McSweeney, T. and Hough, M. (2000b) *Drug Treatment and Testing Orders: Evaluation Report*, Home Office Research Study No. 212. London: Home Office Research and Statistics Directorate.

Tyler, T.R. (1990) *Why People Obey the Law*. New Haven: Yale University Press.

United States General Accounting Office (1991) *Private Prisons*. Washington DC: US Government Printing Office.

United States General Accounting Office (1996) *Private and Public Prisons: Studies Comparing Operational Costs and/or Quality of Service*. Reference Number GAO/GGD-96-198. Gaithersburg, MD: US General Accounting Office.

Vagg, J. (1991) 'Correcting Manifest Wrongs: Prison Grievance and Inspection

Procedures in England and Wales, France, Germany and the Netherlands' in J. Muncie and R. Sparks (eds), *Imprisonment: European Perspectives*, pp. 146–65. Hemel Hempstead: Harvester Wheatsheaf.

Vennard, J., Hedderman, C. and Sugg, D. (1997) *Changing Offenders' Attitudes and Behaviour: What Works?* Home Office Research Study No. 171. London: Home Office Research and Statistics Directorate.

Voltaire (1947) *Candide*. Harmondsworth: Penguin.

Walker, C. and Wall, D. (1997) 'Imprisoning the Poor: Television Licence Evaders and the Criminal Justice System', [1997] *Criminal Law Review*, 173–86.

Walker, J., Collier, P. and Tarling, R. (1990) 'Why are Prison Sentences in England and Wales Higher than in Australia?', *British Journal of Criminology*, 30: 24–35.

Walker, M. (1988) 'The Court Disposal of Young Males, by Race, in London in 1983', *British Journal of Criminology*, 28: 441–60.

Walker, M., Jefferson, T. and Seneviratne, M. (1990) *Ethnic Minorities, Young People and the Criminal Justice System*, ESRC Project No. E06250023: Main Report.

Walker, N. (1968) *Crime and Punishment in Britain* (revised edn). Edinburgh: University of Edinburgh Press.

Walker, N. (1972) *Sentencing in a Rational Society*. Harmondsworth: Penguin.

Walker, N. (1981) 'Feminists' Extravaganzas', [1981] *Criminal Law Review*, 379–86.

Walker, N. and Marsh, C. (1984) 'Do Sentences Affect Public Disapproval?', *British Journal of Criminology*, 24: 27–48.

Walmsley, R. (2000) *World Prison Population List* (2nd edn), Home Office Research Findings No. 116. London: Home Office.

Walmsley, R., Howard, L. and White, S. (1992) *The National Prison Survey 1991: Main Findings*, Home Office Research Study No. 128. London: HMSO.

Ward, D. (1987) *The Validity of The Reconviction Prediction Score*, Home Office Research Study No. 94. London: HMSO.

Wasik, M. and von Hirsch, A. (1988) 'Non-custodial Penalties and the Principles of Desert', [1988] *Criminal Law Review*, 555–72.

Wasik, M. and von Hirsch, A. (1990) 'Statutory Sentencing Principles: The 1990 White Paper', *Modern Law Review*, 53: 508–15.

Wasik, M. and von Hirsch, A. (1994) 'Section 29 Revisited: Previous Convictions in Sentencing', [1994] *Criminal Law Review*, 409–18.

Watkins, M., Gordon, W. and Jeffries, A. (1998) *The Sentence of the Court*. (2nd edn). Winchester: Waterside Press.

Watkins, M. and Gordon, W. (edited by Gibson, B.) (2000) *The Sentence of the Court* (3rd edn). Winchester: Waterside Press.

Weber, M. (1930) *The Protestant Ethic and the Spirit of Capitalism*. London: George Allen and Unwin.

Weber, M. (1968) *Economy and Society*. New York: Bedminster Press.

West, D.J. (1982) *Delinquency: Its Roots, Careers and Prospects*. London: Heinemann.

Whatmore, P.B. (1987) 'Barlinnie Special Unit: An Insider's View', in A.E. Bottoms and R. Light (eds), *Problems of Long-Term Imprisonment*, pp. 249–60. Aldershot: Gower.

White, P. (1999) *The Prison Population in 1998: A Statistical Review*. Home Office Research Findings No. 94. London: Home Office.

White, P. and Cullen, C. (2000) *Projections of Long Term Trends in the Prison Population to 2007*, Home Office Statistical Bulletin 2/00. London: Home Office.

White, P. and Woodbridge, J. (1998) *The Prison Population in 1997*, Home Office Statistical Bulletin 5/98. London: Home Office.

White, P., Woodbridge, J. and Flack, K. (1999) *Projections of Long Term Trends in the Prison Population to 2006*, Home Office Statistical Bulletin 1/99. London: Home Office.

White, S. (1996) 'The Antecedents of the Mode of Trial Guidelines', [1996] *Criminal Law Review*, 471–6.

Whitfield, D. (1995) 'Crime, Surveillance and Tagging: The Thin End of the White Elephant', *Criminal Justice Matters*, 20: 19.

Whitfield, D. (1997) *Tackling the Tag: the Electronic Monitoring of Offenders*. Winchester: Waterside Press.

Willcock, H.D. and Stokes, J. (1968) *Deterrents and Incentives to Crime Among Boys and Young Men Aged 15–21 Years*. London: HMSO.

Willis, C.F. (1983) *The Use, Effectiveness and Impact of Police Stop and Search Powers*. London: Home Office.

Wilson, J.Q. (1975) *Thinking About Crime*. New York: Basic Books.

Windlesham, D. (1993) *Responses to Crime, Volume 2: Penal Policy in the Making*. Oxford: Clarendon Press.

Winfield, M. (1984) *Lacking Conviction: The Remand System in England and Wales*. London: Prison Reform Trust.

Wolds Board of Visitors (1995) *Annual Report to the Secretary of State for the Home Department, Year Ending 31 December, 1994*. Board of Visitors, HMP Wolds.

Woodbridge, J. (1999) *Review of Comparative Costs and Performance of Privately and Publicly Operated Prisons, 1997–8*, Home Office Statistical Bulletin, 13/99. London: Home Office.

Woodcock, J. (1994) *The Escape from Whitemoor Prison on Friday 9th September 1994 (The Woodcock Enquiry)*, Cm 2741. London: HMSO.

Woolf, H. and Tumim, S. (1991) *Prison Disturbances April 1990*, Cm 1456. London: HMSO.

Worrall, A. and Pease, K. (1986) 'The Prison Population in 1985', *British Journal of Criminology*, 26: 184–7.

Wozniak, E. and McAllister, D. (1991) 'Facilities, Standards and Change in the Scottish Prison Service: The Prison Survey 1990/91'. Paper presented at the British Criminology Conference, University of York, July.

Wright, M. (1991) *Justice for Victims and Offenders*. Buckingham: Open University Press.

Wright, M. and Galaway, B. (eds) (1989) *Mediation and Criminal Justice: Victims, Offenders and Community*, London: Sage Publications.

Wynne, J. (1996) 'Leeds Mediation and Reparation Service: Ten Years' Experience with Victim-Offender Mediation', in B. Galaway and J. Hudson (eds) *Restorative Justice: International Perspectives*. Monsey, NY: Criminal Justice Press and Amsterdam: Kugler Publications.

Young, P. (1987) *The Prison Cell*. London: Adam Smith Institute.

Zedner, L. (1994) 'Reparation and Retribution: Are They Reconcilable?', *Modern Law Review*, 57: 228–50.

Zehr, H. (1985) *Retributive Justice, Restorative Justice*. Elkhart, IN: Mennonite Central Committee, US Office of Criminal Justice.

# Index